If it's APRIL 2003
and you are still using this Directory, it's time to order the NEW Edition.

Please visit our website

www.cabells.com

or contact us at

Cabell Publishing Company
Box 5428, Beaumont, Texas 77726-5428
(409) 898-0575
Fax (409) 866-9554

Cabell's Directory Of Publishing Opportunities In Marketing

EIGHTH EDITION 2001-02

David W. E. Cabell, Editor
McNeese State University
Lake Charles, Louisiana

Deborah L. English, Editor
Brooke S. Abernethy, Assistant Editor

To order additional copies
visit our web site
www.cabells.com

or contact us at

CABELL PUBLISHING CO.
Box 5428, Beaumont, Texas 77726-5428
(409) 898-0575
Fax (409) 866-9554

$89.95 U.S. for addresses in United States

Price includes shipping and handling for U.S.
Add $50 for surface mail to countries outside U.S.
Add $100 for air mail to countries outside U.S.

ISBN # 0-911753-16-8

©2000 by Cabell Publishing Company, Box 5428, Beaumont, Texas 77726-5428.

All rights reserved. No part of this publication may be reproduced, stored in a retrieval system, or transmitted in any form or by any means, electronic, mechanical, photocopying, recording, or otherwise without the prior written permission of the publisher.

Although every reasonable effort has been made to ensure the accuracy of the information contained in this directory, the author cautions the reader that there may be mistakes in the information provided. Thus, the reader is responsible for his or her actions resulting from the use of this information.

TABLE OF CONTENTS

Academy of Marketing Science Review 1
Academy of Marketing Studies Journal 9
Advances in International Marketing 12
Agribusiness: An International Journal 16
Air Force Journal of Logistics 21
American Business Perspectives (NBDC Report) 22
American Demographics 27
American International College Journal of Business 29
Anatolia: An International Journal of Tourism Hospitality and Research 30
Annals of Tourism Research: A Social Sciences Journal 34
Annual Advances in Business Cases 38
Asia Pacific Business Review 44
Asia Pacific Journal of Marketing and Logistics 47
Asian Journal of Business & Entrepreneurship 48
Bank Marketing Magazine 50
British Food Journal 53
Business Case Journal 58
California Management Review 61
Case Research Journal 64
Communication Monographs 67
Communication Research 69
Communication Studies 71
Communications and the Law 73
Cornell Hotel and Restaurant Administration Quarterly 75
Decision Sciences (Journal of) 78
Entrepreneurship Theory and Practice 85
European Journal of Marketing 87
Family Business Review 91
FIU Hospitality Review 94
Global Business and Economic Review 96
Global Competitiveness 98
Global Economy Quarterly (GEQ) 100
Harvard Business Review 102
Health Marketing Quarterly 104
Industrial Marketing Management 109
Interactive Marketing 112
International Academy for Case Studies 115
International Journal of Advertising 119
International Journal of Bank Marketing 122
International Journal of Business 127
International Journal of Business and Economics 129
International Journal of Electronic Commerce (IJEC) 131
International Journal of Hospitality & Tourism Administration 134
International Journal of Hospitality Management 138

International Journal of Logistics: Research and Applications ... 143
International Journal of Physical Distribution & Logistics Management ... 146
International Journal of Research In Marketing ... 150
International Journal of Retail and Distribution Management ... 154
International Journal of Tourism Research ... 158
International Journal of Transport Economics ... 162
International Marketing Review ... 164
International Research in the Business Disciplines ... 168
International Review of Retail, Distribution and Consumer Research ... 171
Internet Research ... 174
Journal of Advertising ... 179
Journal of Advertising Research ... 182
Journal of Brand Management ... 186
Journal of Business ... 189
Journal of Business & Industrial Marketing ... 192
Journal of Business and Behavioral Sciences ... 197
Journal of Business Disciplines ... 198
Journal of Business Education ... 201
Journal of Business Logistics ... 204
Journal of Business, Industry and Economics ... 214
Journal of Business-to-Business Marketing ... 215
Journal of Communication ... 219
Journal of Communication Management ... 221
Journal of Consumer Affairs ... 225
Journal of Consumer Marketing ... 228
Journal of Consumer Policy ... 233
Journal of Consumer Psychology ... 240
Journal of Consumer Research ... 242
Journal of Convention & Exhibition Management ... 246
Journal of Current Issues & Research in Advertising ... 250
Journal of Database Marketing ... 254
Journal of Electronic Commerce ... 257
Journal of Euromarketing ... 260
Journal of Fashion Marketing and Management ... 264
Journal of Financial Services Marketing ... 267
Journal of Food Product Marketing ... 270
Journal of Global Marketing ... 276
Journal of Hospital Marketing ... 284
Journal of Hospitality & Leisure Marketing ... 288
Journal of Hospitality & Tourism Research ... 292
Journal of Interactive Marketing ... 295
Journal of International Academy for Case Studies ... 298
Journal of International Consumer Marketing ... 301
Journal of International Food & Agribusiness Marketing ... 309
Journal of International Marketing ... 317
Journal of Internet Commerce ... 326
Journal of Macromarketing ... 330

Journal of Marketing	335
Journal of Marketing Channels	344
Journal of Marketing Communications	348
Journal of Marketing Education	352
Journal of Marketing for Higher Education	356
Journal of Marketing Management	360
Journal of Marketing Research	364
Journal of Marketing Theory and Practice	373
Journal of Ministry Marketing and Management	377
Journal of Nonprofit & Public Sector Marketing	382
Journal of Nonprofit and Voluntary Sector Marketing	386
Journal of Personal Selling & Sales Management	389
Journal of Pharmaceutical Marketing and Management	393
Journal of Problems of Theory and Practice in Reforms of Regional Economies	396
Journal of Product & Brand Management	397
Journal of Promotion Management	402
Journal of Public Policy & Marketing	406
Journal of Quality Assurance in Tourism & Hospitality	409
Journal of Relationship Marketing (Journal of Customer Service in Mktg. & Mgmt.)	413
Journal of Restaurant & Foodservice Marketing	418
Journal of Retail Banking Services	422
Journal of Retailing	424
Journal of Retailing and Consumer Services	429
Journal of Segmentation in Marketing	434
Journal of Selling and Major Account Management	438
Journal of Services Marketing	443
Journal of Sport Management	447
Journal of Strategic Marketing	450
Journal of Targeting, Measurement, and Analysis for Targeting	454
Journal of the Academy of Marketing Science	457
Journal of the Market Research Society	460
Journal of Transport Economics and Policy	462
Journal of Transportation Law, Logistics, and Policy	466
Journal of Transportation Management	470
Journal of Travel & Tourism Marketing	475
Journal of Travel Research	480
Journal of Vacation Marketing	485
Journal of World Business	488
Logistics Information Management	491
Management Science	495
Marketing Education Review	516
Marketing Educator	519
Marketing Health Services	520
Marketing Intelligence & Planning	524
Marketing Letters	528
Marketing Management	531
Marketing Management Journal	535

Mountain Plains Journal of Business and Economics	537
North Central Business Journal	538
Operations Research	540
Pennsylvania Journal of Business and Economics	547
Psychology and Marketing	550
Qualitative Market Research: An International Journal	553
Research in Consumer Behavior	557
Retail Education Today	563
Service Industries Journal (The)	564
Services Marketing Quarterly	569
Sloan Management Review	573
Southwest Business & Economics Journal	578
Southwestern Business Administration Journal	580
Sport Marketing Quarterly	583
Tourism Analysis	586
Tourism and Hospitality Research: The Surrey Quarterly Review	589
Tourism Management	593
Transportation	597
Transportation Journal	601
Transportation Research Part E: Logistics and Transportation Review	603
Transportation Science Journal	606
Western Journal of Communication	609
World Transport Policy & Practice	611
Written Communication	615
INDEX	617

Preface

The objective of *Cabell's Directory of Publishing Opportunities in Marketing* is to help you publish your ideas.

The *Directory* contains the editor's name(s), address(es), phone and fax number(s), and e-mail and web address(es) for over 160 journals.

To help you in selecting those journals that are most likely to publish your manuscripts the **Index** classifies the journals into twenty-five different topic areas. In addition, the Index provides information on the journal's type of review process, number of external reviewers and acceptance rate.

To further assist you in organizing and preparing your manuscripts, the *Directory* includes extensive information on the style and format of most journals. If a journal has its own set of manuscript guidelines, a copy of these guidelines is published in the *Directory*. Also, each entry indicates the use of a standard set of publication guidelines by a journal. For example, some journals use the *Chicago Manual of Style* or the *Publication Manual of the American Psychological Association*.

Furthermore, the *Directory* describes the type of review process used by the editor(s) of a journal, type of review, number of reviewers, acceptance rate, time required for review, availability of reviewers comments, fees charged to review or publish the manuscript, copies required and manuscript topics. Information on the journal's circulation, readership and subscription prices are also provided.

Although this *Directory* focuses on journals in the specialized area of **Marketing**, other directories focus on **Management, Accounting,** and **Economics and Finance**. The division of business journals into these four directories more appropriately meets the researcher's need for publishing in his area of specialization.

The decision to place journals in their respective directory is based on the manuscript topics selected by the editor as well as the journals' guidelines for authors. If you wish to find the most current information on the *Directory*, visit **www.cabells.com**. Please contact us for the login registration procedure.

Also, the *Directory* includes a section titled **"What is a Refereed Article?"** which tends to emphasize the value of a blind review process and use of external reviewers. However, this section cautions individuals using these criteria to also consider a journal's reputation for quality. Additionally, it indicates that differences in acceptance rates may be the result of different methods used to calculate these percentages and the number of people associated with a particular area of specialization.

How To Use the Directory

TABLE OF CONTENTS
Table of Contents provides over 160 journals to help your locate a publication.

INDEX
Index classifies the journals according to twenty-five (25) different manuscript topics. It also includes information on the type of review, number of external reviewers, acceptance rate and page number of each journal.

ADDRESS FOR SUBMISSION
Address for Submission provides: the Editor's Name(s), Mailing Address(es), Telephone and Fax numbers(s), and E-mail and Web address(es).

PUBLICATION GUIDELINES
Manuscript Length refers to the length of the manuscript in terms of the number of double-spaced typescript pages.

Copies Required indicates the number of manuscript copies you should submit to the editor.

Computer Submission indicates whether the journal prefers hardcopy (paper) or electronic submissions such as disk, e-mail attachment, or a combination of methods.

Format refers to the type of word processing programs or computer programs the journal requires for reviewing the manuscript. Some examples of these programs are Microsoft Word, Word Perfect, or ASCII.

Fees to Review refers to whether the journal charges a fee to review the manuscript. Knowing this item permits the author to send the required funds with the manuscript.

Manuscript Style refers to the overall style guide the journal uses for text, references within the text and the bibliography. This is usually either the *Chicago Manual of Style* or the *Publication Manual of the American Psychological Association (APA)*.

REVIEW INFORMATION
Type of Review specifies blind, editorial, or optional review methods. A blind review indicates the reviewer(s) does not know who wrote the manuscript. An editorial review indicates the reviewer knows who wrote the manuscript. The term "optional" indicates the author may choose either one of these types of review.

No. of External Reviewers and *No. of In House Reviewers*
These two items refer to the number of reviewers who review the manuscript prior to making a decision regarding the publication of the manuscript. Although the editor attempted to determine whether the reviewers were on the staff of the journal or were outside reviewers, many of the respondents had trouble distinguishing between internal and external reviewers. Thus it may be more accurate to add these two categories and determine the total number of reviewers.

Acceptance Rate refers to the number of manuscripts accepted for publication relative to the number of manuscripts submitted within the last year. The method of calculating acceptance rates varies among journals.

Time to Review indicates the amount of time that passes between the submission of a manuscript and notification to the author regarding the results of the review process.

Reviewer's Comments indicates whether the author can obtain a copy of the reviewer's comments. In some cases, the author needs to request that the editor send these remarks.

Invited Articles indicates the percentage of articles for which the editor requests an individual to write specifically for publication in the journal. The percentage is the number of invited articles relative to the total number of articles that appeared in a journal within the past year.

Fees to Publish refers to whether the journal charges a fee to publish the manuscript. Knowing this item assists the author in his decision to place the manuscript into the review process.

CIRCULATION DATA
Reader indicates the predominant type of reader the publication seeks to attract. These are divided into a group designated as practitioners and professionals, or another group referred to as researchers and academics in the accounting discipline.

Frequency of Issue indicates the number of times a journal will be published in a year.

Copies per Issue indicates the number of copies the journal distributes per issue.

Sponsor/Publisher indicates the journal's affiliation with a professional association, educational institution, governmental agency, and/or publishing company.

Subscribe Price indicates the cost to order a year's subscription unless otherwise indicated.

MANUSCRIPT TOPICS
Manuscript Topics indicates those subjects the journal emphasizes.

MANUSCRIPT GUIDELINES/COMMENTS
Manuscript Guidelines/Comments provides information on the journal's objectives, style and format for references and footnotes that the editor expects the author to follow in preparing his manuscript for submission.

How the Directory Helps You Publish

Although individuals must communicate their ideas in writing, the *Directory* helps the author determine which journal will most likely accept the manuscript. In making this decision, it is important to compare the characteristics of your manuscript and the needs of each journal. The following table provides a framework for making this comparison.

Information Provided by the Directory for Each Journal	Manuscript Characteristics
Topic(s) of Articles Manuscript Guidelines	Theme
Acceptance Rate Percentage of Invited Articles	Significance of Theme
Type of Reader	Methodology and Style
Circulation Review Process	Prestige
Number of Reviewers Availability of Reviewers Comments Time Required for Reviewer	Results of Review

This framework will help the author determine a small number of journals that will be interested in publishing the manuscript. The *Directory* can assist the author in determining these journals, yet a set of unwritten and written laws prevent simultaneous submission of a manuscript to more than one journal. However, a manuscript can be sent to another journal in the event of a rejection by any one publication.

Furthermore, copyright laws and editorial policy of a given publication often require the author to choose only one journal. Consequently, some journals will require the author to sign a statement indicating the manuscript is not presently under review by another publication.

Publication of the manuscript in the proceedings of a professional association does not prevent the author from sending it to a journal, however there usually are some restrictions attached. Most professional associations require that the author acknowledge the presentation of the manuscript at the associate meeting.

Since the author is limited to submission of a manuscript to only one journal and the review process for each journal requires a long period of time, a "query" letter may help the author determine the journal most likely to publish the manuscript.

The query letter contains the following information:
- Topic, major idea or conclusion of the manuscript
- The subject sample, research setting conceptual framework, methodology type of organization or location
- The reasons why the author thinks the journal's readers would be interested in your proposed article
- Asks the editor to make comments or suggestions on the usefulness of this type of article to the journal

While the query letter is helpful in selecting a journal that will be likely to publish the manuscript, the author could use the *Directory* and the framework presented to develop a set of journals which would be likely to publish the manuscript. With this number of possible journals, it makes the sending of a query letter more feasible and tends to achieve the objective of finding the journal most likely to publish the manuscript.

Relating the Theme of the Manuscript to the Topics of Articles Published by Each Journal

To begin the process of choosing the journals to receive the "query" letter and, at some future time, the manuscript, the author needs to examine the similarity between the theme of the manuscript and the editor's needs. The *Directory* describes these needs by listing the topics each publication considers important and the manuscript guidelines. To find those journals that publish manuscripts in any particular area, refer to the topic index.

In attempting to classify the theme, the author should limit his choice to a single discipline. With the increasing specialization in the academic world, it is unlikely that reviewers, editors, or readers will understand an article that requires knowledge of two different disciplines. If these groups do not understand a manuscript, the journal will reject it.

If a manuscript emphasizes an interdisciplinary approach, it is important to decide who will be reading the article. The approach should be to explain the theoretical concepts of one discipline to the specialist in another discipline. The author should not attempt to resolve theoretical issues present in his discipline and explain their implications for specialists in another discipline.

Although the discipline classifications indicate the number of journals interested in your manuscript topic, the manuscript guidelines help the author determine the journals that will most likely have the greatest interest in the manuscript. The manuscript guidelines provide a detailed statement of the criteria for judging manuscripts, the editorial objectives, the readership and the journal's content and approach. This information makes it possible to determine more precisely the congruence between the manuscript and the type of articles the journal publishes. **The *Directory* contains the manuscript guidelines for a large number of journals.**

The Relationship Between the Journal's Acceptance Rate and Significance of the Theme of the Manuscript

In addition to determining the similarity between the topic of the manuscript and the topic of articles published by the journal, an examination of the significance of the theme to the discipline is also an important criterion in selecting a journal. The journals with the lowest acceptance rate will tend to publish those manuscripts that make the most significant contributions to the advancement of the discipline. Since these journals receive a large number of manuscripts, the editors distinguish those manuscripts likely to make a significant contribution to the reader's knowledge.

Defining newness or the contribution of any one study to the understanding of a discipline is difficult. However, it is possible to gain some insights into this definition by asking the following questions:

1. Is the author stating the existence of a variable, trend or problem, not previously recognized by the literature?

2. Is the author testing the interactions of a different set of variables or events?

3. Is the author presenting a new technique to cope with a problem or test an idea not previously presented in the literature?

4. Is the author using a subject sample with different characteristics than previously presented in the literature?

If the manuscript does not satisfy one of the first two categories, it is unlikely that a journal with a low acceptance rate will accept it for publication. Thus, the author should send the manuscript to those journals where the acceptance rate is higher.

Although the *Directory* provides the acceptance rates of manuscripts for many different journals, it is important to examine the data on percentage of invited articles for each journal. A high acceptance rate may result because the editor has asked leaders in the discipline to write articles on a particular subject. These invited articles are usually accepted. Since the author of an unsolicited manuscript competes with the leaders in the discipline, the manuscript will have to make a significant contribution to receive the editor's approval.

The Relationship of the Manuscript's Style and Methodology to the Journal's Readership

Another factor in selecting the journal to receive the manuscript is the journal's readership. The readers of each journal include either, practitioners and professionals, academics and researchers in accounting, or a combination of these groups.

Since the most important goal for an author is to publish the manuscript, the author should consider the prestige of the journal only after the manuscript has a relatively high probability of being published by more than one journal. This probability is determined by the responses the author received to his query letter and the similarity between the finished manuscript and the needs of the journal.

The method of determining the prestige of a journal varies depending on its readership and the goals of the author. If the readership is primarily administrators or practicing professionals and the goal of the author is to improve the author's image and that of the institution, the journal's circulation would probably be the best indicator of prestige.

In contrast, the author whose goal is to become known among the author's colleagues might consider the type of review process the journal uses as well as its circulation. With a few exceptions, the most prestigious journals with academic readership use a refereed review process.

The Possible Results of the Review Process and the Selection of a Journal to Receive the Manuscript

Despite the fact that a journal with lower prestige would most likely publish the article, the author might be willing to take a chance on a journal with a greater amount of prestige. Since this will decrease the chances of manuscript acceptance, the author should also consider the consequences of rejection. The consequences include the knowledge the author will gain from having his manuscript rejected.

To determine the amount of knowledge the author is likely to gain requires consideration of the number of reviewers the journal uses in the review process, the availability of the reviewer's comments and the time required for the review process. If the journal makes the reviewer's comments available to the author, this provides a great learning opportunity. Also, the more people that review the manuscript, the greater the author's knowledge will be concerning how to improve the present manuscript. Hopefully, the author will transfer the knowledge gained from writing this manuscript to future manuscripts.

Should the review process take a small amount of time relative to a long period of time, the author is provided with a greater opportunity to use this knowledge to revise the manuscript. To assist the author in determining those journals that provide a suitable learning opportunity, each journal in the *Directory* includes information on the number of reviewers, availability of reviewer's comments to the author and time required for review.

Sending the Manuscript

Before sending the manuscript to an editor, the author should write a cover letter, make sure the manuscript is correctly typed, the format conforms to the journal's guidelines and the necessary copies have been included. **The author should always keep a copy of the manuscript.**

The cover letter that is sent with the manuscript makes it easy for the editor to select reviewers and monitor the manuscript while it is in the review process. This letter should include the title of the manuscript, the author name(s), mailing address(es) phone and fax number(s) and e-mail addresses. In addition, this letter should provide a brief description of the manuscript theme, its applicability and significance to the journal's readership. Finally it should request a copy of the reviewer's comments regardless of whether the manuscript is accepted or rejected.

Receipt of the Reviewer's Comments

The reviewers may still reject the article although the author may have followed this procedure and taken every precaution to avoid rejection. When this occurs, the author's attitude should be focused on making those changes that would make the manuscript more understandable to the next editor, and/or reviewer. These changes may include providing additional information and/or presenting the topic in a more concise manner. Also, the author needs to determine whether some error occurred in selecting the journal to receive the manuscript. Regardless of the source of the errors, the author needs to make those changes that will improve the manuscript's chances of being accepted by the next journal to receive it.

Unless the journal specifically requests the author to revise the manuscript for publication, the author should not send the manuscript to the journal that first rejected it. In rejecting the manuscript, the reviewers implied that it could not be revised to meet their standards for publication. Thus, sending it back to them would not improve the likelihood that the manuscript will be accepted.

If your manuscript is accepted, go out and celebrate but write another one very quickly. When you find you're doing something right, keep doing it so you won't forget.

"What is a Refereed Article?"

With some exceptions a refereed article is one that is blind reviewed and has two external reviewers. The blind review requirement and the use of external reviewers are consistent with the research criteria of objectivity and of knowledge.

The use of a blind review process means that the author of the manuscript is not made known to the reviewer. With the large number of reviewers and journals, it is also likely that the name of the reviewers for a particular manuscript is not made known to the author. Thus, creating a double blind review process. Since the author and reviewers are frequently unknown, the manuscript is judged on its merits rather than on the reputation of the author and/or the author's influence on the reviewers.

The use of two (2) reviewers permits specialists familiar with research similar to that presented in the paper to judge whether the paper makes a contribution to the advancement of knowledge. When two reviewers are used it provides a broader perspective for evaluating the research. This perspective is further widened by the discussion between the editor and reviewers in seeking to reconcile these perspectives.

In contrast to these criteria, some journals that have attained a reputation for quality do not use either a blind review process or external reviewers. The most notable is *Harvard Business Review* that uses an editorial review process. Its reputation for quality results from its readership whose continual subscription attests to its quality.

In addition to these criteria, some researchers include the journal's acceptance rate in their definition of a refereed journal. However, the method of calculating acceptance rates varies among journals. Some journals use all manuscripts received as a base for computing this rate. Other journals allow the editor to choose which papers are sent to reviewers and calculate the acceptance rate on those that are reviewed that is less than the total manuscripts received. Also, many editors do not maintain accurate records on this data and provide only a rough estimate.

Furthermore, the number of people associated with a particular area of specialization influences the acceptance rate. If only a few people can write papers in an area, it tends to increase the journal's acceptance rate.

Although the type of review process and use of external reviewers is one possible definition of a refereed article, it is not the only criteria. Judging the usefulness of a journal to the advancement of knowledge requires the reader to be familiar with many journals in their specialization and make their own evaluation.

Academy of Marketing Science Review

ADDRESS FOR SUBMISSION:

Joseph A. Cote, Managing Editor
Academy of Marketing Science Review
Washington State University
14204 NE Salmon Creek Avenue
Vancouver, WA 98686
USA
Phone: 360-546-9753
Fax: 360-546-9037
E-Mail: amsrev@vancouver.wsu.edu
Web: www.amsreview.org
Address May Change:

PUBLICATION GUIDELINES:

Manuscript Length: 16-20
Copies Required: One Electronic Only
Computer Submission: Yes
Format: Wd. Processing Docs.
Fees to Review: 0.00 US$

Manuscript Style:
See Manuscript Guidelines

CIRCULATION DATA:

Reader: Academics
Frequency of Issue: Online/ as accepted
Copies per Issue: 2,001 - 3,000
Sponsor/Publisher: Academy of Marketing Science
Subscribe Price: 0.00 US$ Online

REVIEW INFORMATION:

Type of Review: Blind Review
No. of External Reviewers: 3
No. of In House Reviewers: 0
Acceptance Rate: 11-20%
Time to Review: 1 - 2 Months
Reviewers Comments: Yes
Invited Articles: 0-5%
Fees to Publish: 0.00 US$

MANUSCRIPT TOPICS:
Advertising & Promotion Management; Business Education; Communication; Direct Marketing; Marketing Research; Marketing Theory & Applications; Sales/Selling; Services

MANUSCRIPT GUIDELINES/COMMENTS:

Mission
The *Academy of Marketing Science Review* is a peer-reviewed (double-blind) academic journal publishing high quality theory and measure development articles in the areas of marketing and consumer behavior. The journal has a worldwide audience. The journal's goal is to stimulate the development of marketing and consumer behavior theory worldwide by publishing interesting articles in a highly readable format.

Copyright
The Academy of Marketing Science holds the copyright for all articles appearing in the *AMS Review*. The Academy of Marketing Science allows unlimited copying of *AMS Review* articles for educational purposes (with appropriate acknowledgment). Any other use requires the written permission of the Academy of Marketing Science.

Acceptable Content

AMS Review will evaluate submissions based on contribution and conceptual rigor. Specifically, *AMS Review* seeks intrinsically interesting work, which contributes to the understanding of marketing or consumer behavior. *AMS Review* consists of three sections, *Theory*, *Measurement*, and the *Forum*. *AMS Review* articles should be broadly generalizable and meaningful to an international audience. Contributors should find *AMS Review* open to many different formats. However, *AMS Review* will not publish practitioner-oriented, empirical, modeling-based, or statistical methods articles. If you would like to submit empricially based work, please consider our other journal, the *Journal of the Academy of Marketing Science*.

AMS Review: Theory publishes full-length articles that develop new theory, significantly challenge/clarify current theory, carefully define important constructs, or review the literature. Literature review articles can simply summarize state-of-the-art knowledge, or extend our understanding about an area. Meta analyzes are also an acceptable form of literature review. *AMS Review: Theory* also contains shorter articles that make a substantive contribution to the advancement of theory within a more narrowly focused domain. These shorter articles might rigorously develop a single proposition, clarify a certain aspect of theory, or add a new concept to existing theory. Authors may also critique, extend, or otherwise comment on previous theoretical work in meaningful and constructive ways. Manuscripts that debate conceptual or theoretical premises would also be considered. *AMS Review: Theory* would **not** publish empirical studies or tests of theory.

AMS Review: Measurement publishes full-length articles that develop measures of theoretical constructs. Measurement articles are intended to be a natural extension of the theoretical development process for a construct. As such, all measurement articles must start with a clearly stated and appropriately justified definition of the construct being measured. *AMS Review: Measurement* would **not** consider articles on measurement theory, methodology, or practice including discussions of statistical methods for analyzing data, new measurement methods and techniques, or review articles about the state of the art in measurement methodology.

AMS Review: Forum contains brief commentaries on current research in marketing and consumer behavior. *AMS Review: Forum* commentaries would be timely and address general topics of current interest or research appearing in the academic marketing literature (commentary on articles more than two years old will not be considered). The original authors of a work commented upon would be invited to respond to critiques of their work. *AMS Review: Forum* commentaries should not exceed 1000 words in length with executive summaries no longer than 300 words. The decision to publish commentaries will be made by the editor without additional review.

The *AMS Review* will also not publish manuscripts that have be submitted to, accepted by, or published in other outlets (including published conference proceedings). *AMS Review* will accept papers that have been published on personal web pages, but not other electronic journals.

Instructions to Contributors

All manuscripts must be written in English and submitted as a word processing or HTML document attached to an e-mail message. Authors are encouraged to use hyperlinks in the document, and submit the manuscript in HTML format. The submission should be sent to **amsrev@vancouver.wsu.edu**. A cover letter should accompany all submissions. The cover letter should include the following information:

1. Which section of the journal the paper has been submitted to: Theory, Measurement, or Forum
2. A statement of preferences for the reviewers to be assigned to the paper. No more than one reviewer can be an ad hoc reviewer or not currently a member of the *AMS Review* editorial board.
3. A statement that the paper is not published or under review at other journals, proceedings, or other hard copy or electronic publications.
4. An alternative e-mail address if you will be unavailable at the primary e-mail address for an extended period.

AMS Review encourages authors to take full advantage of the Web format when preparing their papers. This would include material requiring special visual displays, figures, pictures, or photos in color, animated effects, material that includes sounds or music, and material that depends strongly on hyperlinks for its most advantageous presentation. Manuscript length should be reasonable for the contribution offered. **Please proofread the manuscript very carefully** (the editor may require the authors to pay for professional copy editing of accepted manuscripts).

The manuscript should include the following information:

1. Cover page showing title, each author's name, affiliation, complete address, telephone and **e-mail address**.
2. Information about the author(s) up to 100 words each, including terminal degree, written as a paragraph on the cover page.
3. Executive summary of between 500-1000 words.
4. A list of keywords which describe the contents of the manuscript.

The executive summary should be a comprehensive summary of the contents of the manuscript. Unlike a traditional journal abstract, the executive summary must be a stand-alone document. Authors should assume that the executive summary is the only thing a reader will see. Failure to provide an acceptable executive summary will delay publication of the manuscript. The format of the executive summary should mirror the manuscript and contain all the major section headings, and should be limited to 1000 words.

Review Policy - *AMS Review* uses a double-blind review process for all theory and measure development manuscripts. The editor makes all final decisions based on input from 2-3 reviewers. Reviews are normally completed within 45 days. Articles submitted to the Forum section will be reviewed by the editor with no input from reviewers.

Tables and Figures
Table and figure should be placed within text. Tables should be centered on the page and have proper labeling of axes, column headings, and other notations. The table number and title should be typed on separate lines. Tables should be free of cells or other dividing elements unless they are needed for clarity. Figures and artwork must be high quality JPEG or GIF files. The figure title should be typed on a separate line and should **not** be part of the image file.

References Reference citations within the text should consist of the author's last name and date of publication, without punctuation, enclosed within parentheses, and should be inserted before punctuation and/or at a logical break in the sentence. Bookmark links from the citation to a reference are preferred by not required. If several citations are needed, separate them with semicolons, and list alphabetically. Give the page number only if necessary. If the author's name has just been listed in the text, the date in parentheses is sufficient. If two or more works by an author have the same year, distinguish them by placing a, b, etc. after the year. Use et al. for works by four or more authors. For example:

> Jones' latest proposal (1979) has been questioned by some (Boston 1981; Brown 1990), but is generally accepted by others (Fritz 1979; Lang 1979; Rotwang 1984). Investigators (Cockburn et al. 1985; Hodges McCollum, and Hall 1981; Lee and King 1983) have found that...

References should be single-spaced and placed at the end of the manuscript. Works by a single author, list chronologically; two authors, alphabetically and then chronologically; three authors, the same; four or more, list chronologically. References should be in the following format:

Books:
Bagozzi, Richard P. 1980. *Causal Models in Marketing*. New York: Wiley.

Journals:
Singh, Jagdip. 1991. "Understanding the Structure of Consumers' Satisfaction Evaluations of Service Delivery." *Journal of the Academy of Marketing Science 19* (Summer): 223-244.

Three or More Authors:
Zeithaml, Valarie A., Leonard L. Berry, and A. Parasuraman. 1993. "The Nature and Determinants of Customer Experiences of Service." *Journal of the Academy of Marketing Science 21* (Winter): 1-12.

Article in a Book Edited by Another Author:
Levitt, Theodore. 1988. "The Globalization of Markets." In *Multinational Marketing Management*. Eds. Robert D. Buzzell and John A. Quelch. Reading, MA: Addison-Wesley, 186-205.

Unpublished Dissertations:
Paterson, Karen S. 1985. "The Effects of Bilingual Labels in Buyer Behavior." Dissertation. University of California at Irvine.

Mathematical Notation - Notations should be clearly explained within the text. Equations should be centered on the page. If equations are numbered, type the number in parentheses flush with the right margin. Unusual symbols and Greek letters should be identified. For equations that may be too wide to fit in a single column, indicate appropriate breaks.

Ethics Policy - It is expected that authors submitting papers to the *Academy of Marketing Science Review* will have conducted their work in an ethical manner. General guidelines for the conduct of ethical research are available at **http://www.apa.org/ethics/code.html** (see section 6). If evidence comes forward that a published articles violated ethical research guidelines it may be removed from the journal.

Guidelines for Theory Development Articles

The development of good theory must be logical, consistent and explicit. When preparing a theory development paper, make certain you do the following:

1. State and formally define all the constructs in the theory (boxes in a figure). Make certain you maintain consistency in the level of abstraction and unit of analysis. When using multidimensional constructs, be certain to clearly explain all the relevant dimensions.

2. State and justify all the relationships among the constructs (lines in a figure). Make certain to explicitly specify the nature of the relationships (causal, relational, sequential, etc.). Establish a clear link between your theoretical develop and previous research (including alternative perspectives).

3. Explicitly state the underlying assumptions of the theory (e.g., conceptual paradigm).

4. Explicitly state the boundaries of the theory. For whom and under what conditions is the theory appropriate/inappropriate.

5. Make certain the theory can ultimately be tested by empirical research.

6. Clearly state how the theoretical develop changes our understanding of theory and practice. In other words, spend considerable effort establishing the implications of the theoretical developments you suggest.

7. Explain how the proposed theory improves upon existing theory.

Guidelines for Literature Review Articles

There are two acceptable approaches to preparing literature review articles. Traditional literature reviews attempt to summarize and evaluate the literature. Traditional reviews usually present revisions to existing theory and suggest future research streams. In addition to the traditional literature review, *AMS Review* also accepts literature summaries. Literature summaries simply articulate the state-of-the-art for research in a domain of knowledge. Literature summaries are less evaluative than traditional literature reviews in that they do not attempt to expand or revise existing theory. The literature sections of most doctoral dissertations are a good example of a literature summary. You may want to consider reading one of the following books before you submit a literature review.

- Hart, Chris. 1998. *Doing a Literature Review : Releasing the Social Science Research Imagination*. London: Sage Publications.
- Fink, Arlene. 1998. *Conducting Research Literature Reviews : From Paper to the Internet*. Thousand Oaks: Sage Publications.

Whether you are preparing a literature review or summary, keep the following guidelines in mind.

1. Clearly define the domain of the literature review. Don't claim to be conducting a broad review of a topic when you only are covering a single perspective of that domain.

2. Avoid a study-by-study summary of findings. A good literature review should be an integrated discussion of key issues.

3. Organize the literature review around the key issues and clearly state what we know and don't know.

4. Be certain to include both the most recent work and early studies.

5. Attempt to explain inconsistencies in the literature.

6. Where appropriate, discuss how methodological perspectives and limitations explain the inconsistencies and alternative perspectives in the literature.

7. Be balanced in your presentation of alternative perspectives. If you are only interested in a single perspective, make this clear when defining the domain of the review.

8. In addition to the reference section, include a bibliography of readings in the domain.

Guidelines for Measurement Articles
Papers which develop measures, scales, or indicators for latent constructs should describe the procedures used in sufficient detail so that another researcher could duplicate the process. Authors should be certain to include the following:

1. Formally define the construct and state its domain. Provide theoretical justification for the existence of the construct. Failure to adequately define the construct will result in rejection.

2. Formally state and justify whether your measure will be a reflective or a causal (formative) measure of the construct (see Bollen, Kenneth and Richard Lennox. 1991. "Conventional Wisdom on Measurement: A Structural Equation Perspective." *Psychological Bulletin* 110 (2): 305-14 for an explanation of the difference between reflective and causal indicators). Reflective measures are preferred, and authors should have rigorous justification for the use of causal measures.

3. Explain in detail the procedures used to generate items (how were descriptors of the construct, scale anchors, and other phrasing and wording selected). The detail should be sufficiently clear that another researcher can duplicate the procedures.

4. List all the items for which you collected data and provide the covariance matrix for these items.

5. Confirmatory factor analysis should be used to assess the factor structure of the measure. Reliability of the measure should also be reported.

6. If you develop a reflective measure, make certain you test for unidimensionality (see Gerbing, David W. and James C. Anderson. 1988. "An Updated Paradigm for Scale Development Incorporating Unidimensionality and Its Assessment." *Journal of Marketing Research* 25 (May): 186-92). If you develop a formative measure, be clear how you recommend combining items.

7. Provide an assessment of the nomological validity of the scale. It is recommended you use a minimum of two additional constructs in your assessment.

8. Be certain to indicate under what conditions the scale is likely to be valid/invalid.

Guidelines for Forum Articles

Forum articles should be brief commentaries on current research in marketing and consumer behavior (they may or may not be related to a specific piece of research). They must be timely and address general topics of current interest or research appearing in the academic marketing literature. When writing a Forum article, keep the following in mind.

1. Clearly state the major issue and explain why this issue is important

2. Be certain to discuss the implications of your comments. How would our view of the discipline, conduct of research, or interpretation of research in an area/specific study change based on your comments.

3. Be constructive. AMS Review will not publish articles that simply list the faults of previous research.

4. Be concise. Remember, Forum articles are limited to 1000 words.

5. If you are commenting about a specific article, you are encouraged to include a response from the original author in your submission. If a response is not included, *AMS Review* will invite comments from the original author (which will delay publication of the article).

For 'Subject Keywords' see **http://www.amsreview.org/amsrev/submit.htm**

Academy of Marketing Studies Journal

ADDRESS FOR SUBMISSION:

Current Editor's Name/Check Web Page
Academy of Marketing Studies Journal
Submission Address/Check Web Page
Please address other questions to:
 Jim or JoAnn Carland at #'s below
USA
Phone: 828-293-9151
Fax: 828-293-9407
E-Mail: carland@wcu.edu
Web: www.alliedacademies.org
Address May Change:

PUBLICATION GUIDELINES:

Manuscript Length: 16-20
Copies Required: Three
Computer Submission: Yes
Format: MS Word
Fees to Review: 0.00 US$

Manuscript Style:
 American Psychological Association

CIRCULATION DATA:

Reader: Academics
Frequency of Issue: 2 Times/Year
Copies per Issue: Less than 1,000
Sponsor/Publisher: Allied Academies
Subscribe Price: 50.00 US$

REVIEW INFORMATION:

Type of Review: Blind Review
No. of External Reviewers: 2
No. of In House Reviewers: 2
Acceptance Rate: 21-30%
Time to Review: 4 - 6 Months
Reviewers Comments: Yes
Invited Articles: 0-5%
Fees to Publish: 0.00 US$ If member
 50.00 US$ Academy Membership

MANUSCRIPT TOPICS:
Advertising & Promotion Management; Business Law, Public Responsibility & Ethics; Direct Marketing; Marketing Research; Marketing Theory & Applications; Sales/Selling

MANUSCRIPT GUIDELINES/COMMENTS:

Manuscript Topics: Theoretical, Empirical, and Applied or Practical Papers and Cases in Promotion, General Marketing, Consumer Behavior, Marketing Research and Marketing Education.

Comments: All authors of published manuscripts must be members of The Academy. The membership fee is $50.

EDITORIAL POLICY GUIDELINES FOR THEORETICAL AND EMPIRICAL MANUSCRIPTS

The Allied Academies affiliates which handle theoretical and empirical manuscripts include the *Academy of Entrepreneurship*, the *Academy of Accounting and Financial Studies*, the *Academy of Marketing Studies*, the *Academy of Strategic and Organizational Leadership*, the

Academy of Managerial Communications, the *Academy of Educational Leadership*, the *Academy of Information and Management Sciences*, and, the *Academy for Studies in Business Law*. These editorial guidelines reflect the Academies' policy with regard to reviewing theoretical and empirical manuscripts for publication and presentation in each of these affiliates.

The primary criterion upon which manuscripts are judged is whether the research advances the discipline. The specific guidelines followed by referees show the areas of evaluation to which each manuscript is subjected. Key points include currency, interest, and relevancy.

Theoretical manuscripts are particularly vulnerable to problems in literature review. In order for theoretical research to advance a discipline, it must address the literature which exists in the discipline to support conclusions or models which extend knowledge and understanding. Consequently, referees for theoretical manuscripts pay particular attention to completeness of literature review and appropriateness of conclusions drawn from that review.

Empirical manuscripts are particularly vulnerable to methodological problems. In order to advance the literature, empirical manuscripts must employ appropriate and effective sampling and statistical analysis techniques. However, empirical papers must also incorporate thorough literature reviews in order to advance the literature. Referees will pay close attention to the conclusions which are drawn from statistical analyses and their consistency with the literature.

We ask referees to be as specific as possible in indicating what must be done to make a manuscript acceptable for journal publication. This embodies a primary objective of the Academy: to assist authors in the research process.

Our Editorial Policy is one which is supportive, rather than critical. We encourage all authors who are not successful in a first attempt to rewrite the manuscript in accordance with the suggestions of the referees. We will be pleased to referee future versions and rewrites of manuscripts and work with authors in achieving their research goals.

EDITORIAL POLICY GUIDELINES FOR EDUCATIONAL AND PEDAGOGIC MANUSCRIPTS

The Allied Academies affiliates which handle educational and pedagogic manuscripts include the *Academy of Entrepreneurship*, the *Academy of Accounting and Financial Studies*, the *Academy of Marketing Studies*, the *Academy of Strategic and Organizational Leadership*, the *Academy of Managerial Communications*, the *Academy of Educational Leadership*, the *Academy of Information and Management Sciences*, and, the *Academy for Studies in Business Law*. These editorial guidelines reflect the Academies' policy with regard to reviewing educational and pedagogic manuscripts for publication and presentation in each of these affiliates.

The primary criterion upon which manuscripts are judged is whether the research advances the teaching profession. The specific guidelines followed by referees show the areas of evaluation to which each manuscript is subjected. Key points include currency, interest, relevancy and usefulness to educators.

In order for educational or pedagogic manuscripts to be useful to educators, they must address appropriate literature to support conclusions, teaching methodologies or pedagogies. Consequently, referees pay particular attention to completeness of literature review and appropriateness of conclusions drawn from that review.

Pedagogies or teaching methodologies must be well described with sound foundations in order to be useful to educators. Referees will pay particular attention to such issues in judging manuscripts.

In every case, educational or pedagogic manuscripts must embody well developed and well documented ideas in order to be useful to educators. Referees will pay close attention to the ideas presented in the manuscript and how well they are presented and supported.

We ask referees to be as specific as possible in indicating what must be done to make a manuscript acceptable for journal publication. This embodies a primary objective of the Academy: to assist authors in the research process.

Our Editorial Policy is one which is supportive, rather than critical. We encourage all authors who are not successful in a first attempt to rewrite the manuscript in accordance with the suggestions of the referees. We will be pleased to referee future versions and rewrites of manuscripts and work with authors in achieving their research goals.

Advances in International Marketing

ADDRESS FOR SUBMISSION:

S. Tamer Cavusgil, Director
Advances in International Marketing
Michigan State University
International Business Center
7 Eppley Center
East Lansing, MI 48824-1121
USA
Phone: 517-353-4336
Fax: 517-432-1009
E-Mail: fitzge12@pilot.msu.edu
Web: www.jaipress.com
Address May Change:

PUBLICATION GUIDELINES:

Manuscript Length: 20+
Copies Required: Three
Computer Submission: Yes
Format: MS Word or WordPerfect
Fees to Review: 0.00 US$

Manuscript Style:
, Journal of Marketing style

CIRCULATION DATA:

Reader: Business Persons
Frequency of Issue: Yearly
Copies per Issue: Less than 1,000
Sponsor/Publisher: JAI Press, Inc.
Subscribe Price: 82.50 US$
   53.00 Pounds
   45.00 US$

REVIEW INFORMATION:

Type of Review: Blind Review
No. of External Reviewers: 2
No. of In House Reviewers: 0
Acceptance Rate: 11-20%
Time to Review: 1 - 2 Months
Reviewers Comments: Yes
Invited Articles: No Reply
Fees to Publish: 0.00 US$

MANUSCRIPT TOPICS:
Global Business; Marketing Research; Marketing Theory & Applications; Operations Research/Statistics; Organizational Behavior & Theory; Organizational Development; Small Business Entrepreneurship; Strategic Management Policy

MANUSCRIPT GUIDELINES/COMMENTS:

About the Series
The series is a collection of original, high-quality essays in international marketing. Both theoretical/conceptual and empirical contributions are included. Written by scholars from all over the world, these essays address various aspects of export and multinational marketing. While some authors focus on managerial issues in international marketing, others take a public policy or comparative perspective. Similarly, while some authors may confine their analyses to well-established concepts or methodologies in international marketing, others have the opportunity to incorporate new and innovative perspectives.

1. Manuscripts published in the series are lengthy articles which are not suitable for journal publication. Both empirical as well as conceptual/theoretical contributions are solicited.

Previously published material is not acceptable. Submissions from outside the U.S. are especially desirable:

- Managerial issues in international marketing such as positioning, product, innovation, pricing, channel management, and research
- Development of performance measures in international marketing
- Examination of buyer-seller interactions in international marketing
- Collective treatment of company involvement strategies in international marketing
- Marketing selection and expansion strategies
- International marketing activities of trading firms and channel members
- Public policy issues in international marketing
- Comparative/cross cultural studies
- State-of-the-art reviews

2. **Submissions** can be made at any time. Please submit three (3) copies of your manuscript, typed according to the *Journal of Marketing* style guidelines, to our office.

3. If desired, authors may submit a short **abstract** of their paper to the Editor for preliminary review. For further information contact him at 517-353-4336.

4. *Advances In International Marketing* publishes both invited and competitive papers. Submissions are blind-reviewed by a distinguished panel of scholars. Authors of accepted papers may be asked to revise their papers prior to publication. Upon acceptance, each author will be asked to transfer copyright to JAI Press, Inc. Authors are provided with a complimentary copy of the volume in which their work appears and 25 offprints of their article. The senior authors will receive their copy-edited manuscript and a set of galleys for correction prior to publication.

5. **General**: A manuscript will be accepted only on the understanding that it is an original contribution which has not been published previously and is not under consideration for publication elsewhere. Submit four copies of the manuscript to either of the Editors.

Articles submitted to *Advances In International Marketing* are generally of between 4000 and 6000 words in length, excluding figures, tables and references, but longer or shorter articles will be considered. The entire manuscript, including references, should be typed double-spaced with generous margins, complete in all respects. All pages must be numbered consecutively.

The cover page should be a title page stating: title, author(s), affiliations(s), and mailing addresses. The second page of the manuscript should repeat the title and contain an abstract of approximately 100 words.

6. **Style**: A clear and concise style will enhance any paper. Where research data is important to the discussion they should be in a form intelligible to the non-specialist reader. Footnotes should be avoided, and acknowledgements or grant source should be given at the end of the text.

7. **Abbreviations**: If abbreviations are used, the terms should be written out in full when first used, the abbreviations then being given in parentheses. Abbreviations in capitals, without full stops, are preferred.

8. **Tables**: Tables should be numbered consecutively, given adequate titles or headings, typed on separate sheets of paper and attached to the manuscript. The tables must be referred to in text. They should supplement rather than duplicate text data.

9. **Figures**: High quality of reproduction can be obtained only from original artwork or photographs. Do not send negatives or photocopies. Number the figures separately, with the number and author's name in pencil on the back of each figure. Captions should be typed on a separate sheet. Figures must be cited in text as Figure 1, Figure 2, etc.

10. **Permission To Reproduce**: If figures are borrowed from published sources written permissions must be obtained from the copyright holder and a credit line acknowledging the source added to the caption. Such permission must also be obtained and acknowledged for quotations totaling more than 250 words and for tables borrowed verbatim from published sources. Permission letters should accompany the manuscript, but it you have been unable to obtain them, please point this out.
With shorter quotations a bibliographic credit is sufficient.

11. **Reference Citations Within The Text**: Citations in the text should be the author's last name and year in parentheses without punctuation, e.g. (Cateora 1984). If practical, the citation should stand by a punctuation mark. Otherwise, insert it in a logical sentence break. If you use the author's name within the sentence, there is no need to repeat the name in the citation; just use the year of publication in parentheses.

12. **Reference List Style**: References are to be listed alphabetically; surname first, followed by publication date in parentheses. The reference list should be typed double-spaced with a hanging indent, on a separate page.

Reference for books
  Majaro, Simon (1982), International Marketing: A Strategic Approach to World Markets, Revised Edition, London: George Allen & Unwin.

Single and multiple author references for periodicals
  Johansson, Johny K. and Ikujiro Nonako (1983), "Japanese Export Marketing: Structures, Strategies, Counter-strategies", International Marketing Review, 1.2 (Winter), 12-15.

Single and multiple author reference for an article in a book edited by another author
Cavusgil, S. Tamer and John R. Nevin (1981). "State-of-the-Art in International Marketing: An Assessment", in Review of Marketing 1981,

Ben M. Enis and Kenneth J. Roering, eds., Chicago: American Marketing Association, 195-216.

Unpublished works are acceptable only if "in press". References in languages other than English may be published as submitted.

13. **Offprints**: A total of 25 offprints of each paper will be supplied to author(s) free of charge. Additional copies may be purchased at the proof stage on request to the publisher.

14. **Copyright**: Authors submitting a manuscript do so on the understanding that if it is accepted for publication copyright will be assigned to the publisher. The publisher will not put any limitation on the personal freedom of the author to use material contained in the paper in other works which may be published.

Agribusiness: An International Journal

ADDRESS FOR SUBMISSION:

Ronald W. Cotterill, Director
Agribusiness: An International Journal
Food Marketing Policy Center
Agricultural and Resource Economics
U-21
1376 Storrs Road
Storrs, CT 06269-4021
USA
Phone: 860-486-2742
Fax: 860-486-2461
E-Mail: fmpc@canr.cag.uconn.edu
Web: www.interscience.wiley.com
Address May Change:

PUBLICATION GUIDELINES:

Manuscript Length: 16-20
Copies Required: Five paper copies
Computer Submission: Yes Prefer
 Email, 1 copy
Format: Prefer MsWord 6.0, others OK
Fees to Review: 0.00 US$

Manuscript Style:
 See Manuscript Guidelines

CIRCULATION DATA:

Reader: Academics, Industry
Frequency of Issue: Bi-Monthly
Copies per Issue: 1,001 - 2,000
Sponsor/Publisher: John Wiley & Sons
Subscribe Price: 185.00 US$ Individual
 209.00 US$ Individual Outside N.
 Amer.

REVIEW INFORMATION:

Type of Review: Blind Review
No. of External Reviewers: 2
No. of In House Reviewers: 1
Acceptance Rate: 21-30%
Time to Review: 2 - 3 Months
Reviewers Comments: Yes
Invited Articles: 0-5%
Fees to Publish: 0.00 US$

MANUSCRIPT TOPICS:
Advertising & Promotion Management; Agribusiness; Marketing Theory & Applications; Production/Operations; Public Administration; Small Business Entrepreneurship; Strategic Management Policy; Transportation/Physical Distribution

MANUSCRIPT GUIDELINES/COMMENTS:

Aims and Scope
Agribusiness: An International Journal seeks to provide a single forum for the development of specialized research that improves our understanding of how food systems work, how they are evolving, and how public and/or private actions affect the performance of the global agro-industrial complex. Agribusiness covers input industries for agricultural production, post-farmgate industries including the commodity processing, food manufacturing, and food distribution industries, and third party firms that facilitate agribusiness operations, including bankers, brokers, advertising agencies, and market information firms. The journal focuses on the application of economic analysis to the organization and performance of firms and markets in industrial food systems. International, cross-country comparative, and within-country

studies are welcome. The research scope includes applied methods, applied theory, quantitative, and case studies. Subject matter areas include supply and demand analysis, industrial organization analysis, price and trade analysis, marketing studies, and public policy analysis. The journal's Form section will publish position papers, policy studies, and legal economic analyses that facilitate discussion and understanding of agribusiness issues.

Submission Instructions
Submissions by e-mail are preferred; however, surface, air, or expressmail are acceptable. Each submission must indicate the name, address, telephone number, facsimile number, and e-mail address of the author to whom all correspondence is to be addressed. An affiliation must be supplied for each author. If the manuscript has been presented, published, or submitted for publication elsewhere, please inform the Editor-in-Chief. Our primary objective is to publish technical material not otherwise available, but we do occasionally publish papers of unusual merit that have appeared or that will appear elsewhere when there is full justification for this. Prospective authors should submit one copy of the complete manuscript via e-mail, or five paper copies by regular mail to: Ronald W. Cotterill, Director, Food Marketing Policy Center, Agricultural and Resource Economics, U-21, 1376 Storrs Road, Storrs, CT 06269-4021; E-mail: fmpc@canr.cag.uconn.edu; Telephone: 860-486-2742; Fax: 860-486-2461.

Format
Manuscripts should contain: Title; names and complete affiliations of authors, including phone number, facsimile number, and e-mail address. Please provide an informative 150-word abstract at the beginning of your manuscript, and identify no more than five keywords. The abstract should provide an overview of your paper and not a statement of conclusions only. Since abstracts of accepted papers are included in the EconLit citation system, please classify your papers in at least one, and no more than three, EconLit subject matter areas. The EconLit classification of subject matter areas is available at http://www.econlit.org/elsubl.htm. Put the EconLit alphanumeric subject codes at the end of your abstract. If applicable, please provide contract grant sponsor(s); contract grant number(s). Regular manuscripts should be no longer than 30 typed, double-spaced pages, plus references. Notes should be no longer than 10 typed, double-spaced pages, including references. Authors should write succinctly and should note that a significant element of the review process will be its length relative to its content and the clarity of writing. Manuscripts should be subdivided into sections and subsections, numbered with Arabic numerals as in 1.1 or 2.3, to aid readability. For references, tables, list of figure captions, and figure specifications, please see below. Authors of accepted papers will be asked to supply a technical biography. The biography should be in the form used for biographies in professional journals. It should contain information concerning: name, degrees and dates earned, current position, address (including e-mail and phone number), and current research interests.

Instructions for Typists
Manuscripts must be typed double-spaced on a single side only on standard 8½ × 11-inch (21.5 × 28-cm) white paper with one-inch margins. Material intended for footnotes should be inserted in the text as parenthetical material whenever possible. All mathematical symbols, equations, formulas, Greek and/or unusual symbols should be typed. If they must be handwritten, please write clearly and leave ample space above and below for printer's marks. When handwritten symbols are necessary, please provide a separate sheet listing and defining

such symbols. This list will help to distinguish between characters that may otherwise be confused (e.g., b, B, β). Please underscore with a wavy line all vector quantities or use boldface type if available. Please label vector quantities as such the first time they occur in the manuscript. If italic type is unavailable to the typist, please underscore with a straight line anything to be printed in italic type. Please note that the use of italics for emphasis should be used with extreme discretion.

References
Please compile references on a separate sheet at the end of the main body of the text. References to published literature should be quoted in the text by giving author's name, and year of publication. The format for multiple references is either Smith (1997) and Jones and Black (1996) or (Smith, 1997; Jones & Black, 1996). References should be listed alphabetically in the last section of the paper titled "References." Journal references must be complete and include authors' surnames and initials, year of publication in parentheses, title of the paper, name of the journal, volume, pages on which the article appears. Book references must include year of publication, city of publication, publisher. Anthologies and collections must include names of editors and pages on which the reference appears. Books in a series must include series title and number/volume if applicable. Because of the large quantity of conference proceedings available, it is critical to give as much information as possible when citing references from proceedings. Please include the complete title of the meeting, symposium, etc. (*do not abbreviate titles*), and the city and dates of the meeting. If a proceeding has been published, please provide the editors' names, publisher, city, and year of publication, and pages on which the article appears. If a proceeding has *not* been published, please indicate so. Examples follow:

Book:
Senauer, B., Asp, E., & Kinsey, J. (1991). Food trends and the changing consumer. St. Paul, MN: Eagan Press.
Journal:
McCutcheon, M., & Goddard, E.W. (1992). Optimal producer and social payoff from generic advertising--the case of the Canadian supply managed egg sector. Canadian Journal of Agricultural Economics, 4, 141-146.
Chapter in a book:
Ray, S.K. (1991). Instability in Indian agriculture revisited. In P. Narain, O.P. Kathuria, V.K. Sharma, & Prajneshu (Eds.), Recent advances in agricultural statistics research (pp. 11-22), New Delhi: Wiley Eastern Ltd.

Tables
Tables should not be incorporated into the text, but grouped separately after the references. All tables should be numbered consecutively with Arabic numerals and should include an explanatory heading.

Figures
Figures must be numbered consecutively with Arabic numerals. Figures must not be integrated into the text, but must accompany it separately. Please supply a list of figure captions on a separate sheet.

Line Drawings. Figures should be professionally prepared and submitted in a form suitable for reproduction (camera-ready copy). Computer-generated graphs are acceptable only if they have been printed with a high-quality laser printer. Authors are cautioned to provide lettering of graphs and figure labels that are large, clear, and "open" so that letters and numbers do not become illegible when reduced. Likewise, authors are cautioned that very thin lines and other fine details in figures may not successfully reproduce. Original figures should be drawn with these precautions in mind.

Halftones. High-quality photographs are necessary for clear halftone reproduction.

Color Art. High-quality photographs or slides are necessary for clear and accurate reproduction of color figures. Only those illustrations that absolutely must have color to successfully convey the intended information will be considered for color reproduction. Authors willing to totally meet the expense of color art reproduction by themselves or through their institution are welcome to make inquiries with the Editor-in-Chief or the Production Editor.

Electronic Submissions
Authors are to submit the final, accepted version of their manuscript on disk to the Editor-in-Chief. Three hard copies of the manuscript should accompany the disk.

Copyright Information
No article can be published unless accompanied by a signed publication agreement, which serves as a transfer of copyright from author to publisher. A publication agreement may be obtained from the editor or the publisher. A copy of the publication agreement appears in most issues of the journal. Only original papers will be accepted and copyright in published papers will be vested in the publisher. It is the author's responsibility to obtain written permission to reproduce material that has appeared in another publication. A form for this purpose is sent with the manuscript acceptance letter.

Reprints
Reprints can be ordered and purchased by filling out the form provided with the page proofs. Neither the manuscript nor its figures will be returned following publication unless a request for a return is made when the manuscript is originally submitted.

Correspondence
All other correspondence should be addressed to the Publisher, Professional/Trade Group, John Wiley & Sons, Inc., 605 Third Avenue, New York, NY 10158.

DISK SUBMISSION INSTRUCTIONS
Please return your final, revised manuscript on disk as well as hard copy. The hard copy must match the disk.
The Journal strongly encourages authors to deliver the final, revised version of their accepted manuscripts (text, tables, and, if possible, illustrations) on disk. Given the near-universal use of computer word-processing for manuscript preparation, we anticipate that providing a disk will be convenient for you, and it carries the added advantages of maintaining the integrity of

your keystrokes and expediting typesetting. Please return the disk submission slip below with your manuscript and labeled disk(s).

Guidelines for Electronic Submission
Text
Storage medium. 3-1/2" high-density disk in IBM MS-DOS, Windows, or Macintosh format.

Software and format. Microsoft Word 6.0 is preferred, although manuscripts prepared with any other microcomputer word processor are acceptable. Refrain from complex formatting; the Publisher will style your manuscript according to the Journal design specifications. Do not use desktop publishing software such as Adobe PageMaker or Quark XPress. If you prepared your manuscript with one of these programs, export the text to a word processing format. Please make sure your word processing program's "fast save" feature is turned off. Please do not deliver files that contain hidden text: for example, do not use your word processor's automated features to create footnotes or reference lists.

File names. Submit the text and tables of each manuscript as a single file. Name each file with your last name (up to eight letters). Text files should be given the three-letter extension that identifies the file format. Macintosh users should maintain the MS-DOS "eight dot three" file-naming convention.
Labels. Label all disks with your name, the file name, and the word processing program and version used.

Illustrations
All print reproduction requires files for full color images to be in a CMYK color space. If possible, ICC or ColorSync profiles of your output device should accompany all digital image submissions.

Storage medium. Submit as separate files from text files, on separate disks or cartridges. If feasible, full color files should be submitted on separate disks from other image files. 3-1/2" high-density disks, CD, Iomega Zip, and 5 1/4" 44- or 88-MB SyQuest cartridges can be submitted. At authors' request, cartridges and disks will be returned after publication.

Software and format. All illustration files should be in TIFF or EPS (with preview) formats. Do not submit native application formats.

Resolution. Journal quality reproduction will require greyscale and color files at resolutions yielding approximately 300 ppi. Bitmapped line art should be submitted at resolutions yielding 600-1200 ppi. These resolutions refer to the output size of the file; if you anticipate that your images will be enlarged or reduced, resolutions should be adjusted accordingly.

File names. Illustration files should be given the 2- or 3-letter extension that identifies the file format used (i.e., .tif, .eps).
Labels. Label all disks and cartridges with your name, the file names, formats, and compression schemes (if any) used. Hard copy output must accompany all files.

Air Force Journal of Logistics

ADDRESS FOR SUBMISSION:

James C. Rainey, Lt. Col., Editor
Air Force Journal of Logistics
Waxwell AFB
510 Ward Street
Gunter Annex, AL 36114-3236
USA
Phone: 334-416-4088/4087
Fax: 334/416-5890
E-Mail: editor@aflma.gunter.af.mil
Web:
Address May Change:

PUBLICATION GUIDELINES:

Manuscript Length: 11-15
Copies Required: Three
Computer Submission: Yes
Format: MS Word/WdPerfect
Fees to Review: 0.00 US$

Manuscript Style:
 , Gregg Manual

CIRCULATION DATA:

Reader: Academics, Air Force, Military Logistics
Frequency of Issue: Quarterly
Copies per Issue: 5,001 - 10,000
Sponsor/Publisher: United States Air Force
Subscribe Price: 8.50 US$

REVIEW INFORMATION:

Type of Review: Blind Review
No. of External Reviewers: 3
No. of In House Reviewers: 2
Acceptance Rate: 40%
Time to Review: 1 - 2 Months
Reviewers Comments: No
Invited Articles: 6-10%
Fees to Publish: 0.00 US$

MANUSCRIPT TOPICS:
Military History; Military Logistics; Organizational Behavior & Theory; Organizational Development; Services; Strategic Management Policy; Technology/Innovation; Transportation/Physical Distribution

MANUSCRIPT GUIDELINES/COMMENTS:

American Business Perspectives (NBDC Report)

ADDRESS FOR SUBMISSION:

Mary L. Graff, Editor
American Business Perspectives (NBDC Report)
University of Nebraska at Omaha
Nebraska Business Development Center
1313 Farnam-on-the-Mall, Suite 132
Omaha, NE 68182-0248
USA
Phone: 402-595-2381
Fax: 402-595-2385
E-Mail: mary@nbdcoffice.unomaha.edu
Web:
Address May Change:

PUBLICATION GUIDELINES:

Manuscript Length: 11-15
Copies Required: One
Computer Submission: Yes
Format: WdPer 5.1, 6.0, MsWord 6.0, ASCII
Fees to Review: 0.00 US$

Manuscript Style:
  Chicago Manual of Style

CIRCULATION DATA:

Reader: Business Persons, Academics
Frequency of Issue: Monthly
Copies per Issue: 4,001 - 5,000
Sponsor/Publisher: Nebraska Business Development Center
Subscribe Price: 12.00 US$
  12.00 US$ NE Current Subscriber
  12.00 US$ New NE Subscriber

REVIEW INFORMATION:

Type of Review: Editorial Review
No. of External Reviewers: No Reply
No. of In House Reviewers: 1
Acceptance Rate: 11-20%
Time to Review: 1 Month or Less
Reviewers Comments: No
Invited Articles: 6-10%
Fees to Publish: 0.00 US$

MANUSCRIPT TOPICS:

Advertising & Promotion Management; Business Information Systems (MIS); Business Law, Public Responsibility & Ethics; Direct Marketing; Global Business; Labor Relations & Human Resource Mgt.; Marketing Research; Marketing Theory & Applications; Production/Operations; Sales/Selling; Small Business Entrepreneurship; Strategic Management Policy; Technology/Innovation

MANUSCRIPT GUIDELINES/COMMENTS:

American Business Perspectives is a journal bringing the latest ideas and trends in management education to executive managers in privately held, mid-sized companies. Every month, *American Business Perspectives* brings tried and tested practical know-how to business owners and executive managers who must continually and responsibly implement new ideas in the front lines of their growing companies. *American Business Perspectives* is published by the Nebraska Business Development Center, University of Nebraska at Omaha.

Articles cover a wide gamut of disciplines, including: accounting, economics, finance, insurance, human resources management, information technology, international trade, law, operations managements and marketing. Through the new perspectives presented in each of these disciplines, authors share their research with company managers who can apply it at the front lines of American business operations, thus helping to improve operating efficiencies and bottom-line profits.

American Business Perspectives is a new journal; however, it is a follow-on publication that had a solid predecessor, the *NBDC Report*.

Predecessor Publication
Begun in 1977, the *NBDC Report*, was the first publication developed in the U.S. among the eight, pilot-program small business development centers, that attempted to provide business owners and managers with applied research. Over the years, the *NBDC Report* won the respect of small business owners and managers, small business development center directors and their counselors, and faculty who teach small business courses and direct small business programs in colleges and universities across America.

Target Audience
American Business Perspectives, the *NBDC Report's* successor, has a different target audience. The audience is no longer focused solely on owners and managers in small companies, but is focused on executive managers in mid-sized, privately held companies with 100 to 500 employees. The managers in these companies are executives who are responsible for the long-term, as well as the day-to-day operations of the businesses that employ them. The objective of *American Business Perspectives* is to provide the leaders of these companies with practical, thought-provoking concepts that they can implement in daily business operations to help their companies become more profitable.

Each issue of *American Business Perspectives* is eight pages and contains two or three articles. Number of External Reviewers is given upon request.

Applying Research to Business
American Business Perspectives will give executive managers of businesses across America a timely, relevant article each month based upon the applied research of university faculty and other business experts. *American Business Perspectives* will continue bringing the tradition of *NBDC Report's* practical, "how to" focus to mid-sized company executives to help them stay abreast of cutting-edge, interdisciplinary applied research.

Selection and Content of Articles
The editor selects articles for publication in *American Business Perspectives*.

Manuscripts submitted for publication in *American Business Perspectives* may be from any business discipline, but they must have an applied focus and must be relevant to **any type of business in any geographical area**. Manuscripts that will not be considered are those on community affairs and community development. Topics must address business practices as they pertain to industry or business. Should there be any question as to whether an article meets the topic criteria, the editor will decide the issue.

The editor will review submitted manuscripts and respond within 30 days to the author(s) as to whether the manuscript will be published. The time frame for publication may be determined at a later date.

Authors are encouraged to contact the editor prior to submitting or writing for *American Business Perspectives*. The editor will attempt to guide the author in development of topics.

Writing Style

There is no single recommended writing style for *American Business Perspectives*, since the degree of formality or informality in the article's tone will depend upon 1) the author, 2) the discipline, and 3) the targeted audience. Generally, we recommend that the author use a middle-of-the-road approach, being careful not to use vocabulary filled with technical jargon or vocabulary so specific to a discipline that only those individuals knowledgeable in that discipline understand it. Articles will be edited to achieve the tone the editor thinks is consistent with the discipline that is the manuscript's primary focus.

A few suggestions include:
1) Use vocabulary that can be understood by a high school graduate.
2) Write short sentences.
3) Avoid using mathematical equations and complex formulas.
4) Don't "talk down" to the reader; assume the reader has some knowledge of business practices.
5) Other suggestions:
   a) Use the active voice in your selection of verbs.
   b) Use strong action verbs.
   c) Don't use cliches or jargon. and avoid abbreviations. If you must use abbreviations throughout the text, be sure to define them when they appear in the text.
   d) Be enthusiastic in your writing; enthusiastic writing is interesting, and easily read and understood.

Copyright Ownership

Authors are asked to assign ownership of the copyright on their manuscripts to the Nebraska Business Development Center. The Nebraska Business Development Center reserves the right to reprint articles in part or in their entirety, in any of its affiliated publications and to grant permission to other entities and persons to reprint articles in other publications. The Nebraska Business Development Center may charge a fee, which it retains, for granting of these rights. Authors will be provided with five copies of any Nebraska Business Development Center publications in which their articles are reprinted.

Subscriber Audience

Our readers include executives in mid-sized companies, small business owners and managers, small business development center directors, faculty at colleges and universities, and other individuals from both the government and private sectors.

Accordingly, we have created the attached guidelines for authors to follow in writing their articles.

Submission Guidelines For Authors

Manuscripts submitted for possible publication in *American Business Perspectives* should conform to the following specifications.

1. A title page should accompany each manuscript. The title page should contain the following information:
   Title of Article
   Authors' Names
   Primary Author's Location (Name of Institution)
   Street Address or P.O. Box
   City, State and Zip Code
   Daytime Telephone Number & FAX
   E-Mail Address (if available)

2. Authors need submit only one copy of the manuscript.

3. Submit a succinct one paragraph abstract of the manuscript.

4. Manuscripts must be typewritten and double-spaced. In additon, the authors(s) may elect to include with the written manuscript, a 5 1/4" or 3 1/2" diskette containing the manuscript in a WordPerfect (Version 5.1 or higher), Word (Versions 2.0 or higher), or in an ASCII format. Manuscripts will not be returned to authors, but diskettes will be retuned at the request of the author. Published papers become the property of the Nebraska Business Development Center.

5. Margins on manuscripts should be a minimum one inch, left, right, top and bottom.

6. Manuscripts should be no more than 3,000 words, which is approximately 14 double-spaced, typewritten pages, using a 10 pitch pica typeface, such as courier. Because there are many different type fonts used today, we suggest authors use their software's word count as a guide, since some type fonts compress significantly more words into the same number of typewritten pages.

7. Tables, charts, graphs and figures may accompany articles. Each table, chart or graph will count as one, double-spaced page of the manuscript. Therefore, authors should reduce the typewritten manuscript by one page for each table, chart, graph or figure included with the manuscript.

8. Pages should be numbered.

9. Endnotes are preferred over footnotes. The style used for endnote citations should be in the business format. DO NOT abbreviate authors' names. Spell out the authors' full (first and last) names. Include the abbreviation "Vol." for "Volume" and No. for "Number." Sample endnotes are listed for a book and a periodical citation.

   Weston, J. Fred and Eugene F. Brigham, Essentials of Managerial Finance, Chicago, Illinois: The Dryden Press, 1993.

Franklin, Geralyn McClure, A. B. Gresham and Gwen Fontenot, "Aids in the Workplace: Current Practices and Critical Issues," Journal of Small Business Management, Vol. 30, No. 2, 1992, pp. 61-73.

10. At the end of each article, include a brief biographical sketch about each author. The biographical information should be two or three lines, maximum, and should indicate the institution where the author currently is teaching or employed.

11. If you would like to ask the editor about a topic that you would consider developing into a future manuscript, please call the editor at (402) 595-2381.

12. All correspondence should be addressed to the Editor.

American Demographics

ADDRESS FOR SUBMISSION:

Editor
American Demographics
7th Floor North
470 Park Avenue South
New York, NY 10016
USA
Phone:
Fax:
E-Mail: editors@demographics.com
Web: www.demographics.com
Address May Change:

PUBLICATION GUIDELINES:

Manuscript Length: Varies
Copies Required: One
Computer Submission: Yes
Format: Mac/MS Word
Fees to Review: 0.00 US$

Manuscript Style:
    Chicago Manual of Style

CIRCULATION DATA:

Reader: Business Persons
Frequency of Issue: Monthly
Copies per Issue: More than 25,000
Sponsor/Publisher: Intertech/Primedia
    Publishing
Subscribe Price: 69.00 US$ Annual
    US$

REVIEW INFORMATION:

Type of Review: N/A
No. of External Reviewers: 0
No. of In House Reviewers: 0
Acceptance Rate: 6-10%
Time to Review: 1 - 2 Months
Reviewers Comments: No
Invited Articles: 31-50%
Fees to Publish: 0.75 US$ -$1.00/word

MANUSCRIPT TOPICS:
Advertising & Promotion Management; Demographic & Attitudinal Research/Trends; Direct Marketing; Global Business; Marketing Research

MANUSCRIPT GUIDELINES/COMMENTS:

American Demographics is the magazine of consumer markets. The readers of *American Demographics* are marketers, advertisers, strategic planners, and other business people who need information about American consumers.

The articles in *American Demographics* explore the four key elements of a consumer market: its size, its needs and wants, its ability to pay, and how it can be reached. Most articles include specific examples of how companies market to consumers.

If you are interested in submitting an article to *American Demographics*, first query the editor with a story idea and an outline. Include previously published writing samples with your query.

If you get the go-ahead on your query, you should submit an article typed, double-spaced in hard copy or in an email attachment. Most articles are accompanied by tables or graphs. You should submit any tables or graphs that accompany your article in draft form--our art department will create the finished tables and graphs. Most features are also accompanied by photographs chosen by the editors--please do not send photographs with your manuscript. When you submit an article, you should also send copies of your back-up material--tables from reports that you cite in the article; copies of notes you took while talking to a source, etc. These will be used by our factchecker to ensure the accuracy of everything that is published in *American Demographics*.

Thank you for your interest in *American Demographics*.

American International College Journal of Business

ADDRESS FOR SUBMISSION:

Ira Smolowitz, Editor
American International College Journal of Business
American International College
Bureau of Business Research and Program Development
1000 State Street
Springfield, MA 01109-3189
USA
Phone: 413-747-6369
Fax: 413-747-6243
E-Mail: ismolowi@acad.aic.edu
Web:
Address May Change:

PUBLICATION GUIDELINES:

Manuscript Length: 30+
Copies Required: One
Computer Submission: Yes
Format: Disk (Word 97)
Fees to Review: 0.00 US$

Manuscript Style:
American Psychological Association

CIRCULATION DATA:

Reader: Business Persons, Academics
Frequency of Issue: Yearly
Copies per Issue: Less than 1,000
Sponsor/Publisher: American International College
Subscribe Price: 15.00 US$ 2 issues
25.00 US$ 4 issues

REVIEW INFORMATION:

Type of Review: Editorial Review
No. of External Reviewers: 0
No. of In House Reviewers: 3
Acceptance Rate: 90%
Time to Review: 4 - 6 Months
Reviewers Comments: No
Invited Articles: 0-5%
Fees to Publish: 0.00 US$

MANUSCRIPT TOPICS:

Business Law, Public Responsibility & Ethics; Global Business; Marketing Research; Marketing Theory & Applications; Organizational Behavior & Theory; Production/Operations; Sales/Selling; Services; Small Business Entrepreneurship; Strategic Management Policy; Technology/Innovation

MANUSCRIPT GUIDELINES/COMMENTS:

Manuscripts (a) should not have been published elsewhere or be under consideration by another publication, (b) should have an abstract, (c) should include a disk (Word 97), and (d) must address the business theme of the particular issue.

    Theme 1998 Issue: International Marketing
    Theme 1999 Issue: New Directions in Management (The Changing Workplace)
    Theme 2000 Issue: Promoting an Entrepreneurial Organizational Culture

Anatolia: An International Journal of Tourism Hospitality and Research

ADDRESS FOR SUBMISSION:

Nazmi Kozak, Editor-in-Chief
Anatolia: An International Journal of
   Tourism Hospitality and Research
P.K. 589 - 06445
Yenisehir, Ankara,
Turkey
Phone: 90-312-479-1084
Fax: 90-312-479-1084
E-Mail: anatolia@tr-net.net.tr
Web:
Address May Change:

CIRCULATION DATA:

Reader: Academics
Frequency of Issue: 2 Times/Year
Copies per Issue: No Reply
Sponsor/Publisher:
Subscribe Price: 35.00 US$ Individual
   50.00 US$ Institution
   25.00 US$ Student

PUBLICATION GUIDELINES:

Manuscript Length: 4,000-5,000 wds.
Copies Required: Three
Computer Submission: No
Format: N/A
Fees to Review: 0.00 US$

Manuscript Style:
   See Manuscript Guidelines

REVIEW INFORMATION:

Type of Review: Blind Review
No. of External Reviewers: 3
No. of In House Reviewers: 0
Acceptance Rate: 21-30%
Time to Review: 2 - 3 Months
Reviewers Comments: Yes
Invited Articles: 0-5%
Fees to Publish: 0.00 US$

MANUSCRIPT TOPICS:
Global Business; Marketing Research; Marketing Theory & Applications; Organizational Behavior & Theory; Services; Tourism & Hospitality Research

MANUSCRIPT GUIDELINES/COMMENTS:

Website: http://members.tripod.com/~anatoliajournal/

Send manuscripts from North America to:
Sevil F. Sonmez, Department of Recreation Management and Tourism, Arizona State University, PO Box 874905, Tempe, Arizona 85287-4905, USA
Tel: 602-965-8527, Fax: 602-965-5664, Email: sevil@asu.edu

Send all other manuscripts to:
Dr. Nazmi Kozak, Anatolia: An International Journal of Tourism and Hospitality Research
P.K. 589-06445, Yenisehir, Ankara, Turkey
Tel/Fax: 90-312 47910 84, E-mail: anatolia@tr-net.net.tr.

Statement of Purpose

Anatolia is a tourism and hospitality research journal which has been published solely in Turkish since 1990. The overall mission of Anatolia is to provide an outlet for innovative studies that will make a significant contribution to the understanding, practice, and education of tourism and hospitality, Specifically, the objectives of *Anatolia* are to contribute to the dissemination of knowledge through publication of high quality peer-reviewed research papers, reports and book reviews, while serving as a unique forum for case studies for instructional use. Through its updates on Mediterranean tourism, *Anatolia* also aims to heighten awareness of the Mediterranean region as a significant player in international tourism. *Anatolia* is dedicated to the provision of constructive, objective, and timely reviews of research papers through a double-blind review process by internationally well respected scholars

Instruction For Contributors

Anatolia: An International Journal of Tourism and Hospitality Research is published semiannually (Summer and Winter) in Ankara, Turkey. The journal includes articles, case studies, updates on Mediterranean tourism, research notes and reports, thesis/dissertation abstracts, book reviews, and calendar of events. Anatolia is published in English. Neither the Editors nor the Publishers accept responsibility for the views or statements expressed by authors. This journal should be cited as Anatolia.

Manuscripts Reviews:

Submissions will be reviewed by a double-blind review process and will be published based on the recommendations of reviewers and discretion of the editors. Submissions to Anatolia can be processed efficiently only if they are prepared according to these guidelines.

Manuscripts Submission:

Manuscripts must be submitted in triplicate and be prepared to include the following sections: title page, abstract/key words, manuscript text, references, tables/figures, acknowledgements (if applicable). Only one copy of the manuscript should include a title page with manuscript title, author's name, academic degree, present position, complete address (including telephone/fax/e-mail) as well as a brief biography (at the bottom of page) indicating academic field, degree (including year and institution), title and affiliation, and research interests. The cover page for the other two copies should only show article title. Manuscripts should be typewritten on one side of the paper, double spaced (including references), and should be checked carefully. Articles should be no more than 30 pages in length. Submitted manuscripts should not have been published elsewhere. However, if a longer/shorter version or translation of a previously published article is being submitted, a photocopy of the original publication must be included.

Computer Diskette:

Upon acceptance of the manuscript for publication, authors should provide one hard copy (printed format) of the final version of their manuscript and a copy of the manuscript on a 3.5 inch computer diskette. Please follow the following criteria: (1) Specify what software was used, including release (e.g., WordPerfect 6.1/Windows), (2) Specify what computer was used (e.g., McIntosh, IBM compatible), (3) Include both text and file and ASCII file on the disk, and (4) Use the wrap-around end-of-line feature (i.e., on "return" at end of lines). All textual elements should begin flush left, with no paragraph indents. Every element should be followed by two "returns" (i.e., title, headings, paragraphs, etc.).

Abstracts, Key Words, And Summaries:
Authors should include an abstract of 150-200 words and up to 6 key words. Abstracts should contain an abbreviated representation of the content of the manuscript. Major results, conclusions, and/or recommendations should be given, followed by supporting details of method, scope, or purpose as appropriate.

References Within Text:
Citations in the text should include the author's last name, and year of publication enclosed in parentheses without punctuation. For example, (Sönmez 1994) or (Crompton 1979, 1982) or (Yücelt and Marcella 1996) or (Fesenmaier et al. 1994) or (Dener 1995:14-21) (for quoted material). No footnotes or endnotes should be included.

References:
All cited references must be given in full, including the volume, issues, and page numbers. The list of all references should be placed at the end of the paper, arranged in alphabetical order by authors' last names, as shown in examples below.

Periodicals/journals:
Yücelt, U. and Marcella, M. (1996). Services Marketing in the Lodging Industry: An Empirical Investigation, Journal of Travel Research, 34 (4): 32-38.

Books:
Witt, E. S. and Witt, C. A. (1992). Modeling and Forecasting in Tourism. London: Academic Press.

Chapters in edited book:
Uysal, M. and Hagan, L. A. R. (1992). Motivations of Pleasure Travel and Tourism. In M. Khan, M. Olsen, and T. Var (Eds.), VNR's Encyclopedia of Hospitality and Tourism (pp. 798-810). New York: Van Nostrand Reinhold.

Internet:
Jacobson, J. W., Mulick, J. A., & Schwarz, A. A. (1995). A history of facilitated communication: Science, pseudoscience, and antiscience: Science working group on facilitated communication. American Psychologist, 50, 750G765. Retrieved January 25, 1996 from the World Wide Web: http://www.apa.org/journals/jacobson.html

For more information about internet citation look at http://www.apa.org/journals/webref.html

Tables, Illustrations/Diagrams, and Photographs:
All supplements to the manuscript text should be professionally done, should be enclosed on separate pages, and the place where they are to be printed must be clearly marked in the text (i.e., "figure 1 here"). Tables should be intelligible without reference to the text and should include a title caption and headings for columns. Very wide or very long tables should be avoided. Illustrations/diagrams must be clear, suitable for direct reproduction (camera ready),

and should include a title caption. Lettering should be large enough to be legible after reduction to printing size. The first author's name and figure number should be lightly pencilled on the reverse side of the sheet. Captions for illustrations/diagrams should be included on separate pages at the end of the manuscript. Photographs should be submitted unmounted on white glossy paper (slides are not acceptable). These pages should not be numbered.

Page Proofs and Reprints:
Page proofs will be sent to the designated corresponding contributor. A form of ordering reprints and copies of the journal issue in which the article appears will accompany the page proofs. Only minor corrections are allowed at the proof stage.

Annals of Tourism Research: A Social Sciences Journal

ADDRESS FOR SUBMISSION:

Jafar Jafari, Editor-in-Chief
Annals of Tourism Research: A Social
   Sciences Journal
University of Wisconsin-Stout
Department of Hospitality and Tourism
Menomonie, WI 54751
USA
Phone: 715-232-2339
Fax: 715-232-3200
E-Mail: jafari@uwstout.edu
Web:
Address May Change:

PUBLICATION GUIDELINES:

Manuscript Length: 20-35
Copies Required: Five
Computer Submission: Yes
Format: Microsoft Word
Fees to Review: 0.00 US$

Manuscript Style:
   See Manuscript Guidelines

CIRCULATION DATA:

Reader: Academics
Frequency of Issue: Quarterly
Copies per Issue: 1,001 - 2,000
Sponsor/Publisher: Pergamon Press
   /Elsevier Science Publishing
Subscribe Price: 132.00 US$ Individual
   454.00 US$ Institution
   118.44 Euro Indv., 406.59 Euro Inst.

REVIEW INFORMATION:

Type of Review: Blind Review
No. of External Reviewers: 3+
No. of In House Reviewers: 1
Acceptance Rate: 11-20%
Time to Review: 4 - 6 Months
Reviewers Comments: Yes
Invited Articles: 0-5%
Fees to Publish: 0.00 US$

MANUSCRIPT TOPICS:
Business Information Systems (MIS); Global Business; Leisure; Recreation; Socioeconomic Development; Marketing Research; Marketing Theory & Applications; Services; Small Business Entrepreneurship; Strategic Management Policy; Tourism and Social Sciences

MANUSCRIPT GUIDELINES/COMMENTS:

Annals Of Tourism Research is a social sciences journal focusing upon academic perspectives on tourism. While striving for a balance of theory and application, Annals is ultimately dedicated to developing theoretical constructs and new approaches which further an understanding of tourism. Its strategies are to invite and encourage offerings from various disciplines; to serve as a forum through which these may interact; and thus to expand the frontiers of knowledge by contributing to the literature on tourism social science.

To perform its role in the development of a theoretically integrated and methodologically enriched multidisciplinary body of knowledge on tourism, Annals invites manuscripts dealing with various aspects of the tourism phenomenon. Papers on anthropological, ecological, political, economic, educational, geographic, historical, psychological, and sociological aspects of tourism (including theoretical essays, case studies, and industry-oriented expositions) may be submitted for publication in Annals. Purely descriptive manuscripts which do not contribute to the development of knowledge are not considered suitable.

Style: To expedite the review process, all manuscripts must be prepared according to this format. The submission should be divided into the following sections.

Cover Sheet: The coversheet should bear a short informative title (title/subtitle 50 letters maximum). To facilitate blind review, no names or affiliations appear on this sheet.

Title Page: A separate title page, following the coversheet, should include the paper title, all authors' names and affiliations, mailing address for correspondence and page proofs, as well as telephone and fax numbers and email address.

Biographical Note: A short biodata (not exceeding 60 words) about the author(s) appears at the bottom of the title page.

Abstract And Keywords: The abstract (*between* 110-120 words), on the next page, should state concisely what was done and why, what was found, and what was concluded, and ends with a list of keywords pertinent to the central theme. When the paper is accepted for publication, the author will be requested to submit a French resume of the abstract (or *Annals* can make arrangements for its translation).

Text: All parts of the manuscript should be typed (on one side of paper only) double spaced, with ample margins. The text should be subdivided with titled headings, preceded by Introduction and succeeded by Conclusions. No footnotes can be included (they must be incorporated in the body of the text or eliminated). The paper must be written in the third person.

Abbreviations And Terminologies: Abbreviations or terms should be fully spelled out and defined when first used in the text.

References: In the text, references are cited with parentheses using the author date style. *Examples:* (Graburn 1989) or (Dann and Cohen 1991; Sheldon 1984; Smith 1987, 1989). Page numbers for specific points or direct quotations must be given (Graburn 1989:23). The Reference list, placed at the end of the text, must be typed double spaced in alphabetical order of authors:

Dann, Graham, and Erik Cohen
1991 Sociology of Tourism. Annals of Tourism Research 18:155-169.

Graburn, Nelson H.H.
1989 Tourism: The Sacred Journey. In Hosts and Guest: The Anthropology of Tourism (2nd ed.), Valene Smith, editor, pp. 21-36. Philadelphia PA: University of Pennsylvania Press.

Smith, Stephen LJ.
1987 Regional Analysis of Tourism Resources. Annals of Tourism Research 14:254-273.

1989 Tourism Analysis: A Handbook. London: Longman.

For format of other types of publications, please see references in a *recent* issue of *Annals*. Please note that citations such as "personal communication" should not be included in the reference list, but may be added parenthetically in the text.

Tables And Illustrations: Each table should be typed on a separate sheet. The data in tables should be presented in columns with nonsignificant decimal places omitted. The tables and figures should be numbered in Arabic numerals, followed by very brief descriptive titles. Important details should be footnoted under each table or figure, not in the title. In the text, all illustrations, charts and maps should be referred to as Figures. They should be finished drawings (camera-ready, professionally drawn "artworks") not needing further work or typesetting. No tables or figures planned for reproduction can be larger than one page of *Annals*.

Other: The preferred length of an article is 20-35 typewritten pages (about 5,000-9,000 words). The manuscript should be arranged/formatted as follows: cover sheet, title page, abstract, introduction, text (divided into introduction, subdivided discussion, and conclusions) acknowledgements, references, submission dates, and tables and figures.

Submission of a paper requires the assurance that the manuscript is an original work. If the manuscript depends critically on another paper which is not published, a copy of that paper should also be included. Manuscripts incorporating the results of detailed original research should include discussion of the broader significance of the subject matter. All submissions must be in English. Translated papers should be accompanied by a copy of the article in the original language.

Evaluation: *Annals* is a refereed journal. All manuscripts are evaluated by at least three referees from different disciplines. The evaluation is done anonymously (double blind system): communicating via a Coordinating Editor, neither referees nor the authors are aware of each other's identities. To facilitate prompt review, five copies of the manuscript should be submitted.

Copyright And Originality: It is a condition of publication that manuscripts submitted to *Annals* have not been published and will not be simultaneously submitted or published elsewhere. All authors must sign the *Transfer Of Copyright* agreement, available from the Editor-in-Chief or the Coordinating Editor, before the article can be published. (U.S. government officers or employees whose submitted work was prepared as part of their employment are exempt from the transfer requirement, but must certify their status as government writers.) This transfer agreement enables the publisher to protect the copyrighted material for the authors, but does not relinquish the authors' proprietary rights or rights to use their work as they please in the future. The copyright transfer covers the exclusive rights to reproduce and distribute the article, including reprints, photographic reproductions, microform or any other reproductions of similar nature and translations.

Computer Disks: In order to speed publication and ensure accuracy, authors of accepted papers are requested to submit a computer disk (3.50" or 5.25" HD/DD disk) containing the *final* version of the paper along with the *final* manuscript to the editorial office. Please observe the following criteria:

1. Send only hard copy when first submitting your paper.
2. When your paper has been refereed, revised if necessary and accepted, send a disk containing the final version with the final hard copy. **Make sure that the disk and hard copy match exactly.**
3. Specify what software was used, including which release (e.g., WordPerfect 6.0).
4. Specify what computer was used (either IBM compatible PC or Apple Macintosh).
5. Include both the text file and ASCII file, and separate table and illustration files, if available.
6. The file should follow the general instructions on style/arrangement and, in particular, the reference format of this journal.
7. The file should be single-spaced and should use the wrap-around end-of-line feature (i.e., no returns at the end of each line). All textual elements should begin flush left, with no paragraph indents. Place two returns after every element such as title, headings, paragraphs, figure and table callouts, etc.
8. Keep a backup disk for reference and safety.

Commentary And Rejoinders, Research Notes And Reports, Book Reviews, Film Reviews: *Annals* also solicits submission to these Departments. While the above general format applies, for length and other specifics, prospective contributors are asked to contact the respective Associate Editor as identified on the first page of each Department.

Manuscript Submissions: Please send all manuscripts (5 copies) directly to J. Jafari, Editor-in-Chief, *Annals Of Tourism Research*, Department of Hospitality and Tourism, University of Wisconsin Stout, Menomonie WI 54751, USA. Telephone (715) 232-2339, fax (715) 232-3200, telex 13-7328, email 'jafari@uwstout".

Annual Advances in Business Cases

ADDRESS FOR SUBMISSION:

Patricia Ryan, Editor
Annual Advances in Business Cases
Colorado State University
College of Business
Department of Finance & Real Estate-1272
Fort Collins, CO 80523-1272
USA
Phone: 970-491-5670
Fax: 970-491-7665
E-Mail: patryan@lamar.colostate.edu
Web:
Address May Change:

PUBLICATION GUIDELINES:

Manuscript Length: 11-20
Copies Required: Four
Computer Submission: No
Format: N/A
Fees to Review: 0.00 US$

Manuscript Style:
  Chicago Manual of Style

CIRCULATION DATA:

Reader: Academics
Frequency of Issue: Yearly
Copies per Issue: Less than 1,000
Sponsor/Publisher: Professional Association
Subscribe Price: 30.00 US$ Annual Mem.

REVIEW INFORMATION:

Type of Review: Blind Review
No. of External Reviewers: 3
No. of In House Reviewers: 0
Acceptance Rate: 30%
Time to Review: 2 - 3 Months
Reviewers Comments: Yes
Invited Articles: 0-5%
Fees to Publish: 0.00 US$

MANUSCRIPT TOPICS:
Advertising & Promotion Management; Business Education; Business Information Systems (MIS); Business Law, Public Responsibility & Ethics; Direct Marketing; Global Business; Labor Relations & Human Resource Mgt.; Marketing Research; Marketing Theory & Applications; Office Administration/Management; Operations Research/Statistics; Organizational Behavior & Theory; Organizational Development; Production/Operations; Public Administration; Sales/Selling; Services; Small Business Entrepreneurship; Strategic Management Policy; Technology/Innovation; Transportation/Physical Distribution

MANUSCRIPT GUIDELINES/COMMENTS:

EVALUATION CRITERIA FOR BUSINESS CASES

Objectives
Are objective(s) explicitly stated in teaching notes?
  Clarity of stated purpose of objectives.
  Specificity and relevance of case objectives.

Values of Objective(s).
> Is the objective worthwhile in class time and student's preparation time?
> In other words, is the invested time worth the stated objectives?
> Does the case fulfill its stated objectives?
> To what degree does it meet is objectives?

Pedagogy
Suitable topic for college course.
> Level of narration, subject matter, popularity or chance for acceptance by potential users – the market.

Significance to the field of the topic area.

"Teachability"
> Will the students learn from this case?
> Will the stated objective of the case be met?
> Extent of specialized knowledge required...
> by professor?
> by students?
> provided or supplemented by auxiliary material.

Will it make the students think?
Does the case contain issue(s) the reader can focus on?
> Does it have "handles" to grab to begin analysis?
> Is the issue(s) relevant to today's world?
> To what extent is it relevant to other organizations?

Does it aid in understanding valuable theories, concepts, techniques?
How well does it lend itself to use of theory or basic principles?

Writing Mechanics
Format of case presentation. (Is it really a case?)
> This should be answered at the Workshop. Sometimes new case writers create exercises or stories, not cases. However, this should not be used to inhibit imaginative exploration of new formats. Note that "cases" are usually different in law, philosophy, ethics, and other fields.

Is the case well written?
> Does it provide a good "feel" for the organization and situation?
> Clarity – Is it easy to read and understand?
> Are the spelling, grammar, and punctuation proper?
> Are headings used to organize the case?
> Conciseness of the text and numerical presentations.
> Does one topic flow into another?

Organization
> Is the case presented with some logical flow and in a useful sequence?

This does not mean that every case must be laid out in an easy-to-understand sequence for students – life can be messy – but the case should have an inherent logical structure.

Format
Conforming to SCR publication format as follows:
Margins – 1" top; 1-1/2" bottom and sides including figures and tables.
Page 1 identifications.
Top – Title
Bottom:
- Author(s) institution(s)
- Address
- Standard SCR identification
- Required copyright notice
    Note: The law requires a full circle around the little 'c'.

Prestige Elite (or comparable typeface) 12 pitch (6 lines per inch)

Figures, tables, charts.
Each captioned - centered and capitalized
Superior legibility and within margins.
Turned **counter-clockwise**, if rotated.

No page numbers printed.
Pencil lightly on back of original pages.
Teaching notes on back beginning with TN-1.

Overall professional appearance.
After reproduction in a volume, printing and subsequent copying, the material should not only be legible, but should reflect credibly on the author, on his or her institution, and on the SCR. Do not use a dot matrix printer.

Content

Interest – Does this case tell an interesting story?
There are many different ways to do this, of course, and obviously it is subjective – a qualitative dimension – but a good case makes the reader want to finish it; it provides absorbing reading.

Accuracy – Accurately illustrates a particular situation.
Cases should be accurately written from real situations. They should not be works of fiction. They should be modified to preserve the anonymity of individuals and firms (unless explicit permission has been obtained). This often means that some numerical data may be modified. These changes should not modify the inherent nature of the situation.

Completeness and adequacy...
For a proper analysis.
To make a realistic decision.
To develop realistic implementation.

Clarity – of graphs, charts and tables for key data.

Relevance – of case data to implied problems of case.
Everything that is written into a case should be there for a reason, including material that may lead to improper results. There are several good reasons to include material not directly relevant to the problem – or even potentially relevant at the time of the problem. Such reasons involve consideration of prior training and general capability of students, level of course, and instructors' capabilities.

Complexity – is it appropriate to the objectives and course?

Reasonableness of any "red herrings" within case.

Student questions optionally provided.
    Not superficial
    Guides development of in-depth understanding.
    Implies alternative approaches to analysis.
    Elicits specific decisions and action.

Teaching Notes
Opening structure
    Starts with brief synopsis of case situation.
    Presents purpose or objectives of case.
    Describes intended field or course, and level.
    Identifies any specialized knowledge required.

Overall quality of teaching note
    Completeness of the note.
    Utility of note to case adopters.
    Quality of the written presentation – See criteria above for the case.
    Is consistent with case.

Completeness and utility
    Provides help in better understanding the key issues.
    Gives suggestions about ways to use the case in class.
    Enough analysis to be able to lead a class without surprises.
    Points out critical norms or facts of the situation.
    If student questions provided, indicates answers to them.
    Provides sample calculations and key results.

Special background materials, as may be needed:
    Annotated bibliography or references.
    Optional supplementary handouts.

Tells what actually happened, if known.
* * * * C.F. Douds, April 1985

(EXAMPLE OF FORMAT)

TITLE OF CASE

(ALL CAPS, CENTERED)

Generally speaking there are some introductory comments that establish the purpose of the particular case setting and provide the reader with enough information to develop interest. The writer should recognize the need to appeal to the user, author and publisher as well as to provide a basis for discussion. Please use **Prestige Elite** on 12 pitch. Single space throughout. Double space between paragraphs and headings. Margins should be one inch on all four sides of the page. Place page numbers at bottom center beginning with second page.

HEADINGS (ALL CAPS, LEFT JUSTIFIED)

Your case should be separated into various sections to enhance clarity and information flow. The nature of the section will of course vary from case to case but typical ones are: Background Information, Market Situation, Financial Information, etc.

Exhibits, tables and diagrams should be on separate pages and of good quality to aid reproduction of your case for the *Annual Advances In Business Cases*.

This case was prepared by (your name and co-author, if appropriate) of (your school) as a basis for class discussion rather than to illustrate either effective or ineffective handling of an administrative situation.

Presented to the Midwest Society for Case Research Workshop, 1988. All rights reserved to the author(s) and the Midwest Society for Case Research. Copyright c 1988 by (your name and co-author).
(This appears on first page only)

TITLE OF CASE

Teaching note

TEACHING OBJECTIVES

The teaching note is often more important to the user than the case itself since time is short and there are many cases from which to choose. The objectives of the case should be enumerated here

1.

2.

3.

4. etc.

CASE OVERVIEW

A short synopsis of the case should be presented providing the user with the salient points of the case and the basic tasks the student is being asked to do. Usually 1-3 paragraphs.

QUESTIONS

The questions proposed by the case and a discussion of the solutions sought should be presented.

Any references that will aid the user should be footnoted at the bottom of the page.

Statistical solutions, exhibits, etc. should be provided as well.

DISCUSSION

The remainder of your teaching note should continue.

Asia Pacific Business Review

ADDRESS FOR SUBMISSION:

Robert Fitzgerald, Editor
Asia Pacific Business Review
University of London
School of Management
Royal Holloway
Egham, Surrey, TW20 0EX
UK
Phone: +44 0 1784 443780
Fax: +44 0 1784 439854
E-Mail: www.frankcass.com
Web:
Address May Change:

PUBLICATION GUIDELINES:

Manuscript Length: 21-25
Copies Required: Three
Computer Submission: Yes
Format: RTF
Fees to Review: 0.00 US$

Manuscript Style:
   See Manuscript Guidelines

CIRCULATION DATA:

Reader: Academics
Frequency of Issue: Quarterly
Copies per Issue: Less than 1,000
Sponsor/Publisher: Frank Cass & Co., Ltd.
Subscribe Price: 49.00 US$ Individual
   195.00 US$ Institution

REVIEW INFORMATION:

Type of Review: Blind Review
No. of External Reviewers: 3+
No. of In House Reviewers: 0
Acceptance Rate: 21-30%
Time to Review: 4 - 6 Months
Reviewers Comments: Yes
Invited Articles: 11-20%
Fees to Publish: 0.00 US$

MANUSCRIPT TOPICS:
Asia Pacific Business; Business Law, Public Responsibility & Ethics; Global Business; Marketing Theory & Applications; Organizational Behavior & Theory; Organizational Development; Production/Operations; Strategic Management Policy; Technology/Innovation

MANUSCRIPT GUIDELINES/COMMENTS:

About the Journal
The growth of the Asia Pacific region and the rising presence of its multinationals in world markets has raised a number of questions about the origins of national economic success. *Asia Pacific Business Review* addresses these key questions and draws together the lessons of economics, history, politics and culture in order to explore business in the Asia Pacific countries. The *Review* is intended for both academics and interested observers, contains the contributions of recognized experts, and is essential to anyone seeking the latest research on Asia Pacific business in a readily available, approachable form.

Notes for Contributors
Asia pacific Business Review is a refereed journal. Articles submitted to *Asia Pacific Business Review* should be original contributions and should not be under consideration for any other publication at the same time. If another version of the article is under consideration by another publication, or has been, or will be published elsewhere, authors should indicate this clearly at the time of submission.

Each manuscript should be submitted in triplicate. Articles should be typewritten on A4/Letter paper, on one side only, double-spaced with ample margins. All pages (including those containing only diagrams and tables) should be numbered consecutively. There is no standard length for articles but 6-8,000 words (including notes and references) is a useful target. The article should begin with an indented and italicized summary of around 100 words, which should describe the main arguments and conclusions of the article. Details of the author's institutional affiliation, full address and other contact information should be included on a separate cover sheet. Any acknowledgements should be included on the cover sheet as should a note of the exact length of the article.

All diagrams, charts and graphs should be referred to as figures and consecutively numbered. Tables should be kept to a minimum and contain only essential data. Each figure and table must be given an Arabic numeral, followed by a heading, and be referred to in the text.

Following acceptance for publication, articles should be submitted on high density 3½ inch disks (IBM PC or Macintosh compatible) in rich text format (.RTF) together with a hard copy. To facilitate the typesetting process, notes should be grouped together at the end of the file. Tables should also be placed at the end of the file. Tables should be saved as text using the appropriate function within your word processor. If this function is not available then tables should be prepared using tabs. Any diagrams or maps should be copied to a separate disk separately in uncompressed .TIF or .JPG formats in individual files. These should be prepared in black and white. Tints should be avoided, use open patterns instead. If maps and diagrams cannot be prepared electronically, they should be presented on good quality white paper. If mathematics are included 1/2 is preferred over ½.

Each disk should be labeled with the journal's name, article title, lead author's name and software used. It is the author's responsibility to ensure that where copyright materials are included within an article the permission of the copyright holder has been obtained. Confirmation of this should be included on a separate sheet included with the disk.

Authors are entitled to 25 free offprints and a copy of the issue in which their article appears. Copyright in articles published in *Asia Pacific Business Review* rests with the publisher.

Style
British spellings throughout. Use -ize rather than -ise (recognize).
Numbers: one-ten; 11 etc.
Dates: 1 January 1996 (but Aug.-Feb. in notes); the 1920s, 1945-48.
Capitalization: use sparingly, generally in titles.

Harvard referencing system to be used (author-date in brackets).

Simple references to be inserted within text: (Ludlow, 1992: 85), for example.

Endnotes should be kept to a minimum, and indicated consecutively through the article by raised numerals corresponding to the list of notes placed at the end of the manuscript.

References: bibliographical list to appear after the endnotes, containing all the works referred to. For example:

    Chandler, A.D. (1990), *Scale and Scope: The Dynamics of Industrial Capitalism.* Cambridge, MA: Harvard University Press.

    Porter, M.E. (1991), 'Towards a Dynamic Theory of Strategy', *Strategic Management Journal,* Vol.12, No.1, pp.95-105.

    Redding, S.G. (1991), 'Weak Organisations and Strong Linkages' in G.G. Hamilton fed.), *Business Networks and Economic Development in East and South East Asia.* Hong Kong: University of Hong Kong, pp.30-47.

Foreign words should be shown in italics. Authors whose first language is not English should ensure that a draft of their article has been read and corrected by a competent person whose first language is English.

Authors are responsible for ensuring that their manuscripts conform to the journal style. The Editors will not undertake retyping of manuscripts before publication. A guide to style and presentation is obtainable from the Editors, or from the publisher, Frank Cass & Co. Ltd., Newbury House. 900 Eastern Avenue, Newbury House, London IG2 7HH, England; Fax: +44 (0)181 599 0984; Email: editors@frankcass.com.

Asia Pacific Journal of Marketing and Logistics

ADDRESS FOR SUBMISSION:

Oliver H. M. Yau, Editor
Asia Pacific Journal of Marketing and
  Logistics
City University of Hong Kong
Associate Dean (Academic)
Faculty of Business
83 Tat Chee Avenue, Kow Loon
Hong Kong,
Phone: 852-2788 7888
Fax: 852-2788 7182
E-Mail: bmyau@cityu.edu.hk
Web:
Address May Change:

PUBLICATION GUIDELINES:

Manuscript Length: 16-20
Copies Required: Three
Computer Submission: No
Format: N/A
Fees to Review: US$
  US$

Manuscript Style:
  No Reply

CIRCULATION DATA:

Reader: Academics
Frequency of Issue: 2 Times/Year
Copies per Issue: No Reply
Sponsor/Publisher: Bamarick Publications
  Ltd.
Subscribe Price: 750.00 US$
  US$
  US$

REVIEW INFORMATION:

Type of Review: Blind Review
No. of External Reviewers: No Reply
No. of In House Reviewers: 1
Acceptance Rate: 11-20%
Time to Review: 2 - 3 Months
Reviewers Comments: Yes
Invited Articles: No Reply
Fees to Publish: 0.00 US$

MANUSCRIPT TOPICS:
Advertising & Promotion Management; Business Education; Direct Marketing; Global Business; Marketing Research; Marketing Theory & Applications; Sales/Selling; Services; Technology/Innovation; Transportation/Physical Distribution

MANUSCRIPT GUIDELINES/COMMENTS:

Asia Pacific Journal of Marketing and Logistics is published by Barmarick Publications.

Asian Journal of Business & Entrepreneurship

ADDRESS FOR SUBMISSION:

Man Kee Choe, Editor
Asian Journal of Business & Entrepreneurship
Keimyung University
Research Institute for Business and Entrepreneurship
2139 Dae Myung-dong, Nam-Gu
Taegu, 705-701,
Korea
Phone: +82-53-620-2394
Fax: +82-53-626-4241
E-Mail: manchoe@kmucc.keimyung.ac.kr
Web:
Address May Change:

PUBLICATION GUIDELINES:

Manuscript Length: 21-25
Copies Required: Three
Computer Submission: Yes
Format: MS Word
Fees to Review: 0.00 US$

Manuscript Style:
, Academy of Management of Journal

CIRCULATION DATA:

Reader: Academics
Frequency of Issue: 2 Times/Year
Copies per Issue: Less than 1,000
Sponsor/Publisher: Research Institute for Business and Entrepreneurship, Keimyung University
Subscribe Price: 15.00 US$ Individual
30.00 US$ Institution
10.00 US$ Student

REVIEW INFORMATION:

Type of Review: Blind Review
No. of External Reviewers: 2
No. of In House Reviewers: 1
Acceptance Rate: 21-30%
Time to Review: 2 - 3 Months
Reviewers Comments: Yes
Invited Articles: 0-5%
Fees to Publish: 0.00 US$

MANUSCRIPT TOPICS:
Business Information Systems (MIS); Global Business; Labor Relations & Human Resource Mgt.; Marketing Research; Marketing Theory & Applications; Organizational Behavior & Theory; Organizational Development; Production/Operations; Small Business Entrepreneurship; Strategic Management Policy; Technology/Innovation

MANUSCRIPT GUIDELINES/COMMENTS:

Call for Papers
In order to meet the increasing demand among international scholars for published English-language research on Asian business issues, the *Asian Journal of Business and Entrepreneurship* began publication in 1998. The Journal accepts quality original English-language manuscripts in any field of business administration including but not exclusive to management, tourism, MIS, marketing, accounting. economics, production management, finance, human resources management, and international trade. Papers should emphasize the

development of new business theories and practices or the enrichment of existing ones, and should preferably focus on entrepreneurship, business start-up, and venture management.

The editorial board members believe that creative insight often occurs outside traditional research approaches and topic areas, and the Journal can help integrate the diverse strands of business and entrepreneurship research. Although manuscripts motivated strictly by data collection and analysis will be considered, preference will be given to authors who describe theoretical concepts that give meaning to date, and show how these concepts are relevant to the business and entrepreneurship problems identified. Manuscripts will not be given discriminative treatment because of their research methodologies. If warranted, commentary, reports, descriptive studies and literature reviews will be published.

All manuscripts should be submitted on by email and on 3.5-inch floppy diskettes in MS-Word format accompanied by 3 paper copies of the manuscript. The authors name should appear only on the title page. Manuscripts should be sent to the address above.

Review Process
(1) Decisions regarding the publication of submitted manuscripts will be based on the recommendation of members of the Journal's editorial board or other qualified reviewers.

(2) All articles published in the Journal are subject to a blind review process. Obvious self-citations that make known an author's identity should be avoided whenever possible.

(3) Reviewers will evaluate manuscripts on their significance to the field, conceptual adequacy, technical adequacy, appropriateness of content, and clarity of presentation.

(4) Reviewers' comments will be made available to authors.

Bank Marketing Magazine

ADDRESS FOR SUBMISSION:

Mike Campbell, Associate Editor
Bank Marketing Magazine
1120 Connecticut Ave, N.W.
Washington, D.C., 20036
USA
Phone: 202-663-5268
Fax: 202-828-4540
E-Mail: michaelc@aba.com
Web:
Address May Change:

PUBLICATION GUIDELINES:

Manuscript Length: 10-15
Copies Required: One
Computer Submission: Yes
Format: N/A
Fees to Review: 0.00 US$

Manuscript Style:
    Associated Press Stylebook

CIRCULATION DATA:

Reader: Business Persons
Frequency of Issue: Monthly
Copies per Issue: 5,001 - 10,000
Sponsor/Publisher: American Bankers
    Association
Subscribe Price: 98.00 US$
    80.00 US$ Members
    125.00 US$ Foreign

REVIEW INFORMATION:

Type of Review: Editorial Review
No. of External Reviewers: 0
No. of In House Reviewers: 3
Acceptance Rate: 50%
Time to Review: 2 - 3 Months
Reviewers Comments: Yes
Invited Articles: 31-50%
Fees to Publish: 0.00 US$

MANUSCRIPT TOPICS:
Advertising & Promotion Management; Communication; Direct Marketing; Marketing Research; Marketing Theory & Applications; Organizational Behavior & Theory; Organizational Development; Sales/Selling; Services; Small Business Entrepreneurship; Technology/Innovation

MANUSCRIPT GUIDELINES/COMMENTS:

1. *AP Style Manual*

2. Articles should take one of the following approaches:
    1) The case history;
    2) The "how-to-do-it" article or
    3) The general or comprehensive article dealing with principles of marketing or marketing thought.

3. Copy should be well-written (preferably in the third person), accurate, original, and exclusive to *Bank Marketing Magazine*. Footnotes should be avoided, if possible, and references properly documented within the article.

4. Average article length is approximately 2,500 words or 10 typed pages, double-spaced.

5. Deadline for receipt of final manuscripts is ten weeks before date of publication. For example, copy of the magazine's March issue would be due December 15.

6. Support material—separate from the body copy but helpful for illustrative purposes (photos, graphs, overviews, etc.)—is requested. Such documentation, however, should be brief, concise, and properly identified.

7. The BMA Magazine Group reserves the right to accept or reject any manuscript submitted for publication. Common cause for rejection would be lack of substantial editorial content, poorly written copy, or copy that is blatantly commercial.

8. Unless otherwise stipulated in writing in advance, BMA does not pay for manuscripts.

9. BMA will provide the author with two complimentary copies of the issue in which his or her article appears.

10. Prospective authors are required to sign a terms of publication form and return it with their manuscript.

11. Terms of Publication

    To:

    Bank Marketing Association "BMA" is pleased to have the privilege of publishing your article in *Bank Marketing Magazine*, now entitled " ", subject to your acceptance of the following terms of publication.

1. Whereas BMA is undertaking to publish the article, of which the undersigned is the sole author and in which the undersigned is the sole owner of copyright, the author hereby grants and assigns exclusively to BMA for its use any and all rights of whatsoever kind of nature now or hereafter protected by the copyright laws of the United States (common or statutory) and all foreign countries in all languages in and to the article, including all subsidiary rights. BMA, in turn, grants to the author the right to republication (without charge) in any book of which he is the author or editor after it has been published in *Bank Marketing Magazine*, subject only to his giving proper credit in the book to the original publication of the article by BMA.

2. The author warrants the article submitted for publication in *Bank Marketing Magazine* contains no matter libelous or otherwise unlawful or which invades individual privacy or which infringes any proprietary rights (including, without limitation, any copyrights). It is understood that author will receive no royalty or other monetary compensation from BMA or its use of the article. BMA will publish the article at its own cost and expense.

3. The author warrants that the article is an original work and that he has full power to make this assignment. Author further warrants that the article has not been previously published

elsewhere, in whole or in part; otherwise, the author represents that if the article has been previously published in whole or in part permission has been obtained for publication in *Bank Marketing Magazine* and the author has attached hereto a copy of the permission release and copy for credit lines.

4. The author agrees to indemnify and hold harmless BMA, its officers, directors, agents, and employees, from and against any and all claims, actions, losses, demands, costs, attorneys fees and all other expenses relating to or arising directly or indirectly from the inaccuracy or breach of any of the above-referenced warranties of author.

If foregoing terms are satisfactory, please sign and date this form, and return it to BMA at the following address:

1120 Connecticut Avenue NW
Washington, DC 20036

13. **Articles Of Summary**

Important: Please complete the following and return with query to:
The Editor, *Bank Marketing Magazine*, 1120 Connecticut Avenue, N.W., Washington, DC 20036. (202) 663-5268.

Name, address, phone number of Author:
Proposed Title of Article:
Proposed Magazine Issue:

In two or three sentences EACH, please complete the following:

1. This article is important for *Bank Marketing* readers because:

2. What three major points does the article cover?

3. Background information - origin of article, duties of author, size of bank or type of company, plus any unusual but pertinent data:

A more detailed outline is strongly preferred. Discussing the article idea with the Editor in advance is strongly recommended.

British Food Journal

ADDRESS FOR SUBMISSION:

S. Henson and D. Jukes, Co-Editors
British Food Journal
The University of Reading
Dept. of Agricultural Food Economics
4 Earley Gate, Whiteknights Road
Reading, RG6 6AR
USA
Phone: 44 0 1734 875123
Fax: 44 0 1734 310080
E-Mail: aeshensn@rdg.ac.uk
Web: www.mcb.co.uk
Address May Change:

PUBLICATION GUIDELINES:

Manuscript Length: 3,000 to 5,000 words
Copies Required: Three
Computer Submission: Yes If accepted
Format: N/A
Fees to Review: 6799.00 US$
    8499.00 AUS$

Manuscript Style:
    Uniform System of Citation (Harvard Blue Book)

CIRCULATION DATA:

Reader: Business Persons, Academic, & Practitioner
Frequency of Issue: 11Times/Year
Copies per Issue: No Reply
Sponsor/Publisher: MCB Press
Subscribe Price: 0.00 US$

REVIEW INFORMATION:

Type of Review: Blind Review
No. of External Reviewers: 2
No. of In House Reviewers: 1
Acceptance Rate: 50%
Time to Review: 1 - 2 Months
Reviewers Comments: No Reply
Invited Articles: 11-20%
Fees to Publish: 0.00 US$

MANUSCRIPT TOPICS:
Food Marketing/Development; Marketing Theory & Applications

MANUSCRIPT GUIDELINES/COMMENTS:

About the journal
The British Food Journal is highly respected worldwide for its broad, interdisciplinary coverage of food-related research. With its independent analysis and informed insights, it provides a vital communications link between all sectors of this dynamic industry, keeping you fully abreast of the latest issues and emerging trends. What is the real story behind bovine spongiform encephalopathy (BSE)? How should we be responding to the rising incidence of E. coli 0157 infections? All these topics and more are examined within the journal's pages. Covering every conceivable aspect of food, including production, processes, food safety, consumption and marketing, it provides new perspectives to advance your knowledge in the field.

Unique Attributes Disseminates food-related research of the highest academic quality to an international multidisciplinary audience. The research arises from work in all areas of food production, processes, consumption and marketing. Legal issues are covered in depth. A double-blind review process ensures the academic relevance and integrity of the papers.

Topicality
The journal's coverage of major issues is augmented by its reliably fast reporting on new legislation and a widely acclaimed Enforcements and Law Reports section which keeps readers up to date with key cases, legal liabilities, rights and duties.

Key Benefits
British Food Journal's independent analysis of current concerns, trends and developments means it commands the serious attention of a wide industry readership, and provides a vital communications link between all sectors of this dynamic industry. Practitioners who depend on authoritative information on issues such as food scares, health and diet trends, tampering during manufacture or packaging, food poisoning and production procedures will find *BFJ* an invaluable resource.

Key Journal Audiences
- Academic and research institutes
- Catering managers
- Food manufacturers and retailers
- Food marketing executives and consumer groups
- Nutrition, health and hygiene experts
- Regulatory bodies and environmental health officers
- Senior production and distribution staff
- Trading standards authorities

Coverage
- Catering in public and private sectors
- Consumer affairs
- Food and sales law
- Food marketing
- Health and hygiene
- Nutrition
- Production
- Retailing and distribution
- Technology

Articles submitted to the journal should be original contributions and should not be under consideration for any other publication at the same time. Authors submitting articles for publication warrant that the work is not an infringement of any existing copyright and will indemnify the publisher against any breach of such warranty. For ease of dissemination and to ensure proper policing of use, papers and contributions become the legal copyright of the publisher unless otherwise agreed. Submissions should be sent to: The Editors, Dr Spencer Henson and Dr David Jukes, at the above address.

Editorial objectives

The aim of the journal is to provide a vehicle for the dissemination of food-related research of the highest academic quality to an international multi-disciplinary audience.

Editorial scope

Work on any aspect of food will be considered for publication provided it is of a high academic standard. Authors should take into account the international readership of the journal when drafting papers. The aim of the journal is to present work in a manner which is accessible to a readership from a variety of backgrounds, including different academic disciplines and non-academics. Thus, where research of a highly technical nature is reported, the text should be written in a form which is clear to non-specialists in the area of enquiry. However, if required for clarification, the text can be supported by a technical annexe at the end of the paper. Where possible, authors should spell out the implications of their work for those who produce and retail food and regulate the food system.

The reviewing process

Each paper is reviewed by the editor and, if it is judged suitable for this publication, it is then sent to two referees for double blind peer review. Based on their recommendations, the editor then decides whether the paper should be accepted as is, revised or rejected.

Manuscript requirements

Three copies of the manuscript should be submitted in double line spacing with wide margins. All authors should be shown and author's details must be printed on a separate sheet and the author should not be identified anywhere else in the article.

As a guide, articles should be between 3,000 and 5,000 words in length. A title of not more than eight words should be provided. A brief **autobiographical note** should be supplied including full name, affiliation, e-mail address and full international contact details. Authors must supply an **abstract** of 100-150 words. Up to six **keywords** should be included which encapsulate the principal subjects covered by the article.

Where there is a **methodology**, it should be clearly described under a separate heading. **Headings** must be short, clearly defined and not numbered. **Notes** or **Endnotes** should be used only if absolutely necessary and must be identified in the text by consecutive numbers, enclosed in square brackets and listed at the end of the article.

Figures, charts and diagrams should be kept to a minimum. They must be black and white with minimum shading and numbered consecutively using arabic numerals with a brief title and labelled axes. In the text, the position of the figure should be shown by typing on a separate line the words "take in Figure 2". Good quality originals must be provided.

Tables should be kept to a minimum. They must be numbered consecutively with roman numerals and a brief title. In the text, the position of the table should be shown by typing on a separate line the words "take in Table IV".

Photos and illustrations must be supplied as good quality black and white original half tones with captions. Their position should be shown in the text by typing on a separate line the words "take in Plate 2".

References to other publications should be complete and in Harvard style. They should contain full bibliographical details and journal titles should not be abbreviated. For multiple citations in the same year use a, b, c immediately following the year of publication. References should be shown within the text by giving the author's last name followed by a comma and year of publication all in round brackets, e.g. (Fox, 1994). At the end of the article should be a reference list in alphabetical order as follows

for books
surname, initials and year of publication, title, publisher, place of publication, e.g.Casson, M. (1979), *Alternatives to the Multinational Enterprise*, Macmillan, London.
for chapter in edited book
surname, initials and year, "title", editor's surname, initials, title, publisher, place, pages, e.g.Bessley, M. and Wilson, P. (1984), "Public policy and small firms in Britain", in Levicki, C. (Ed.), *Small Business Theory and Policy*, Croom Helm, London, pp.111-26. Please note that the chapter title must be underlined.
for journals
surname, initials, (year) "title", journal, volume, number, pages, e.g. Fox, S. (1994) "Empowerment as a catalyst for change: an example from the food industry", Supply Chain Management, Vol 2 No 3, pp. 29-33

If there is more than one author list surnames followed by initials. All authors should be shown.

Electronic sources should include the URL of the electronic site at which they may be found, as follows:
Neuman, B.C.(1995), "Security, payment, and privacy for network commerce", IEEE Journal on Selected Areas in Communications, Vol. 13 No.8, October, pp.1523-31. Available (IEEE SEPTEMBER)
http://www.research.att.com/jsac/

Notes/Endnotes should be used only if absolutely necessary. They should, however, always be used for citing Web sites. They should be identified in the text by consecutive numbers enclosed in square brackets and listed at the end of the article. Please then provide full Web site addresses in the end list.

Final submission of the article
Once accepted for publication, the final version of the manuscript must be provided, accompanied by a 3.5" disk of the same version labelled with: disk format; author name(s); title of article; journal title; file name.

Each article must be accompanied by a completed and signed Journal Article Record Form available from the Editor or on http://www.literaticlub.co.uk/

The manuscript will be considered to be the definitive version of the article. The author must ensure that it is complete, grammatically correct and without spelling or typographical errors.

In preparing the disk, please use one of the following formats: Word, Word Perfect, Rich text format or TeX/LaTeX. Figures which are provided electronically must be in tif, gif or pic file extensions. All figures and graphics must also be supplied as good quality originals.

Final submission requirements
Manuscripts must:
- be clean, good quality hard copy and;
- include an abstract and keywords
- have Harvard style references
- include any figures, photos and graphics as good quality originals
- be accompanied by a labelled disk
- be accompanied by a completed Journal Article Record Form

Technical assistance is available from MCB's World Wide Web Literati Club on http://www.literaticlub.co.uk/ or contact Mike Massey at MCB, e-mail mmassey@mcb.co.uk

Business Case Journal

ADDRESS FOR SUBMISSION:

Peter Goulet, Editor
Business Case Journal
University of Northern Iowa
College of Business Administration
Department of Management
Cedar Falls, IA 50614-0130
Phone: 319-273-7350
Fax: 319-273-7512
E-Mail: katherine.cota@uni.edu
Web:
Address May Change:

PUBLICATION GUIDELINES:

Manuscript Length: Any
Copies Required: Four
Computer Submission: No
Format: N/A
Fees to Review: 0.00 US$

Manuscript Style:
    See Manuscript Guidelines

CIRCULATION DATA:

Reader: Academics
Frequency of Issue: 2 Times/Year
Copies per Issue: Less than 1,000
Sponsor/Publisher: McGraw Hill
Subscribe Price: 40.00 US$

REVIEW INFORMATION:

Type of Review: Blind Review
No. of External Reviewers: 2
No. of In House Reviewers: 1
Acceptance Rate: 21-30%
Time to Review: 2 - 3 Months
Reviewers Comments: Yes
Invited Articles: 0-5%
Fees to Publish: 0.00 US$

MANUSCRIPT TOPICS:
Accounting; Business Education; Business Information Systems (MIS); Business Law, Public Responsibility & Ethics; Finance & Investments; Global Business; Health Care Administration; Labor Relations & Human Resource Mgt.; Marketing Theory & Applications; Non Profit Organizations; Operations Research/Statistics; Organizational Behavior & Theory; Organizational Development; Production/Operations; Real Estate; Small Business Entrepreneurship; Strategic Management Policy

MANUSCRIPT GUIDELINES/COMMENTS:

Editorial Policy
The *Business Case Journal* is established by the Society for Case Research to publish business cases and research related to case writing or teaching with cases. The first issue was published in November, 1993. Two issues will be published each year.

The Journal publishes cases based on field research or research from secondary sources. Cases may pertain to any business discipline, and will be evaluated on the basis of relevance to and adequacy for clearly stated teaching or research goals. Other requirements are suitable writing style, complexity, and completeness. An instructors' manual or teaching notes must accompany each case. Teaching notes will not be published but will be used to aid reviewers in evaluating the case.

The purpose of the journal is to encourage the creation and use of high quality business cases. Results of research contributing to the process of case writing or the use of cases also will be considered for publication. Manuscripts will be evaluated for both technical and theoretical suitability.

Submissions are subject to an initial editorial review. Manuscripts which meet the minimum standards of the *BCJ* will receive a blind review from two or more members of the editorial board. Cases or articles that have been published previously or are under review elsewhere should not be submitted to *BCJ*. Cases may be released for publication in other outlets after a publication date has been set by the *BCJ* editor.

Submission Guidelines
Contributors should submit four paper copies of each manuscript (case and teaching note) for review.

Manuscripts (case and teaching note) should be double-spaced with 1" margins. Names of authors should not appear on the case or teaching note, but should appear with the name, affiliation, address, mailing address, and phone number for each author on a cover sheet.

Manuscripts (case and teaching note) should be accompanied by a letter of transmittal containing the name of the author to contact for final copy editing.

Authors of cases based on field research must submit a copy of written authorization for the use of the case from an appropriate officer in the subject organization before the case will be released for publication.

Manuscripts (case and teaching note) should be sent to: Peter Goulet, Editor, Business Case Journal, College of Business Administration, University of Northern Iowa, Cedar Falls, IA 50614-0130. No submission fees are required.

Publication Guidelines

Attention: Authors must adhere to these guidelines to ensure publication.
Questions concerning these guidelines should be directed to Katherine Cota, Managing Editor, at (319) 273-7350 or katherine.cota@uni.edu.

All manuscripts (case and teaching note) must be submitted on virus-free 3 ½" disks with two paper copies of the manuscript. WordPerfect 5.1, WordPerfect 6.1 and Word 7.0 are the only acceptable formats for publication.

- Manuscripts (case and teaching note) should be double-spaced with 1" margins.

- Keep formatting of text elements simple. Do not use boxes, frames, elaborate indentation, etc.

- For WordPerfect programs, use the column table function for creating tables instead of the tab and space bar.

- Do not mix text and illustration files.

- Avoid templates and "style sheets".

- Do not use automatic footnote systems. Please type the footnotes at the end of the document and use a superscript number in the text that corresponds to that footnote.

- Photographs and other exhibits not readily adaptable to the word processing format should be submitted as separate pages in camera-ready copy.

- Names of authors should not appear on the case or teaching note, but should appear with the name, affiliation, address, mailing address, and phone number for each author on a cover sheet.

- Manuscripts (case and teaching note) should be accompanied by a letter of transmittal containing the name, affiliation, address, mailing address, and phone number for each author. Be certain to note which author should be contacted for final copy editing.

- Authors of cases based on field research must submit a copy of written authorization for the use of the case from an appropriate officer in the subject organization before the case will be released for publication.

- Materials should be sent to: Peter Goulet, Editor, Business Case Journal, College of Business Administration, University of Northern Iowa, Cedar Falls, IA 50614-0130.

California Management Review

ADDRESS FOR SUBMISSION:

David Vogel, Editor
California Management Review
University of California
5549 Haas School of Business #1900
Berkeley, CA 94720-1900
USA
Phone: 510-642-7159
Fax: 510-642-1318
E-Mail: cmr@haas.berkeley.edu
Web:
Address May Change:

PUBLICATION GUIDELINES:

Manuscript Length: 16-25
Copies Required: Three
Computer Submission: No
Format: N/A
Fees to Review: 0.00 US$

Manuscript Style:
   Chicago Manual of Style

CIRCULATION DATA:

Reader: Business Persons, Academics
Frequency of Issue: Quarterly
Copies per Issue: 5,001 - 10,000
Sponsor/Publisher: Haas School of
   Business, University of California
Subscribe Price: 65.00 US$ Individual
   90.00 US$ Institution
   105.00 US$ Foreign, $35 Student

REVIEW INFORMATION:

Type of Review: Blind Review
No. of External Reviewers: 3
No. of In House Reviewers: 1
Acceptance Rate: 6-10%
Time to Review: 2 - 3 Months
Reviewers Comments: Yes
Invited Articles: 0-5%
Fees to Publish: 0.00 US$

MANUSCRIPT TOPICS:

Business Education; Business Information Systems (MIS); Business Law, Public Responsibility & Ethics; Communication; Global Business; Labor Relations & Human Resource Mgt.; Marketing Research; Marketing Theory & Applications; Non Profit Organizations; Operations Research/Statistics; Organizational Behavior & Theory; Organizational Development; Production/Operations; Public Administration; Services; Strategic Management Policy; Technology/Innovation

MANUSCRIPT GUIDELINES/COMMENTS:

CMR publishes articles from a number of different disciplines, including economics, psychology, history, political science, sociology, law, philosophy, business administration, and education. We interpret management broadly, to include subject matter taught in business schools as well as work in other fields that is applicable to management functions and practices.

CMR is particularly interested in manuscripts that focus on Business and Public Policy, Strategy and Organization, and International Trade and Competitiveness. CMR is also interested in point-of-view pieces, Book-Review essays that discuss several recent books on a particular topic or theme, and articles on Marketing, Accounting, and Finance.

Articles that present the results of original research and analysis are given high priority, but we also invite reports on business surveys, analyses or descriptions of new or revised business techniques, and perspectives on contemporary social, economic, and political issues. We welcome articles written for and by practitioners. CMR will also consider publishing excerpts from forthcoming books as well as revisions of papers originally prepared for academic conferences.

Submissions and query letters will be promptly acknowledged. Authors can normally expect a publication decision within six to twelve weeks. Manuscripts will not be returned. Authors whose work is accepted for publication in CMR will receive further instructions with their acceptance letter.

CMR does not accept multiple submissions (manuscripts simultaneously submitted to other publications). The manuscript may not be previously copyrighted nor accepted for publication (or published) elsewhere unless specific permission is received from the editor.

Format:
The submission package should consist of a cover letter addressed to the editor and three copies of the manuscript. Each copy should include a one-paragraph summary (abstract) of its basic argument. The author(s)'s name should not appear anywhere on the manuscript except on the first (cover) page.

Manuscripts should run between twenty and thirty pages, double-spaced. Please inquire with the editor before submitting articles of greater length.

Footnotes, citations, and references should be numbered in the text and compiled at the end of the manuscript.

Tables, charts, and diagrams should be placed on separate pages.

Style:
Articles should be as jargon-free as possible. Terminology and acronyms that are not common knowledge should be defined. Technical material should be placed in footnotes whenever possible.

Three discending levels of headings should be used periodically and consistently, throughout the article. They should be descriptive, but brief.

Tables, charts, diagrams, and other graphic materials should be used for providing necessary information or clarificatin of central concepts. They should be clean and uncluttered and should appear on separate pages. In most cases, multiple page tables or tables that have more than six columns are discouraged.

Footnotes should also be kept to a minimum. Citation order should be author(s) (first name first), title of work, complete publication information (city, state, publisher, date) in parentheses, and page number references. The accuracy of the citations in the footnotes is the responsibility of the author(s).

For more specific style questions, consult a recent issue of CMR. CMR uses the *Chicago Manual of Style* as primary reference source.

Case Research Journal

ADDRESS FOR SUBMISSION:

Linda E. Swayne, Editor
Case Research Journal
University of North Carolina, Charlottte
Department of Marketing
9201 University City Blvd.
Charlotte, NC 28223-0001
USA
Phone: 704-547-2849
Fax: 704-510-6463
E-Mail: leswayne@email.uncc.edu
Web:
Address May Change:

PUBLICATION GUIDELINES:

Manuscript Length: Any
Copies Required: Four
Computer Submission: No
Format: N/A
Fees to Review: 50.00 US$ Membership

Manuscript Style:
, Turabian

CIRCULATION DATA:

Reader: Academics
Frequency of Issue: Quarterly
Copies per Issue: Less than 1,000
Sponsor/Publisher: North American Case Research Association (NACRA)
Subscribe Price: 75.00 US$
 50.00 US$ Member in NACRA

REVIEW INFORMATION:

Type of Review: Blind Review
No. of External Reviewers: 3
No. of In House Reviewers: 1
Acceptance Rate: 11-20%
Time to Review: 2 - 3 Months
Reviewers Comments: Yes
Invited Articles: 0-5%
Fees to Publish: 0.00 US$

MANUSCRIPT TOPICS:
Accounting, Economics, & Finance; Advertising & Promotion Management; Business Education; Business Information Systems (MIS); Business Law, Public Responsibility & Ethics; Communication; Direct Marketing; Educational Administration; Engineering Management; Global Business; Health Care Administration; Hospitaltity Management; Labor Relations & Human Resource Mgt.; Marketing Research; Marketing Theory & Applications; Non Profit Organizations; Operations Research/Statistics; Organizational Behavior & Theory; Organizational Development; Production/Operations; Public Administration; Sales/Selling; Services; Small Business Entrepreneurship; Strategic Management Policy; Technology/Innovation

MANUSCRIPT GUIDELINES/COMMENTS:

Editorial Comments
The Type of Review is double-blind. The Reviewer's Comments are comprehensive. No Fees are charged to review the manuscript; however, at least one author must belong to North American Case Research Association. Membership fee is $50/year.

Manuscript Topics:
The *Case Research Journal* publishes outstanding decision-oriented cases drawn from research in real organizations, dealing with issues in all management-related disciplines including business, health care, education, technology, hospitality, and p0ublic administration. Usually, cases will be framed around problems facing some decision-maker in the organization. The Journal emphasizes cases based on field research but also accepts secondary-source cases. Occasionally, the Journal also publishes papers concerning case writing or teaching.

Previously published cases or articles (except those appearing in Proceedings or workshop presentations) are not eligible for consideration. Cases must not be under simultaneous consideration for textbook adoption. The Journal does not accept fictional works or cases synthesized from author experience.

Manuscript Guidelines

1. The North American Case Research Association (NACRA), publisher of the *Case Research Journal*, encourages the widest possible reproduction and use of the cases developed through its workshops and the Journal's review process, always with appropriate notice of copyright. NACRA members in non-profit institutions are encouraged to photocopy these cases for distribution to their own students, without requesting permission or paying fees. The NACRA membership receipt is also a permission to copy. Other faculty should contact the editor.

2. All other rights, including the right to use the cases in printed or electronically produced textbooks, are reserved to NACRA and the authors, who share copyright for these purposes. NACRA charges permission fees for these publication rights, in order to fund its continuing faculty development programs.

3. Cases must be accompanied by a comprehensive "Instructor's Manual," which identifies the case's intended course(s), audience, and the specific teaching objectives; lists assignment questions for student preparation; and analyzes each question. The Manual should discuss the research methodology for gathering case data and should state what disguises (if any) have been imposed. If possible, an epilogue or follow-on information about the decision actually taken should be included.

4. Cases submitted may be single- or double-spaced. Articles must be double-spaced.

5. Figures and Tables essential to student understanding of the case content should be embedded in the text and numbered separately. Exhibits should be grouped at the end of the case.

6. Wherever possible, citations should be embedded in the text, with bibliographic information restricted to a "Reference List" at the end of the case. All exhibits should state their sources in detail.

7. Authors' full names and positions, addresses, telephone and fax numbers, should be listed on a separate cover sheet. The corresponding author should be clearly identified.

No author identification should appear on either the case itself or the Instructor's Manual.

8. The corresponding author's cover letter should include the following paragraph:

In submitting this case to the *Case Research Journal* for widespread distribution in print and electronic media, I (we) certify that it is original work, based on real events in a real organization. It has not been published and is not under review elsewhere. Copyright holders have given written permission for the use of any material not permitted by the "Fair Use Doctrine." Where research has included field interviews, the host organization has signed a release authorizing the publication of the case and all data gathered with understandings of confidentiality.

9. The following notice should appear at the bottom of the first page of the manuscript:

"Review copy for use of the *Case Research Journal*. Not for reproduction or distribution. Dated (date of submission)."

10. Four copies of all manuscripts should be submitted.

11. It is expected that at least one author will be a member of the North American Case Research Association. Membership applications are available from the editor or from NACRA's treasurer, Robert N. Carter, PhD, 1117 13th Street, Columbus, Georgia 31901. Membership dues are currently $50 per year; a check payable to NACRA may be sent directly to the treasurer.

Communication Monographs

ADDRESS FOR SUBMISSION:

Michael J. Beatty, Editor
Communication Monographs
University of Missouri-St. Louis
Department of Communication
8001 Natural Bridge Road
St. Louis, MO 63121-4499
USA
Phone: 314-516-6725
Fax: 314-516-5816
E-Mail: beatty@umsl.edu
Web:
Address May Change:

PUBLICATION GUIDELINES:

Manuscript Length: 30
Copies Required: Four
Computer Submission: No
Format: N/A
Fees to Review: 0.00 US$

Manuscript Style:
American Psychological Association

CIRCULATION DATA:

Reader: Academics
Frequency of Issue: Quarterly
Copies per Issue: 4,001 - 5,000
Sponsor/Publisher: National Communication Association
Subscribe Price: No Reply

REVIEW INFORMATION:

Type of Review: Blind Review
No. of External Reviewers: 2
No. of In House Reviewers: 0
Acceptance Rate: 0-5%
Time to Review: 2 - 3 Months
Reviewers Comments: Yes
Invited Articles: 0-5%
Fees to Publish: 0.00 US$

MANUSCRIPT TOPICS:
Communication; Organization, Group, Mass Communication; Persuasion

MANUSCRIPT GUIDELINES/COMMENTS:

Editorial Policy
Communication Monographs historically has published original research dealing with processes which are central to communication. It will continue to do so. Although the journal is not restricted to particular conceptual perspectives or research paradigms, it is the responsibility of contributors to articulate dear and defensible rationales for the theoretical and methodological approaches employed in their research. Moreover, it is incumbent on contributors to explain precisely how their research findings advance our understanding of communication. Manuscripts dealing with quantitative research should report and discuss implications of obtained effect sizes within the context of theory (predictive power, parsimony, etc.) and the procedures employed in the study (reliability and validity of measures, relative strength of experimental manipulations, etc.). Priority will be given to research reports which have the broadest and most compelling implications for communication theory. Manuscripts that make limited contributions to our understanding of

communication, apply only to narrow contexts, or principally voice ideological concerns should be directed to more appropriate, specialized journals. The tradition of high standards and rigorous review associated with the journal will continue. In keeping with that tradition, only the very best of the manuscripts received are accepted for publication. All manuscripts are evaluated by at least two, and often three, qualified reviewers. The decision to publish a manuscript is made by the Editor, and all decisions are final.

Manuscript Submission
Authors should submit four copies of the manuscript and retain the original. Manuscripts should not be under review at any other publication while under consideration at Monographs. No material identifying the author(s) should appear anywhere except on the title page, which should include (1) a title and identification of the author(s); (2) professional title, address, telephone number, and electronic mail address (if available) and; (3) information concerning the manuscript's history. Historical information should include previous public presentation, publication of any part of the data set or portion of the manuscript, any NCA journals to which the manuscript previously has been submitted, and, if the manuscript is based on a thesis or dissertation, the advisor's name. The title page should be followed by an abstract of 200 or fewer words. Manuscript and reference style (including the preparation of tables and figures) should conform to the Publication Manual of the American Psychological Association, 4th Edition (1994). Contributors are encouraged to familiarize themselves with the criteria set forth in that manual before submitting to Monographs. Manuscripts that deviate substantially from APA style will not be forwarded to reviewers. Cost factors prohibit returning inappropriate manuscripts to contributors. Manuscripts, in general, should not exceed 30 pages or approximately 9,000 words (including references, notes, figures, and tables). Manuscripts should include tables only when they are the most efficient way to present data.

By submitting to Monographs contributors agree to sign copyright of their manuscripts, if accepted, to NCA. Authors should send four copies to: Michael J. Beatty, Editor, Communication Monographs, Department of Communication, University of Missouri-St. Louis, 8001 Natural Bridge Road, St. Louis, MO 63121.

Communication Research

ADDRESS FOR SUBMISSION:

Pamela J. Shoemaker, Co-editor
Communication Research
Syracuse University
S.I. Newhouse School of
  Public Communications
215 University Place
Syracuse, NY 13244-2100
USA
Phone: 315-443-1922
Fax: 315-443-1107
E-Mail: commre@summail.syr.edu
Web:
Address May Change:

PUBLICATION GUIDELINES:

Manuscript Length: 20-30
Copies Required: Four
Computer Submission: No
Format: N/A
Fees to Review: 0.00 US$

Manuscript Style:
    American Psychological Association

CIRCULATION DATA:

Reader: Academics
Frequency of Issue: Bi-Monthly
Copies per Issue: 1,001 - 2,000
Sponsor/Publisher: Sage
Subscribe Price: 51.00 US$ Individual
    177.00 US$ Institution
    9.00 US$ Add for Outside USA

REVIEW INFORMATION:

Type of Review: Blind Review
No. of External Reviewers: 3
No. of In House Reviewers: 2
Acceptance Rate: 21-30%
Time to Review: 1 - 2 Months
Reviewers Comments: Yes
Invited Articles: 0-5%
Fees to Publish: 0.00 US$

MANUSCRIPT TOPICS:
Communication; Interpersonal/Human Communication; Mass Communication

MANUSCRIPT GUIDELINES/COMMENTS:

Co-Editors: Michael E. Roloff & Pamela J. Shoemaker

Empirical research in communication began in. the 20th century, and there are more researchers pursuing answers to communication questions today than at any other time. The editorial goal of *Communication Research* is to offer a special opportunity for reflection and change in the impending millennium. To qualify for publication, research should, first, be explicitly tied to some form of communication; second, be theoretically driven with results that inform theory; third, use the most rigorous empirical methods; and fourth, be directly linked to the most important problems and issues facing humankind. Our criteria do not privilege any particular context; indeed, we believe that the key problems facing humankind occur tux close relationships, groups, organizations, and cultures. Hence, we hope to publish research conducted across a wide variety of levels and units of analysis.

The coeditors and editorial board make every effort to review manuscripts thoroughly and promptly. One of the coeditors initially determines whether the content of the manuscript is appropriate for the journal and whether there is sufficient publication to proceed with anonymous reviews. Manuscripts that do not pass this initial screening are returned immediately. If a manuscript is sent out for review, the process is typically completed in six weeks. Authors are encouraged to obtain and incorporate editorial advice of their colleagues prior to submitting their works to *Communication Research*.

Manuscripts should be prepared ire accordance with the *Publication Manual of the American Psychological Association*, 4th edition (1994). In particular, the entire manuscript should be double spaced, and manuscripts should have one and a half inch margins on all four sides. Tables should be clear and understandable without the text. Figures should be sent camera ready, clear, and legible when reduced. References should be carefully edited to ensure consistency with APA guidelines. Reliability estimates should be provided for measures. Effect size estimates should accompany reports of all statistically significant differences. Submissions should include current addresses, phone and FAX numbers, and e-mail addresses of all authors as well as author biographies of 100 words maximum for all authors. In addition, we request an abstract of no more than 150 words.

We require that authors report standard deviations with means, and that authors report measures of strength of association with tests of significance. Authors are responsible for gaining permission for including any copyrighted material that needs permission, including quotations of more than 300 words. A copy of the final revised manuscript on a computer disk should be included with The final revised hard copy.

Submission of a manuscript implies commitment to publish in the journal. Authors submitting manuscripts to the journal should not simultaneously submit them to another journal, nor should manuscripts have been published elsewhere in substantially similar form or with substantially similar content. Authors in doubt about what constitutes prior publication should consult the editor. *Four copies* of submitted manuscripts should be sent to Pamela J. Shoemaker, Coeditor, Communication Research, S. I, Newhouse School of Public Communications, Syracuse University, 215 University Place, Syracuse, New York 13244-2100.

Communication Studies

ADDRESS FOR SUBMISSION:

Paul Mongeau, Editor
Communication Studies
Miami University
Department of Communication
Oxford, OH 45056
USA
Phone: 513-529-7413
Fax: 513-529-1268
E-Mail: mongeapa@muohio.edu
Web:
Address May Change: 12/31/00

PUBLICATION GUIDELINES:

Manuscript Length: 21-25
Copies Required: Four
Computer Submission: No
Format: N/A
Fees to Review: 0.00 US$

Manuscript Style:
American Psychological Association

CIRCULATION DATA:

Reader: Academics
Frequency of Issue: Quarterly
Copies per Issue: 2,001 - 3,000
Sponsor/Publisher: Central State
  Communication Association
Subscribe Price: 45.00 US$ CSCA Mem.
  25.00 US$ Student/Emeritus Member
  90.00 US$ Dept.Member, $50 Library

REVIEW INFORMATION:

Type of Review: Blind Review
No. of External Reviewers: 3
No. of In House Reviewers: No Reply
Acceptance Rate: 11-20%
Time to Review: 2 - 3 Months
Reviewers Comments: Yes
Invited Articles: 0-5%
Fees to Publish: 6.00 US$

MANUSCRIPT TOPICS:
Communication

MANUSCRIPT GUIDELINES/COMMENTS:

Information For Contributors
Communication Studies is committed to publishing high-quality original scholarship focused centrally on human communication processes. Articles published in *Communication Studies* should represent the diversity of scholarship that composes the study of human communication, regardless of philosophical, theoretical, or methodological underpinnings. Published essays and reports of studies should make important and noteworthy contributions to the advancement of human communication scholarship. *Communication Studies* supports research and writing free of sexism and other biases.

The Editor assumes that manuscripts submitted to *Communication Studies* are original, unpublished, and not under consideration by other publication outlets. *Communication Studies* follows a policy of masked peer review. To ensure such a masked review, include no author-identifying information beyond the title page.

Authors should submit four copies of the manuscript to the Editor. Authors should retain a copy as manuscripts will not be returned. Double-space manuscripts on 8½ by 11 inch paper. An abstract of 120 or fewer words should accompany the manuscript. Manuscript preparation, source citations, and reference style should conform to the fourth edition of the *Publication Manual of the American Psychological Association*. Upon acceptance of the manuscript for publication, authors must submit high quality camera-ready copy for all artwork and figures and must assign, copyright to the Central States Communication Association. *Communication Studies* will not publish any material for which the assignment of copyright to the Central States Communication Association is withheld.

A separate title page must accompany each manuscript. In addition to the title and author(s) of the manuscript, the title page should include a short biographical summary of each author, including full name, professional title, address, telephone number, and electronic mail address (if available). If any portion of the manuscript has been presented in other forms (e.g., speech or colloquy) or in other forums (e.g., convention), include details on the occasion on the title page. Finally, indicate on the title page whether the manuscript is drawn, in whole or part, from a thesis or dissertation, with the name of the director of the study identified.

Communication Studies (formerly the Central Stares Speech Journal) is a quarterly publication (Spring, Summer, Fall, and Winter) of the Central States Communication Association. Annual subscriptions to *Communication Studies* are $45.00 which includes a regular CSCA membership, $25.00 which includes student and emeritus membership. $90.00 which includes departmental membership, and $50.00 for libraries.

Send questions about membership, subscriptions, orders for back issues, and/or inquiries into reprinting *Communication Studies* or Central States Speech Journal articles to the Executive Director, Lynn Turner, *Communication Studies*, Marquette University. Milwaukee, WI 53201. Send requests for advertising rates to the Advertising Manager, Renee Meyers, Department of Communication, University of Wisconsin, Milwaukee, WI 53201.

Communication Studies is printed by Science Press. Ephrata. PA 17522.

Communications and the Law

ADDRESS FOR SUBMISSION:

The Honorable Theodore R. Kupferman
Communications and the Law
 Editor-in-Chief
425 Park Avenue
New York, NY 10022
USA
Phone: 212-583-0500
Fax: 212-583-0412
E-Mail:
Web:
Address May Change:

PUBLICATION GUIDELINES:

Manuscript Length: 21-25
Copies Required: Two
Computer Submission: Yes
Format: IBM Compatible/Prefer WP
Fees to Review: 0.00 US$

Manuscript Style:
 Chicago Manual of Style, & Uniform
 System of Citation for footnotes

CIRCULATION DATA:

Reader: Business Persons, Academics &
 Lawyers
Frequency of Issue: Quarterly
Copies per Issue: 1,001 - 2,000
Sponsor/Publisher: Fred B. Rotham & Co.
Subscribe Price: 115.00 US$
    250.00 US$

REVIEW INFORMATION:

Type of Review: Editorial Review
No. of External Reviewers: 0
No. of In House Reviewers: 1
Acceptance Rate: 50%
Time to Review: 1 - 2 Months
Reviewers Comments: Yes
Invited Articles: 6-10%
Fees to Publish: 0.00 US$

MANUSCRIPT TOPICS:
Advertising & Promotion Management; Business Law, Public Responsibility & Ethics; Communication; Labor Relations & Human Resource Mgt.; Technology/Innovation

MANUSCRIPT GUIDELINES/COMMENTS:

This quarterly journal provides in-depth articles on issues such as privacy, libel, freedom of speech, censorship, defamation, expanding technologies, aggressive use of the media by business, public opinion formation by government, and a host of other issues facing our information society.

1. Manuscript should be submitted in duplicate and cannot be returned. If article is accepted, a disk will be required (IBM-compatible, WordPerfect preferred). Manuscript and disk should be sent to the Editor.

2. Submission is a representation that the manuscript has not been published previously and is not currently under consideration tor publication elsewhere.

A statement transferring copyright from the authors (or their employers, if they hold the copyright) to Fred B. Rothman & Co. will be required before the manuscript can be accepted for publication. The publisher will provide the necessary forms for this transfer. Such a written transfer of copyright, which previously was assumed to be implicit in the act of submitting a manuscript, is necessary under the U.S. copyright law effective 1978 in order for the publisher to carry through the dissemination of information and reviews as widely and effectively as possible.

3. Papers should average between 5,000 and 10,000 words in length. Pages should be numbered sequentially, with the total number of pages indicated on each page in the upper right corner (i.e., 1 of 22, 2 of 22, etc.).

4. Use 8 1/2 x 11-inch paper, one side of the sheet only, and double space throughout. Allow at least 1 1/4-inch margin left and right.

5. Footnotes should be submitted on separate sheets, at the end of the manuscript, double spaced.

6. Use *A Uniform System of Citation*, Fifteenth Edition for legal footnote style. Use The *Chicago Manual of Style*, Fourteenth Edition for general style.

7. The publisher will provide seven copies of the issue in which the contribution appears to the senior author of the paper. Additional issues and individual reprints are available to authors and may be ordered from the publisher.

Cornell Hotel and Restaurant Administration Quarterly

ADDRESS FOR SUBMISSION:

Glenn Withiam, Executive Editor
Cornell Hotel and Restaurant
  Administration Quarterly
Cornell University
School of Hotel & Restaurant Admin.
Statler Hall
Ithaca, NY 14853
USA
Phone: 607-255-3025
Fax: 607-255-4179
E-Mail: cornell_hraq@cornell.edu
Web: www.elsevier.nl
Address May Change:

PUBLICATION GUIDELINES:

Manuscript Length: Any
Copies Required: Three
Computer Submission: Yes
Format: MAC
Fees to Review: 0.00 US$

Manuscript Style:
  Chicago Manual of Style

CIRCULATION DATA:

Reader: Business Persons
Frequency of Issue: Bi-Monthly
Copies per Issue: 5,001 - 10,000
Sponsor/Publisher: Elsevier Science
  Publishing Co.
Subscribe Price: 85.00 US$ Individual
  230.00 US$ Institution

REVIEW INFORMATION:

Type of Review: Blind Review
No. of External Reviewers: 2
No. of In House Reviewers: 7
Acceptance Rate: 50%
Time to Review: 4 - 6 Months
Reviewers Comments: No
Invited Articles: 0-5%
Fees to Publish: 0.00 US$

MANUSCRIPT TOPICS:
Advertising & Promotion Management; Hospitaltity Management; Human Resources; Marketing Research; Marketing Theory & Applications; Organizational Behavior & Theory; Sales/Selling; Services; Technology/Innovation

MANUSCRIPT GUIDELINES/COMMENTS:

Description
The Cornell Hotel and Restaurant Administration Quarterly is the premier publication of the hospitality and food service industries.

It is dedicated to advancing the reader's understanding of the industry and of new management principles relevant to the field. The Cornell Quarterly's articles provide practical advice on management concerns, in-depth analyses of major trends, and recommendations for career development.

Audience
Executives, mid-level Managers, and Consultants in the lodging, resort and food service industry, as well as Academics and Students in business and hotel and restaurant management schools.

Submission Procedure
Submission of manuscripts to *The Cornell Quarterly* is open to anyone who has a message of interest for managers in the hospitality industry. Prospective authors are welcome to query the editors regarding potential topics, but that is not required.

To submit a paper, send three copies to the address above. The print must be double-spaced and margins should be generous. The editors will read the paper for general acceptability and send it for review to two members of the Quarterly editorial board, which comprises Cornell faculty and outside volunteer experts. The review is double blind, that is, the author does not know who the judges are and the judges do not know who the author is. Based on the reviewers' recommendation, the editors make a final decision regarding publication. The review process can take anywhere from three to 12 months.

You may be asked to revise the paper based on the reviewers' suggestions. If you choose to make the revisions and resubmit the paper, it may still be subject to the review process. Papers deemed not suitable for publication are usually rejected without prejudice, meaning that the author make seek to make amendments that would make the paper acceptable. Once again, resubmissions are subject to the review process.

Once your paper is accepted, the editors will request a diskette containing the article. This disk can be formatted in any IBM- or Macintosh-readable format, although Mac is preferred, and we can read files from nearly any application. If there is any question, send an ASCII file or text file. You may also send the manuscript via e-mail.

Your paper will be edited for style and readability. Issues of logic or fact that have not been resolved during the review process will be resolved in the editing process. Should an issue arise that has somehow been overlooked in the review process, The Quarterly reserves the right to suspend publication of the paper until all issues are resolved.

When the editing process is complete, you will receive a final draft for your approval. The purpose of this step is serve as a check on the editing process, to ensure no errors were inadvertently introduced. This step is not an invitation to revise your thinking or substantially rewrite the paper.

Accepted papers generally appear within four to six months of acceptance. The editors reserve the right to schedule the appearance of accepted papers.

Style and footnotes
The Quarterly generally uses the writing conventions set forth in the *Chicago Manual of Style*. Citations should follow the CMS format, and should appear as endnotes or footnotes on the manuscript. Make sure to include all publisher information, page numbers, dates of

publication, and the like. Please avoid the commonly used American Psychological Association (APA) style, although its use alone will not cause a paper to be rejected.

As a professional journal, The Quarterly prefers a direct, vigorous writing style that employs simple, declarative sentences. In particular, authors should use the active voice rather than passive voice in their sentence structure. The Quarterly's purpose is to share information clearly, and active voice does that job well. On the other hand, passive voice is anything but clear and usually serves to disguise information (or a paucity thereof).

Thank you for your interest in The Cornell Quarterly. Without the continuing strong support of volunteer authors, The Quarterly would not be able to continue its mission of disseminating management-level information to the hospitality industry and academia

Decision Sciences (Journal of)

ADDRESS FOR SUBMISSION:

Ram Narasimhan, Editor
Decision Sciences (Journal of)
Michigan State University
Eli Broad Graduate School of Management
Department of Marketing & Supply Chain
 Management, N370 Business Complex
East Lansing, MI 48824-1122
USA
Phone: 517-432-4664
Fax: 517-432-4665
E-Mail: decsci@pilot.msu.edu
Web: dsi.gsu.edu
Address May Change:

PUBLICATION GUIDELINES:

Manuscript Length: 18-20
Copies Required: Five
Computer Submission: No
Format: N/A
Fees to Review: 50.00 US$ Non Members
 25.00 US$ Dec. Sci. Institute Member

Manuscript Style:
 Chicago Manual of Style

CIRCULATION DATA:

Reader: Academics
Frequency of Issue: Quarterly
Copies per Issue: 3,001 - 4,000
Sponsor/Publisher: Decision Sciences
 Institute
Subscribe Price: 20.00 US$
 80.00 US$

REVIEW INFORMATION:

Type of Review: Blind Review
No. of External Reviewers: 2
No. of In House Reviewers: 2
Acceptance Rate: 11-20%
Time to Review: 2 - 3 Months
Reviewers Comments: Yes
Invited Articles: No Reply
Fees to Publish: 0.00 US$

MANUSCRIPT TOPICS:
Business Information Systems (MIS); Health Care Administration; Marketing Research; Marketing Theory & Applications; Operations Research/Statistics; Organizational Behavior & Theory; Production/Operations; Purchasing/Materials Management; Strategic Management Policy; Technology/Innovation

MANUSCRIPT GUIDELINES/COMMENTS:

Submission
Five copies of the manuscript should be submitted to the Editor at the above address.

Your submission of a paper certifies that none of the contents are copyrighted, published or accepted for publication by another journal, under review by another journal, or submitted to another journal while under review by *Decision Sciences*. All manuscripts should be printed in Times Roman (12 pt), double-spaced on 8 1/2 x 11 paper, accompanied by an abstract of not more than 180 words, and an author's vita of not more than 150 words. The author's name and affiliation should appear on a separate page.

All equations should be set on separate lines, centered, and numbered consecutively in parentheses that appear flush with the right margin of the page. Figures and charts, as well as tables, should be consecutively numbered in arabic. *Decision Sciences* does not allow the use of footnotes or end notes. A copy of all referenced forthcoming papers should accompany the submitted manuscript. References should be listed alphabetically by author at the end of the paper and referred to in the body of the text by Name (date). While the "Name (date)" style is new to *Decision Sciences,* the general format remains the same. It would do prospective authors no great harm to scrutinize past issues of the journal prior to preparing manuscripts for submission. However, conformity to exact page layout is not the responsibility of the authors.

To facilitate the reviewing process, authors **must** indicate appropriate key words for their papers. Papers submitted to *Decision Sciences* without key words will suffer a delay in the assignment of reviewers and associate editors. The key word list presently in use at *Decision Sciences* follows after the next page, although authors can specify other key words if that list is not adequate. Authors should specify as many key words as apply to their papers, however key words must be specified in at least one functional area and at least one methodological area.

Should the manuscript be accepted for publication, the author will be asked to submit a copy of the disc containing the final post-review version of the paper. The word processing file (or ASCII text file) will be used in the typesetting process.

There is a nonrefundable submission fee of $25 for Institute members and $50 for nonmembers.

Editorial Philosophy
The central theme of the Decision Sciences Institute is not problem solving per se, but decision making in public and private organizations utilizing behavioral, economic, and quantitative methods of analysis. *Decision Sciences* articles, therefore, must have a decision-making orientation and address problems of managerial significance. A reasonable case should be made for the importance of the problem. Under this aegis, the Editor's objective is to attain a broad coverage of topics at a level of sophistication that will place the journal within the grasp of the entire membership.

Educational research papers and tutorials that are not merely reportorial but make a unique contribution to the decision sciences and to the teaching of decision sciences will be welcome. Articles on new course designs or improved approaches to education in the decision sciences should, as a general rule, include evidence that the new designs or methods are indeed superior to other approaches. Conceptual and theoretical articles should make clear how their contents contribute to the decision-making process or our understanding of that process. Articles posing new methodologies or improvements over existing ones should make clear why they are important for decision makers to consider, and what important problems they address. Papers concerned with the development of algorithms that are not directly related to a specific decision problem will not be published in *Decision Sciences*.

There is no restriction on the length of articles, particularly on the down side. However, conciseness will be considered a virtue. Articles must be written in the English language as *Decision Sciences* does not have the capability to do foreign language translations.

Reviewing Process
Each article submitted to *Decision Sciences* is subjected to the following reviewing process:

1. An initial screening by the Editor to determine the suitability of the article for the Journal. Assuming it is suitable, it is assigned to two referees, according to its functional and methodological content.

2. A careful review by two referees, each of whom makes a recommendation to the Editor and supplies comments, of varying detail, for the author.

3. An appraisal of the reviews by the Editor, who makes an initial decision regarding the disposition of the paper. If in the Editor's judgment the paper should proceed in the review process, the paper and the reviews are assigned to an Associate Editor for blind review and a recommendation. If the Editor feels the paper has potential for publication, the author is invited to make revisions according to the suggestions of the reviewers and the Associate Editor, who will also process the revised paper.

4. A critique by the Associate Editor who reviews the revised paper, the original paper, and the comments of the referees. The Associate Editor provides the Editor with a recommendation regarding publication and may indicate that further revisions are necessary.

5. A final decision made by the Editor, who appraises the entire review process, making certain that all revisions suggested by the referees and the Associate Editor prerequisite to publication have been made.

The Editor reserves the right to deviate from the above procedures when the situation warrants and as it is deemed appropriate.

Decision Sciences **Journal**
Functional Areas

To facilitate the review process, authors should indicate the appropriate functional and methodological areas into which their paper fits. The areas should be chosen from the following list.

ACCOUNTING

Accounting Education
Accounting Information Systems
Accounting Policy
Activity-Based Costing
Audit
Audit Evidence

Financial Accounting
Foreign Currency
Internal Control
Leases
Leverage
Litigation

Auditor Judgment
Capital Budgeting
Cost Accounting
Cost Benefit Analysis
Disclosure
Errors
Ethics
Expectation Theory
Expert Systems

Management Accounting
Market Efficiency
Pensions
Performance Evaluation
Reporting Decisions
Sampling
Tax
Tests of Controls

BUSINESS STRATEGY & ENTREPRENEURSHIP

Agency Theory
Cognitive Decision Models
Cost Leadership Strategies
Diversification Strategies

Joint Ventures
Strategic Alliances
Strategic Decision Making
Strategic Groups

ECONOMICS

Budget & Planning
Capital Budget
Cash Flow
Econometrics
Economic Analysis
Efficiency Analysis
Incentives

Inflation
Monetary Policy
Privatization
Risk
Strategy and Policy
Utility

FINANCE

Agency Costs
Arbitrage Pricing
Asset Valuation
Bankruptcy/Financial Distress
Capital/Asset Pricing
Capital Budgeting
Capital Structure
Carve Outs
Corporate Finance
Cost of Capital
Divestitures
Ethics
Financial DSS
Financial Markets
Financial Models

Futures
Initial Public Offerings
Investment Banking
Market Timing
Merger/Acquisition
Net Present Value
Optimal Contracting
Options
Portfolio
Securities
Signaling
Speculation
Spin-offs
Stocks/Bonds
Term Structure

HEALTH CARE SYSTEMS

Capacity
Cost
DRG's

Hospital Management
Planning & Scheduling

EDUCATION RESEARCH
- Academic Computing
- Budgeting
- Computer Applications
- Cost Management
- Course/Instructor Evaluation
- Enrollment Management
- Ethics
- Faculty Assignment/Course Scheduling
- Faculty Development Issues
- Faculty/Student Evaluation
- Group Formation
- Implementation
- Information Use
- Learning Theory
- Multimedia Instruction
- Pedagogy

INTERNATIONAL BUSINESS AND GLOBALIZATION
- Cultural Efforts
- Globalization
- Location
- Monetary Analysis
- Negotiation
- Sourcing
- Strategic Issues
- Trade Agreements & Regulations

MARKETING
- Advertising and Promotion
- Brand Management
- Brand Switching
- Choice Process
- Consumer Behavior
- Cross Cultural
- Direct and Mail Marketing
- Distribution Channels
- Ethics
- Framing
- Market Research/Strategy
- Performance
- Pricing
- Product Design/Planning
- Psychometrics
- Sales Analysis

MIS/DSS & COMPUTER SYSTEMS
- Artificial Intelligence
- Computer Hardware
- Computer Networks
- Database Management
- Decision Support Systems
- Distributed Data Processing
- Electronic Data Interchange (EDI)
- Executive Information Systems (EIS)
- End-User Computing
- Expert Systems (ES)
- Global Information Systems
- Group Decision Support System (GDSS)
- Human/Computer Interaction
- Hypermedia/Hypertext
- Information Search Strategies
- IS Implementation
- Inter-Organizational Systems
- Knowledge Acquisition
- Knowledge-Based Systems
- Management Information Systems
- Organizational Learning Systems
- Strategic Information Systems (SIS)
- Systems Development Methodologies
- Telecommunications
- User-Analyst Reference
- Virtual Reality Systems

ORG. BEHAVIOR/ORG. DESIGN
- Bias
- Diversity Issues
- Employee Discipline
- Ethics
- Expectancy Theory
- Motivation
- Networks
- Organizational Commitment
- Organizational Structure
- Organizational Theory

Feedback
Gain Sharing
Gender Studies
Job Satisfaction
Labor/Staff Relations
Leadership
Merit Pay
Participation
Performance Appraisal
Planning/Strategy
Reengineering
Social Issues
Team Building

OPERATIONS AND LOGISTICS MANAGEMENT

Aggregate Planning
Assembly Systems
Automation-Robotics
Benchmarking
Business Process Reengineering
Capacity Planning
Cellular Manufacturing
Computer Integrated Manufacturing (CIM)
Distribution/Logistics
Ethics
Facility Layout
Flexible Manufacturing Systems (FMS)
Global Operations Management
Group Technology
Hierarchical Planning
Inventory Management
Inventory Theory
Job Shop Scheduling
Just-In-Time Systems
Labor and Staff Planning
Learning
Location
Lot Sizing
Machine Scheduling and Sequencing
Management of R&D
Manufacturing Strategy
Manufacturing Technology
Master Production Scheduling
Materials Management
Materials Requirement Planning (MRP)
New Product Introduction
Operations Strategy
Process Choice/Design
Product Planning
Production and Inventory Control Systems
Productivity
Project Management
Purchasing
Quality
Repetitive Manufacturing
Service Operations
Shop Floor Control
Supply Chain Management
Technology Management
Theory of Constraints
Total Quality Management (TQM)
Work Teams
Workforce Scheduling

Decision Sciences Journal
Methodological Area

Analytic Hierarchy Process (AHP)
Artificial Intelligence
Box-Jenkins
Case Study
Chaotic Systems (Chaos Theory)
Choice Simulation
Cluster Analysis/Hierarchical Grouping
Computer Science
Conjoint Analysis
Correspondence Analysis
Mathematical Programming Optimization
Mathematics
Meta-Analysis
Multi-Attribute Utility Theory
Multi-Criteria Decision Making (MCDM)
Multi-Dimensional Scaling
Multivariate Statistics
Multivariate Time Series
Network Theory
Neural Networks

- Curve Fitting
- Data Envelopment Analysis
- Decision Analysis
- Dynamic Programming
- Experimental Design
- Fuzzy Logic
- Game Theory
- Goal Programming
- Heuristics
- Integer/Binary Program
- Judgment Analysis
- Linear Programming
- Linear Regression
- Logic Modeling
- Markov Processes/Chains
- Nonlinear Dynamic Systems
- Nonlinear Regression
- Optimal Control Theory
- Parameter Estimation
- Probability Models
- Queuing Theory
- Risk Analysis
- Sampling
- Simulation
- Statistical Process Control
- Statistics
- Stochastic Processes
- Structural Equation Models
- Survey Research/Design
- Time Series Forecasting

Entrepreneurship Theory and Practice

ADDRESS FOR SUBMISSION:

D. Ray Bagby, Executive Editor
Entrepreneurship Theory and Practice
Baylor University
Hankamer School of Business
Waco, TX 76798-8011
USA
Phone: 254-710-4156
Fax: 254-710-2271
E-Mail: ray_bagby@baylor.edu
Web:
Address May Change:

PUBLICATION GUIDELINES:

Manuscript Length: 21-25
Copies Required: Four hardcopies
Computer Submission: Yes ,e-mail attachment
Format: MsWord 6.0 compatible
Fees to Review: 0.00 US$

Manuscript Style:
See Manuscript Guidelines

CIRCULATION DATA:

Reader: Academics
Frequency of Issue: Quarterly
Copies per Issue: 1,001 - 2,000
Sponsor/Publisher: Baylor University
Subscribe Price: 55.00 US$ Individual
90.00 US$ Institution in N. America
73.00 US$ & 108 US$ Outside N.Amer.

REVIEW INFORMATION:

Type of Review: Blind Review
No. of External Reviewers: 2
No. of In House Reviewers: 0
Acceptance Rate: 11-20%
Time to Review: 2 - 3 Months
Reviewers Comments: Yes
Invited Articles: 11-20%
Fees to Publish: 0.00 US$

MANUSCRIPT TOPICS:
Small Business Entrepreneurship

MANUSCRIPT GUIDELINES/COMMENTS:

Our purpose is to publish manuscripts that significantly advance the entrepreneurship field. Entrepreneurship includes but is not limited to: management of small firms; and issues in family businesses. Other areas considered within the journal's scope are: international and cross-cultural studies; entrepreneurship in the not-for-profit sector; interdisciplinary approaches to the study of entrepreneurship; an public policy issues impacting entrepreneurial ventures.

Review Process
All manuscripts will be reviewed by two members of the Editorial Review Board, including ad hoc reviewers when necessary and/or appropriate. Authors will be informed of the decision, including any relevant comments, within y60 days of the receipt of the paper in acceptable format. Neither authors nor reviewers will be identified in the review process. Manuscripts are not returned to authors.

Copyright
The copyright of published articles will belong to the publisher. Therefore, only unpublished, noncopyrighted manuscripts should be submitted. Revised versions of papers published in Proceedings are acceptable, if the author has retained the copyright. Authors will be granted permission to reprint or otherwise use portions of their published papers.

What To Submit
Original manuscripts of either a conceptual or empirical nature that are the result of scholarly research and which contribute to the mission above will be considered. The Journal also publishes teaching cases, research notes and dissertation abstracts.

Format
Title Page. A page containing the title of the manuscript and the name, position/title, affiliation, address and telephone number of each author should accompany the submission. This page should also contain any acknowledgements of assistance and notice of prior or pending presentations of the paper.

First Page. The first page of the manuscript should contain a short descriptive title, an abstract of not more than 100 words (single spaced), and the beginning of the text.

Body. The manuscript must be typed, double-spaced (except for the abstract) on one side of the paper only. Appropriate headings (centered) and sub-headings (left justified) should be used to segment the manuscript to enhance readability.

Footnotes. Footnotes should be used only for clarification that is not appropriate for the body of the manuscript. If used they should be numbered consecutively, marked at the appropriate place in the text, but listed under the heading Footnotes, at the end of the manuscript.

Tables, Etc. Tables, charts, and graphs should be included only when they contribute materially to an understanding of the written presentation. They should be numbered consecutively and placed at the end of the manuscript with an appropriate notice in the text to indicate approximate placement, i.e.,

----
Insert Table 1 About Here

References. Citations in the text should be accomplished using author's(s') last name(s), year of publication, and, when quoting, the page numbers. All publications cited in the text should be listed alphabetically by first author's last name in the References section at the end of the paper. Both citations and references should conform to the latest edition of the Publication Manual of the American Psychological Association.

Where To Submit
One copy of the paper, in a format compatible with Word for Windows 6.0 should be submitted to the Executive Editor as an attachment to e-mail at ray_bagby@baylor.edu or send four (4) paper copies to the address above. Authors of manuscripts accepted for publication will receive reprints of the article.

European Journal of Marketing

ADDRESS FOR SUBMISSION:

David J. Carson, Editor
European Journal of Marketing
University of Ulster
School of Management
Shore Road
Newtownabbey, Co. Antrim, BT37 0QB
Northern Ireland
Phone: 353-232-365131
Fax: 44 1274 785200
E-Mail: rneedham@mcb.co.uk
Web: www.mcb.co.uk
Address May Change:

PUBLICATION GUIDELINES:

Manuscript Length: 3,000-6,000 words
Copies Required: Three
Computer Submission: No
Format: N/A
Fees to Review: 0.00 US$

Manuscript Style:
  See Manuscript Guidelines

CIRCULATION DATA:

Reader: Academics, Practitioners
Frequency of Issue: Monthly
Copies per Issue: No Reply
Sponsor/Publisher: MCB University Press
Subscribe Price: 7439.00 US$

REVIEW INFORMATION:

Type of Review: Blind Review
No. of External Reviewers: No Reply
No. of In House Reviewers: No Reply
Acceptance Rate: 28%
Time to Review: 2 - 3 Months
Reviewers Comments: Yes
Invited Articles: No Reply
Fees to Publish: 0.00 US$

MANUSCRIPT TOPICS:
Advertising & Promotion Management; Communication; Direct Marketing; Marketing Research; Marketing Theory & Applications; Sales/Selling

MANUSCRIPT GUIDELINES/COMMENTS:

About the journal
The European Journal of Marketing provides a platform for contemporary ideas in marketing, the thinking, theory and practice. It aims to facilitate information among researchers on a worldwide basis and keep up to date with developments in European marketing and Europe in the global context. The journal contains leading edge marketing theory - supported by evidence-based research, from the world's leading marketing thinkers. Every article published in the European Journal of Marketing has been subject to a double blind peer review process to ensure its relevance and quality. The science of strategic marketing covers many areas of human and organizational experience, so as you'd expect, the European Journal of Marketing also covers a wide range of topics.

Coverage
- Marketing strategy
- Globalization
- Marketing theory development
- Marketing research
- Marketing communications
- Consumerism
- Relationship Marketing

Notes for Contributors

Copyright
Articles submitted to the journal should be original contributions and should not be under consideration for any other publication at the same time. Authors submitting articles for publication warrant that the work is not an infringement of any existing copyright and will indemnify the publisher against any breach of such warranty. For ease of dissemination and to ensure proper policing of use, papers and contributions become the legal copyright of the publisher unless otherwise agreed. Submissions should be sent to:

The Editor, Professor David J. Carson (see address above), or
Associate Editor, Dr A. Gilmore, School of Management, University of Ulster, Shore Road, Newtownabbey, Co. Antrim, BT37 0QB.

Editorial objectives
To provide a platform for new ideas in marketing - the thinking, theory and practice - and a forum for debating issues that arise. In this way the journal seeks to:
1. facilitate the interchange of information among researchers on a worldwide basis;
2. assist both academics and practitioners to keep up-to-date with developments in marketing in Europe and Europe in the global context.

General principles
a. It is our intention to publish well-written readable articles with broad appeal and a truly international relevance.
b. Contributors are encouraged to focus on either conceptual or empirical work to outline practical implications for marketing. Topics should always relate to some aspect of marketing.
c. New and first-time authors are particularly encouraged.
d. At the European Journal of Marketing we are keen to publish more good papers which emanate from Europe, or focus on Europe in the global context.

The reviewing process
Each paper is reviewed by the editor and, if it is judged suitable for this publication, it is then sent to two referees for double blind peer review. Based on their recommendations, the editor then decides whether the paper should be accepted as is, revised or rejected.

Manuscript requirements
Three copies of the manuscript should be submitted in double line spacing with wide margins. All authors should be shown and author's details must be printed on a separate sheet and the author should not be identified anywhere else in the article.

As a guide, articles should be between 3,000 and 6,000 words in length. A title of not more than eight words should be provided. A brief **autobiographical note** should be supplied including full name, affiliation, e-mail address and full international contact details. Authors must supply an **abstract** of 100-150 words. Up to six **keywords** should be included which encapsulate the principal subjects covered by the article.

Where there is a **methodology**, it should be clearly described under a separate heading. **Headings** must be short, clearly defined and not numbered. **Notes** or **Endnotes** should be used only if absolutely necessary and must be identified in the text by consecutive numbers, enclosed in square brackets and listed at the end of the article.

Figures, charts and **diagrams** should be kept to a minimum. They must be black and white with minimum shading and numbered consecutively using arabic numerals with a brief title and labelled axes. In the text, the position of the figure should be shown by typing on a separate line the words "take in Figure 2". Good quality originals must be provided.

Tables should be kept to a minimum. They must be numbered consecutively with roman numerals and a brief title. In the text, the position of the table should be shown by typing on a separate line the words "take in Table IV".

Photos and **illustrations** must be supplied as good quality black and white original half tones with captions. Their position should be shown in the text by typing on a separate line the words "take in Plate 2".

References to other publications should be complete and in Harvard style. They should contain full bibliographical details and journal titles should not be abbreviated. For multiple citations in the same year use a, b, c immediately following the year of publication. References should be shown within the text by giving the author's last name followed by a comma and year of publication all in round brackets, e.g. (Fox, 1994). At the end of the article should be a reference list in alphabetical order as follows

(a) *for books*
surname, initials and year of publication, title, publisher, place of publication, e.g.Casson, M. (1979), Alternatives to the Multinational Enterprise, Macmillan, London.

(b) *for chapter in edited book*
surname, initials and year, "title", editor's surname, initials, title, publisher, place, pages, e.g.Bessley, M. and Wilson, P. (1984), "Public policy and small firms in Britain", in Levicki, C. (Ed.), Small Business Theory and Policy, Croom Helm, London, pp.111-26. Please note that the chapter title must be underlined.

(c) *for articles*
surname, initials, year "title", journal, volume, number, pages, e.g.Fox, S. (1994) "Empowerment as a catalyst for change: an example from the food industry", Supply Chain Management, Vol 2 No 3, pp. 29-33

If there is more than one author list surnames followed by initials. All authors should be shown.

Electronic sources should include the URL of the electronic site at which they may be found, as follows:
Neuman, B.C.(1995), "Security, payment, and privacy for network commerce", IEEE Journal on Selected Areas in Communications, Vol. 13 No.8, October, pp.1523-31. Available (IEEE SEPTEMBER) http://www.research.att.com/jsac/

Notes/Endnotes should be used only if absolutely necessary. They should, however, always be used for citing Web sites. They should be identified in the text by consecutive numbers enclosed in square brackets and listed at the end of the article. Please then provide full Web site addresses in the end list.

Final submission of the article
Once accepted for publication, the final version of the manuscript must be provided, accompanied by a 3.5" **disk** of the same version labelled with: disk format; author name(s); title of article; journal title; file name.

Each article must be accompanied by a completed and signed **Journal Article Record Form** available from the Editor or on http://www.literaticlub.co.uk/

The manuscript will be considered to be the definitive version of the article. The author must ensure that it is complete, grammatically correct and without spelling or typographical errors. In preparing the disk, please use one of the following formats: Word, Word Perfect, Rich text format or TeX/LaTeX. Figures which are provided electronically must be in tif, gif or pic file extensions. All figures and graphics must also be supplied as good quality originals.

Final submission requirements
Manuscripts must be clean, good quality hard copy and;
- include an abstract and keywords
- have Harvard style references
- include any figures, photos and graphics as good quality originals
- be accompanied by a labelled disk
- be accompanied by a completed Journal Article Record Form

Technical assistance is available from MCB's World Wide Web Literati Club on http://www.literaticlub.co.uk/ or contact Mike massey at MCB, e-mail mmassey@mcb

Family Business Review

ADDRESS FOR SUBMISSION:

Joseph H. Astrachan, Editor
Family Business Review
Kennesaw State College
Family Enterprise Center
1000 Chastain Road
Kennesaw, GA 30144-5591
USA
Phone: 770423-6045
Fax: 770-423-6721
E-Mail: jastrach@ksumail.kennesaw.edu
Web:
Address May Change:

PUBLICATION GUIDELINES:

Manuscript Length: 20+
Copies Required: Five
Computer Submission: Yes
Format: If accepted
Fees to Review: 0.00 US$

Manuscript Style:
　See Manuscript Guidelines

CIRCULATION DATA:

Reader: Academics, Professionals
　(e.g.Consultants)
Frequency of Issue: Quarterly
Copies per Issue: 1,001 - 2,000
Sponsor/Publisher: The Familly Firm
　Institute
Subscribe Price: 55.00 US$ Indiv,2 Yrs
　84.00 US$ Institution, 2 Years

REVIEW INFORMATION:

Type of Review: Blind Review
No. of External Reviewers: 3
No. of In House Reviewers: 2
Acceptance Rate: 21-30%
Time to Review: 2 - 3 Months
Reviewers Comments: Yes
Invited Articles: 6-10%
Fees to Publish: 0.00 US$

MANUSCRIPT TOPICS:
Business Law, Public Responsibility & Ethics; Communication; Family Business; Family Systems Theory; Global Business; Labor Relations & Human Resource Mgt.; Marketing Theory & Applications; Operations Research/Statistics; Organizational Behavior & Theory; Organizational Development; Small Business Entrepreneurship; Strategic Management Policy

MANUSCRIPT GUIDELINES/COMMENTS:

Family Business Review seeks high-quality manuscripts on new research findings, frameworks, and methodologies for business in family firms; development of theories and research on how business and organizational factors affect family dynamics and vice versa; applications of organizational and management theory to family firms of all sizes; international aspects of family businesses; gender issues in family businesses; and legal and financial issues specific to family businesses.

Manuscripts fifteen to twenty-five pages long will be considered for publication and must be original work. Shorter works on new issues in family business practice are acceptable. Four copies of each manuscript must be submitted to the editor. No fax copies will be accepted for review. Articles accepted, published, or submitted for publication elsewhere cannot be accepted by FBR.

Selection of articles for publication is made by the editor, who relies primarily on the recommendations of reviewers. Manuscripts appropriate for consideration receive two or more independent blind reviews by members of the editorial board or other professional authorities. Reviewers evaluate manuscripts on their significance in advancing the understanding of family firms; development of general theory in family business; conceptual soundness; originality; logical and analytical qualities; provocativeness; and relevance for consultants, academics, and high-level executives in family businesses.

FBR also publishes reviews of current books in the field and innovations in family business consulting. Reviews are by invitation of the Book Review Editor, and innovations are selected by the Innovations Editor. Reviews and innovations should not exceed ten double-spaced pages.

Special issues of FBR will be published under the editorship of the associate editors. Submit manuscripts for regular issues to the Editor. For information call, fax or e-mail the Editor.

Manuscript Preparation. Type all copy - including references, extracts, tables, and exhibits - double-spaced in 12-point Times Roman font, leaving one-inch margins on all sides. Right margin should be ragged right (non justified). Pages should be numbered. The title page should include (1) title of the article; (2) names and primary affiliations of the author(s); (3) authors' home and office telephone numbers, fax numbers and e-mail addresses; (4) a brief abstract of no more than 100 words; and (5) several key words indicating content of the article. To facilitate the blind review process, please ensure that information about authors appears only on the title page.

Citations and References. Do not use footnotes; incorporate all such material in the text. For literature citations in the text, supply author surname and date of publication, and include the original page number for each direct quotation and statistic; for example, (Knight, 1973) or Knight and Jones (1975, p. 74). Provide a double-spaced alphabetical list of only those references cited in the text. References without corresponding text citations will be omitted. Follow the reference style in the *Publicaiton Manual of The American Psychological Association*, 4th edition, 1994, as illustrated in the following examples:

Journal Article
Welsch, J. H. M. (1933). The impact of family ownership and involvement on the process of management succession. Family Business Review, 6(1), 32-54.

Book
Ward, J. L. (1987). Keeping the family business healthy: How to plan for continuing growth, profitability, and family leadership. San Francisco: Jossey-Bass.

Chapter in a Book
Smith, W. A. & Jones, W. B. (1988). "Successes and failures of joint ventures in developing countries: Lessons from experience." In A. J. Black & P. White (Eds.), Cooperative strategies in international businesses (pp. 517-522). Hillsdale, NJ: Erlbaum.

Figures and Tables. Clean copies of figures should accompany the manuscript, each on a separate sheet. On acceptance of the manuscript for publication, authors must provide camera-ready artwork (original illustrations or photostat copies). Tables should be double-spaced on separate pages. Table notes should be keyed to the body of the table with letters rather than numbers. All figures and tables should have short descriptive titles and should include source notes if applicable.

Permissions. Authors are responsible for obtaining necessary written permission from publisher or copyright holder for reproduction of figures and tables and for extensive text quotations. If an article contains material reproduced from other sources, the necessary written permission must accompany the manuscript.

Publication Process. When a manuscript is accepted for publication, authors are asked to sign a letter of agreement granting the publisher the right to copyedit, publish, and copyright the material. FBR editors are responsible for reviewing the copyediting for each issue and will only contact authors if clarification is needed. Copyedited manuscripts will not be returned to authors. Authors must ensure the accuracy of all statements-particularly data, quotations, and references-before submitting manuscripts. Final manuscripts should be submitted on a 3.5-inch, IBM-compatible disk, in Microsoft Word for Windows, along with a hard copy that exactly matches the file on disk. One or two sentences, placed after the reference list and stating the author's primary affiliations, should also be included.

FIU Hospitality Review

ADDRESS FOR SUBMISSION:

William O'Brien, Editor
FIU Hospitality Review
Florida Internatinal University
School of Hospitality Management
3000 Northeast 151 ST Street
North Miami, FL 33181
USA
Phone: 305-919-4553
Fax: 305-919-4555
E-Mail: review@flu.edu
Web:
Address May Change:

CIRCULATION DATA:

Reader: Business Persons
Frequency of Issue: 2 Times/Year
Copies per Issue: 1,001 - 2,000
Sponsor/Publisher: Florida International
   University
Subscribe Price: 10.00 US$

PUBLICATION GUIDELINES:

Manuscript Length: 26-30
Copies Required: Two
Computer Submission: Yes
Format: Microsoft Word
Fees to Review: 0.00 US$

Manuscript Style:
   , Turabian's Manual or MLA Style Sheet

REVIEW INFORMATION:

Type of Review: N/A
No. of External Reviewers: 2
No. of In House Reviewers: 2
Acceptance Rate: 21-30%
Time to Review: 4 - 6 Months
Reviewers Comments: Yes
Invited Articles: 6-10%
Fees to Publish: 0.00 US$

MANUSCRIPT TOPICS:
Business Education; Global Business; Hospitaltity Management; Marketing Research; Operations Research/Statistics; Organizational Behavior & Theory; Services; Small Business Entrepreneurship; Strategic Management Policy; Technology/Innovation

MANUSCRIPT GUIDELINES/COMMENTS:

Fiu Hospitaity Review encourages the submission of manuscripts on topics relevant to the hospitality industry. The following guidelines will assist authors in preparing articles for publication. Manuscripts must:

• be typed, double-spaced, on a letter-quality printer or typewriter. In addition, authors must include a diskette (5 1/4" or 3 1/2"), labeled with the article's file name and the name of the word processing program used (ability to convert to Wordperfect required), along with the hard copy.

• have a cover sheet with an article title and the name, title, school and address of business affiliation of author(s).

- have a preface, usually two to three sentences, which summarizes the article. This is printed on the first page of the article prior to the text.

- be written in the third person. The policy of the *FIU Hospitality Review* is not to print first or second person articles.

- include a minimum number of tables, charts or exhibits, with a preferred vertical format which must not exceed 35 lines in depth and 40 characters in width so each can fit on a single page.

- follow standard footnote/endnote format, which the *FIU Hospitality Review* runs as "References." Use consecutive numbers in the text and follow the style set forth in the *MLA Stylesheet* or *Kate L. Turabian, "A Manual for Writers of Term Papers, Theses and Dissertations,"* 5th ed., (Chicago: University of Chicago Press, 1987). The *Fiu Hospitality Review* will not accept articles with internal footnote citations or textnotes.

- not include bibliographic references.

- range from 10 to 25 pages, with references and tables included.

- include major subheads within text; each should consist of a subject/verb construction and be short.

- E-mail submission is preferred and given faster turn-around than printed manuscripts.

Global Business and Economic Review

ADDRESS FOR SUBMISSION:

Demetri Kantarelis, Editor
Global Business and Economic Review
64 Holden Street
Worcester, MA 01605-3109
USA
Phone: 508-767-7557
Fax: 508-767-1780
E-Mail: dkantar@assumption.edu
Web: see Guidelines
Address May Change:

CIRCULATION DATA:

Reader: Academics, Practitioners
Frequency of Issue: 3 Times/Year
Copies per Issue: Less than 1,000
Sponsor/Publisher: Business & Economic
   Society International
Subscribe Price: 120.00 US$

PUBLICATION GUIDELINES:

Manuscript Length: 11-15
Copies Required: Four
Computer Submission: Yes
Format: Microsoft Word
Fees to Review: 0.00 US$

Manuscript Style:
   See Manuscript Guidelines

REVIEW INFORMATION:

Type of Review: Blind Review
No. of External Reviewers: 3+
No. of In House Reviewers: 3+
Acceptance Rate: 22-25%
Time to Review: 2 - 3 Months
Reviewers Comments: Yes
Invited Articles: 0-5%
Fees to Publish: 0.00 US$

MANUSCRIPT TOPICS:
Advertising & Promotion Management; Direct Marketing; Global Business; Marketing Research; Marketing Theory & Applications; Sales/Selling; Services; Strategic Management Policy; Technology/Innovation; Transportation/Physical Distribution

MANUSCRIPT GUIDELINES/COMMENTS:

Written Communication is an international multidisciplinary journal that publishes theory and research in writing from fields including anthropology, English, history, journalism, linguistics, psychology, and rhetoric. Among topics of interest are the nature of writing ability; the assessment of writing; the impact of technology on writing (and of writing on technology); social and political consequences of writing and writing instruction; nonacademic writing; literacy (including workplace and emergent literacy and the effects of classroom processes on literacy development); social construction of knowledge; cognition and composing; the structure of written text and written communication; relationships among gender, race, class, and writing; and connections among writing, reading, speaking, and listening. Also of interest are review essays and reviews of research on topics important to writing researchers. No worthy topic in writing is beyond the scope of the journal. Published articles will collectively represent a wide range of methodologies, but the methodology of each study must be handled expertly.

Guidelines For Submission: Prospective authors are strongly urged to acquaint themselves with previously published issues of the journal, particularly the Editors' Comments in Vol. 11, No. 1 (January 1994). Submitting an article indicates that the work reported has not been previously published, that the article - in present or revised form - is not being considered for publication in other journals or in edited volumes, and that the author(s) will not allow the article to be so considered before notification in writing of an editorial decision by *Written Communication*. Submissions should generally not exceed 9,000 words and must follow the American Psychological Association's 1994 guidelines for publication.

When submitting a manuscript:
(a) Send four copies (double-sided if possible) to Editors, *Written Communication*, in care of the University of Wisconsin-Madison, Department of English, 6185E Helen C. White Hall, 600 North Park Street, Madison, WI 53706-1475 or in care of Kent State University, Department of English, P.O. Box 5190, Kent, OH 44242.

(b) Include with each copy an abstract of 100-150 words.

(c) Provide on a separate sheet the title of the submission and the name(s), institutional affiliation(s), mailing address(es), home and office telephone number(s), fax number(s) and e-mail address(es), and a three-to-four-sentence biographical statement for each author.

(d) Include unattached postage stamps (American authors) or international postage coupons, available at local post offices (international authors) sufficient to cover separate first-class mailings of the four copies of the manuscript. Special note to international authors: Exchange value of international postage coupons need not exceed 9USD.

(e) Note that the entire manuscript should be double-spaced, including the abstract, block quotations, tables, notes, and references. Written Communication does not normally return submitted manuscripts to authors. A copy of the final revised manuscript saved on an IBM-compatible disk should be included with the final revised hard copy.

Written Communication (ISSN 0741-0883) is published four times annually - in January, April, July, and October - by Sage Publications, Inc., 2455 Teller Road, Thousand Oaks, CA 91320. Telephone: (805) 499-0721; FAX/Order Line: (805) 499-0871. Copyright 1997 by Sage Publications, Inc. All rights reserved. No portion of the contents may be reproduced in any form without written permission of the publisher.

Global Competitiveness

ADDRESS FOR SUBMISSION:

Abbas J. Ali, Editor
Global Competitiveness
PO Box 1658
Indiana, PA 15705
USA
Phone: 724-357-5759
Fax: 724-357-5743
E-Mail: aaali@grove.iup.edu
Web:
Address May Change:

PUBLICATION GUIDELINES:

Manuscript Length: 16-20
Copies Required: Three
Computer Submission: Yes
Format: WordPerfect 6-7 or MS Word 97
Fees to Review: 0.00 US$

Manuscript Style:
   American Psychological Association

CIRCULATION DATA:

Reader: Academics, Business Persons
Frequency of Issue: 1-2 Times/Year
Copies per Issue: Less than 1,000
Sponsor/Publisher: American Society for
   Competitiveness
Subscribe Price: 40.00 US$

REVIEW INFORMATION:

Type of Review: Blind Review
No. of External Reviewers: 2
No. of In House Reviewers: 1
Acceptance Rate: 50%
Time to Review: 2 - 3 Months
Reviewers Comments: Yes
Invited Articles: 21-30%
Fees to Publish: 0.00 US$ up to 20pgs
   8.00 US$ per pg over 20 pgs

MANUSCRIPT TOPICS:

Business Education; Business Information Systems (MIS); Business Law, Public Responsibility & Ethics; Global Business; International Trade Competition; Labor Relations & Human Resource Mgt.; Marketing Research; Marketing Theory & Applications; Non Profit Organizations; Organizational Development; Purchasing/Materials Management; Sales/Selling; Services; Small Business Entrepreneurship; Strategic Management Policy; Technology/Innovation; Transportation/Physical Distribution

MANUSCRIPT GUIDELINES/COMMENTS:

Editor's Comment
Various topics on competitiveness, competition and firm performance are sought. The objective is to provide authors with an outlet to publish their research on a timely basis. Most of the articles that are published in the journal were presented at the American Society for Competitiveness Conference. All papers are reviewed by two outside reviewers. A special issue of the Journal is actually utilized to publish invited papers on a specific topic or event.

References and Bibliographies
The style guidelines for references and bibliographies must follow the publications manual of the *American Psychological Association*. Titles of journals or books will be italicized instead

of underlined. **Please note**: Reference styles must be observed, otherwise the paper will not be included. Below are examples.

Journal Articles
Author. (Date). Title of article - lowercase. Title of Journal - italicized, volume(number), pages.
Paivio, A. (1988). Perceptual comparisons through the mind's eye. *Memory and Cognition* 3(5), 653-668.

Chapter in Book
Author. (Date). Title of chapter - lowercase. In editor's name(s) (Ed.), Title of book - italicized and lowercase (pp. 000-000). City: Publisher.
Hartley, J. T., Harker, J. O., & Walsh, D. A. (1980). Contemporary issues and new directions in adult development. In L. W. Poon (Ed.), *Aging in the 1980's* (pp. 234-278). Washington, DC: American Psychological Association.

Entire Book
Author or Editor in Chief. (Date). Title of book - italicized. City: Publisher.
Bernstein, T. M. (1965). *The careful writer: a modern guide to English usage*. New York: Atheneum
Letheridege, S., & Cannon, C. R. (Eds.). (1980). *Bilingual education: teaching English as a second language*. New York: Praeger.

Global Economy Quarterly (GEQ)

ADDRESS FOR SUBMISSION:

Khosrow Fatemi, Editor
Global Economy Quarterly (GEQ)
PO Box 3547
Calexico, CA 92232-3547
USA
Phone: 760-768-5591
Fax: 760-768-5592
E-Mail: geq@sdsu.edu
Web:
Address May Change:

PUBLICATION GUIDELINES:

Manuscript Length: 16-25
Copies Required: Four
Computer Submission: Yes
Format: WordPerfect 8.0 or higher
Fees to Review: 0.00 US$

Manuscript Style:
    See Manuscript Guidelines

CIRCULATION DATA:

Reader: Academics
Frequency of Issue: Quarterly
Copies per Issue: Less than 1,000
Sponsor/Publisher: International Trade and
    Finance Association
Subscribe Price: 190.00 US$ Institution
    45.00 US$ Included with Membership
    49.00 US$ Individual Copy

REVIEW INFORMATION:

Type of Review: Blind Review
No. of External Reviewers: 2
No. of In House Reviewers: 1
Acceptance Rate: 11-20%
Time to Review: 2 - 3 Months
Reviewers Comments: Yes
Invited Articles: 11-20%
Fees to Publish: 0.00 US$

MANUSCRIPT TOPICS:
Business Education; Global Business; Strategic Management Policy

MANUSCRIPT GUIDELINES/COMMENTS:

Aim and Scope
The mission of the *Global Economy Quarterly* is to provide a forum for the exchange of scholarly ideas within different sectors of the global economy. Its scope includes public-policy, managerial, and macro-economic issues. It is a refereed journal which encourages publication of both theoretical and conceptual research findings as well as the perspectives of the practitioners' of the global economy. The *Global Economy Quarterly*'s scope includes, but is not limited to the following fields:

International Trade	Regulatory Issues
International Finance	Fiscal Policy
Pedagogical Issues	Foreign Exchange Rates
Cross-Cultural Management	Economic Integration
International Public Policy	Economic Development
Multinational Corporations	International Human Resource Management
Cross-Cultural Communication	Comparative Studies

Commercial Policy
International Marketing
Managerial Decision Making
International Monetary Policy

Regionalism
Internationalism
Theoretical Studies
National and Regional Studies

The *Global Economy Quarterly* is a publication of the International Trade and Finance Association and the Imperial Valley Campus of San Diego State University.

Intended Audience
The *Global Economy Quarterly* will be of interest to academic researchers at both graduate and undergraduate levels. Furthermore, its audience includes public policy makers, corporate decision makers and general practitioners of the different sectors of the global economy.

Typing Guidelines
The Typing and Editorial Instruction for the Perspective Authors of the *Global Economy Quarterly* can be found at www.rtedwards.com/joumals/GEQ

Harvard Business Review

ADDRESS FOR SUBMISSION:

Editor
Harvard Business Review
60 Harvard Way
Boston, MA 02163
USA
Phone: 617-495-6800
Fax: 617-495-9933
E-Mail: hbr_editorial@hbsp.harvard.edu
Web: www.hbsp.harvard.edu
Address May Change:

CIRCULATION DATA:

Reader: Business Persons
Frequency of Issue: Bi-Monthly
Copies per Issue: More than 25,000
Sponsor/Publisher: Harvard University
Subscribe Price: 95.00 US$ USA
  105.00 US$ Canada

PUBLICATION GUIDELINES:

Manuscript Length: See Guidelines
Copies Required: See Guidelines
Computer Submission:
Format:
Fees to Review: 0.00 US$

Manuscript Style:
  Chicago Manual of Style

REVIEW INFORMATION:

Type of Review: Editorial Review
No. of External Reviewers: 0
No. of In House Reviewers: 3+
Acceptance Rate: 0-5%
Time to Review: 1 - 2 Months
Reviewers Comments: No
Invited Articles: 31-50%
Fees to Publish: 0.00 US$

MANUSCRIPT TOPICS:
Advertising & Promotion Management; Direct Marketing; Global Business; Marketing Research; Marketing Theory & Applications; Non Profit Organizations; Sales/Selling; Services; Strategic Management Policy; Technology/Innovation; Transportation/Physical Distribution

MANUSCRIPT GUIDELINES/COMMENTS:

Author Guidelines
The purpose of the *Harvard Business Review is* to advance the theory and practice of management. *Harvard Business Review* articles fulfill this purpose in several ways:
- They offer important new ideas and original thinking to help senior managers establish an intellectual agenda for discussion within their companies.
- They provide best-practice models and hands-on techniques from companies around the world.
- They report on cutting-edge research by academics, consultants, and management analysts. They give firsthand insight into how companies work and how managers respond to demanding challenges in the workplace.

Published articles cover a wide range of management topics and practices in different industries, sectors, management functions, and geographic locations. They develop themes such as globalization, business and social issues, service and quality, corporate restructuring, and managing change. But regardless of the subject, *Harvard Business Review* articles share certain characteristics. They are written for senior managers by experts whose authority comes from careful analysis and study of an issue or from deep personal experience, and who demonstrate a mastery of the material presented. Their ideas have been tested in the real world of business and can be translated into management action in most instances.

Harvard Business Review readers are overwhelmingly managers: almost 95 percent of *Harvard Business Review*'s 200,000-plus subscribers are managers in organizations of all sizes and kinds. Their interests—in improving their performance, in learning and benefiting from the thinking and experience of experts—shape what *Harvard Business Review* editors look for in reviewing submissions. Proposals for articles that demonstrate clear and bold thinking, fresh and useful ideas, accessible and jargon-free expression, and unambiguous authority and expertise are most likely to meet such readers' needs.

The best way to inquire about *Harvard Business Review*'s potential interest in a topic is to send a letter with a two-page proposal and a full sentence outline. Because of the volume of inquiries about publishing in *Harvard Business Review,* it is not our policy to read complete manuscripts, and we cannot guarantee a response if they are submitted. The proposal should clearly and succinctly answer the following questions:

What is the message of the article you propose to write? What are the implications of the message? Or, as *Harvard Business Review* editors often say, What's the "so what"? Why should a busy manager stop and read your article? What is new, unusual, useful, counterintuitive, or important about your message? Who is the targeted audience? What research have you conducted to support the argument or logic in your article? What company examples can you cite to support your argument? What is the authority or expertise that you will draw on to make your argument convincing?

After you have answered these questions, outline the manuscript, offering enough detail for an editor to be able to understand the article's main points and the evidence or examples that will support those points. You should also write a draft of the first few paragraphs of the article, which contains the central message of the piece.

Send the letter, the outline, and the introduction to *Harvard Business Review,* 60 Harvard Way, Boston, MA 02163.

We will review the proposal and get back to you as quickly as we can. The volume of proposals is so large, however, that it can take four to six weeks for *Harvard Business Review* to complete the review of a proposal. We appreciate your interest in *Harvard Business Review* and ask for your patience.

Unsolicited materials will be returned only if accompanied by a self-addressed, stamped envelope.

Health Marketing Quarterly

ADDRESS FOR SUBMISSION:

David P. Paul, III, Co-Editor
Health Marketing Quarterly
Monmouth University
School of Business Administration
Marketing & Health Care Management
West Long Branch, NJ 07764
USA
Phone: 732-263-5336
Fax: 732-263-5128
E-Mail: dpaul@monmouth.edu
Web:
Address May Change: 1/1/04

PUBLICATION GUIDELINES:

Manuscript Length: 18 Minimum/No Max.
Copies Required: One
Computer Submission: Yes Prefer Electronic
Format: Microsoft Word
Fees to Review: 0.00 US$

Manuscript Style:
American Psychological Association

CIRCULATION DATA:

Reader: Academics
Frequency of Issue: Quarterly
Copies per Issue: 4,001 - 5,000
Sponsor/Publisher: Haworth Press, Inc.
Subscribe Price: 75.00 US$ Individual
125.00 US$ Institution
475.00 US$ Library

REVIEW INFORMATION:

Type of Review: Blind Review
No. of External Reviewers: 2
No. of In House Reviewers: 1
Acceptance Rate: 40%
Time to Review: 1 - 2 Months
Reviewers Comments: Yes
Invited Articles: 0-5%
Fees to Publish: 0.00 US$

MANUSCRIPT TOPICS:
Health Care Administration; Marketing Research; Marketing Theory & Applications

MANUSCRIPT GUIDELINES/COMMENTS:

Co-Editor: Earl D. Honeycutt, Jr., Professor of Marketing, Department of Business Administration, Old Dominion University, Norfolk, VA 23529-0220.
(757) 683-4988, Fax (757) 683-5639, Email: ehoneycu@odu.edu

About the Journal
Health Marketing Quarterly endeavors to be the primary academic journal for health care marketing. The journal will consider original research, either conceptual or empirical or both. Literature reviews would be considered, however, they must clearly explain and justify suggestions for directions of future research. Applied case studies will also be considered for publication. The journal encourages articles on a broad range of health care marketing topics, from the micro (e.g., factors to consider in determining the most appropriate location for a practitioner's office) to the macro (e.g., effects of managed care on health care marketing). Articles should focus on health care marketing management issues, especially

planning/forecasting, strategy, segmentation/targeting/positioning, and relationship building. Specific services/products/industries could be considered in depth, perhaps examining strategy, brand management, new product development, and customer value and service. Additional topic areas which readers could find interesting would include the more traditional areas of marketing (as applied to health care): retailing, channels of distribution, pricing, promotion/advertising, and personal selling/sales management.

The editorial goals of *Health Marketing Quarterly* are two fold: (1) to advance the current state of health care marketing research and practice, and (2) to transfer knowledge between health care academics and the practitioners. While health care marketing management is the primary domain of the journal, articles integrating concepts from such related fields as health care economics, health care finance, health care ethics, health care information systems, etc. will be considered insofar as they apply to health care marketing management.

While the bulk of the journal will consist of original research, it is anticipated that a Book Review Section and a Review of Current Literature Section will be added as quickly as possible.

The journal will be referred (by the Editors) and peer-reviewed. Each article will be reviewed by at least 3 Members of the Editorial Review Board. Articles utilizing relatively sophisticated statistical techniques will be reviewed by at least one methodologist, to ensure appropriateness of both experimental design and analysis of results. A double blind Review process will be utilized so as to protect both authors and Reviewers from bias, and to ensure academic integrity in the reviewing process. Ad-hoc Reviewers may also be employed at the discretion of the Editors. The final decision regarding acceptance for each paper is made solely by the Editors, after considering the recommendations and comments of the Reviewers.

The Editors strongly encourage electronic submission of manuscripts, in order to keep the "turn around time" required by the refereeing process to a minimum.

Instructions for Authors

1. **Manuscripts.** Manuscripts should be submitted to the Editor.

2. **Original Articles Only.** Submission of a manuscript to this Journal represents a certification on the part of the author(s) that it is an original work, and that neither this manuscript nor a version of it has been published elsewhere nor is being considered for publication elsewhere.

3. **Copyright. Copyright owner ship of your manuscript must be transferred officially to The Haworth Press, Inc.** before we can begin the peer-review process. The Editor's letter acknowledging receipt of the manuscript will be accompanied by a form fully explaining this. All authors must sign the form and return the original to the Editor as soon as possible. Failure to return the copyright form in a timely fashion will result in delay in review and subsequent publication.

4. **Manuscript Length.** Your manuscript may be approximately 15 typed pages double-spaced (including references and abstract). Lengthier manuscripts may be considered, but only

at the discretion of the Editor. Sometimes, lengthier manuscripts may be considered if they can be divided up into sections for publication in successive Journal issues.

5. **Manuscript Style**. References, citations, and general style of manuscripts for this Journal should follow the APA style (as outlined in the latest edition of the *Publication of the American Psychological Association*). References should be double-spaced and placed in alphabetical order.

If an author wishes to submit a paper that has been already prepared in another style, he or she may do so. However, if the paper is accepted (with or without reviewer's alterations), the author is fully responsible for retyping the manuscript in the correct style as indicated above. Neither the Editor nor the Publisher is responsible for re-preparing manuscript copy to adhere to the Journal's style.

6. **Manuscript Preparation**.
Margins: leave at least a one-inch margin on all four sides.
Paper: use clean white, 8-1/2" x 11" bond paper.
Number of Copies: 4 (the original plus three photocopies).
Cover Page: Important - staple a cover page to the manuscript, indicating only the article title (this is used for anonymous refereeing) and the ABSTRACT.
Second "Title Page": enclose a regular title page but do not staple it to the manuscript. Include the title again, plus:
- full authorship
- an ABSTRACT of about 100 words
- 5 or 6 keywords that identify article content;
- an introductory footnote with authors' academic degrees, professional titles, affiliations, mailing addresses, and any desired acknowledgement of research support or other credit.
- a header or footer on each page with abbreviated title and pg. number of total (e.g., pg. 2 of 7).

7. **Return Envelopes**. When you submit your four manuscript copies, also include:
- a 9" x 12" envelope, self-addressed and stamped (with sufficient postage to ensure return of your manuscript);
- a regular envelope, stamped and self-addressed. This is for the Editor to send you an "acknowledgement of receipt" letter.

8. **Spelling, Grammar, and Punctuation**. You are responsible for preparing manuscript copy which is clearly written in acceptable scholarly English, and which contains no errors of spelling, grammar, or punctuation. Neither the Editor nor the Publisher is responsible for correcting errors of spelling and grammar: the manuscript, after acceptance by the Editor, must be immediately ready for typesetting as it is finally submitted by the author(s). Also, check the accuracy of all arithmetic calculations statistics, numerical data, text citations, and references. **Inconsistencies Must Be Avoided**. Be sure you are consistent in your use of abbreviations, terminology, and in citing references, from one part of your paper to another.

9. **Preparation of Tables, Figures, and Illustrations.** All tables, figures, illustrations, etc. must be "camera-ready." That is, they must be cleanly typed or artistically prepared so that they can be used either exactly as they are or else used after a photographic reduction in size. (Please note that dot-matrix type is often unacceptable for artwork.)

10. **Tables will be printed as is and will not be typeset.** If submitted art cannot be used, the Publisher reserves the right to redo the art and to charge the author a fee of $35.00 per hour for this service. The Haworth Press, Inc. is not responsible for errors incurred in the preparation of new camera-ready artwork. Figures, tables, and illustrations must be prepared on separate sheets of paper. Always use black ink and professional drawing instruments. On the back of these items, write your article title and the journal title lightly in pencil, so they do not get misplaced. In the text, skip extra lines and indicate where these figures and tables are to be placed (please do not write on face of art). Photographs are considered part of the acceptable manuscript and remain with the publisher for use in additional printings.

10. **Alterations Required By Referees and Reviewers.** Many times a paper is accepted by the Editor contingent upon changes that are mandated by anonymous specialist referees and members of the Editorial Board. If the Editor returns your manuscript for revisions you are responsible for retyping any sections of the paper to incorporate these revisions (if applicable, revisions should also be put on disk).

11. **Typesetting.** You will not be receiving galley proofs of your article. Editorial revisions, if any, must therefore be made while your article is still in manuscript. The final version of the manuscript will be the version you see published. Typesetting errors will be corrected by the production staff of The Haworth Press. Authors are expected to submit manuscripts, disks, and art that are free from error.

11. **Electronic Media.** Haworth's in-house typesetting unit will now be able to utilize your final manuscript material as prepared on most personal computers and word processors. This will minimize typographical errors and decrease overall production time.

Please send your first draft and final draft copies of your manuscript to the journal Editor in print format for his/her final review and approval; after approval of your final manuscript, please submit the final approved version both on printed format ("hard copy") and floppy diskette. On the outside of the disk package write:
    A. the brand name of your computer or word processor
    B. the word-processing program that you used
    C. the title of your article
    D. file name

Note: Disk and hard copy must agree. In case of discrepancies, it is The Haworth Press' policy to follow hard copy. Authors are advised that no revisions of the manuscript can be made after acceptance by the Editor for publication. The benefits of this procedure are many with speed and accuracy being the most obvious. We look forward to working with you on this, knowing we will be able to serve you more efficiently in the future.

The benefits of this procedure are many with speed and accuracy being the most obvious. We look forward to working with you on this, knowing we will be able to serve you more efficiently in the future.

14. **Reprints**. The senior author will receive two copies of the journal issue and 25 complimentary reprints several weeks after the issue is published. The junior author will receive two copies of the issue. An order form will be sent to the corresponding author for the purchase of additional reprints at this time. (Approximately 4-6 weeks is necessary for the preparation of reprints.) Please do not query the Journal's Editor about reprints. All such questions should be directed to The Haworth Press, Inc., Production Department, 21 East Broad Street, West Hazleton, PA 18201-3809. To order additional reprints, please contact The Haworth Document Delivery Service, The Haworth Press, Inc., 10 Alice Street, Binghamton, NY 13904-1580 USA, 1-800-342-9678 or Fax 1-607-722-6362.

15. **Copyright and Permissions**. For permission to reprint articles that have appeared in Haworth journals, please contact: Copyright & Permissions Department, The Haworth Press, Inc., 10 Alice Street, Binghamton, NY 13904-1580.

Industrial Marketing Management

ADDRESS FOR SUBMISSION:

Peter LaPlaca, Editor
Industrial Marketing Management
University of Vermont
24 Quarry Drive, Suite 201
Vernon, CT 06066-4917
USA
Phone: 860-875-8017
Fax: 860-875-2318
E-Mail: plaplaca@portone.com
Web: www.elsevier.nl
Address May Change:

PUBLICATION GUIDELINES:

Manuscript Length: 15-40
Copies Required: Four
Computer Submission: No
Format: N/A
Fees to Review: 0.00 US$

Manuscript Style:
   No Reply

CIRCULATION DATA:

Reader: Business Persons, Academic
Frequency of Issue: Bi-Monthly
Copies per Issue: 1,600
Sponsor/Publisher: Elsevier Science
   Publishing, Co.
Subscribe Price: 468.00 US$ Instituion
   75.00 US$ Individual

REVIEW INFORMATION:

Type of Review: Blind Review
No. of External Reviewers: 3
No. of In House Reviewers: 1
Acceptance Rate: 20-25%
Time to Review: 3 - 6 months
Reviewers Comments: Yes
Invited Articles: 2 or 3/Year
Fees to Publish: 0.00 US$

MANUSCRIPT TOPICS:
Advertising & Promotion Management; Business Information Systems (MIS); Direct Marketing; E-commerce; Global Business; Marketing Research; Marketing Theory & Applications; Purchasing/Materials Management; Sales/Selling; Services; Strategic Management Policy; Technology/Innovation; Transportation/Physical Distribution

MANUSCRIPT GUIDELINES/COMMENTS:

Articles must be based on sound theoretical and methodological models and must provide a section dealing with applicability to practicing industrial marketers.

We seek manuscripts that are scholarly, applied, and provide information that is at the edge of management practice with regard to marketing between companies.

Industrial Marketing Management provides a medium for exchange of information within the broadly defined field of industrial marketing management. The readership consists primarily of business people and scholars concerned with product and market planning, marketing research, product, management, buyer behavior, forecasting, sales management, and business research and planning. Articles should be timely, providing guidelines, techniques, and suggestions for problem solving in industrial marketing. The use of conceptual, analytical, or in-depth case histories is encouraged.

Manuscripts should be submitted in quadruplicate (the original and three copies) to Editor-in-Chief, Dr. Peter J. LaPlaca.

All material should be typed double-spaced, single column text on 8½ x 11 inch bond paper (one sided). Reference lists, tabular material, and figure legends should be typed on separate sheets. References to the literature and indicated in the text by full size Arabic numbers in brackets, i.e., [1]. Footnotes to the text are indicated by superior numbers, and are placed at the bottom of the page on which they are cited. An abstract (Summary) of 150 words or less should be included. The title page should include the full names of the author(s), with the complete address for proofs and correspondence. A brief biographical sketch for each author must be included. Please indicate the date of submission on the article cover page to facilitate future revisions.

Mathematical Notation. Use typewritten letters, numbers, and symbols wherever possible. Identify boldface, script letters, etc., the first time they occur. Distinguish between arabic "1" and the letter "l" and between zero and the letter "O", capital or lower case, wherever confusion might result.

The following reference style should be observed:

Article: Easton, Allan, Sales Quota Achievement Indices for Multi-Product Firms, Industrial Marketing Management 5, 77-88 (1976).

Book: Steele, Lowell W., Innovative in Big Business. Elsevier North-Holland, New York, 1975, Chap. 1, pp. 5-7.

Chapter in edited book: Ayre, Robert U., and Shapanka, Adele, Explicit Technological Substitution Forecasts in Long-Range Input-Output Models, in Technological Substitution: Forecasting Techniques and Applications, Harold A. Linstone and Devendra Sahal, eds., Elsevier, New York, 1976.

Theses, reports, and other unpublished material: Style as journal article with as much source information as possible.

Figures should be submitted as separate (not embedded between text) **Original illustrations** or glossy **photostats** or originals (as professionally done as possible), complete and ready for photoreproduction. Lettering and data points should be large enough so when reduced to fit on the journal page (maximum 7 x 9 inch) they can be read with ease.

Proofs and reprints. Authors receive proofs, which should be proofread, corrected and returned **within 48 hours of receipt**. Instructions for ordering reprints are included with proofs.

Copyright. Upon acceptance of an article by the journal, the author(s) will be asked to transfer copyright in the article to the publisher. This transfer will insure the widest possible dissemination of information under the U.S. Copyright Law.

Interactive Marketing

ADDRESS FOR SUBMISSION:

Derek Holder & Robin Fairlie, Co-Editors
Interactive Marketing
Henry Stewart Publications
Museum House
25 Museum Street
London, WC1A 1JT
U.K.
Phone: +44 2073 232916
Fax: +44 2073 232918
E-Mail: submissions@hspublications.co.uk
Web: www.henrystewart.com
Address May Change:

PUBLICATION GUIDELINES:

Manuscript Length: 11-30
Copies Required: Three
Computer Submission: Yes
Format: Word
Fees to Review: 0.00 US$

Manuscript Style:
    Uniform System of Citation (Harvard Blue Book)

CIRCULATION DATA:

Reader: No Reply
Frequency of Issue: Quarterly
Copies per Issue: 1,001 - 2,000
Sponsor/Publisher: Henry Stewart Publications
Subscribe Price: 190.00 US$ Institution
    95.00 US$ Individual/Academic

REVIEW INFORMATION:

Type of Review: Blind Review
No. of External Reviewers: 2
No. of In House Reviewers: 1
Acceptance Rate: 21-30%
Time to Review: 1 - 2 Months
Reviewers Comments: Yes
Invited Articles: No Reply
Fees to Publish: 0.00 US$

MANUSCRIPT TOPICS:

Advertising & Promotion Management; Communication; Direct Marketing; Global Business; Marketing Research; Marketing Theory & Applications; Organizational Behavior & Theory; Organizational Development; Strategic Management Policy; Technology/Innovation

MANUSCRIPT GUIDELINES/COMMENTS:

About the Journal

Old-model marketing once added value. It now adds costs. Little wonder that marketing is the hot seat in today's boardroom. Every other cost has been pruned, leaving about 40% of a product's cost consumed by the information and transaction cost of getting it to market.

Now, emerging new-model marketers are fighting back. They're already driving down costs. And they're finding new ways to add value. These are the Interactive Marketers.

A major international journal, *Interactive Marketing* provides a forum for these up-and-coming stars of marketing to share experience, ideas and case histories.

Notes for Contributors

1. Contributions should be between 2,000 and 5,000 words in length. All submissions should be typewritten and double-spaced.

2. The Journal's Editors and Editorial Board particularly welcome submissions which present case study material, new approaches, techniques, empirical research or conceptual papers.

3. All articles should be accompanied by a short abstract outlining the paper's aims and subject matter.

4. All articles should be accompanied by up to six keywords.

5. Articles should be accompanied by a short (about 80 words) description of the author(s) and, if appropriate, the organization of which he or she is a member.

6. Authors should not seek to use the Journal as a vehicle for marketing any specific product or service.

7. Authors should avoid the use of language or slang which is not in keeping with the professional and academic style of the Journal.

8. Titles of organizations etc should be written out first in full and thereafter in initials.

9. Articles should be supported by references. For all Henry Stewart Journals excluding *Corporate Reputation Review, Tourism and Hospitality Research, Journal of Fashion Marketing and Management, Journal of Small Business and Enterprise Development, Journal of Asset Management and International Journal of Police Science Management*, these should be set out in accordance with the Vancouver referencing system. References for the Journals listed above should be set out in accordance with the Harvard referencing system.

10. Photographs and illustrations supporting articles should be submitted where appropriate. Photographs should be good quality positives, printed from the original negatives and preferably in black and white only. Figures and other line illustrations should be submitted in good quality originals and a copy of the data should also be included.

11. Authors must ensure that references to named people and/or organizations are accurate, not racist or sexist and without libellous implications.

12. All contributions sent to the Publisher, whether invited or not, will be submitted to the Journal's Editors and Editorial Board. Any such contribution must bear the author's full name and address, even if this is not for publication. Contributions, whether published pseudonymously or not, are accepted on the strict understanding that the author is responsible for the accuracy of all opinion, technical comment, factual report, data, figures, illustrations and photographs. Publication does not necessarily imply that these are the opinions of the Editorial Board, Editors or the Publisher, nor does the Board, Editors or Publisher accept any liability for the accuracy of such comment, report and

other technical and factual information. The Publisher will, however, strive to ensure that all opinion, comments, reports, data, figures, illustrations and photographs are accurate, insofar as it is within its abilities to do so. The Publisher reserves the right to edit, abridge or omit material submitted for publication.

13. All Articles submitted for publication will be subject to a double-blind refereeing procedure.

14. The author bears the responsibility for checking whether material submitted is subject to copyright or ownership rights, eg photographs, illustrations, trade literature and data. Where use is so restricted, the Publisher must be informed with the submission of the material.

15. No contribution will be accepted which has been published elsewhere, unless it is expressly invited or agreed by the Publisher. Articles and contributions published become the copyright of the Publisher, unless otherwise agreed.

16. All reasonable efforts are made to ensure accurate reproduction of text, photographs and illustrations. The Publisher does not accept responsibility for mistakes, be they editorial or typographical, nor for consequences resulting from them.

17. Submissions should be sent to Henry Stewart Publications, Museum House, 25 Museum Street, London WC1A 1JT, email: submissions@hspublications.co.uk. **Please clearly state for which journal you are contributing**

International Academy for Case Studies

ADDRESS FOR SUBMISSION:

Current Editor's Name/Check Web Page
International Academy for Case Studies
Submission Address/Check Web Page
Please address other questions to:
  Jim or JoAnn Carland at #'s below
USA
Phone: 828-293-9151
Fax: 828-293-9407
E-Mail: jcarlalnd@dnet.net
Web: www.alliedacademies.org
Address May Change:

PUBLICATION GUIDELINES:

Manuscript Length: 26-30
Copies Required: Five
Computer Submission: Yes
Format: WdPerfect or MS Word attachment
Fees to Review: 0.00 US$

Manuscript Style:
    American Psychological Association

CIRCULATION DATA:

Reader: Academics
Frequency of Issue: 2 Times/Year
Copies per Issue: Less than 1,000
Sponsor/Publisher: Allied Academies
Subscribe Price: 50.00 US$

REVIEW INFORMATION:

Type of Review: Blind Review
No. of External Reviewers: 3
No. of In House Reviewers: 2
Acceptance Rate: 21-30%
Time to Review: 4 - 6 Months
Reviewers Comments: Yes
Invited Articles: 0-5%
Fees to Publish: 50.00 US$ Membership

MANUSCRIPT TOPICS:
All types of cases; Business Education; Business Information Systems (MIS); Business Law; Public Responsibility & Ethics; Communication; Direct Marketing; Global Business; Health Care Administration; Labor Relations & Human Resource Mgt.; Office Administration/Management; Organizational Behavior & Theory; Sales/Selling; Services; Small Business Entrepreneurship; Strategic Management Policy; Technology/Innovation

MANUSCRIPT GUIDELINES/COMMENTS:

Editorial Policy Guidelines For Cases

The International Academy for Case Studies is the Allied Academies affiliate which handles cases, publishes proceedings and the *Journal of the International Academy for Case Studies*. These editorial guidelines reflect the Academy's policy with regard to reviewing cases for publication and presentation.

The Academy is interested in cases in any discipline, any area, and any subject. Cases may be any length and any level of difficulty. The Academy strongly believes that any subject and any course can benefit from well-prepared cases. To that end, we judge submissions to conferences and for journal consideration on the value of the case as a teaching tool.

Cases may be presented in narrative style or in dialogue. The case should provide sufficient information to be able to accomplish the case objectives, and should be written in a fashion to draw and hold student attention. Cases should focus upon a decision point and should lead a reader to a point at which some decision or series of strategies must be developed. The student's task should be to analyze the case and any outside information which is pertinent and to formulate a course of action. Referees will be most concerned about the development of a strong decision point. Cases must be accompanied by an Instructor's Note, which will be described in following sections.

Cases may be any length and need not conform to any specific guidelines. We encourage case authors to use writing styles and approaches which they believe will be useful in making the case an appropriate teaching tool. Cases may be drawn from field research. In such cases, publication permission from an appropriate officer in the business should be obtained. Cases may also be drawn from library research, public or published sources. Finally, cases may be designed by the case writer to illustrate a specific point or problem or to facilitate student mastery of concepts.

Cases must begin with a description of the case which identifies the area, difficulty level, and length of the case. It is important that authors choose a single subject for the primary focus of the case. Please be aware that a case appropriate for any given level can also be used by higher levels. The reverse is not necessarily true. A case appropriate for use at the graduate level would be appropriate for advanced seniors, but not for typical seniors. Authors should be guided in their classification by considering appropriateness for typical college students at the various levels of study. The case description should follow the format described in the following section.

Case Description

The primary subject matter of this case concerns (choose one discipline or subject). Secondary issues examined include (list as many secondary issues as the case contains). The case has a difficulty level of (choose one of the following: one, appropriate for freshman level courses; two, appropriate for sophomore level courses; three, appropriate for junior level courses; four, appropriate for senior level courses; five, appropriate for first year graduate students; six, appropriate for second year graduate students; seven, appropriate for doctoral students). The case is designed to be taught in (indicate how many) class hours and is expected to require (indicate how many) hours of outside preparation by students.

Information About the Case Synopsis

The Editors encourage authors to be creative in this section. Use of selected dialogue from the case, comments about class usefulness or student responses to use of the case, or any other information which authors feel is valuable may be used. The synopses should capture the attention and interest of users. The synopsis should follow the format described in the following section.

Case Synopsis
In this section, present a brief overview of the case. The synopsis should be a maximum of 300 words. Be creative. This section will be the primary selling point of your case. Use this section to sell your case.

Body of the Case
The body of the case should follow the synopsis. This section should use headings to divide the case as appropriate. The body- should be well organized and flow through to the decision point and the closure of the case.

Instructor's Notes
Instructor's Notes may be the most important aspect of a case. They lead an instructor through the case and support the design and execution of the teaching of the case. They should be designed for less experienced case users and should make teaching the case an interesting and successful process. The note should conform to a standard approach and should contain sections as described in the following subheadings.

Introduction
Case Notes should begin with a repeat of the case title and authors. The Note should include a description of the case and present any pertinent information about the case or how it was developed. Explain how the case might be used in a class and discuss specific strategies and recommendations for teaching approaches, student assignments, or presentation methods.

Case Overview
The Note should continue with a case overview. Describe for the instructor what the case contains, point out pertinent information or issues, and review the material presented. This is an important aspect of the Note because it allows instructors to see what students should be extracting as they read the case.

Discussion Questions
Some users like to have questions included in a case to start discussion. Others like to devise their own approach to using an individual case. Consequently, the Editors recommend that discussion questions appear in the Instructor's Note. This allows a case user to make an individual choice about utilizing or assigning questions. Present questions which can be used as student assignments or in class discussions of the case. For each question, provide an answer or response. Arrange the questions so that answers immediately follow each question. Discussion questions often take the form of an analysis. Financial analyses, environmental analyses, market assessments, etc., frequently are valuable aspects of teaching a case. If an analytic question is posed, case authors should include complete analyses as the answer for that question. For open ended or broad discussion questions, include possible answers or responses which could occur and describe how such questions can be used in the classroom.

Additional Exhibits
If additional information is provided, such as industry notes, industry averages, comparison data, etc., include it in the Note as exhibits. Explain the information included, and describe its use in teaching the case.

Epilogue
If appropriate, include an epilogue which describes what actually happened or displays any information which you think might be of interest to instructors or students. An epilogue might not be appropriate for all cases, so feel free to omit this section.

Referee Guidelines
The exhibit on the following page displays the referee guidelines for reviewing cases and instructor's notes. As the guidelines suggest, primary importance is placed on readability, interest, and usefulness as a teaching tool.

Referee Support
As the last question on the referee guidelines suggests, we ask referees to be as specific as possible in indicating what must be done to make a case acceptable for journal publication. This embodies a primary objective of the Academy: to assist authors in the research process.

Our Editorial Policy is one which is supportive, rather than critical. We encourage all authors who are not successful in a first attempt to rewrite the manuscript in accordance with the suggestions of the referees. We will be pleased to referee future versions and rewrites of manuscripts and work with authors in achieving their research goals.

International Journal of Advertising

ADDRESS FOR SUBMISSION:

Katharine Goldsmith, Production Editor
International Journal of Advertising
NTC Publications Ltd.
Farm Road, Henley-On-Thames
Oxfordshire, RG9 1EJ
UK
Phone: 44 1491 411000
Fax: 44 1491 521188
E-Mail: ijoa@ntc.co.uk
Web:
Address May Change:

PUBLICATION GUIDELINES:

Manuscript Length: 4,000-6,000 Words
Copies Required: Four
Computer Submission: Yes
Format: ASCII/Common Wd. Processor
Fees to Review: 0.00 US$

Manuscript Style:
    See Manuscript Guidelines

CIRCULATION DATA:

Reader: Academics, Practitioners, & Policy Makers
Frequency of Issue: Quarterly
Copies per Issue: Less than 1,000
Sponsor/Publisher: NTC Publications Ltd.
Subscribe Price: 132.00 US$ Individuals
    254.00 US$ Institutions

REVIEW INFORMATION:

Type of Review: Blind Review
No. of External Reviewers: 3+
No. of In House Reviewers: 0
Acceptance Rate: 35%
Time to Review: 2 - 3 Months
Reviewers Comments: Yes
Invited Articles: 6-10%
Fees to Publish: 0.00 US$

MANUSCRIPT TOPICS:
Advertising & Promotion Management; Business Law, Public Responsibility & Ethics; Communication; Direct Marketing; Global Business; International Marketing Communications; Marketing Research; Marketing Theory & Applications

MANUSCRIPT GUIDELINES/COMMENTS:

International Journal Of Advertising (IJOA) publishes original contributions on all aspects of marketing communications from the academic, practitioner and public policy perspective based on new research, case studies, 'state-of-the-art' practice and historical review.

It includes: media and direct advertising, public relations, sales promotion and sponsorship; domestic, business and government targets; the roles, behavior and interaction of advertisers/sponsors, agencies, the media and target audiences; the economic, social, technological and regulatory environment and research and measurement of the effects and effectiveness of campaigns. Studies with international application are preferred to the domestic issues of a single country.

Editorial: Correspondence and manuscripts for submission should be sent to the Editor above. A manuscript will be accepted only on the understanding that it is an original contribution which has not been published previously and is not under consideration for publication elsewhere. Contributions are independently refereed prior to publication decision.

Book Reviews: Books for review should be sent to The Editor, as above.

Manuscript Specifications: Articles accepted to the journal are generally of between 4000 and 6000 words in length, excluding illustrations, tables and bibliography, but shorter articles will be considered. The entire manuscript, including reference list and Figure captions, should be presented as A4 double-spaced typescript with generous margins, complete in all respects. All pages must be numbered consecutively. On separate sheets please give (a) the full title of the paper, author's name and affiliation(s) in the exact form required for publication, and an abstract not exceeding 150 words; (b) author's name, full address and telephone number (office hours) for contact re copy-editor's queries, proofs and offprints, and not more than 100 words author biography and current interests for the 'About the authors' page. A word count would be helpful.

The complete original typescript and illustrations should be sent to the Editor together with two complete Photocopies. A disk will be welcome in addition to the hard copies, if compatible with IBM, Apple Mackintosh or ASCII with 'flags'.

Style should be clear and concise. A journal is not a textbook or a thesis. Short papers have more chance of acceptance. Numbers of references should be appropriate to the length of the paper. Make complex technical or statistical data intelligible to non-specialists (e.g. by diagrams, charts and tables). Describe sample surveys and other data collection methods in enough detail for an expert to assess their validity, perhaps in an Appendix. Avoid footnotes and make necessary acknowledgements at the beginning or end. Number (1, 2, 3) main headings and up to two orders of subheadings within the text. We render spunks generally consistent with the Oxford English Dictionary.

Abbreviations: if used, the terms should first be written out in full followed by their abbreviation in parenthesis, preferably in capitals without full stops.

Tables: Tables should be numbered consecutively, given adequate titles or headings, typed on separate sheets of paper and attached to the manuscript. The tables must be referred to in text. They should supplement rather than duplicate text data.

Illustrations: High quality of reproduction can be obtained only from original artwork or photographs. Please do not send negatives or photocopies. If roughs are presented, however, they should be drawn large and dearly, and on separate sheets. Number the illustrations separately, with the number and author's name in pencil on the back of each illustration. Captions should be typed on a separate sheet, illustrations must be cited in text as Figure 1, Figure 2, etc.

Permission To Reproduce: If illustrations are borrowed from published sources written permission must be obtained from the copyright holder and a credit line acknowledging the source added to the caption. Such permission must also be obtained and acknowledged for quotations totalling more than 250 words and for tables borrowed verbatim from published sources. Permission letters should accompany the manuscript, but if you have been unable to obtain them please point this out. With shorter quotations a bibliographic credit is sufficient.

References: If an author is cited in text a date should follow in brackets, with the full details given in a reference list in alphabetical order at the end of the text. Multiple entries by one author or a set of authors in the same year should be post scripted a, b, c (1981a, 1981b, 1981c), etc. The list of references should follow the conventions illustrated by the following examples:

1. Journal articles
Jones, J. & Zufryden, E (1981) Relating deal purchases and consumer characteristics to repeat purchase probability. Journal of the Market Research Society, 23, 84-99.

2. Books
Fulop, C. (1981) Advertising, Competition and Consumer Behaviour. London: Holt, Rinehart and Winston.

3. Articles in books
Plummer, J. (1978) A theoretical view of advertising communication. In Marketing Management and Administrative Action (Ed.) Britt, S. & Boyd, H. 4th Edition, pp. 376-382. New York: McGraw-Hill.

References which have not been published are acceptable only if 'in press'. References in languages other than English may be published as submitted.

Proofs: Page proofs will be sent to the author for correction of typographical errors and other essential changes only. In the case of two or more authors please indicate to whom the proofs should be sent.

Offprints: One copy of the issue in which their article appears will be sent to each named contributor. Additional copies and a minimum of fifty offprints may be purchased at proof stage.

International Journal of Bank Marketing

ADDRESS FOR SUBMISSION:

Christine Ennew, Associate Editor
International Journal of Bank Marketing
University of Nottingham
School of Management & Finance
Nottingham, NG7 2RD
UK
Phone:
Fax: 44 0 11595 15259
E-Mail: watkins@vax.sbu.ac.uk
Web: www.mcb.co.uk
Address May Change:

PUBLICATION GUIDELINES:

Manuscript Length: 16-20
Copies Required: Three
Computer Submission: No
Format: N/A
Fees to Review: 0.00 US$

Manuscript Style:
    See Manuscript Guidelines

CIRCULATION DATA:

Reader: Administrators
Frequency of Issue: 7 Times/Year
Copies per Issue: No Reply
Sponsor/Publisher: MCB University Press
    Limited - UK
Subscribe Price: 9979.00 US$
    12559.00 A$

REVIEW INFORMATION:

Type of Review: Blind Review
No. of External Reviewers: 2
No. of In House Reviewers: 1
Acceptance Rate: 21-30%
Time to Review: 1 - 2 Months
Reviewers Comments: Yes
Invited Articles: 11-20%
Fees to Publish: 0.00 US$

MANUSCRIPT TOPICS:
Advertising & Promotion Management; Direct Marketing; Financial Services Marketing; Marketing Research; Marketing Theory & Applications

MANUSCRIPT GUIDELINES/COMMENTS:

Editor
Professor Trevor Watkins, Deputy Vice Chancellor and Deputy Chief Executive, South Bank University, 103 Borough Road, London, SE1 OAA. Email: watkinst@vax.sbu.ac.uk

Unique Attributes
The International Journal of Bank Marketing for the financial services sector, aims to present the latest thinking, practice and research findings on issues of current and future concern for financial services marketers worldwide. Each paper submitted to *IJBM* is subject to a double-blind review process.

Topicality
Financial institutions sell essential products and services in a fiercely competitive arena, governed by strict codes of practice. Intense market pressures mean they have developed some

of the most sophisticated and ingenious marketing strategies ever seen. This journal brings together the experiences of marketers in the field, providing valuable insights into the problem-solving initiatives employed by financial institutions all over the world to win customers-and keep them.

Key Journal Audiences
Marketing personnel in other financial institutions
Marketing practitioners in banks
Senior and middle bank management
Teachers, researchers and students of financial services and marketing, and libraries supplying their needs

Coverage
- Competition from non-banking institutions
- Corporate attitudes towards bank services
- Corporate banking requirements
- Development of marketing audits
- Financial service marketing abstracts
- Internationalization of bank services
- Marketing communications and bank services
- Measurement of in-branch customer service
- Personal selling and sales professionals
- Strategic planning policies
- Success of foreign banks

Copyright
Articles submitted to the journal should be original contributions and should not be under consideration for any other publication at the same time. Authors submitting articles for publication warrant that the work is not an infringement of any existing copyright and will indemnify the publisher against any breach of such warranty. For ease of dissemination and to ensure proper policing of use, papers and contributions become the legal copyright of the publisher unless otherwise agreed. Submissions should be sent to the Associate Editor.

Editorial objectives
The purpose of the International Journal of Bank Marketing is to present the latest thinking, practice and research findings on issues of current and future concern for financial services marketers. The focus of the journal is on the adoption and implementation of aspects of marketing management and marketing planning in the personal, corporate and international sectors of the financial services sector and which include the present nature and acceptability of marketing ideas among practitioners, together with longer-term marketing activities and challenges.

Editorial scope
a. It is hoped that contributors will comprise both academics and practicing marketing managers in the financial services sector.

b. It is our intention that published articles will be a mix of conceptualization of marketing challenges facing financial services, empirically based work, and discussion articles on topical issues.

c. Contributors are encouraged to spell out the practical implications of their work for those involved in marketing in the financial services sector.

d. Articles will only be considered for publication if they have not been published, submitted or accepted for publication elsewhere.

The reviewing process
Each paper is reviewed by the editor and, if it is judged suitable for this publication, it is then sent to two referees for double blind peer review. Based on their recommendations, the editor then decides whether the paper should be accepted as is, revised or rejected.

Manuscript requirements
Three copies of the manuscript should be submitted in double line spacing with wide margins. All authors should be shown and author's details must be printed on a separate sheet and the author should not be identified anywhere else in the article.

As a guide, articles should be between 3,000 and 6,000 words in length. A title of not more than eight words should be provided. A brief **autobiographical note** should be supplied including full name, affiliation, e-mail address and full international contact details. Authors must supply an **abstract** of 100-150 words. Up to six **keywords** should be included which encapsulate the principal subjects covered by the article.

Where there is a **methodology**, it should be clearly described under a separate heading. **Headings** must be short, clearly defined and not numbered. **Notes** or **Endnotes** should be used only if absolutely necessary and must be identified in the text by consecutive numbers, enclosed in square brackets and listed at the end of the article.

Figures, charts and **diagrams** should be kept to a minimum. They must be black and white with minimum shading and numbered consecutively using arabic numerals with a brief title and labelled axes. In the text, the position of the figure should be shown by typing on a separate line the words "take in Figure 2". Good quality originals must be provided.

Tables should be kept to a minimum. They must be numbered consecutively with roman numerals and a brief title. In the text, the position of the table should be shown by typing on a separate line the words "take in Table IV".

Photos and **illustrations** must be supplied as good quality black and white original half tones with captions. Their position should be shown in the text by typing on a separate line the words "take in Plate 2".

References to other publications should be complete and in Harvard style. They should contain full bibliographical details and journal titles should not be abbreviated. For multiple citations in the same year use a, b, c immediately following the year of publication.

References should be shown within the text by giving the author's last name followed by a comma and year of publication all in round brackets, e.g. (Fox, 1994). At the end of the article should be a reference list in alphabetical order as follows

(a) for books
surname, initials and year of publication, title, publisher, place of publication, e.g.Casson, M. (1979), *Alternatives to the Multinational Enterprise*, Macmillan, London.

(b) for chapter in edited book
surname, initials and year, "title", editor's surname, initials, title, publisher, place, pages, e.g.Bessley, M. and Wilson, P. (1984), "Public policy and small firms in Britain", in Levicki, C. (Ed.), Small Business Theory and Policy, Croom Helm, London, pp.111-26. Please note that the chapter title must be underlined.

(c) for journals
surname, initials, year "title", journal, volume, number, pages, e.g.Fox, S. (1994) "Empowerment as a catalyst for change: an example from the food industry", Supply Chain Management, Vol 2 No. 3, pp. 29-33

If there is more than one author list surnames followed by initials. All authors should be shown.

Electronic sources should include the URL of the electronic site at which they may be found, as follows:

Neuman, B.C.(1995), "Security, payment, and privacy for network commerce", IEEE Journal on Selected Areas in Communications, Vol. 13 No.8, October, pp.1523-31. Available (IEEE SEPTEMBER) http://www.research.att.com/jsac/

Notes/Endnotes should be used only if absolutely necessary. They should, however, always be used for citing Web sites. They should be identified in the text by consecutive numbers enclosed in square brackets and listed at the end of the article. Please then provide full Web site addresses in the end list.

Final submission of the article
Once accepted for publication, the final version of the manuscript must be provided, accompanied by a 3.5" **disk** of the same version labelled with: disk format; author name(s); title of article; journal title; file name.

Each article must be accompanied by a completed and signed **Journal Article Record Form** available from the Editor or on http://www.literaticlub.co.uk/

The manuscript will be considered to be the definitive version of the article. The author must ensure that it is complete, grammatically correct and without spelling or typographical errors.

In preparing the disk, please use one of the following formats: Word, Word Perfect, Rich text format or TeX/LaTeX. Figures which are provided electronically must be in tif, gif or pic file extensions. All figures and graphics must also be supplied as good quality originals.

Final submission requirements
Manuscripts must:
- be clean, good quality hard copy and;
- include an abstract and keywords
- have Harvard style references
- include any figures, photos and graphics as good quality originals
- be accompanied by a labelled disk
- be accompanied by a completed Journal Article Record Form

Technical assistance is available from MCB's World Wide Web Literati Club on http://www.literaticlub.co.uk/ or contact Mike Massey at MCB, e-mail mmassey@mcb.co.uk

International Journal of Business

ADDRESS FOR SUBMISSION:

K. C. Chen, Editor
International Journal of Business
California State University
Craig School of Business
Fresno, CA 93740-8001
USA
Phone: 559-278-5646
Fax: 559-278-5220
E-Mail: kchen@csufresno.edu
Web:
Address May Change:

PUBLICATION GUIDELINES:

Manuscript Length: No Reply
Copies Required: Three
Computer Submission: Yes
Format: MS Word 97
Fees to Review: 25.00 US$

Manuscript Style:
   Chicago Manual of Style

CIRCULATION DATA:

Reader: Academics
Frequency of Issue: 2 Times/Year
Copies per Issue: Less than 1,000
Sponsor/Publisher: Premier Publishing
Subscribe Price: 120.00 US$ Institution
   35.00 US$ Individual
   10.00 US$ Add for airmail Outside USA

REVIEW INFORMATION:

Type of Review: Blind Review
No. of External Reviewers: 2
No. of In House Reviewers: 0
Acceptance Rate: 11-20%
Time to Review: 2 - 3 Months
Reviewers Comments: Yes
Invited Articles: 6-10%
Fees to Publish: 0.00 US$

MANUSCRIPT TOPICS:
Advertising & Promotion Management; Business Education; Business Information Systems (MIS); Direct Marketing; Global Business; Labor Relations & Human Resource Mgt.; Marketing Research; Marketing Theory & Applications; Office Administration/Management; Operations Research/Statistics; Organizational Behavior & Theory; Organizational Development; Purchasing/Materials Management; Sales/Selling; Services; Small Business Entrepreneurship; Strategic Management Policy

MANUSCRIPT GUIDELINES/COMMENTS:

International Journal of Business (IJB) is a refereed professional journal published by Craig School of Business at California State University, Fresno, in collaboration with Premier Publishing. IJB will serve and provide a forum for exchange of ideas among business executives and academicians concerned with global business and economic issues. With the rapid evolution of corporate business from international to global in recent years, general business has been one of the areas of greatest added complexity and concern for corporate managers. Almost every single topic that can be studied in general business now has global dimensions that are equally important. As such, practitioners and academicians, each with a unique perspective on global business, must go beyond the presently limited sharing of information and ideas.

IJB is intended to be an academic journal combining academic inquiry and informed business practices. It will publish empirical, analytical, review, and survey articles, as well as case studies related to all areas of global business and economics. Emphasis is placed on instructiveness, clarity, and the direct applicability of the paper to business practices. IJB will solicit high-quality applied-research papers from all disciplines including:

- Accounting
- Finance
- International Business
- Marketing
- Economics
- General Management
- Management Information Systems
- Other Contemporary Business Issues

IJB will publish two issues per year. All manuscripts will be reviewed anonymously. Please submit three copies of your manuscript with a submission fee of $25 (waived for IJB subscribers) to: Professor K. C. Chen, Editor at the submission address above.

For subscription information, please contact Dr. K.C. Chen.

International Journal of Business and Economics

ADDRESS FOR SUBMISSION:

Atul Gupta, Editor
International Journal of Business and Economics
PO Box 11172
Lynchburg, VA 24506
USA
Phone: 800-462-2631
Fax: 804-385-1842
E-Mail: FFORUM@msn.com
Web:
Address May Change: 1/1/04

PUBLICATION GUIDELINES:

Manuscript Length: 3000-5000 wds.
Copies Required: Four
Computer Submission: No
Format: N/A
Fees to Review: 0.00 US$

Manuscript Style:
  Chicago Manual of Style

CIRCULATION DATA:

Reader: Business Persons, Academics
Frequency of Issue: 3 Times/Year
Copies per Issue: 1,001 - 2,000
Sponsor/Publisher: Orbit Publishing Co.
Subscribe Price: 50.00 US$ Individual
  75.00 US$ Library

REVIEW INFORMATION:

Type of Review: Blind Review
No. of External Reviewers: 2
No. of In House Reviewers: No Reply
Acceptance Rate: 11-20%
Time to Review: 4 - 6 Months
Reviewers Comments: Yes
Invited Articles: 0-5%
Fees to Publish: 0.00 US$

MANUSCRIPT TOPICS:
Accounting; Business Education; Business Information Systems (MIS); Business Law, Public Responsibility & Ethics; Economics; Finance & Investments; General Management & Business Research; Global Business; Labor Relations & Human Resource Mgt.; Marketing Theory & Applications; Operations Research/Statistics; Organizational Behavior & Theory; Production/Operations; Strategic Management Policy; Technology/Innovation

MANUSCRIPT GUIDELINES/COMMENTS:

1. Submit four (4) copies of. all manuscript to editorial office. Manuscripts will not be returned.

2. To maintain anonymity, only the title should appear on the manuscript. Attach a cover page with title of the manuscript, the author(s) and affiliation(s).

3. Include an abstract of 150 words or less.

4. Type all copy – including abstract, quotations, tabular material, notes, and references- double spaces, allowing a 1-inch margin on all sides.

5. Type all tables, using a standard word processing program, on separate pages, numbered consecutively, with brief descriptive titles, and place at the end of the manuscript following references.

6. Illustrations and charts should be referred to as "Figures" in text. They must be provided on disk using Adobe Illustrator, Quark Xpress, Photoshop, or PowerPoint graphics program.

7. Notes should be sequentially numbered in the text and listed as separate appendix titled "Notes." Do not use the footnote features available on most computer software programs. Notes should be kept a minimum and used only for substantive observation. Source citations are made in text, not the notes.

8. References to published work must be cited in text according to the author/date system and listed alphabetically as separate appendix titled "References" at the end of the manuscript. Al citations must be referenced and all references must be cited in the text. All references will adhere to *Chicago Manual of Style*, 14th edition.

9. Articles accepted for publication must be submitted on diskette in MS Word 7.0, in addition to hard copy when in final form.

10. Each author will receive a bound copy of the issue in which their article appears; arrangements to purchase offprint may be made with the International Association of Business and Economics.

International Journal of Electronic Commerce (IJEC)

ADDRESS FOR SUBMISSION:

Vladimir Zwass, Editor-in-Chief
International Journal of Electronic
  Commerce (IJEC)
19 Warewoods Road
Saddle River, NJ 07458
USA
Phone: 201-327-9239
Fax: 201-327-3682
E-Mail: zwass@alpha.fdu.edu
Web:
Address May Change:

PUBLICATION GUIDELINES:

Manuscript Length: 21-25
Copies Required: Five
Computer Submission: No
Format: N/A
Fees to Review: 0.00 US$

Manuscript Style:
  See Manuscript Guidelines

CIRCULATION DATA:

Reader: Academics, Business Persons
Frequency of Issue: Quarterly
Copies per Issue: Less than 1,000
Sponsor/Publisher: M.E. Sharpe
Subscribe Price: 66.00 US$ Individual
  315.00 US$ Institution

REVIEW INFORMATION:

Type of Review: Blind Review
No. of External Reviewers: 3
No. of In House Reviewers: 1
Acceptance Rate: 11-20%
Time to Review: 2 - 3 Months
Reviewers Comments: Yes
Invited Articles: 0-5%
Fees to Publish: 0.00 US$

MANUSCRIPT TOPICS:
Business Information Systems (MIS); Global Business; Marketing Research; Marketing Theory & Applications; Organizational Development; Sales/Selling; Technology/Innovation

MANUSCRIPT GUIDELINES/COMMENTS:

The *International Journal of Electronic Commerce* (IJEC) began its publication in the summer of 1996 as the first scholarly journal devoted exclusively to advancing the understanding and practice of electronic commerce. IJEC publishes significantly novel contributions from multiple disciplines to offer an integrated view of the field. Management information systems, computer science, economics, marketing, as well as sociology, are only some of these disciplines.

Electronic commerce is sharing of business information, maintaining business relationships, and conducting business transactions by means of wide-area computer networks. The area is undergoing explosive growth and calls for rethinking of many aspects of commerce and of societal relationships, as well as for the adaptation and application of several essential information technologies.

The Journal appears quarterly and will maintain stringent refereeing standards. Principal areas of interest will be:

- the marketplace and the organizational effects of electronic commerce
- the Internet as the infrastructure for electronic commerce
- effects of the Internet and World-Wide Web use on the organizational structure and processes
- changes in interorganizational relationships caused by electronic commerce
- internet-based marketplaces and supply chains
- economics of electronic commerce
- role of electronic commerce in business globalization
- social dynamics of the Internet-style communications
- security and privacy of transactions and information
- advanced electronic data interchange
- electronic funds transfer
- standardization in electronic commerce
- marketing on the Internet
- on-line screen-based trading
- smart cards and other access technologies
- intelligent agents, browsers, and spiders

Information For Contributors

The *International Journal Of Electronic Commerce* (IJEC) is the first scholarly journal devoted to advancing, the understanding and practice of electronic commerce. IJEC, using a multi-disciplinary approach, offers an integrated view of the field covering the areas of management information systems, computer science, economics, and sociology, as well as other related disciplines. The Journal will appear quarterly and will maintain stringent refereeing standards. Empirical and interpretive papers, espousing multiple methodologies and perspectives, as well as paradigmatic designs will be published.

Manuscripts may be submitted to the Editor-in-chief.

Form of Manuscripts

Five copies of manuscripts should be submitted. The text should be double-spaced on one side of good quality paper, allowing ample margins. All illustrations, tables, etc. should be placed on separate sheets, included with each copy. Their approximate placement should be indicated in the text. The covering letter should provide full affiliation and the address and telephone number(s) of the corresponding author. Brief biographical statements of all authors are also requested. The title page should include the paper title and the names and affiliations of authors. Every manuscript should contain an abstract (up to 150 words) and a set of key words and phrases to serve as indicators of the paper's content. A footnote on the first page should acknowledge any funding sources. If the paper relies on the use of questionnaires or similar research instruments that are not included in the text, five copies of the instrument should be submitted. All resubmissions should include five copies of the revised paper. Authors are encouraged to enclose a note explaining the revisions. The final submission of an accepted paper should include three copies of the manuscript and a diskette with the complete text, including the biographical statements.

References
The reference list should be provided at the end of the paper. The references should be arranged alphabetically according to the name of the first author or editor, and numbered. Citations in text, referring to this list, should be made as numbers in square brackets, e.g., [7]. References should be provided as follows.

References To Items In Periodicals: These should take the form: author(s), title, journal (italicized or underlined), volume and issue number, date, inclusive pages. For all authors, last names are given first; likewise for editors, with the names followed by "(ed.)". The name of the last author ends with a period. More than two authors (but not editors) are separated by semi-colons. The title has only the first word and proper names (or their derivatives) starting with capital letters, and it ends with a period. The date is given in parentheses.

Example: 19. Davenport. T.H., and Beers. M.C. Managing information about processes. *Journal of Management Information Systems*, 12, 1 Summer 1995), 57-80.

References To Books: Author(s)—same style as in periodicals. Title--all principal words are capitalized and the title is italicized or underlined. The title ends with a period and is followed by city, ":", publisher, year.

Figures and Tables
In preparing an accepted manuscript for publication, figures should be submitted as original drawings, complete and ready for photo reproduction. Tables submitted as cleanly printed copy may also be reproduced photographically. All lettering and figure elements should be large enough to be readable when the figure has been reduced to fit the journal page. All figures and tables must be specifically referred to within the text. All figures and tables should have brief, descriptive captions.

Proofs and Reprint
Authors will receive page proofs of their papers, which must be returned to the publisher within three working days. Each author will receive a free copy of the issue in which his or her paper appears. Additional copies of the journal and/or reprints may be ordered at the time the proofs are returned.

IJEC is sponsored and published by M.E. Sharpe, Inc., 30 Business Park Drive, Armonk, New York 10504.

International Journal of Hospitality & Tourism Administration

ADDRESS FOR SUBMISSION:

John C. Crotts, Editor
International Journal of Hospitality &
  Tourism Administration
College of Charleston
School of Business and Economics
Hospitality & Tourism Management
9 Liberty Street
Charleston, SC 29424-0001
USA
Phone: 843-953-6916
Fax:
E-Mail: crottsj@cofc.edu
Web:
Address May Change:

PUBLICATION GUIDELINES:

Manuscript Length: 21-25
Copies Required: Three
Computer Submission: Yes
Format: MS Word
Fees to Review: 0.00 US$

Manuscript Style:
  American Psychological Association

CIRCULATION DATA:

Reader: Academics
Frequency of Issue: Quarterly
Copies per Issue: Less than 1,000
Sponsor/Publisher: Haworth Press, Inc.
Subscribe Price: 36.00 US$ Individual
  48.00 US$ Institution
  85.00 US$ Library

REVIEW INFORMATION:

Type of Review: Blind Review
No. of External Reviewers: 2
No. of In House Reviewers: 0
Acceptance Rate: 50%
Time to Review: 1 - 2 Months
Reviewers Comments: Yes
Invited Articles: 6-10%
Fees to Publish: 0.00 US$

MANUSCRIPT TOPICS:
Advertising & Promotion Management; Business Law, Public Responsibility & Ethics; Global Business; Marketing Research; Marketing Theory & Applications; Non Profit Organizations; Organizational Behavior & Theory; Small Business Entrepreneurship; Strategic Management Policy; Transportation/Physical Distribution

MANUSCRIPT GUIDELINES/COMMENTS:

This is an exciting and challenging time to be in the hospitality and tourism field. Dynamic market forces such as global competition, changing customer expectations, and new communication technology—combined with career challenges due to ongoing industry consolidation and corporate restructuring—requires the continuous learning and sharing of ideas. The *International Journal of Hospitality & Tourism Administration* is an applied, internationally oriented, hospitality and tourism management journal designed to help practitioners and researchers stay abreast of the latest developments in the field as well as facilitate the exchange of ideas. The journal's goal is to address the critical competency areas needed to succeed today and tomorrow.

The *International Journal of Hospitality & Tourism Administration* publishes refereed articles on the best practices of hospitality and tourism management, applied research studies, and critical reviews on major issues affecting the hospitality and tourism sectors. The journal's scope includes but is not limited to
- managing guest's expectations and experiences
- marketing management
- human resource management
- managing cultural diversity in the workplace and in consumer markets
- information technologies
- strategic alliances
- security and safety
- energy management and resource conservation
- host quality of life

Original Articles Only. Submission of a manuscript to this Journal represents a certification on the part of the author(s) that it is an original work, and that neither this manuscript nor a version of it has been published elsewhere nor is being considered for publication elsewhere.

2. Manuscript Length. Your manuscript may be approximately **5-50 typed pages** double spaced (including references and abstract). Lengthier manuscripts may be considered, but only at the discretion of the Editor. Sometimes, lengthier manuscripts maybe considered if they can be divided up into sections for publication in successive journal issues.

3. Manuscript Style. References, citations, and general style of manuscripts for this Journal should follow the Chicago style (as outlines in the latest edition of the *Manual of Style* of the University of Chicago Press). References should be double-spaced and placed in alphabetical order.

If an author wishes to submit a paper that has been already prepared in another style, he or she may do so. However, if the paper is accepted (with or without reviewer's alterations), the author is fully responsible for retyping the manuscript in the correct style as indicated above. Neither the Editor nor the Publisher is responsible for re-preparing manuscript copy to adhere to the Journal's style.

4. Manuscript Preparation.
Margins: leave at least a one-inch margin on all four sides.
Paper: use clean white, 8-1/2" x 11" bond paper.
Number of copies: 4 (the original plus three photocopies).
Cover page: *Important* -- staple a cover page to the manuscript, indicating only the article title (this is used for anonymous refereeing).
Second "title page": enclose a regular title page but do not staple it to the manuscript. Include the title again, plus:
- full authorship

- an ABSTRACT of about 100 words. (Below the abstract provide 3-1 0 key words for index purposes).
- an introductory footnote with authors' academic degrees, professional titles, affiliations, mailing addresses, and any desired acknowledgment of research support or other credit.

5. Return Envelopes. When you submit your four manuscript copies, also include:
- A regular envelope, stamped and self-addressed. This is for the Editor to send you an "acknowledgement of receipt" letter.
- Manuscripts will not be returned.

6. Spelling, Grammar, and Punctuation. You are responsible for preparing manuscript copy which is clearly written in acceptable scholarly English, and which contains no errors of spelling, grammar, or punctuation. Neither the Editor nor the Publisher is responsible for correcting errors of spelling and grammar: the manuscript, after acceptance by the Editor, must be immediately ready for typesetting as it is finally submitted by the author(s). Check your paper for the following common errors:
- dangling modifiers
- misplaced modifiers
- unclear antecedents
- incorrect or inconsistent abbreviations

Also, check the accuracy of all arithmetic calculations, statistics, numerical data, text citations, and references.

7. Inconsistencies Must Be Avoided. Be sure you are consistent in your use of abbreviations, terminology, and in citing references, from one part of your paper to another.

8. Preparation of Tables, Figures, and Illustrations. All tables, figures, illustrations, etc. must be "camera-ready." That is, they must be cleanly typed or artistically prepared so that they can be used either exactly as they are or else used after a photographic reduction in size. Figures, tables, and illustrations must be prepared on separate sheets of paper. Always use black ink and professional drawing instruments. On the back of these items, write your article title and the journal title lightly in pencil, so they do not get misplaced. In text, skip extra lines and indicate where these figures and tables are to be placed (please **do not write** on face of art). Photographs are considered part of the acceptable manuscript and remain with Publisher for use in additional printings. If submitted art cannot be used, the Publisher reserves the right to redo the art and to charge the author a fee of $35.00 per hour for this service.

9. Alterations Required By Referees And Reviewers. Many times a paper is accepted by the Editor contingent upon changes that are mandated by anonymous specialist referees and members of the Editorial Board. If the Editor returns your manuscript for revisions, you are responsible for retyping any sections of the paper to incorporate these revisions (if applicable, revisions should also be put on disk).

10. Typesetting. You will not be receiving galley proofs of your article. Editorial revisions, if any, must therefore be made while your article is still in manuscript. The final version of the manuscript will be the version you see published. The production staff of The Haworth Press will correct typesetter's errors. Authors are expected to submit manuscripts, disks, and art that are free from error.

11. Electronic Media. Haworth's in-house typesetting unit is able to utilize your final manuscript material as prepared on most personal computers and word processors. This will minimize typographical errors and decrease overall production time lag. Please send the first draft and final draft copies of your manuscript to the journal Editor in print format for his/her final review and approval. **After approval of** your final manuscript, please submit the final approved version both on printed format ("hard copy") and floppy diskette. On the outside of the diskette package write:
A. the brand name of your computer or word processor
B. the word-processing program that you used
C. the title of your article, and
D. file name

Note: Disk and hard copy must agree. In case of discrepancies, it is The Haworth Press's policy to follow hard copy. Authors are advised that no revisions of the manuscript can be made after acceptance by the Editor for publication. The benefits of this procedure are many with speed and accuracy being the most obvious. We look forward to working with you on this, knowing we will be able to serve you more efficiently in the future.

12. Reprints. The senior author will receive two copies of the journal issue and 25 complimentary reprints of his or her article. The junior author will receive two copies of the journal issue. These are sent several weeks after the journal issue is published and in circulation. An order form for the purchase of additional reprints will also be sent to all authors at this time. (Approximately 4-6 weeks is necessary for the preparation of reprints.) Please do not query the Journal's Editor about reprints. All such questions should be sent directly to: **The Haworth Press, Inc., Production Department, 21 East Broad Street, West Hazleton, PA 18201**

To order additional reprints (minimum: 50 copies), please contact:
The Haworth Document Delivery Center, 10 Alice Street, Binghamton, NY 13904-1580
1-800-342-9678 or Fax (607) 722-6362.

13. Copyright. Copyright ownership of your manuscript must be transferred officially to The Haworth Press, Inc., before we can begin the peer-review process. The Editor's letter acknowledging receipt of the manuscript will be accompanied by a form fully explaining this. All authors must sign the form and return the original to the Editor as soon as possible. Failure to return the copyright form in a timely fashion will result in delay in review and subsequent publication

International Journal of Hospitality Management

ADDRESS FOR SUBMISSION:

Abraham Pizam, Editor-North America
International Journal of Hospitality
  Management
University of Central Florida
Department of Hospitality Management
PO Box 161400
Orlando, FL 32816-1400
USA
Phone: 407-823-6202
Fax: 407-823-5696
E-Mail: abraham.pizam@bus.ucf.edu
Web:
Address May Change:

PUBLICATION GUIDELINES:

Manuscript Length: 11-15
Copies Required: Three
Computer Submission: Yes
Format: Only after acceptance
Fees to Review: 0.00 US$

Manuscript Style:
  American Psychological Association

CIRCULATION DATA:

Reader: Academics
Frequency of Issue: Quarterly
Copies per Issue: 1,001 - 2,000
Sponsor/Publisher: Pergamon, Elsevier
  Science Publishing Co.
Subscribe Price: 157.00 US$ Individual
  463.00 US$ Institution
  139.76 Euro Indv., 413.39 Euro Inst.

REVIEW INFORMATION:

Type of Review: Blind Review
No. of External Reviewers: 2
No. of In House Reviewers: 1
Acceptance Rate: 21-30%
Time to Review: 4 - 6 Months
Reviewers Comments: Yes
Invited Articles: 6-10%
Fees to Publish: 0.00 US$

MANUSCRIPT TOPICS:
Advertising & Promotion Management; Business Education; Business Information Systems (MIS); Business Law, Public Responsibility & Ethics; Communication; Global Business; Hotels, Tourism, Food Service; Labor Relations & Human Resource Mgt.; Marketing Research; Marketing Theory & Applications; Organizational Behavior & Theory; Organizational Development; Purchasing/Materials Management; Sales/Selling; Services; Strategic Management Policy

MANUSCRIPT GUIDELINES/COMMENTS:

International Journal of Hospitality Management is published with the support of the International Association of Hotel Management Schools

Description
The *International Journal of Hospitality Management* discusses major trends and developments in a variety of disciplines as they apply to the hospitality industry. The range of topics covered by the journal includes:

- human resources management;
- consumer behaviour and marketing;
- business forecasting and applied economics;
- operational management;
- financial management;
- planning and design;
- information processing;
- education and training;
- technological developments;
- national and international legislation.

The journal also contains research papers, state-of-the-art reviews and analyses of business practice within the industry. It is also intended to include papers on the hospitality industry in different national contexts. As well as the refereed papers and Research Notes, the journal publishes Discussion Papers, Viewpoints, letters to the Editor, book reviews and reports on conferences.

Submission of Papers
Three typescript copies should be submitted to facilitate refereeing. All communications, except Research Notes and manuscripts from North America, must be sent to the Editor-in-Chief, John O'Connor, 4 Feilden Grove, Headington, Oxford OX3 0DU, UK. Manuscripts from authors in the USA and Canada should be addressed to the Associate Editor North America, Professor Abraham Pizam, Department of Hospitality Management, University of Central Florida, Orlando, Florida 32816, USA. Research Notes should also be sent to Professor A. Pizam at the above address.Manuscripts will be referred to acknowledged experts in the subject. All main papers are refereed by the double-blind process. Only those receiving favourable recommendation from referees will be published at the discretion of the Editor-in-Chief.

Articles for the Discussion Paper or Viewpoint section should not exceed 3000 words and will be published at the discretion of the Editor-in-Chief. Articles may be presented in a form intended to stimulate discussion through the expression of informed opinion. Such articles should be headed Viewpoint or Discussion Paper.

Submission of a paper implies that it has not been published previously, that it is not under consideration for publication elsewhere, and that if accepted it will not be published elsewhere in the same form, in English or in any other language, without the written consent of the publisher.

Manuscript Preparation
General: Manuscripts must be typewritten in English, with the lines double spaced on one side of good quality paper. Use a font size of 10 or 12 pt. Allow a reasonable left-hand margin. The corresponding author should be identified (include a Fax number and E-mail address). Full postal addresses must be given for all co-authors. Authors should consult a recent issue of the journal for style if possible. An electronic copy of the paper should accompany the **final** version. The Editors reserve the right to adjust style to certain standards of uniformity. Authors should retain a copy of their manuscript since we cannot accpet

responsibility for damage or loss of papers. Original manuscripts are discarded one month after publication unless the Publisher is asked to return original material after use.

Paper length: Manuscripts should not normally exceed 6000 words.

Abstracts: A short abstract (up to 100 words) in English should immediately precede the introduction. Abstracts should be most informative, giving a clear indication of the nature and range of results in the paper and should be accompanied by not more than six keywords which define the subject matter. Wherever possible the practical application of results should be cited.

Text: Follow this order when typing manuscripts: Title, Authors, Affiliations, Abstract, Keywords, Main text, Acknowledgements, Appendix, References, Vitae, Figure captions, Figures and then Tables. Do not import the Figures or Tables into your text. The Introduction should define clearly the nature of the problem being considered. The corresponding author should be identified with an asterisk and footnote. All other footnotes (except for table footnotes) should be identified with superscript Arabic numerals. A brief biography should also be supplied on a separate manuscript page as should the Title, Authors and Affiliations to facilitate blind refereeing.

Standard usage: The Concise Oxford English Dictionary is used as a reference for all spellings and hyphenations. Statistics should be given in figures, e.g. 10 minutes, 40 metres, except where the number begins a sentence. When the number does not refer to a unit of measurement it is spelt out in full, e.g. twenty guests, except where the number is more than one hundred, e.g. 103 bedrooms. Abbreviations should not be used except for SI units, e.g. kg (kilogram).

References: References should be made to previously published pertinent papers, accenting the major original contributions. Only papers closely related to the author's work should be included; exhaustive lists should be avoided.

All publications cited in the text should be present in a list of references following the text of the manuscript. In the text refer to the author's name (without initials) and year of publication, e.g. "Since Peterson (1993) has shown that..." or "This is in agreement with results obtained later (Kramer, 1994)". For three or more authors use the first author followed by "et al." in the text. The list of references should be arranged alphabetically by authors' names. The manuscript should be carefully checked to ensure that the spelling of authors' names and dates are exactly the same in the text as in the reference list. Names of journals must be given in full.

References should be given in the following form:
Barge, P., 1993. International management contracts. In: Jones, P., Pizam, A. (Eds.), The International Hospitality Industry: Organizational and Operational Issues. Pitman, London, pp. 117-125.

Edgar, D., Taylor, S., 1996. Strategic management research in hospitality: from slipstream to mainstream? In: Proceedings of 5th Annual CHME Research Conference. Nottingham Trent Polytechnic, Nottingham, UK, 10-11 April, pp. 264-278.

Guerrier, Y., Deery, M., 1998. Research in hospitality human resource management and organizational behaviour. International Journal of Hospitality Management 17 (2), 145-160.

Hill, T., 1983. Production operation management. Prentice Hall, London, pp. 10-19.

Illustrations: All illustrations should be provided in camera-ready form, suitable for reproduction (which may include reduction) without retouching. Photographs, charts and diagrams should be referred to as "Figure(s)" and should be numbered consecutively in the order to which they are referred. They should accompany the manuscript, but should not be included within the text. All illustrations should be clearly marked on the back with the figure number, the name(s) of the author(s) and an arrow pointing to the top of the figure. All figures are to have a caption. Captions should be supplied on a separate sheet.

Line drawings: Good quality printouts on white paper produced in black ink are required. All lettering, graph lines and points on graphs should be sufficiently large and bold to permit reproduction when the diagram has been reduced to a size suitable for inclusion in the journal. Dye-line prints or photocopies are not suitable for reproduction. Do not use any type of shading on computer-generated illustrations.

Photographs: Original photographs must be supplied as they are to be reproduced (e.g. black and white). If necessary, a scale should be marked on the photograph. Please note that photocopies of photographs are not acceptable.

Colour: Authors will be charged for colour at current printing costs.

Tables: Tables should be as few as possible and include only essential data. Tables should be numbered consecutively and given a suitable caption and each table typed on a separate sheet. Footnotes to tables should be typed below the table and should be referred to by superscript lower case letters. No vertical rules should be used. Tables should not duplicate results presented elsewhere in the manuscript (e.g. in graphs).

Electronic Submission
Authors should submit an electronic copy of their paper with the final version of the manuscript. The electronic copy should match the hard copy exactly.

Always keep a backup copy of the electronic file for reference and safety. Full details of electronic submission and formats can be obtained from http://www.elsevier.nl.locate/disksub or from Author Services at Elsevier Science. For authors using LaTeX, the document style files, as well as the instructions "Preparing articles with LaTeX" in the form of a dvi file, can be obtained free of charge from any host on the Comprehensive TeX Archive Network (CTAN) using anonymous ftp. The primary CTAN hosts are ftp.dante.de and ftp.tex.ac.uk. The Elsevier macros are in /pub/tex/macros/latex/contrib/supported/elsevier. These can also be downloaded from the Internet site: http://www.tex.ac.uk.

Proofs
Proofs will be sent to the author (first named author of multi-authored papers if no corresponding author is identified) and should be returned within 48 hours of receipt. Corrections should be restricted to typesetting errors; any others may be charged to the author. Any queries should be answered in full. Please note that authors are urged to check their proofs carefully before return, since the inclusion of late corrections cannot be guaranteed. Proofs are to be returned to the Log-in Department, Elsevier Science Limited, Stover Court, Bampfylde Street, Exeter, Devon EX1 2AH, UK.

Offprints
Fifty offprints will be supplied free of charge with 100 extra free offprints in cases of paid colour. Additional offprints and copies of the issue can be ordered at a specially reduced rate using the order form sent to the corresponding author after the manuscript has been accepted. Orders for reprints (produced after publication of an article) will incur a 50% surcharge.

Copyright
All authors must sign the "Transfer of Copyright" agreement before the article can be published. This transfer agreement enables Elsevier Science Ltd to protect the copyrighted material for the author, without the author relinquishing his/her proprietary rights. The copyright transfer covers the exclusive rights to reproduce and distribute the article, including reprints, photographic reproductions, microfilm or any other reproductions of a similar nature, and translations. It also includes the right to adapt the article for use in conjunction with computer systems and programs, including reproduction or publication in machine-readable form and incorporation in retrieval systems. Authors are responsible for obtaining from the copyright holder permission to reproduce any material for which copyright already exists.

Author Services
For queries relating to the general submission of manuscripts (including electronic text and artwork) and the status of accepted manuscripts, please contact Author Services, Log-in Department, Elsevier Science Limited, The Boulevard, Langford Lane, Kidlington, Oxford OX5 1GB, UK. E-mail: authors@elsevier.co.uk, Fax: +44 (0)1865 843905, Tel: +44 (0)1865 843900. Authors can also keep a track of the progress of their article through our OASIS system on the Internet. For information on an article go to the Internet page: http://www.elsevier.nl/oasis and key in the corresponding author's name and the Elsevier reference number.

International Journal of Logistics: Research and Applications

ADDRESS FOR SUBMISSION:

Peter Hines, Editor-in-Chief
International Journal of Logistics: Research and Applications
Cardiff Business School
Lean Enterprise Research Center
45 Park Place
Cardiff, CF1 3AS
UK
Phone: 44 1222 876005
Fax: 44 1222 874544
E-Mail: hinespa@cardiff.ac.uk
Web:
Address May Change:

PUBLICATION GUIDELINES:

Manuscript Length: 16-25
Copies Required: Four
Computer Submission: No Only Final Version
Format: Not Specified
Fees to Review: 0.00 US$

Manuscript Style:
See Manuscript Guidelines

CIRCULATION DATA:

Reader: Academics
Frequency of Issue: 3 Times/Year
Copies per Issue: Less than 1,000
Sponsor/Publisher: UK Institute of Logistics/Carfax
Subscribe Price: 262.00 US$ Institute
70.00 US$ Individual
24.00 Pounds Members: UK. Inst. of Log.

REVIEW INFORMATION:

Type of Review: Blind Review
No. of External Reviewers: 2
No. of In House Reviewers: 1
Acceptance Rate: 40%
Time to Review: 2 - 3 Months
Reviewers Comments: Yes
Invited Articles: 0-5%
Fees to Publish: 0.00 US$

MANUSCRIPT TOPICS:
Production/Operations; Purchasing/Materials Management; Strategic Management Policy

MANUSCRIPT GUIDELINES/COMMENTS:

International Journal of Logistics: Research & Applications will publish original and challenging work that has a clear applicability to the business world. As a result the journal concentrates on articles of an academic journal standard but aimed at the practitioner as much as the academic. The term 'logistics' is taken in its broadest context with articles crossing the various traditional functional boundaries of the complete supply-chain.

Articles are drawn from, but not restricted to:

1. The Logistics Sub-Process Areas of:
    Distribution (including third-party distribution); Manufacturing; Marketing; Material Management; Purchasing; Stock Management; Transport; Warehousing

2. The Logistics and Supply-Chain Process

3. Specific Areas within Logistics such as:
   New Technology - EDI, EPOS, 4 Fields Mapping
   Systems - DRIP, MRP I/II, OPT, JIT, JIT 2
   Methods - Cross Docking, Intermodal Transport, Supplier Associations,
   Vendor Managed Inventory, Quality Function Deployment

4. People Related Issues in the Supply-Chain
   Logistics training and education
   Motivation and competences

Bearing in mind the focus of the journal, papers submitted may be of a theoretical nature, be based on practical experience; report a case study or an experimental result.

Manuscripts to be considered for publication should be submitted to the Editor-in-Chief. All submissions will be independently judged by at least two referees. Authors should consult the Notes for Contributors' overleaf before sending a manuscript.

Notes for Contributors
In order to meet the needs of the target audience articles will be no more than 5,000 words in length and written in a clear way. Manuscripts should be submitted to Professor Peter Hines, International Journal of Logistics: Research & Applications, Lean Enterprise Research Centre, Cardiff Business School, 45 Park Place, Cardiff CF1 3AS, UK.

Articles can only be considered if four complete copies of each manuscript are submitted. They should be typed on one side of the paper, double-spaced, with ample margins, and bear the title of the contribution and the addresses where the work was carried out. Each article should be accompanied by an abstract/summary of 100-150 words on a separate sheet, and a short note of biographical details. The full postal address, telephone, fax, and e-mail numbers of the author who will check proofs and receive correspondence and offprints should also be included. All pages should be numbered. Footnotes to the text should be kept to a minimum.

Contributors should bear in mind that they are addressing an international audience. Jargon should be avoided wherever possible. Authors should also define their choice of terms clearly. Bearing in mind the focus of the journal, papers submitted may be of a theoretical nature, be based on practical experience, report a case study or an experimental result. Within this articles should:

1. Make an original contribution to the field
2. Be directly relevant to the management of logistics
3. Contain elements with general applicability
4. Be within the general scope of coverage of the journal
5. Not have been published elsewhere except in a very limited circulation

Tables and figures should be completely understandable independent of the text. Tables must be typed on separate sheets and not included as part of the text. The captions to illustrations should be gathered together and typed on a separate sheet. The approximate position of tables and figures should be indicated in the manuscript. Please supply clear copies of artwork in a finished form suitable for reproduction. Figures will not normally be redrawn by the publisher.

References should be indicated in the manuscript by giving the author's name, with the year of publication in parentheses, eg Whiteoak (1993) or (Whiteoak 1993) as appropriate. If several publications are cited by the same author and from same year, a. b, c etc. should be put after the year of publication. All references cited in the text should be listed in full at the end of the paper in the following standard form:

For books: Lambert D. and Stock J. (1993) Strategic Logistics Management, 3rd Edition, Richard D. Irwin Inc., Homewood

For articles: Whiteoak P. (1993) 'The Realities of Quick Response in the Grocery Sector', International Journal of Retail & Distribution Management, Vol. 21, No. 8, pp. 3-10

Titles of journals should not be abbreviated. Copyright will reside with the journal as a condition of acceptance of submitted papers. Proofs will be sent to authors if there is sufficient time to do so. They should be corrected and returned to the editor within three days. Major alterations to the text cannot be accepted.

Fifty offprints of each paper are supplied free of charge. Additional copies may be purchased and should be ordered when proofs are returned. Offprints, together with a complete copy of the relevant journal issue, are sent by accelerated surface post about three weeks after publication.

International Journal of Physical Distribution & Logistics Management

ADDRESS FOR SUBMISSION:

James R. Stock, Editor
International Journal of Physical
 Distribution & Logistics Management
University of South Florida
Department of Marketing
Tampa, FL 33620-5500
USA
Phone: 813-974-6173
Fax: 813-974-6175
E-Mail: jstock@coba.usf.edu
Web:
Address May Change:

PUBLICATION GUIDELINES:

Manuscript Length: 3,000-6,000 words
Copies Required: Four
Computer Submission: Yes
Format: Most Software
Fees to Review: 0.00 US$

Manuscript Style:
 Uniform System of Citation (Harvard Blue Book)

CIRCULATION DATA:

Reader: Business Persons, Academic
Frequency of Issue: 10 Times/Year
Copies per Issue: Less than 1,000
Sponsor/Publisher: MCB Unviversity Press
Subscribe Price: 9159.00 US$
 11559.00 AUS$

REVIEW INFORMATION:

Type of Review: Blind Review
No. of External Reviewers: 3
No. of In House Reviewers: 0
Acceptance Rate: 21-30%
Time to Review: 2 - 3 Months
Reviewers Comments: Yes
Invited Articles: 0-5%
Fees to Publish: 0.00 US$

MANUSCRIPT TOPICS:
Business Information Systems (MIS); Global Business; Marketing Theory & Applications; Organizational Behavior & Theory; Production/Operations; Purchasing/Materials Management; Transportation/Physical Distribution

MANUSCRIPT GUIDELINES/COMMENTS:

About the journal
The International Journal of Physical Distribution & Logistics Management (IJPDLM) has been number one in its field since 1970, the result of its astoundingly wide and deep coverage of key issues and the latest developments in distribution and logistics management. Carefully aligning the academic and practical elements of its subject, this prestigious journal offers sound guidance and good ideas to business planners and researchers worldwide. Within its pages, you will find innovative solutions to a host of distribution and logistics problems, as well as expert knowledge to broaden your understanding and provide a platform for the development of new research and theories.

Coverage

- Channel management and relationships
- Distribution planning and costing
- Information technology
- Materials and purchasing management
- Order processing systems
- Transport and inventory management
- Service logistics
- Outsourcing

NOTES FOR CONTRIBUTORS

Copyright

Articles submitted to the journal should be original contributions and should not be under consideration for any other publication at the same time. Authors submitting articles for publication warrant that the work is not an infringement of any existing copyright and will indemnify the publisher against any breach of such warranty. For ease of dissemination and to ensure proper policing of use, papers and contributions become the legal copyright of the publisher unless otherwise agreed. Submissions should be sent to

The Editor, Professor James R. Stock (address above)

European Editor, Professor Remko van Hoek, Erasmus University of Rotterdam, H14-05, 3000DR Rotterdam, The Netherlands. Email: Remko.van.hoek@wxs.nl

Australian and Far East Editor, Professor David Walters, Division of Economic and Financial Studies, MacQuarie University, Ryde, NSW 2109, Australia.
Email: dwalters@efs.mq.edu.au

Editorial objectives

To provide business practitioners, consultants and academics with leading edge information and discussions of current developments in the fields of physical distribution and logistics. To facilitate the interchange of information about physical distribution and logistics management among business planners and researchers on a worldwide basis. To provide a platform for new thinking on the problems and techniques of physical distribution and logistics management.

The reviewing process

Each paper is reviewed by the editor and, if it is judged suitable for this publication, it is then sent to two referees for double blind peer review. Based on their recommendations, the editor then decides whether the paper should be accepted as is, revised or rejected.

Manuscript requirements

Three copies of the manuscript should be submitted in double line spacing with wide margins. All authors should be shown and author's details must be printed on a separate sheet and the author should not be identified anywhere else in the article.

As a guide, articles should be between 3,000 and 6,000 words in length. A title of not more than eight words should be provided. A brief **autobiographical note** should be supplied including full name, affiliation, e-mail address and full international contact details. Authors must supply an **abstract** of 100-150 words. Up to six **keywords** should be included which encapsulate the principal subjects covered by the article.

Where there is a **methodology**, it should be clearly described under a separate heading. **Headings** must be short, clearly defined and not numbered. **Notes** or **Endnotes** should be used only if absolutely necessary and must be identified in the text by consecutive numbers, enclosed in square brackets and listed at the end of the article.

Figures, charts and **diagrams** should be kept to a minimum. They must be black and white with minimum shading and numbered consecutively using arabic numerals with a brief title and labelled axes. In the text, the position of the figure should be shown by typing on a separate line the words "take in Figure 2". Good quality originals must be provided.

Tables should be kept to a minimum. They must be numbered consecutively with roman numerals and a brief title. In the text, the position of the table should be shown by typing on a separate line the words "take in Table IV".

Photos and **illustrations** must be supplied as good quality black and white original half tones with captions. Their position should be shown in the text by typing on a separate line the words "take in Plate 2".

References to other publications should be complete and in Harvard style. They should contain full bibliographical details and journal titles should not be abbreviated. For multiple citations in the same year use a, b, c immediately following the year of publication. References should be shown within the text by giving the author's last name followed by a comma and year of publication all in round brackets, e.g. (Fox, 1994). At the end of the article should be a reference list in alphabetical order as follows

(a) for books
surname, initials and year of publication, title, publisher, place of publication, e.g.Casson, M. (1979), Alternatives to the Multinational Enterprise, Macmillan, London.

(b) for chapter in edited book
surname, initials and year, "title", editor's surname, initials, title, publisher, place, pages, e.g.Bessley, M. and Wilson, P. (1984), "Public policy and small firms in Britain", in Levicki, C. (Ed.), Small Business Theory and Policy, Croom Helm, London, pp.111-26. Please note that the chapter title must be underlined.

(c) for articles
surname, initials, year "title", journal, volume, number, pages, e.g.Fox, S. (1994) "Empowerment as a catalyst for change: an example from the food industry", Supply Chain Management, Vol 2 No 3, pp. 29-33

If there is more than one author list surnames followed by initials. All authors should be shown.

Electronic sources should include the URL of the electronic site at which they may be found, as follows:
Neuman, B.C.(1995), "Security, payment, and privacy for network commerce", IEEE Journal on Selected Areas in Communications, Vol. 13 No.8, October, pp.1523-31. Available (IEEE SEPTEMBER) http://www.research.att.com/jsac/

Notes/Endnotes should be used only if absolutely necessary. They should, however, always be used for citing Web sites. They should be identified in the text by consecutive numbers enclosed in square brackets and listed at the end of the article. Please then provide full Web site addresses in the end list.

Final submission of the article
Once accepted for publication, the final version of the manuscript must be provided, accompanied by a 3.5" **disk** of the same version labelled with: disk format; author name(s); title of article; journal title; file name.

Each article must be accompanied by a completed and signed **Journal Article Record Form** available from the Editor or on http://www.literaticlub.co.uk/

The manuscript will be considered to be the definitive version of the article. The author must ensure that it is complete, grammatically correct and without spelling or typographical errors. In preparing the disk, please use one of the following formats: Word, Word Perfect, Rich text format or TeX/LaTeX. Figures which are provided electronically must be in tif, gif or pic file extensions. All figures and graphics must also be supplied as good quality originals.

Final submission requirements
Manuscripts must:
- be clean, good quality hard copy
- include an abstract and keywords
- have Harvard style references
- include any figures, photos and graphics as good quality originals
- be accompanied by a labelled disk
- be accompanied by a completed Journal Article Record Form

Technical assistance is available from MCB's World Wide Web Literati Club on http://www.literaticlub.co.uk/ or contact Mike Massey at MCB, e-mail mmassey@mcb.co.uk

International Journal of Research In Marketing

ADDRESS FOR SUBMISSION:

J. E. B. M. Steenkamp, Editor
International Journal of Research In
  Marketing
Tilburg University
Room B638
Department of Marketing
PO Box 90153
NL-5000 LE Tilburg,
The Netherlands
Phone: 31 13 466 9111
Fax:
E-Mail: ijrm@kub.nl
Web: www.elsevier.nl
Address May Change:

PUBLICATION GUIDELINES:

Manuscript Length: 50 maximum
Copies Required: Six
Computer Submission: No
Format: N/A
Fees to Review: 0.00 US$

Manuscript Style:
  See Manuscript Guidelines

CIRCULATION DATA:

Reader: Academics
Frequency of Issue: Quarterly
Copies per Issue: 1,001 - 2,000
Sponsor/Publisher: Elsevier Science
  Publishing Co.
Subscribe Price: 463.00 US$
  912.00 NLG$
  413.85 Euro

REVIEW INFORMATION:

Type of Review: Blind Review
No. of External Reviewers: 2
No. of In House Reviewers: 1
Acceptance Rate: 11-20%
Time to Review: 2 - 3 Months
Reviewers Comments: No Reply
Invited Articles: 0%
Fees to Publish: 0.00 US$

MANUSCRIPT TOPICS:
Advertising & Promotion Management; Business Information Systems (MIS); Communication; Direct Marketing; Global Business; Marketing Research; Marketing Theory & Applications; Sales/Selling

MANUSCRIPT GUIDELINES/COMMENTS:

Description
The purpose of the *International Journal of Research in Marketing (IJRM)* is to provide a high-quality medium, through which both developments in marketing theory and thought and results of empirical research can be communicated to those active in marketing research as well as those wishing to be informed about progress in the field. *IJRM* aims to contribute to the body of knowledge about research in marketing by performing an integrative function, publishing theoretical and empirical articles from all countries and with different disciplinary approaches. *IJRM* covers the entire area of marketing: profit as well as non-profit marketing, consumer behavior, product decisions, pricing marketing communication, marketing channels,

strategic marketing planning, industrial marketing, international marketing etc. Methodological subject areas to be covered are, for example, the philosophical basis of marketing theory and research, the confrontation of different research traditions, and theoretical reflections on the nature, scope, and boundaries of marketing. Special attention will be paid to topics such as comparative marketing, cross-cultural aspects of marketing, the relationship between government and marketing, and marketing and society.

Guide for Authors

(1) Papers must be in English. Preferably, the length of a paper should not exceed 7000 words.

(2) Papers for publication should be sent in sixfold to the Editor at the above address.

Submission of a paper will be held to imply that it contains original unpublished work and is not being submitted for publication elsewhere. The Editor does not accept responsibility for damage or loss of papers submitted. Upon acceptance of an article, author(s) will be asked to transfer copyright of the article to the publisher. This transfer will ensure the widest possible dissemination of information.

(3) Submission of accepted papers as electronic manuscripts, i.e., on disk with accompanying manuscript, is encouraged. Electronic manuscripts have the advantage that there is no need for rekeying of text, thereby avoiding the possibility of introducing errors and resulting in reliable and fast delivery of proofs. The preferred storage medium is a 5.25 or 3.5-inch disk in MS-DOS format, although other systems are welcome, e.g., Macintosh (in this case, save your file in the usual manner; do not use the option 'save in MS-DOS format'). Do not submit your original paper as electronic manuscript but hold on to the disk until asked for this by the Editor (in case your paper is accepted without revisions). Do submit the accepted version of your paper as electronic manuscript. Make absolutely sure that the file on the disk and the printout are identical. Please use a new and correctly formatted disk and label this with your name; also specify the software and hardware used as well as the title of the file to be processed. Do not convert the file to plain ASCII. Ensure that the letter 'l' and digit '1', and also the letter 'O' and digit '0' are used properly, and format your article (tabs, indents, etc.) consistently. Characters not available on your word processor (Greek letters, mathematical symbols, etc.) should not be left open but indicated by a unique code (e.g. gralpha, α, @, etc., for the Greek letter α). Such codes should be used consistently throughout the entire text; a list of codes used should accompany the electronic manuscript. Do not allow your word processor to introduce word breaks and do not use a justified layout. Please adhere strictly to the general instructions below on style, arrangement and, in particular, the reference style of the journal.

(4) Manuscripts should be double spaced, with wide margins, and printed on one side of the paper only. All pages should be numbered consecutively. Titles and subtitles should be short. References, tables, and legends for the figures should be printed on separate pages.

(5) The first page of the manuscript should contain the following information: (i) the title; (ii) the name(s) and institutional affiliation(s) of the author(s); (iii) an abstract of not more than 100 words. A footnote on the same sheet should give the name, address, and telephone and fax numbers of the corresponding author [as well as an e-mail address]. In addition, up to five key words should be supplied.

(6) Acknowledgements and information on grants received can be given before the References.

(7) Footnotes should be kept to a minimum and numbered consecutively throughout the text with superscript Arabic numerals. They should be double-spaced and not include displayed formulae or tables.

(8) Displayed formulae should be numbered consecutively throughout the manuscript as (1), (2), etc. against the right-hand margin of the page. In cases where the derivation of formulae has been abbreviated, it is of great help to the referees if the full derivation can be presented on a separate sheet (not to be published).

(9) References to publications should be as follows: 'Smith (1992) reported that...' or 'This problem has been studied previously (e.g., Smith et al., 1969)'. The author should make sure that there is a strict one-to-one correspondence between the names and years in the text and those on the list. The list of references should appear at the end of the main text (after any appendices, but before tables and legends for figures). It should be double spaced and listed in alphabetical order by author's name. References should appear as follows:

For books:
Schulz, R. and A. Zoltners, 1981. Marketing decision models. Amsterdam: North-Holland.

For articles in collected volumes:
Goldberg, M.E. and G.J. Gorn, 1983. Researching the effects of television advertising on children: A methodological critique. In: M. Howe (ed.), Learning from television, 125-151. London: Academic Press.

For articles in journals:
Graham, J.L. 1984. A comparison of Japanese and American business negotiations. International Journal of Research in Marketing 1, 45- 62.

Note that journal titles should not be abbreviated.

(10) Illustrations will be reproduced photographically from originals supplied by the author; they will not be redrawn by the publisher. Please provide all illustrations in sixfold (one high-contrast original and five photocopies). Care should be taken that lettering and symbols are of a comparable size. The illustrations should not be inserted in the text, and should be marked on the back with figure number, title of paper, and author's name. All graphs and diagrams should be referred to as figures, and should be numbered consecutively in the text in Arabic numerals. Illustration for papers submitted as electronic manuscripts should be in traditional form.

(11) Tables should be numbered consecutively in the text in Arabic numerals and printed on separate sheets.

Any manuscript which does not conform to the above instructions may be returned for the necessary revision before publication.

Page proofs will be sent to the corresponding author. Proofs should be corrected carefully; the responsibility for detecting errors lies with the author. Corrections should be restricted to instances in which the proof is at variance with the manuscript. Extensive alterations will be charged. Twenty-five reprints of each paper are supplied free of charge to the corresponding author; additional reprints are available at cost if they are ordered when the proof is returned.

All articles published in IJRM will be in English. However, a paper may be submitted in Japanese, French or German. In that case the reviewing process is carried out in two rounds. If the result of the first round is a provisional acceptance, the paper is to be translated into English. (This is the responsibility of the author(s).) In the second round the English version of the paper is put through the regular review process. In this process additional revisions may be required from the author, before the paper is definitely accepted.

International Journal of Retail and Distribution Management

ADDRESS FOR SUBMISSION:

John Fernie, Editor
International Journal of Retail and
 Distribution Management
Heriot-Watt University
School of Management
Edinburgh, EH14 4AS
UK
Phone: 44 0 131-451-3880
Fax: 44 0 131-451-3498
E-Mail: j.fernie@hw.ac.uk
Web: www.mcb.co.uk
Address May Change:

PUBLICATION GUIDELINES:

Manuscript Length: 16-20
Copies Required: Three
Computer Submission: Yes
Format: Word for Windows
Fees to Review: 0.00 US$

Manuscript Style:
 Uniform System of Citation (Harvard Blue Book)

CIRCULATION DATA:

Reader: Business Persons, Academics
Frequency of Issue: Monthly
Copies per Issue: No Reply
Sponsor/Publisher: MCB University Press
 Limited-UK
Subscribe Price: 6799.00 US$

REVIEW INFORMATION:

Type of Review: Blind Review
No. of External Reviewers: 2
No. of In House Reviewers: 1
Acceptance Rate: 21-30%
Time to Review: 1 - 2 Months
Reviewers Comments: Yes
Invited Articles: 6-10%
Fees to Publish: 0.00 US$

MANUSCRIPT TOPICS:
Retailing; Transportation/Physical Distribution

MANUSCRIPT GUIDELINES/COMMENTS:

Unique Attributes
The *International Journal of Retail & Distribution Management* focuses on issues of strategic significance in retailing and distribution worldwide and provides a forum for researchers in academia, business, consultancy and management. All academic articles are refereed anonymously.

Topicality
The competitive retail sector is under pressure to provide efficient services to hold its share of the market. As consumers demand higher levels of service and supply, they are simultaneously wooed by other alternatives like mail order and out of-town-shopping. The *International Journal of Retail & Distribution Management* provides a link between production and consumer, and by understanding their relationship it allows retail personnel to study operations practice in other organizations, and to compare methodologies.

Key Benefits
Because the journal is not connected to any retail or distribution organization, it remains totally impartial and can publish controversial material as well as highlight special concerns in an objective manner. This makes it an especially valuable resource for a worldwide readership committed to the improvement of standards in retail distribution.

Key Journal Audiences
- Consultants
- Libraries supplying practising managers and researchers
- Retail strategists, researchers and students
- Retail managers
- Suppliers and contractors to the retail industry

Coverage
- Abstracts drawn from over 300 international publications
- Case studies and industry reports
- Information and reviews
- Leading edge research institute papers

NOTES FOR CONTRIBUTORS

Copyright
Articles submitted to the journal should be original contributions and should not be under consideration for any other publication at the same time. Authors submitting articles for publication warrant that the work is not an infringement of any existing copyright and will indemnify the publisher against any breach of such warranty. For ease of dissemination and to ensure proper policing of use, papers and contributions become the legal copyright of the publisher unless otherwise agreed. Submissions should be sent to:

Editorial objectives
To provide a forum for researchers in academia, business, consultancy, and management. In particular to focus on issues of strategic significance in retailing and distribution, worldwide.

General principles

a. It is our intention to encourage communication between retail managers, teachers and researchers.
b. Contributors are encouraged to spell out the practical implications of their work for those involved in retailing and distribution.
c. Articles based on experience and evidence rather than just philosophical speculation will receive particular encouragement.

The reviewing process
Articles written by academics will be refereed anonymously.

Manuscript requirements

Three copies of the manuscript should be submitted in double line spacing with wide margins. All authors should be shown and author's details must be printed on a separate sheet and the author should not be identified anywhere else in the article.

As a guide, articles should be between 3,000 and 6,000 words in length. A title of not more than eight words should be provided. A brief **autobiographical note** should be supplied including full name, affiliation, e-mail address and full international contact details. Authors must supply an abstract of 100-150 words. Up to six keywords should be included which encapsulate the principal subjects covered by the article.

Where there is a **methodology**, it should be clearly described under a separate heading. **Headings** must be short, clearly defined and not numbered. **Notes** or **Endnotes** should be used only if absolutely necessary and must be identified in the text by consecutive numbers, enclosed in square brackets and listed at the end of the article.

Figures, charts and **diagrams** should be kept to a minimum. They must be black and white with minimum shading and numbered consecutively using arabic numerals with a brief title and labelled axes. In the text, the position of the figure should be shown by typing on a separate line the words "take in Figure 2". Good quality originals must be provided.

Tables should be kept to a minimum. They must be numbered consecutively with roman numerals and a brief title. In the text, the position of the table should be shown by typing on a separate line the words "take in Table IV".

Photos and **illustrations** must be supplied as good quality black and white original half tones with captions. Their position should be shown in the text by typing on a separate line the words "take in Plate 2".

References to other publications should be complete and in Harvard style. They should contain full bibliographical details and journal titles should not be abbreviated. For multiple citations in the same year use a, b, c immediately following the year of publication. References should be shown within the text by giving the author's last name followed by a comma and year of publication all in round brackets, e.g. (Fox, 1994). At the end of the article should be a reference list in alphabetical order as follows

(a) *for books*
surname, initials and year of publication, title, publisher, place of publication, e.g.Casson, M. (1979), *Alternatives to the Multinational Enterprise*, Macmillan, London.
(b) *for chapter in edited book*
surname, initials and year, "title", editor's surname, initials, title, publisher, place, pages, e.g.Bessley, M. and Wilson, P. (1984), "Public policy and small firms in Britain", in Levicki, C. (Ed.), Small Business Theory and Policy, Croom Helm, London, pp.111-26. Please note that the chapter title must be underlined.
(c) *for articles*

surname, initials, year "title", journal, volume, number, pages, e.g.Fox, S. (1994) "Empowerment as a catalyst for change: an example from the food industry", Supply Chain Management, Vol 2 No 3, pp. 29-33

If there is more than one author list surnames followed by initials. All authors should be shown.

Electronic sources should include the URL of the electronic site at which they may be found, as follows:
Neuman, B.C.(1995), "Security, payment, and privacy for network commerce", IEEE Journal on Selected Areas in Communications, Vol. 13 No.8, October, pp.1523-31. Available (IEEE SEPTEMBER) http://www.research.att.com/jsac/

Notes/Endnotes should be used only if absolutely necessary. They should, however, always be used for citing Web sites. They should be identified in the text by consecutive numbers enclosed in square brackets and listed at the end of the article. Please then provide full Web site addresses in the end list.

Final submission of the article

Once accepted for publication, the final version of the manuscript must be provided, accompanied by a 3.5" **disk** of the same version labelled with: disk format; author name(s); title of article; journal title; file name.

Each article must be accompanied by a completed and signed **Journal Article Record Form** available from the Editor or on http://www.literaticlub.co.uk/

The manuscript will be considered to be the definitive version of the article. The author must ensure that it is complete, grammatically correct and without spelling or typographical errors. In preparing the disk, please use one of the following formats: Word, Word Perfect, Rich text format or TeX/LaTeX. Figures which are provided electronically must be in tif, gif or pic file extensions. All figures and graphics must also be supplied as good quality originals.

Final submission requirements

Manuscripts must:
- be clean, good quality hard copy
- include an abstract and keywords
- have Harvard style references
- include any figures, photos and graphics as good quality originals
- be accompanied by a labelled disk
- be accompanied by a completed Journal Article Record Form

Technical assistance is available from MCB's World Wide Web Literati Club on http://www.literaticlub.co.uk/ or contact Mike Massey at MCB, e-mail mmassey@mcb.co.uk

International Journal of Tourism Research

ADDRESS FOR SUBMISSION:

C. Cooper, Editor
International Journal of Tourism Research
Bournemouth University
PO Box 2816
Poole BH12 5YT, Dorset,
UK
Phone: 44 120 2595 158
Fax: 44 120 2595 228
E-Mail: ccooper@bournemouth.ac.uk
Web:
Address May Change:

PUBLICATION GUIDELINES:

Manuscript Length: 26-30+
Copies Required: Three
Computer Submission: Yes
Format: Any
Fees to Review: 0.00 US$

Manuscript Style:
    See Manuscript Guidelines

CIRCULATION DATA:

Reader: Academics
Frequency of Issue: Bi-Monthly
Copies per Issue: Less than 1,000
Sponsor/Publisher: John Wiley & Sons
Subscribe Price: 225.00 US$ Individual
    345.00 US$ Institution

REVIEW INFORMATION:

Type of Review: Blind Review
No. of External Reviewers: 2
No. of In House Reviewers: 0
Acceptance Rate: 50%
Time to Review: 2 - 3 Months
Reviewers Comments: Yes
Invited Articles: 0-5%
Fees to Publish: 0.00 US$

MANUSCRIPT TOPICS:
Advertising & Promotion Management; Business Education; Global Business; Marketing Research; Marketing Theory & Applications; Sales/Selling; Services; Small Business Entrepreneurship; Tourism & Hospitality Research

MANUSCRIPT GUIDELINES/COMMENTS:

Aims & Scope
The *International Journal of Tourism Research* promotes and enhances research developments in the field of tourism. The journal provides an international platform for debate and dissemination of research findings whilst also facilitating the discussion of new research areas and techniques. IJTR represents a vibrant and exciting channel for those interested in tourism research developments. This function is further enhanced by the provision of regular book, conference and web site reviews in addition to the delivery of review articles. The provision of regular statistical features including trends and characteristics maintains an empirical interest and adds to other data sources currently available to researchers.

The scope of the journal is international and encompasses research into tourism aspects as well as the development of new research approaches. It includes high quality research papers in any area of tourism including:
Reviews of literature in the field; empirical papers on tourism issues; incubator papers involving new ideas and concepts; commentaries of recently published materials on concepts and methodologies; cutting edge papers drawn from Ph.D. research; reviews of classic papers as well as the regular review and statistical-based sections.

The journal welcomes submissions based upon both primary research and reviews including papers in areas that may not directly be tourism based but concern a topic that is of interest to researchers in the field of tourism, such as economics, marketing, sociology and statistics.

All papers are subject to strict double blind peer review by the international research community.

Instructions to Authors
Initial Manuscript Submission. Submit three copies of the manuscript (including copies of tables and illustrations) to - The Editors.

Authors must also supply:
- an electronic copy of the final version (see section below),
- a Copyright Transfer Agreement with original signature - without this, we are unable to accept the submission, and
- permission letters - it is the author's responsibility to obtain written permission to reproduce (in all media, including electronic) material which has appeared in another publication.

Submission of a manuscript will be held to imply that it contains original unpublished work and is not being submitted for publication elsewhere at the same time. Submitted material will not be returned to the author, unless specifically requested.

Electronic submission. The electronic copy of the final, revised manuscript must be sent to the Editor together with the paper copy. Disks should be PC or Mac formatted; write on the disk the software package used, the name of the author and the name of the journal. We are able to use most word processing packages, but prefer Word or WordPerfect and TeX or one of its derivatives.

Illustrations must be submitted in electronic format where possible. Save each figure as a separate file, in TIFF or EPS format preferably, and include the source file. Write on the disk the software package used to create them; we favor dedicated illustration packages over tools such as Excel or PowerPoint.

Manuscript style. The language of the journal is English. All submissions including book reviews must have a title, be printed on one side of the paper, be double-line spaced and have a margin of 3cm all round. Illustrations and tables must be printed on separate sheets, and not be incorporated into the text.

- The **title page** must list the full title, short title and names and affiliations of all authors. Give the full address, including email, telephone and fax, of the author who is to check the proofs.
- Include the name(s) of any **sponsor(s)** of the research contained in the paper, along with **grant number(s)**.
- Supply a summary of up to 100 words for all articles [except book reviews]. A summary is a concise summary of the whole paper, not just the conclusions, and is understandable without reference to the rest of the paper. It should contain no citation to other published work.
- Include up to six **keywords** that describe your paper for indexing purposes.
- Papers submitted for publication should normally be between 4,000 to 7,000 words.

Reference style. References should be quoted in the text as name and year within brackets and listed at the end of the paper alphabetically. Where reference is made to more than one work by the same author published in the same year, identify each citation in the text as follows: (Collins, 1998a), (Collins, 1998b). Where three or more authors are listed in the reference list, please cite in the text as (Collins *et al.*, 1998)

All references must be complete and accurate. Online citations should include date of access. If necessary, cite unpublished or personal work in the text but do not include it in the reference list. References should be listed in the following style:

> Beaver H, Kettler P, Scholes M. 1970. The association between market determined and accounting determined risk measures. *Accounting Review* 45(3):654-682
>
> Drucker P. 1992. In *Managing for the Future*. Butterworth-Heinemann: Oxford.

Illustrations. Supply each illustration on a separate sheet, with the lead author's name and the figure number, with the top of the figure indicated, on the reverse. Supply original photographs; photocopies or previously printed material will not be used. Line artwork must be high-quality laser output (not photocopies). Tints are not acceptable; lettering must be of a reasonable size that would still be clearly legible upon reduction, and consistent within each figure and set of figures. Supply artwork at the intended size for printing.

The cost of printing color illustrations in the journal will be charged to the author. If color illustrations are supplied electronically in either TIFF or EPS format, they may be used in the PDF of the article at no cost to the author, even if this illustration was printed in black and white in the journal. The PDF will appear on the *Wiley InterScience* site.

Copyright. To enable the publisher to disseminate the author's work to the fullest extent, the author must sign a Copyright Transfer Agreement, transferring copyright in the article from the author to the publisher, and submit the original signed agreement with the article presented for publication. A copy of the agreement to be used (which may be photocopied) can be found in the first issue of each volume of the *International Journal of Tourism Research*. Copies may also be obtained from the journal editor or publisher, or may be printed from this website.

Further Information. Proofs will be sent to the corresponding author for checking. This stage is to be used only to correct errors that may have been introduced during the production process. Prompt return of the corrected proofs, preferably within two days of receipt, will minimize the risk of the paper being held over to a later issue. 25 complimentary offprints and one copy of the journal in which the article appeared will be provided to the author who checked the proofs, unless otherwise indicated. Further offprints and copies of the journal may be ordered. There is no page charge to authors.

International Journal of Transport Economics

ADDRESS FOR SUBMISSION:

Gianrocco Tucci, Editor
International Journal of Transport
   Economics
Via G. A. Guatanni, 8
00161 Rome,
Italy
Phone: +39 06 499 10691
Fax: +39 06 445 3870
E-Mail: See guidelines
Web:
Address May Change:

PUBLICATION GUIDELINES:

Manuscript Length: 16-20
Copies Required: Two
Computer Submission: Yes
Format: ASCII
Fees to Review: 0.00 US$

Manuscript Style:
   See Manuscript Guidelines

CIRCULATION DATA:

Reader: Academics
Frequency of Issue: 3 Times/Year
Copies per Issue: Less than 1,000
Sponsor/Publisher: Instituti Editorialie
   Poligrafici Internationali -Pisa, Italy
Subscribe Price: 125.00 US$

REVIEW INFORMATION:

Type of Review: Blind Review
No. of External Reviewers: 1
No. of In House Reviewers: 1
Acceptance Rate: 11-20%
Time to Review: 2 - 3 Months
Reviewers Comments: Yes
Invited Articles: 31-50%
Fees to Publish: 0.00 US$

MANUSCRIPT TOPICS:
Transportation Economics; Transportation/Physical Distribution

MANUSCRIPT GUIDELINES/COMMENTS:

Aims of the Review
The main aim of the review is to bring together the research work being done in the field of Transport Economics and arrange it organically in the form of a synthesis between theory and fact.

The situation facing transport economics is one in which old problems remain to be solved and new ones have been created by a wider range of information and improved methods of analysis.

In addition, foreseeable development in the internal logic of theories and the formulation of fresh hypotheses to interpret complex phenomena, both economic and non-economic, are becoming the object of further research for which the review is intended to be a median of expression and comparison. It is important in this respect to stress the fact that transport economics is prepared to take advantage of contributions from allied sciences and combine with them in providing a more convincing interpretation of realities together with solutions to concrete problems. Within this framework the contributions to the review from inside and outside Italy, though differing in standpoint and cultural background, will at be expected to maintain a rigorous standard of scientific scholarship.

Information for Contributors
Manuscripts should be submitted to the editor in two typed copies with double-spacing and with a wide left-hand margin. They will be examined on the understanding that their content has not been already published and is not being submitted for publication elsewhere. Each paper should be summarized in do abstract of about 400 words so as to enable the reader to know whether the paper is pertinent to his needs.

The Language of the Journal Is English.

Communications and research notes as a rule should not exceed 15 printed pages including diagrams and tables.

The author is requested to provide the editor with any information that might be worthwhile including in the section: "Contributors to this issue".

Names of journals and titles of books should be underlined (Italics).

Figures must be submitted in a form suitable for good reproduction, have a brief descriptive title and be professionally drawn so that they will be clear and legible when reduced to final size. If halftone reproductions are included, the author is requested to submit glossy prints.

Tables should have a brief descriptive title and should be clearly headed in order to be fully Understandable even without reference to the text.

The author will be asked to incorporate least cost mathematical notation, avoid circumflexes, bars, dots, and tildes, so far as possible, because these must be set by hand; superscripts or subscripts are to be preferred. Fractions should, whenever possible, be written in the form $(a + bQ) / (2pj)$. Roots should be written as fractional powers.

Reprints. A total of 25 reprints of each paper will be supplied free of charge. Additional copies may be ordered.

International Marketing Review

ADDRESS FOR SUBMISSION:

Jeryl Whitelock, Editor
International Marketing Review
University of Salford
The Crescent
Salford, M5 4WT
UK
Phone: 44 0 1619 5987
Fax: 44 0 1619 5556
E-Mail: j.m.whitelock@salford.ac
Web: www.mcb.co.uk.imr.htm
Address May Change:

PUBLICATION GUIDELINES:

Manuscript Length: 16-20
Copies Required: Four
Computer Submission: Yes
Format: PC or MAC in ASCII
Fees to Review: 0.00 US$

Manuscript Style:
    See Manuscript Guidelines

CIRCULATION DATA:

Reader: Academics, Practitioners
Frequency of Issue: 6 Times/Year
Copies per Issue: No Reply
Sponsor/Publisher: MCB University Press Limited-UK
Subscribe Price: 5899.00 US$

REVIEW INFORMATION:

Type of Review: Blind Review
No. of External Reviewers: 2
No. of In House Reviewers: 1
Acceptance Rate: 21-30%
Time to Review: 2 - 3 Months
Reviewers Comments: Yes
Invited Articles: 31-50%
Fees to Publish: 0.00 US$

MANUSCRIPT TOPICS:
Advertising & Promotion Management; All International Marketing Topics; Global Business; Marketing Research; Marketing Theory & Applications; Sales/Selling; Transportation/Physical Distribution

MANUSCRIPT GUIDELINES/COMMENTS:

About the journal
The International Marketing Review provides a platform for contemporary ideas in international marketing, the thinking, theory and practice. It is not a home for general marketing papers, but delivers research based on empirical studies of marketing strategy issues as well as comparative studies of markets and marketing practice with a purely 'International' flavour. The *International Marketing Review* seeks to publish papers that are academically robust, hence the double blind peer review process it adopts, but also papers that communicate effectively and therefore really contribute to international marketing.

Coverage
- Global marketing strategy
- Market research and techniques

- International marketing communications
- Market segmentation
- Exporting
- National cultures

Copyright
Articles submitted to the journal should be original contributions and should not be under consideration for any other publication at the same time. Authors submitting articles for publication warrant that the work is not an infringement of any existing copyright and will indemnify the publisher against any breach of such warranty. For ease of dissemination and to ensure proper policing of use, papers and contributions become the legal copyright of the publisher unless otherwise agreed. Submissions should be sent either to

The Editor, Jeryl Whitelock (address above) or
The Deputy Editor, Marylyn Carrigan, Department of Commerce, University of Birmingham Business School, Edgbaston, Birmingham B15 2TT, UK.

Editorial objectives
The principal aims of International Marketing Review (IMR) are to push back the boundaries of the thinking theory, and practice in international marketing and to provide a forum to explore these developments. It is NOT a home for general marketing papers nor single country studies. To achieve these aims, IMR is interested in publishing papers based on empirical studies of marketing strategy issues (such as approaches to market entry and globalization) as well as comparative studies of markets and marketing practice (providing they go beyond the descriptive and parochial). But it also means that IMR looks to publish papers based on theoretical explanations, methodological developments and modelling. Furthermore, there is also a place for the synthesizing literature review, when it enhances understanding in the way the literature is analysed. As a forum, IMR invites responses to articles that are published and is also willing to publish controversial articles to stimulate debate. To facilitate this, in addition to standard articles, IMR also publishes "viewpoints" and "notes". These are short papers (up to 2,000 words) that explore, or comment on, an issue in a way which is useful, interesting, worthwhile, relevant and, ideally, provocative. The decision to publish a note is made by the Editor, it is not peer reviewed.

While IMR seeks to publish papers which are academically robust, hence the rigorous review process described below, it also seeks to publish papers that communicate effectively. It is interesting, well written and, therefore, readable papers that really contribute to international marketing. Papers to IMR should, therefore, keep technical jargon and statistical formulae within papers to a minimum and always aim to present material, however complex, simply and clearly.

The reviewing process
Each paper is reviewed by the editor and, if it is judged suitable for this publication, it is then sent to two referees for double blind peer review. Based on their recommendations, the editor then decides whether the paper should be accepted as is, revised or rejected.

Manuscript requirements
Three copies of the manuscript should be submitted in double line spacing with wide margins. All authors should be shown and author's details must be printed on a separate sheet and the author should not be identified anywhere else in the article.

As a guide, articles should be between 3,000 and 6,000 words in length. A title of not more than eight words should be provided. A brief **autobiographical note** should be supplied including full name, affiliation, e-mail address and full international contact details. Authors must supply an **abstract** of 100-150 words. Up to six **keywords** should be included which encapsulate the principal subjects covered by the article.

Where there is a **methodology**, it should be clearly described under a separate heading. **Headings** must be short, clearly defined and not numbered. **Notes** or **Endnotes** should be used only if absolutely necessary and must be identified in the text by consecutive numbers, enclosed in square brackets and listed at the end of the article.

Figures, charts and **diagrams** should be kept to a minimum. They must be black and white with minimum shading and numbered consecutively using arabic numerals with a brief title and labelled axes. In the text, the position of the figure should be shown by typing on a separate line the words "take in Figure 2". Good quality originals must be provided.

Tables should be kept to a minimum. They must be numbered consecutively with roman numerals and a brief title. In the text, the position of the table should be shown by typing on a separate line the words "take in Table IV".

Photos and **illustrations** must be supplied as good quality black and white original half tones with captions. Their position should be shown in the text by typing on a separate line the words "take in Plate 2".

References to other publications should be complete and in Harvard style. They should contain full bibliographical details and journal titles should not be abbreviated. For multiple citations in the same year use a, b, c immediately following the year of publication. References should be shown within the text by giving the author's last name followed by a comma and year of publication all in round brackets, e.g. (Fox, 1994). At the end of the article should be a reference list in alphabetical order as follows

(a) for books
surname, initials and year of publication, title, publisher, place of publication, e.g. Casson, M. (1979), Alternatives to the Multinational Enterprise, Macmillan, London.

(b) for chapter in edited book
surname, initials and year, "title", editor's surname, initials, title, publisher, place, pages, e.g. Bessley, M. and Wilson, P. (1984), "Public policy and small firms in Britain", in Levicki, C. (Ed.), Small Business Theory and Policy, Croom Helm, London, pp.111-26. Please note that the chapter title must be underlined.

(c) for articles
surname, initials, year "title", journal, volume, number, pages, e.g.Fox, S. (1994) "Empowerment as a catalyst for change: an example from the food industry", Supply Chain Management, Vol 2 No 3, pp. 29-33

If there is more than one author list surnames followed by initials. All authors should be shown.

Electronic sources should include the URL of the electronic site at which they may be found, as follows:

Neuman, B.C.(1995), "Security, payment, and privacy for network commerce", IEEE Journal on Selected Areas in Communications, Vol. 13 No.8, October, pp.1523-31. Available (IEEE SEPTEMBER) http://www.research.att.com/jsac/

Notes/Endnotes should be used only if absolutely necessary. They should, however, always be used for citing Web sites. They should be identified in the text by consecutive numbers enclosed in square brackets and listed at the end of the article. Please then provide full Web site addresses in the end list.

Final submission of the article
Once accepted for publication, the final version of the manuscript must be provided, accompanied by a 3.5" **disk** of the same version labelled with: disk format; author name(s); title of article; journal title; file name.

Each article must be accompanied by a completed and signed **Journal Article Record Form** available from the Editor or on http://www.literaticlub.co.uk/

The manuscript will be considered to be the definitive version of the article. The author must ensure that it is complete, grammatically correct and without spelling or typographical errors. In preparing the disk, please use one of the following formats: Word, Word Perfect, Rich text format or TeX/LaTeX. Figures which are provided electronically must be in tif, gif or pic file extensions. All figures and graphics must also be supplied as good quality originals.

Final submission requirements
Manuscripts must be clean, good quality hard copy and;
- include an abstract and keywords
- have Harvard style references
- include any figures, photos and graphics as good quality originals
- be accompanied by a labelled disk
- be accompanied by a completed Journal Article Record Form

Technical assistance is available from MCB's World Wide Web Literati Club on http://www.literaticlub.co.uk/ or contact Mike Massey at MCB, e-mail mmassey@mcb.co.uk

International Research in the Business Disciplines

ADDRESS FOR SUBMISSION:

Mike H. Ryan, Editor
International Research in the Business
  Disciplines
Bellarmine University
Rubel School of Business
2001 Newburg Road
Louisville, KY 40205
USA
Phone: 502-452-8247
Fax: 502-452-8013
E-Mail: mryan@bellarmine.edu
Web:
Address May Change:

PUBLICATION GUIDELINES:

Manuscript Length: 16-20 average
Copies Required: Five
Computer Submission: Yes
Format: MS Word or WdPerfect
Fees to Review: 0.00 US$

Manuscript Style:
    American Psychological Association

CIRCULATION DATA:

Reader: Academics
Frequency of Issue: 2 Times/Year
Copies per Issue: 2,001 - 3,000
Sponsor/Publisher: Elsevier Science
  Publishing Co.
Subscribe Price: 90.00 US$ Paperback
  140.00 US$ Hardback

REVIEW INFORMATION:

Type of Review: Blind Review
No. of External Reviewers: 2
No. of In House Reviewers: 2
Acceptance Rate: 11-20%
Time to Review: 1 - 2 Months
Reviewers Comments: Yes
Invited Articles: 0-5%
Fees to Publish: 0.00 US$

MANUSCRIPT TOPICS:
Business Law, Public Responsibility & Ethics; Cross Disciplinary & with International Flavor; Global Business; Labor Relations & Human Resource Mgt.; Marketing Research; Non Profit Organizations; Organizational Development; Public Administration; Sales/Selling; Services; Small Business Entrepreneurship; Strategic Management Policy; Technology/Innovation

MANUSCRIPT GUIDELINES/COMMENTS:

Style Sheet and Order of Material for Submissions:

Title Page: Title of paper, name and station of author(s), author(s) complete current address(es) and telephone number(s) e-mail addresses, and any acknowledgement of assistance. For multiple author papers, please indicate contact author.

Abstract: Title of paper author(s) name(s) andd a brief abstract of no more than 150 words summarizing the article and its findings/conclusions.

Main Text: Title of paper without author(;) name(;)

Acknowledgements:

Appendix:

References:

Figure Legends: Numbered consecutively in tire order in which they are first mentioned in the text.

Tables: Numbered consecutively in the order in which they are first mentioned in the text.

Other Issues for Preparing g Your Manuscript.
Use 11-point Times Roman or Times New Roman for all text and tables.

When typing:
- Distinguish between the digit 1 and the letter l (also 0 and O).
- Use tabs for indents, not spaces.
- Display titles and headings in a consistent manner.
- Double space between all lines of the manuscript. Single spacing is only acceptable on tables.

References should follow the APA (American Psychological Association) standard.

- References should be indicated by giving (in parenthesis) tire author's name followed by the date of the paper or book; or with the date in parenthesis, as in 'suggested by Fletohing (1975)'. In the text, use the form Olsen et al 1975 where there are more than two authors, but list all authors in the references. Quotations of more than one line of text from cited works should be indented and citation should include the page number of the quotation; e.g. (Thomas 1979: 5b).

- References should be listed in one alphabetical sequence at the end of the text:
  - For journals: Thornthwaite, C. W. and Mather, J. R. (1955). The Water Balance. *Climatology* 8, 1-104.
  - For Books: Zeleny M, (1982). *Multiple criteria decision making*, New York'. McGraw-Hill
  - For a Thesis: Gait-ide, S. (1994). *Helplessness and depression*. Unpublished doctoral dissertation, McGill University, Montreal.
  - For papers from Conference Proceedings, chapters from book, etc.:
  - Smith, I. J. K. (1977). Liberal theories of the state. in P. Shed (Ed.), *Alternative Perspectives of the State* (pp. 170-82). Boston MA: Back Bay Press.

Tables and Figures: Begin each table or figure on a separate page. In text, indicate the approximate placement of each table by a clear break in the text inserting:

TABLE 1/FIGURE 1 ABOUT HERE
Set off by double spacing above and below.
(all figures and table should be numbered consecutively (e.g. table 1, figure 1)

Accepted papers will be required to be submitted if) electronic from Microsoft Word (for Macintosh or Windows) or Word Perfect is preferred.

International Review of Retail, Distribution and Consumer Research

ADDRESS FOR SUBMISSION:

John Dawson, Editor
International Review of Retail, Distribution
   and Consumer Research
University of Edinburgh
William Robertson Building
Department of Business Studies
50 George Square
Edinburgh, EH8 9JY
UK
Phone:
Fax: 44 131 668-3053
E-Mail: john.dawson@ed.ac.uk
Web: www.routledge.com
Address May Change:

PUBLICATION GUIDELINES:

Manuscript Length: 21-25
Copies Required: Three
Computer Submission: No
Format: N/A
Fees to Review: 0.00 US$

Manuscript Style:
   Uniform System of Citation (Harvard Blue Book)

CIRCULATION DATA:

Reader: Academics
Frequency of Issue: Quarterly
Copies per Issue: Less than 1,000
Sponsor/Publisher: Routledge Journals
Subscribe Price: 55.00 US$ Individual
   405.00 US$ Institution
   38.00 Pounds Indv., 245 Pounds Inst.

REVIEW INFORMATION:

Type of Review: Blind Review
No. of External Reviewers: 2
No. of In House Reviewers: 1
Acceptance Rate: 33%
Time to Review: 2 - 3 Months
Reviewers Comments: Yes
Invited Articles: 0-5%
Fees to Publish: 0.00 US$

MANUSCRIPT TOPICS:
Consumer Behavior; Marketing Research; Marketing Theory & Applications; Organizational Behavior & Theory; Organizational Development; Retailing; Services; Transportation/Physical Distribution

MANUSCRIPT GUIDELINES/COMMENTS:

Aims and Scope:
The *International Review of Retail, Distribution and Consumer Research* is the only academic, fully refereed journal of its kind published from the UK. Launched in 1990 it has quickly developed a reputation for innovative and original research. The Review is international in scope and content, it publishes articles of a conceptual, theoretical and empirical nature.

In particular the Review includes:

- results of research into strategic and operational applications.
- analyses and statements of their managerial applications.
- substantial reviews and critiques of existing knowledge.
- theoretical, conceptual and empirical analyses of the retail and distribution industry.
- issues of both national and international character.
- book reviews, notes and observations.
- pointers to expanding and new research topics.

All articles are rigorously reviewed double-blind by an international panel of research scholars to ensure that their quality matches the high standards of the journal.

Instructions for Authors:
Authors should submit three complete copies of their text, tables and figures, with any original illustrations, to: Professor John A. Dawson [at the above address].

1. The submission should include a cover page showing the author's name, the department where the work was done, an address for correspondence, if different, telephone numbers, e-mail address and any acknowledgements.

2. Submissions should be in English, typed in double spacing with wide margins, on one side only of the paper, preferably of A4 size. The title, but not the author's name should appear on the first page of the manuscript.

3. Articles should normally be as concise as possible and preceded by an abstract of not more than 100-25 words and a list of up to 6 keywords for on-line searching purposes.

4. Within the manuscript there may be up to three levels of heading.

5. Tables and figures should not be inserted in the pages of the manuscript but should be on separate sheets. They should be numbered consecutively in Arabic numerals with a descriptive caption. The desired position in the text for each table and figure should be indicated in the margin of the manuscript.

6. Use the Harvard system of referencing which gives the name of the author and the date of publication as a key to the full bibliographical details which are set out in the list of references. When the author's name is mentioned in the text, the date is inserted in the parentheses immediately after the name, as in Aldcroft (1964)'. When a less direct reference is made to one or more authors, both name and date are bracketed, with the references separated by a semi-colon, as in 'several authors have noted this trend (Rimmer 1960; Pollard 1965; Mckendrick 1970)'. Where appropriate, page numbers should also be provided (Roberts 1956: 56). When the reference is to a work of dual or multiple authorship, use 'Harvey and Press (1988)' or 'Yamey *et al.* (1963)' respectively, if an author has two references published in the same year, add lower case letters after the date to distinguish them, as in 'Johnson 1984a, 1984b). Always use the minimum number of figures in page numbers, dates, etc., e.g. 22-4, 105-6 (but 112-13 for 'teen numbers) and 1968-9.

7. Direct quotations of 40 words or more should start on a separate line and be indented.

8. Footnotes should be used only where necessary to avoid interrupting the continuity of the text. They should be numbered consecutively using superscript Arabic numerals. They should appear at the end of the main text, immediately before the list of references.

9. Submissions should include a reference list, in alphabetical order, at the end of the article, the content and format should conform to the following examples. Jones, K. and Simmons, J. (1987) *Location, Location, Location,* Toronto: Methuen.
Whysall, P. (1989) 'Service uses in a major shopping centre: change in Nottingham', *Services Industries Journal*, 9(3): 420-38.

10. For any other matters of presentation not covered by the above notes, please refer to the usual custom and practice as indicated by the last few issues of the Journal.

11. On acceptance for publication, authors will be requested to provide a copy of their paper in exact accordance with the conventions listed in the preceding notes. If the final version of the paper is *not* submitted in accordance with these conventions then publication may be delayed by the need to return manuscripts to authors for necessary revisions. Authors should note that, following acceptance for publication, they will be required to provide not only a hard copy of the final version, but also a copy on a virus-free disk, preferably in MS-Word 6 format, if possible. Authors will also be required to complete a Publishing Agreement form assigning copyright to the Publisher.

12. Page proofs will be sent for correction to a first-named author, unless otherwise requested, the difficulty and expense involved in making amendments at the page proof stage make it essential for authors to prepare their typescript carefully; any alteration to the original text is strongly discouraged.

Internet Research

ADDRESS FOR SUBMISSION:

David G. Schwartz, Editor
Internet Research
Bar-Ilan University
Graduate School of Business Admin.
Information Systems Division Head
Israel
Phone: 972-3-531-8909
Fax: 972-3-535-3182
E-Mail: dschwar@mail.biu.ac.il
Web: www.mcb.co.uk
Address May Change:

PUBLICATION GUIDELINES:

Manuscript Length: 11-15
Copies Required: Two
Computer Submission: Yes
Format: MS Word/Windows compatible
Fees to Review: 0.00 US$

Manuscript Style:
    See Manuscript Guidelines

CIRCULATION DATA:

Reader: Academics, Business Persons
Frequency of Issue: 5 Times/Year
Copies per Issue: 1,001 - 2,000
Sponsor/Publisher: MCB University Press Limited-UK
Subscribe Price: 369.00 US$ Electronic
    869.00 US$ Paper + Electronic

REVIEW INFORMATION:

Type of Review: Blind Review
No. of External Reviewers: 2
No. of In House Reviewers: 0
Acceptance Rate: 35%
Time to Review: 1 - 2 Months
Reviewers Comments: Yes
Invited Articles: 0-5%
Fees to Publish: 0.00 US$

MANUSCRIPT TOPICS:
Business Information Systems (MIS); Strategic Management Policy; Technology/Innovation

MANUSCRIPT GUIDELINES/COMMENTS:

About the Journal
Internet Research: Electronic Networking, Applications and Policy was the first publication to seriously debate the Internet as a powerful resource and still leads the field in fostering understanding of telecommunication networks in society. In addition to looking at the technological developments which facilitate their increasing use, this journal also examines the social, ethical, economic and political implications which arises from mass public access to a wealth of information. If you need to be on the cutting edge of international research and find practical advice on systems capabilities and use, Internet Research: Electronic Networking, Applications and Policy will keep you at the forefront of your profession.

Coverage
- Use and impacts of electronic networks in research and education
- Managerial and organizational concerns
- Standards

- Technical consideration in the design and operations of networks
- Public and private sector roles
- Network development
- Social and behavioral roles
- Resource reviews

Call for Case Studies

The *Journal of Internet Research* is an international, refereed journal that aims to describe, assess and foster understanding of the role of wide-area, multi-purpose computer networks such as the Internet. As the Internet continues to gather influence and momentum, it is increasingly important to be aware of the potential applications of this powerful resource throughout professional, political, personal and academic life.

Internet Research covers the full scope of topics in its field including: Electronic networks in research and education - Managerial and organizational issues - Standards - Network design and operation - Public and private sector roles and responsibility - Security concerns. As well as looking at the technological developments which facilitate the use of wide-area networks, the journal examines the social, ethical, economic and organizational implications which arise from mass public access to information resources.

Maximising the benefits of Internet Research

During the 2000 volume *Internet Research* will introduce a regular Case Study section to demonstrate how industry is responding to the challenges and opportunities of Internet developments to remain competitive in increasingly dynamic and complex global markets. A clear understanding of the technological and developmental possibilities afforded by the Internet is now vital if organisations are to succeed. This new section will allow readers to discover how others have translated the theoretical research and development into practical business solutions. It will be international in scope and multi-disciplinary focusing on such areas as marketing, promotion, data collection, customer service, publishing, legal and security issues.

The Editor now invites authors to submit Case Study articles of between 2,000 and 6,000 words with an abstract and keywords. Full Notes for Contributors can be found at: http://www.mcb.co.uk/portfolio/intr/notes.htm

NOTES FOR CONTRIBUTORS
Copyright

Articles submitted to the journal should be original contributions and should not be under consideration for any other publication at the same time. Authors submitting articles for publication warrant that the work is not an infringement of any existing copyright and will indemnify the publisher against any breach of such warranty. For ease of dissemination and to ensure proper policing of use, papers and contributions become the legal copyright of the publisher unless otherwise agreed. **Submissions should be sent to the Editor.**

(Articles created in Microsoft or compatible format may be submitted by e-mail attachment.)

Editorial objectives
Internet Research: Electronic Networking Applications and Policy, established in 1991, was the first scholarly journal to devote itself to collecting serious research about the Internet and its applications and uses, specifically organizational.

The journal aims to discuss, assess and foster understanding of the role of wide-area multipurpose computer networks, specifically the Internet.

Editorial scope
The primary focus is business and organizational applications of the Internet, such as marketing, promotion, data collection, research, customer service, publishing, educational, legal and security issues.

The Editor encourages a wide range of submissions and contributions, including research findings, critical essays, trend analyses, anecdotal experiences, product and service reviews and commentaries, book and other publication reviews, and other areas of interest.
Subscribers to the journal include executives, educators and researchers in commercial, academic, government and library organizations.

The reviewing process
Papers are normally reviewed by two or more members of the journal's review board. Where possible, submissions will be blind-reviewed using electronic network technology.

For this reason, all manuscripts should be accompanied by a copy of the article on disk or should also be submitted by e-mail.

Manuscript requirements
The manuscript should be submitted as a Word or rtf document, formatted with double spacing and wide margins. All authors should be shown and author's details must be printed on a separate sheet and the author should not be identified anywhere else in the article.

As a guide, articles should be between 2,000 and 6,000 words in length. A title of not more than eight words should be provided. A brief **autobiographical note** should be supplied including full name, affiliation, e-mail address and full international contact details. Authors must supply an **abstract** of 100-150 words. Up to six **keywords** should be included which encapsulate the principal subjects covered by the article.

Where there is a **methodology**, it should be clearly described under a separate heading. **Headings** must be short, clearly defined and not numbered. **Notes** or **Endnotes** should be used only if absolutely necessary and must be identified in the text by consecutive numbers, enclosed in square brackets and listed at the end of the article.

Figures, **charts** and **diagrams** should be kept to a minimum. They must be black and white with minimum shading and numbered consecutively using arabic numerals with a brief title and labelled axes. In the text, the position of the figure should be shown by typing on a separate line the words "take in Figure 2". Good quality originals must be provided.

Tables should be kept to a minimum. They must be numbered consecutively with roman numerals and a brief title. In the text, the position of the table should be shown by typing on a separate line the words "take in Table IV".

Photos and **illustrations** must be supplied as good quality black and white original half tones with captions. Their position should be shown in the text by typing on a separate line the words "take in Plate 2".

References to other publications should be complete and in Harvard style. They should contain full bibliographical details and journal titles should not be abbreviated. For multiple citations in the same year use a, b, c immediately following the year of publication. References should be shown within the text by giving the author's last name followed by a comma and year of publication all in round brackets, e.g. (Fox, 1994). At the end of the article should be a reference list in alphabetical order as follows

(a) for books
surname, initials and year of publication, title, publisher, place of publication, e.g.Casson, M. (1979), Alternatives to the Multinational Enterprise, Macmillan, London.
(b) for chapter in edited book
surname, initials and year, "title", editor's surname, initials, title, publisher, place, pages, e.g.Bessley, M. and Wilson, P. (1984), "Public policy and small firms in Britain", in Levicki, C. (Ed.), Small Business Theory and Policy, Croom Helm, London, pp.111-26. Please note that the chapter title must be underlined.
(c) for articles
surname, initials, year "title", journal, volume, number, pages, e.g.Fox, S. (1994) "Empowerment as a catalyst for change: an example from the food industry", Supply Chain Management, Vol 2 No 3, pp. 29-33

If there is more than one author list surnames followed by initials. All authors should be shown.

Electronic sources should include the URL of the electronic site at which they may be found, as follows:
Neuman, B.C.(1995), "Security, payment, and privacy for network commerce", IEEE Journal on Selected Areas in Communications, Vol. 13 No.8, October, pp.1523-31. Available (IEEE SEPTEMBER) http://www.research.att.com/jsac/

Notes/Endnotes should be used only if absolutely necessary. They should, however, always be used for citing Web sites. They should be identified in the text by consecutive numbers enclosed in square brackets and listed at the end of the article. Please then provide full Web site addresses in the end list.

Final submission of the article
Once accepted for publication, the final version of the manuscript must be provided, accompanied by a 3.5" disk of the same version labelled with: disk format; author name(s); title of article; journal title; file name.

Each article must be accompanied by a completed and signed **Journal Article Record Form** available from the Editor or on http://www.literaticlub.co.uk/

The manuscript will be considered to be the definitive version of the article. The author must ensure that it is complete, grammatically correct and without spelling or typographical errors. In preparing the disk, please use one of the following formats: Word, Word Perfect, Rich text format or TeX/LaTeX. Figures which are provided electronically must be in tif, gif or pic file extensions. All figures and graphics must also be supplied as good quality originals.

Final submission requirements
Manuscripts must be clean, good quality hard copy and;
- include an abstract and keywords
- have Harvard style references
- include any figures, photos and graphics as good quality originals
- be accompanied by a labelled disk
- be accompanied by a completed Journal Article Record Form

Technical assistance is available from MCB's World Wide Web Literati Club on http://www.literaticlub.co.uk/ or contact Mike Massey at MCB, e-mail mmassey@mcb.co.uk.

Journal of Advertising

ADDRESS FOR SUBMISSION:

Ron Faber, Editor
Journal of Advertising
University of Minnesota
School of Journalism & Mass
 Communication
111 Murphy Hall
Minneapolis, MN 55455
USA
Phone: 612-626-0888
Fax: 612-626-8165
E-Mail:
Web:
Address May Change:

PUBLICATION GUIDELINES:

Manuscript Length: Any
Copies Required: Six
Computer Submission: Yes
Format: MS Word or WordPerfect
Fees to Review: 0.00 US$

Manuscript Style:
 See Manuscript Guidelines

CIRCULATION DATA:

Reader: Academics
Frequency of Issue: Quarterly
Copies per Issue: 1,001 - 2,000
Sponsor/Publisher: American Academy of
 Advertising
Subscribe Price: 0.00 US$

REVIEW INFORMATION:

Type of Review: Blind Review
No. of External Reviewers: 3
No. of In House Reviewers: 1
Acceptance Rate: 11-20%
Time to Review: 1 - 2 Months
Reviewers Comments: Yes
Invited Articles: 0-5%
Fees to Publish: 0.00 US$

MANUSCRIPT TOPICS:
Advertising & Promotion Management; Communication; Direct Marketing; Global Business; Non Profit Organizations; Services

MANUSCRIPT GUIDELINES/COMMENTS:

The *Journal's* space is reserved for original contributions of quality. A submitted manuscript or similar version of it **must not** have been previously published, accepted for publication or be currently submitted for publication elsewhere.

Authors' other work on the same topic: Every manuscript submitted to *The Journal of Advertising* should:

1. reference all previously published work reporting the same data or parts thereof, including *Journal* articles, portions of books, proceedings papers, unpublished conference papers, working papers, and/or a dissertation or thesis;

2. describe the similarities and differences between the submitted manuscript and any previously written works by any of the authors based on the same data set or on the same topic using the same methodology.

Reports of empirical research should include:
1. a description of the population from which the sample was drawn and the method by which the respondents (or subjects) were selected;
2. a description of the operationalization and/or manipulation of the major variables;
3. a description of and/or sample items from any measurement instruments not previously published;
4. tables of means, degrees of freedom, and other applicable statistics;
5. 5.a discussion of the generalizability of the study's findings;
6. ads or variations of ads used or referred to (copies, scripts, storyboards, etc.);
7. the availability and source of methodological details not included in this manuscript or referenced from other publications.

Length: Up to 20 double-spaced type-written pages including tables and exhibits. References must be double-spaced, but do not count in the 20-page length. Submitted manuscripts are to be "letter quality."

Copies: Send six copies of the manuscript to the Editor - please keep the original.

Abstract: Manuscripts must be accompanied by an abstract of 100-120 words in length, on a separate sheet of paper. Write the title of your paper at the top of this page followed by "Abstract" centered at the top of this page. Do not identify the author(s) on this page.

Author identification: Given the blind review process, it is inappropriate for the author(s) to be identified or discernible in the body of the paper. Authors' names, institution from which they received their highest degree, academic rank/professional title, and affiliation should appear **only** on the title page of the manuscript which will be torn off before mailing to the reviewers. The full name, address and telephone number of each author must appear on this page. Also, at the time of submission, authors are asked to fully disclose all funding sources which have contributed to the development of the manuscript. Affiliation with, or interest in, any entity that could benefit from the publication of the research should also be acknowledged. This should generally appear on the title page of the submission. This information will be held in confidence by the editor and will not influence the review process. Prior to publication, the editor and the author will discuss if, and how, such information should be communicated to the readers.

References: Reference cites in the text of a manuscript should be in parentheses, by author's last name and year of publication [e.g., (Smith 1980)]. If an author's name is used within a sentence, the name should be followed by the year of publication [e.g.,...work by Smith (1983)]. If a page is cited, it should be noted within the parentheses [e.g., (Smith 1985, p.35)]. For multiple-authored publications, up to three authors, should be cited; publications with four or more authors should be cited by the first author's name, followed by "et al." [e.g., (Smith et al. 1985)]. Do not use punctuation within parentheses, except when there is a string of references [e.g., (Smith 1985, Jones 1983, Wilson et al. 1985)]. References are to be listed alphabetically, surname first, followed by publication date in parentheses. Ensure that the first names of all authors are completely spelled out and that the references are typed double spaced.

References for **periodicals** are to include author(s) name, publication date, article title, name of periodical, volume number, issue or month, and page numbers. For example: Sternthal, Brian and C. Samuel Craig (1974), "Fear Appeals: Revisited and Revised," *Journal of Consumer Research*, 1 (December), 23-24.

References for **books** are to include author(s) name, publication date, title of book, and location and name of publisher. For example: Rossiter, John R. and Larry Percy (1987), *Advertising and Promotion Management*, New York: McGraw Hill, Inc.

References for works published in an **edited book** or proceedings are to include volume number if applicable, name of editor(s), location and name of publisher, and page numbers. For example: Carey, James W. (1960), "Advertising: An Institutional Approach," in the Role of Advertising in Society, C.H. Sandage and Vernon Fryburger, eds., Homewood, IL: Richard D. Irwin, 3-17.

Works published in the same year by the same author(s) are to be differentiated by letters after the date (e.g., Smith 1983a, 1983b).

For more specific details consult the most recent *A Manual of Style*, University of Chicago Press.

Footnotes: *The Journal of Advertising* does not use footnotes. All material must be incorporated within the body of the text. Acknowledgments are discouraged but may be used.

Computer readable files: Upon acceptance, authors will be responsible for providing the completed manuscript in computer readable form. Most major word processing programs on IBM compatible and Macintosh systems are supported.

Copyrighted material: Copyright law prohibits a manuscript from appearing in more than one copyrighted publication. Allowing an article to be published in *The Journal of Advertising* is a guarantee that it has not been nor will be published in any other copyrighted publication.

Authors are responsible for obtaining permission to use any material in their manuscripts which is copyrighted.

Journal of Advertising Research

ADDRESS FOR SUBMISSION:

Arthur J. Kover, Editor
Journal of Advertising Research
c/o William Martin, Editorial Assistant
641 Lexington Avenue
New York, NY 10022
USA
Phone: 212-715-5656 Ext. 225
Fax: 212-319-5265
E-Mail: journal@arfsite.org
Web:
Address May Change:

PUBLICATION GUIDELINES:

Manuscript Length: 24
Copies Required: Three
Computer Submission: Yes
Format: MS Word
Fees to Review: 0.00 US$

Manuscript Style:
American Psychological Association

CIRCULATION DATA:

Reader: Business Persons, Academics
Frequency of Issue: Bi-Monthly
Copies per Issue: 5,001 - 10,000
Sponsor/Publisher: Advertising Research Foundation, Inc.
Subscribe Price: 110.00 US$

REVIEW INFORMATION:

Type of Review: Blind Review
No. of External Reviewers: 2
No. of In House Reviewers: 1
Acceptance Rate: 21-30%
Time to Review: 2 - 3 Months
Reviewers Comments: Yes
Invited Articles: 21-30%
Fees to Publish: 0.00 US$

MANUSCRIPT TOPICS:
Advertising & Promotion Management; Communication; Marketing Research; Media Research

MANUSCRIPT GUIDELINES/COMMENTS:

Because we try to promote publication of research by practitioners as well as academics, and practitioners are less motivated to submit manuscripts, we often solicit authors who have interesting research in progress and have given speeches to ARF conferences. Consequently, the publication rate for practitioners is higher than that for academics. Among practitioners the acceptance rate is about 33% while among academics it is 21%.

Editorial Policy Statement
The *Journal of Advertising Research* is primarily a vehicle for the reporting of primary field and laboratory research on advertising. Secondly, it reports issues of major relevance on research methodology and advertising effectiveness. Tertiarily, it provides a forum for senior statespersons to share perspectives and concerns about major trends occurring in the industry.

Mission
The mission of the JAR is to enhance the state of the art of advertising research by providing a forum for sharing research findings, their applications, and statements of need and avenues of solution. Its primary audience is the practitioner--at all levels. The JAR encourages dialogue between practitioners and academics to expand the scientific body of knowledge about advertising research and to facilitate the translation of that knowledge into the practice of advertising and its research.

Types of Articles
It is preferable that the subject of the research has "news" value and isn't "obvious" or irrelevant to practitioners. First preference is given to articles which report actual field or laboratory research to document the authors' assertions or offer models and analyses of substantive or widely-recognized datasets.

Case studies are acceptable if they are representative of a broad set of circumstances affecting JAR readers. Preferably, two or three cases will be reported in an article to assure the generalizability of the case findings.

"Point of view" articles are published when the issues addressed are substantive and relevant to a meaningfully large segment of the JAR readership. The style and tonality of point-of-view articles should be thoughtful and considerate of the diversity of views represented by the broad JAR constituency.

Short technical notes will probably not be published unless they have unusual "news" value, are very well-written and fit into the shorter article format of the **observations** section.

Editorial Review
Manuscripts are submitted to blind review. An academic and a practitioner reviewer are sent a copy of the manuscript without author identification along with a brief questionnaire. If either reviewer recommends rejection of the manuscript, it will usually be turned down.

Sampling
Research published in the JAR is expected to have practical value. Sampling populations used should offer sufficient breadth of generalizability of the findings to ensure relevance for practitioners. Research with student populations usually fails to provide that generalizability.

Sample size should be large enough that the sample findings have a high likelihood of being able to be replicated. The sample size should be adequately large that differences big enough to be of practical importance are likely to be found statistically significant.

The authors should make clear what the sampling frame was, why it was selected, and what the response rate was. Because many practitioners have relevant information about individual cities and metro areas, we encourage the identification by name of places where studies were executed.

Statistical Significance

The Neyman-Pearson approach to statistical deduction will be followed. Null hypotheses should be established and statistical tests used to reject them and accept or implicitly "support" the alternative hypotheses. Unless the author offers a reasonable argument for a different level of significance, the standard alpha=.05 will be used for all tests. In most instances, authors should avoid discussions of findings that only "approach significance".

Statistical tests should usually attempt to minimize alpha errors, but sometimes in practice beta errors ought to be kept small. Typically, multivariate and other tests of overall findings should be found significant before lower-level comparisons are made. If two-way interactions are found significant, discussion of those would usually be given precedence over the related main effects.

Style

The editor offers broad latitude in overall layout, but the purpose and logical structure of the article need to be very clear to the reader. It is recommended, but not required, that a background description be provided in the introductory portion of the manuscript.

Appropriate items for the **Introduction** are: industry needs; previous solution attempts; methodological strengths and/or weaknesses in previous research; how the situation might be improved and the contribution(s) that would make to the industry; objective(s) of the present research, observation or point of view.

Short simple sentences and paragraphs reduce the reader's workload and improve readability. Clear logical flow and ample use of **subheadings** also aid communication with the reader. Methodological, theoretical and statistical jargon should be minimized because it restricts readership among practitioners.

Literature Reviews are an important means of framing the present study and of providing additional sources of reference for interested readers. They should be kept current. If several months pass between the initial writing of a manuscript and its submission to the JAR, the literature review should be updated. Because JAR readers are typically familiar with previous research published in the JAR, citation of relevant prior articles from the JAR can help readers comprehend the present article more readily.

In the **results** section, summarize findings first in simple English sentences. Then reference Tables, Figures and detailed statistical test results. Let the logical organization of the findings follow that of the introductory section or the hypotheses under evaluation. Statistical or methodological aspects of the analysis should not dictate the order of presentation of the findings.

It is important that the findings themselves and the authors' interpretations of those findings be distinguishable. It is not essential to have separate **results** and **discussion** sections, but separating those topics adds clarity. Authors who choose to mix them must exercise caution and provide the reader clear indications of which are the "facts" and which are the interpretations.

Short, impactful titles draw in more readers. Short topic headings are recommended to ease the reader through longer sections. Practical suggestions and a concise summary make the **conclusion** section more actionable and memorable. A brief **abstract** of 50-60 words should accompany each article along with a 15-20 word abridged abstract for the table of contents page.

Preparing the Manuscript

1. Manuscripts should be typed double-spaced (including references), with pages numbered consecutively and having at least a one-inch margin on all four sides on 8 1/2 x 11 inch paper.

2. Three (3) nonreturnable copies for review should be sent to the Editor.

3. A cover sheet should include the title of the paper, author(s)' names, complete address(es), and any acknowledgement of financial or technical assistance.

4. Do not use footnotes. All references should be included and listed alphabetically by author's last name at the end of the paper.
Example of references:

Books: Cox, Keith K., and Ben M. Enis. Experimentation for Marketing Decisions. Scranton, PA: International Textbooks, 1969.

Articles: San Augustine, Andre J., and William F. Foley. "How Large Advertisers Set Budgets." Journal of Advertising Research (Vol.) 15, (No.) 5 (1975) :11-16

In making reference to these sources in the text, use authors' last names and date only in parentheses. Example: (Cox and Enis, 1959).

5. All tables and figures should have titles and must be numbered consecutively throughout. Charts and graphs should be labeled as figures. Tables and figures should be typed on separate pages, not interspersed with the text of the paper. If there is complicated art work, this should be provided in camera-ready form.

Upon acceptance of the manuscript for publication, a 5"x7" glossy black-and-white photograph of each author is required. Authors receive 10 complimentary copies of the issue in which their paper appears. Letters of comment and criticism are invited. Publication in the *Journal of Advertising Research* implies no endorsement of the writer's purpose, methods, or views by the Advertising Research Foundation, its board of directors, or any of its councils.

Journal of Brand Management

ADDRESS FOR SUBMISSION:

Brenda Rouse, Editor
Journal of Brand Management
Henry Stewart Publications
Museum House
25 Museum Street
London, WC1A 1JT
UK
Phone: 44 0 171 323-2916
Fax: 44 0 171 323-2918
E-Mail: brenda@hspublications.co.uk
Web:
Address May Change:

PUBLICATION GUIDELINES:

Manuscript Length: 2,500-5,000 words
Copies Required: Three
Computer Submission: Yes
Format: Word/WordPerfect
Fees to Review: 0.00 US$

Manuscript Style:
, Cambridge

CIRCULATION DATA:

Reader: Business Persons, 65%, Academic, 35%
Frequency of Issue: Bi-Monthly
Copies per Issue: 1,001 - 2,000
Sponsor/Publisher: Henry Stewart Publcations
Subscribe Price: 360.00 US$

REVIEW INFORMATION:

Type of Review: Blind Review
No. of External Reviewers: 3
No. of In House Reviewers: 2
Acceptance Rate: 50%
Time to Review: 1 - 2 Months
Reviewers Comments: Yes
Invited Articles: 31-50%
Fees to Publish: 0.00 US$

MANUSCRIPT TOPICS:
Communication; Direct Marketing; Global Business; Marketing Research; Marketing Theory & Applications; Non Profit Organizations; Strategic Management Policy

MANUSCRIPT GUIDELINES/COMMENTS:

1. Contributions should be between 2,000 and 5,000 words in length. All submissions should be typewritten and double-spaced.

2. The Journal's Editors and Editorial Board particularly welcome submissions which present case study material, new approaches, techniques, empirical research or conceptual papers.

3. All articles should be accompanied by a short abstract outlining the paper's aims and subject matter.

4. All articles should be accompanied by up to six keywords.

5. Articles should be accompanied by a short (about 80 words) description of the author(s) and, if appropriate, the organization of which he or she is a member.

6. Authors should not seek to use the Journal as a vehicle for marketing any specific product or service.

7. Authors should avoid the use of language or slang which is not in keeping with the professional and academic style of the Journal.

8. Titles of organizations etc should be written out first in full and thereafter in initials.

9. Articles should be supported by references. For all Henry Stewart Journals excluding Corporate Reputation Review, Tourism and Hospitality Research, Journal of Fashion Marketing and Management, Journal of Small Business and Enterprise Development, Journal of Asset Management and International Journal of Police Science Management, these should be set out in accordance with the Vancouver referencing system. References for the Journals listed above should be set out in accordance with the Harvard referencing system.

10. Photographs and illustrations supporting articles should be submitted where appropriate. Photographs should be good quality positives, printed from the original negatives and preferably in black and white only. Figures and other line illustrations should be submitted in good quality originals and a copy of the data should also be included.

11. Authors must ensure that references to named people and/or organizations are accurate, not racist or sexist and without libellous implications.

12. All contributions sent to the Publisher, whether invited or not, will be submitted to the Journal's Editors and Editorial Board. Any such contribution must bear the author's full name and address, even if this is not for publication. Contributions, whether published pseudonymously or not, are accepted on the strict understanding that the author is responsible for the accuracy of all opinion, technical comment, factual report, data, figures, illustrations and photographs. Publication does not necessarily imply that these are the opinions of the Editorial Board, Editors or the Publisher, nor does the Board, Editors or Publisher accept any liability for the accuracy of such comment, report and other technical and factual information. The Publisher will, however, strive to ensure that all opinion, comments, reports, data, figures, illustrations and photographs are accurate, insofar as it is within its abilities to do so. The Publisher reserves the right to edit, abridge or omit material submitted for publication.

13. All Articles submitted for publication will be subject to a double-blind refereeing procedure.

14. The author bears the responsibility for checking whether material submitted is subject to copyright or ownership rights, eg photographs, illustrations, trade literature and data. Where use is so restricted, the Publisher must be informed with the submission of the material.

15. No contribution will be accepted which has been published elsewhere, unless it is expressly invited or agreed by the Publisher. Articles and contributions published become the copyright of the Publisher, unless otherwise agreed.

16. All reasonable efforts are made to ensure accurate reproduction of text, photographs and illustrations. The Publisher does not accept responsibility for mistakes, be they editorial or typographical, nor for consequences resulting from them.

17. Submissions should be sent to Henry Stewart Publications, Museum House, 25 Museum Street, London WC1A 1JT, email: submissions@hspublications.co.uk. **Please clearly state for which journal you are contributing.**

Journal of Business

ADDRESS FOR SUBMISSION:

Douglas W. Diamond, Editor
Journal of Business
University of Chicago
Graduate School of Business
1101 East 58th Street
Chicago, IL 60637
USA
Phone: 773-702-7140
Fax: 773-702-0458
E-Mail: job@gsb.uchicago.edu
Web:
Address May Change:

PUBLICATION GUIDELINES:

Manuscript Length: No Reply
Copies Required: Two
Computer Submission: No
Format: N/A
Fees to Review: 50.00 US$

Manuscript Style:
 See Manuscript Guidelines

CIRCULATION DATA:

Reader: Academics
Frequency of Issue: Quarterly
Copies per Issue: 2,001 - 3,000
Sponsor/Publisher: University of Chicago Press
Subscribe Price: 27.00 US$

REVIEW INFORMATION:

Type of Review: Blind Review
No. of External Reviewers: 2
No. of In House Reviewers: 1
Acceptance Rate: 11-20%
Time to Review: 2 - 3 Months
Reviewers Comments: Yes
Invited Articles: 0-5%
Fees to Publish: 0.00 US$

MANUSCRIPT TOPICS:
Accounting; Banking; Business Education; Economics; Finance; Global Business; Labor Relations & Human Resource Mgt.; Marketing Research; Marketing Theory & Applications; Money; Public Administration

MANUSCRIPT GUIDELINES/COMMENTS:

1. **All manuscripts must be double-spaced** (text, references footnotes, etc.). Allow right and left-hand margins of at least 1-1/2 inches each.

2. **First page of manuscript**
   A. Title should be at least 2 inches from the topic edge of the page.
   B. Allow 1-inch space, and on a separate line type the name(s) of the author(s).
   C. One inch below this, on a separate line, type author(s) affiliation.
   D. On a separate sheet, an abstract of not more than 100 words.

3. **References follow the text**. They should be typed on a separate page or pages in alphabetical order by authors' last names. Each line after the first line of each reference should

be indented 1/2 inch. All references must be referred to in the text by author's name and year of publication. Note that journal titles should not be abbreviated. Reference style is as follows:

A. For periodicals
Jones, R.Y., and Brown, E.B. 1985. Transactions costs and the stock market. Journal of Business 23 (April): 178-85.
Smith, J.D. 1960. Economic theory. Journal of Political Economy 67 (May): 126-42.

B. For a book title
Donahue, C.L. The Economics of Western Europe. 2 vols. New York: Oxford University Press.

C. For contributions to collective works
Smith, J.D. 1942. Predictions in economic theory. In C.E. Lang (ed.), Sociology as a Force. 2d ed. New York: Farrar & Rinehart.

In the text, references should appear as follows: "Smith (1942) showed that ..." For multiple references by the same author in the same year, alphabetize by article title, adding a after the first reference date, b after the second, etc. For example:

Jones, C.D. 1971a. Social Trends. Boston: Beacon Press.
Jones, C.D. 1971 b. Tax deductions. Finance 7 (December): 218-35.
In the text they are referred to as Jones (1971a), or (Jones 1971a).

4. **Footnotes** (typed paragraph style) should be placed together on typed sheets following the references. They should be numbered in order and correspond with the numbers in the text. In both places, footnote numbers should be shown as superscripts (i.e., slightly above the line). For example:

(Text) ...in that study [3] (footnote)
[3] Numerous studies have shown that

Footnotes are not necessary if only used to refer to a work cited. In this case, the information should be placed in the text in parenthesis. Example: (see Jones 1956, pp. 8-15). Footnotes are only necessary for further explanation of something within the text. An acknowledgement footnote should be unnumbered and should precede any numbered footnotes.

5. **Tabular material.** Each table should be on a separate sheet of paper following the footnotes. Each table should be numbered and should be referred to in order in the text.

6. **Illustrations.** Each illustration (figure) should be on a separate sheet of paper and should follow the tabular material. Legends for the illustrations should be typed in order on a sheet of paper which should accompany the illustrations. All illustrations should be referred to in order in the text as figure 1, figure 2, etc.

7. **Miscellaneous.** Any unusual symbols or abbreviations in the text should be identified in the margin (in pencil). **Please prepare one original typescript (not a carbon) and one clear xerox copy of the manuscript.**

8. **Instructions for preparation of figures.** Illustrations are expensive; be certain that yours are essential and do not repeat material presented in the text.

9. Cite all illustrations in the text (as Figure X), numbering them in one consecutive series. A circled note in the margin, enables the editor or printer to place the figure correctly in the text.

10. Art work submitted with the manuscript ordinarily should be 8-1/2 by 11 inches or smaller. Plan line drawings for reduction of 50% or more; this will minimize flows. Remember that not only the overall dimensions but also the thickness of individual lines, spaces, and letters will be reduced proportionally.

Journal of Business & Industrial Marketing

ADDRESS FOR SUBMISSION:

Wesley J. Johnston, Editor
Journal of Business & Industrial Marketing
Georgia State University
College of Business Administration
Department of Marketing
University Plaza
Atlanta, GA 30303-3083
USA
Phone: 404-651-4184
Fax: 404-651-4198
E-Mail: wesleyj@gsu.edu
Web: www.mcb.co.uk
Address May Change:

PUBLICATION GUIDELINES:

Manuscript Length: 3,000-6,000 wds
Copies Required: Three
Computer Submission: Yes if accepted
Format: MS Word, WordPerfect
Fees to Review: 0.00 US$

Manuscript Style:
   See Manuscript Guidelines

CIRCULATION DATA:

Reader: Business Persons, Academics
Frequency of Issue: Quarterly
Copies per Issue: No Reply
Sponsor/Publisher: MCB University Press
Subscribe Price: 799.00 US$
   2899.00 AUS$

REVIEW INFORMATION:

Type of Review: Blind Review
No. of External Reviewers: 3
No. of In House Reviewers: 1
Acceptance Rate: 21-30%
Time to Review: 2 - 3 Months
Reviewers Comments: Yes
Invited Articles: 0-5%
Fees to Publish: 0.00 US$

MANUSCRIPT TOPICS:
Business-to-Business Marketing; Marketing Theory & Applications

MANUSCRIPT GUIDELINES/COMMENTS:

About the journal
The *Journal of Business & Industrial Marketing* explores all aspects of marketing and offers in-depth research articles that enrich the practice of business & industrial marketing, while simultaneously making significant contributions to the body of knowledge. Combined with case analyses, conceptual arguments, industry reviews and executive summaries of each article, make this an invaluable resource. Those seeking to keep pace with the latest knowledge and identify further research opportunities will find the in-depth analysis, lively discussion and practical recommendations extremely valuable. Every article published in the Journal of Business & Industrial Marketing has been subject to a double blind review process to ensure its relevance and quality.

Coverage
- Sales management
- Strategic alliances
- New technology & innovation
- Marketing communications
- Environmental issues
- Market segmentation
- Supplier relationships

NOTES FOR CONTRIBUTORS
Copyright
Articles submitted to the journal should be original contributions and should not be under consideration for any other publication at the same time. Authors submitting articles for publication warrant that the work is not an infringement of any existing copyright and will indemnify the publisher against any breach of such warranty. For ease of dissemination and to ensure proper policing of use, papers and contributions become the legal copyright of the publisher unless otherwise agreed. Submissions should be sent to the Editor.

Regional Editors,
(Africa), Kofi Dadzie, same address as editor.

(Australia), Ian Wilkinson, University of Western Sydney, 158-160 Hawkesbury Road, Westmead, NSW 2145, Australia.

(Europe) Professor Dr Hans George Gemuenden, Technical University Berlin, D-10263 Berlin, Germany

(Southeast Asia and India) Professor George T Haley, School of Business, University of New Haven, 300 Orange Avenue, West Haven, CT06516, USA

Editorial objectives
The objective of this journal is to provide both academics teaching marketing and practitioners of marketing with new ideas concerning business-to-business marketing. That is, how one company or organization markets its goods/services/ideas to another company or organization. The ideal article would be one that could be used in the classroom to educate graduate students on the theory and practice of business-to-business marketing and read by managers interested in the state-of-the-art thinking in this area. Each article, therefore, must put forth recommendations as to how the material contained in the article can be utilized in business practice and at the same time provide teachers of marketing with examples of how the theories taught in the classroom work in the real world.

The basis of an article may be research, but it is not intended that the Methodology or Methods section be extensive. If the methodology is so unique as to warrant detailed attention, it will be added as an appendix. But research is not the only basis for an article. Cases, conceptual arguments, and industry reviews and practices may be put forth with equal acceptability. In addition, we will publish opinions of industry professionals, when available, in a section entitled Commentary. Book reviews will also be published when available.

The reviewing process
Each paper is reviewed by the editor and, if it is judged suitable for this publication, it is then sent to two referees for double blind peer review. Based on their recommendations, the editor then decides whether the paper should be accepted as is, revised or rejected.

Manuscript requirements
Three copies of the manuscript should be submitted in double line spacing with wide margins. All authors should be shown and author's details must be printed on a separate sheet and the author should not be identified anywhere else in the article.

As a guide, articles should be between 3,000 and 6,000 words in length. A title of not more than eight words should be provided. A brief **autobiographical note** should be supplied including full name, affiliation, e-mail address and full international contact details. Authors must supply an **abstract** of 100-150 words. Up to six **keywords** should be included which encapsulate the principal subjects covered by the article.

Where there is a **methodology**, it should be clearly described under a separate heading. **Headings** must be short, clearly defined and not numbered. **Notes** or **Endnotes** should be used only if absolutely necessary and must be identified in the text by consecutive numbers, enclosed in square brackets and listed at the end of the article.

Figures, charts and **diagrams** should be kept to a minimum. They must be black and white with minimum shading and numbered consecutively using arabic numerals with a brief title and labelled axes. In the text, the position of the figure should be shown by typing on a separate line the words "take in Figure 2". Good quality originals must be provided.

Tables should be kept to a minimum. They must be numbered consecutively with roman numerals and a brief title. In the text, the position of the table should be shown by typing on a separate line the words "take in Table IV".

Photos and **illustrations** must be supplied as good quality black and white original half tones with captions. Their position should be shown in the text by typing on a separate line the words "take in Plate 2".

References to other publications should be complete and in Harvard style. They should contain full bibliographical details and journal titles should not be abbreviated. For multiple citations in the same year use a, b, c immediately following the year of publication. References should be shown within the text by giving the author's last name followed by a comma and year of publication all in round brackets, e.g. (Fox, 1994). At the end of the article should be a reference list in alphabetical order as follows

(a) for books
surname, initials and year of publication, title, publisher, place of publication, e.g.Casson, M. (1979), Alternatives to the Multinational Enterprise, Macmillan, London.

(b) for chapter in edited book
surname, initials and year, "title", editor's surname, initials, title, publisher, place, pages, e.g.Bessley, M. and Wilson, P. (1984), "Public policy and small firms in Britain", in Levicki, C. (Ed.), Small Business Theory and Policy, Croom Helm, London, pp.111-26. Please note that the chapter title must be underlined.

(c) for articles
surname, initials, year "title", journal, volume, number, pages, e.g.Fox, S. (1994) "Empowerment as a catalyst for change: an example from the food industry", Supply Chain Management, Vol 2 No 3, pp. 29-33

If there is more than one author list surnames followed by initials. All authors should be shown.

Electronic sources should include the URL of the electronic site at which they may be found, as follows:

Neuman, B.C.(1995), "Security, payment, and privacy for network commerce", IEEE Journal on Selected Areas in Communications, Vol. 13 No.8, October, pp.1523-31. Available (IEEE SEPTEMBER) http://www.research.att.com/jsac/

Notes/Endnotes should be used only if absolutely necessary. They should, however, always be used for citing Web sites. They should be identified in the text by consecutive numbers enclosed in square brackets and listed at the end of the article. Please then provide full Web site addresses in the end list.

Final submission of the article
Once accepted for publication, the final version of the manuscript must be provided, accompanied by a 3.5" **disk** of the same version labelled with: disk format; author name(s); title of article; journal title; file name.

Each article must be accompanied by a completed and signed **Journal Article Record Form** available from the Editor or on http://www.literaticlub.co.uk/

The manuscript will be considered to be the definitive version of the article. The author must ensure that it is complete, grammatically correct and without spelling or typographical errors.

In preparing the disk, please use one of the following formats: Word, Word Perfect, Rich text format or TeX/LaTeX. Figures which are provided electronically must be in tif, gif or pic file extensions. All figures and graphics must also be supplied as good quality originals.

Final submission requirements
Manuscripts must be clean, good quality hard copy and;
- include an abstract and keywords
- have Harvard style references
- include any figures, photos and graphics as good quality originals

- be accompanied by a labelled disk
- be accompanied by a completed Journal Article Record Form

Technical assistance is available from MCB's World Wide Web Literati Club on http://www.literaticlub.co.uk/ or contact Mike Massey at MCB, e-mail mmassey@mcb.co.uk

Journal of Business and Behavioral Sciences

ADDRESS FOR SUBMISSION:

Wali I. Mondal, Ediltor
Journal of Business and Behavioral
  Sciences
ASBBS
PO Box 10367
San Bernardino, CA 92423-0367
USA
Phone: 909-748-6287
Fax: 909-335-9279
E-Mail: mondal@asbbs.org
Web:
Address May Change:

PUBLICATION GUIDELINES:

Manuscript Length: 16-20
Copies Required: Four
Computer Submission: No
Format: N/A
Fees to Review: 50.00 US$

Manuscript Style:
  American Psychological Association

CIRCULATION DATA:

Reader: Academics
Frequency of Issue: 2 Times/Year
Copies per Issue: 1,001 - 2,000
Sponsor/Publisher: American Society of
  Business & Behavioral Sciences
Subscribe Price: 50.00 US$

REVIEW INFORMATION:

Type of Review: Blind Review
No. of External Reviewers: 3
No. of In House Reviewers: 2
Acceptance Rate: 11-20%
Time to Review: 4 - 6 Months
Reviewers Comments: Yes
Invited Articles: 0-5%
Fees to Publish: 100.00 US$ 1st 10 pgs.
  20.00 US$ for Each Additional Page

MANUSCRIPT TOPICS:
Accounting, Economics, & Finance; Advertising & Promotion Management; Business Information Systems (MIS); Business Law, Public Responsibility & Ethics; Communication; Direct Marketing; Global Business; Health Care Administration; Labor Relations & Human Resource Mgt.; Marketing Research; Marketing Theory & Applications; Non Profit Organizations; Office Administration/Management; Operations Research/Statistics; Organizational Behavior & Theory; Organizational Development; Production/Operations; Public Administration; Purchasing/Materials Management; Sales/Selling; Services; Small Business Entrepreneurship; Strategic Management Policy; Technology/Innovation; Transportation/Physical Distribution

MANUSCRIPT GUIDELINES/COMMENTS:

Manuscripts in any area of Management and Marketing will be considered for publication. Papers must be prepared in double space and must accompany an abstract not to exceed 250 words. Authors should follow the APA guidelines in preparing their manuscripts. Guidelines for final submission to the Journal will be sent only if a paper is accepted after review.

Journal of Business Disciplines

ADDRESS FOR SUBMISSION:

Douglas K. Barney, Editor
Journal of Business Disciplines
Indiana University, SE
School of Business
4201 Grant Line Road
New Albany, IN 47150
USA
Phone: 812-941-2532
Fax: 812-941-2672
E-Mail: dbarney@ius.edu
Web:
Address May Change:

PUBLICATION GUIDELINES:

Manuscript Length: 11-20
Copies Required: Four
Computer Submission: No
Format: N/A
Fees to Review: 25.00 US$

Manuscript Style:
   See Manuscript Guidelines

CIRCULATION DATA:

Reader: Academics
Frequency of Issue: 2 Times/Year
Copies per Issue: Less than 1,000
Sponsor/Publisher: Academy of Business Disciplines/ Indiana University SE School of Business
Subscribe Price: 25.00 US$ Individual
   50.00 US$ Library

REVIEW INFORMATION:

Type of Review: Blind Review
No. of External Reviewers: 3
No. of In House Reviewers: 2
Acceptance Rate: 11-20%
Time to Review: 1 - 2 Months
Reviewers Comments: Yes
Invited Articles: 11-20%
Fees to Publish: 0.00 US$

MANUSCRIPT TOPICS:

Advertising & Promotion Management; Business Education; Business Information Systems (MIS); Business Law, Public Responsibility & Ethics; Communication; Direct Marketing; Global Business; Health Care Administration; Labor Relations & Human Resource Mgt.; Marketing Research; Marketing Theory & Applications; Office Administration/Management; Operations Research/Statistics; Organizational Behavior & Theory; Organizational Development; Production/Operations; Purchasing/Materials Management; Sales/Selling; Services; Small Business Entrepreneurship; Strategic Management Policy; Technology/Innovation; Transportation/Physical Distribution

MANUSCRIPT GUIDELINES/COMMENTS:

Goal
To increase and share business knowledge.

Aim and Scope
The Journal is dedicated to publishing quality applied business articles designed to inform business practitioners and business academics. Articles should be of current importance and

can be either empirical or theoretical in approach. General readability of the articles is of critical importance. (i.e. Manuscripts submitted should not be so technical or specialized that they are of interest only to specialists in that area. Manuscripts should be free of technical jargon or should define terms used. Also, manuscripts should not be focused on or overly dwell on an issue that is not of practical importance.) Possible application areas include:

Accounting	Finance
Applied Business Economics	Information Systems
Business History	International Business
Business Education	Management
E-Commerce	Marketing
Entrepreneurship	Small Business
Ethics	

Manuscripts will be subjected to external blind reviews.

Submit only original, unpublished manuscripts that are not under review elsewhere:

Manuscript Guidelines
Submit four copies of the manuscript on 8 ½ x 11 inch paper and a check for $25 payable to the *Journal of Business Disciplines*. If you are submitting an article or if your article has been accepted for publication, please adhere to the following guidelines.

Guidelines include:
Title page listing all authors and contact information for corresponding author (for submission purposes only)

Title page includes no personal titles for authors (for submission purposes only)

Title should be limited to 8 words

Body of the text starts on new page with title and no author identification (for accepted manuscripts, authors are listed below the title and the first footnote(s) should provide information about the author(s))

Margins of 1 inch and full justification

First level headings (title) centered, initial capitalization, bold 16 point font

Second level headings (major captions, eg. Introduction . . .) centered, initial capitalization, bold 14 point font

Third level headings, left justified, initial capitalization, bold 12 point font

Fourth level headings, indented, initial capitalization, bold 10 point font

The text should be in 10 point font

Single space text (double space for submission purposes only)

Bullet points - consistency within each group of bullet points, no bold, italicize opening phrases of lengthy bullets

Use footnotes

Number tables sequentially, label and describe

In-text references include (author, year, page) notation

Reference section at the end of the text:

> Reference only works cited in the text
>
> Reference multiple works by the same author(s) using a, b, c
>
> Reference as follows: Author, Date, Title, Publisher (or if no identifiable authors) Title, Date, Publisher
>
>> Journal: Platt, ILD., Platt, M.B., 1991. A note on the use of industry-relative ratios in bankruptcy prediction. *Journal of Banking and Finance* 15 (6), 1183-1194.
>>
>> Book: Wasserman, P.D., 1989. Neural Computing: Theory and Practice. Van Nostrand Reinhold, New York.
>>
>> Institute Publication: US Congress, 1985. Public Law 99-198. 99 United States Statutes as Large 1325. US Government Printing Office, Washington, DC.

If your work is accepted to the Journal submit the manuscript in MS Word.

Journal of Business Education

ADDRESS FOR SUBMISSION:

Jean L. Heck, Editor
Journal of Business Education
Villanova University
College of Commerce and Finance
Villanova, PA 19085
USA
Phone: 610-519-4325
Fax: 610-519-6881
E-Mail: abe@villanova.edu
Web:
Address May Change:

PUBLICATION GUIDELINES:

Manuscript Length: Any
Copies Required: Four
Computer Submission: No
Format: N/A
Fees to Review: 50.00 US$ Non-Member

Manuscript Style:
See Manuscript Guidelines

CIRCULATION DATA:

Reader: Academics
Frequency of Issue: 2 Times/Year
Copies per Issue: Less than 1,000
Sponsor/Publisher: Academy of Business Education
Subscribe Price: 0.00 US$ Member
75.00 US$ Institution
30.00 US$ Individual

REVIEW INFORMATION:

Type of Review: Blind Review
No. of External Reviewers: 2
No. of In House Reviewers: 0
Acceptance Rate: 11-20%
Time to Review: 1 - 2 Months
Reviewers Comments: Yes
Invited Articles: 0-5%
Fees to Publish: 0.00 US$

MANUSCRIPT TOPICS:

Accounting, Economics, & Finance; Business Education; Business Information Systems (MIS); Business Law, Public Responsibility & Ethics; Global Business; Marketing Theory & Applications; Office Administration/Management; Production/Operations; Sales/Selling

MANUSCRIPT GUIDELINES/COMMENTS:

The *Journal of Business Education* is a multi-disciplinary journal seeking the following kinds of papers:

1) Educational research - empirical research that tests teaching practices, student performance and learning environments;
2) Pedagogy - papers offering interesting or unique approaches to teaching or delivering business education
3) Curriculum - papers addressing interesting or unique approaches to curriculum development and discipline integration
4) Literature reviews - papers that offer extensive reviews of current relevant research and thought;

5) Mufti-disciplinary - papers emphasizing mufti-disciplinary/interdisciplinary approaches to business education
6) Ethics and Moral Values - papers offering guidance in the integration of ethics and moral values in business education

Submission Guidelines

There are few strict layout requirements for submitting a manuscript for review. Specific style instructions for publication will be provided upon acceptance of manuscript. Style and format requirements that are important for publication are often not suitable for reviewing. However, the following are guidelines helpful in preparing your manuscript for submission:

1) Manuscripts should be typed, double-spaced in an easy to read font e.g., Times Roman (12 point) or Courier (10 point);
2) Cover page should include paper title, authors' names and affiliations and phone number and email address of manuscript contact person. Authors' names should appear no where else in manuscript;
3) First page of manuscript should begin with paper title, followed by an abstract of no more than 100 words, then followed by the first section of the paper that should be called "INTRODUCTION";
4) Sections - There should be no more than three levels of headings in body of paper:
   Level One headings should be left justified and all caps;
   Level Two headings should begin each word with capital letter and left justified;
   Level Three headings same as Level Two, but italicized.
5) End Notes - Use end notes only, not foot notes. Number them consecutively throughout the manuscript with superscripted Arabic numerals. Place all end notes together at end of manuscript before the REFERENCES section;
6) Equations - Number all equations consecutively and place number in parentheses at the right margin of equation. If you use equation editor, place equation number outside of equation box;
7) Tables - Except for very small tables, tables should be placed at end of manuscript. Make very effort to avoid "landscape" orientations, but we understand this is not always possible. Tables should have centered headings as: Table 1: Title of Table Should Look Like This Note in body of paper approximately where table or figure should be placed, as:

Place Table 1 about here

8) Figures - All figures should be headed as in the tables described above, except use the word "Figure" in place of "Table." Each figure must ultimately be provided in camera ready form on a separate sheet;
9) References - References should appear alphabetically by author's last name at end of paper. Citations in body of paper should be in [brackets]. Only include references actually cited in paper. Examples:
   Smith, R. J. "Learning by Doing: Teaching Can Be Fun," Journal of Business Education, 22 (Spring, 1994),77-81.
   Jones, R. R., Carol King and Sidney Slack. "Team Teaching Via the Internet," Journal of Educational Design, 7 (No. 2, 1993), 123-144.
In the body of the paper show citations like this [Smith, 1994] or [Jones et al., 1993].

10) There is no submission fee for members (only one author need be an ABE member). For non-ABE members there is a $50 submission fee. Submit four (4) copies of the manuscript along with the submission fee (for non-members) payable to the "Academy of Business Education" to, Jean L. Heck, Editor, College of Commerce and Finance, Villanova University, Villanova, PA 19085.

Journal of Business Logistics

ADDRESS FOR SUBMISSION:

David J. Closs, Editor
Journal of Business Logistics
Michigan State University
Department of Marketing and Supply
 Chain Management
N 370 Business College Complex
East Lansing, MI 48824
USA
Phone: 517-353-6381
Fax: 517-432-1112
E-Mail: closs@pilot.msu.edu
Web:
Address May Change:

PUBLICATION GUIDELINES:

Manuscript Length: 16-20
Copies Required: Five
Computer Submission: Yes
Format: MS Word
Fees to Review: 0.00 US$

Manuscript Style:
 Chicago Manual of Style, Turabian
 Manual of Style

CIRCULATION DATA:

Reader: Business Persons
Frequency of Issue: 2 Times/Year
Copies per Issue: 10,001 - 25,000
Sponsor/Publisher: Council of Logistics
 Management
Subscribe Price: 35.00 US$

REVIEW INFORMATION:

Type of Review: Blind Review
No. of External Reviewers: 3+
No. of In House Reviewers: 2
Acceptance Rate: 21-30%
Time to Review: 2 - 3 Months
Reviewers Comments: Yes
Invited Articles: 0-5%
Fees to Publish: 0.00 US$

MANUSCRIPT TOPICS:
Business Information Systems (MIS); Production/Operations; Transportation/Physical Distribution

MANUSCRIPT GUIDELINES/COMMENTS:

Publication Office
Council of Logistics Management
2805 Butterfield Road
Suite 200
Oak Brook, IL 60521
Ph: (630) 574-0985
Fax: (630) 574-0989
E-mail: clmadmin@clm1.org
Fax: (517) 432-1112
e-mail: closs@pilot.msu.edu

Editorial Office
David J. Closs, Editor
Department of Marketing and
Supply Chain Management
N370 Business College Complex
Michigan State University
East Lansing, MI 48824
Ph: (517) 353-6381

The *Journal of Business Logistics* is published by the Council of Logistics Management. It is published twice yearly in the Spring and Autumn and is directed toward the needs of practitioners, executives, researchers, students and teachers of logistics.

EDITORIAL POLICY

The *Journal of Business Logistics* is designed as a forum for current research, opinion, and identification of trends in logistics and supply chain management. The opinions expressed are those of the authors and do not necessarily reflect the opinions of the Editor, Editorial Review Board or the Council of Logistics Management.

All published material is copyrighted by the Council of Logistics Management, with future use rights reserved. This, however, does not limit the author's right to use his or her own material.

Objectives

The editorial objectives of the *Journal of Business Logistics* are to advance knowledge and science and to stimulate greater thought and effort in the fields of logistics and supply chain management by providing readers with:
- new and helpful information;
- new logistics and supply chain management theory or techniques;
- research generalizations about logistics and supply chain management thought and practice;
- creative views and syntheses of dispersed concepts in logistics and supply chain management; and
- articles in subject areas which have significant current impact on thought and practice in logistics and supply chain management which present challenges for the future.

Content

Journal articles include four categories of material. *First* are articles that report empirical research based on management surveys. Such survey research must justify its contribution to the discipline. *Second* are articles that report on the development of methodologies and techniques that can enhance logistics decision-making. *Third* are articles reporting the application of decision tools to generic or specific logistics problems. Such applications must either generalize current insight or extend the application of such decision tools. The *final* category includes invited articles from acknowledged leaders in the logistics discipline and winners of the Grosvenor Plowman Award given at the Logistics Educators' Conference.

Manuscripts should be between 4,000 and 6,000 words, typically 15-20 double-spaced, typewritten pages. Articles of shorter length are also acceptable. Only rarely will it be possible to publish a manuscript of more than 6,000 words.

Review

Articles are considered for publication if they have not been published or accepted for publication elsewhere and are not being concurrently considered elsewhere. Authors will usually be notified of acceptance, rejection or need for revision within 12 weeks of submission.

When editing by Journal staff is extensive, articles are returned to the author(s) for review prior to being typeset.

No manuscript is accepted for the *Journal of Business Logistics* until it has been reviewed by the Editor or one of the Associate Editors and at least three outside reviewers who are experts in their respective fields. In most cases, the reviewers are drawn from the Review Board and represent a combination of practitioners and academics. Manuscripts are reviewed simultaneously by geographically separated reviewers.

The authors' name(s) and credentials (i.e., the cover page) are removed prior to review to maximize objectivity and ensure that the manuscripts are judged solely on the basis of content, clarity and contribution to the field. The authors' name(s) should not appear anywhere except the cover page.

All manuscripts are judged on their contribution to the advancement of the science and/or practice of logistics or supply chain management. Journal editors expect all manuscripts to follow accepted standards for scholarly work.

Manuscripts are judged not only on depth and scope of ideas presented and their contribution to the field, but also on their clarity, organization, readability and comprehensibility. Manuscripts should be written in a manner that is interesting and readable to both practitioners and academics. It is beneficial to include a section regarding managerail implications and discussing the consequences of applying the proposed ideas. Technical terms should be defined.

MANUSCRIPT PREPARATION
Manuscripts should be typed double-spaced, including references, in 12-point type using Times Roman or similar type. Do not use single spacing anywhere. Number every page at the bottom center. Please allow the text to wrap, rather than entering a RETURN or LINEFEED after every line.

For details of manuscript preparation not covered in these Guidelines, see *The Chicago Manual of Style*, 14th Edition (Chicago and London: University of Chicago Press, 1993) and review recent issues of the Journal.

Five copies of each manuscript should be submitted to the Editor.

The sections of the manuscript should be placed in the following order: Cover page, Author biography, Title page, Abstract, Body, Appendices, Endnotes, Tables and Figures. Each section should begin on a new page.

Cover Page
The cover page should include the title of the manuscript and the authors' name(s) in the order in which they should be printed. Please indicate which author will serve as the primary contact for the Journal and provide a facsimile number and E-mail address for this person.

In addition to any acknowledgment of financial or technical assistance, this page should include each author's title, present position and complete address and telephone number. Please keep professional titles succinct.

Author Biography
Please include a brief biography--usually not over 75 words--entitled "About the Author(s)" for each author. This may include the current title and position and a statement of qualifications for writing this article. The listing of prior publications should be held to a minimum. Please include degrees received, field and institution.

Title Page
The title page should include the title of the article, without the authors' name(s).

Abstract
Include an "Abstract" for the manuscript--usually not over 50 words. The Abstract is a "teaser" or "come-on." It is not to be a summary of the article and should not state the final conclusions. Simply describe the content of the article and give just enough indication regarding the content of the article to encourage the reader's interest. The "Abstract" can be placed on the "Title" page.

Body
Center major (Level 1) headings on the page and subheadings (Level 2) flush with the left margin. Level 1 headings should be centered, capitalized and bold. Level 2 headings should be left alligned and bold. The Journal recognizes a maximum of two heading levels.

Use tab indents to set indentations for paragraphs and lists, rather than spaces.

Citations in the text should use the standard author-date system.

Brand names and registered trademark names (including those of computer equipment and software packages) should always be capitalized in text and illustrations. The symbols © and TM are not necessary in Journal articles.

In the text, refer to tables and figures by their numbers. The numbers of each should begin with 1 and proceed sequentially. Avoid using "above," "below," "preceding," and similar terms. On a separate line between text paragraphs, indicate approximate placement of each table and figure. Each table and figure must be labeled with the table or figure number centered above the title.

Type text left and right justified. Do not break words with hyphens at the end of lines.

Regarding Mathematical Notation
The percent sign (%) should be used in the text and in tables.

Mathematical notation must be clear within the text and illustrations.

All equations must be very clearly typed. Display (separate line) equations should be aligned to the left margin.

Italic type is used for letters in equations, except for trigonometric functions and logarithm abbreviations, which are plain (normal) type. Matrices and vectors are in boldface type. (If these cannot be typed in italic and boldface, italic type can be indicated by a hand-drawn straight underline and boldface by a wavy underline).

Unusual and Greek symbols should be typed in the text using the Symbol capability. If no Symbol capability is possible, such special characters should be identified by name in a marginal note. (This is important; the editor may be not familiar with these symbols and may have difficulty producing the correct one without a marginal note.)

For equations that might be too long to type in a 6" column, indicate appropriate breaks.

Appendices
Each appendix should begin on a separate page.

If any mathematical proof or development is used but not critical to the exposition of the main argument of the manuscript, authors should include it in an appendix. An appendix may also be used for the mathematical material than may be beyond the level of the average reader. Keep in mind that the majority of Journal readers are practitioners.

Endnotes
Endnotes should be used for reference purposes only and should not be employed for discussion. Ideas not worth stating in the body of the manuscript should be omitted. Endnotes should be numbered consecutively throughout the manuscript and appear listed at the end of the manuscript.

Every reference to an article should provide specific information in the following order: The author's complete name (first name, middle initial, last name); title of the article (in quotation marks); name of the publication (in italics or underlined); volume number; date of publication; both beginning and ending page numbers of the article; and (where applicable) specific page references.

Example: Farouk A. Saleh and C. Das, "Transport Service Choice: Punctuality or Choice," *International Journal of Physical Distribution*, 4:5 (1974), pp. 297-304.

Every reference to a book should provide specific information in the following order: The author's complete name (first name, middle initial, last name); title of book (in italics or underlined); place of publication, name of publisher, and year in parenthesis; and (where applicable) specific page references. If there is more than one volume or edition, this information must also be given.

Example: Donald J. Bowersox and David J. Closs. Logistical Management: *The Integrated Supply Chain Process* (New York: Mc-Graw Hill Companies, 1996), pg. 190.

See *A Manual of Style, A Manual for Writers*, or previous editions of the Journal for other kinds of examples.

Subsequent references to a preceeding endnote should be indicated as follows: Same reference as Note ____ (#) and p. ____ (#).

The Endnotes list should be typed double-spaced in 12-point type. Please let the Endnotes wrap rather than using tabs or returns at the end of internal lines. Completeness and accuracy of Endnotes are the responsibility of the author(s). Reader's questions and comments about incomplete and inaccurate Endnotes will be referred to the article authors with a follow-up by the Editor. Text citations should be carefully checked against the Endnotes list. All authors of a referenced work should be listed; et al. should not be used in the Endnotes list. Undefined acronyms should not be used.

Illustrations (Tables and Figures)
When submitting a manuscript, include photocopies of the tables and figures used. Please do not submit camera-ready copies (high quality copies, using Journal styles, suitable for direct professional printing) of illustrations unless they are requested. (See the section on Camera-Ready Copy).

Each illustration should be on a separate page and should be numbered consecutively within its series type (Table 1, Table 2, Figure 1, Figure 2). If illustrations appear in appendices, they should be numbered consecutively, but separately from body illustrations (e.g., Table A-1, Figure A-1). All Tables and Figures must have titles. Titles for each Table and Figure should be descriptive but not lengthy. The title should be in ALL CAPITAL letters at the top of the Table or Figure. Tables and Figures should be called "TABLE" or "FIGURE" X in and should be followed by the title for the table or figure also in ALL CAPITAL letters at the top of the table or figure.

For Journal purposes, tables and figures are defined as follows: a table is comprised of rows and columns of numbers and/or text; A figure is a chart, graph, diagram, map, drawing, or any other nontext item that is not a table.

Tables should be typed in the following style:

TABLE 1
SELLING ACTIVITY IN TWO TIME PERIODS [a]

Definition	First Period	Second Period
	(Body of Table)	

[a] Footnotes (if any)

While tables and figures are numbered in separate consecutive series, the guidelines for each type of artwork are similar.

General Design
For more effective communication and better quality reproduction when printed, tables and figures should be kept as simple and uncluttered as possible, while conveying all necessary information.

When designing an illustration, please keep the size and verticalness of Journal pages in mind. An illustration that will cover more than one full page when typeset should be designed to be readily and logically divided into two or more pages. Excessive reduction of illustrations results in poor printing and poor readability.

Consistency is very important, both for the effectiveness of illustrations and for the standards of the Journal. This involves consistency of details within each illustration, between the illustrations and the manuscript, and between the illustrations and the textual references to them. Similar types of illustrations should have the same orientation, similar design, and consistent presentation of elements.

A very complex illustration is often better presented in a series of simpler, related illustrations.

A series of related illustrations should be numbered separately and subtitled to indicate relationships. For example, Figure 3 - Vertical and Lateral Relationships in Boyd's Model could become Figure 3 - Boyd's Model, Vertical Relationships and Figure 4 - Boyd's Model, Lateral Relationships (not Figures 3a and 3b).

Please see recent issues of the Journal for examples of the sizing and design of illustrations.

Details
Footnotes should appear directly below illustrations, flush with the left edge, and they should be designated by small letters, rather than asterisks or numerals. Column or row heads should be footnoted only if the footnote applies to all items in the column or row.

Complete source information must be provided for illustrations copied or derived from other sources. This complete information should be provided and an author-date citation should be given in a source note on the illustration. (Source notes are sized and placed like footnotes, below any footnotes for the illustration.)

If elements on an illustration are not labeled, but represent certain categories, items, or amounts, a complete key (legend) should be included.

Make sure that necessary measures of statistical significance are reported with each illustration.

Designate units (percent, dollars, hours, etc.) in column and row headings (tables) or in element labels or keys (figures).

Separate from each figure, give numerical values for all points, bars, pie slices, etc., so that they can be readily reproduced by the typesetter, if necessary.

Double-check formulae and mathematical terms and equations for consistency, readability and accuracy. Add extra space between characters to clarify and separate the terms, and be sure that sub- and superscript relationships are clear. Check for opening and closing parenthesis and brackets. Write the names of Greek and special characters in the margin.

Use tab indents or column alignment, rather than spaces, to align columns and indent headings.

American spelling should be used; foreign terms not commonly used in American English should be italicized.

Camera-ready Copy
For complex tables and figures, Journal staff may ask the author(s) to provide two camera-ready copies that follow these guidelines.

Camera-ready illustrations must be provided in black and white.

All elements of an illustration must be very clear and readable.

Camera-ready illustrations should be laser printed on heavy paper.

If the item is copied from another source (book, journal, proceedings, etc.), the copy should be done using scanning equipment and image processing software that will produce a clear image that can be laser printed on heavy paper.

Sometimes, excellent photocopies can make extremely clear, sharp images with minimal distortion on heavy-weight paper from completely flat sources; this is unusual and should be used only as a last resort.

However it is produced, the Journal will be able to use a camera-ready copy only if it provides a sharp, crisp image of all elements of the illustration.

Use Times Roman for all text and labels.

The preferred size range for type is between 9 and 12 points. No type smaller than 7 points should be used for any purpose. If the illustration will have to be reduced to fit a column or page, no type smaller than 9 points should be used. (No illustration should require more than a 20% reduction.)

For examples of head and label type on tables, please review recent issues of the Journal.

Hairlines do not print well: lines should be 0.5 point (thin), 1 point (single) and 2 points (thick) with patterned lines styles in the same size range.

On camera-ready copy of formulae or mathematical terms or equations, all numbers and all Greek and special characters must be very clear and distinct.

Graph axis labels should always be outside the axes and centered relative to them.

Permissions

Submitting a manuscript to the Journal of Business Logistics constitutes an assignment of copyright to the Journal and a guarantee that the work is original, that the author(s) own it, and that no part of it has been previously published in substantially the same form, that it is not being published or considered for publication elsewhere, and that any use of others' materials is by permission or falls within fair use standards of copyright law. The author(s) are responsible for obtaining any necessary permissions from copyright holders and for paying any necessary fees.

Fair use standards are exceeded whenever a significant portion of any published or unpublished item belonging to another (e.g., model, graph, table poem, essay, chapter, abstract, database, or more than about one hundred words in text) is reproduced with little modification. Extensive paraphrasing is considered disguised copying; permission is required.

Portions of an item, such as some of the data from a table, a few stanzas from a song, or part of a graphic representation of a model, can be used without permission if they are properly credited with full and exact source information and do not comprise a significant portion of the submitted article.

For a discussion of copyright law and fair use, see the Chicago Manual of Style, 14th Edition, items 4.43 through 4.73.

Copies of written permissions should be submitted with the final manuscript.

Electronic Submission

Initial submission must be in hard copy, or paper, form; facsimiles, electronically mailed copies, and files on disks will not be accepted for the initial review stage.

When the authors are notified of acceptance, they will be asked to provide the final, accepted version of the article on disk(s) containing the article text files and files for any illustrations that were produced on a computer, with a disk submission form (see below).

The Journal can accept most 3.5" disks produced in Macintosh, MS-DOS, or Windows formats. The manuscript should be provided in either Word or Word Perfect format. Write the manuscript number and an abbreviated, but clear version of the article title on the disk labels. File names should include key words or abbreviations from the article title (not, e.g., Article.jbl). The disk label should also identify the word processing system and the version number used. Tables and figures should be provided in separate files from the text. Tables can be provided in either Spreadsheet (Excel or Lotus) format and figures and other graphics can be provided in PowerPoint or Freelance format.

Notes

Use tabs, rather than spaces, for indentations and for column alignment.

Use the word wrap feature rather than hitting the "RETURN" key at the end of each line.

If formulae or equations are produced with separate software, rather than with the word processor used for the text, please copy them into the appropriate places in the text (to show location) and also provide them in a separate formula or equation file.

Mailing Disks
Please mail your article disk(s) to the Editor as soon as your article has been accepted.

The article disk(s) should be accompanied by a Disk Submission Form and should be sent with paper copies of the final, approved manuscript to the Editor.

The Disk Submission Form is very important and must be filled out completely and mailed with the disk(s).

Write protect disks before mailing them.

The disk(s) sent to the Journal should contain a copy of each file used to produce the manuscript; authors should retain their original files.

Mailed disks should be well-protected and well-supported through the use of a disk mailer; envelopes and homemade cardboard covers may result in disk damage:

Application of these guidelines and prompt response to inquiries and requests from the Editor and Journal staff will facilitate the timely production and distribution of the Journal and will ensure the inclusion of each article in its assigned issue.

MANUSCRIPT SUBMISSION
All correspondence regarding submission of manuscripts should be directed to: David J. Closs, Editor at the above address.

Journal of Business, Industry and Economics

ADDRESS FOR SUBMISSION:

Keith Atkinson, Editor
Journal of Business, Industry and
   Economics
Delta State University
Box 3222
Cleveland, MS 38733
USA
Phone: 662-846-4217
Fax: 662-846-4215
E-Mail: katkinsn@dsu.deltast.edu
Web:
Address May Change:

PUBLICATION GUIDELINES:

Manuscript Length: 6-10
Copies Required: Three
Computer Submission: Yes
Format: No Reply
Fees to Review: 50.00 US$

Manuscript Style:
   No Reply

CIRCULATION DATA:

Reader: Academics
Frequency of Issue: 2 Times/Year
Copies per Issue: Less than 1,000
Sponsor/Publisher: Delta State University
Subscribe Price: No Reply

REVIEW INFORMATION:

Type of Review: Blind Review
No. of External Reviewers: 2
No. of In House Reviewers: No Reply
Acceptance Rate: 70%
Time to Review: 2 - 3 Months
Reviewers Comments: Yes
Invited Articles: 0-5%
Fees to Publish: 0.00 US$

MANUSCRIPT TOPICS:

Advertising & Promotion Management; Direct Marketing; Global Business; Marketing Research; Marketing Theory & Applications; Sales/Selling; Services; Strategic Management Policy; Transportation/Physical Distribution

MANUSCRIPT GUIDELINES/COMMENTS:

Journal of Business-to-Business Marketing

ADDRESS FOR SUBMISSION:

J. David Lichtenthal, Editor
Journal of Business-to-Business Marketing
Baruch College
Zicklin School of Business
City University of New York Box E-0821
17 Lexington Avenue
New York, NY 10010
USA
Phone: 212-802-6516
Fax: 212-802-6483
E-Mail: david_lichtenthal@baruch.cuny.ed
Web:
Address May Change:

PUBLICATION GUIDELINES:

Manuscript Length: 20-50
Copies Required: Four
Computer Submission: Yes
Format: 3.5 disk
Fees to Review: 0.00 US$

Manuscript Style:
, Journal of Marketing Style Sheet

CIRCULATION DATA:

Reader: Academics, Business Persons
Frequency of Issue: Quarterly
Copies per Issue: Less than 1,000
Sponsor/Publisher: Haworth Press, Inc.
Subscribe Price: 45.00 US$ Individual
60.00 US$ Institution
150.00 US$ Library

REVIEW INFORMATION:

Type of Review: Blind Review
No. of External Reviewers: 3
No. of In House Reviewers: 0
Acceptance Rate: 21-25%
Time to Review: 2 - 3 Months
Reviewers Comments: Yes
Invited Articles: 0-5%
Fees to Publish: 0.00 US$

MANUSCRIPT TOPICS:

Business-to-Business Marketing; Marketing Research; Marketing Theory & Applications; Purchasing/Materials Management

MANUSCRIPT GUIDELINES/COMMENTS:

Manuscript Topics: The domain of business-to-business marketing encompasses all transactions except the final consumer transaction. JBBM will publish manuscripts that address any topic within this broad definition. We encourage potential authors to consider JBBM as an outlet for their work. We are concerned with the contribution to the science and practice of business marketing.

The JBBM will actively encourage diversity in research approaches and methodology for business-to-business marketing theory development and practice. The Editor and Editorial Board are charged with maintaining high standards of scholarship across diverse approaches.

Broad coverage within business-to-business marketing (transactions and exchange relationships: Industrial Marketing, Business Marketing Theory & Applications, Marketing Research, Advertising & Promotion Management, Direct Marketing, Sales/Selling, Purchasing/Materials Management, Technology/Innovation, Strategic Management Policy, Business Information Systems (MIS), Global Business, Business Education.)

The mission of the *Journal of Business-To-Business Marketing* is to further the science and practice of marketing among businesses. The Journal will encourage and publish quality research that reflects the state of scholarship and practice throughout the world. The Editorial Board is comprised of out standing scholars who have international reputations. This will ensure that the JBBM maintains high standards of scholarship.

Original Manuscripts Only. Submission of a manuscript to this Journal represents a certification on the part of the author(s) that it is an original work, and that neither this Manuscript nor a version of it has been published elsewhere nor is being considered for publication elsewhere.

Manuscript Length. Your manuscript may be approximately 20-50 typed pages double-spaced (including references and abstract). Lengthier manuscripts may be considered, but only at the discretion of the Editor.

Manuscript Style. References, citations, and general style of manuscripts for this Journal should follow the Chicago style (as outlined in the latest edition of the *Manual of Style* of The University of Chicago Press). References should be double-spaced and placed in alphabetical order.

If an author wishes to submit a paper that has already been prepared in another style, he or she may do so. However, if the paper is accepted (with or without reviewer's alterations), the author is fully responsible for retyping the manuscript in the correct style as indicated above. Neither the Editor nor the Publisher is responsible for re-preparing manuscript copy to adhere to the Journal's style.

Manuscript Preparation.
Margins: leave at least a one-inch margin on all four sides.
Paper: use clean, white, 8 ½ " x 11" bond paper.
Number of Copies: 4
Cover Page: Important – indicating only the article title, plus:
- an introductory footnote with authors' academic degrees, professional titles, affiliations, mailing addresses, and any desired acknowledgement of research support or other credit.

Second "Title Page": enclose an additional title page. Include the title again, plus:
- an **abstract** of about 100 words. (Below the abstract provide 3-10 key words for index purposes).

Spelling, Grammar, And Punctuation. You are responsible for preparing manuscript copy which is clearly written in acceptable scholarly English, and which contains no errors of spelling, grammar, or punctuation. Neither the Editor nor the Publisher is responsible for correcting errors of spelling and grammar: the manuscript, after acceptance by the Editor,

must be immediately ready for typesetting as it is finally submitted by the author(s). Check your paper for the following common errors:
- dangling modifiers
- misplaced modifiers
- unclear antecedents
- incorrect or inconsistent abbreviations

Also, check the accuracy of all arithmetic calculations, statistics, numerical data, text citations, and references.

Inconsistencies Must Be Avoided. Be sure you are consistent in your use of abbreviations, terminology, and in citing references, from one part of your paper to another.

Preparation of Tables, Figures, And Illustrations. All tables, figures, illustrations, etc. must be "camera-ready." That is, they must be cleanly typed or artistically prepared so that they can be used either exactly as they are or else used after a photographic reduction in size. **Tables will be printed as is and will not be reset.** Figures, tables, and illustrations must be prepared on separate sheets of paper. Always use black ink and professional drawing instruments. On the back of these items, write your article title and the journal title lightly in pencil, so they do not get misplaced. In text skip extra lines and indicate where these figures and tables are to be placed (please do not write on face of art).

Artwork. (Please note that dot-matrix type is often unacceptable for artwork.) If submitted art cannot be used, the Publisher reserves the right to redo the art and to charge the author a fee of $35.00 per hour for this service. The Haworth Press, Inc. is not responsible for errors incurred in the preparation of new camera-ready artwork.

Alterations Required By the Editor or Reviewers. Many times a paper is accepted by the Editor contingent upon changes that are mandated by anonymous specialist referees and members of the Editorial Board. If the Editor returns your manuscript for revisions, you are responsible for retyping any sections of the paper to incorporate these revisions (if applicable, revisions should also be put on disk).

Typesetting. You will not receive galley proofs of your article. Editorial revisions if any, must therefore be made while your article is still in manuscript. The final version of the manuscript will be the version you see in published form. Typesetter's errors will be corrected by the production staff of The Haworth Press, Inc. Authors are expected to submit manuscripts, disks, and art that are free of error.

Electronic Media. Haworth's in-house typesetting unit is able to utilize your final manuscript material as prepared on most personal computers and word processors. This will minimize typographical errors and decrease overall production timelag. Please send the first draft and final draft copies of your manuscript to the journal Editor in print format for his/her final review and approval.

After Approval of your final manuscript, please submit the final approved version both on printed format ("hard copy") and floppy diskette. On the outside of the diskette package write:
A. the brand name of your computer or word processor
B. the word-processing program that you used
C. the title of your article, and
D. file name

NOTE: Disk and hard copy must agree. In case of discrepancies, it is The Haworth Press's policy to follow hard copy. Authors are advised that no revisions of the manuscript can ve made after acceptance by the Editor for publication. The benefits of this procedure are many with speed and accuracy being the most obvious. We look forward to working with you on this, knowing we will be able to serve you more efficiently in the future.

Reprints. The senior author will receive two copies of the journal issue and ten complimentary reprints of his or her article. The junior author will receive two copies of the issue. These are sent several weeks after the journal issue is published and in circulation. An order form for the purchase of additional reprints will also be sent to authors at this time. (Approximately 4-6 weeks is necessary for the preparation of reprints) Please do not query the Journal's Editor about reprints. All such questions should be sent directly to The Haworth Press, Inc, Production Department, 21 East Broad Street, West Hazelton, PA 18201. To order additional reprints (minimum 50 copies), please contact The Haworth Document Delivery Center, 10 Alice Street, Binghamton, NY 13904-1580; 1-800-342-9678 or Fax (607) 722-6362.

Copyright. Copyright ownership must be transferred officially to The Haworth Press, Inc. before we can begin the peer-review process. The Editor's letter acknowledging receipt of the manuscript will be accompanied by a form fully explaining this. All authors must sign the form and return the original to the Editor as soon as possible. Failure to return the copyright form in a timely fashion will result in delay in review and subsequent publication.

Journal of Communication

ADDRESS FOR SUBMISSION:

Alan M. Rubin, Editor
Journal of Communication
Kent State University
School of Communication Studies
PO Box 5190
Kent, OH 44242-0001
USA
Phone: 330-672-4609
Fax: 330-672-4547
E-Mail: joc@kent.edu
Web:
Address May Change:

PUBLICATION GUIDELINES:

Manuscript Length: 25
Copies Required: Four
Computer Submission: No
Format: N/A
Fees to Review: 0.00 US$

Manuscript Style:
American Psychological Association

CIRCULATION DATA:

Reader: Academics
Frequency of Issue: Quarterly
Copies per Issue: 5,001 - 10,000
Sponsor/Publisher: International Communication Association /Oxford University Press
Subscribe Price: 25.00 US$
  20.00 US$ Institution

REVIEW INFORMATION:

Type of Review: Blind Review
No. of External Reviewers: 3
No. of In House Reviewers: 0
Acceptance Rate: 11-20%
Time to Review: 3 - 4 Months
Reviewers Comments: Yes
Invited Articles: 0-5%
Fees to Publish: 0.00 US$

MANUSCRIPT TOPICS:
Communication; Organizational Behavior & Theory; Technology/Innovation

MANUSCRIPT GUIDELINES/COMMENTS:

Manuscript Topics: The *Journal of Communication* publishes articles and book reviews that examine a broad range of issues in communication theory and research. The Journal seeks to be a general forum for communication scholarship and is especially interested in research whose significance crosses subdisciplinary boundaries. The Journal maintains a broad scholarly focus and seeks to publish the best available scholarship on all aspects of communication.

Manuscript Guidelines: Manuscripts should be original work and not be under consideration by any other publication. Because manuscripts are evaluated blindly, author identification should only appear on the title page.

Manuscripts must be prepared in strict accordance with the 4th edition of the *Publication Manual of the American Psychological Association*. Tables and footnotes should be kept to a minimum. All parts of the manuscript should be double-spaced. Submissions are seldom longer than 30 pages, including tables and references, plus an abstract of 100 words. Authors should submit four (4) copies of their manuscripts. Manuscripts will not be returned to authors.

The *Journal of Communication* is an official publication of the International Communication Association. It is edited in cooperation with the School of Communication Studies at Kent State University and is published quarterly by Oxford University Press.

Journal of Communication Management

ADDRESS FOR SUBMISSION:

Julie Simmons
Journal of Communication Management
Henry Stewart Publications
Museum House
25 Museum Street
London, WC1A 1JT
Phone: 0 171 323-2916
Fax: 0 171 323-2918
E-Mail: submissions@hspublications.co.uk
Web:
Address May Change:

PUBLICATION GUIDELINES:

Manuscript Length: 2,000-5,000 words
Copies Required: Three
Computer Submission: Yes
Format: MS Word/WordPerfect
Fees to Review: 0.00 US$

Manuscript Style:
, Cambridge Handbook

CIRCULATION DATA:

Reader: , 65% Business, 35% Academic
Frequency of Issue: Quarterly
Copies per Issue: 1,001 - 2,000
Sponsor/Publisher: Henry Stewart Publications
Subscribe Price: 260.00 US$ Full Rate
110.00 US$ Academic
208.00 US$ IPR/PRCA/IABC

REVIEW INFORMATION:

Type of Review: Blind Review
No. of External Reviewers: 3
No. of In House Reviewers: 2
Acceptance Rate: 50%
Time to Review: 1 - 2 Months
Reviewers Comments: Yes
Invited Articles: 31-50%
Fees to Publish: 0.00 US$

MANUSCRIPT TOPICS:
Advertising & Promotion Management; Business Education; Communication; Direct Marketing; Global Business; Health Care Administration; Marketing Research; Non Profit Organizations; Operations Research/Statistics; Organizational Behavior & Theory; Organizational Development; Strategic Management Policy

MANUSCRIPT GUIDELINES/COMMENTS:

About the Journal
Journal of Communication Management is a must-read for those responsible for the management of PR, public affairs, investor relations, internal communication, corporate advertising, sponsorship, community relations, environmental issues, crisis management and risk management.

Both on paper and online, the journal provides in-depth, peer-reviewed, practitioner-oriented articles from leading consultants and agents, blue-chips and academics at the forefront of practice and theory of stakeholder communication, so you can:
- set the agenda
- minimise negative and maximise positive exposure

- attain loyalty and good will

Journal of Communication Management is published in association with the *Institute of Public Relations* and the *International Association of Business Communicators (Europe and Africa)*, and is authoritative and directly relevant to practitioners and academics alike.

By publishing longer, in-depth articles and papers that PR magazines do not provide and by bridging the gap between cutting-edge practice and academic research, Journal of Communication Management offers a unique opportunity to benefit from the experiences of others.

- **Fully referenced articles** by leading practitioners, consultants and academics on latest thinking and techniques
- **Case studies** from communicators world-wide, detailing their practical experiences, the problems overcome and the lessons learned
- **Book reviews** providing a summary of content and and assessment of their relevance to communication specialists

This information is authoritative, accessible and cutting edge, the journal
- is guided by an **International Editorial Board** of leading client-side practitioners, consultants and academics...
- publishes only articles that have been subjected to **double-blind peer review** and have been judged pertinent and of the highest standard, ensuring that...
- only the **genuinely useful, challenging and thought-provoking articles and case studies are published in the Journal of Communication Management.**

Notes for Contributors

1. Contributions should be between 2,000 and 5,000 words in length. All submissions should be typewritten and double spaced.

2. The Journal's Editors and Editorial Board particularly welcome submissions which present case study material, new approaches, techniques, empirical research or conceptual papers.

3. All articles should be accompanied by a short abstract outlining the paper's aims and subject matter.

4. All articles should be accompanied by up to six keywords.

5. Articles should be accompanied by a short (about 80 words) description of the author(s) and, if appropriate, the organization of which he or she is a member.

6. Authors should not seek to use the Journal as a vehicle for marketing any specific product or service.

7. Authors should avoid the use of language or slang which is not in keeping with the professional and academic style of the Journal.

8. Titles of organizations etc should be written out first in full and thereafter in initials.

9. Articles should be supported by references. For all Henry Stewart Journals excluding Corporate Reputation Review, Tourism and Hospitality Research, Journal of Fashion Marketing and Management, Journal of Small Business and Enterprise Development, Journal of Asset Management and International Journal of Police Science Management, these should be set out in accordance with the Vancouver referencing system. References for the Journals listed above should be set out in accordance with the Harvard referencing system.

10. Photographs and illustrations supporting articles should be submitted where appropriate. Photographs should be good quality positives, printed from the original negatives and preferably in black and white only. Figures and other line illustrations should be submitted in good quality originals and a copy of the data should also be included.

11. Authors must ensure that references to named people and/or organizations are accurate, not rascist or sexist and without libellous implications.

12. All contributions sent to the Publisher, whether invited or not, will be submitted to the Journal's Editors and Editorial Board. Any such contribution must bear the author's full name and address, even if this is not for publication. Contributions, whether published pseudonymously or not, are accepted on the strict understanding that the author is responsible for the accuracy of all opinion, technical comment, factual report, data, figures, illustrations and photographs. Publication does not necessarily imply that these are the opinions of the Editorial Board, Editors or the Publisher, nor does the Board, Editors or Publisher accept any liability for the accuracy of such comment, report and other technical and factual information. The Publisher will, however, strive to ensure that all opinion, comments, reports, data, figures, illustrations and photographs are accurate, insofar as it is within its abilities to do so. The Publisher reserves the right to edit, abridge or omit material submitted for publication.

13. All Articles submitted for publication will be subject to a double-blind refereeing procedure.

14. The author bears the responsibility for checking whether material submitted is subject to copyright or ownership rights, eg photographs, illustrations, trade literature and Page 2 of 2 data. Where use is so restricted, the Publisher must be informed with the submission of the material.

15. No contribution will be accepted which has been published elsewhere, unless it is expressly invited or agreed by the Publisher. Articles and contributions published become the copyright of the Publisher, unless otherwise agreed.

16. All reasonable efforts are made to ensure accurate reproduction of text, photographs and illustrations. The Publisher does not accept responsibility for mistakes, be they editorial or typographical, nor for consequences resulting from them.

17. Submissions should be sent to Henry Stewart Publications, Museum House, 25 Museum Street, London WC1A UT, email: submissions@hspublications.co.uk. Please clearly state for which journal you are contributing.

Journal of Consumer Affairs

ADDRESS FOR SUBMISSION:

Claudia J. Peck-Heath, Editor
Journal of Consumer Affairs
University of Kentucky
College of Environmental Sciences
102 Erikson Hall
Lexington, KY 40506-0050
USA
Phone: 606-257-4080
Fax: 606-257-4095
E-Mail: cjpeck@pop.uky.edu
Web:
Address May Change:

PUBLICATION GUIDELINES:

Manuscript Length: 10
Copies Required: Four
Computer Submission: Yes
Format: Microsoft Word
Fees to Review: 70.00 US$ Nonmember
          35.00 US$ Member ACCI

Manuscript Style:
      Chicago Manual of Style

CIRCULATION DATA:

Reader: Academics
Frequency of Issue: 2 Times/Year
Copies per Issue: 2,001 - 3,000
Sponsor/Publisher: W I Press/American
    Council on Consumer Interests
Subscribe Price: 15.00 US$

REVIEW INFORMATION:

Type of Review: Blind Review
No. of External Reviewers: 3
No. of In House Reviewers: 2
Acceptance Rate: 21-30%
Time to Review: 2 - 3 Months
Reviewers Comments: Yes
Invited Articles: 5%
Fees to Publish: 0.00 US$

MANUSCRIPT TOPICS:
Business Law, Public Responsibility & Ethics; Communication; Consumer Behavior; Consumer Policy and Education; Marketing Research; Marketing Theory & Applications

MANUSCRIPT GUIDELINES/COMMENTS:

Editorial Policy

1. The purpose of the *Journal of Consumer Affairs* is to foster and disseminate professional thought and scholarly research advancing the consumer interest. The Journal serves as a forum for communication, discourse, and debate on consumer affairs and consumer protection issues.

2. The scope of the Journal includes consumer policy, consumer education, consumer economics, and consumer behavior. Acceptable manuscripts may be theoretical, empirical, philosophical, or historical in perspective. They should, however, have clear implications for government, household, or business policy.

In a cover letter please indicate:
3. That the material in the manuscript, so far as the author knows, will not infringe upon any statutory copyright.

4. The paper will not be submitted elsewhere, while under JCA review.

Manuscript Preparation
5. Submit 4 copies – one original and two copies on 8 ½" x 11" paper with 1-1/4" margins. Double space throughout, including footnotes and quoted matter.

6. The manuscript should include a separate title page, with the title of the paper, the author's title and affiliation, and any acknowledgements. This page will be removed before review to ensure anonymity.

7. Manuscripts submitted for publication should include a headnote not exceeding 75 words. Headnotes are not necessary for papers to be included in the "Viewpoints and Communications" Section.

8. Citations in the text must be by the author's last name and year of publication, enclosed in parentheses and without punctuation, e.g., (Smith 1984). In the case of multiple authors, use all of the authors' last names for up to three authors. For four or more authors, use the first author's name followed by et al.

9. References are to be listed alphabetically by surname of the author, followed by the publication date in parentheses. Author(s) complete name(s) should be given. The list should be single spaced with a double space between each entry. Entitle the page "REFERENCES." An example style of a book and periodical entry is listed below:

> Smith, Joe G. (1979), *Consumer Protection to Dwarf Terrapins*, New York: ASPCA Publishing Company.
>
> Washington, Michael and Herbert W. Johnson (1982), "The Effects of Radio on Children," *Journal of Behavior*, 19 (No. 11; June): 267-272.

If an author or team of authors appear more than once, introduce a short line for the repeated authors' names. Retain the complete names of additional authors. If two or more works by the same author have the same publication date, they should be differentiated by letters after the date. This letter should also appear in the text citation. The following is an example: Smith, Joe G. (1984a).

10. Footnotes should be numbered consecutively throughout the paper and included on a separate page placed following the text and references.

11. Each table, graph, figure, or chart should be placed on a separate page and included at the end of the manuscript. Omit all vertical lines. Use letters for footnotes to tables, and asterisks for statistical significance levels.

12. The typical JCA article is about 4000 - 6000 words. Longer papers are published under exceptional circumstances.

Processing Fee

13. A $35.00 processing fee is charged for manuscripts submitted by members of ACCI. A $70.00 processing fee is charged for manuscripts submitted by non-members of ACCI. A check or money order payable to "American Council on Consumer Interests" should be included with all submissions.

Other Information

14. Manuscripts submitted to the JCA are refereed by the editorial board and reviewers selected by the Editor. Manuscripts cannot be returned.

15. There is no page charge. Authors may purchase reprints. Requests for JCA reprints should be sent directly to authors.

16. Acceptance of a manuscript for JCA publication gives the ACCI the right to publish and copyright the material. Republication elsewhere is contingent upon written approval from the Editor.

Journal of Consumer Marketing

ADDRESS FOR SUBMISSION:

Richard C. Leventhal, Editor
Journal of Consumer Marketing
7678 Upham Street
Arvada, CO 80003
USA
Phone:
Fax: 303-727-4038
E-Mail:
Web: www.mcb.co.uk
Address May Change:

PUBLICATION GUIDELINES:

Manuscript Length: 16-20
Copies Required: Four
Computer Submission: No only accepted
Format: N/A
Fees to Review: 0.00 US$

Manuscript Style:
  Uniform System of Citation (Harvard Blue Book)

CIRCULATION DATA:

Reader: Academics, Practitioners, Consultants
Frequency of Issue: Bi-Monthly
Copies per Issue: No Reply
Sponsor/Publisher: MCB University Press, Limited UK
Subscribe Price: 799.00 US$
  2899.00 AUS$

REVIEW INFORMATION:

Type of Review: Blind Review
No. of External Reviewers: 3
No. of In House Reviewers: 1
Acceptance Rate: 21-27%
Time to Review: 2 - 3 Months
Reviewers Comments: Yes
Invited Articles: 6-10%
Fees to Publish: 0.00 US$

MANUSCRIPT TOPICS:
Business Law, Public Responsibility & Ethics; Communication; Consumer Behavior; Consumer Policy and Education; Direct Marketing; Franchising Research; Internet Marketing; Marketing Research; Sales/Selling; Services

MANUSCRIPT GUIDELINES/COMMENTS:

Unique Attributes
The Journal of Consumer Marketing is written by practitioners, consultants and marketing academics and is edited for people in marketing who desire to develop further insight into how people behave as consumers worldwide.

Each paper submitted to this journal is subject to a double-blind reviewing process.

Topicality
Consumers are fickle, demanding and capricious, changing attitudes, spending patterns and needs just when you think you've got them worked out. Keeping abreast of these sea changes, which can wreck or precipitate months of planning, is essential if you are to maintain and increase corporate profitability and professional credibility – and keep ahead of the

competition. The journal offers incisive and authoritative material on all aspects of marketing to consumers to help professionals devise appropriate sales initiatives.

Key Benefits
Written by acknowledged experts in the field, this journal makes an invaluable companion in an aggressive marketing world. It helps you to determine when you need a new idea, and when you simply need a new application, and offers invaluable practical guidance that can create the spark of inspiration that will outwit your competitors - and delight your prospects and customers.

Key Journal Audiences

- Academics wanting the latest research findings or classroom examples
- Consultants advising corporations with consumer markets
- Marketing directors, business strategists, advertising managers and all practitioners in consumer marketing or sales management
- Students

Coverage

- Consumer behaviour
- Customer policy and service
- Practical case studies to illustrate concepts
- The latest thinking and research in marketing planning
- The marketing of services worldwide

Notes for Contributors

Copyright
Articles submitted to the journal should be original contributions and should not be under consideration for any other publication at the same time. Authors submitting articles for publication warrant that the work is not an infringement of any existing copyright and will indemnify the publisher against any breach of such warranty. For ease of dissemination and to ensure proper policing of use, papers and contributions become the legal copyright of the publisher unless otherwise agreed.

Submissions should be sent to the Editor.

Editorial Objectives
Journal of Consumer Marketing is a journal written by practitioners, consultants and marketing academics and is edited for marketers who desire to develop further insight into how people behave as consumers worldwide. Consumption is a key element of much of human behaviour. Understanding consumer behaviour is the key to creating effective marketing strategies. We are committed to publishing not only research, but cases, new concepts and/or practices, as well as commentary which reflect personal opinion. JCM seeks to blend both theory and practice.

Franchising Research Section Editor
Dianne H B Welsh PhD, Eastern Washington University, 668 North Riverpoint, Suite A, Spokane, WA 99202-1660, USA. E-mail: dwelsh@ewu.edu

Franchising Research Editorial objectives
The editorial aim is to publish Franchising Research articles with the emphasis on marketing. The Franchising Research Section will strongly favour international articles to promote a better understanding of the cultures in which franchising operates.

Article content
The bases of an article may be research, but research is not the only basis for an article. Cases, concepts and industry reviews and practices may be put forth with equal acceptability. In addition, we have provided a section for Commentary, which need be little more than personal opinion.

Each article should contain:
1. Background and some short references to previous articles, if they are pertinent. Specifically omit endless strings of quotations by other authors, especially if the ideas are currently well accepted. This is particularly true of citations in the literature that are five or more years old. If previous material is pertinent, please paraphrase it and eliminate endnotes and authors. Citations should be used only for significant and timely contributions. Also, standard textbooks should not be used as references.

2. Basic premise, major thoughts, problems or concept.

3. A discussion of the theory incorporating any research.
   A case example of clear argument supporting the basic premise or concept.

4. A summary to wrap-up the key ideas. Then a section titled Managerial Implications and applications for the information presented in the article.

The reviewing process
Each paper is reviewed by the editor and, if it is judged suitable for this publication, it is then sent to three referees for double blind peer review. Based on their recommendations, the editor then decides whether the paper should be accepted as is, revised or rejected.

Manuscript requirements
Four copies of the manuscript should be submitted in double line spacing with wide margins. All authors should be shown and author's details must be printed on a separate sheet and the author should not be identified anywhere else in the article.

As a guide, articles should be between 4,000 and 6,000 words in length. A title of not more than eight words should be provided. A brief autobiographical note should be supplied including full name, affiliation, e-mail address and full international contact details. Authors must supply an abstract of 100-150 words. Up to six keywords should be included which encapsulate the principal subjects covered by the article.

Where there is a **methodology**, it should be clearly described under a separate heading. **Headings** must be short, clearly defined and not numbered. **Notes** or **Endnotes** should be used only if absolutely necessary and must be identified in the text by consecutive numbers, enclosed in square brackets and listed at the end of the article.

Figures, charts and **diagrams** should be kept to a minimum. They must be black and white with minimum shading and numbered consecutively using arabic numerals with a brief title and labelled axes. In the text, the position of the figure should be shown by typing on a separate line the words "take in Figure 2". Good quality originals must be provided.

Tables should be kept to a minimum. They must be numbered consecutively with roman numerals and a brief title. In the text, the position of the table should be shown by typing on a separate line the words "take in Table IV".

Photos and **illustrations** must be supplied as good quality black and white original half tones with captions. Their position should be shown in the text by typing on a separate line the words "take in Plate 2".

References to other publications should be complete and in Harvard style. They should contain full bibliographical details and journal titles should not be abbreviated. For multiple citations in the same year use a, b, c immediately following the year of publication. References should be shown within the text by giving the author's last name followed by a comma and year of publication all in round brackets, e.g. (Fox, 1994). At the end of the article should be a reference list in alphabetical order as follows

(a) for books
surname, initials (year) *title*, publisher, place of publication, e.g.Casson, M. (1979), *Alternatives to the Multinational Enterprise*, Macmillan, London.
(b) for chapter in edited book
surname, initials (year) "title", editor's surname, initials, title, publisher, place, pages, e.g.Bessley, M. and Wilson, P. (1984), "Public policy and small firms in Britain", in Levicki, C. (Ed.), Small Business Theory and Policy, Croom Helm, London, pp.111-26. Please note that the chapter title must be underlined.
(c) for articles
surname, initials, (year) "title", journal, volume, number, pages, e.g. Fox, S. (1994) "Empowerment as a catalyst for change: an example from the food industry", Supply Chain Management, Vol. 2 No 3, pp. 29-33

If there is more than one author list surnames followed by initials. All authors should be shown.

Electronic sources should include the URL of the electronic site at which they may be found, as follows:

Neuman, B.C.(1995), "Security, payment, and privacy for network commerce", IEEE Journal on Selected Areas in Communications, Vol. 13 No.8, October, pp.1523-31. Available (IEEE SEPTEMBER) http://www.research.att.com/jsac/

Notes/Endnotes should be used only if absolutely necessary. They should, however, always be used for citing Web sites. They should be identified in the text by consecutive numbers enclosed in square brackets and listed at the end of the article. Please then provide full Web site addresses in the end list.

Final submission of the article
Once accepted for publication, the final version of the manuscript must be provided, accompanied by a 3.5" **disk** of the same version labelled with: disk format; author name(s); title of article; journal title; file name.

Each article must be accompanied by a completed and signed **Journal Article Record Form** available from the Editor or on http://www.literaticlub.co.uk/

The manuscript will be considered to be the definitive version of the article. The author must ensure that it is complete, grammatically correct and without spelling or typographical errors.

In preparing the disk, please use one of the following formats: Word, Word Perfect, Rich text format or TeX/LaTeX. Figures which are provided electronically must be in tif, gif or pic file extensions. All figures and graphics must also be supplied as good quality originals.

Final submission requirements
Manuscripts must be clean, good quality hard copy and;
- include an abstract and keywords
- have Harvard style references
- include any figures, photos and graphics as good quality originals
- be accompanied by a labelled disk
- be accompanied by a completed Journal Article Record Form

Technical assistance is available from MCB's World Wide Web Literati Club on http://www.literaticlub.co.uk/ or contact Mike Massey at MCB, e-mail mmassey@mcb.co.uk

Journal of Consumer Policy

ADDRESS FOR SUBMISSION:

Heiner Imkamp, Associate Editor
Journal of Consumer Policy
University of Hohenheim (530/1)
Editorial Office
D-70593
Stuttgart 70,
Germany
Phone:
Fax:
E-Mail: imkamp@uni-hohenheim.de
Web: www.wkap.nl
Address May Change:

CIRCULATION DATA:

Reader: Academics
Frequency of Issue: Quarterly
Copies per Issue: Less than 1,000
Sponsor/Publisher: Kluwer Academic Publishers
Subscribe Price: 307.00 US$
675.00 NLG

PUBLICATION GUIDELINES:

Manuscript Length: 11-15
Copies Required: Four hardcopy & a diskette
Computer Submission: Yes
Format: MS Word or Word Perfect
Fees to Review: 0.00 US$

Manuscript Style:
American Psychological Association

REVIEW INFORMATION:

Type of Review: Blind Review
No. of External Reviewers: 3
No. of In House Reviewers: 3+
Acceptance Rate: No Reply
Time to Review: 2 - 3 Months
Reviewers Comments: Yes
Invited Articles: 6-10%
Fees to Publish: 0.00 US$

MANUSCRIPT TOPICS:
Advertising & Promotion Management; Consumer Behavior; Consumer Policy and Education; Marketing Research; Marketing Theory & Applications

MANUSCRIPT GUIDELINES/COMMENTS:

Aims and Scope

The *Journal of Consumer Policy* is a refereed, international journal which encompasses a broad range of issues concerned with consumer affairs. It looks at the consumer's dependence on existing social and economic structures, helps to define the consumer's interest, and discusses the ways in which consumer welfare can be fostered – or restrained – through actions and policies of consumers, industry, organizations, government, educational institutions, and the mass media.

The *Journal of Consumer Policy* publishes theoretical and empirical research on consumer and producer conduct, emphasizing the implications for consumers and increasing communication between the parties in the marketplace.

Articles cover consumer issues in law, economics, and behavioural sciences. Current areas of topical interest include the impact of new information technologies, the economics of information, the consequences of regulation or deregulation of markets, problems related to an increasing internationalization of trade and marketing practices, consumers in less affluent societies, the efficacy of economic cooperation, consumers and the environment, problems with products and services provided by the public sector, the setting of priorities by consumer organizations and agencies, gender issues, product safety and product liability, and the interaction between consumption and associated forms of behaviour such as work and leisure.

The *Journal of Consumer Policy* reports regularly on developments in legal policy with a bearing on consumer issues. It covers the integration of consumer law in the European Union and other transnational communities and analyzes trends in the application and implementation of consumer legislation through administrative agencies, courts, trade associations, and consumer organizations. It also considers the impact of consumer legislation on the supply side and discusses comparative legal approaches to similar issues of consumer policy taken throughout the world.

The *Journal of Consumer Policy* informs readers on a broad array of consumer policy issues by publishing regularly both extended book reviews and brief, non-evaluative book notes on new publications in the field.

Manuscript Submission
Kluwer Academic Publishers prefer the submission of manuscripts and figures in electronic form in addition to a hard-copy printout. The preferred storage medium for your electronic manuscript is a 3 ½ inch diskette. Please label your diskette properly, giving exact details on the name(s) of the file(s), the operating system and software used. Always save your electronic manuscript in the word processor format that you use; conversions to other formats and versions tend to be imperfect. In general, use as few formatting codes as possible. For safety's sake, you should always retain a backup copy of your file(s). **After acceptance**, please make absolutely sure that you send the latest (i.e., revised) version of your manuscript, both as hard-copy printout and on diskette.

Kluwer Academic Publishers prefer articles submitted in word processing packages such as MS Word, WordPerfect, etc. running under operating systems MS DOS, Windows and Apple Macintosh, or in the file format LaTeX. Articles submitted in other software programs, as well as articles for conventional typesetting, can also be accepted.

For submission in LaTeX, *Kluwer Academic Publishers* have developed a Kluwer LaTeX class file, which can be downloaded from: www.wkap.nl/kaphtml.htm/IFAHOME. Use of this class file is highly recommended. Do not use versions downloaded from other sites. Technical support is available at: texhelp@wkap.nl. If you are not familiar with TeX/LaTeX, the class file will be of no use to you. In that case, submit your article in a common word processor format.

For the purpose of reviewing, articles for publication should be submitted as hard-copy printout (four-fold) and on diskette to **Heiner Imkamp, Associate Editor.**

Book Review Editors:
Suzanne Beckmann, Copenhagen Business School, (Economics and Behavioural Sciences), Department of Marketing, Struenseegade 7-9, DK-2200, Copenhagen N, Denmark
(E-mail: suz.beckmann@cbs.dk)

Stephen Weatherill, University of Oxford (Law), Sommerville College, Oxford OX2 6HD U.K.

Manuscript Presentation
The journal's language is English. British English or American English spelling and terminology may be used, but either one should be followed consistently throughout the article. Articles in French may also be considered for publication, if accompanied with an abstract in English. Manuscripts submitted for consideration as general articles should be not more than 20 double-spaced pages, and should be formatted in APA style see the Publication Manual of the American Psychological Association, 4th ed. (1994). Manuscripts submitted as general articles should not exceed 5000 words (or 10 12 pages, double spaced). Brief papers can be considered based on conference presentations, counselling issues, or counselling cases. Brief papers are occasionally published in a section of the *International Journal for the Advancement of Counselling* that is designed for brief articles. Manuscripts submitted for brief articles should not exceed 7 double-spaced pages. Manuscripts should be printed or typewritten on A4 or US Letter bond paper, one side only, leaving adequate margins (2.5 centimeters or 1 inch) on all sides to allow reviewers' remarks. The font size or size of print should be 12 points. Please double-space all material, including notes and references. Quotations of more than 40 words should be set off clearly, either by indenting the left-hand margin or by using a smaller typeface. Use double quotation marks for direct quotations and single quotation marks for quotations within quotations and for words or phrases used in a special sense.

Number the pages consecutively with the first page containing:
- running head (shortened title)
- article type
- title
- author(s)
- affiliation(s)
- full address for correspondence, including telephone and fax number and e-mail address

Abstract
Please provide a short abstract of 100 to 250 words. The abstract should not contain any undefined abbreviations or unspecified references. Abstracts in other languages may be published if submitted by authors.

Figures and Tables
Submission of electronic figures
In addition to hard-copy printouts of figures, authors are encouraged to supply the electronic versions of figures in either Encapsulated PostScript (EPS) or TIFF format. Many other

formats, e.g., Microsoft Postscript, PiCT (Macintosh) and WMF (Windows), cannot be used and the hard copy will be scanned instead.

Figures should be saved in separate files without their captions, which should be included with the text of the article. Files should be named according to DOS conventions, e.g., 'figure1.eps'. For vector graphics, EPS is the preferred format. Lines should not be thinner than 0.25pts and in-fill patterns and screens should have a density of at least 10%. Font-related problems can be avoided by using standard fonts such as Times Roman and Helvetica. For bitmapped graphics, TIFF is the preferred format but EPS is also acceptable. The following resolutions are optimal: black-and-white line figures - 600 - 1200 dpi; line figures with some grey or coloured lines - 600 dpi; photographs - 300 dpi; screen dumps - leave as is. Higher resolutions will not improve output quality but will only increase file size, which may cause problems with printing; lower resolutions may compromise output quality. Please try to provide artwork that approximately fits within the typeset area of the journal. Especially screened originals, i.e. originals with grey areas, may suffer badly from reduction by more than 10-15%.

Avoiding Problems With Eps Graphics
Please always check whether the figures print correctly to a PostScript printer in a reasonable amount of time. If they do not, simplify your figures or use a different graphics program.
If EPS export does not produce acceptable output, try to create an EPS file with the printer driver (see below). This option is unavailable with the Microsoft driver for Windows NT, so if you run Windows NT, get the Adobe driver from the Adobe site (www.adobe.com).
If EPS export is not an option, e.g., because you rely on OLE and cannot create separate files for your graphics, it may help us if you simply provide a PostScript dump of the entire document.

How To Set Up For Eps And Postscript Dumps Under Windows
Create a printer entry specifically for this purpose: install the printer 'Apple Laserwriter Plus' and specify 'FILE': as printer port. Each time you send something to the 'printer' you will be asked for a filename. This file will be the EPS file or PostScript dump that we can use.

The EPS export option can be found under the PostScript tab. EPS export should be used only for single-page documents. For printing a document of several pages, select 'Optimise for portability' instead. The option 'Download header with each job' should be checked.

Submission of hard-copy figures
If no electronic versions of figures are available, submit only high-quality artwork that can be reproduced as is, i.e., without any part having to be redrawn or re-typeset. The letter size of any text in the figures must be large enough to allow for reduction. Photographs should be in black-and-white on glossy paper. If a figure contains colour, make absolutely clear whether it should be printed in black-and-white or in colour. Figures that are to be printed in black-and-white should not be submitted in colour. Authors will be charged for reproducing figures in colour.

Each figure and table should be numbered and mentioned in the text. The approximate position of figures and tables should be indicated in the margin of the manuscript. On the

reverse side of each figure, the name of the (first) author and the figure number should be written in pencil; the top of the figure should be clearly indicated. Figures and tables should be placed at the end of the manuscript following the Reference section. Each figure and table should be accompanied by an explanatory legend. The figure legends should be grouped and placed on a separate page. Figures are not returned to the author unless specifically requested.
In tables, footnotes are preferable to long explanatory material in either the heading or body of the table. Such explanatory footnotes, identified by superscript letters, should be placed immediately below the table.

Section Headings
First-, second-, third-, and fourth-order headings should be clearly distinguishable but not numbered.

Appendices
Supplementary material should be collected in an Appendix and placed before the Notes and Reference sections.

Notes
Please use endnotes rather than footnotes. Explanatory notes should be avoided and incorporated in the text whenever possible. Notes should be numbered consecutively in the text with a superscript numeral without parentheses. A source reference note should be indicated by means of an asterisk after the title. This note should be placed at the bottom of the first page.

Cross-Referencing
In the text, a reference identified by means of an author's name should be followed by the date of the reference in parentheses and page number(s) where appropriate. When there are more than two authors, only the first author's name should be mentioned, followed by 'et al.'. In the event that an author cited has had two or more works published during the same year, the reference, both in the text and in the reference list, should be identified by a lower case letter like 'a' and 'b' after the date to distinguish the works.
Examples:
Winograd (1986, p. 204)
(Winograd 1986a, b)
(Winograd 1986; Flores et al. 1988)
(Bullen & Bennett 1990)

Acknowledgements
Acknowledgements of people, grants, funds, etc. should be placed in a separate section before the References.

References
References to books, journal articles, articles in collections and conference or workshop proceedings, and technical reports should be listed at the end of the article in **alphabetical** order. Articles in preparation or articles submitted for publication, unpublished observations, personal communications, etc. should not be included in the reference list but should only be mentioned in the article text (e.g., T. Moore, personal communication).

References to books should include the author's name; year of publication; title; page numbers where appropriate; publisher; place of publication, in the order given in the example below.

Clausius, K. (1997). *Vertragskontinuitat und Anpassungsbedarf.* Bonn: Zentrum fur Europaisches Wirtschaftsrecht. Nr. 87.

References to articles in an edited collection should include the author's name; year of publication; article title; editor's name; title of collection; first and last page numbers; publisher; place of publication., in the order given in the example below.

Tajfel, H., & Turner, J.C. (1979). An integrative theory of inter-group conflict. In: W.G. Austin & S. Worchel (Eds.), *The social psychology of inter-group relations*, pp. 33-57. Monterey (CA): Brooks/Cole.

References to articles in conference proceedings should include the author's name; year of publication; article title; editor's name (if any); title of proceedings; first and last page numbers; place and date of conference; publisher and/or organization from which the proceedings can be obtained; place of publication, in the order given in the example below.

Hess, T., & Vonk, T. (1988). Developing a new instrument for quantitative research into financial services. In: *Research for financial services conference proceedings*, pp. 55-74. Amsterdam: ESOMAR.

References to articles in periodicals should include the author's name; year of publication; article title; full title of periodical; volume number (issue number where appropriate); first and last page numbers, in the order given in the example below.

Gunnarson, J., & Wahlund, R. (1997). Household financial strategies in Sweden: An exploratory study. *Journal of Economic Psychology*, 18, 201-234.

References to technical reports or doctoral dissertations should include the author's name; year of publication; title of report or dissertation; institution; location of institution.

Nyhus, E.K. (1996). *The VSB-CentER Savings Project: Data collection methods, questionnaires and sampling procedures.* Tilburg: CentER for Economic Research. VSB-CentER Savings Project Progress Report 42.

Proofs
Proofs will be sent to the corresponding author. One corrected proof, together with the riginal, edited manuscript, should be returned to the Publisher within three days of receipt by mail (airmail overseas).

Offprints
Fifty offprints of each article will be provided free of charge. Additional offprints can be ordered by means of an offprint order form supplied with the proofs. An order form for additional offprints will be sent to the corresponding author.

Page Charges and Colour Figures
No page charges are levied on authors or their institutions. Colour figures are published at the author's expense only.

Copyright
Authors will be asked, upon acceptance of an article, to transfer copyright of the article to the Publisher. This will ensure the widest possible dissemination of information under copyright laws.

Permissions
It is the responsibility of the author to obtain written permission for a quotation from unpublished material, or for all quotations in excess of 250 words in one extract or 500 words in total from any work still in copyright, and for the reprinting of figures, tables or poems from unpublished or copyrighted material.

Additional Information
Additional information can be obtained from:
Acquisition Editor *Journal of Consumer Policy* Business & Economics Kluwer Academic Publishers, P.O. Box 990, 3300 AA Dordrecht, The Netherlands
Tel.: +31 (0)78 6392157, Fax: +31 (0)78 6392350

or from the homepage of the *Journal of Consumer Policy* at:
http://www.wkap.nl/journalhome.htm/0342-5843

Journal of Consumer Psychology

ADDRESS FOR SUBMISSION:

Paul Herr, Editor
Journal of Consumer Psychology
University of Colorado
Graduate School of Business
Department of Marketing
Box 419
Boulder, CO 80309-0419
USA
Phone: 303-492-2379
Fax: 303-492-5692
E-Mail: paul.herr@colorado.edu
Web: www.erlbaum.com/journals
Address May Change:

PUBLICATION GUIDELINES:

Manuscript Length: 30+
Copies Required: Five
Computer Submission: No
Format: N/A
Fees to Review: 0.00 US$

Manuscript Style:
American Psychological Association

CIRCULATION DATA:

Reader: Academics
Frequency of Issue: Quarterly
Copies per Issue: Less than 1,000
Sponsor/Publisher: Lawrence Erlbaum
  Associates
Subscribe Price: 75.00 US$ Individual
  575.00 US$ Institution
  67.50 US$ Individual/Electronic

REVIEW INFORMATION:

Type of Review: Blind Review
No. of External Reviewers: 3
No. of In House Reviewers: 0
Acceptance Rate: 11-20%
Time to Review: 2 - 3 Months
Reviewers Comments: Yes
Invited Articles: 0-5%
Fees to Publish: 0.00 US$

MANUSCRIPT TOPICS:
Consumer Behavior; Marketing Research; Marketing Theory & Applications

MANUSCRIPT GUIDELINES/COMMENTS:

Editorial Scope
This journal is devoted to advancing consumer psychology as a dynamic discipline by disseminating knowledge generated and contributed by scholars from a variety of backgrounds, substantive fields, and methodological orientations. It publishes papers providing theoretical analyses, critical reviews, original empirical reports, as well as methodological contributions that shape thought and practice in the discipline of consumer psychology. Topics covered include: the role of advertising, the development and change of consumer attitudes; judgment, choice and decision processes; direct brand experience; post-purchase evaluations; social cognition research; consumer socialization; motivational processes; salespersons' influences; and behavioral decision research.

Audience

Professionals in advertising, marketing, and public relations; researchers in social psychology and related disciplines.

Instructions to Contributors

Manuscripts should be prepared following the style in the *Publication Manual of the American Psychological Association (4th ed.)*. All components of the manuscript should be typed double-spaced, including title page, abstract, text, quotes, acknowledgments, references, appendices, tables, figure captions, and footnotes. The abstract should be no more than 1,000 characters in length (counting spaces between words). A stamped, self-addressed envelope should be included for acknowledgment that a manuscript has been received.

Journal of Consumer Psychology follows a double-blind review policy. To facilitate anonymous review, only the article title should appear on the first page of the manuscript. An attached cover page must contain the title, authorship, and an introductory footnote with professional titles and mailing addresses of the authors and any statements of credit to research support.

Authors are responsible for all statements made in their work and for obtaining permission from copyright owners to reprint or adapt a table or figure or reprint a quotation of 500 words or more. Authors should write to the original author(s) and publisher to request nonexclusive world rights in all languages to use the material in the article and in future editions. Provide copies of all languages and of all permissions and credit lines.

In a cover letter, authors should state that the findings reported in the manuscript have not been published previously and that the manuscript is not being simultaneously submitted elsewhere. Authors should also state that they have complied with American Psychological Association ethical standards in the treatment of their samples.

Four complete title pages, along with four copies of the manuscript prepared for blind review should be submitted to the Editor at the above address.

Journal of Consumer Research

ADDRESS FOR SUBMISSION:

David Glen Mick, Editor
Journal of Consumer Research
University of Wisconsin
School of Business
975 University Avenue
Madison, WI 53706
USA
Phone: 608-263-4264
Fax: 608-262-0394
E-Mail: dmick@bus.wisc.edu
Web:
Address May Change: 12/31/02

PUBLICATION GUIDELINES:

Manuscript Length: 40 Maximum
Copies Required: Five
Computer Submission: No
Format: N/A
Fees to Review: 0.00 US$

Manuscript Style:
    See Manuscript Guidelines

CIRCULATION DATA:

Reader: Academics
Frequency of Issue: Quarterly
Copies per Issue: 3,001 - 4,000
Sponsor/Publisher: 12 Professional
    Academic Associations
Subscribe Price: 90.00 US$
    45.00 US$ Member
    25.00 US$ Student

REVIEW INFORMATION:

Type of Review: Blind Review
No. of External Reviewers: 3
No. of In House Reviewers: 0
Acceptance Rate: 11-20%
Time to Review: 2 - 3 Months
Reviewers Comments: Yes
Invited Articles: 0-5%
Fees to Publish: 0.00 US$

MANUSCRIPT TOPICS:
Advertising & Promotion Management; Communication; Cross Discipline Studies of Consumer Behavior; Direct Marketing; Global Business; Marketing Research; Marketing Theory & Applications; Non Profit Organizations; Organizational Behavior & Theory; Services; Technology/Innovation

MANUSCRIPT GUIDELINES/COMMENTS:

The Journal
Twenty-five years ago in the inaugural issue of the *Journal of Consumer Research*, Ronald Frank, the first editor, stated that the journal's "primary objective is to serve as an interdisciplinary communications vehicle for theory, empirical research, and methodology of the study of consumer behavior" (1974, p. iv). Over the years, the goal of interdisciplinarity has endured as the journal's principal strength (Kernan 1995). Although opinions differ about the extent to which this goal is being met, there is unmistakable evidence from the last decade that JCR is increasingly drawing from, and striving harder to contribute to, a diversity of perspectives, topics, and methods across the social sciences, humanities, and professional areas. Because of its ecumenical spirit and uncompromising standards-fostered by its

founders, policy board, editors, reviewers, and authors--the *Journal of Consumer Research* has achieved an indisputable prestige as the premier international outlet for inquiry on consumer behavior.

As I undertake the editor's role in July 1999, I intend to reinforce and, where possible, improve upon this tradition. The journal will continue to seek manuscripts reflecting the broadest possible range of cutting-edge consumer research; evaluate each according to rigorous and paradigmatically-appropriate criteria; and publish those that present the most impactful new learning about consumer behavior. The foremost criterion in judging submitted manuscripts will be the degree to which knowledge of important consumer behavior issues has been extended. As always, JCR will continue to champion those manuscripts that aspire to major and long-lasting, rather than incremental and short-term, advances.

The Review Process
The structure of the review process--involving a dedicated team of associate editors--will parallel the one implemented by the two most recent editors, Brian Sternthal and Robert Burnkrant. The primary merit of this structure is to ensure high-quality reviews, fair and justifiable decisions, and constructive feedback for authors. Nine associate editors, whose expertise in consumer research spans an array of theoretical, substantive, and methodological domains, will assist me in the review process. They are Punam Anand Keller, Eric Arnould, William Bearden, Merrie Brucks, John Deighton, Wayne Hoyer, Joel Huber, Michael Johnson, and Wagner Kamakura. I am pleased and fortunate to have these experienced scholars join me in carrying out the journal's editorial duties.

When a manuscript is received, I will assign it to an associate editor and choose appropriate reviewers after consultation with the associate editor. Typically, three reviewers will be assigned to a manuscript, although as few as two or as many as four may be used in some cases. After the reviews are completed, the associate editor will develop a report based on the reviews and the associate editor's independent assessment of the manuscript. Combining these inputs with my own reading of the manuscript, I will then decide whether to accept, reject, or invite revision of the manuscript. This decision and its basis will be communicated to the authors, reviewers, and associate editor. The chief objectives in all feedback to authors will be to provide clear explanation for the decision and to offer explicit guidance, if appropriate, on how the manuscript might be improved.

Enhancing Value and Innovativeness
My top priority in editing JCR will be to enhance its value and innovativeness for all authors and readers. Although the journal rightfully prides itself on being the most interdisciplinary and path-breaking source of new knowledge on consumer behavior, these revered qualities could be further cultivated. They are especially important to nurture at this time as the number of total pages per issue has been compressed in recent years.

Following past trends, theoretically-oriented empirical work is likely to remain the modal category of articles appearing in the journal. However, I particularly want to encourage and publish research of the following kinds:

- Innovative conceptual papers and integrative literature reviews, as both of these types of articles have been among the most influential in the journal historically

- Cross-paradigmatic, transdisciplinary, or multimethod projects, i.e., melding different doctrines, techniques, or types of data

- Research that addresses conventional or "matured" topics (e.g., decision making and choice, advertising response, diffusion of innovations) in novel or unusual ways

- Articles that introduce, develop, and apply new theories

- Research that draws increased attention to, and expands understanding of, previously undervalued substantive topics

- Articles that focus on the welfare of consumers, broadly construed

- Meta-analyses of large or growing streams of research

- Articles that provide new methods (data collection or analysis, quantitative or qualitative) that are demonstrated to have key advantages over existing methods

During the next several months I will also be considering and planning some new developments at the journal to increase its intellectual benefits. Two of these come under the rubric of reviews and reflections. The first would involve invited essays by leading consumer scholars on new books that have had a significant impact on their current thinking and research. The second would involve invited essays by distinguished researchers who have not published before in JCR, but whose pioneering work in their respective fields (e.g., economics, psychology, philosophy, folklore, women's studies) has definitive relevance to consumer behavior. They will summarize their past and present work as it relates to theoretical and substantive knowledge of consumer behavior, and propose valuable directions for future research. Among other positive outcomes, both forms of these invited essays should have the salutary effect of enlarging the circle of interactions and insights among all consumer researchers.

Conclusion

Details about the submission of new or revised manuscripts, as the transition of the editorial office is finalized, will appear in the front pages of the June 1999 issue of JCR. In the meantime, I must acknowledge that it is an immense honor and responsibility to be entrusted with the editorship of the Journal of Consumer Research. We all owe considerable gratitude to Bob Burnkrant and the prior editors for their legacies of leadership and scholarship at JCR. I also have appreciated their helpful advice as the journal prepares to move to a new editorial home. I am inspired by the opportunity to make a contribution to the field of consumer behavior and to be a part of the rich heritage of our esteemed journal.

David Glen Mick
Editor

References

Frank, Ronald E. (1974), "The Journal of Consumer Research: An Introduction," *Journal of Consumer Research*, 1 (1), iv-v.

Kernan, Jerome B. (1995), "Framing a Rainbow, Focusing the Light: JCR's First Twenty Years," in *Advances in Consumer Research*, Volume 22, eds. Frank R. Kardes and Mita Sujan, Provo, UT: Association for Consumer Research, 488-496.

Journal of Convention & Exhibition Management

ADDRESS FOR SUBMISSION:

JeAnna Lanza Abbott, Editor
Journal of Convention & Exhibition
 Management
University of Houston
Conrad N. Hilton College
4800 Calhoun
Houston, TX 77204-3902
USA
Phone: 713-743-2413
Fax: 713-743-2552
E-Mail: jabbot@uh.edu
Web:
Address May Change:

PUBLICATION GUIDELINES:

Manuscript Length: 16-20
Copies Required: Four
Computer Submission: Yes
Format: MS Word 95
Fees to Review: 0.00 US$

Manuscript Style:
 American Psychological Association

CIRCULATION DATA:

Reader: Business Persons, Academic
Frequency of Issue: Quarterly
Copies per Issue: 5,001 - 10,000
Sponsor/Publisher: Haworth Press, Inc.
Subscribe Price: 145.00 US$

REVIEW INFORMATION:

Type of Review: Blind Review
No. of External Reviewers: 3
No. of In House Reviewers: 1
Acceptance Rate: 11-20%
Time to Review: 1 - 2 Months
Reviewers Comments: Yes
Invited Articles: 0-5%
Fees to Publish: 0.00 US$

MANUSCRIPT TOPICS:
Advertising & Promotion Management; Convention/Exhibition; Direct Marketing; Global Business; Marketing Research

MANUSCRIPT GUIDELINES/COMMENTS:

1. Original Articles Only. Submission of a manuscript to this Journal represents a certification on the part of the author(s) that it is an original work, and that neither this manuscript nor a version of it has been published elsewhere nor is being considered for publication elsewhere.

2. Manuscript Length. Your manuscript may be approximately 5-50 typed pages double-spaced (including references and abstract.) Lengthier manuscripts may be considered, but only at the discretion of the Editor. Sometimes, lengthier manuscripts may be considered if they can be divided up into sections for publication in successive journal issues.

3. Manuscript Style. References, citations, and general style of manuscripts for this Journal should follow the APA style (as outlined in the lates edition of the *Publication Manual of the American Psychological Association* Fourth Edition, 1994). References should be double-spaced and placed in alphabetical order.

If an author wishes to submit a paper that has been already prepared in another style, he or she may do so. However, if the paper is accepted (with or without reviewer's alterations), the author is fully responsible for retyping the manuscript in the correct style as indicated above. Neither the Editor nor the Publisher is responsible for re-preparing manuscript copy to adhere to the Journal's style.

4. Manuscript Preparation.
Margins: leave at least a one-inch margin on all four sides.
Paper: use clean white, 8-1/2" x 11" bond paper.
Number of copies: 4 (the original plus three photocopies).
Cover page: *Important*—staple a cover page to the manuscript, indicating only the article title (this is used for anonymous refereeing).
Second "title page": enclose a regular title page but do not staple it to the manuscript. Include the title again, plus:
- full authorship
- an ABSTRACT of about 100 words. (Below the abstract provide 3-1 0 key words for index purposes).
- an introductory footnote with authors' academic degrees, professional titles, affiliations, mailing addresses, and any desired acknowledgment of research support or other credit.

5. Return Envelopes. When you submit your four manuscript copies, also include:
- A regular envelope, stamped and self-addressed. This is for the Editor to send you an "acknowledgement of receipt" letter.
- Manuscripts will not be returned.

6. Spelling, Grammar, and Punctuation. You are responsible for preparing manuscript copy which is clearly written in acceptable scholarly English, and which contains no errors of spelling, grammar, or punctuation. Neither the Editor nor the Publisher is responsible for correcting errors of spelling and grammar: the manuscript, after acceptance by the Editor, must be immediately ready for typesetting as it is finally submitted by the author(s). Check your paper for the following common errors:
- dangling modifiers
- misplaced modifiers
- unclear antecedents
- incorrect or inconsistent abbreviations

Also, check the accuracy of all arithmetic calculations, statistics, numerical data, text citations, and references.

7. Inconsistencies Must Be Avoided. Be sure you are consistent in your use of abbreviations, terminology, and in citing references, from one part of your paper to another.

8. Preparation Of Tables, Figures, and Illustrations. All tables, figures, illustrations, etc. must be "camera-ready." That is, they must be cleanly typed or artistically prepared so that they can be used either exactly as they are or else used after a photographic reduction in size. Figures, tables, and illustrations must be prepared on separate sheets of paper. Always use black ink and professional drawing instruments. On the back of these items, write your article title and the journal title lightly in pencil, so they do not get misplaced. In text, skip extra lines and indicate where these figures and tables are to be placed (please **do not write** on face of art). Photographs are considered part of the acceptable manuscript and remain with Publisher for use in additional printings. If submitted art cannot be used, the Publisher reserves the right to redo the art and to charge the author a fee of $35.00 per hour for this service.

9. Alterations Required By Referees And Reviewers. Many times a paper is accepted by the Editor contingent upon changes that are mandated by anonymous specialist referees and members of the Editorial Board. If the Editor returns your manuscript for revisions, you are responsible for retyping any sections of the paper to incorporate these revisions (if applicable, revisions should also be put on disk).

10. Typesetting. You will not be receiving galley proofs of your article. Editorial revisions, if any, must therefore be made while your article is still in manuscript. The final version of the manuscript will be the version you see published. Typesetter's errors will be corrected by the production staff of The Haworth Press. Authors are expected to submit manuscripts, disks, and art that are free from error.

11. Electronic Media. Haworth's in-house type-setting unit is able to utilize your final manuscript material as prepared on most personal computers and word processors. This will minimize typographical errors and decrease overall production time lag. Please send the first draft and final draft copies of your manuscript to the journal Editor in print format for his/her final review and approval. **After approval of** your final manuscript, please submit the final approved version both on printed format ("hard copy") and floppy diskette. On the outside of the diskette package write:
A. the brand name of your computer or word processor
B. the word-processing program that you used
C. the title of your article, and
D. file name

Note: Disk and hard copy must agree. In case of discrepancies, it is The Haworth Press's policy to follow hard copy. Authors are advised that no revisions of the manuscript can be made after acceptance by the Editor for publication. The benefits of this procedure are many with speed and accuracy being the most obvious. We look forward to working with you on this, knowing we will be able to serve you more efficiently in the future.

12. Reprints. The senior author will receive two copies of the journal issue and 25 complimentary reprints of his or her article. The junior author will receive two copies of the journal issue. These are sent several weeks after the journal issue is published and in circulation. An order form for the purchase of additional reprints will also be sent to all authors at this time. (Approximately 4-6 weeks is necessary for the preparation of reprints.)

Please do not query the Journal's Editor about reprints. All such questions should be sent directly to:

The Haworth Press, Inc., Production Department, 21 East Broad Street, West Hazleton, PA 18201

To order additional reprints (minimum: 50 copies), please contact:
The Haworth Document Delivery Center, 10 Alice Street, Binghamton, NY 13904-1580
1-800-342-9678 or Fax (607) 722-6362.

13. Copyright. Copyright ownership of your manuscript must be transferred officially to The Haworth Press, Inc., before we can begin the peer-review process. The Editor's letter acknowledging receipt of the manuscript will be accompanied by a form fully explaining this. All authors must sign the form and return the original to the Editor as soon as possible. Failure to return the copyright form in a timely fashion will result in delay in review and subsequent publication.

Journal of Current Issues & Research in Advertising

ADDRESS FOR SUBMISSION:

Claude R. Martin, Jr., Co-Editor and
Journal of Current Issues & Research in
   Advertising
James H. Leigh, Co-Editor
1116 Aberdeen Drive
Ann Arbor, MI 48104
USA
Phone: 734-971-1897
Fax: 734-971-1897
E-Mail: crmartin@umich.edu
Web:
Address May Change:

PUBLICATION GUIDELINES:

Manuscript Length: 16-30
Copies Required: Five
Computer Submission: Yes
Format: Mac/Dos/OCA/RTF
Fees to Review: 0.00 US$

Manuscript Style:
   See Manuscript Guidelines

CIRCULATION DATA:

Reader: Academics, Business Persons,
   Government
Frequency of Issue: 2 Times/Year
Copies per Issue: 1,001 - 2,000
Sponsor/Publisher: CTC Press
Subscribe Price: 20.00 US$ to 40 US$

REVIEW INFORMATION:

Type of Review: Blind Review
No. of External Reviewers: 3
No. of In House Reviewers: 2
Acceptance Rate: 6-10%
Time to Review: 2 - 3 Months
Reviewers Comments: Yes
Invited Articles: 6-10%
Fees to Publish: 0.00 US$

MANUSCRIPT TOPICS:
Advertising & Promotion Management; Communication; Direct Marketing; Services

MANUSCRIPT GUIDELINES/COMMENTS:

The process of typesetting *The Journal of Current Issues and Research in Advertising* is computerized. Thus, authors are requested to submit the final copy of their manuscript in computer readable format. Below are the specifications for doing so.

Alternatives for Manuscript Submission
The vast majority of accepted articles for JCIRA were prepared on personal computers. In most cases, the files created for these documents can be read directly into the typesetting program. Papers can be submitted in most word processing formats commonly used on either the Macintosh or IBM/Compatible families of computers.

For the IBM/Compatible computers, files can be submitted on a 3½" floppy (either 750K or 1.44M). Files created on the following word processors are acceptable: Word Perfect,

Multimate, Word Star, Microsoft Word, and XYWrite In addition, DCA and RTF files are acceptable.

Macintosh files can be submitted on a 3 ½" floppy (either 400 or 8110 K). Files created on the following word processors are acceptable: Microsoft Word, Word Perfect, and MacWrite. In addition, DCA and RTF files are acceptable. It is possible that other word processing files are acceptable. Please call CtC Press should you have questions regarding the software package used to create your documents.

If you do not have access to an IBM/Compatible or Macintosh computer (or for some other reason, wish not to submit your manuscript on diskette), a hard copy of the paper may be submitted. CtC will key in the manuscript (at the price of $7.00 per typed, double-spaced page). If you choose this option, please send the typed paper and your prepayment to CtC Press.

Preparing the File
The original word processing file used to produce the document should be adequate for submission. There is no need to adjust margins, tab stops, etc., since these are not retained in the file translation. The hard copy may follow any formal you choose; however, a few simple rules must be followed in formatting the disk:

- Make absolutely sure all references are in the proper style (see examples below).

- If possible, save without "hard returns" at the end of each line.

- Type everything in upper/lower case letters (e.g., titles should not be in all caps). Please do not set titles in bold face or italics (on disk).

- Avoid using footnotes. All material should be integrated into the text of the manuscript. If this creates major problems for the readability of the manuscript, place them at the end of the paper under the heading "Endnotes."

- Create two additional tiles. One should contain the abstract of the paper (no more than 100 words), and the other should contain the authors' description (in paragraph form, the name of the author, position/title, institutional affiliation, and acknowledgments).

References
References should be entered in accordance with the following examples:

Crissy, William J. E. and Robert M. Kaplan (1969), <u>Salesmanship The Personal Force in Marketing</u>, New York: John Wiley & Sons.

Enis, Ben M. and Lawrence B. Chonko (1979), "A Review of Personal Selling: Implications for Managers and Researchers," In <u>Review of Marketing</u>: 1978. Gerald Zaltman and Thomas V. Bonoma, eds., Chicago: American Marketing Association, 23-32.

Ingram, Thomas N. and Danny N. Bellenger (1983), "Personal and Organizational Variables: Their Relative Effect on Reward Valences of Industrial Salespeople," *Journal of Marketing Research*, 20 (May), 198-205.

Please note the month and not the number is used in designating issues.
Also, publication titles are underlined but not placed in bold, or in all caps,

Figures and Tables
In most cases, the camera-ready art for tables/figures will be created by CtC Press. To assist in this process, please submit a separate word processing file for each figure with all of the text contained in the figure (i.e., type Into this file the titles, labels, etc., without concern for any boxes, circles, arrows, etc.). This text will then be used to create the figure. If complex figures are to be used, please submit an original laser copy (preferably 600 dpi or greater) along with your hard copy.

Each table should be Included as a separate file. Within each row, numbers or text tram one column should be separated from numbers or text in the next column by tabs. If a table editor has been used to create your table(s), you must remove them from this format and make certain that your columns are separated by tabs in their correct order. This may look incorrect when formatting your disk, but CtC will use your hard copy to align columns correctly in the formatted version.

In some cases it may be necessary to use your original hard copy for tables or figures. Please submit the highest resolution copy possible for all tables and figures.

Final Checklist
Please make sure that you have enclosed the disk containing the appropriate number of files appropriately formatted.

Label this disk with:
- The name, address, telephone and fax number, and e-mail address of the contact person;
- The word processor and version used to create the file;
- The words "The Journal of Current Issues and Research in Advertising."

Send one hard copy of the paper and the computer disk to CtC Press/ Publisher Services, P.O. Box 936, Winnsboro, SC 29180. It is not necessary to express mail manuscripts to CtC Press unless requested by the editor. In such cases, please contact CtC Press for the correct street address for express mail packages.

Send one hard copy of the paper to the editor of JCIRA.

Publisher Notes
Failure to prepare manuscript according to these guidelines may result in delays in its publication.

The contact author will be given the opportunity to inspect the entire formatted manuscript prior to publication. It shall be the responsibility of the contact author to fax the manuscript to other authors, if necessary. Do not ask CtC to fax the article to multiple authors.

Please do not contact CtC regarding publication dates for manuscripts. Such information may be obtained by contacting the editor(s).

Journal of Database Marketing

ADDRESS FOR SUBMISSION:

May Cornfield, Editor
Journal of Database Marketing
Henry Stewart Publications
Museum House
25 Museum Street
London, WC1A 1JT
UK
Phone: 44 171 323 2916
Fax: 44 171 323 2918
E-Mail: submissions@hspublications.co.uk
Web: www.henrystewart.com/journals
Address May Change:

CIRCULATION DATA:

Reader: , 65% Business, 35% Academic
Frequency of Issue: Quarterly
Copies per Issue: 1,001 - 2,000
Sponsor/Publisher: Henry Stewart Publications
Subscribe Price: 300.00 US$ N. America
190.00 Pounds Europe
205.00 Pounds Rest of World

PUBLICATION GUIDELINES:

Manuscript Length: 2,500-5,000 words
Copies Required: Three
Computer Submission: Yes
Format: MS Word/WordPerfect
Fees to Review: 0.00 US$

Manuscript Style:
, Vancouver Referencing System

REVIEW INFORMATION:

Type of Review: Blind Review
No. of External Reviewers: 3
No. of In House Reviewers: 2
Acceptance Rate: 50%
Time to Review: 1 - 2 Months
Reviewers Comments: Yes
Invited Articles: 31-50%
Fees to Publish: 0.00 US$

MANUSCRIPT TOPICS:

Advertising & Promotion Management; Business Education; Communication; Direct Marketing; Global Business; Marketing Theory & Applications; Non Profit Organizations; Operations Research/Statistics; Organizational Behavior & Theory; Organizational Development; Strategic Management Policy

MANUSCRIPT GUIDELINES/COMMENTS:

1. Contributions should be between 2,000 and 5,000 words in length. All submissions should be typewritten and double-spaced.

2. The Journal's Editors and Editorial Board particularly welcome submissions which present case study material, new approaches, techniques, empirical research or conceptual papers.

3. All articles should be accompanied by a short abstract outlining the paper's aims and subject matter.

4. All articles should be accompanied by up to six keywords.

5. Articles should be accompanied by a short (about 80 words) description of the author(s) and, if appropriate, the organization of which he or she is a member.

6. Authors should not seek to use the Journal as a vehicle for marketing any specific product or service.

7. Authors should avoid the use of language or slang which is not in keeping with the professional and academic style of the Journal.

8. Titles of organizations etc should be written out first in full and thereafter in initials.

9. Articles should be supported by references. For all Henry Stewart Journals excluding *Corporate Reputation Review*, *Tourism and Hospitality Research*, *Journal of Fashion Marketing and Management*, *Journal of Small Business and Enterprise Development*, *Journal of Asset Management* and *International Journal of Police Science Management*, these should be set out in accordance with the Vancouver referencing system. References for the Journals listed above should be set out in accordance with the Harvard referencing system.

10. Photographs and illustrations supporting articles should be submitted where appropriate. Photographs should be good quality positives, printed from the original negatives and preferably in black and white only. Figures and other line illustrations should be submitted in good quality originals and a copy of the data should also be included.

11. Authors must ensure that references to named people and/or organizations are accurate, not rascist or sexist and without libellous implications.

12. All contributions sent to the Publisher, whether invited or not, will be submitted to the Journal's Editors and Editorial Board. Any such contribution must bear the author's full name and address, even if this is not for publication. Contributions, whether published pseudonymously or not, are accepted on the strict understanding that the author is responsible for the accuracy of all opinion, technical comment, factual report, data, figures, illustrations and photographs. Publication does not necessarily imply that these are the opinions of the Editorial Board, Editors or the Publisher, nor does the Board, Editors or Publisher accept any liability for the accuracy of such comment, report and other technical and factual information. The Publisher will, however, strive to ensure that all opinion, comments, reports, data, figures, illustrations and photographs are accurate, insofar as it is within its abilities to do so. The Publisher reserves the right to edit, abridge or omit material submitted for publication.

13. All Articles submitted for publication will be subject to a double-blind refereeing procedure.

14. The author bears the responsibility for checking whether material submitted is subject to copyright or ownership rights, eg photographs, illustrations, trade literature and data. Where use is so restricted, the Publisher must be informed with the submission of the material.

15. No contribution will be accepted which has been published elsewhere, unless it is expressly invited or agreed by the Publisher. Articles and contributions published become the copyright of the Publisher, unless otherwise agreed.

16. All reasonable efforts are made to ensure accurate reproduction of text, photographs and illustrations. The Publisher does not accept responsibility for mistakes, be they editorial or typographical, nor for consequences resulting from them.

17. Submissions should be sent to Henry Stewart Publications. **Please clearly state for which journal you are contributing.**

Journal of Electronic Commerce

ADDRESS FOR SUBMISSION:

Dan Ferguson, Editor
Journal of Electronic Commerce
Faulkner & Gray EC Research
300 South Wacker Drive
Chicago, IL 60606-6680
USA
Phone: 312-983-6138
Fax: 312-922-3363
E-Mail: dferguson@mediaone.net
Web:
Address May Change:

PUBLICATION GUIDELINES:

Manuscript Length: 6-10
Copies Required: One
Computer Submission: Yes
Format: PC/MS Word/WdPerfect
Fees to Review: 0.00 US$

Manuscript Style:
    Chicago Manual of Style

CIRCULATION DATA:

Reader: Business Persons
Frequency of Issue: Quarterly
Copies per Issue: 5,001 - 10,000
Sponsor/Publisher: Faulkner & Gray
Subscribe Price: 195.00 US$ 1 Year
    650.00 US$ Ref.Library+ 1yr.Subscript

REVIEW INFORMATION:

Type of Review: Editorial Review
No. of External Reviewers: 0
No. of In House Reviewers: 1
Acceptance Rate: 21-30%
Time to Review: 4 - 6 Months
Reviewers Comments: No
Invited Articles: 50% +
Fees to Publish: 0.00 US$

MANUSCRIPT TOPICS:
Business Information Systems (MIS); E-commerce; Electronic Data Interchange; Internet Commerce

MANUSCRIPT GUIDELINES/COMMENTS:

Tapping into the knowledge of the seasoned professionals, *The Journal of Electronic Commerce* is the premier professional journal serving the EDI and EC market place. The sharing of information and experience is the cornerstone of electronic commerce and 3-business, and *The Journal of Electronic Commerce* is the industry leader, providing insight, in-depth analysis of emerging technologies and comprehensive case studies of EDI and electronic commerce technology implementations. Only the Journal provides you with access to the most objective analytical and professionally written documentation of EDI and electronic commerce issues and experiences that affect you and your business.

How To Contribute An Article to EDI Forum: the Journal of Electronic Commerce
Start by contacting one of the Forum's editors and submitting to them an article outline or an abstract that describes the topic and the scope of the issues you plan to cover. Following this submission, an editor will contact you in order to let you know if the subject matter is

appropriate for the journal. If the article idea is accepted, the editor will establish a working schedule with you for its publication. If you are interested in submitting an article, please contact the forum at least four months prior to the issue of publication. In general, the deadline for articles is three months prior to the issue of publication. All articles submitted should include a typed version of the manuscript, all appropriate photographs and/or diagrams, a diskette copy (WordPerfect or ASCII format) of the manuscript, and a photo of the author.

Article Guidelines: Contributed features generally range from 3,000 to 6,000 words (10 to 20 typed, double spaced pages). They should be as long as necessary to cover the topic fully and in-depth. These articles should be accurate, original, logical, and focus on the technology or application being covered in a non-commercial manner.

The types of articles published in the Forum typically fall into one of six categories:

Application or Case History: This type of article presents an example of how a technology is being applied in a real-world setting. Feature articles of this type should generally focus on: How is EDI or electronic commerce being done at the present time (or prior to using the technology)? What alternatives were explored? What stages of development did you have to go through? What were some of the problems encountered when implementing? What benefits are now being reaped?

History and Standards: Articles of this type focus on the development and therefore the history of electronic data interchange and electronic commerce. They also can cover issues relating to standards setting, including features on individual transaction sets in X12 or EDIFACT, issues in standards development, and proprietary or industry standards.

Technology Focus or Update: This type of article focuses on a specific technology and provides information on what the technology is, how it works, its features and benefits, and what are its uses and application in the field of EDI and electronic commerce. These articles should provide an unbiased review of significant techniques or technology. These articles often provide actual examples of how the technology is being utilized in a real-world environment.

Comparative Technology: Articles of this type generally focus on comparing the strengths/weaknesses, features, benefits, advantages/disadvantages, and applications of different technologies. These articles should give special attention to the different types of applications for which each technology compared is best suited.

Research Findings: This type of article presents the key findings to research done in the areas of electronic commerce and EDI. The methods of research should be presented as well as analysis given to how these findings might impact the future of the technology.

Global Insights: These articles present news of EDI and electronic commerce activity outside the United States and discuss those global EDI issues that directly affect EDI implementors in the United States. Its can also discuss the use of electronic commerce in cross-border applications. Significant savings are often realized through the implementation of EDI in international trade and transport. We seek to publish the stories behind these implementations.

As mentioned previously, if you are interested in writing on one of these topics, contact a Forum editor at least 4 months prior to the issue of publication. The deadline for articles submitted is three months prior to the issue of publication.

Authors warrant, that unless otherwise stated, the work they submit is original.

Photography and Artwork: Any photography, charts, diagrams, tables. etc., that will enhance the reader's understanding of the information being presented should be included with the finished manuscript. Photography, either color or black and white, can be accepted in any format. (High quality, 35-mm. slides or transparencies preferred.) Artwork should be sent in a camera-ready format, if possible. However, if this is not possible, our production houses can usually recreate a camera-ready version of the figure. Please discuss this with the editor with whom you are working. Authors should provide captions for all artwork submitted on a separate piece of paper. Do not write on the front surface of the artwork.

Journal of Euromarketing

ADDRESS FOR SUBMISSION:

Erdener Kaynak, Executive Editor
Journal of Euromarketing
International Business Press Journals
PO Box 399
Middletown, PA 17057
USA
Phone: 717-566-3054
Fax: 717-566-8589
E-Mail: k9x@psu.edu
Web: www.haworthpress.com
Address May Change:

PUBLICATION GUIDELINES:

Manuscript Length: 5-20
Copies Required: Three
Computer Submission: Yes
Format: WordPerfect 5.1 or above
Fees to Review: 0.00 US$

Manuscript Style:
    American Psychological Association

CIRCULATION DATA:

Reader: Academics
Frequency of Issue: Quarterly
Copies per Issue: Less than 1,000
Sponsor/Publisher: Haworth Pres, Inc.
Subscribe Price: 65.00 US$ Individual
    125.00 US$ Institution
    300.00 US$ Library

REVIEW INFORMATION:

Type of Review: Blind Review
No. of External Reviewers: 2
No. of In House Reviewers: 1
Acceptance Rate: 21-30%
Time to Review: 1 - 2 Months
Reviewers Comments: Yes
Invited Articles: 0-5%
Fees to Publish: 0.00 US$

MANUSCRIPT TOPICS:
Advertising & Promotion Management; Communication; Direct Marketing; European Marketing; Global Business; Marketing Research; Marketing Theory & Applications; Sales/Selling; Services

MANUSCRIPT GUIDELINES/COMMENTS:

Aims

The *Journal of Euromarketing* aims to meet the needs of academicians, practitioners, and public policymakers in the discussion of marketing issues pertaining to Europe. It helps to increase our understanding of the strategic planning aspects of marketing in Europe and the marketing aspects of the trading relationship between European and foreign firms.

Currently, there is a vacuum in the marketing literature which needs to be filled by relating the Europe factor to the global marketing scene, emphasizing the horizontal dimension as well as the inter- and intra-trade and marketing activities in Europe. As such, the *Journal of Euromarketing* covers the following areas of inquiry:

- functional areas of marketing in Europe and comparisons with the practices of those in other regions
- the dynamics that account for the linkage of European national markets into markets of the developing world, North and Latin America, the Far East, and Africa
- the best methods available for marketing goods and services in different socioeconomic, cultural, and legal-political environments of Europe at national and regional levels
- the method by which European marketing institutions are linked together into viable and coherent business systems
- the type of environmental factors prevailing in different European countries of the region which force changes in the marketing structure of the area countries
- the efficiency of the marketing system in performing its universal functions in the countries of Europe and strategies to overcome the weaknesses of the marketing system of the region
- the various stages of market and marketing system development in Europe as a working device for generalizing and possibly predicting likely developments in marketing in individual countries of the region

Instructions for Authors

1. Original Articles Only. Submission of a manuscript to this Journal represents a certification on the part of the author(s) that it is an original work, and that neither this manuscript nor a version of it has been published elsewhere nor is being considered for publication elsewhere.

2. Manuscript Length. Your manuscript may be approximately 5-20 typed pages double-spaced (including references and abstract). Lengthier manuscripts may be considered, but only at the discretion of the Editor. Sometimes, lengthier manuscripts may be considered if they can be divided up into sections for publication in successive Journal issues.

3. Manuscript Style. References, citations, and general style of manuscripts for this Journal should follow the Chicago style (as outlined in the latest edition of the *Manual of Style* of the University of Chicago Press). References should be double spaced and placed in alphabetical order.

4. Manuscript Preparation.
Margins: leave at least a one-inch margin on all four sides.
Paper: use clean white, 8 ½ " x 11" bond paper.
Number of copies: 4 (the original plus three photocopies).
Cover page: *Important* -- staple a cover page to the manuscript, indicating only the article title (this is used for anonymous refereeing).
Second "title page": enclose a regular title page but do not staple it to the manuscript. Include the title again, plus:
- full authorship
- an **abstract** of about 100 words. (Below the abstract provide 3-1 0 key words for index purposes).

- an introductory footnote with authors' academic degrees, professional titles, affiliations, mailing addresses, and any desired acknowledgment of research support or other credit.

5. Return Envelopes. When you submit your four manuscript copies, also include:
- a 9" by 12" envelope, self-addressed and stamped with sufficient postage to ensure return of your manuscript
- a regular envelope stamped and self-addressed. This is for the Editor to send you an "acknowledgement of receipt" letter.

6. Spelling, Grammar, and Punctuation. You are responsible for preparing manuscript copy which is clearly written in acceptable scholarly English, and which contains no errors of spelling, grammar, or punctuation. Neither the Editor nor the Publisher is responsible for correcting errors of spelling and grammar: the manuscript, after acceptance by the Editor, must be immediately ready for typesetting as it is finally submitted by the author(s). Check your paper for the following common errors:
- dangling modifiers
- misplaced modifiers
- unclear antecedents
- incorrect or inconsistent abbreviations

Also, check the accuracy of all arithmetic calculations, statistics, numerical data, text citations, and references.

7. Inconsistencies Must Be Avoided. Be sure you are consistent in your use of abbreviations, terminology, and in citing references, from one part of your paper to another.

8. Preparation of Tables, Figures, And Illustrations. All tables, figures, illustrations, etc. must be "camera-ready." That is, they must be cleanly typed or artistically prepared so that they can be used either exactly as they are or else used after a photographic reduction in size. Figures, tables, and illustrations must be prepared on separate sheets of paper. Always use black ink and professional drawing instruments. On the back of these items, write your article title and the journal title lightly in pencil, so they do not get misplaced. In text, skip extra lines and indicate where these figures and tables are to be placed (please **do not write** on face of art). Photographs are considered part of the acceptable manuscript and remain with Publisher for use in additional printings. If submitted art cannot be used, the Publisher reserves the right to redo the art and to charge the author a fee of $35.00 per hour for this service.

9. Alterations Required By Referees and Reviewers. Many times a paper is accepted by the Editor contingent upon changes that are mandated by anonymous specialist referees and members of the Editorial Board. If the Editor returns your manuscript for revisions, you are responsible for retyping any sections of the paper to incorporate these revisions (if applicable, revisions should also be put on disk).

10. Typesetting. You will not be receiving galley proofs of your article. Editorial revisions, if any, must therefore be made while your article is still in manuscript. The final version of the manuscript will be the version you see published. Typesetter's errors will be corrected by the production staff of The Haworth Press. Authors are expected to submit manuscripts, disks, and art that are free from error.

11. Electronic Media. Haworth's in-house type-setting unit is able to utilize your final manuscript material as prepared on most personal computers and word processors. This will minimize typographical errors and decrease overall production timelag. Please send the first draft and final draft copies of your manuscript to the journal Editor in print format for his/her final review and approval. **After approval of** your final manuscript, please submit the final approved version both on printed format ("hard copy") and floppy diskette. On the outside of the diskette package write:

A. the brand name of your computer or word processor
B. the word-processing program that you used
C. the title of your article, and
D. file name

Note: Disk and hard copy must agree. In case of discrepancies, it is The Haworth Press's policy to follow hard copy. Authors are advised that no revisions of the manuscript can be made after acceptance by the Editor for publication. The benefits of this procedure are many with speed and accuracy being the most obvious. We look forward to working with you on this, knowing we will be able to serve you more efficiently in the future.

12. Reprints. The senior author will receive two copies of the journal issue and 25 complimentary reprints of his or her article. The junior author will receive two copies of the journal issue. These are sent several weeks after the journal issue is published and in circulation. An order form for the purchase of additional reprints will also be sent to all authors at this time. (Approximately 4-6 weeks is necessary for the preparation of reprints.) Please do not query the Journal's Editor about reprints. All such questions should be sent directly to:

The Haworth Press, Inc., Production Department, 21 East Broad Street, West Hazleton, PA 18201

To order additional reprints (minimum: 50 copies), please contact: The Haworth Document Delivery Center, 10 Alice Street, Binghamton, NY 13904-1580 Phone: 1-800-342-9678 or Fax (607) 722-6362.

13. Copyright. Copyright ownership of your manuscript must be transferred officially to The Haworth Press, Inc., before we can begin the peer-review process. The Editor's letter acknowledging receipt of the manuscript will be accompanied by a form fully explaining this. All authors must sign the form and return the original to the Editor as soon as possible. Failure to return the copyright form in a timely fashion will result in delay in review and subsequent publication

Journal of Fashion Marketing and Management

ADDRESS FOR SUBMISSION:

Richard Jones, Editor
Journal of Fashion Marketing and Management
Manchester Metropolitan University
Dept. of Clothing Design & Technology
Old Hall Lane, Hollings Faculty
Manchester, M14 6HR
UK
Phone: 44 171 404 3040
Fax: 44 161 247 6329
E-Mail: submissions@hspublications.com
Web: www.henrystewart.co.uk
Address May Change:

PUBLICATION GUIDELINES:

Manuscript Length: 2,500-5,000 words
Copies Required: Three
Computer Submission: Yes
Format: MS Word/WordPerfect
Fees to Review: 0.00 US$

Manuscript Style:
  Uniform System of Citation (Harvard Blue Book)

CIRCULATION DATA:

Reader: , 65% Business, 35% Academic
Frequency of Issue: Quarterly
Copies per Issue: 1,001 - 2,000
Sponsor/Publisher: Henry Stewart Publications
Subscribe Price: 250.00 US$ Institution
  95.00 US$ Academic

REVIEW INFORMATION:

Type of Review: Blind Review
No. of External Reviewers: 3
No. of In House Reviewers: 2
Acceptance Rate: 50%
Time to Review: 1 - 2 Months
Reviewers Comments: Yes
Invited Articles: 31-50%
Fees to Publish: 0.00 US$

MANUSCRIPT TOPICS:
Advertising & Promotion Management; Direct Marketing; Global Business; Logistics; Marketing Research; Marketing Theory & Applications; Organizational Behavior & Theory; Public Administration; Sales/Selling; Small Business Entrepreneurship; Strategic Management Policy

MANUSCRIPT GUIDELINES/COMMENTS:

1. Contributions should be between 2,000 and 5,000 words in length. All submissions should be typewritten and double spaced.

2. The Journal's Editors and Editorial Board particularly welcome submissions which present case study material, new approaches, techniques, empirical research or conceptual papers.

3. All articles should be accompanied by a short abstract outlining the paper's aims and subject matter.

4. All articles should be accompanied by up to six keywords.

5. Articles should be accompanied by a short (about 80 words) description of the author(s) and, if appropriate, the organization of which he or she is a member.

6. Authors should not seek to use the Journal as a vehicle for marketing any specific product or service.

7. Authors should avoid the use of language or slang which is not in keeping with the professional and academic style of the Journal.

8. Titles of organizations etc should be written out first in full and thereafter in initials.

9. Articles should be supported by references. For all Henry Stewart Journals excluding *Corporate Reputation Review, Tourism and Hospitality Research, Journal of Fashion Marketing and Management, Journal of Small Business and Enterprise Development, Journal of Asset Management* and *International Journal of Police Science Management*, these should be set out in accordance with the Vancouver referencing system. References for the Journals listed above should be set out in accordance with the Harvard referencing system.

10. Photographs and illustrations supporting articles should be submitted where appropriate. Photographs should be good quality positives, printed from the original negatives and preferably in black and white only. Figures and other line illustrations should be submitted in good quality originals and a copy of the data should also be included.

11. Authors must ensure that references to named people and/or organizations are accurate, not racist or sexist and without libellous implications.

12. All contributions sent to the Publisher, whether invited or not, will be submitted to the Journal's Editors and Editorial Board. Any such contribution must bear the author's full name and address, even if this is not for publication. Contributions, whether published pseudonymously or not, are accepted on the strict understanding that the author is responsible for the accuracy of all opinion, technical comment, factual report, data, figures, illustrations and photographs. Publication does not necessarily imply that these are the opinions of the Editorial Board, Editors or the Publisher, nor does the Board, Editors or Publisher accept any liability for the accuracy of such comment, report and other technical and factual information. The Publisher will, however, strive to ensure that all opinion, comments, reports, data, figures, illustrations and photographs are accurate, insofar as it is within its abilities to do so. The Publisher reserves the right to edit, abridge or omit material submitted for publication.

13. All Articles submitted for publication will be subject to a double-blind refereeing procedure.

14. The author bears the responsibility for checking whether material submitted is subject to copyright or ownership rights, eg photographs, illustrations, trade literature and data. Where use is so restricted, the Publisher must be informed with the submission of the material.

15. No contribution will be accepted which has been published elsewhere, unless it is expressly invited or agreed by the Publisher. Articles and contributions published become the copyright of the Publisher, unless otherwise agreed.

16. All reasonable efforts are made to ensure accurate reproduction of text, photographs and illustrations. The Publisher does not accept responsibility for mistakes, be they editorial or typographical, nor for consequences resulting from them.

17. Submissions should be sent to Henry Stewart Publications, Museum House, 25 Museum Street, London WC1A 1JT, email: submissions@hspublications.co.uk. **Please clearly state for which journal you are contributing.**

Journal of Financial Services Marketing

ADDRESS FOR SUBMISSION:

Janet Noble, Editor
Journal of Financial Services Marketing
Henry Stewart Publications
Museum House
25 Museum Street
London, WC1A 1JT
UK
Phone: 44 (0) 171-323 2916
Fax: 44 (0) 171-323 2918
E-Mail: janet@hspublications.co.uk
Web: www.henrystewart.com/journals/
Address May Change:

PUBLICATION GUIDELINES:

Manuscript Length: 2,000-5,000 Words
Copies Required: Three
Computer Submission: Yes
Format: Word/Word Perfect
Fees to Review: 0.00 US$

Manuscript Style:
, Cambridge

CIRCULATION DATA:

Reader: , 65% Business, 35% Academic
Frequency of Issue: Quarterly
Copies per Issue: 1,001 - 2,000
Sponsor/Publisher: Henry Stewart Publications
Subscribe Price: 240.00 US$

REVIEW INFORMATION:

Type of Review: Blind Review
No. of External Reviewers: 3
No. of In House Reviewers: 2
Acceptance Rate: 50%
Time to Review: 1 - 2 Months
Reviewers Comments: Yes
Invited Articles: 31-50%
Fees to Publish: 0.00 US$

MANUSCRIPT TOPICS:

Advertising & Promotion Management; Direct Marketing; Financial Services Marketing; Global Business; Marketing Research; Marketing Theory & Applications; Production/Operations; Sales/Selling; Services

MANUSCRIPT GUIDELINES/COMMENTS:

1. Contributions should be between 2,000 and 5,000 words in length. All submissions should be typewritten and double spaced.

2. The Journal's Editors and Editorial Board particularly welcome submissions which present case study material, new approaches, techniques, empirical research or conceptual papers.

3. All articles should be accompanied by a short abstract outlining the paper's aims and subject matter.

4. All articles should be accompanied by up to six keywords.

5. Articles should be accompanied by a short (about 80 words) description of the author(s) and, if appropriate, the organization of which he or she is a member.

6. Authors should not seek to use the Journal as a vehicle for marketing any specific product or service.

7. Authors should avoid the use of language or slang which is not in keeping with the professional and academic style of the Journal.

8. Titles of organizations etc should be written out first in full and thereafter in initials.

9. Articles should be supported by references. For all Henry Stewart Journals excluding *Corporate Reputation Review, Tourism and Hospitality Research, Journal of Fashion Marketing and Management, Journal of Small Business and Enterprise Development, Journal of Asset Management* and *International Journal of Police Science Management*, these should be set out in accordance with the Vancouver referencing system. References for the Journals listed above should be set out in accordance with the Harvard referencing system.

10. Photographs and illustrations supporting articles should be submitted where appropriate. Photographs should be good quality positives, printed from the original negatives and preferably in black and white only. Figures and other line illustrations should be submitted in good quality originals and a copy of the data should also be included.

11. Authors must ensure that references to named people and/or organizations are accurate, not rascist or sexist and without libellous implications.

12. All contributions sent to the Publisher, whether invited or not, will be submitted to the Journal's Editors and Editorial Board. Any such contribution must bear the author's full name and address, even if this is not for publication. Contributions, whether published pseudonymously or not, are accepted on the strict understanding that the author is responsible for the accuracy of all opinion, technical comment, factual report, data, figures, illustrations and photographs. Publication does not necessarily imply that these are the opinions of the Editorial Board, Editors or the Publisher, nor does the Board, Editors or Publisher accept any liability for the accuracy of such comment, report and other technical and factual information. The Publisher will, however, strive to ensure that all opinion, comments, reports, data, figures, illustrations and photographs are accurate, insofar as it is within its abilities to do so. The Publisher reserves the right to edit, abridge or omit material submitted for publication.

13. All Articles submitted for publication will be subject to a double-blind refereeing procedure.

14. The author bears the responsibility for checking whether material submitted is subject to copyright or ownership rights, eg photographs, illustrations, trade literature and data. Where use is so restricted, the Publisher must be informed with the submission of the material.

15. No contribution will be accepted which has been published elsewhere, unless it is expressly invited or agreed by the Publisher. Articles and contributions published become the copyright of the Publisher, unless otherwise agreed.

16. All reasonable efforts are made to ensure accurate reproduction of text, photographs and illustrations. The Publisher does not accept responsibility for mistakes, be they editorial or typographical, nor for consequences resulting from them.

17. Submissions should be sent to Henry Stewart Publications, Museum House, 25 Museum Street, London WC1A 1JT, email: submissions@hspublications.co.uk. **Please clearly state for which journal you are contributing.**

Journal of Food Product Marketing

ADDRESS FOR SUBMISSION:

John L. Stanton, Editor
Journal of Food Product Marketing
Saint Joseph's University
College of Business Administration
Department of Food Marketing
5600 City Avenue
Philadephia, PA 19131-1395
USA
Phone:
Fax: 610-660-1997
E-Mail: jstanton@sju.edu
Web:
Address May Change:

PUBLICATION GUIDELINES:

Manuscript Length: 16-20
Copies Required: Three
Computer Submission: Yes
Format: ASCII/IBM Compatible
Fees to Review: 0.00 US$

Manuscript Style:
    Uniform System of Citation (Harvard Blue Book)

CIRCULATION DATA:

Reader: Academics
Frequency of Issue: Quarterly
Copies per Issue: Less than 1,000
Sponsor/Publisher: Haworth Press
Subscribe Price: 60.00 US$ Individual
    95.00 US$ Institution
    175.00 US$ Library

REVIEW INFORMATION:

Type of Review: Blind Review
No. of External Reviewers: 3
No. of In House Reviewers: 1
Acceptance Rate: 50%
Time to Review: 4 - 6 Months
Reviewers Comments: No
Invited Articles: 50% +
Fees to Publish: 0.00 US$

MANUSCRIPT TOPICS:

Advertising & Promotion Management; Any Business in the Food Industry; Business Law, Public Responsibility & Ethics; Communication; Direct Marketing; Global Business; Labor Relations & Human Resource Mgt.; Marketing Research; Marketing Theory & Applications; Operations Research/Statistics; Organizational Behavior & Theory; Organizational Development; Production/Operations; Purchasing/Materials Management; Sales/Selling; Services; Small Business Entrepreneurship; Strategic Management Policy; Technology/Innovation; Transportation/Physical Distribution

MANUSCRIPT GUIDELINES/COMMENTS:

About The Journal
The *Journal of Food Products Marketing* is the only journal devoted entirely to the full range of food products marketing, covering the entire range from food promotion and advertising through new food product development and consumer behavior research.

The goal of the *Journal of Food Products Marketing* is to provide timely and practical articles that will keep food marketers on the cutting edge of their profession. In order to accomplish this task, the journal will include both refereed research studies as well as opinions, guidelines, and speeches by practitioners which contribute to the better practice and understanding of food marketing.

This comprehensive journal aims to provide a single forum for both food marketing academicians and food marketing scholars.
- Papers submitted to the research section of the journal will be blind reviewed by outstanding academicians and researchers in food marketing.
- Papers submitted to the application section will be reviewed by food marketing executives from leading food manufacturers in the United States and around the world.

Editorial Content Areas
Research and application articles will cover break-away areas of food products marketing including

- Updates on basic principles in food marketing
- New food production development
- New developments in food products distribution channels
- Economics of the food industry
- Food retailing and food wholesaling management
- Food product policy
- Legal and societal aspects of food marketing
- Physical distribution in the food industry
- Personal selling in the food industry
- Sales management in the food industry
- Food and consumer behavior research
- Food pricing studies

Special research reports will also provide rapid publication of such topical areas as

- Consumer taste and flavor preference studies
- Top management involvement with new food products
- Health claims in food advertising
- Ethnicity and food marketing
- Inner city food marketing
- Suburban food marketing
- Retail advertising in high and low income areas
- National versus generic food brands
- Vertical food merchandising
- Coupon-clipping customers
- Personalized interactive video in food marketing
- Supermarket promotional strategies

Instructions For Authors

1. **Original articles only.** Submissions of a manuscript to this Journal represents a certification on the part of the author(s) that it is an original work, and that neither this manuscript nor a version of it has been published elsewhere nor is being considered for publication elsewhere.

2. **Manuscript Length.** Your manuscript may be no longer than 15-25 typed pages double-spaced (including references and abstract). Lengthier manuscripts may be considered, but only at the discretion of the Editor. Sometimes, lengthier manuscripts may be considered if they can be divided up into sections for publication in successive Journal issues.

3. **Manuscript Style.** References, citations, and general style of manuscripts for this Journal should follow the APA style (as outlined in the latest edition of the *Publication Manual of The American Psychological Association*). Reference should be placed in alphabetical order.

If an author wishes to submit a paper that had already been prepared in another style, he or she may do so. However, if the paper is accepted (with or without reviewer's alterations) the author is fully responsible for retyping the manuscript in the correct style as indicated above. Neither the Editor nor the Publisher is responsible for re-preparing manuscript copy to adhere to the Journal's style.

Electronic media. Articles may be submitted on electronic media limited to 5-1/4 inch floppy disks (double or high density, 40 or 80 track single or double sided) using ASCII files from IBM compatible word processors such as Microsoft Word, Word Perfect, and Multimate or on 40 track, single sided, double density 5-1/4 inch floppies using Superscript files for the TRS-80 Model III/IV. Due to the volatility of electronic media, authors are encouraged to include a printout of the file. Floppy disks will not be returned unless requested.

4. **Manuscript Preparation.**
Margins: leave at least a one-inch margin on all four sides.
Paper: use clean white, 8-1/2- x 11- bond paper.
Number Of Copies: 3 (the original plus two photocopies).
Cover Page: Important - staple a cover page to the manuscript, indicating only the article title (this is used for anonymous refereeing).
Second "Title Page": enclose a regular title page but do not staple it to the manuscript. Include the title again, plus:
- full authorship
- an ABSTRACT of about 100 words
- an introductory footnote with authors' academic degrees, professional titles, affiliations, mailing addresses, and any desired acknowledgement of research support or other credit.

5. **Return Envelopes.** When you submit your three manuscript copies, also include:
- a 9" x 12" envelope, self-addressed and stamped (with sufficient postage to ensure return of your manuscript.)
- a regular envelope, stamped and self-addressed. This is for the Editor to send you an "acknowledgement of receipt" letter.

6. **Spelling, Grammar, and Punctuation**. You are responsible for preparing manuscript copy which is clearly written in acceptable scholarly English, and which contains no errors of spelling, grammar, or punctuation. Neither the Editor nor the Publisher is responsible for correcting errors of spelling and grammar: the manuscript, after acceptance by the Editor, must be immediately ready for typesetting as it is finally submitted by the author(s). Check your paper for the following common errors:
- dangling modifiers
- misplaced modifiers
- unclear antecedents
- incorrect and inconsistent abbreviations
- Also, check the accuracy of all arithmetic calculations, statistics, numerical data, and references.

7. **Inconsistencies Must Be Avoided**. Be sure you are consistent in your use of abbreviations, terminology, and in citing references, from one part of your paper to another.

8. **Preparation of Tables, Figures, and Illustrations**. All tables, figures, illustrations, etc. must be "camera-ready." That is, they must be cleanly typed or artistically prepared so that they can be used either exactly as they are or else used after a photographic reduction in size. Figures, tables, and illustrations must be prepared on separate sheets of paper. Always use black ink and professional drawing instruments. On the back of these items, write your article title and the journal title lightly in pencil, so they do not get misplaced. In text, skip extra spaces and indicate where these figures and tables are to be placed.

9. **Alterations Required By Referees and Reviewers**. Many times a paper is accepted by the Editor contingent upon changes that are mandated by anonymous specialist referees and members of the Editorial Board. If the Editor returns your manuscript for revisions, you are responsible for retyping any sections of the paper to incorporate these revisions.

10. **Typesetting**. You will not be receiving galley proofs of your article. Editorial revisions, if any, must therefore be made while your article is still in manuscript. The final version of the manuscript will be the version you see published. Printer's errors will be corrected by the production staff of The Haworth Press. Authors are expected to submit manuscripts that are free from error.

11. **Reprints**. The senior author will receive one copy of the journal issue and 10 complimentary reprints of his or her article. The junior author will receive one copy of the issue. These are sent several weeks after the journal issue is published and in circulation. An order form for the purchase of additional reprints will also be sent to all authors at this time. (Approximately 10-12 weeks is necessary for the preparation of reprints.) Please do not query the Journal's Editor about reprints. All such questions should be sent directly to The Haworth Press, Inc., Production Department, 16-22 Alice Street, Binghamton, NY 13904, U.S.A.

12. **Copyright**. If your manuscript is accepted for publication, copyright ownership must be transferred officially to The Haworth Press, Inc. The Editor's acceptance letter will include a

form fully explaining this. The form must be signed by all authors and returned to the Editor at that time.

13. **Examples To Format**

Examples of Reference To Periodicals:
1. Journal Article: One Author:
Levitt, T. (1983). The Globalization of Markets, Harvard Business Review. (May-June), 61 (3), 92-102.

2. Journal Article: Multiple Authors.
Kaynak, E. and Mitchell A.L. (1981). Analysis of Marketing Strategies Used in Diverse Cultures, Journal of advertising Research (June), 21 (3), 25-32.

3. Magazine Article.
Tinnin, D.B. (1981, November 16) The Heady Success of Holland's Heineken, Fortune, pp. 158-164.

4. Newspaper Article.
The opportunity of world brands, (1984, June 3). The New York Times, p. 6F.

5. Monograph.
Franko, L.G. (1979). A Survey of the impact of Manufactured Exports From Industrializing Countries in Asia and Latin America, Changing International Realities (Monograph) No. 6.

Examples of References To Books:
1. Reference to an Entire Book.
Kaynak, E. (1986) Marketing and Economic Development, New York: Praeger Publishers Inc.

2. Book with a Corporate Author.
Committee For Economic Development (1981) Transnational Corporations for Developing Countries, New York: Author.

3. Edited Book.
Kaynak, E. (ed.) (1985) Global Perspectives in Marketing, New York: Praeger Publishers Inc.

4. Book with No Author or Editor.
Marketing Opportunities in Japan (1978). London: Dentsu Incorporated.

5. Article or Chapter in an Edited Book.
Bucklin, L.P. (1986). Improving Food Retailing in Less Developed Asian Countries. In E. Kaynak (Ed.) World Food Marketing Systems (pp.73-81) London: Butterworth Scientific Publishers.

Proceedings of Meetings and Symposia:
1. Published Proceedings, Published Contributions to a Symposium.

Lee, K.H. (1981). From Production Orientation to Marketing Orientation-Hong Kong in the International Trade Setting. In D.B. Yeaman (Ed.) Developing Global Corporate Strategies (pp. 753-766). Conference held at the University of Navarra, Barcelona, Spain, 2 (December 17-19).

2. Unpublished Paper Presented at a Meeting.
Yucelt, U. (1987). Tourism Marketing Planning in Developing Economies. Paper presented at the annual meeting of the Academy of Marketing Science, Bal Harbour, Florida.

Doctoral Dissertations:
1. Unpublished Doctoral Dissertation.
Czintoka, M.F. (1980). An Analysis of Export Development Strategies in Selected U.S. Industries. Dissertations Abstract International (University Microfilms No. 50-15, 865).

For reference to unpublished manuscripts, publications of limited circulation, reviews and interviews and nonprint media please refer to the latest edition of *Publication Manual of American Psychological Association*.

Journal of Global Marketing

ADDRESS FOR SUBMISSION:

Erdener Kaynak, Editor
Journal of Global Marketing
International Business Press
PO Box 399
Middletown, PA 17057
USA
Phone: 717-566-3054
Fax: 717-566-8589
E-Mail: k9x@psu.edu
Web: www.haworthpress.com
Address May Change:

PUBLICATION GUIDELINES:

Manuscript Length: 21-25
Copies Required: Three
Computer Submission: Yes
Format: WdPerfect 6.1 or above
Fees to Review: 0.00 US$

Manuscript Style:
   American Psychological Association

CIRCULATION DATA:

Reader: Academics
Frequency of Issue: Quarterly
Copies per Issue: 1,001 - 2,000
Sponsor/Publisher: Haworth Press, Inc.
Subscribe Price: 126.00 US$ Individual
    189.00 US$ Institution
    577.50 US$ Libraries

REVIEW INFORMATION:

Type of Review: Blind Review
No. of External Reviewers: 2
No. of In House Reviewers: 1
Acceptance Rate: 11-20%
Time to Review: 1 - 2 Months
Reviewers Comments: Yes
Invited Articles: 0-5%
Fees to Publish: 0.00 US$

MANUSCRIPT TOPICS:
Advertising & Promotion Management; Business Information Systems (MIS); Communication; Direct Marketing; Global Business; Marketing Research; Marketing Theory & Applications; Sales/Selling; Services

MANUSCRIPT GUIDELINES/COMMENTS:

About The Journal
Secure an edge in competitive global markets with this exciting journal. Created to address marketing challenges, opportunities, and problems encountered by firms, industries, and governments on a global scale, the *Journal of Global Marketing* contains significant contributions to the fields of global marketing from scholars, practitioners, and public policymakers at all levels.

This high quality journal benefits academic and business researchers and consultants by providing them with new and improved methods, approaches, and techniques of global marketing management. In addition to treating North American and European aspects, the journal places special emphasis on the perspectives of contributors from other areas of the globe, particularly Asia, Africa, East and Central Europe, and Australia. Comparative marketing studies and marketing case studies on individual countries, regions, and industries form the foundation of the *Journal of Global Marketing.*

Instructions For Authors
1. Original Articles Only. Submission of a manuscript to this journal represents a certification on the part of the author(s) that it is an original work, and that neither this manuscript nor a version of it has been published elsewhere nor is being considered for publication elsewhere.

2. Manuscript Length. Your manuscript may be approximately 15-25 typed pages double-spaced (including references and abstract). Lengthier manuscripts may be considered, but only at the discretion of the Editor. Sometimes, lengthier manuscripts may be considered if they can be divided up into sections for publication in successive Journal issues.

3. **Manuscript Style.** References, citations, and general style of manuscripts for this Journal should follow the APA style (as outlined in the latest edition of the *Publication Manual of The American Psychological Association*). References should be double-spaced and placed in alphabetical order.

If an author wishes to submit a paper that has been already prepared in another style, he or she may do so. However, if the paper is accepted (with or without reviewer's alterations), the author is fully responsible for retyping the manuscript in the correct style as indicated above. Neither the Editor nor the Publisher is responsible for re-preparing manuscript copy to adhere to the Journal's style.

4. **Manuscript Preparation.**
Margins: leave at least a one-inch margin on all four sides.
Paper: use clean white, 8 1/2 " x 11" bond paper.
Number of Copies: 4 (the original plus three photocopies).
Cover Page: Important--staple a cover page to the manuscript, indicating only the article title (this is used for anonymous refereeing).
Second "Title Page": enclose a regular title page but do not staple it to the manuscript. Include the title again, plus:
- full authorship
- an ABSTRACT of about 100 words. (Below the abstract provide 3-10 key words for index purposes).
- an introductory footnote with authors' academic degrees, professional titles, affiliations, mailing addresses, and any desired acknowledgment of research support or other credit.

5. **Return Envelopes.** When you submit your four manuscript copies, also include:
- a 9" x 12" envelope, self-addressed and stamped (with sufficient postage to ensure return of your manuscript);
- a regular envelope, stamped and self-addressed. This is for the Editor to send you an "acknowledgement of receipt" letter.

6. **Spelling, Grammar, and Punctuation**. You are responsible for preparing manuscript copy which is clearly written in acceptable scholarly English, and which contains no errors of spelling, grammar, or punctuation. Neither the Editor nor the Publisher is responsible for correcting errors of spelling and grammar: the manuscript, after acceptance by the Editor, must be immediately ready for typesetting as it is finally submitted by the author(s). Check your paper for the following common errors:
- dangling modifiers
- misplaced modifiers
- unclear antecedents
- incorrect or inconsistent abbreviations

Also, check the accuracy of all arithmetic calculations, statistics, numerical data, text citations, and references.

7. **Inconsistencies Must Be Avoided**. Be sure you are consistent in your use of abbreviations, terminology, and in citing references, from one part of your paper to another.

8. **Preparation of Tables, Figures, and Illustrations**. All tables and figures, illustrations, etc. must be "camera-ready". That is, they must be cleanly typed or artistically prepared so that they can be used either exactly as they are or else used after a photographic reduction in size. Figures, tables, and illustrations must be prepared on separate sheets of paper. Always use black ink and professional drawing instruments. On the back of these items, write your article title and the journal title lightly in pencil, so they do not get misplaced. In test, skip extra lines and indicate where these figures and tables are to be placed (please **do not write** on the face of art). Photographs are considered part of the acceptable manuscript and remain with the publisher for use in additional printings.

9. **Alterations Required By Referees And Reviewers**. Many times a paper is accepted by the Editor contigent upon changes that are mandated by anonymous specialist referees and members of the Editorial Board. If the Editor returns your manuscript for revisions, you are responsible for retyping any sections of the paper to incorporate these revisions (if applicable, revisions should also be put on disk).

10. **Typesetting**. You will not be receiving galley proofs o your article. Editorial revisions, if any, must therefore be made while your article is still in manuscript. the final version of the manuscript will be the version you see published. Typesetter's errors will be corrected by the production staff of The Haworth Press. Authors are expected to submit manuscripts, disks, and art that are free from error.

11. **Electronic Media**. Haworth's in-house type-setting unit is able to utilize your final manuscript material as prepared on most personal computers and word processors. This will minimize typographical errors and decrease overall production timelag. Please send the first draft and final draft copies of you manuscript to the journal Editor in print format for his/her final review and approval.

After approval of your final manuscript, please submit the final approved version both on printed format ("hard copy") and floppy diskette. On the outside of the diskette package write:
A. the brand name of your computer or word processor
B. the word-processing program that you used
C. the title of your article, and
D. file name

Note: Disk and hard copy must agree. In case of discrepancies, it is The Haworth Press' policy to follow hard copy. Authors are advised that **No Revisions** of the manuscript can be made after acceptance by the Editor for publication. The benefits of this procedure are many with speed and accuracy being the most obvious. We look forward to working with you on this, knowing we will be able to serve you more efficiently in the future.

12. **Reprints**. The senior author will receive two copies of the journal issue and 10 complimentary reprints of his or her article. The junior author will receive two copies of the journal issue and 10 complimentary reprints of his or her article. The junior author will receive two copies of the journal issue. These are sent several weeks after the journal issue is published and in circulation. An order form for the purchase of additional reprints will also be sent to all authors at this time. (Approximately 4-6 weeks is necessary for the preparation of reprints.) Please do not query the Journal's Editor about reprints. All such questions should be sent directly to The Haworth Press, Inc. Production Department, 21 East Broad Street, West Hazleton, PA 18201 USA. To order additional reprints (minimum: 50 copies), please contact The Haworth Document Delivery Center, 10 alice Street, Binghamton, NY 13904-1580 USA; 1-800-342-9678, (607) 722-5857 or Fax (607) 722-6362.

13. **Copyright**. Copyright ownership of your manuscript must be transferred officially to The Haworth Press, Inc. before we can begin the peer-review process. The Editor's letter acknowledging receipt of the manuscript will be accompanied by a form fully explaining this. All authors must sign the form and return the original to the Editor as soon as possible. Failure to return the copyright form in a timely fashion will result in delay in review and subsequent publication.

14. **Examples To Format**.
Examples of Reference to Periodicals:
1. Journal Article: One Author.
Levitt, T. (1983). The Globalizatin of Markets, Harvard Business Review. (May-June), 61 (3), 92-102.
2. Journal Article: Multiple Authors.
Kaynak, E. and Mitchell A.L. (1981). Analysis of Marketing Strategies Used in Diverse Cultures, Journal of Advertising Research (June), 21 (3), 25-32.
3. Magazine Article.
Tinnin, D.B. (1981, November 16) The Heady Success of Holland's Heineken, Fortune, pp. 158-164.
4. Newspaper Article.
The opportunity of world brands, (1984, June 3), The New York Times, p. 6F.
5. Monograph.

Franko, L.G. (1979). A Survey of the Impact of Manugactured Exports From Industrializing Countries in Asia and Latin America, Changing International Realities [Monograph] No. 6.

Examples of References to Books:
1. Reference to an Entire Book.
Kaynak, E. (1986) Marketing and Economic Development, New York: Praeger Publishers Inc.
2. Book with a Corporate Author.
Committee For Economic Development (1981) Transnational Corporatin for Developing Countries, New York: Author.
3. Edited Book.
Kaynak, E. (ed.) (1985) Global Perspectives in Marketing, New York: Praeger Publishers Inc.
4. Book with No Author or Editor.
Marketing Opportunities in Japan (1978). London: Dentsu Incorporated.
5. Article or Chapter in an Edited Book.
Bucklin, L.P. (1986). Improving Food Retailing in Less Developed Asian Countries. In E. Daynak (Ed.) World Food Marketing Systems (pp. 73-81) London: Butterworth Scientific Publishers.

Proceedings of Meetings and Symposia:
1. Published Proceedings, Published Contributions to a Symposium.
Lee, K.H. (1981). From Production Orientation to Marketing Orientation-Hong Kong in the Internatinal Trade Setting. In D.B. Yeaman (Ed.) Developing Global Corporate Strategies (pp. 753-766). Conference held at the University of Navarra, Barcelona, Spain, 2 (December 17-19).
2. Unpublished Paper Presented at a Meeting.
Yucelt, U. (1987). Tourism Marketing Planning in Developing Economies. Paper presented at the annual meeting of the Academy of Marketing Science, Bal harbour, Florida.

Doctoral Dissertations:
1. Unpublished Doctoral Dissertation.
Czintoka, M.F. (1980). An Analysis of Export Development Strategies in Selected U.S. Industries. Dissertations Abstract International (University Microfilms No. 80-15, 865).

For reference to unpublished manuscripts, publications of limited circulation, reviews and interviews and nonprint media please refer to the latest edition of *Publication Manual of American Psychological Association.*

Publication Agreement
(This form must be completed and must accompany all manuscripts submitted for review.)
1. **Copyright**: In consideration for review and possible subsequent publication of our Work in the journal noted on the reverse side of this page, the Author(s) agree to transfer copyright of the work to The Haworth Press, Inc., including full and exclusive rights to publication in all media now known or later developed, including but not limited to electronic databases and microfilm, and in anthologies of any kind. **(Note to U.S. Government employees: see your exemption, paragraph 5 below.)**

2. **Author Re-Use Of Work**: As a professional courtesy, the authors retain the right to reprint their article submitted again, after publication in the journal in any work for which they are sole Author, or in any edited work for which the author is Senior Editor. No further permission is necessary in writing from The Haworth Press, Inc., nor will the Press require fees of any kind for the reprinting. This statement is intended to provide full copyright release for the purposes listed above, and a photocopy of the release may be used when another Publisher requires a written release.

3. **Author Warranties**: The author(s) represent(s) and warrant(s):
a) that the manuscript submitted is his/her (their) own work;
b) that the work has been submitted only to this journal and that it has not been previously published;
c) that the article contains no libelous or unlawful statements and does not infringe upon the civil rights of others;
d) that the author(s) is (are) not infringing upon anyone else's copyright.
The authors agree that if there is a breach of any of the above representations and warranties that (s)he (they) will indemnify the Publisher and Editor and hold them harmless.

4. **Author Retention of Patents**: The author(s) may have, within their article, descriptions of their own proprietary patents. It is not the intention of the Editor or Publisher to require copyright transfer of such materials. If any of these materials appear in the work, the authors may add their personal copyright notice to patents, with this understanding:

a) the author(s) retain copyright for said patents, with full and exclusive rights to their publication, not to include any other material from the article/publication;
b) the Publisher retains full and exclusive rights to publication to the article/publication in any format, including patents when published as part of the entire article or publication.
c) photographs are considered part of the acceptable manuscript and remain with the Publisher for use in additional printings.

5. **Note for u.s. Government employees**: If the article is single-authored by a U.S. government employee as part of his/her official duties, it is understood that the article is not copyrightable. It is called a "Work of the U.S. Government." However, if the article was not part of the employee's official duties, it may be copyrighted. If the article was jointly written, the authors understand that they are delegating the right of copyright to the nongovernmental employee, who must sign this agreement.

6. **"Work For Hire" Authors**: If the article was written by an author who was hired by another person or company to do so, the article is called a "Work for Hire" manuscript. This agreement must then be signed by the "employer" who hired the author, as well as the author.

7. **No Amendments**: No amendments or modifications of the terms of this Agreement are permissible unless same shall be in writing and signed by a duly authorized officer of The Haworth Press, Inc. No Journal Editor, Guest Editor or Special Issue Editor is authorized to waive, amend or modify any of the procedures or other provisions of this Agreement. This form is not valid if the Author(s) add any additional constraints and amendments. Please

submit the article elsewhere for publication if the Author(s) do not sign this Agreement without alteration.

8. **Integration**: This Agreement embodies the entire agreement and understanding between the Author and The Haworth Press, Inc. and supersedes all other agreements and understandings, whether oral or written, relating to the subject matter hereof.

Name and **Exact** Mailing Address of Contributor:

Special note: this will be used for mailing reprints. You must include exact street address, name of your department if at a university, and ZIP CODE. The Haworth Press cannot be responsible for lost reprints if you do not Provide us with your exact mailing address.

In Reference To Your Journal Article:

___ If this box is checked...

Thank you for your article submission! Please allow 10-15 weeks for the review process. Before sending out your article for review, however, the Publisher requires us to obtain your signature(s) confirming that you have read the PUBLICATION AGREEMENT on the reverse side of this page.

All co-authors must sign and return the ORIGINAL signed copy.

IT IS CONFIRMED that I/we have read the PUBLICATION AGREEMENT on the reverse side of the page, and agree and accept all conditions:

author's signature	date
author's signature	date
author's signature	date

Other Comments: _____

_____

Please reply to

( ) Journal Editor: Erdener Kaynak, PhD, DSc
                     Executive Editor
                     P.O. Box 231
                     Middletown, PA 17057
                     phone 717-566-3054
                     fax: 717-566-8589
                     e-mail: K9X@PSU.EDU

( ) Guest Editor / Special Issue Editor:

_____

___ It this box is checked...

Your article has been favorably reviewed. Our reviewers, however, require certain revisions which are indicated on the attached sheets. Please review and incorporate their suggestions, and return your manuscript/disk retyped within 14 days. A decision about publication will he made at that time. Thank you for your help and cooperation.

_____

___ If this box is checked...

We are pleased to inform you that your article has been accepted for publication in the journal noted above, or (if noted) by a special issue/ edition/monographic supplement to the journal.

Please note the following:

1. **Publication**: Your article is currently scheduled to appear in

Volume: _____ Number: _____

Published during this season: _____

2. **Typesetting**: Your article will be sent to the Production Department of The Haworth Press, Inc., 21 East Broad Street, West Hazleton, PA 18201. They will typeset your article (preferably from your computer disk) exactly as submitted. Please note that you will not be receiving galley proofs. The production staff will proofread the galleys for typesetting errors against the final version of the manuscript as submitted. No revisions are allowed.

3. **Reprints**: Shortly after publication you will receive an order form for purchasing quantities of reprints. (About three weeks after publication, the senior author will receive two complimentary copies of the issue and ten copies of the article, and the junior author(s) will receive two complimentary copies of the issue.) Please note that preparation of reprints takes about eight weeks additional time after the actual issue is printed and in circulation.

_____

___ If this box is checked...

We are sorry, but the reviewers for this journal did not agree that your article was appropriate for publication in this periodical. If the reviewers consented in having their comments forwarded to you, their critiques are attached. Your submission is appreciated, and we hope that you will contribute again in the future.

Journal of Hospital Marketing

ADDRESS FOR SUBMISSION:

Kathy Rutz, Interim Editor
Journal of Hospital Marketing
Haworth Press, Inc.
10 Alice Street
Binghamton, NY 13904
USA
Phone: 607-656-7981
Fax: 607-722-6362
E-Mail:
Web:
Address May Change:

PUBLICATION GUIDELINES:

Manuscript Length: 16-20
Copies Required: Four
Computer Submission: Yes
Format: Any standard w/hardcopy
Fees to Review: 0.00 US$

Manuscript Style:
   Chicago Manual of Style, or APA

CIRCULATION DATA:

Reader: Administrators, Academics,
   Business Persons
Frequency of Issue: 2 Times/Year
Copies per Issue: 3,001 - 4,000
Sponsor/Publisher: Haworth Press, Inc.
Subscribe Price: 60.00 US$ Individual
   125.00 US$ Institution
   300.00 US$ Library

REVIEW INFORMATION:

Type of Review: Editorial Review
No. of External Reviewers: 4
No. of In House Reviewers: 1
Acceptance Rate: 50%
Time to Review: 2 - 3 Months
Reviewers Comments: No Reply
Invited Articles: 6-10%
Fees to Publish: 0.00 US$

MANUSCRIPT TOPICS:
Health Care Administration; Hospital System Marketing; Joint Venture & Merger; Marketing Planning; Marketing Research; Marketing Theory & Applications; Strategic Management Policy

MANUSCRIPT GUIDELINES/COMMENTS:

About The Journal
This dynamic journal disseminates pertinent and practical information for hospital marketing professionals on new and effective ways of marketing hospital services. Hospitals are requiring new management tools to deal with increasing competition and other social and economic pressures. As a result, hospital marketing has quickly become a sophisticated specialty that is being recognized at the executive level inmost hospitals around the country. The *Journal of Hospital Marketing* shares current marketing concepts, methodologies, tools, and applied case studies used in hospitals throughout the country, making it a unique and valuable resource for hospital marketers, consultants, educators, fund raisers, advertisers, and community and public relations professionals.

The Editor welcomes articles that will assist practitioners in enhancing their productivity and effectiveness in marketing hospital services, such as

strategic market planning	hospital economics
strategy development	staff development from
fund development	a marketing perspective
recruitment	contracting
internal marketing	mergers/acquisitions
joint venturing	advertising
market analysis	new service development
competitive advantage	and planning
managed care/contracting	target analysis
marketing research and auditing	data-support systems and microcomputer applications
public relations	financial planning in marketing
community relations	
patient liaison activities	working with marketing consultants
lobbying/regulatory affiliation	

Instructions For Authors

1. **Original Articles Only.** Submission of a manuscript to this Journal represents a certification on the part of the author(s) that it is an original work, and that neither this manuscript nor a version of it has been published elsewhere nor is being considered for publication elsewhere.

2. **Manuscript Length.** Your manuscript may be approximately 15 typed pages double-spaced (including references and abstract). Lengthier manuscripts may be considered, but only at the discretion of the Editor. Sometimes, lengthier manuscripts may be considered if they can be divided up into sections for publication in successive Journal issues.

3. **Manuscript Style.** References, citations, and general style of manuscripts for this Journal should follow the "Chicago" style (as outlined in the latest edition of the *Manual of Style* of the university of Chicago Press). References should be double-spaced and placed in alphabetical order.

If an author wishes to submit a paper that has been already prepared in another style, he or she may do so. However, if the paper is accepted (with or without reviewer's alterations), the author is fully responsible for retyping the manuscript in the correct style as indicated above. Neither the Editor nor the Publisher is responsible for re-preparing manuscript copy to adhere to the Journal's style.

4. **Manuscript Preparation.**
Margins: leave at least a one-inch margin on all four sides.
Paper: use clean white, 8-1/2" x 11" bond paper.
Number Of Copies: 4 (the original plus three photocopies).

Cover Page: Important - staple a cover page to the manuscript, indicating only the article title (this is used for anonymous refereeing).
Second "Title Page": enclose a regular title page but do not staple it to the manuscript. Include the title again, plus:
- full authorship
- an **abstract** of about 100 words
- an introductory footnote with authors' academic degrees, professional titles, affiliations, mailing addresses, and any desired acknowledgement of research support or other credit.

5. **Return Envelopes**. When you submit your four manuscript copies, also include:
- a 9" x 12" envelope, self-addressed and stamped (with sufficient postage to ensure return of your manuscript);
- a regular envelope, stamped and self-addressed. This is for the Editor to send you an "acknowledgement of receipts letter.

6. **Spelling, Grammar, And Punctuation**. You are responsible for preparing manuscript copy which is clearly written in acceptable scholarly English, and which contains no errors of spelling, grammar, or punctuation. Neither the Editor nor the Publisher is responsible for correcting errors of spelling and grammar: the manuscript, after acceptance by the Editor, must be immediately ready for typesetting as it is finally submitted by the author(s). Check your paper for the following common errors:
- dangling modifiers
- misplaced modifiers
- unclear antecedents
- incorrect or inconsistent abbreviations

Also, check the accuracy of all arithmetic calculations statistics, numerical data, text citations, and references.

7. **Inconsistencies Must Be Avoided**. Be sure you are consistent in your use of abbreviations, terminology, and in citing references, from one part of your paper to another.

8. **Preparation of Tables, Figures, And Illustrations**. All tables, figures, illustrations, etc. must be "camera-ready." That is, they must be cleanly typed or artistically prepared so that they can be used either exactly as they are or else used after a photographic reduction in size. Figures, tables, and illustrations must be prepared on separate sheets of paper. Always use black ink and professional drawing instruments. On the back of these items, write your article title and the journal title lightly in pencil, so they do not get misplaced. In text, skip extra lines and indicate where these figures and tables are to be placed (please do not write on face of art).

9. **Alterations Required By Referees and Reviewers**. Many times a paper is accepted by the Editor contingent upon changes that are mandated by anonymous specialist referees and members of the Editorial Board. If the Editor returns your manuscript for revisions you are responsible for retyping any sections of the paper to incorporate these revisions (if applicable, revisions should also be put on disk).

10. **Typesetting**. You will not be receiving galley proofs of your article. Editorial revisions, if any, must therefore be made while your article is still in manuscript. The final version of the manuscript will be the version you see published. Typesetter's errors will be corrected by the production staff of The Haworth Press. Authors are expected to submit manuscripts, disks, and art that are free from error.

11. **Electronic Media**. Haworth's in-house typesetting unit will now be able to utilize your final manuscript material as prepared on most personal computers and word processors. This will minimize typographical errors and decrease overall production time lag.

A. Please continue to send your first draft and final draft copies of your manuscript to the journal Editor in print format for his/her final review and approval;
B. Only after the journal editor has approved your final manuscript, you may submit the final approved version both on:
printed format ("hard copy")
floppy diskette
C. Please make sure that the disk version and the hard copy printed copy) are exactly the same.
D. Wrap your floppy diskettes in a strong diskette wrapper or holder, and write on the outside of the package:

- the brand name of your computer or word processor
- the word-processing program that you used to create your article, book chapter, or book
- the title of your article
- file name

The benefits of this procedure are many with speed and accuracy being the most obvious. We look forward to working with you on this, knowing we will be able to serve you more efficiently in the future.

12. **Reprints**. The senior author will receive one copy of the journal issue and 10 complimentary reprints of his or her article. The junior author will receive one copy of the issue. These are sent several weeks after the journal issue is published and in circulation. An order form for the purchase of additional reprints will also be sent to all authors at this time. (Approximately 4-6 weeks is necessary for the preparation of reprints.) Please do not query the Journal's Editor about reprints. All such questions should be sent directly to The Haworth Press, Inc., Production Department, 10 Alice Street, Binghamton, NY 13904-1580.

13. **Copyright**. If your manuscript is accepted for publication, copyright ownership must be transferred officially to The Haworth Press, Inc. The Editor's acceptance letter will include a form fully explaining this. The form must be signed by all authors and returned to the Editor at that time.

14. **Computer Disk**. Article must arrive as hardcopies (3) and on 3 1/2" or 5 1/4" computer disk in any standard wordprocessor format.

Journal of Hospitality & Leisure Marketing

ADDRESS FOR SUBMISSION:

Bonnie J. Knutson, Editor
Journal of Hospitality & Leisure Marketing
Michilgan State University
Eli Broad College of Business
Eli Broad Graduate School of Management
235 Eppley Center
East Lansing, MI 48814-1121
USA
Phone: 517-353-9211
Fax: 517-432-1170
E-Mail: drbonnie@msu.edu
Web: www.haworthpressinc.com
Address May Change:

PUBLICATION GUIDELINES:

Manuscript Length: 16-25
Copies Required: Three
Computer Submission: Yes
Format: Word and WordPerfect
Fees to Review: 0.00 US$

Manuscript Style:
 Chicago Manual of Style

CIRCULATION DATA:

Reader: Academics
Frequency of Issue: Quarterly
Copies per Issue: No Reply
Sponsor/Publisher: Haworth Press, Inc.
Subscribe Price: 75.00 US$ Individual
 125.00 US$ Institution

REVIEW INFORMATION:

Type of Review: Blind Review
No. of External Reviewers: 2
No. of In House Reviewers: 1
Acceptance Rate: 50%
Time to Review: 1 - 2 Months
Reviewers Comments: Yes
Invited Articles: 0-5%
Fees to Publish: 0.00 US$

MANUSCRIPT TOPICS:

Advertising & Promotion Management; Communication; Direct Marketing; Hospitaltity Management; Hotels, Tourism, Food Service; Marketing Research; Marketing Theory & Applications; Non Profit Organizations; Sales/Selling; Services; Strategic Management Policy; Technology/Innovation

MANUSCRIPT GUIDELINES/COMMENTS:

1. **Original Articles Only**. Submission of a manuscript to the *Journal of Segmentation In Marketing* represents a certification on the part of the author(s) that it is an original work, and that neither this manuscript nor a version of it has been published elsewhere nor is being considered for publication elsewhere.

2. **Manuscript Length**. Your manuscript may be approximately 20 typed pages double-spaced (including references and abstract). Lengthier manuscripts may be considered, but only at the discretion of the Editor. Sometimes, lengthier manuscripts may be considered if they

can be divided up into sections for publication in successive Journal issues. Shorter manuscripts (e.g. 10-15 pages) are acceptable for case studies and commentaries.

3. **Manuscript Style**. References, citations, and general style of manuscripts for the *Journal of Segmentation In Marketing* should follow the Chicago style (as outlined in the latest edition of the *Manual of Style* of the University of Chicago Press). References should be double-spaced and placed in alphabetical order.

If an author wishes to submit a paper that has been already prepared in another style, he or she may do so. However if the paper is accepted (with or without reviewer's alterations, the author is fully responsible for retyping the manuscript in the correct style as indicated above. Neither the Editor nor the Publisher is responsible for re-preparing manuscript copy to adhere to the Journal's style.

4. **Manuscript Preparation**.
Margins: leave at least a one-inch margin on all four sides.
Paper: use clean white 8 ½ x 11" bond paper.
Number of copies: 4 (the original plus three photocopies).
Cover page: **Important**--staple a cover page to the manuscript, indicating only the article title (this is used for anonymous refereeing).
Second "title page": enclose a regular title page but do not staple it to the manuscript. Include the title again, plus:
- full authorship
- an ABSTRACT of about 100-150 words. (Below the abstract provide 4-6 key words for index purposes).
- an introductory footnote with authors' academic degrees professional titles, affiliations, mailing addresses, and any desired acknowledgment of research support or other credit.

5. **Return Envelopes**. When you submit your four manuscript copies, also include:
- a 9" x 12" envelope, self-addressed and stamped (with sufficient postageto ensure return of your manuscript)
- a regular envelope, stamped and self-addressed. This is for the Editor to send you an "acknowledgement of receipt" letter.

6. **Spelling grammar, and punctuation**. You are responsible for; preparing manuscript copy which is clearly written in acceptable scholarly English, and which contains no errors of spelling, grammar, or punctuation. Neither the Editor nor the Publisher is responsible for correcting errors of spelling and grammar: the manuscript, after acceptance by the Editor, must be immediately ready for typesetting as it is finally submitted by the author(s). Check your paper for the following common errors:
- dangling modifiers
- misplaced modifiers
- unclear antecedents
- incorrect or inconsistent abbreviations

Also, check the accuracy of all arithmetic calculations, statistics, numerical data, text citations, and references.

7. **Inconsistencies must be avoided.** Be sure you are consistent in your use of abbreviations, terminology, and in citing references, from one part of your paper to another.

8. **Preparation of tables and figures.** All tables, figures, etc. must be "camera-ready." That is, they must be cleanly typed or artistically prepared so that they can be used either exactly as they are or else used after a Photographic reduction in size. Figures and tables must be prepared on separate sheets of paper. Always use black ink and professional drawing instruments. On the back of these items, write your article title and the journal title lightly in pencil, so they do not get misplaced. In text, skip extra lines and indicate where these figures and tables are to be placed (please do not write on face of art).

9. **Alterations required by reviewers.** Many times a paper is accepted by the Editor contingent upon changes that are mandated by anonymous reviewers and members of the Editorial Board. If the Editor returns your manuscript for revisions, you are responsible for retyping any sections of the paper to incorporate these revisions (if applicable, revisions should also be put on disk).

10. **Typesetting.** You will not be receiving galley proofs of your article. Editorial revisions, if any, must therefore be made while your article is still in manuscript. The final version of the manuscript will be the version you see published. Typesetter's errors will be corrected by the production staff of The Haworth Press. Authors are expected to submit manuscripts, disks, and art that are free from error.

11. **Electronic Media.** Haworth's in-house type-setting unit is able to utilize your final manuscript material as prepared on most personal computers and word processors. This will minimize typographical errors and decrease overall production timelag. Please send the first draft and final draft copies of your manuscript to the journal Editor in print format for his/her final review and approval. After approval of your final manuscript please submit the final approved version both on printed format ("hard copy") and floppy diskette. On the outside of the diskette package write:

A. the brand name of your computer or word processor
B. the word-processing program that you used
C. the title of your article, and
D. file name

Note: Disk and hard copy must agree. In case of discrepancies, it is The Haworth Press's policy to follow hard copy. Authors are advised that no revisions of the manuscript can be made after acceptance by the Editor for publication. The benefits of this procedure are many with speed and accuracy being the most obvious. We look forward to working with you on this, knowing we will be able to serve you more efficiently in the future.

12. **Reprints.** The senior author will receive two copies of the journal issue and 10 complimentary reprints of his or her article. The junior author will receive two copies of the

journal issue. These are sent several weeks after the journal issue is published and in circulation. An order form for the purchase of additional reprints will also be sent to all authors at this time. (Approximately 4-6 weeks is necessary for the preparation of reprints.) Please do not query the Journal's Editor about reprints. All such questions should be sent directly to The Haworth Press, Inc., Production Department, 21 East Broad Street, West Hazleton, PA 18201. To order additional reprints (minimum: 50 copies), please contact The Haworth Document Delivery Center, 10 Alice Street, Binghamton, NY 1 3904-1580; 1-800-342-9678 or Fax (607) 722-6362.

13. **Copyright**. Copyright ownership of your manuscript must be transferred officially to The Haworth Press, Inc. before we can begin the peer-review process. The Editor's letter acknowledging receipt of the manuscript will be accompanied by a form fully explaining this. All authors must sign the form and return the original to the Editor as soon as possible. Failure to return the copyright form in a timely fashion will result in delay in review and subsequent publication.

Journal of Hospitality & Tourism Research

ADDRESS FOR SUBMISSION:

K.S.(Kaye) Chon, Editor
Journal of Hospitality & Tourism Research
Hong Kong Polytechnic University
Department of Hotel and Tourism Mgt.
Hung Hom
Kowloon,
Hong Kong
Phone: 852 -276-6632
Fax:
E-Mail: kchon@uh.edu
Web: www.sagepub.com
Address May Change:

PUBLICATION GUIDELINES:

Manuscript Length: 21-25
Copies Required: Four
Computer Submission: No
Format: N/A
Fees to Review: 0.00 US$

Manuscript Style:
American Psychological Association

CIRCULATION DATA:

Reader: Academics
Frequency of Issue: Quarterly
Copies per Issue: 2,001 - 3,000
Sponsor/Publisher: Sage Publishing Co.
Subscribe Price: 71.00 US$ Individual
157.00 US$ Institution

REVIEW INFORMATION:

Type of Review: Blind Review
No. of External Reviewers: 3
No. of In House Reviewers: 0
Acceptance Rate: 11-20%
Time to Review: 1 - 2 Months
Reviewers Comments: Yes
Invited Articles: 0-5%
Fees to Publish: 0.00 US$

MANUSCRIPT TOPICS:
Advertising & Promotion Management; Business Information Systems (MIS); Business Law, Public Responsibility & Ethics; Direct Marketing; Global Business; Labor Relations & Human Resource Mgt.; Marketing Research; Marketing Theory & Applications; Office Administration/Management; Operations Research/Statistics; Organizational Behavior & Theory; Organizational Development; Production/Operations; Public Administration; Sales/Selling; Services; Small Business Entrepreneurship; Strategic Management Policy; Technology/Innovation

MANUSCRIPT GUIDELINES/COMMENTS:

Description:
The *Journal of Hospitality & Tourism Research* publishes high-quality, refereed scholarship which advances the knowledge base of the hospitality and tourism field. Featuring conceptual, empirical research, and applied research articles as well as book and software reviews, research notes, industry viewpoints, and conference reviews, JHTR keeps educators, researchers, and professionals in travel and hospitality up to date with the latest and most vital findings in the field.

At the forefront of hospitality scholarship for over 20 years, *Journal of Hospitality and Tourism Research* is now published by Sage Publications, Inc. JHTR's prestige as a premier journal in hospitality and tourism research is further enhanced by its new relationship with Sage, an international leader in professional and scholarly publishing for the social sciences and business.

Journal Submission Guidelines
Manuscripts submitted to JHTR should be original contributions not under consideration for any other publication at the same time. If an article is under consideration by another publication, authors should clearly indicate this at the time of submission. Manuscripts should normally not exceed 7,000 words and must be written in English. Articles for the Viewpoints and Commentary, Publications in Review, and Research Notes and Industry Viewpoints sections should not exceed 3,000 words. The Rejoiners section of the journal is intended to publish short articles, commentaries, and rebuttals on the contents of JHTR. Authors should submit such contributions immediately after each issue of JHTR appears so that they are published in the subsequent issue.

Manuscripts should be typed double-spaced, including references. Submit four (4) copies of each manuscript. The author's name should not appear anywhere except on the cover page (to preserve anonymity during the review process). All general editorial formats, abbreviations, use of statistics in text, citations, and references should conform to the *Publication Manual of the American Psychological Association* (4th edition).

On the first page please include name of author(s) and title; author(s) note, including present position, complete address, telephone/fax numbers, e-mail address, and any acknowledgement of financial or technical assistance. The second page should feature the title of paper (without author's name), a list of no more than six keywords that define the subject matter, and a brief abstract of no more than 150 words substantively summarizing the article.

Body - The text, with major headings centered on the page and subheadings flush with the left margin. Major headings should use all uppercase letters; side subheadings should be typed in upper and lowercase letters.

Tables and Figures - Each table or figure should be prepared on a separate page and grouped together at the end of the manuscript. The data in tables should be arranged so that columns of like materials read down, not across. Nonsignificant decimal places in tabular data should be omitted. The tables and figures should be numbered in Arabic numerals, followed by brief descriptive titles. Authors should indicate in text where tables and figures should appear.

Additional details should be footnoted under the table not in the title. In the text, all illustrations and charts should be referred to as figures.
Figures must be clean, crisp, black-and-white, camera-ready copies. Please avoid the use of gray-scale shading; use hatchmarks, dots, or lines instead.

References - References should be typed double-spaced in alphabetical order by author's last name and should appear in APA style.

REFERENCE LIST STYLE
List references alphabetically, principal author's surname first, followed by publication date in parentheses. The reference list should be typed double-spaced, with a hanging indent, on a separate page. Do not number references. Be sure that all titles cited in the text appear in the reference list and vice versa. Please see the specific examples below.

Specth, M.L., and Wilkie, D.M. (1985). Subjective shortening: A model of pigeon's memory for even Duration. Journal of Experimental Psychology: Animal Behavior Processes, 9, 14-30.

Tardener, H. (1981, December). Do babies sing a universal song? Psychology Today, 70-76

Weinstein, T.M.K. (1991). The careful writer: A modern guide to the English usage. New York: Atheneum.

Zachary, A.S., & Kniskern, D.P. (1988). Family therapy outcome research: Knowns and unknowns. In A.S. Gurman & D.P. Kniskern (Eds.), Handbook of family therapy (pp.742-775).New York: Brunner/Mazel.

Authors of final manuscripts accepted for publication should provide both a hard copy of the final version of their article and a matching version on a 3.5-inch computer disk. Please send all manuscripts to
    Professor K.S. (Kaye) Chon, Executive Editor
    Journal of Hospitality & Tourism Research
    Conrad N. Hilton College of Hotel and Restaurant Management
    Univerisity of Houston
    4800 Calhoun Road, Houston, TX 77204-3902
    Telephone: 713-743-2458, Fax: 713-743-2427
    e-mail: Kchon@uh.edu, http://www.hrm.uh.edu/Faculty/KChon/chon1.html

All published material is copyrighted by the Council on Hotel, Restaurant and Institutional Education. Every author and coauthor must sign a contract before an article can be published.

Journal of Interactive Marketing

ADDRESS FOR SUBMISSION:

Ellen R. Foxman, Associate Editor
Journal of Interactive Marketing
Bentley College
Department of Marketing
Waltham, MA 02452-4705
USA
Phone: 781-891-2796
Fax: 781-891-3410
E-Mail: efoxman@bentley.edu
Web: www.interscience.wiley.com
Address May Change:

PUBLICATION GUIDELINES:

Manuscript Length: 21-25
Copies Required: Five
Computer Submission: Yes
Format: Wd. 5.0 or later
Fees to Review: 0.00 US$

Manuscript Style:
American Psychological Association

CIRCULATION DATA:

Reader: Academics
Frequency of Issue: Quarterly
Copies per Issue: 1,001 - 2,000
Sponsor/Publisher: Direct Marketing Educational Foundation/ John Wiley & Sons
Subscribe Price: 169.00 US$ Individual
550.00 US$ Institute

REVIEW INFORMATION:

Type of Review: Blind Review
No. of External Reviewers: 2
No. of In House Reviewers: 0
Acceptance Rate: 11-20%
Time to Review: 2 - 3 Months
Reviewers Comments: Yes
Invited Articles: 0-5%
Fees to Publish: 0.00 US$

MANUSCRIPT TOPICS:
Communication; Direct Marketing; Interactive Marketing; Internet Marketing; Marketing Theory & Applications; Technology/Innovation

MANUSCRIPT GUIDELINES/COMMENTS:

The *Journal of Interactive Marketing* is an important and timely undertaking in the evolution of the marketing discipline. It is the expectation that the *Journal* will become a major catalyst for helping shape the issues and ideas associated with the emerging interactive/electronic commercial environment, while elevating the level of research conducted around more traditional direct marketing concerns. The *Journal* seeks original research in interactive marketing, broadly defined. Indeed, it is expected that the *Journal* will be instrumental in helping define the term "interactivity" and in setting the research agenda. The areas addressed include, but are not limited to:

- the strategic use of information and information technology as corporate assets
- the analysis of interactive databases
- network-based communications
- customer and managerial behavior in interactive environments

- the evolution of interactive institutions
- the design and testing of interactive marketing decisions

The *Journal of Interactive Marketing* is sponsored by the Direct Marketing Educational Foundation (a unit of the Direct Marketing Association).

Call For Papers
The *Journal of Interactive Marketing* invites papers for upcoming issues. The policy of *Journal of Interactive Marketing* is to publish significant manuscripts–papers that may change the way direct marketing is viewed, studied, and practiced. If this invitation speaks to the potential *Journal of Interactive Marketing* author in you, take us up on it: RSVP.

Manuscript Guidelines
Manuscripts should be typed double-spaced, with pages numbered consecutively. Allow margins of at least one inch on all four sides. Tables and references should be typed on separate pages. Indicate their placement in the text.

Copies. Send 5 copies of the manuscript. Keep the original.

Length. Up to 25 double-spaced typewritten pages, including charts, tables, exhibits, and references. Shorter manuscripts are appreciated. Manuscripts should be accompanied by an abstract of 100 to 125 words on a separate sheet of paper.

Footnotes. The use of footnotes should be **avoided**. If the author feels that a footnote would clarify, extend a point, or improve the readability of the text, a *few* footnotes may be included but never for reference sources. They should appear double-spaced on a separate page and be numbered consecutively throughout the text.

References. References are to be arranged in numbered alphabetical order at the end of the body of the paper, beginning on a separate page. Reference notation in the body of the paper is in parentheses, by number, and may include page numbers. For example, (12) means reference number 12. Two references are separated by a comma, e.g., (12, 16). Page numbers are indicated by a colon, e.g., (12:7), which means reference 12, Page 7.

Disk Submission Instructions
Please return your final, revised manuscript on disk as well as hard copy. The hard copy must match the disk.
The Journal strongly encourages authors to deliver the final, revised version of their accepted manuscripts (text, tables, and, if possible, illustrations) on disk. Given the near-universal use of computer word-processing for manuscript preparation, we anticipate that providing a disk will be convenient for you, and it carries the added advantages of maintaining the integrity of your keystrokes and expediting typesetting. Please return the disk submission slip below with your manuscript and labeled disk(s).

Guidelines For Electronic Submission
Text
Storage medium. 3-1/2" high-density disk in IBM MS-DOS, Windows, or Macintosh format.

Software and format. Microsoft Word 6.0 is preferred, although manuscripts prepared with any other microcomputer word processor are acceptable. Refrain from complex formatting; the Publisher will style your manuscript according to the Journal design specifications. Do not use desktop publishing software such as Aldus PageMaker or Quark XPress. If you prepared your manuscript with one of these programs, export the text to a word processing format. Please make sure your word processing program's "fast save" feature is turned off. Please do not deliver files that contain hidden text: for example, do not use your word processor's automated features to create footnotes or reference lists.

File names. Submit the text and tables of each manuscript as a single file. Name each file with your last name (up to eight letters). Text files should be given the three-letter extension that identifies the file format. Macintosh users should maintain the MS-DOS "eight dot three" file-naming convention.

Labels. Label all disks with your name, the file name, and the word processing program and version used.

Illustrations

All print reproduction requires files for full color images to be in a CMYK color space. If possible, ICC or ColorSync profiles of your output device should accompany all digital image submissions.

Storage medium. Submit as separate files from text files, on separate disks or cartridges. If feasible, full color files should be submitted on separate disks from other image files. 3-1/2" high-density disks, CD, Iomega Zip, and 5 1/4" 44- or 88-MB SyQuest cartridges can be submitted. At authors' request, cartridges and disks will be returned after publication.

Software and format. All illustration files should be in TIFF or EPS (with preview) formats. Do not submit native application formats.

Resolution. Journal quality reproduction will require greyscale and color files at resolutions yielding approximately 300 ppi. Bitmapped line art should be submitted at resolutions yielding 600-1200 ppi. These resolutions refer to the output size of the file; if you anticipate that your images will be enlarged or reduced, resolutions should be adjusted accordingly.

File names. Illustration files should be given the 2- or 3-letter extension that identifies the file format used (i.e., .tif, .eps).

Labels. Label all disks and cartridges with your name, the file names, formats, and compression schemes (if any) used. Hard copy output must accompany all files.

[Print Diskette Label form at www.interscience.wiley.com/jpages/1094-9968/authors.html]

Journal of International Academy for Case Studies

ADDRESS FOR SUBMISSION:

Current Editor's Name/Check Web Page
Journal of International Academy for Case Studies
Submission Address/Check Web Page
Address other Questions to:
  Jim or JoAnn Carland at #'s below
USA
Phone: 828-293-9151
Fax: 828-293-9407
E-Mail: carland@wcu.edu
Web: www.alliedacademies.org
Address May Change:

PUBLICATION GUIDELINES:

Manuscript Length: 16-20
Copies Required: Three
Computer Submission: Yes
Format: WordPerfect 6.1
Fees to Review: 0.00 US$

Manuscript Style:
  American Psychological Association

CIRCULATION DATA:

Reader: Academics
Frequency of Issue: 2 Times/Year
Copies per Issue: Less than 1,000
Sponsor/Publisher: Allied Academies
Subscribe Price: 50.00 US$

REVIEW INFORMATION:

Type of Review: Blind Review
No. of External Reviewers: 2
No. of In House Reviewers: 2
Acceptance Rate: 11-20%
Time to Review: 4 - 6 Months
Reviewers Comments: Yes
Invited Articles: 0-5%
Fees to Publish: 50.00 US$ Membership

MANUSCRIPT TOPICS:

Advertising & Promotion Management; Business Education; Business Information Systems (MIS); Business Law, Public Responsibility & Ethics; Cases in Discipline; Communication; Direct Marketing; Global Business; Health Care Administration; Labor Relations & Human Resource Mgt.; Marketing Research; Marketing Theory & Applications; Non Profit Organizations; Office Administration/Management; Operations Research/Statistics; Organizational Behavior & Theory; Organizational Development; Public Administration; Purchasing/Materials Management; Sales/Selling; Services; Small Business Entrepreneurship; Strategic Management Policy; Technology/Innovation; Transportation/Physical Distribution

MANUSCRIPT GUIDELINES/COMMENTS:

EDITORIAL POLICY GUIDELINES FOR THEORETICAL AND EMPIRICAL MANUSCRIPTS

The Allied Academies affiliates which handle theoretical and empirical manuscripts include the *Academy of Entrepreneurship*, the *Academy of Accounting and Financial Studies*, the *Academy of Marketing Studies*, the *Academy of Strategic and Organizational Leadership*, the

Academy of Managerial Communications, the *Academy of Educational Leadership*, the *Academy of Information and Management Sciences*, and, the *Academy for Studies in Business Law*. These editorial guidelines reflect the Academies' policy with regard to reviewing theoretical and empirical manuscripts for publication and presentation in each of these affiliates.

The primary criterion upon which manuscripts are judged is whether the research advances the discipline. The specific guidelines followed by referees show the areas of evaluation to which each manuscript is subjected. Key points include currency, interest, and relevancy.

Theoretical manuscripts are particularly vulnerable to problems in literature review. In order for theoretical research to advance a discipline, it must address the literature which exists in the discipline to support conclusions or models which extend knowledge and understanding. Consequently, referees for theoretical manuscripts pay particular attention to completeness of literature review and appropriateness of conclusions drawn from that review.

Empirical manuscripts are particularly vulnerable to methodological problems. In order to advance the literature, empirical manuscripts must employ appropriate and effective sampling and statistical analysis techniques. However, empirical papers must also incorporate thorough literature reviews in order to advance the literature. Referees will pay close attention to the conclusions which are drawn from statistical analyses and their consistency with the literature.

We ask referees to be as specific as possible in indicating what must be done to make a manuscript acceptable for journal publication. This embodies a primary objective of the Academy: to assist authors in the research process.

Our Editorial Policy is one which is supportive, rather than critical. We encourage all authors who are not successful in a first attempt to rewrite the manuscript in accordance with the suggestions of the referees. We will be pleased to referee future versions and rewrites of manuscripts and work with authors in achieving their research goals.

EDITORIAL POLICY GUIDELINES FOR EDUCATIONAL AND PEDAGOGIC MANUSCRIPTS

The Allied Academies affiliates which handle educational and pedagogic manuscripts include the *Academy of Entrepreneurship*, the *Academy of Accounting and Financial Studies*, the *Academy of Marketing Studies*, the *Academy of Strategic and Organizational Leadership*, the *Academy of Managerial Communications*, the *Academy of Educational Leadership*, the *Academy of Information and Management Sciences*, and, the *Academy for Studies in Business Law*. These editorial guidelines reflect the Academies' policy with regard to reviewing educational and pedagogic manuscripts for publication and presentation in each of these affiliates.

The primary criterion upon which manuscripts are judged is whether the research advances the teaching profession. The specific guidelines followed by referees show the areas of evaluation to which each manuscript is subjected. Key points include currency, interest, relevancy and usefulness to educators.

In order for educational or pedagogic manuscripts to be useful to educators, they must address appropriate literature to support conclusions, teaching methodologies or pedagogies. Consequently, referees pay particular attention to completeness of literature review and appropriateness of conclusions drawn from that review.

Pedagogies or teaching methodologies must be well described with sound foundations in order to be useful to educators. Referees will pay particular attention to such issues in judging manuscripts.

In every case, educational or pedagogic manuscripts must embody well developed and well documented ideas in order to be useful to educators. Referees will pay close attention to the ideas presented in the manuscript and how well they are presented and supported.

We ask referees to be as specific as possible in indicating what must be done to make a manuscript acceptable for journal publication. This embodies a primary objective of the Academy: to assist authors in the research process.

Our Editorial Policy is one which is supportive, rather than critical. We encourage all authors who are not successful in a first attempt to rewrite the manuscript in accordance with the suggestions of the referees. We will be pleased to referee future versions and rewrites of manuscripts and work with authors in achieving their research goals.

Editorial Comments: All authors of published manuscripts must be members of The Academy. The membership fee is $50.

Journal of International Consumer Marketing

ADDRESS FOR SUBMISSION:

Erdener Kaynak, Executive Editor
Journal of International Consumer
 Marketing
International Business Press
PO Box 399
Middltown, PA 17057
USA
Phone: 717-566-3054
Fax: 717-566-8589
E-Mail: k9x@psu.edu
Web:
Address May Change:

PUBLICATION GUIDELINES:

Manuscript Length: 21-25
Copies Required: Three
Computer Submission: Yes
Format: WdPerfect 5.1 or above
Fees to Review: 0.00 US$

Manuscript Style:
 Chicago Manual of Style

CIRCULATION DATA:

Reader: Academics
Frequency of Issue: Quarterly
Copies per Issue: 1,001 - 2,000
Sponsor/Publisher: Haworth Press, Inc.
Subscribe Price: 54.00 US$ Individual
 81.00 US$ Institutions
 525.00 US$ Libraries

REVIEW INFORMATION:

Type of Review: Blind Review
No. of External Reviewers: 2
No. of In House Reviewers: 1
Acceptance Rate: 11-20%
Time to Review: 1 - 2 Months
Reviewers Comments: Yes
Invited Articles: 0-5%
Fees to Publish: 0.00 US$

MANUSCRIPT TOPICS:
Advertising & Promotion Management; Communication; Direct Marketing; Global Business; Marketing Research; Marketing Theory & Applications; Sales/Selling; Services

MANUSCRIPT GUIDELINES/COMMENTS:

About The Journal

Articles of highest quality, written by practitioners and public policymakers as well as academicians from a variety of countries, offer managerial insights to other practitioners and policymakers to enable them to formulate need-oriented action programs and policies. The journal caters to all professionals who are dealing with overseas customers and/or catering to the needs of international consumers. The journal also benefits teachers of marketing and international business, consultants, and business researchers with "insiders' information" on cross-cultural/national consumer marketing issues.

In particular, persons working within the following fields would find the journal very useful: international marketing departments, trading companies, banks and other financial institutions, government departments and international organizations of dealing with trade, commerce and industry, academics teaching or with research interests in international consumer behavior, research institutions, professional and commercial organizations, firms, and publicly owned international corporations.

Instructions For Authors
1. **Original Articles Only.** Submission of a manuscript to this journal represents a certification on the part of the author(s) that it is an original work, and that neither this manuscript nor a version of it has been published elsewhere nor is being considered for publication elsewhere.

2. **Manuscript Length.** Your manuscript may be approximately 15-25 typed pages double-spaced (including references and abstract). Lengthier manuscripts may be considered, but only at the discretion of the Editor. Sometimes, lengthier manuscripts may be considered if they can be divided up into sections for publication in successive Journal issues.

3. **Manuscript Style.** References, citations, and general style of manuscripts for this Journal should follow the APA style (as outlined in the latest edition of the *Publication Manual of The American Psychological Association*). References should be double-spaced and placed in alphabetical order.

If an author wishes to submit a paper that has been already prepared in another style, he or she may do so. However, if the paper is accepted (with or without reviewer's alterations), the author is fully responsible for retyping the manuscript in the correct style as indicated above. Neither the Editor nor the Publisher is responsible for re-preparing manuscript copy to adhere to the Journal's style.

4. **Manuscript Preparation.**
Margins: leave at least a one-inch margin on all four sides.
Paper: use clean white, 8 1/2 " x 11" bond paper.
Number of Copies: 4 (the original plus three photocopies).
Cover Page: Important--staple a cover page to the manuscript, indicating only the article title (this is used for anonymous refereeing).
Second "Title Page": enclose a regular title page but do not staple it to the manuscript. Include the title again, plus:
- full authorship
- an ABSTRACT of about 100 words. (Below the abstract provide 3-10 key words for index purposes)
- an introductory footnote with authors' academic degrees, professional titles, affiliations, mailing addresses, and any desired acknowledgment of research support or other credit.

5. **Return Envelopes.** When you submit your four manuscript copies,also include:
- a 9" x 12" envelope, self-addressed and stamped (with sufficient postage to ensure return of your manuscript);
- a regular envelope, stamped and self-addressed. This is for the Editor to send you an "acknowledgement of receipt" letter.

6. **Spelling, Grammar, and Punctuation.** You are responsible for preparing manuscript copy which is clearly written in acceptable scholarly English, and which contains no errors of spelling, grammar, or punctuation. Neither the Editor nor the Publisher is responsible for correcting errors of spelling and grammar: the manuscript, after acceptance by the Editor, must be immediately ready for typesetting as it is finally submitted by the author(s). Check your paper for the following common errors:

- dangling modifiers
- misplaced modifiers
- unclear antecedents
- incorrect or inconsistent abbreviations

Also, check the accuracy of all arithmetic calculations, statistics, numerical data, text citations, and references.

7. **Inconsistencies Must Be Avoided.** Be sure you are consistent in your use of abbreviations, terminology, and in citing references, from one part of your paper to another.

8. **Preparation of Tables, Figures, and Illustrations.** All tables and figures, illustrations, etc. must be "camera-ready". That is, they must be cleanly typed or artistically prepared so that they can be used either exactly as they are or else used after a photographic reduction in size. Figures, tables, and illustrations must be prepared on separate sheets of paper. Always use black ink and professional drawing instruments. On the back of these items, write your article title and the journal title lightly in pencil, so they do not get misplaced. In test, skip extra lines and indicate where these figures and tables are to be placed (please do not write on the face of art). Photographs are considered part of the acceptable manuscript and remain with the publisher for use in additional printings.

9. **Alterations Required By Referees And Reviewers.** Many times a paper is accepted by the Editor contigent upon changes that are mandated by anonymous specialist referees and members of the Editorial Board. If the Editor returns your manuscript for revisions, you are responsible for retyping any sections of the paper to incorporate these revisions (if applicable, revisions should also be put on disk).

10. **Typesetting.** You will not be receiving galley proofs o your article. Editorial revisions, if any, must therefore be made while your article is still in manuscript. the final version of the manuscript will be the version you see published. Typesetter's errors will be corrected by the production staff of The Haworth Press. Authors are expected to submit manuscripts, disks, and art that are free from error.

11. **Electronic Media.** Haworth's in-house type-setting unit is able to utilize your final manuscript material as prepared on most personal computers and word processors. This will minimize typographical errors and decrease overall production timelag. Please send the first draft and final draft copies of you manuscript to the journal Editor in print format for his/her final review and approval.

After approval of your final manuscript, please submit the final approved version both on printed format ("hard copy") and floppy diskette. On the outside of the diskette package write:
A. the brand name of your computer or word processor
B. the word-processing program that you used
C. the title of your article, and
D. file name

Note: Disk and hard copy must agree. In case of discrepancies, it is The Haworth Press' policy to follow hard copy. Authors are advised that No Revisions of the manuscript can be made after acceptance by the Editor for publication. The benefits of this procedure are many with speed and accuracy being the most obvious. We look forward to working with you on this, knowing we will be able to serve you more efficiently in the future.

12. **Reprints**. The senior author will receive two copies of the journal issue and 10 complimentary reprints of his or her article. The junior author will receive two copies of the journal issue and 10 complimentary reprints of his or her article. The junior author will receive two copies of the journal issue. These are sent several weeks after the journal issue is published and in circulation. An order form for the purchase of additional reprints will also be sent to all authors at this time. (Approximately 4-6 weeks is necessary for the preparation of reprints.) Please do not query the Journal's Editor about reprints. All such questions should be sent directly to The Haworth Press, Inc. Production Department, 21 East Broad Street, West Hazleton, PA 18201 USA. To order additional reprints (minimum: 50 copies), please contact The Haworth Document Delivery Center, 10 alice Street, Binghamton, NY 13904-1580 USA; 1-800-342-9678, (607) 722-5857 or Fax (607) 722-6362.

13. **Copyright**. Copyright ownership of your manuscript must be transferred officially to The Haworth Press, Inc. before we can begin the peer-review process. The Editor's letter acknowledging receipt of the manuscript will be accompanied by a form fully explaining this. All authors must sign the form and return the original to the Editor as soon as possible. Failure to return the copyright form in a timely fashion will result in delay in review and subsequent publication.

14. **Examples To Format**.

Examples of Reference to Periodicals:
1. Journal Article: One Author.
Levitt, T. (1983). The Globalizatin of Markets, Harvard Business Review. (May-June), 61 (3), 92-102.
2. Journal Article: Multiple Authors.
Kaynak, E. and Mitchell A.L. (1981). Analysis of Marketing Strategies Used in Diverse Cultures, Journal of Advertising Research (June), 21 (3), 25-32.
3. Magazine Article.
Tinnin, D.B. (1981, November 16) The Heady Success of Holland's Heineken, Fortune, pp. 158-164.
4. Newspaper Article.
The opportunity of world brands, (1984, June 3), The New York Times, p. 6F.
5. Monograph.

Franko, L.G. (1979). A Survey of the Impact of Manugactured Exports From Industrializing Countries in Asia and Latin America, Changing International Realities [Monograph] No. 6.

Examples of References to Books:
1. Reference to an Entire Book.
Kaynak, E. (1986) Marketing and Economic Development, New York: Praeger Publishers Inc.
2. Book with a Corporate Author.
Committee For Economic Development (1981) Transnational Corporatin for Developing Countries, New York: Author.
3. Edited Book.
Kaynak, E. (ed.) (1985) Global Perspectives in Marketing, New York: Praeger Publishers Inc.
4. Book with No Author or Editor.
Marketing Opportunities in Japan (1978). London: Dentsu Incorporated.
5. Article or Chapter in an Edited Book.
Bucklin, L.P. (1986). Improving Food Retailing in Less Developed Asian Countries. In E. Daynak (Ed.) World Food Marketing Systems (pp. 73-81) London: Butterworth Scientific Publishers.

Proceedings of Meetings and Symposia:
1. Published Proceedings, Published Contributions to a Symposium.
Lee, K.H. (1981). From Production Orientation to Marketing Orientation-Hong Kong in the Internatinal Trade Setting. In D.B. Yeaman (Ed.) Developing Global Corporate Strategies (pp. 753-766). Conference held at the University of Navarra, Barcelona, Spain, 2 (December 17-19).
2. Unpublished Paper Presented at a Meeting.
Yucelt, U. (1987). Tourism Marketing Planning in Developing Economies. Paper presented at the annual meeting of the Academy of Marketing Science, Bal harbour, Florida.

Doctoral Dissertations:
1. Unpublished Doctoral Dissertation.
Czintoka, M.F. (1980). An Analysis of Export Development Strategies in Selected U.S. Industries. Dissertations Abstract International (University Microfilms No. 80-15, 865).

For reference to unpublished manuscripts, publications of limited circulation, reviews and interviews and nonprint media please refer to the latest edition of *Publication Manual of American Psychological Association.*

Publication Agreement
(This form must be completed and must accompany all manuscripts submitted for review.)
1. **Copyright**: In consideration for review and possible subsequent publication of our Work in the journal noted on the reverse side of this page, the Author(s) agree to transfer copyright of the work to The Haworth Press, Inc., including full and exclusive rights to publication in all media now known or later developed, including but not limited to electronic databases and microfilm, and in anthologies of any kind. (Note to U.S. Government employees: see your exemption, paragraph 5 below.)

2. Author Re-Use Of Work: As a professional courtesy, the authors retain the right to reprint their article submitted again, after publication in the journal in any work for which they are sole Author, or in any edited work for which the author is Senior Editor. No further permission is necessary in writing from The Haworth Press, Inc., nor will the Press require fees of any kind for the reprinting. This statement is intended to provide full copyright release for the purposes listed above, and a photocopy of the release may be used when another Publisher requires a written release.

3. **Author Warranties**: The author(s) represent(s) and warrant(s):
a) that the manuscript submitted is his/her (their) own work;
b) that the work has been submitted only to this journal and that it has not been previously published;
c) that the article contains no libelous or unlawful statements and does not infringe upon the civil rights of others;
d) that the author(s) is (are) not infringing upon anyone else's copyright.
The authors agree that if there is a breach of any of the above representations and warranties that (s)he (they) will indemnify the Publisher and Editor and hold them harmless.

4. Author Retention of Patents: The author(s) may have, within their article, descriptions of their own proprietary patents. It is not the intention of the Editor or Publisher to require copyright transfer of such materials. If any of these materials appear in the work, the authors may add their personal copyright notice to patents, with this understanding:

a) the author(s) retain copyright for said patents, with full and exclusive rights to their publication, not to include any other material from the article/publication;
b) the Publisher retains full and exclusive rights to publication to the article/publication in any format, including patents when published as part of the entire article or publication.
c) photographs are considered part of the acceptable manuscript and remain with the Publisher for use in additional printings.

5. **Note for u.s. Government employees**: If the article is single-authored by a U.S. government employee as part of his/her official duties, it is understood that the article is not copyrightable. It is called a "Work of the U.S. Government." However, if the article was not part of the employee's official duties, it may be copyrighted. If the article was jointly written, the authors understand that they are delegating the right of copyright to the nongovernmental employee, who must sign this agreement.

6. **"Work For Hire" Authors**: If the article was written by an author who was hired by another person or company to do so, the article is called a "Work for Hire" manuscript. This agreement must then be signed by the "employer" who hired the author, as well as the author.

7. **No Amendments**: No amendments or modifications of the terms of this Agreement are permissible unless same shall be in writing and signed by a duly authorized officer of The Haworth Press, Inc. No Journal Editor, Guest Editor or Special Issue Editor is authorized to waive, amend or modify any of the procedures or other provisions of this Agreement. This form is not valid if the Author(s) add any additional constraints and amendments. Please

submit the article elsewhere for publication if the Author(s) do not sign this Agreement without alteration.

8. Integration: This Agreement embodies the entire agreement and understanding between the Author and The Haworth Press, Inc. and supersedes all other agreements and understandings, whether oral or written, relating to the subject matter hereof.

COPYRIGHT TRANSFER FORM

Name of journal:

Name and **Exact** Mailing Address of Contributor:

Special note: this will be used for mailing reprints. You must include exact street address, name of your department if at a university, and ZIP CODE. The Haworth Press cannot be responsible for lost reprints if you do not Provide us with your exact mailing address.

In Reference To Your Journal Article:

___ **If this box is checked...**

Thank you for your article submission! Please allow 10-15 weeks for the review process. Before sending out your article for review, however, the Publisher requires us to obtain your signature(s) confirming that you have read the PUBLICATION AGREEMENT on the reverse side of this page.

All co-authors must sign and return the ORIGINAL signed copy.

IT IS CONFIRMED that I/we have read the PUBLICATION AGREEMENT on the reverse side of the page, and agree and accept all conditions:

author's signature	date
author's signature	date
author's signature	date

Other Comments: _____

Please reply to
( ) Journal Editor: Erdener Kaynak, PhD, DSc
 Executive Editor
 International Business
 P.O. Box 399
 Middletown, PA 17057

( ) Guest Editor / Special Issue Editor:

___ **It this box is checked...**

Your article has been favorably reviewed. Our reviewers, however, require certain revisions which are indicated on the attached sheets. Please review and incorporate their suggestions, and return your manuscript/disk retyped within 14 days. A decision about publication will he made at that time. Thank you for your help and cooperation.

___ **If this box is checked...**

We are pleased to inform you that your article has been accepted for publication in the journal noted above, or (if noted) by a special issue/ edition/monographic supplement to the journal.

Please note the following:

1. Publication: Your article is currently scheduled to appear in

Volume: _____ Number: _____

Published during this season: _____

2. **Typesetting**: Your article will be sent to the Production Department of The Haworth Press, Inc., 21 East Broad Street, West Hazleton, PA 18201. They will typeset your article (preferably from your computer disk) exactly as submitted. Please note that you will not be receiving galley proofs. The production staff will proofread the galleys for typesetting errors against the final version of the manuscript as submitted. No revisions are allowed.

3. **Reprints**: Shortly after publication you will receive an order form for purchasing quantities of reprints. (About three weeks after publication, the senior author will receive two complimentary copies of the issue and ten copies of the article, and the junior author(s) will receive two complimentary copies of the issue.) Please note that preparation of reprints takes about eight weeks additional time after the actual issue is printed and in circulation.

___ **If this box is checked...**

We are sorry, but the reviewers for this journal did not agree that your article was appropriate for publication in this periodical. If the reviewers consented in having their comments forwarded to you, their critiques are attached. Your submission is appreciated, and we hope that you will contribute again in the future.

Journal of International Food & Agribusiness Marketing

ADDRESS FOR SUBMISSION:

Erdener Kaynak, Executive Editor
Journal of International Food &
   Agribusiness Marketing
International Business Press
PO Box 399
Middeltown, PA 17057
USA
Phone: 717-566-3054
Fax: 717-566-8589
E-Mail: k9x@psu.edu
Web: www.haworthpress.com
Address May Change:

PUBLICATION GUIDELINES:

Manuscript Length: 15-25
Copies Required: Three
Computer Submission: Yes
Format: WordPerfect 5.1 or above
Fees to Review: 0.00 US$

Manuscript Style:
   Chicago Manual of Style

CIRCULATION DATA:

Reader: Academics
Frequency of Issue: Quarterly
Copies per Issue: Less than 1,000
Sponsor/Publisher: Haworth Pres, Inc.
Subscribe Price: 60.00 US$ Individual
   75.00 US$ Institution
   175.00 US$ Library

REVIEW INFORMATION:

Type of Review: Blind Review
No. of External Reviewers: 2
No. of In House Reviewers: 1
Acceptance Rate: 21-30%
Time to Review: 1 - 2 Months
Reviewers Comments: Yes
Invited Articles: 0-5%
Fees to Publish: 0.00 US$

MANUSCRIPT TOPICS:

Business Information Systems (MIS); Communication; Direct Marketing; Food & Agribusiness; Global Business; Marketing Research; Purchasing/Materials Management; Sales/Selling; Transportation/Physical Distribution

MANUSCRIPT GUIDELINES/COMMENTS:

About The Journal

Here is a timely journal that serves as a forum for the exchange and dissemination of food and agribusiness marketing knowledge and experiences on an international scale. Designed to study the characteristics and workings of food and agribusiness marketing systems around the world, the *Journal of International Food & Agribusiness Marketing* critically examines marketing issues in the total food business chain prevailing in different parts of the globe by using a systems and cross-cultural/national approach to explain the many facets of food marketing in a range of socioeconomic and political systems.

Scholars, practitioners, and public policymakers share up-to-date and insightful information - both descriptive and analytical - on international food and agribusiness marketing theory and practice. In particular, they place a special emphasis on the exporting and importing of food products between developed and developing countries. Methods for improving food and agribusiness marketing practices in developing countries and the transfer of food marketing technology from advanced countries are discussed.

Instructions For Authors

1. **Original Articles Only**. Submission of a manuscript to this journal represents a certification on the part of the author(s) that it is an original work, and that neither this manuscript nor a version of it has been published elsewhere nor is being considered for publication elsewhere.

2. **Manuscript Length**. Your manuscript may be approximately 15-25 typed pages double-spaced (including references and abstract). Lengthier manuscripts may be considered, but only at the discretion of the Editor. Sometimes, lengthier manuscripts may be considered if they can be divided up into sections for publication in successive Journal issues.

3. **Manuscript Style**. References, citations, and general style of manuscripts for this Journal should follow the APA style (as outlined in the latest edition of the *Publication Manual of The American Psychological Association*). References should be double-spaced and placed in alphabetical order.

If an author wishes to submit a paper that has been already prepared in another style, he or she may do so. However, if the paper is accepted (with or without reviewer's alterations), the author is fully responsible for retyping the manuscript in the correct style as indicated above. Neither the Editor nor the Publisher is responsible for re-preparing manuscript copy to adhere to the Journal's style.

4. **Manuscript Preparation**.
Margins: leave at least a one-inch margin on all four sides.
Paper: use clean white, 8 1/2 " x 11" bond paper.
Number of Copies: 4 (the original plus three photocopies).
Cover Page: Important--staple a cover page to the manuscript, indicating only the article title (this is used for anonymous refereeing).
Second "Title Page": enclose a regular title page but do not staple it to the manuscript. Include the title again, plus:
- full authorship
- an ABSTRACT of about 100 words. (Below the abstract provide 3-10 key words for index purposes)
- an introductory footnote with authors' academic degrees, professional titles, affiliations, mailing addresses, and any desired acknowledgment of research support or other credit.

5. **Return Envelopes**. When you submit your four manuscript copies, also include:
- a 9" x 12" envelope, self-addressed and stamped (with sufficient postage to ensure return of your manuscript);
- a regular envelope, stamped and self-addressed. This is for the Editor to send you an "acknowledgement of receipt" letter.

6. **Spelling, Grammar, and Punctuation.** You are responsible for preparing manuscript copy which is clearly written in acceptable scholarly English, and which contains no errors of spelling, grammar, or punctuation. Neither the Editor nor the Publisher is responsible for correcting errors of spelling and grammar: the manuscript, after acceptance by the Editor, must be immediately ready for typesetting as it is finally submitted by the author(s). Check your paper for the following common errors:
- dangling modifiers
- misplaced modifiers
- unclear antecedents
- incorrect or inconsistent abbreviations

Also, check the accuracy of all arithmetic calculations, statistics, numerical data, text citations, and references.

7. **Inconsistencies Must Be Avoided.** Be sure you are consistent in your use of abbreviations, terminology, and in citing references, from one part of your paper to another.

8. **Preparation of Tables, Figures, and Illustrations.** All tables and figures, illustrations, etc. must be "camera-ready". That is, they must be cleanly typed or artistically prepared so that they can be used either exactly as they are or else used after a photographic reduction in size. Figures, tables, and illustrations must be prepared on separate sheets of paper. Always use black ink and professional drawing instruments. On the back of these items, write your article title and the journal title lightly in pencil, so they do not get misplaced. In test, skip extra lines and indicate where these figures and tables are to be placed (please do not write on the face of art). Photographs are considered part of the acceptable manuscript and remain with the publisher for use in additional printings.

9. **Alterations Required By Referees And Reviewers.** Many times a paper is accepted by the Editor contigent upon changes that are mandated by anonymous specialist referees and members of the Editorial Board. If the Editor returns your manuscript for revisions, you are responsible for retyping any sections of the paper to incorporate these revisions (if applicable, revisions should also be put on disk).

10. **Typesetting.** You will not be receiving galley proofs o your article. Editorial revisions, if any, must therefore be made while your article is still in manuscript. the final version of the manuscript will be the version you see published. Typesetter's errors will be corrected by the production staff of The Haworth Press. Authors are expected to submit manuscripts, disks, and art that are free from error.

11. **Electronic Media.** Haworth's in-house type-setting unit is able to utilize your final manuscript material as prepared on most personal computers and word processors. This will minimize typographical errors and decrease overall production timelag. Please send the first draft and final draft copies of you manuscript to the journal Editor in print format for his/her final review and approval.

After approval of your final manuscript, please submit the final approved version both on printed format ("hard copy") and floppy diskette. On the outside of the diskette package write:
A. the brand name of your computer or word processor
B. the word-processing program that you used
C. the title of your article, and
D. file name

Note: Disk and hard copy must agree. In case of discrepancies, it is The Haworth Press' policy to follow hard copy. Authors are advised that No Revisions of the manuscript can be made after acceptance by the Editor for publication. The benefits of this procedure are many with speed and accuracy being the most obvious. We look forward to working with you on this, knowing we will be able to serve you more efficiently in the future.

12. **Reprints**. The senior author will receive two copies of the journal issue and 10 complimentary reprints of his or her article. The junior author will receive two copies of the journal issue and 10 complimentary reprints of his or her article. The junior author will receive two copies of the journal issue. These are sent several weeks after the journal issue is published and in circulation. An order form for the purchase of additional reprints will also be sent to all authors at this time. (Approximately 4-6 weeks is necessary for the preparation of reprints.) Please do not query the Journal's Editor about reprints. All such questions should be sent directly to The Haworth Press, Inc. Production Department, 21 East Broad Street, West Hazleton, PA 18201 USA. To order additional reprints (minimum: 50 copies), please contact The Haworth Document Delivery Center, 10 alice Street, Binghamton, NY 13904-1580 USA; 1-800-342-9678, (607) 722-5857 or Fax (607) 722-6362.

13. **Copyright**. Copyright ownership of your manuscript must be transferred officially to The Haworth Press, Inc. before we can begin the peer-review process. The Editor's letter acknowledging receipt of the manuscript will be accompanied by a form fully explaining this. All authors must sign the form and return the original to the Editor as soon as possible. Failure to return the copyright form in a timely fashion will result in delay in review and subsequent publication.

14. **Examples To Format**.

Examples of Reference to Periodicals:
1. Journal Article: One Author.
Levitt, T. (1983). The Globalizatin of Markets, Harvard Business Review. (May-June), 61 (3), 92-102.
2. Journal Article: Multiple Authors.
Kaynak, E. and Mitchell A.L. (1981). Analysis of Marketing Strategies Used in Diverse Cultures, Journal of Advertising Research (June), 21 (3), 25-32.
3. Magazine Article.
Tinnin, D.B. (1981, November 16) The Heady Success of Holland's Heineken, Fortune, pp. 158-164.
4. Newspaper Article.
The opportunity of world brands, (1984, June 3), The New York Times, p. 6F.
5. Monograph.

Franko, L.G. (1979). A Survey of the Impact of Manugactured Exports From Industrializing Countries in Asia and Latin America, Changing International Realities [Monograph] No. 6.

Examples of References to Books:
1. Reference to an Entire Book.
Kaynak, E. (1986) Marketing and Economic Development, New York: Praeger Publishers Inc.
2. Book with a Corporate Author.
Committee For Economic Development (1981) Transnational Corporatin for Developing Countries, New York: Author.
3. Edited Book.
Kaynak, E. (ed.) (1985) Global Perspectives in Marketing, New York: Praeger Publishers Inc.
4. Book with No Author or Editor.
Marketing Opportunities in Japan (1978). London: Dentsu Incorporated.
5. Article or Chapter in an Edited Book.
Bucklin, L.P. (1986). Improving Food Retailing in Less Developed Asian Countries. In E. Daynak (Ed.) World Food Marketing Systems (pp. 73-81) London: Butterworth Scientific Publishers.

Proceedings of Meetings and Symposia:
1. Published Proceedings, Published Contributions to a Symposium.
Lee, K.H. (1981). From Production Orientation to Marketing Orientation-Hong Kong in the Internatinal Trade Setting. In D.B. Yeaman (Ed.) Developing Global Corporate Strategies (pp. 753-766). Conference held at the University of Navarra, Barcelona, Spain, 2 (December 17-19).
2. Unpublished Paper Presented at a Meeting.
Yucelt, U. (1987). Tourism Marketing Planning in Developing Economies. Paper presented at the annual meeting of the Academy of Marketing Science, Bal harbour, Florida.

Doctoral Dissertations:
1. Unpublished Doctoral Dissertation.
Czintoka, M.F. (1980). An Analysis of Export Development Strategies in Selected U.S. Industries. Dissertations Abstract International (University Microfilms No. 80-15, 865).

For reference to unpublished manuscripts, publications of limited circulation, reviews and interviews and nonprint media please refer to the latest edition of *Publication Manual of American Psychological Association*.

Publication Agreement
(This form must be completed and must accompany all manuscripts submitted for review.)
1. **Copyright**: In consideration for review and possible subsequent publication of our Work in the journal noted on the reverse side of this page, the Author(s) agree to transfer copyright of the work to The Haworth Press, Inc., including full and exclusive rights to publication in all media now known or later developed, including but not limited to electronic databases and microfilm, and in anthologies of any kind. (Note to U.S. Government employees: see your exemption, paragraph 5 below.)

2. Author Re-Use Of Work: As a professional courtesy, the authors retain the right to reprint their article submitted again, after publication in the journal in any work for which they are sole Author, or in any edited work for which the author is Senior Editor. No further permission is necessary in writing from The Haworth Press, Inc., nor will the Press require fees of any kind for the reprinting. This statement is intended to provide full copyright release for the purposes listed above, and a photocopy of the release may be used when another Publisher requires a written release.

3. Author Warranties: The author(s) represent(s) and warrant(s):
a) that the manuscript submitted is his/her (their) own work;
b) that the work has been submitted only to this journal and that it has not been previously published;
c) that the article contains no libelous or unlawful statements and does not infringe upon the civil rights of others;
d) that the author(s) is (are) not infringing upon anyone else's copyright.
The authors agree that if there is a breach of any of the above representations and warranties that (s)he (they) will indemnify the Publisher and Editor and hold them harmless.

4. Author Retention of Patents: The author(s) may have, within their article, descriptions of their own proprietary patents. It is not the intention of the Editor or Publisher to require copyright transfer of such materials. If any of these materials appear in the work, the authors may add their personal copyright notice to patents, with this understanding:

a) the author(s) retain copyright for said patents, with full and exclusive rights to their publication, not to include any other material from the article/publication;
b) the Publisher retains full and exclusive rights to publication to the article/publication in any format, including patents when published as part of the entire article or publication.
c) photographs are considered part of the acceptable manuscript and remain with the Publisher for use in additional printings.

5. Note for u.s. Government employees: If the article is single-authored by a U.S. government employee as part of his/her official duties, it is understood that the article is not copyrightable. It is called a "Work of the U.S. Government." However, if the article was not part of the employee's official duties, it may be copyrighted. If the article was jointly written, the authors understand that they are delegating the right of copyright to the nongovernmental employee, who must sign this agreement.

6. "Work For Hire" Authors: If the article was written by an author who was hired by another person or company to do so, the article is called a "Work for Hire" manuscript. This agreement must then be signed by the "employer" who hired the author, as well as the author.

7. No Amendments: No amendments or modifications of the terms of this Agreement are permissible unless same shall be in writing and signed by a duly authorized officer of The Haworth Press, Inc. No Journal Editor, Guest Editor or Special Issue Editor is authorized to waive, amend or modify any of the procedures or other provisions of this Agreement. This form is not valid if the Author(s) add any additional constraints and amendments. Please

submit the article elsewhere for publication if the Author(s) do not sign this Agreement without alteration.

8. Integration: This Agreement embodies the entire agreement and understanding between the Author and The Haworth Press, Inc. and supersedes all other agreements and understandings, whether oral or written, relating to the subject matter hereof.

COPYRIGHT TRANSFER FORM

Name of journal:

Name and **Exact** Mailing Address of Contributor:

Special note: this will be used for mailing reprints. You must include exact street address, name of your department if at a university, and ZIP CODE. The Haworth Press cannot be responsible for lost reprints if you do not Provide us with your exact mailing address.

In Reference To Your Journal Article:

___ **If this box is checked...**

Thank you for your article submission! Please allow 10-15 weeks for the review process. Before sending out your article for review, however, the Publisher requires us to obtain your signature(s) confirming that you have read the PUBLICATION AGREEMENT on the reverse side of this page.

All co-authors must sign and return the ORIGINAL signed copy.

IT IS CONFIRMED that I/we have read the PUBLICATION AGREEMENT on the reverse side of the page, and agree and accept all conditions:

author's signature	date
author's signature	date
author's signature	date

Other Comments: _____

_____

Please reply to
( ) Journal Editor: Erdener Kaynak, PhD, DSc
　　　　　　　　　Executive Editor
　　　　　　　　　International Business
　　　　　　　　　P.O. Box 399
　　　　　　　　　Middletown, PA 17057

( ) Guest Editor / Special Issue Editor:

___ **It this box is checked...**

Your article has been favorably reviewed. Our reviewers, however, require certain revisions which are indicated on the attached sheets. Please review and incorporate their suggestions, and return your manuscript/disk retyped within 14 days. A decision about publication will he made at that time. Thank you for your help and cooperation.

___ **If this box is checked...**

We are pleased to inform you that your article has been accepted for publication in the journal noted above, or (if noted) by a special issue/ edition/monographic supplement to the journal.

Please note the following:

1. Publication: Your article is currently scheduled to appear in

Volume: _____ Number: _____

Published during this season: _____

2. **Typesetting**: Your article will be sent to the Production Department of The Haworth Press, Inc., 21 East Broad Street, West Hazleton, PA 18201. They will typeset your article (preferably from your computer disk) exactly as submitted. Please note that you will not be receiving galley proofs. The production staff will proofread the galleys for typesetting errors against the final version of the manuscript as submitted. No revisions are allowed.

3. **Reprints**: Shortly after publication you will receive an order form for purchasing quantities of reprints. (About three weeks after publication, the senior author will receive two complimentary copies of the issue and ten copies of the article, and the junior author(s) will receive two complimentary copies of the issue.) Please note that preparation of reprints takes about eight weeks additional time after the actual issue is printed and in circulation.

___ **If this box is checked...**

We are sorry, but the reviewers for this journal did not agree that your article was appropriate for publication in this periodical. If the reviewers consented in having their comments forwarded to you, their critiques are attached. Your submission is appreciated, and we hope that you will contribute again in the future.

Journal of International Marketing

ADDRESS FOR SUBMISSION:

Bodo Schlegelmilch, Editor-In-Chief
Journal of International Marketing
Wirtschaftuniversitat Wien
Augasse 206
1090 Vienna,
Austria
Phone: 43 1 313 365103
Fax: 43 1 313 36793
E-Mail: bodo.schlegelmilch@wu-wien.ac.at
Web: www.ama.org
Address May Change:

PUBLICATION GUIDELINES:

Manuscript Length: 35 Maximum
Copies Required: Four
Computer Submission: No
Format: N/A
Fees to Review: 0.00 US$

Manuscript Style:
 See Manuscript Guidelines,
 References/Chicago Manual, 14th ed.

CIRCULATION DATA:

Reader: Academics, & Practitioners
Frequency of Issue: Quarterly
Copies per Issue: Less than 1,000
Sponsor/Publisher: American Marketing
 Association
Subscribe Price: 125.00 US$ Institution
 40.00 US$ AMA Member with ID#
 75.00 US$ Non-Member of AMA

REVIEW INFORMATION:

Type of Review: Blind Review
No. of External Reviewers: 2
No. of In House Reviewers: 1
Acceptance Rate: 20%
Time to Review: 1 - 2 Months
Reviewers Comments: Yes
Invited Articles: No Reply
Fees to Publish: 0.00 US$

MANUSCRIPT TOPICS:
Global Business; Marketing Research; Marketing Theory & Applications; Small Business Entrepreneurship; Strategic Management Policy

MANUSCRIPT GUIDELINES/COMMENTS:

Introduction

As the globalization of markets continues at a rapid pace, business practitioners and educators alike face the challenge of staying current with the developments. Marketing managers require a source of new information and insights on international business events. International marketing educators require a forum for disseminating their thoughts and research findings.
Journal of International Marketing (JIM) is designed to serve both the practitioner and educator audiences. Its primary mission is to contribute to the advancement of international marketing practice and theory. JIM brings to the readership a selection of original articles, executive insights, and book reviews. The journal is published quarterly with issues appearing spring, summer, fall and winter.

EDITORIAL GUIDELINES

Journal of International Marketing is an international, peer-reviewed journal dedicated to advancing international marketing practice, research, and theory. Contributions addressing any aspect of international marketing management are welcome. The journal presents scholarly and managerially relevant articles on international marketing. Aimed at both international marketing/business scholars and practitioners at senior and middle level international marketing positions, the prime objective is to bridge the gap between theory and practice in international marketing.

The editors encourage scholars and practitioners from around the world to submit articles with a diverse approach to international marketing. They welcome traditional empirical articles on important international marketing management issues, thoughtful essays on international marketing trends and practices, in-depth case studies of individual companies or industries, and integrative research reviews. These articles can be traditional narrative reviews or meta-analyses that result in theories, models, or further research agenda. Articles should be written in a clear, concise, and logical manner.

All submissions are subject to a double-blind refereeing process. Journal of International Marketing strives to publish work of the highest quality. Synthesis, replication with advancement, systematic extension, and work that disconfirms assumptions about international marketing are appropriate for submission. Managerial relevance is a key criterion in the final decision process.

The JIM Editorial Board is committed to providing authors with timely and constructive reviews. Turnaround time for most manuscripts is seven weeks. Manuscript acceptance rate for the past year is 21 percent.

Editorial Philosophy
The following provides a more specific articulation of the editorial position of JIM:

The domain is international marketing management. The principal topical area is marketing aspects of global business operations. The journal strives to give special emphasis to mainstream issues in international marketing management and strategy such as market entry, segmentation, positioning, pricing, channel development, product/service innovation, customer service, company organization, and globalization.

JIM's Audience includes educators and students of international marketing, thoughtful practitioners of business enterprises engaged in international business activities, and those involved in formulating public policy for international marketing activity.

Coverage is managerial. The ultimate criterion for publication in JIM is relevance for international marketing practice. Does the work offer rich managerial insights? Will it have some impact on practice? Please note that purely comparative studies are not appropriate for JIM. Comparisons of marketing institutions, concepts, etc., are not automatically suitable for JIM unless they explore an issue of importance for the international marketing manager and develop some broader conceptual insights.

The focus is on firm strategy and practice, not consumer behavior. JIM prefers to publish articles about business enterprises engaged in international marketing, such as manufacturers, service firms, intermediaries, trading companies, franchisors, licensors, and facilitators in international business (e.g., freight forwarders). Equal attention is given to small and large company players (e.g., multinationals) as well as to all modes of international business entry (e.g., exporting, contractual arrangements, and direct investment). Discussion of newer forms of cross-border business activity such as strategic alliances and global sourcing is also encouraged.

Although the typical consumer behavior studies may not meet the editorial objectives of JIM, this does not imply indifference to consumer needs and wants. On the contrary, such issues as the implications of customer orientation in multinational business, cross-cultural market segmentation, and market research are of concern to international marketing management and, therefore, to JIM.

The approach is interdisciplinary. In practice, marketing functions are intertwined with other business activities such as corporate strategy, procurement, logistics, human resource management, research and development, manufacturing, etc. Therefore, JIM especially encourages articles that provide holistic views of international marketing phenomena and those that explore interrelationships between marketing and other business functions.

Article formats are diverse. JIM publishes works in a variety of formats. First, traditional empirical articles on important international marketing management issues are welcome. Second, thoughtful essays on international marketing trends and practices are desirable. Third, in-depth case studies of individual companies or industries are welcome. Fourth, integrative research reviews are also of interest. These articles can be traditional narrative reviews or meta-analyses that result in theories, models, or further research agenda. Fifth, JIM encourages "Executive Insights"--pieces that report and express opinions on important and timely issues in international marketing practice-- and "Educator Insights"--articles that are useful teaching tools.

The writing style is non-technical. Although the articles published must meet rigorous methodological criteria, the JIM editorial board strives to publish works that are written in an interesting, highly readable style. Articles should be written in a clear, concise, and logical manner. The text should appeal to a wide audience by avoiding the use of methodological/technical jargon wherever possible. It may be more appropriate to include technical details in an appendix rather than in the body of the article.

MANUSCRIPT GUIDELINES

Manuscript and Disk Preparation
Submit four (4) paper copies of your manuscript to the Editor. (Do not submit disk copies until directed to do so by the editor.)

Keep an extra, exact copy for future reference.

Manuscripts should not exceed thirty-five (35) pages, inclusive of all text, tables, figures, appendices, etc. Manuscripts should be typed double spaced throughout (including references) on 8 1/2 x 11 inch white, nonerasable paper.

Allow margins of at least one inch on all four sides and do not justify your right-hand margin. Type on one side of the paper only.

What Goes Where
First page: Name of author(s) and title; authors(s) footnote, including present position, complete address, telephone number, fax number, and e-mail address (if available). Also include any acknowledgment of financial or technical assistance.

Second page: Title of paper (without author's name) and a brief abstract of no more than 50 words substantively summarizing the article. It should be informative, giving the reader a "taste" of the article.

Next: The text with major headings centered on the page and subheadings flush with the left margin.

Then: Technical appendices if applicable.

Followed by: Endnotes numbered consecutively on a separate page. JIM does not use footnotes.

Then: Tables, numbered consecutively, each on a separate page. If tables appear in an appendix, they should be numbered separately and consecutively, as in Table A-1, A-2, and so on.

Last: References, typed double spaced in alphabetical order by author's last name.

MATHEMATICAL NOTATION
JIM discourages the use of mathematical notations in the body of the article. If essential, these can be included in an endnote or appendix.

TABLES
Tables should consist of at least four columns and four rows; otherwise they should be left as in-text tabulations or their results should be integrated in the text.
The table number and title should be typed on separate lines, centered.
Use only horizontal rules.
Designate units (e.g., %, $) in column headings.
Align all decimals.
Refer to tables in text by number. Avoid using "above," "below," and "preceding."
If possible, combine closely related tables.
Indicate placement in text.
Make sure the necessary measures of statistical significance are reported with the table.

FIGURES AND CAMERA-READY ARTWORK
Figures should be prepared professionally on disk and as camera-ready copy. PhotoShop, Illustrator, and PowerPoint formats are preferred.

Label both vertical and horizontal axes. The ordinate label should be centered above the ordinate axis; the abscissa label should be placed beneath the abscissa.

Place all calibration tics inside the axis lines, with the values outside the axis lines. The figure number and title should be typed on separate lines, centered.

Once a manuscript has been accepted, complex tables and all figures must be on disk and camera-ready. Table and figure headings should be typed on a separate page and attached to the appropriate camera-ready art. These titles will be set in our own typeface.

Lettering should be large enough to be read easily with 50% reduction.

Do not submit camera-ready art until your manuscript has been accepted. When the artwork is completed, submit photocopies.

Reference Citations Within the Text
Citations in the text should be by the author's last name and year of publication enclosed in parentheses without punctuation: "(Thorelli 1960)." If practical, the citation should stand by a punctuation mark. Otherwise, insert it in a logical sentence break. If you use the author's name within the sentence, there is no need to repeat the name in the citation; just use the year of publication in parentheses, as in "...The Howard Harris Program (1966)."

If a particular page, section, or equation is cited, it should be placed within the parentheses: "(Thorelli 1960, p. 112)." For multiple authors, use the full citation for up to three authors; for four or more, use the first author's name followed by "et al." (no italics). A series of citations should be listed in alphabetical order and separated by semicolons: (Terpstra 1961; Thorelli 1960; Welch 1981).

Reference List Style
References are to be listed alphabetically, last name first, followed by publication date in parentheses. Use full first name, not just initials. The reference list should be typed double spaced on a separate page. Do not use indents or tabs. Put two hard returns between each reference. Limit the references to only those that are essential.

Authors are responsible for the accuracy of their references. Check them carefully.

Single- and multiple-author reference for books:
Terpstra, Vern and Ravi Sarathy (1991), International Marketing. Chicago: The Dryden Press.

Single- and multiple-author reference for periodicals (include author's name, publication date, article title, complete name of periodical, volume number, month of publication, and page numbers):

Green, Robert T. and A.W. Allaway (1981), "Identification of Export Opportunities: A Shift-share Approach," Journal of Marketing, 49 (Winter), 83-88.

Single- and multiple-author reference for an article in a book edited by another author(s):
Cavusgil, S. Tamer (1982), "Country of Origin Effects on Product Evaluations: A Sequel to Bilkey and Ness," in Export Management-An International Context, Michael R. Czinkota and George Tesar, eds. New York: Praeger Publishers, 276-86.

If an author appears more than once, substitute four hyphens (this will appear as a 1-inch line when typeset) for each author's name (do not use underlines):
Bartlett, Christopher A. and Sumantra Ghoshal (1986), "Tap Your Subsidiary for Global Reach," Harvard Business Review, (November-December), 87-97.
---- and ---- (1987a), "Managing Across Borders: New Strategic Requirements," Sloan Management Review, (Summer), 7-17.

If two or more works by the same author have the same publication date, they should be differentiated by letters after the date. The letter also should appear with the citation in the text:
---- and ---- (1987b), "Managing Across Borders: New Organizational Requirements," Sloan Management Review, (Fall), 43-53.

References to unpublished works, such as doctoral dissertations and working papers, should be included in the reference list as follows:
Katcher, Max (1975), "An Analysis of the Effectiveness of the Overseas Trade Fair Program of the U.S. Department of Commerce as an Exporter Promotion," doctoral dissertation, The George Washington University.

Papers printed in published proceedings of meetings:
Cavusgil, S. Tamer and John R. Nevin (1981), "State-of-the Art in International Marketing: An Assessment," in Review of Marketing 1981, Ben M. Enis and Kenneth J. Roering, eds. Chicago: American Marketing Association, 195-216.

Technical Appendix
To improve the readability of the manuscript, any mathematical proof or development that is not critical to the exposition of the main part of the text may be placed in a technical appendix.

Readability
JIM manuscripts are judged not only on the depth and scope of the ideas presented and their contributions to the field, but also on their clarity and whether they can be read and understood. JIM readers have varied backgrounds and include many practitioners. Hence, the following guidelines should be followed:

- Write in an interesting, readable manner with varied sentence structure.
- Reduce the discussion of methodology to a minimum. JIM readers are most interested in implication for managerial action.
- Avoid using technical terms that few readers are likely to understand. If you use these terms, include definitions. Remember: The journal is designed to be read, not deciphered.

- Keep sentences short so the reader does not get lost before the end of a sentence.

Review Procedure

The procedures guiding the selection of articles for publication in JIM require that no manuscript be accepted until after is has been reviewed by the editor and at least two members of the editorial review board. The decision of the editor to publish the manuscript is influenced considerably by the judgments of these advisors, who are experts in their respective fields. The author's name and credentials are removed prior to forwarding a manuscript to reviewers to maximize objectivity and ensure that a manuscript is judged solely on the basis of its content and contribution to the field.

ACCEPTANCE CRITERIA

All manuscripts are judged on their contributions to the advancement of the science and/or practice of marketing. All articles are expected to follow the rules for scholarly work, namely:

- Use references to previous work when developing your arguments. Do not assume other work on the subject does not exist, giving yourself credit for all the ideas in your manuscript.

- When data collection is discussed, consider the relevance of the sample to the subject matter. Carefully chosen sample groups are preferable to haphazardly chosen subjects who have little knowledge of or relevance to the subject being studied.

- Give as much information as possible about the characteristics of the sample and its representativeness of the population being studied.

- Do not ignore the nonrespondents. They might have different characteristics than the respondents.

- Give consideration to the limitations of your study, model, and/or concepts and discuss them explicitly in your manuscript. Be objective.

- Use appropriate statistical procedures.

- Address the reliability and validity of any empirical findings.

PREPARING THE FINAL VERSION

After a manuscript is accepted for publication, the final version must be submitted on 3.5-inch disk. The disk copy should contain the entire manuscript, including tables, figures, endnotes, and references. Although authors can prepare the disk copy using any work processing software that is Macintosh or IBM compatible, submission of the disk copy using Microsoft Word 6.0 for Windows is required. Save Word 7.0 files as Word 6.0. Please adhere to the following guidelines when preparing the final version.

1. Type everything in upper and lower case letters.

2. Footnotes are not accepted. If necessary to improve the readability of the text, a few endnotes may be included. They should appear double spaced on a separate page and be numbered consecutively throughout the text. Do not use foot-note feature in your word processing program.

3. Begin each new paragraph with a single hard return, not a tab. Also, use only a single space after each period, not a double space. Use the italic attribute rather than the underline attribute.

4. Write the name of the software program used on the disk submitted.

OTHER INFORMATION

All published material is copyrighted by the American Marketing Association with future-use rights reserved. This does not limit the author's right to use his or her own material in future works.

For details on manuscript preparation not covered here, see Chicago Manual of Style: The Essential Guide for Authors, Editors, and Publishers, 14th edition, Chicago: University of Chicago Press, 1993. For specific questions on content or editorial policy, contact the editor.

AMA Journals Editorial Policy

The following policies are applicable to the Journal of Marketing, Journal of Marketing Research, Journal of International Marketing and Journal of Public Policy & Marketing.

1. Replication and/or Extension of Results

The American Marketing Association supports the meaningful exchange of information to help create an environment for constructive criticism and free exchange of ideas. Such an environment requires the authors of AMA manuscripts to share their research findings and insights. Authors of manuscripts that report data dependent results will make available, upon request, exact information regarding their procedures, materials (excluding data), and stimuli during the editorial review process. The same information will also be made available, upon request, for at least five years after the date of publication for the benefit of researchers interested in replicating or extending their results.

Authors of articles published in AMA journals are required to footnote the availability of their research instruments and other stimuli as appropriate and provide information on how the materials may be obtained. Authors of manuscripts based on proprietary data sets or other restricted material must so notify the editor at the time a manuscript is submitted. The editor will then decide whether to accept the manuscript for review. Published articles in this genre will contain a footnote stating that the data or other elements of the research process as identified are proprietary.

2. Concurrent Reviews

AMA policy prohibits an article under review at an AMA journal from being concurrently reviewed at another journal without prior discussion with and written permission from the involved AMA journal editor.

3. Multiple Submissions

Multiple reports based on essentially the same data and results should not be submitted for publication in AMA journals. The publication of a manuscript in a non-AMA journal or other publication outlet precludes publication in an AMA journal if the manuscript is based on essentially the same data set and analysis as the AMA publication. Upon request, the AMA journal editor will make a binding decision about whether a manuscript submitted to an AMA journal is too similar to a previous publication elsewhere based on the same data set to warrant review for possible publication. Each article published must also contain references to the previously published papers.

4. Conflicts of Interest

Conflicts of interest may arise in a variety of situations. A conflict of interest may exist when a manuscript under review puts forth a position contrary to the reviewer's published work or when a manuscript reviewer has a substantial direct or indirect financial interest in the subject matter of a published manuscript. Since it is AMA policy to engage in a double-blind review process, a conflict of interest may also exist when a reviewer knows the author of a manuscript. The reviewer should consult the journal editor in such situations to decide whether to review the manuscript. A conflict of interest does not exist when an author disagrees with a reviewer's assessment that a problem is unimportant or disagrees with an editorial outcome.

Journal of Internet Commerce

ADDRESS FOR SUBMISSION:

Ron Berry, Editor
Journal of Internet Commerce
University of Louisiana at Monroe
Department of C.I.S.
700 University Avenue
Monroe, LA 71209-0120
USA
Phone: 318-342-1137
Fax: 318-342-1149
E-Mail: ciberry@ulm.edu
Web:
Address May Change:

PUBLICATION GUIDELINES:

Manuscript Length: 16-20
Copies Required: Four
Computer Submission: Yes
Format: Word or WdPerfect
Fees to Review: 0.00 US$

Manuscript Style:
　　Chicago Manual of Style

CIRCULATION DATA:

Reader: Academics
Frequency of Issue: Quarterly
Copies per Issue: New Journal
Sponsor/Publisher: The Haworth Press:
　New York
Subscribe Price: 48.00 US$

REVIEW INFORMATION:

Type of Review: Blind Review
No. of External Reviewers: 3
No. of In House Reviewers: 1
Acceptance Rate: New J
Time to Review: 1 - 2 Months
Reviewers Comments: Yes
Invited Articles: No Reply
Fees to Publish: 0.00 US$

MANUSCRIPT TOPICS:

Business Information Systems (MIS); Internet Commerce; Marketing Theory & Applications; Technology/Innovation

MANUSCRIPT GUIDELINES/COMMENTS:

1. Original Articles Only. Submission of a manuscript to this Journal represents a certification on the part of the author(s) that it is an original work, and that neither this manuscript nor a version of it has been published elsewhere nor is being considered for publication elsewhere.

2. Manuscript Length. Your manuscript may be approximately 5-30 typed pages double-spaced (including references and abstract.) Lengthier manuscripts may be considered, but only at the discretion of the Editor. Sometimes, lengthier manuscripts may be considered if they can be divided up into sections for publication in successive journal issues.

3. Manuscript Style. References, citations, and general style of manuscripts for this Journal should follow the Chicago style (as outlined in the latest edition of the *Manual of Style* of the

University of Chicago Press.) References should be double-spaced and placed in alphabetical order.

If an author wishes to submit a paper that has been already prepared in another style, he or she may do so. However, if the paper is accepted (with or without reviewer's alterations), the author is fully responsible for retyping the manuscript in the correct style as indicated above. Neither the Editor nor the Publisher is responsible for re-preparing manuscript copy to adhere to the Journal's style.

4. Manuscript Preparation.
Margins: leave at least a one-inch margin on all four sides.
Paper: use clean white, 8-1/2" x 11" bond paper.
Number of copies: 4 (the original plus three photocopies).
Cover page: *Important* -- staple a cover page to the manuscript, indicating only the article title (this is used for anonymous refereeing).
Second "title page": enclose a regular title page but do not staple it to the manuscript. Include the title again, plus:
- full authorship
- an ABSTRACT of about 100 words. (Below the abstract provide 3-1 0 key words for index purposes).
- an introductory footnote with authors' academic degrees, professional titles, affiliations, mailing addresses, and any desired acknowledgment of research support or other credit.

5. Return Envelopes. When you submit your four manuscript copies, also include:
- A regular envelope, stamped and self-addressed. This is for the Editor to send you an "acknowledgement of receipt" letter.
- Manuscripts will not be returned.

6. Spelling, Grammar, and Punctuation. You are responsible for preparing manuscript copy which is clearly written in acceptable scholarly English, and which contains no errors of spelling, grammar, or punctuation. Neither the Editor nor the Publisher is responsible for correcting errors of spelling and grammar: the manuscript, after acceptance by the Editor, must be immediately ready for typesetting as it is finally submitted by the author(s). Check your paper for the following common errors:
- dangling modifiers
- misplaced modifiers
- unclear antecedents
- incorrect or inconsistent abbreviations
- Also, check the accuracy of all arithmetic calculations, statistics, numerical data, text citations, and references.

7. Inconsistencies Must Be Avoided. Be sure you are consistent in your use of abbreviations, terminology, and in citing references, from one part of your paper to another.

8. Preparation Of Tables, Figures, and Illustrations. All tables, figures, illustrations, etc. must be "camera-ready." That is, they must be cleanly typed or artistically prepared so that they can be used either exactly as they are or else used after a photographic reduction in size. Figures, tables, and illustrations must be prepared on separate sheets of paper. Always use black ink and professional drawing instruments. On the back of these items, write your article title and the journal title lightly in pencil, so they do not get misplaced. In text, skip extra lines and indicate where these figures and tables are to be placed (please **do not write** on face of art). Photographs are considered part of the acceptable manuscript and remain with Publisher for use in additional printings. If submitted art cannot be used, the Publisher reserves the right to redo the art and to charge the author a fee of $35.00 per hour for this service.

9. Alterations Required By Referees And Reviewers. Many times a paper is accepted by the Editor contingent upon changes that are mandated by anonymous specialist referees and members of the Editorial Board. If the Editor returns your manuscript for revisions, you are responsible for retyping any sections of the paper to incorporate these revisions (if applicable, revisions should also be put on disk).

10. Typesetting. You will not be receiving galley proofs of your article. Editorial revisions, if any, must therefore be made while your article is still in manuscript. The final version of the manuscript will be the version you see published. Typesetter's errors will be corrected by the production staff of The Haworth Press. Authors are expected to submit manuscripts, disks, and art that are free from error.

11. Electronic Media. Haworth's in-house type-setting unit is able to utilize your final manuscript material as prepared on most personal computers and word processors. This will minimize typographical errors and decrease overall production time lag. Please send the first draft and final draft copies of your manuscript to the journal Editor in print format for his/her final review and approval. **After approval of** your final manuscript, please submit the final approved version both on printed format ("hard copy") and floppy diskette. On the outside of the diskette package write:
A. the brand name of your computer or word processor
B. the word-processing program that you used
C. the title of your article, and
D. file name

Note: Disk and hard copy must agree. In case of discrepancies, it is The Haworth Press's policy to follow hard copy. Authors are advised that no revisions of the manuscript can be made after acceptance by the Editor for publication. The benefits of this procedure are many with speed and accuracy being the most obvious. We look forward to working with you on this, knowing we will be able to serve you more efficiently in the future.

12. Reprints. The senior author will receive two copies of the journal issue and 25 complimentary reprints of his or her article. The junior author will receive two copies of the journal issue. These are sent several weeks after the journal issue is published and in circulation. An order form for the purchase of additional reprints will also be sent to all authors at this time. (Approximately 4-6 weeks is necessary for the preparation of reprints.) Please do not query the Journal's Editor about reprints. All such questions should be sent directly to:

The Haworth Press, Inc., Production Department, 21 East Broad Street, West Hazleton, PA 18201

To order additional reprints (minimum: 50 copies), please contact:
The Haworth Document Delivery Center, 10 Alice Street, Binghamton, NY 13904-1580
1-800-342-9678 or Fax (607) 722-6362.

13. Copyright. Copyright ownership of your manuscript must be transferred officially to The Haworth Press, Inc., before we can begin the peer-review process. The Editor's letter acknowledging receipt of the manuscript will be accompanied by a form fully explaining this. All authors must sign the form and return the original to the Editor as soon as possible. Failure to return the copyright form in a timely fashion will result in delay in review and subsequent publication.

Journal of Macromarketing

ADDRESS FOR SUBMISSION:

Luis V. Dominguez, Editor
Journal of Macromarketing
Florida Atlantic University
College of Business
Reubin O'D. Askew Tower
220 S. E. Second Avenue
Fort Lauderdale, FL 33301
USA
Phone: 954-762-5221
Fax: 954-762-5245
E-Mail: ldomingu@fau.edu
Web:
Address May Change:

PUBLICATION GUIDELINES:

Manuscript Length: 16-30
Copies Required: Four
Computer Submission: No
Format: N/A
Fees to Review: 0.00 US$

Manuscript Style:
    Chicago Manual of Style

CIRCULATION DATA:

Reader: Academics
Frequency of Issue: 2 Times/Year
Copies per Issue: Less than 1,000
Sponsor/Publisher: Sage Publications
Subscribe Price: 46.00 US$ Individual
    115.00 US$ Institution

REVIEW INFORMATION:

Type of Review: Blind Review
No. of External Reviewers: 3
No. of In House Reviewers: 1
Acceptance Rate: 11-20%
Time to Review: 2 - 3 Months
Reviewers Comments: Yes
Invited Articles: 0-5%
Fees to Publish: 0.00 US$

MANUSCRIPT TOPICS:
Business Law, Public Responsibility & Ethics; Macromarketing; Marketing & Economic Development; Marketing Behavior; Marketing History; Marketing Theory & Applications; Public Policy Regarding Marketing; Quality of Life Studies

MANUSCRIPT GUIDELINES/COMMENTS:

The *Journal of Macromarketing* focuses on important societal issues as they are affected by marketing and on how society affects the conduct of marketing. The journal covers macromarketing areas such as marketing and public policy, marketing and development, marketing and the quality of life, and the history of marketing.

Four kinds of material are published in the *Journal of Macromarketing*. Feature articles explain relationships, analyze data, or examine methodological concepts, tests, or approaches to a problem. Reader response letters confirm or challenge viewpoints expressed in feature articles. Reviews and communications summarize and evaluate books and published research

Articles studies. Seminar abstracts summarize papers presented at the annual Macromarketing Conference.

should cover subjects listed in the current Guide to the Selection of Manuscript Topics (available from the editor). Articles may involve explanatory theory, empirical studies, or methodological treatment of tests.

The procedures guiding the selection of articles for publication in the journal require that no manuscript be accepted until it has been reviewed by the editor, the section editor (if applicable), and at least three outside reviewers who are experts in their respective fields (often members of the Editorial Review Board). Manuscripts are reviewed simultaneously by geographically separated reviewers. It is journal policy to remove the author's name and credentials prior to forwarding a manuscript to a reviewer to maximize objectivity and ensure that manuscripts are judged solely on the basis of content, clarity, and contribution to the field. All manuscripts are judged on their contribution to the advancement of science, the practice of macromarketing, or both. Articles should be written in an interesting, readable manner, and technical terms should be defined. In some highly exceptional circumstances, the journal will publish an invited manuscript from a noted scholar on a topic deemed of particular interest to the development of the field of macromarketing.

Manuscripts submitted to the journal can be processed most expeditiously if they are prepared according to these instructions.

Manuscript Preparation
Manuscripts should be typed double-spaced, including references. Do not use single spacing anywhere, except on tables and figures. Page numbers are to be placed in the upper right-hand corner of every page. A tab indent should begin each paragraph. Please allow the text to wrap, rather than placing a hard return after every line. Manuscripts ordinarily should be between 4,000 and 6,000 words (ca.15 typewritten pages of text) using Times New Roman 12-point type or larger. Articles of shorter length are also acceptable and encouraged.

Submit four (4) copies of each manuscript. The author's name should not appear anywhere except on the cover page. The author should keep an extra, exact copy for future reference.

For details of manuscript preparation not covered in the following sections, see *The Chicago Manual of Style*, 14th edition, Chicago and London: University of Chicago Press, 1993, and review issues of the journal.

1. **What goes where?**
The sections of the manuscript should be placed in the following order: cover page, title page, body, appendixes, endnotes, reference list, tables, figures. Each section should begin on a new page.

Cover Page – Article title, with full name of author(s), present position, organization affiliation, full address including postal code and country, telephone/fax numbers, and e-mail address. Authors must be listed in the order in which they are to appear in the published article. Please clearly indicate which author will serve as the primary contact for the journal and be especially sure to provide a fax number and e-mail address for this person. A 50-word (maximum) narrative on each author's specialty or interests should also appear on this page, as should any acknowledgment of financial or technical assistance. (This page will be removed prior to sending the manuscript to reviewers.)

Title Page - Title of paper, without author(s) name(s), and a brief abstract of no more than 150 words substantively summarizing the article.

Body - The text, with major headings centered on the page and subheadings flush with the left margin. Major headings should use all uppercase letters; side subheadings should be typed in upper and lowercase letters. Do not use footnotes in the body of the manuscript. If used, please place endnotes in a numbered list after the body of the text and before the reference list; however, avoid endnotes wherever possible because they interrupt the flow of the manuscript.

Tables and Figures - Each table or figure should be prepared on a separate page and grouped together at the end of the manuscript. The data in tables should be arranged so that columns of like materials read down, not across. Nonsignificant decimal places in tabular data should be omitted. The tables and figures should be numbered in Arabic numerals, followed by brief descriptive titles.

Additional details should be footnoted under the table, not in the title. In the text, all illustrations and charts should be referred to as figures.

Figures must be clean, crisp, black-and-white, camera-ready copies. Please avoid the use of gray-scale shading; use hatchmarks, dots, or lines instead.

References - References should be typed double-spaced in alphabetical order by author's last name (see 3).

2. Reference Citations Within Text
Citations in the text should include the author's last name and year of publication enclosed in parentheses without punctuation, for example, (Kinsey 1960). If practical, the citation should be placed immediately before a punctuation mark. Otherwise, insert it in a logical sentence break

If a particular page, section, or equation is cited, it should be placed within the parentheses, for example, (Kinsey 1960, p.112). For multiple authors, use the full, formal citation for up to three authors, but for four or more use the first author's name with "et al." For example, use (White and Smith 1977) and (Brown, Green, and Stine 1984). For more than three authors, use (Hunt et al. 1975) unless another work published in that year would also be identified as (Hunt et al. 1975); in that case, list all authors, for example, (Hunt, Bent, Marks, and West 1975).

3. Reference List Style
List references alphabetically, principle author's surname first, followed by publication date in parentheses. The reference list should be typed double-spaced, with a hanging indent, on a separate page. Do not number references. Please see the reference examples below as well as

reference lists in recent issues. Be sure that all titles cited in the text appear in the reference list and vice versa.

Book:
Unwin, L.P., and Joseph Galloway. 1984. A History of the Eastern Roman Empire. Boston: No Such Press.

Article in a book:
Roy, Allen. 1993. The Viking marketer. In Marketing History, marketing's greatest empirical experiment, edited by Kathleen M. Rassuli, Stanley C. Hollander, and Terence R. Nevett, 190-203. Austin: University of Texas.

Journal articles:
Jackson, Richard. 1989. Running down the up-escalator: Regional inequality in Papua New Guinea. Australian Geographer 14 (May): 175-85.

4. Mathematical Notation
Mathematical notation must be clear within the text. Equations should be centered on the page. If equations are numbered, type the number in the parentheses flush with the right margin. For equations that may be too wide to fit in a single column, indicate appropriate breaks. Unusual symbols and Greek letters should be identified by a marginal note.

5. Permission Guidelines
Authors are solely responsible for obtaining all necessary permissions and for paying any association fees. Permission must be granted in writing by the copyright holder and must accompany the submitted manuscript. Authors are responsible for the accuracy of facts, opinions, and interpretations expressed in the article.

Permission is required to reprint, paraphrase, or adapt the following in a work of scholarship or research:

- Any piece of writing or other work that is used in its entirety (e.g. poems, tables, figures, charts, graphs, photographs, drawings, illustrations, book chapters, journal articles, newspaper or magazine articles, radio/television broadcasts);

- Portions of articles or chapters of books or of any of the items in the preceding paragraph , if the portion used is a sizable amount in relation to the item as a whole, regardless of size, or if it captures the "essence" or the "heart" of the work;

- Any portion of a fictional, creative, or other nonfactual work (e.g., opinion, editorial, essay, lyrics,commentary, plays, novels, short stories); and

- Any portion of an unpublished work.

Manuscript Submission
Please send all manuscripts to Luis V. Dominguez, Editor.

All published material is copyrighted by Sage Publications, Inc. Every author and coauthor must sign an agreement before an article can be published.

Submission of Final Manuscripts

Authors of final manuscripts accepted for publication should provide both a hard copy of the final version of their article and a matching version on a 3.5-inch computer disk. Please group all sections of the article in one file on the disk; do not use separate files for tables, references, and so forth. Please do not include figures on disk. Figures are acceptable as camera-ready copy only.

Journal of Marketing

ADDRESS FOR SUBMISSION:

Dave W. Stewart, Editor
Journal of Marketing
Universtiy of Southern California
Marshall School of Business
ACC306B
Los Angeles, CA 90089-1421
USA
Phone: 213-740-6892
Fax: 213-740-6297
E-Mail: jmarket@bus.usc.edu
Web: www.ama.org
Address May Change:

PUBLICATION GUIDELINES:

Manuscript Length: 50 Maximum
Copies Required: Five
Computer Submission: No
Format: Disk only on request by Editor
Fees to Review: 0.00 US$

Manuscript Style:
  Chicago Manual of Style

CIRCULATION DATA:

Reader: Academics, 80% Marketing Practitioners
Frequency of Issue: Quarterly
Copies per Issue: 5,001 - 10,000
Sponsor/Publisher: American Marketing Association
Subscribe Price: 80.00 US$ Individual
  200.00 US$ Institution
  45.00 US$ AMA Member

REVIEW INFORMATION:

Type of Review: Blind Review
No. of External Reviewers: 3
No. of In House Reviewers: 1
Acceptance Rate: 6-10%
Time to Review: 2 - 3 Months
Reviewers Comments: Yes
Invited Articles: 0-5%
Fees to Publish: 0.00 US$

MANUSCRIPT TOPICS:
Advertising & Promotion Management; Direct Marketing; Marketing Theory & Applications; Sales/Selling; Services

MANUSCRIPT GUIDELINES/COMMENTS:

AMA Journals Editorial Policy
The following policies are applicable to the *Journal of Marketing*, *Journal of Marketing Research*, *Journal of International Marketing* and *Journal of Public Policy & Marketing*.

1. **Replication and/or Extension of Results**
The American Marketing Association supports the meaningful exchange of information to help create an environment for constructive criticism and free exchange of ideas. Such an environment requires the authors of AMA manuscripts to share their research findings and insights. Authors of manuscripts that report data dependent results will make available, upon request, exact information regarding their procedures, materials (excluding data), and stimuli during the editorial review process. The same information will also be made available, upon

request, for at least five years after the date of publication for the benefit of researchers interested in replicating or extending their results.

Authors of articles published in AMA journals are required to footnote the availability of their research instruments and other stimuli as appropriate and provide information on how the materials may be obtained. Authors of manuscripts based on proprietary data sets or other restricted material must so notify the editor at the time a manuscript is submitted. The editor will then decide whether to accept the manuscript for review. Published articles in this genre will contain a footnote stating that the data or other elements of the research process as identified are proprietary.

2. Concurrent Reviews

AMA policy prohibits an article under review at an AMA journal from being concurrently reviewed at another journal without prior discussion with and written permission from the involved AMA journal editor.

3. Multiple Submissions

Multiple reports based on essentially the same data and results should not be submitted for publication in AMA journals. The publication of a manuscript in a non-AMA journal or other publication outlet precludes publication in an AMA journal if the manuscript is based on essentially the same data set and analysis as the AMA publication. Upon request, the AMA journal editor will make a binding decision about whether a manuscript submitted to an AMA journal is too similar to a previous publication elsewhere based on the same data set to warrant review for possible publication. Each article published must also contain references to the previously published papers.

4. Conflicts of Interest

Conflicts of interest may arise in a variety of situations. A conflict of interest may exist when a manuscript under review puts forth a position contrary to the reviewer's published work or when a manuscript reviewer has a substantial direct or indirect financial interest in the subject matter of a published manuscript. Since it is AMA policy to engage in a double-blind review process, a conflict of interest may also exist when a reviewer knows the author of a manuscript. The reviewer should consult the journal editor in such situations to decide whether to review the manuscript. A conflict of interest does not exist when an author disagrees with a reviewer's assessment that a problem is unimportant or disagrees with an editorial outcome.

EDITORIAL GUIDELINES

Editorial Statement

The *Journal of Marketing* (JM), a quarterly publication of the American Marketing Association (AMA), is one of the premier refereed scholarly journals of the marketing discipline. Since its founding in 1936, JM has played a significant role in the dissemination of marketing knowledge grounded in scholarly research, as well as in shaping the content and boundaries of the discipline.

Two AMA objectives have a direct bearing on the publication policies of JM: (1) to lead in the development, dissemination, and implementation of marketing concepts, practice, and information and (2) to probe and promote the use of marketing concepts by business, not-for-profit, and other institutions for the betterment of society.

Editorial Goals
The editorial goals of JM are:
1. the advancement of the science and practice of marketing (to make a difference by adding to what we know about marketing phenomena and changing how we study and practice marketing).
2. to serve as a bridge between the scholarly and the practical, each of which has a vital stake in what's happening on the other side.

Primary Reader Targets
Thoughtful marketing practitioners and educators concerned with marketing theory and practice.

Positioning
Every discipline needs a broad-based journal that can serve as a vehicle for the publication of papers that have the potential to make a significant contribution to knowledge in any area of marketing. JM is positioned as the premier, broad-based, scholarly journal of the marketing discipline focusing on substantive issues in marketing and marketing management.

The target audience for JM articles are the thoughtful marketing academicians and practitioners. The word "thoughtful" in the statement of target audience has important implications. It implies that the reader, whether academician or practitioner, is knowledgeable about the state-of-the-art of the topic areas covered in JM.

Implications of Goals and Positioning for Editorial Content
By design, JM will publish articles on a variety of topics contributing to the advancement of the science and/or practice of marketing. However, in accordance with the formal policies established by the Board of Directors of the American Marketing Association regarding the nature of articles appropriate for publication in JM and it sister publication *Journal of Marketing Research* (JMR), articles whose primary focus is on marketing research methodology and/or models will not be considered for publication in JM. Methodological aspects published in JM articles serve to support the contribution to marketing knowledge, but are not the central feature of articles published in JM. Authors are encouraged to submit such articles to JMR for review and publication consideration. Also, manuscripts whose primary focus is on general management issues, rather that marketing issues, will not be considered for publication in JM.

Given JM's positioning as a broad-based journal of the discipline, and a readership comprised of heterogeneous groups of academics and practitioners with diverse substantive areas of interest and philosophical orientations, JM cannot devote a disproportionate amount of space to any one area. The mix of articles published in any issue of JM will vary markedly in their orientation, level of sophistication, nature of contribution to the field and segment appeal.

Appropriate Editorial Content

As a literature-based scholarly journal, JM is committed to publishing a broad spectrum of conceptual and empirical articles that make a new theoretical and/or substantive contribution to the field. The following is a partial list of the nature of articles appropriate for submission to the journal for review and publication consideration:

Articles focusing on any substantive area that falls within the field of marketing, addressing problems or issues deemed significant by one or more of JM's constituencies.

- Articles providing critical syntheses and reviews of relevant areas within marketing.
- Articles reporting generalizable empirical findings.
- Articles focusing on neglected areas of marketing.
- Articles that critically reexamine existing concepts and theories in marketing.
- Articles focusing on important forces, events, and trends affecting the present and future of marketing.
- Articles that provide insights into emerging and evolving concepts and theories in marketing.
- Articles that lead the discipline—push marketing into new frontiers.
- Articles that have the potential to stimulate further research and, by doing so, alter the nature and scope of marketing's foundation.
- Articles focusing on substantive areas characterized by a dearth of research, emerging and evolving areas that might potentially impact on the boundaries and frontier of the discipline, and areas that currently lack a theory base but constitute substantive issues that merit serious inquiry by marketing scholars.
- Articles integrating concepts from allied disciplines such as economics, strategic management, finance, accounting, organizational behavior, sociology, psychology and anthropology into marketing.

MANUSCRIPT GUIDELINES

Manuscript and Disk Preparation

1. Submit five (5) paper copies of your manuscript to the Editor. (Do not submit disk copies until directed to do so by the editor.)
2. Keep an extra, exact copy for future reference.
3. Manuscripts should not exceed fifty (50) pages, inclusive of all text, tables, figures, appendices, etc.
4. Manuscripts should be typed double spaced throughout (including references) on 8 1/2 x 11 inch white, nonerasable paper.
5. Allow margins of at least one inch on all four sides and do not justify your right-hand margin. Use a 12 pt. font.
6. Type on one side of the paper only.

What Goes Where?

1. First page: Name of author(s) and title; author(s) footnote, including present positions, complete address, telephone number, fax number, email address, and any acknowledgment of financial or technical assistance.

2. Second page: Title of paper (without author's name) and a brief abstract of no more than 50 words substantively summarizing the article. It should be informative, giving the reader a "taste" of the article.
3. Next: The text with major headings centered on the page and subheadings flush with the left margin.
4. Then: Tables, numbered consecutively, each on a separate page. If tables appear in an appendix, they should be numbered separately and consecutively, as in Table A-1, A-2, and so on.
5. Next: Figures, numbered consecutively, each placed on a separate page. If tables appear in an appendix, they should be numbered separately, as in Figure A-1, A-2, etc.
6. Last: References, typed double spaced in alphabetical order by author's last name.

Mathematical Notation
1. Mathematical notation must be clear within the text.
2. Equations should be centered on the page. If equations are numbered, type the number in parentheses flush with the left margin.
3. Unusual symbols and Greek letters should be identified by a marginal note. If equations are too wide to fit in a single column, indicate appropriate breaks.

Tables
1. Tables should consist of at least four columns and four rows; otherwise they should be left as in-text tabulations or their results should be integrated in the text.
2. The table number and title should be typed on separate lines, centered.
3. Use only horizontal rules.
4. Designate units (e.g., %, $) in column headings.
5. Align all decimals.
6. Refer to tables in text by number. Avoid using "above," "below," and "preceding."
7. If possible, combine closely related tables.
8. Indicate placement in text.
9. Make sure the necessary measures of statistical significance are reported with the table.

Figures and Camera-Ready Artwork
1. Figures should be prepared professionally on disk and as camera-ready copy.
2. Label both vertical and horizontal axes. The ordinate label should be centered above the ordinate axis; the abscissa label should be placed beneath the abscissa.
3. Place all calibration tics inside the axis lines, with the values outside the axis lines.
4. The figure number and title should be typed on separate lines, centered.
5. Once a manuscript has been accepted, complex tables and all figures must be on disk and camera-ready. Table and figure headings should be typed on a separate page and attached to the appropriate camera-ready art. These titles will be set in our own typeface.
6. Lettering should be large enough to be read easily with 50% reduction. Any art not done on a computer graphics program should be professionally drafted in India ink.
7. Do not submit camera-ready art until your manuscript has been accepted. If the artwork is completed, submit photocopies.

Reference Citations Within the Text

1. Citation in the text should be by the author's last name and year of publication, enclosed in parentheses without punctuation: "(Kinsey 1960)." If practical, the citation should stand by a punctuation mark. Otherwise, insert it in a logical sentence break. If you use the author's name within the sentence, there is no need to repeat the name in the citation; just use the year of publication in parentheses, as in "...The Howard Harris Program (1966)."

2. If a particular page, section, or equation is cited, it should be placed within the parentheses: "(Kinsey 1960, p. 112)." For multiple authors, use the full citation for up to three authors; for four or more, use the first author's name followed by "et al." (no italics). A series of citations should be listed in alphabetical order and separated by semicolons: (Donnelly 1961; Kinsey 1960; Wensley 1981).

Reference List Style

1. References are to be listed alphabetically, last name first, followed by publication date in parentheses. Use full first name, not just initials. The reference list should be typed double spaced on a separate page. Do not use indents, tabs, or symbols to delineate your paragraphs. Instead, use two hard returns between each reference.

2. Authors are responsible for the accuracy of their references. Check them carefully.

3. *Single- and multiple-author references for books:*

   Donnelly, James H. and William R. George (1981), Marketing of Services. Chicago: American Marketing Association.

4. *Single- and multiple-author reference for periodicals* (include author's name, publication date, article title, complete name of periodical, volume number, month of publication, and page numbers):

   Wensley, Robin (1981), "Strategic Marketing: Betas, Boxes, or Basics," Journal of Marketing, 45 (Summer), 173-82.

5. *Single- and multiple-author reference for an article in a book edited by another author(s):*

   Nevin, John R. and Ruth A. Smith (1981), "The Predictive Accuracy of a Retail Gravitation Model: An Empirical Evaluation," in The Changing Marketing Environment, Kenneth Bernhardt et al., eds. Chicago: American Marketing Association.

6. *If an author appears more than once, substitute four hyphens* (this will appear as a 1-inch line when typeset) for each author's name (do not use underlines):

   Fornell, Claes and David F. Larcher (1981a), "Evaluating Structural Equation Models with Unobservable Variables and Measurement Error," Journal of Marketing Research, (February), 39-50.

----and---- (1981b), "Structural Equation Models with Unobservable Variables and Measurement Error: Algebra and Statistics," Journal of Marketing Research, 18 (August).

7. *If two or more works by the same author have the same publication date*, they should be differentiated by letters after the date. The letter also should appear with the citation in the text:

Day, George (1981a), "Analytical Approaches to Strategic Market Planning," in Review of Marketing 1981, Ben Enis and Kenneth J. Roering, eds. Chicago: American Marketing Association.

----(1981b), "The Product Life Cycle: Analysis and Applications Issues," Journal of Marketing, 45 (Fall), 60-67.

8. *References to unpublished works*, such as doctoral dissertations and working papers, should be included in the references list as follows:

Coughlin, Maureen (1980), "Fear of Success: Reaction to Advertising Stimuli and Intention to Purchase," doctoral dissertation, City University of New York.

Technical Appendix
To improve the readability of the manuscript, any mathematical proof or development that is not critical to the exposition of the main part of the text my be placed in a technical appendix.

Readability
JM manuscripts are judged not only on the depth and scope of the ideas presented and their contributions to the field, but also on their clarity and whether they can be read and understood. Readers have varied backgrounds. Hence, the following guidelines should be followed:

- Write in an interesting, readable manner with varied sentence structure. Use as little passive voice as possible.

- Avoid using technical terms that few readers are likely to understand. If you use these terms, include definitions. Remember: The journal is designed to be read, not deciphered.

- Keep sentences short so the reader does not get lost before the end of a sentence.

Review Procedure
The procedures guiding the selection of articles for publication in JM require that no manuscript be accepted until after it has been reviewed by the editor and at least two members of the editorial review board. The decision of the editor to publish the manuscript is influenced considerably by the judgments of these advisors, who are experts in their respective fields. The author's name and credentials are removed prior to forwarding a manuscript to reviewers to maximize objectivity and ensure that a manuscript is judged solely on the basis of it content and contribution to the field.

Acceptance Criteria
All manuscripts are judged on their contributions to the advancement of the science and/or practice of marketing. All articles are expected to follow the rules for scholarly work, namely:

- Use references to previous work when developing your model or theory. Do not assume other work on the subject does not exist, giving yourself credit for all the ideas in your manuscript.

- When data collection is discussed, consider the relevance of the sample to the subject matter. Carefully chosen sample groups are preferable to haphazardly chosen subjects who have little knowledge of or relevance to the subject being studied.

- Give as much information as possible about the characteristics of the sample and its representativeness of the population being studied.

- Do not ignore the nonrespondents. They might have different characteristics than the respondents.

- Give consideration to the limitations of your study, model, and/or concepts and discuss these in your manuscript. Be objective.

- Use appropriate statistical procedures.

- Address the reliability and validity of any empirical findings.

Preparing the Final Paper and Disk Versions
After a manuscript is accepted for publication, the final version must be submitted on a 3.5-inch disk, along with three copies on 8 ½ x 11 inch white, nonerasable paper. All copies should contain the entire manuscript, including tables, figures, footnotes, and references. Although authors may prepare the disk copy using any word processing software that is Macintosh or IBM compatible, submission of the disk copy using Microsoft Word 97 for Windows is preferred. Please adhere to the following additional guidelines when preparing the final disk and paper versions.

1. Review all references and footnotes to be certain they fully comply with the "Manuscript Guidelines." Pay careful attention to consistency, accuracy, and formatting.
2. Type everything in upper and lower case letters, using a 12 pt. font.
3. Paragraphs will be identified by spacing -- not tab indention. At the CLOSE of each paragraph, use two hard returns (hit ENTER or RETURN two times). This, in effect, puts 4 line spaces between paragraphs. Example:

> This is the end of paragraph one. <ENTER><ENTER>
>
> This is the beginning of paragraph two.

4. Double space the entire paper, including the abstract, references, and footnotes.

5. Footnotes should not be used for reference purposes and should be avoided if possible. If necessary to improve the readability to the text, a few footnotes may be included. They should appear double spaced on a separate page and be numbered consecutively throughout the text.

6. Use the italics function when it is appropriate (e.g., titles of publications, for emphasis, etc.).

7. Submit graphics as PowerPoint, Illustrator, Photoshop, or QuarkXpress application files, and/or EPS, high resolution *.tif or *.bmp files, and camera-ready copy.

8. Write the name of the software program used on the disk submitted.

Other Information

All published material is copyrighted by the American Marketing Association with future-use rights reserved. This does not limit the author's right to use his or her own material in future works.

For details on manuscript preparation not covered here, see Chicago Manual of Style: The Essential Guide for Authors, Editors, and Publishers, 14th edition, Chicago: University of Chicago Press, 1993. For specific questions on content or editorial policy, contact the editor.

Journal of Marketing Channels

ADDRESS FOR SUBMISSION:

Lou E. Pelton, Editor
Journal of Marketing Channels
University of North Texas
College of Business Administration
PO Box 31196
Denton, TX 76203-1396
USA
Phone: 940-565-3124
Fax: 940-565-3837
E-Mail: pelton@unt.edu
Web: www.haworthpress.com
Address May Change:

PUBLICATION GUIDELINES:

Manuscript Length: 21-25
Copies Required: Four
Computer Submission: No
Format: N/A
Fees to Review: 0.00 US$

Manuscript Style:
    American Psychological Association

CIRCULATION DATA:

Reader: Academics
Frequency of Issue: Quarterly
Copies per Issue: Less than 1,000
Sponsor/Publisher: Haworth Press, Inc.
Subscribe Price: 60.00 US$ Individual
    75.00 US$ Institution
    200.00 US$ Library

REVIEW INFORMATION:

Type of Review: Blind Review
No. of External Reviewers: 2
No. of In House Reviewers: 0
Acceptance Rate: 21-30%
Time to Review: 2 - 3 Months
Reviewers Comments: Yes
Invited Articles: 0-5%
Fees to Publish: 0.00 US$

MANUSCRIPT TOPICS:

Channels of Distribution; Direct Marketing; Marketing Channels; Transportation/Physical Distribution

MANUSCRIPT GUIDELINES/COMMENTS:

About the Journal

The purpose of the Journal of Marketing Channels is to provide the knowledge and tools needed to develop superior distribution systems, strategies, and management. Leading authorities from around the world will present the most up-to-date and in-depth thought, analysis, and research on these topics in this refereed international quarterly.

Each article will provide solid information, insights, or tools of analysis for dealing with such crucial marketing channel issues as

- How will changing economic, competitive, and technological developments affect marketing channels?
- How can marketing channels be designed to provide superior customer service while enhancing profitability?

- How can effective channel partnerships be created through the selection of channel members?
- How can distributors, dealers, and other channel members be motivated to do a more effective selling job?
- How can the performance of marketing channels be evaluated more accurately and effectively?
- How can cooperation in marketing channels be fostered and conflict reduced?
- How can marketing channel strategy be used to gain a competitive advantage?
- How can marketing channels be used to gain access to international markets?

Instructions for Authors

1. Original articles only. Submission of a manuscript to this Journal represents a certification on the part of the author(s) that it is an original work, and that neither this manuscript nor a version of it has been published elsewhere nor is being considered for publication elsewhere.

2. Manuscript Length. 20-25 typed pages.

3. Manuscript style. *Chicago Manual of Style.*

4. Manuscript Preparation.
Margins: leave at least a one-inch margin on all four sides.
Paper: use clean white, 8-1/2" x 11" bond paper.
Number of copies: 4 (the original plus three photocopies).
Cover page: *Important* -- staple a cover page to the manuscript, indicating only the article title (this is used for anonymous refereeing).
Second "title page": enclose a regular title page but do not staple it to the manuscript. Include the title again, plus:
- full authorship
- an **abstract** of about 100 words. (Below the abstract provide 3-1 0 key words for index purposes).
- an introductory footnote with authors' academic degrees, professional titles, affiliations, mailing addresses, and any desired acknowledgment of research support or other credit.

5. Return envelopes. When you submit your four manuscript copies, also include:
- A regular envelope, stamped and self-addressed. This is for the Editor to send you an "acknowledgement of receipt" letter.
- Manuscripts will not be returned.

6. Spelling, grammar, and punctuation. You are responsible for preparing manuscript copy which is clearly written in acceptable scholarly English, and which contains no errors of spelling, grammar, or punctuation. Neither the Editor nor the Publisher is responsible for correcting errors of spelling and grammar: the manuscript, after acceptance by the Editor, must be immediately ready for typesetting as it is finally submitted by the author(s). Check your paper for the following common errors:
- dangling modifiers
- misplaced modifiers

- unclear antecedents
- incorrect or inconsistent abbreviations

Also, check the accuracy of all arithmetic calculations, statistics, numerical data, text citations, and references.

7. Inconsistencies must be avoided. Be sure you are consistent in your use of abbreviations, terminology, and in citing references, from one part of your paper to another.

8. Preparation of tables, figures, and illustrations. All tables, figures, illustrations, etc. must be "camera-ready." That is, they must be cleanly typed or artistically prepared so that they can be used either exactly as they are or else used after a photographic reduction in size. Figures, tables, and illustrations must be prepared on separate sheets of paper. Always use black ink and professional drawing instruments. On the back of these items, write your article title and the journal title lightly in pencil, so they do not get misplaced. In text, skip extra lines and indicate where these figures and tables are to be placed (please **do not write** on face of art). Photographs are considered part of the acceptable manuscript and remain with Publisher for use in additional printings. If submitted art cannot be used, the Publisher reserves the right to redo the art and to charge the author a fee of $35.00 per hour for this service.

9. Alterations required by referees and reviewers. Many times a paper is accepted by the Editor contingent upon changes that are mandated by anonymous specialist referees and members of the Editorial Board. If the Editor returns your manuscript for revisions, you are responsible for retyping any sections of the paper to incorporate these revisions (if applicable, revisions should also be put on disk).

10. Typesetting. You will not be receiving galley proofs of your article. Editorial revisions, if any, must therefore be made while your article is still in manuscript. The final version of the manuscript will be the version you see published. Typesetter's errors will be corrected by the production staff of The Haworth Press. Authors are expected to submit manuscripts, disks, and art that are free from error.

11. Electronic media. Haworth's in-house type-setting unit is able to utilize your final manuscript material as prepared on most personal computers and word processors. This will minimize typographical errors and decrease overall production timelag. Please send the first draft and final draft copies of your manuscript to the journal Editor in print format for his/her final review and approval. **After approval of** your final manuscript, please submit the final approved version both on printed format ("hard copy") and floppy diskette. On the outside of the diskette package write:

A. the brand name of your computer or word processor
B. the word-processing program that you used
C. the title of your article, and
D. file name

Note: Disk and hard copy must agree. In case of discrepancies, it is The Haworth Press's policy to follow hard copy. Authors are advised that no revisions of the manuscript can be made after acceptance by the Editor for publication. The benefits of this procedure are many with speed and accuracy being the most obvious. We look forward to working with you on this, knowing we will be able to serve you more efficiently in the future.

12. Reprints. The senior author will receive two copies of the journal issue and 25 complimentary reprints of his or her article. The junior author will receive two copies of the journal issue. These are sent several weeks after the journal issue is published and in circulation. An order form for the purchase of additional reprints will also be sent to all authors at this time. (Approximately 4-6 weeks is necessary for the preparation of reprints.) Please do not query the Journal's Editor about reprints. All such questions should be sent directly to: **The Haworth Press, Inc., Production Department, 21 East Broad Street West Hazleton, PA 18201**

To order additional reprints (minimum: 50 copies), please contact:
The Haworth Document Delivery Center, 10 Alice Street, Binghamton, NY 13904-1580
1-800-342-9678 or Fax (607) 722-6362.

13. Copyright. Copyright ownership of your manuscript must be transferred officially to The Haworth Press, Inc., before we can begin the peer-review process. The Editor's letter acknowledging receipt of the manuscript will be accompanied by a form fully explaining this. All authors must sign the form and return the original to the Editor as soon as possible. Failure to return the copyright form in a timely fashion will result in delay in review and subsequen' publication.

Journal of Marketing Communications

ADDRESS FOR SUBMISSION:

Phillip J. Kitchen, Editor
Journal of Marketing Communications
Queen's University of Belfast
Queen's School of Management
Lanyon Building
Belfast, BT7 1NN
Northern Ireland
Phone: 44 0 1232 273782
Fax: 44 0 1232 248372
E-Mail: p.kitchen@qub.ac.uk
Web: www.routledge.co
Address May Change:

CIRCULATION DATA:

Reader: Academics
Frequency of Issue: Quarterly
Copies per Issue: No Reply
Sponsor/Publisher: Routlege Journals
Subscribe Price: 68.00 US$ Individual
    498.00 US$ Institution
    60.00 US$ Members of MEG

PUBLICATION GUIDELINES:

Manuscript Length: 21-25
Copies Required: Four
Computer Submission: No
Format: N/A
Fees to Review: 0.00 US$

Manuscript Style:
    See Manuscript Guidelines

REVIEW INFORMATION:

Type of Review: Blind Review
No. of External Reviewers: 2
No. of In House Reviewers: 0
Acceptance Rate: 40%
Time to Review: 1 - 2 Months
Reviewers Comments: Yes
Invited Articles: 0-5%
Fees to Publish: 0.00 US$

MANUSCRIPT TOPICS:
Advertising & Promotion Management; Communication; Direct Marketing; Global Business; Internet & Database Marketing; Marketing Theory & Applications; Public Relations; Sales/Selling; Services

MANUSCRIPT GUIDELINES/COMMENTS:

Associate Editors:
Don E. Schultz - *Integrated Marketing Communications, Medill School of Journalism, Northwestern University, 1908 Sheridan Road,, Evanston, Illinois 60208-1290, USA*

Professor Charles H. Patti - *(Pacific Rim) Head - School of Communication, Queensland University of Technology, Level 10, Z Block, 2 George Street, Brisbane, Queensland 4001, Australia*

W. Fred van Raaij - *Faculty of Social and Behavioural Sciences, Katholicke Universiteit Brabant, Warandelaan 2, PO Box 90153, 5000 Tilberg, The Ntherlands*

Book Reviews Editor:
Gill Rolls-Willson - *Kingston Business School, Kingston University, Kingston Hill, Kingston, Surrey KT2 7LB, UK*

Aims and Scope:
The Journal of Marketing Communications is devoted to publishing research papers and information concerning all aspects of marketing communications and promotion management. It is a channel for discussing emergent issues such as relationship marketing and integrated marketing communications together with behavioural foundations of marketing communications and promotional management.

Issues that the journal covers include:

- Marketing communications - communications via any or all of the marketing mix elements.
- The way(s) the marketing mix elements are operationalized and interrelated for communication purposes in marketing plans.
- Promotional management - this would not only include the bedrock of advertising, sales promotion, publicity and personal selling, but would also include emergent areas such as marketing public relations, direct marketing and sponsorship.
- The mechanism or process of developing effective communications or promotion via specific case studies.
- Behavioural foundations of marketing communications and promotion management including semiotics, consumer behaviour, attitudes and persuasion, source and message factors, diffusion of innovations and adoption factors.
- Effects of changing environmental circumstance on marketing communications and promotional strategy - altered budget allocation, messages. and media vehicles adopted.
- Exploration of the trends toward integrated marketing communications, marketing public relations, and relationship marketing.
- Examples of sound or innovative teaching or training practice in relation to the marketing communications or promotional management.
- The interface between corporate and marketing public relations.
- The relationship between marketing and corporate communications.

Instructions for Authors:
All papers are subject to a double-blind refereeing process. There is no submission fee and no page charge. If a paper is considered suitable, it will be passed to an Associate Editor and thus to the review process. The Editor will make the final decision as to acceptability after taking into account reports from Associate Editors and referees. Authors will be provided with copies of the referees' reports.

Submission. Authors should submit four copies of their manuscript together with original illustrations and a covering letter to the Editor or to one of the Associate Editors. It is assumed that the author will keep one copy. Articles should be between 4000 and 6000 words. Submission of manuscripts in electronic form is also encouraged. Word, WordPerfect or ASCII files are acceptable, however four hard copies must be supplied.

The Manuscript. Manuscripts must be typed double-spaced on one side of A4 paper only, with a 4cm left-hand margin. Permission to reproduce previously published material or to use illustrations that identify individuals must be obtained by the author prior to submission. Information on the transfer of copyright will be sent to authors on acceptance of their manuscript for publication. The transfer of copyright from author(s) to publisher must be stated in writing before any manuscript can be published.

Title page. The title page must include the following information: the full title; the affiliation and full addresses of all authors; a running title (maximum 50 characters); indication of the author responsible for correspondence and correction of proofs; a brief biographical outline.

Abstract and keywords. The abstract should be comprehensible without reference to the text and should not exceed 200 words. The main findings and new and important aspects of the study should be emphasized. Up to five keywords or phrases must be submitted for indexing purposes.

References. The Harvard system is used. When quoted in the text the style is: ...Jones (1991) or (Smith and Jones, 1991). For three or more authors: Jones et al., (1991) or (Jones et al., 1991). References to papers by the same author(s) in the same year are distinguished in text and reference list by the letters a, b etc: Smith (1989a). References are listed at the end of the paper in alphabetical order giving the title of the paper and journal titles in full, together with the first and last page numbers. References to books and reports must include the year of publication, title, edition, editor(s), place of publication and publisher in that order.

Tables. Each table should be typed on a separate sheet, numbered consecutively and provided with a brief title. Tables should be comprehensible without reference to the text, but repetition of methods that have been described in the text are not necessary. Explanatory material should be placed as a footnote to the table. When results are expressed as percentages, the absolute value(s) that correspond to 100% should be stated.

Illustrations. Line drawings should be supplied at double the intended size. Illustrations should not be inserted in the pages of the manuscript, but supplied separately with the typescript. Typewritten or handwritten annotations are not acceptable. Illustrations must be presented either as: (1) high resolution, well-contrasted glossy photographs or (2) high quality laser printed computer output. Colour illustrations should be supplied as colour prints grouped into plates; costs of colour printing will be charged to the author.

Footnotes. These should not be used unless absolutely essential. If included they should be kept to a minimum, and numbered separately on separate sheets.

Proofs. Proofs will be sent to the corresponding author for correction. The proofs must be corrected within three days of receipt and returned to the publisher. Alteration to proofs other than the correction of printer's errors may be charged to the authors.

Offprints. Each corresponding author will receive 25 free offprints and a bound copy of the journal.

Copyright. Submission of a paper to the Journal of Marketing Communications will be taken to imply that it presents original unpublished work, not under consideration for publication elsewhere. By submitting a manuscript, the authors agree that the copyright for their article is transferred to Taylor Francis Ltd if and when the article is accepted for publication. The copyright covers the exclusive rights to reproduce and distribute the article, including electronic distribution, reprints, photographic reproductions, microfilm or any other reproductions of a similar or any nature, and translations. Permission to publish illustrations must be obtained by the author before submission and any acknowledgements should be included in the captions.

Journal of Marketing Education

ADDRESS FOR SUBMISSION:

Craig A. Kelley, Editor
Journal of Marketing Education
California State University
School of Business Administration
600 J. Street
Sacramento, CA 95819-6088
USA
Phone: 916-278-7199
Fax: 916-278-5437
E-Mail: kelleyca@csus.edu
Web: www.sagepub.com
Address May Change:

PUBLICATION GUIDELINES:

Manuscript Length: 15-30
Copies Required: Five
Computer Submission: No
Format: N/A
Fees to Review: 0.00 US$

Manuscript Style:
    Chicago Manual of Style

CIRCULATION DATA:

Reader: Academics
Frequency of Issue: 3 Times/Year
Copies per Issue: 1,001 - 2,000
Sponsor/Publisher: Western Marketing
    Educator's Assn. /Sage Publications
Subscribe Price: 46.00 US$ Individual
    115.00 US$ Institution

REVIEW INFORMATION:

Type of Review: Blind Review
No. of External Reviewers: 3+
No. of In House Reviewers: 0
Acceptance Rate: 11-20%
Time to Review: 2 - 3 Months
Reviewers Comments: Yes
Invited Articles: 0-5%
Fees to Publish: 0.00 US$

MANUSCRIPT TOPICS:
Advertising & Promotion Management; Business Education; Business Law, Public Responsibility & Ethics; Communication; Direct Marketing; Marketing Education; Marketing Research; Marketing Theory & Applications; Sales/Selling; Services; Technology/Innovation; Transportation/Physical Distribution

MANUSCRIPT GUIDELINES/COMMENTS:

Journal Submission Guidelines
The *Journal of Marketing Education* is the leading international scholarly journal devoted to issues in marketing education. The objective of the journal is to publish articles focusing on the latest techniques in marketing education, emphasizing new course content and teaching methods. Its purpose is to provide a forum for the exchange of ideas, information, and experiences related to the process of educating students of marketing and advertising.

Our audience is largely composed of marketing faculty members at institutions of higher education where teaching is an important component of the assignment. The readership of the Journal of Marketing Education is international in scope, with a significant representation in university libraries. In addition to the subscriber base, the journal is available to researchers on microfilm, microfiche, CD-ROM, and various electronic databases.

The *Journal of Marketing Education* strives to enhance excellence in instruction by providing our readership with innovative plans for effective methods of teaching. First priority for publication goes to articles that specifically address this objective. The journal also publishes articles that address various professional issues of importance to marketing faculty members. Development of the curriculum, career development, and the state of the profession are examples of such areas of interest.

Submission Of Initial Manuscripts
To expedite initial consideration of your manuscript, please prepare and submit manuscripts according to the following guidelines:

Prior Publication
Manuscripts are considered for publication only of they have not been published or accepted for publication elsewhere and are not concurrently being reviewed for publication elsewhere. Publication of a one-page abstract of the manuscript in a conference proceedings will not preclude consideration for publication in the journal.

Manuscript Length and Selection Criteria
Manuscripts ordinarily should be between 4,000 and 7,000 words (15-30 pages), in addition to appropriate references, tables, and other supporting materials. Shorter articles are also acceptable. Authors should strive for conciseness, readability, and a high density of contribution per page.

Manuscripts are judged on the significance of their potential contribution to the literature and relevance to marketing educators. Additional criteria include clarity of presentation and technical adequacy. Articles should be interesting and readable. Copies of the Guidelines for Reviewers are available from the editor.

Style Guidelines
The entire manuscript, including references, should be double-spaced. Use only standard, 12-point type. Place the sections of the manuscript in the following order: cover page, title page with abstract, body, appendices, footnotes, reference list, tables, exhibits, maps, and figures. Begin each section on a new page.

Use standard author-date citations within the text. Please do not identify the author(s) in the body of the paper, either directly or by citation. Note with item number and title where tables, exhibits, and so forth, should appear in the body of the text (e.g. between two paragraphs: Table 1 about here).

Consult recent issues of the journal for appropriate style and formatting of references, tables, and so forth. When in doubt, consult the latest edition of *The Chicago Manual of Style*.

Neither the names(s) nor the university affiliation(s) of the author(s) should appear anywhere in the manuscript. A separate cover sheet should provide this information and indicate a contact author and her or his full mailing address, telephone number, fax number, and e-mail address (where available).

Select a single category for the manuscript to be reviewed under and indicate this category on the cover page. Consult recent issues of the annual index for examples of topics within these categories.

- Pedagogy / Marketing Education
- Student
- Projects and Advising
- Faculty Issues
- Curriculum
- Course Content/Innovation (please specify course(s)

Submit five (5) laser-printed originals, or very clean copies, of each manuscript. Do not submit any computer files or camera-ready materials with the initial manuscript.

Send manuscripts to Craig A. Kelley, Editor.

Please note that we cannot accept manuscripts by either fax or e-mail. Thank you for your consideration.

Editorial Review Procedures
Manuscripts are normally desk reviewed by the editor and acknowledged within 2 weeks of receipt. Initial manuscript reviews are usually completed within 10 weeks, and accepted manuscripts are published within 1 year of acceptance. At the present time, the journal publishes approximately one in four manuscripts received for review.

The journal uses a double-blind review process. Neither the author nor the reviewers know the identities of any other party. Any manuscript accepted for the journal has been reviewed by the editor and at least three outside reviewers who are experts in their respective fields. In some instances, one reviewer will be from outside of North America.

Publisher and Sponsors
The Journal of Marketing Education is published three times a year by Sage Publications. The journal is sponsored by the Western Marketing Educators' Association with additional financial support for the editor provided by the Department of Management, California State University, Sacramento.

Copyrights
All published material is copyrighted by the *Journal of Marketing Education*, and the publisher reserves future use rights. (This does not limit authors' rights to use their own material.) Authors must obtain any necessary permissions and agree to incur any related expense.

Submission of Final Manuscripts
A detailed set of guidelines for the final version of the manuscript will be sent to authors upon acceptance of their manuscript for publication, or a copy may be requested directly from either the editor or the publisher.

Authors of final manuscripts accepted for publication will provide two hard copies and one 3.5-inch computer disk. The manuscript should be written in a widely used word processing program. Camera-ready copies of graphic elements should be provided promptly when requested by journal staff or publisher.

Journal of Marketing for Higher Education

ADDRESS FOR SUBMISSION:

Thomas J. Hayes, Editor
Journal of Marketing for Higher Education
Xavier University
Department of Marketing
3800 Victory Parkway
Cincinnati, OH 45207-3214
USA
Phone: 513-745-3059
Fax: 513-745-3692
E-Mail: hayes@xu.edu
Web: www.haworthpress.com
Address May Change:

PUBLICATION GUIDELINES:

Manuscript Length: 5-50 typed pages.
Copies Required: Three
Computer Submission: No
Format: N/A
Fees to Review: 0.00 US$

Manuscript Style:
    Chicago Manual of Style

CIRCULATION DATA:

Reader: Academics
Frequency of Issue: Quarterly
Copies per Issue: Less than 1,000
Sponsor/Publisher: Haworth Press, Inc.
Subscribe Price: 60.00 US$ Individual
    120.00 US$ Institution
    250.00 US$ Library

REVIEW INFORMATION:

Type of Review: Blind Review
No. of External Reviewers: 3
No. of In House Reviewers: 0
Acceptance Rate: 35%
Time to Review: 4 - 6 Months
Reviewers Comments: Yes
Invited Articles: 6-10%
Fees to Publish: 0.00 US$

MANUSCRIPT TOPICS:

Direct Marketing; Higher Education Administration & Management; Marketing Research; Marketing Theory & Applications; Organizational Behavior & Theory; Strategic Management Policy

MANUSCRIPT GUIDELINES/COMMENTS:

About the Journal

This journal provides guidance for marketing, admissions, public relations, development, and planning professionals who have the responsibility for enrollments and image enhancement at institutions of higher education. A further goal of the journal is to provide a focus through which the many aspects of marketing for higher education can be integrated into a coherent discipline.

The *Journal of Marketing For Higher Education* welcomes the submission of articles dealing with all phases of admissions, institutional research, planning, public relations, development and academic administration that contribute to the marketing of higher education. Of special interest are papers that aim to combine all or some of the appropriate elements from these separate functions into a formal marketing structure. The journal welcomes papers by practitioners as well as academics and particularly welcomes reports which cover both the positive and negative outcomes of projects that have been implemented, with retrospective discussion designed to aid colleagues who involved in similar projects.

Instructions for Authors

1. Original articles only. Submission of a manuscript to this Journal represents a certification on the part of the author(s) that it is an original work, and that neither this manuscript nor a version of it has been published elsewhere nor is being considered for publication elsewhere.

2. Manuscript Length. 5-50 typed pages.

3. Manuscript Style. *Chicago Manual of Style.*

4. Manuscript Preparation.
Margins: leave at least a one-inch margin on all four sides.
Paper: use clean white, 8-1/2" x 11" bond paper.
Number of copies: 4 (the original plus three photocopies).
Cover page: *Important* -- staple a cover page to the manuscript, indicating only the article title (this is used for anonymous refereeing).
Second "title page": enclose a regular title page but do not staple it to the manuscript. Include the title again, plus:
- full authorship
- an abstract of about 100 words. (Below the abstract provide 3-1 0 key words for index purposes).
- an introductory footnote with authors' academic degrees, professional titles, affiliations, mailing addresses, and any desired acknowledgment of research support or other credit.

5. Return Envelopes. When you submit your four manuscript copies, also include:
- A regular envelope, stamped and self-addressed. This is for the Editor to send you an "acknowledgement of receipt" letter.
- Manuscripts will not be returned.

6. Spelling, Grammar, and Punctuation. You are responsible for preparing manuscript copy which is clearly written in acceptable scholarly English, and which contains no errors of spelling, grammar, or punctuation. Neither the Editor nor the Publisher is responsible for correcting errors of spelling and grammar: the manuscript, after acceptance by the Editor, must be immediately ready for typesetting as it is finally submitted by the author(s). Check your paper for the following common errors:
- dangling modifiers
- misplaced modifiers
- unclear antecedents
- incorrect or inconsistent abbreviations

Also, check the accuracy of all arithmetic calculations, statistics, numerical data, text citations, and references.

7. Inconsistencies must be avoided. Be sure you are consistent in your use of abbreviations, terminology, and in citing references, from one part of your paper to another.

8. Preparation of tables, figures, and illustrations. All tables, figures, illustrations, etc. must be "camera-ready." That is, they must be cleanly typed or artistically prepared so that they can be used either exactly as they are or else used after a photographic reduction in size. Figures, tables, and illustrations must be prepared on separate sheets of paper. Always use black ink and professional drawing instruments. On the back of these items, write your article title and the journal title lightly in pencil, so they do not get misplaced. In text, skip extra lines and indicate where these figures and tables are to be placed (please **do not write** on face of art). Photographs are considered part of the acceptable manuscript and remain with Publisher for use in additional printings. If submitted art cannot be used, the Publisher reserves the right to redo the art and to charge the author a fee of $35.00 per hour for this service.

9. Alterations required by referees and reviewers. Many times a paper is accepted by the Editor contingent upon changes that are mandated by anonymous specialist referees and members of the Editorial Board. If the Editor returns your manuscript for revisions, you are responsible for retyping any sections of the paper to incorporate these revisions (if applicable, revisions should also be put on disk).

10. Typesetting. You will not be receiving galley proofs of your article. Editorial revisions, if any, must therefore be made while your article is still in manuscript. The final version of the manuscript will be the version you see published. Typesetter's errors will be corrected by the production staff of The Haworth Press. Authors are expected to submit manuscripts, disks, and art that are free from error.

11. Electronic media. Haworth's in-house type-setting unit is able to utilize your final manuscript material as prepared on most personal computers and word processors. This will minimize typographical errors and decrease overall production timelag. Please send the first draft and final draft copies of your manuscript to the journal Editor in print format for his/her final review and approval. **After approval of** your final manuscript, please submit the final approved version both on printed format ("hard copy") and floppy diskette. On the outside of the diskette package write:
A. the brand name of your computer or word processor
B. the word-processing program that you used
C. the title of your article, and
D. file name

Note: Disk and hard copy must agree. In case of discrepancies, it is The Haworth Press's policy to follow hard copy. Authors are advised that no revisions of the manuscript can be made after acceptance by the Editor for publication. The benefits of this procedure are many with speed and accuracy being the most obvious. We look forward to working with you on this, knowing we will be able to serve you more efficiently in the future.

12. Reprints. The senior author will receive two copies of the journal issue and 25 complimentary reprints of his or her article. The junior author will receive two copies of the journal issue. These are sent several weeks after the journal issue is published and in circulation. An order form for the purchase of additional reprints will also be sent to all authors at this time. (Approximately 4-6 weeks is necessary for the preparation of reprints.) Please do not query the Journal's Editor about reprints. All such questions should be sent directly to: **The Haworth Press, Inc., Production Department, 21 East Broad Street, West Hazleton, PA 18201.**

To order additional reprints (minimum: 50 copies), please contact:
The Haworth Document Delivery Center,10 Alice Street, Binghamton, NY 13904-1580
1-800-342-9678 or Fax (607) 722-6362.

13. Copyright. Copyright ownership of your manuscript must be transferred officially to The Haworth Press, Inc., before we can begin the peer-review process. The Editor's letter acknowledging receipt of the manuscript will be accompanied by a form fully explaining this. All authors must sign the form and return the original to the Editor as soon as possible. Failure to return the copyright form in a timely fashion will result in delay in review and subsequent publication

Journal of Marketing Management

ADDRESS FOR SUBMISSION:

Susan Hart, Editor
Journal of Marketing Management
University of Strathclyde
Department of Marketing
173 Cathedral Street
Glasgow, G4 0RQ
Scotland
Phone: 44 0 1415 484927
Fax: 44 0 1415 522802
E-Mail:
Web: www.westburn.co.uk
Address May Change:

CIRCULATION DATA:

Reader: Academics
Frequency of Issue: 5 Times/ Year
Copies per Issue: 2,001 - 3,000
Sponsor/Publisher: Westburn Publishers, Ltd.
Subscribe Price: 245.00 Pounds Institution
115.00 Pounds Personal
60.00 Pounds Member

PUBLICATION GUIDELINES:

Manuscript Length: 21-30+
Copies Required: Three + Electronic Version
Computer Submission: No Reply
Format: No Reply
Fees to Review: 0.00 US$

Manuscript Style:
See Manuscript Guidelines

REVIEW INFORMATION:

Type of Review: Blind Review
No. of External Reviewers: 2
No. of In House Reviewers: 1
Acceptance Rate: 11-20%
Time to Review: 2 - 3 Months
Reviewers Comments: Yes
Invited Articles: 0-5%
Fees to Publish: 0.00 US$

MANUSCRIPT TOPICS:
Advertising & Promotion Management; Communication; Direct Marketing; Global Business; Marketing Research; Marketing Theory & Applications; Purchasing/Materials Management; Sales/Selling; Services; Small Business Entrepreneurship; Strategic Management Policy; Technology/Innovation; Transportation/Physical Distribution

MANUSCRIPT GUIDELINES/COMMENTS:

In accordance with its policy, the *Journal of Marketing Management* welcomes contributions from theoreticians and practitioners in the following areas:

- **State of the art papers on particular topics**
  e.g. portfolio planning, sales management, pricing

- **Management of the marketing mix**
  the practical issues of managing product, price, place and promotion efficiently and effectively

- **Customer behavior**
  how and why both corporate and ultimate customers behave in the way they do

- **Marketing intelligence**
  the establishment and maintenance of marketing information systems and everything associated with them

- **Case studies**
  how an organization has tackled an important marketing problem

- **Meta marketing**
  how marketing ideas and techniques are applied to the less- or non-traditional areas of services, public and non-profit organizations

In addition to these core areas the journal also attracts
- Marketing education and training papers
- Conference reports and commentaries
- Books reviews and abstracts
- Letters

Submissions (3 copies) should be of 4000-6000 words (excluding display material and references) typed double-spaced on A4 paper. The first page should consist of the title, authors' names, addresses and an indication of author for correspondence with his/her telephone/fax number. The second page should comprise an abstract of the paper (c. 150 words) and a biography (c. 150 words) detailing the authors' background, affiliations and interests. Display material must be numbered, captioned and cited in the text. Authors should avoid identifying themselves in the main body of the text

References
References are indicated in the text by the Harvard (name and date) system: Either "Recent work (Smith 1970)" or "Recently Smith (1970) has found ..". All such references should then be listed in alphabetical order at the end of the paper in accordance with the following conventions:

1. **Books**
Baker, Michael J. and Hart, Susan J. (1989), Marketing and Competitive Success, Hemel Hempstead, Philip Allen.

2. **Journal Articles**
Star, Steven H. (1989), "Marketing and its Discontents", Harvard Business Review, November/December 1989 No.6, pp. 148-154.

3. **Contributions in books, proceedings, etc.**
Doyle, Peter (1990), "Managing the Marketing Mix". In: The Marketing Book 2nd Edition. (Ed.)Baker, Doyle, peter (1990), "Managing the Marketing Mix." In: The Marketing Book 2nd Editorn. (Ed.) Baker, Michael J. (London), William Heinemann Ltd, pp.227-267.

Copyright offprints: Authors submitting a manuscript do so on the understanding that if it is accepted for publication, copyright in the paper exclusive shall be assigned to the Publisher. In consideration of the assignment of copyright 20 reprints of each paper, and a copy of the journal will be supplied. Further reprints may be ordered at extra cost, The Publisher will not put any limitations on the personal freedom of the author to use material contained in the paper in other works. Papers are accepted for the Journal on the understanding that they have not been or will not be published elsewhere in the same form, in any language.

Manuscripts on Disc

When supplying the final version of your article please include a disc of your manuscript prepared on PC compatible or Apple Macintosh computers along with one hard copy print-out. 3.5" sized discs, and 100MB Iomega Zip Discs and most word processing packages are acceptable, although any version of Microsoft Word or WordPerfect is preferred.

Please follow these guidelines carefully

- Include one copy of the word-processed article in its original format (e.g. Word), including figures and tables.

- Also include an .rtf copy of the file (Rich Text Format), with all the diagrams etc. included. If the article includes a figure which is a photograph, or a particularly complex illustration, this should be saved in a separate .tif file. All diagrams and figures should be in black and white. If prepared on an Apple, include the file in ASCII format.

- Ensure that the files are not saved as read-only.

- Manuscripts prepared on discs must be accompanied by one hard copy, including all figures, printed with double spacing and which may be used if setting from the disc proves impracticable.

- Ensure the final version of the hard copy and the file on disc are the same. It is the author's responsibility to ensure complete compatibility. If there are differences the hard copy will be used.

- The directives for preparing the paper in the style of the journal as set out in the Instructions to Authors must be followed; i.e. ensure the document is in the following order. Title; Authors; Addresses; Abstract; Running heads; Introduction; Materials and methods; Results; Discussion; Acknowledgements; References; Appendices; Figure legends; Tables; Footnotes; Abbreviations.

- The operating system and the word processing software used to produce the article should be noted on the disc (e.g. Win 98/Word 2000), as well as all file names. The disc should be labelled with the journal reference number (if known) and author name(s).

- Do not include copyright material, e.g. word processing software or operating system files, on the disc because this can create difficulties with Customs clearance.

- Package floppy discs in such a way as to avoid damage in the post.

Additional points to note
- Use two carriage returns to end headings and paragraphs.
- Type text without end of line hyphenation, except for compound words.
- Do not use lower case "1" for "1" or "0" for "0". (They have different typesetting values.)
- Be consistent with punctuation and only insert a single space between words and after punctuation.
- Please include a list of any special characters you have had to use, e.g. Greek, maths.

Please note that all articles should be submitted to the Editor for review:

Professor Susan Hart
Editor, Journal of Marketing Management, Department of Marketing, University of Strathclyde, 173 Cathedral Street, Glasgow, G4 ORQ, Scotland
Tel: +44 141 548 4927, Fax: +44 141 552 2802, E-mail: susan.hart@strath.ac.uk

All other enquiries and accepted papers and accompanying disks should be directed to:

Westburn Publishers Ltd, Westburn, Helensburgh, Argyll, G84 9NH, Scotland
Tel: +44 1436 678 699, Fax: +44 1436 670 328, E-Mail: jmm@westburn.co.uk

All of this information and more can be found on our Website at:
http)://www.westburn.co.uk

Journal of Marketing Research

ADDRESS FOR SUBMISSION:

Wagner A. Kamakura, Editor
Journal of Marketing Research
University of Iowa
College of Business Administration
Department of Marketing
108 Pappajohn Bus. Adm. Bldg.
Iowa City, IA 52242-1000
USA
Phone: 319-335-1013
Fax: 319-335-3690
E-Mail: wagner-kamakura@uiowa.edu
Web: www.ama.org
Address May Change:

PUBLICATION GUIDELINES:

Manuscript Length: 20-40
Copies Required: Five
Computer Submission: Yes
Format: ASCII, MS Word
Fees to Review: 0.00 US$

Manuscript Style:
    Chicago Manual of Style

CIRCULATION DATA:

Reader: Academics
Frequency of Issue: Quarterly
Copies per Issue: 5,001 - 10,000
Sponsor/Publisher: American Marketing
   Association
Subscribe Price: 75.00 US$ Individual
   150.00 US$ Institution
   40.00 US$ AMA Member

REVIEW INFORMATION:

Type of Review: Blind Review
No. of External Reviewers: 3
No. of In House Reviewers: 1
Acceptance Rate: 11-20%
Time to Review: 1 - 2 Months
Reviewers Comments: Yes
Invited Articles: 0-5%
Fees to Publish: 6.00 US$

MANUSCRIPT TOPICS:
Marketing Research; Marketing Theory & Applications

MANUSCRIPT GUIDELINES/COMMENTS:

AMA Journals Editorial Policy
The following policies are applicable to the Journal of Marketing, Journal of Marketing Research, Journal of International Marketing and Journal of Public Policy & Marketing.

1. Replication and/or Extension of Results
The American Marketing Association supports the meaningful exchange of information to help create an environment for constructive criticism and free exchange of ideas. Such an environment requires the authors of AMA manuscripts to share their research findings and insights. Authors of manuscripts that report data dependent results will make available, upon request, exact information regarding their procedures, materials (excluding data), and stimuli during the editorial review process. The same information will also be made available, upon

request, for at least five years after the date of publication for the benefit of researchers interested in replicating or extending their results.

Authors of articles published in AMA journals are required to footnote the availability of their research instruments and other stimuli as appropriate and provide information on how the materials may be obtained. Authors of manuscripts based on proprietary data sets or other restricted material must so notify the editor at the time a manuscript is submitted. The editor will then decide whether to accept the manuscript for review. Published articles in this genre will contain a footnote stating that the data or other elements of the research process as identified are proprietary.

2. Concurrent Reviews
AMA policy prohibits an article under review at an AMA journal from being concurrently reviewed at another journal without prior discussion with and written permission from the involved AMA journal editor.

3. Multiple Submissions
Multiple reports based on essentially the same data and results should not be submitted for publication in AMA journals. The publication of a manuscript in a non-AMA journal or other publication outlet precludes publication in an AMA journal if the manuscript is based on essentially the same data set and analysis as the AMA publication. Upon request, the AMA journal editor will make a binding decision about whether a manuscript submitted to an AMA journal is too similar to a previous publication elsewhere based on the same data set to warrant review for possible publication. Each article published must also contain references to the previously published papers.

4. Conflicts of Interest
Conflicts of interest may arise in a variety of situations. A conflict of interest may exist when a manuscript under review puts forth a position contrary to the reviewer's published work or when a manuscript reviewer has a substantial direct or indirect financial interest in the subject matter of a published manuscript. Since it is AMA policy to engage in a double-blind review process, a conflict of interest may also exist when a reviewer knows the author of a manuscript. The reviewer should consult the journal editor in such situations to decide whether to review the manuscript. A conflict of interest does not exist when an author disagrees with a reviewer's assessment that a problem is unimportant or disagrees with an editorial outcome.

EDITORIAL GUIDELINES
Mission
The *Journal of Marketing Research* (JMR) is a quarterly journal striving to publish the best manuscripts available dealing with research in marketing and marketing research practice. JMR is a scholarly and professional journal. It does not attempt to serve the generalist in marketing management, but it does strive to appeal to the professional in marketing research.

Primary Reader Targets
Technically oriented marketing researchers and educators concerned with marketing research. In this context, "technically oriented" is included but is not limited to quantitative treatments.

Article Guidelines
The following article guidelines are appropriate:
- New marketing research related methods and techniques,
- Applications of new and current marketing research methods and techniques,
- Clarifications of marketing research methodology and practice, and
- State of the art articles in marketing research.

Articles may be occasionally published outside the established article guidelines. These articles should never exceed one article in any one issue.

Editorial Objectives
The objective of the JMR is to publish the highest quality empirical, theoretical, and methodological marketing research. Because JMR is the major academic journal for research in marketing, articles published in the journal must make a significant contribution to the marketing discipline, provide a basis for stimulating additional research, and meet high standards of scholarship.

Nature of JMR Research
JMR publishes articles representing the entire spectrum of research in marketing, ranging from analytical models of marketing phenomena to descriptive studies using ethnographic methodologies. However, most of the research currently published in JMR fits into the following two categories: (1) empirical research testing a theory or describing and evaluating a management practice and (2) methodological research presenting new approaches for analyzing data or addressing marketing research problems.

Empirical Research
The empirical research published in JMR typically begins with a conceptual framework in which constructs are identified and defined and their interrelationships are hypothesized. The hypothesized interrelationships are supported by prior research and/or logical reasoning. Then the framework, or a portion of the framework, is tested by collecting and analyzing primary or secondary data.

JMR empirical studies often involve complex experimental designs and multivariate techniques for examining the relationships between variables. However, authors are encouraged to focus on the potential substantive contributions of their research and not overemphasize the sophistication of their methodology. To facilitate a basic understanding of the research findings, authors should report important descriptive statistics-cell, row, and column means in experimental designs or the means, standard deviations, and correlation matrix for variables in survey research.

Empirical research should be reported in sufficient detail that readers can evaluate and replicate the methodology. Measures developed for the research should be described completely in the body of the article or in a measurement appendix.

Finally, authors are encouraged to use the concluding discussion section of empirical papers to provide guidance to readers interested in exploring issues presented in the article. Frequently, discussion sections go beyond a simple summary of the statistical results and provide an interpretation of those results. Limitations in the research design and implementation should be noted to guide the interpretation of results and the development of further research. Although authors should not make assertions that are unsupported by their finding, they may have developed valuable insights while undertaking the research. By sharing and clearly identifying their informed speculations, authors can play a valuable part in stimulating further research.

Methodological Research
The explosive growth in market data has stimulated the development of methodologies for converting such data into managerially useful information. JMR maintains a long tradition for publishing research on state-of-the-art methodological contributions.

In addition to describing the benefits and advantages of new methods, methodological articles must indicate their relevance in a marketing context. Limitations of the method should be fully disclosed.

Finally, methodological articles must go beyond a simple presentation of a new method. The new method should be compared with alternative approaches for attacking a problem. The article should indicate the circumstances under which the new method is superior and why it is superior. Authors are encouraged to include empirical illustrations comparing a new method with current methods.

Review Articles
JMR encourages the submission of articles reviewing and integrating research in marketing. Such articles have had a high impact on the marketing discipline--the majority of O'Dell award winning articles are review articles, even though the review articles account for a small percentage of the research published in JMR.

Review articles published in JMR must go beyond a summary of previous research in a substantive or methodological area. A review article should advance the marketing discipline by providing a critical and integrative evaluation of prior research, developing a conceptual framework to explain contradictory findings, and suggesting directions for further research.

Comments and Rejoinders
JMR publishes comments on previously published articles and rejoinders by the authors(s) of the focal article. A comment on an article should be submitted as soon as possible after the publication of the focal article. Comments undergo the standard review process. If a comment is accepted for publication, the author(s) of the focal paper will be given the opportunity to prepare and submit a rejoinder. The rejoinder must also pass through the review process. Typically, comments and rejoinders are shorter than 15 pages.

MANUSCRIPT GUIDELINES
Manuscript and Disk Preparation
1. Submit five copies of your manuscript to Wagner A. Kamakura.
   (Do not submit disk copies until directed to do so by the editor.)
2. Keep an extra, exact copy for future reference.

3. Manuscripts should not exceed fifty (50) pages, inclusive of all text, tables, figures, appendices, etc.
4. Manuscripts should be typed double spaced throughout (including references) on 8 1/2 x 11 inch white, nonerasable paper.
5. Allow margins of at least one inch on all four sides and do not justify your right-hand margin. Use a 12 pt. font.
6. Type on one side of the paper only.

What Goes Where?
1. First page: Name of author(s) and title; author(s) footnote, including present positions, complete address, telephone number, fax number, email address, and any acknowledgment of financial or technical assistance.
2. Second page: Title of paper (without author's name) and a brief abstract of no more than 50 words substantively summarizing the article. It should be informative, giving the reader a "taste" of the article.
3. Next: The text with major headings centered on the page and subheadings flush with the left margin.
4. Then: Tables, numbered consecutively, each on a separate page. If tables appear in an appendix, they should be numbered separately and consecutively, as in Table A-1, A-2, and so on.
5. Next: Figures, numbered consecutively, each placed on a separate page. If tables appear in an appendix, they should be numbered separately, as in Figure A-1, A-2, etc.
6. Last: References, typed double spaced in alphabetical order by author's last name.

Mathematical Notation
1. Mathematical notation must be clear within the text.
2. Equations should be centered on the page. If equations are numbered, type the number in parentheses flush with the left margin.
3. Unusual symbols and Greek letters should be identified by a marginal note. If equations are too wide to fit in a single column, indicate appropriate breaks.

Tables
1. Tables should consist of at least four columns and four rows; otherwise they should be left as in-text tabulations or their results should be integrated in the text.
2. The table number and title should be typed on separate lines, centered.
3. Use only horizontal rules.
4. Designate units (e.g., %, $) in column headings.
5. Align all decimals.
6. Refer to tables in text by number. Avoid using "above," "below," and "preceding."
7. If possible, combine closely related tables.
8. Indicate placement in text.
9. Make sure the necessary measures of statistical significance are reported with the table.

Figures and Camera-Ready Artwork

1. Figures should be prepared professionally on disk and as camera-ready copy.

2. Label both vertical and horizontal axes. The ordinate label should be centered above the ordinate axis; the abscissa label should be placed beneath the abscissa.

3. Place all calibration tics inside the axis lines, with the values outside the axis lines.

4. The figure number and title should be typed on separate lines, centered.

5. Once a manuscript has been accepted, complex tables and all figures must be on disk and camera-ready. Table and figure headings should be typed on a separate page and attached to the appropriate camera-ready art. These titles will be set in our own typeface.

6. Lettering should be large enough to be read easily with 50% reduction. Any art not done on a computer graphics program should be professionally drafted in India ink.

7. Do not submit camera-ready art until your manuscript has been accepted. If the artwork is completed, submit photocopies.

Reference Citations Within the Text

1. Citation in the text should be by the author's last name and year of publication, enclosed in parentheses without punctuation: "(Kinsey 1960)." If practical, the citation should stand by a punctuation mark. Otherwise, insert it in a logical sentence break. If you use the author's name within the sentence, there is no need to repeat the name in the citation; just use the year of publication in parentheses, as in "...The Howard Harris Program (1966)."

2. If a particular page, section, or equation is cited, it should be placed within the parentheses: "(Kinsey 1960, p. 112)." For multiple authors, use the full citation for up to three authors; for four or more, use the first author's name followed by "et al." (no italics). A series of citations should be listed in alphabetical order and separated by semicolons: (Donnelly 1961; Kinsey 1960; Wensley 1981).

Reference List Style

1. References are to be listed alphabetically, last name first, followed by publication date in parentheses. Use full first name, not just initials. The reference list should be typed double spaced on a separate page. Do not use indents, tabs, or symbols to delineate your paragraphs. Instead, use two hard returns between each reference.

2. Authors are responsible for the accuracy of their references. Check them carefully.

3. *Single- and multiple-author references for books*:

   Donnelly, James H. and William R. George (1981), Marketing of Services. Chicago: American Marketing Association.

4. *Single- and multiple-author reference for periodicals* (include author's name, publication date, article title, complete name of periodical, volume number, month of publication, and page numbers):

   Wensley, Robin (1981), "Strategic Marketing: Betas, Boxes, or Basics," Journal of Marketing, 45 (Summer), 173-82.

5. *Single- and multiple-author reference for an article in a book edited by another author(s):*

   Nevin, John R. and Ruth A. Smith (1981), "The Predictive Accuracy of a Retail Gravitation Model: An Empirical Evaluation," in The Changing Marketing Environment, Kenneth Bernhardt et al., eds. Chicago: American Marketing Association.

6. *If an author appears more than once, substitute four hyphens* (this will appear as a 1-inch line when typeset) for each author's name (do not use underlines):

   Fornell, Claes and David F. Larcher (1981a), "Evaluating Structural Equation Models with Unobservable Variables and Measurement Error," Journal of Marketing Research, (February), 39-50.

   ----and---- (1981b), "Structural Equation Models with Unobservable Variables and Measurement Error: Algebra and Statistics," Journal of Marketing Research, 18 (August).

7. *If two or more works by the same author have the same publication date*, they should be differentiated by letters after the date. The letter also should appear with the citation in the text:

   Day, George (1981a), "Analytical Approaches to Strategic Market Planning," in Review of Marketing 1981, Ben Enis and Kenneth J. Roering, eds. Chicago: American Marketing Association.

   ----(1981b), "The Product Life Cycle: Analysis and Applications Issues," Journal of Marketing, 45 (Fall), 60-67.

8. *References to unpublished works*, such as doctoral dissertations and working papers, should be included in the references list as follows:

   Coughlin, Maureen (1980), "Fear of Success: Reaction to Advertising Stimuli and Intention to Purchase," doctoral dissertation, City University of New York.

Technical Appendix
To improve the readability of the manuscript, any mathematical proof or development that is not critical to the exposition of the main part of the text my be placed in a technical appendix.

Readability

JM manuscripts are judged not only on the depth and scope of the ideas presented and their contributions to the field, but also on their clarity and whether they can be read and understood. Readers have varied backgrounds. Hence, the following guidelines should be followed:

- Write in an interesting, readable manner with varied sentence structure. Use as little passive voice as possible.
- Avoid using technical terms that few readers are likely to understand. If you use these terms, include definitions. Remember: The journal is designed to be read, not deciphered.
- Keep sentences short so the reader does not get lost before the end of a sentence.

Review Procedure

The procedures guiding the selection of articles for publication in JM require that no manuscript be accepted until after it has been reviewed by the editor and at least two members of the editorial review board. The decision of the editor to publish the manuscript is influenced considerably by the judgments of these advisors, who are experts in their respective fields. The author's name and credentials are removed prior to forwarding a manuscript to reviewers to maximize objectivity and ensure that a manuscript is judged solely on the basis of it content and contribution to the field.

Acceptance Criteria

All manuscripts are judged on their contributions to the advancement of the science and/or practice of marketing. All articles are expected to follow the rules for scholarly work, namely:

- Use references to previous work when developing your model or theory. Do not assume other work on the subject does not exist, giving yourself credit for all the ideas in your manuscript.

- When data collection is discussed, consider the relevance of the sample to the subject matter. Carefully chosen sample groups are preferable to haphazardly chosen subjects who have little knowledge of or relevance to the subject being studied.

- Give as much information as possible about the characteristics of the sample and its representativeness of the population being studied.

- Do not ignore the nonrespondents. They might have different characteristics than the respondents.

- Give consideration to the limitations of your study, model, and/or concepts and discuss these in your manuscript. Be objective.

- Use appropriate statistical procedures.

- Address the reliability and validity of any empirical findings.

Preparing The Final Paper And Disk Versions

After a manuscript is accepted for publication, the final version must be submitted on a 3.5-inch disk, along with three copies on 8 1/2 x 11 inch white, nonerasable paper. All copies should contain the entire manuscript, including tables, figures, footnotes, and references. Although authors may prepare the disk copy using any word processing software that is Macintosh or IBM compatible, submission of the disk copy using Microsoft Word 97 for Windows is preferred. Please adhere to the following additional guidelines when preparing the final disk and paper versions.

1. Review all references and footnotes to be certain they fully comply with the "Manuscript Guidelines." Pay careful attention to consistency, accuracy, and formatting.

2. Type everything in upper and lower case letters, using a 12 pt. font.

3. Paragraphs will be identified by spacing -- not tab indention. At the CLOSE of each paragraph, use two hard returns (hit ENTER or RETURN two times). This, in effect, puts 4 line spaces between paragraphs. Example:

    This is the end of paragraph one. <ENTER><ENTER>

    This is the beginning of paragraph two.

4. Double space the entire paper, including the abstract, references, and footnotes.

5. Footnotes should not be used for reference purposes and should be avoided if possible. If necessary to improve the readability to the text, a few footnotes may be included. They should appear double spaced on a separate page and be numbered consecutively throughout the text.

6. Use the italics function when it is appropriate (e.g., titles of publications, for emphasis, etc.).

7. Submit graphics as PowerPoint, Illustrator, Photoshop, or QuarkXpress application files, and/or EPS, high resolution *.tif or *.bmp files, and camera-ready copy.

8. Write the name of the software program used on the disk submitted.

Other Information
All published material is copyrighted by the American Marketing Association with future-use rights reserved. This does not limit the author's right to use his or her own material in future works.

For details on manuscript preparation not covered here, see *Chicago Manual of Style*: The Essential Guide for Authors, Editors, and Publishers, 14th edition, Chicago: University of Chicago Press, 1993. For specific questions on content or editorial policy, contact the editor.

Journal of Marketing Theory and Practice

ADDRESS FOR SUBMISSION:

Thomas N. Ingram, Editor
Journal of Marketing Theory and Practice
Colorado State University
College of Business
Department of Marketing
Fort Collins, CO 80523-1278
USA
Phone: 970-491-5063
Fax: 970-491-5956
E-Mail: tingram@lamar.colostate.edu
Web: www.biz.colostate.edu/jmtp
Address May Change:

PUBLICATION GUIDELINES:

Manuscript Length: Unlimited
Copies Required: Four
Computer Submission: No
Format:
Fees to Review: 0.00 US$

Manuscript Style:
  See Manuscript Guidelines

CIRCULATION DATA:

Reader: Academics
Frequency of Issue: Quarterly
Copies per Issue: 1,001 - 2,000
Sponsor/Publisher: Assn. of Marketing
  Theory and Practice, Inc.
Subscribe Price: 50.00 US$ Individual
  60.00 US$ Library

REVIEW INFORMATION:

Type of Review: Blind Review
No. of External Reviewers: 3
No. of In House Reviewers: 0
Acceptance Rate: 11-20%
Time to Review: 2 - 3 Months
Reviewers Comments: Yes
Invited Articles: 0-5%
Fees to Publish: 10.50 US$ per page

MANUSCRIPT TOPICS:
Advertising & Promotion Management; Direct Marketing; Global Business; Marketing Research; Marketing Theory & Applications; Sales/Selling; Services; Technology/Innovation; Transportation/Physical Distribution

MANUSCRIPT GUIDELINES/COMMENTS:

The purpose of the *Journal of Marketing Theory and Practice* is to publish manuscripts that encourage the application of established marketing theories or the development of new marketing theories that improve the understanding of business practices and the prediction of business behavior and outcomes. In addition, manuscripts addressing the contributions of other disciplines to marketing are encouraged.

Manuscripts from all areas of marketing will be actively solicited including, but not limited to:

1. Consumer Behavior;
2. Strategy;
3. Ethics;
9. Marketing Research;
10. Services Marketing;
11. Macro-Marketing;

    4. Logistics/Transportation
    5. Electronic Commerce
    6. Marketing Management;
    7. Sales Management;
    8. Industrial Marketing;
    12. Entrepreneurship;
    13. Pricing
    14. International & Global Marketing;
    15. Integrated Marketing Communication
    16. Sales Promotion

Many of these areas will be addressed in special journal issues of the Journal with selected issue editors.

Sponsorship

The Association of Marketing Theory and Practice, Inc.
Central Office - College of Business Administration
Department of Marketing
Georgia Southern University
Statesboro, GA 30460-8154

MANUSCRIPT GUIDELINES

Manuscripts should be typed, double-spaced (including references) on 8 ½ by 11 inch white paper with margins of at least one inch on all four sides. Submit four (4) non-returnable copies of the manuscript to the Editor.

Order of Material

Front matter
First Page: Title of paper, name and position of author(s), author(s') complete address(es) and telephone number(s), and any acknowledgement of assistance.

Second Page: A brief biographical sketch of each author including name, degree(s) held, title or position, organization or institution, previous publications, and areas of research interest.

Third Page: Title of paper without author(s') name(s) and a brief abstract of no more than 100 words summarizing the article. The abstract is used on the Contents page and serves to generate reader interest in the full article.

Body of Text
The text begins on page four, with major headings centered, all caps. All sub-headings are typed with upper and lower case and bolded. Footnotes are not used for reference purposes. The order of material is an example of proper format.

Managerial Implications
It is the editorial policy of the JMTP that manuscripts must include a section pertaining to the managerial implications of the research. Researchers are encouraged to utilize realistic examples, case studies, or proposed extensions to current administrative practices in the development of this section. Manuscripts that do not explicitly address the implications of research to practicing marketers will not be reviewed.

Tables and Figures
Each table or figure should be placed on a separate page and numbered consecutively beginning with Table 1 and Figure 1, again using DR 10 pt. or a point size appropriate for the table or figure. A table or figure should not be included unless it is referred to in the text of the article. Placement in the text should be indicated as follows:

Table 2 About Here

Footnotes in tables or figures should be designated by lower case letters. Table or figure number and title should be typed on two separate lines, using upper case, as follows:

TABLE 1
TASK ENVIRONMENT OF THEORY
PRACTICE INTERACTION

References
References within the text should include the author's last name and year of publication enclosed in parentheses, e.g. (Feyerabend 1968; Robin and Reidenbach 1987). If more than one cite, references should be in chronological order. If there is more than one cite for the same year, then those references should be alphabetized. For example (Bales 1955; Spence 1979; Bem 1981; Orlofsky 1981; Feather 1984). If practical, place the citation just ahead of a punctuation mark. If the author's name is used within the text sentence, just place the year of publication in parentheses, e.g., "According to Robin and Reidenbach (1987)...,". if a particular page or section is cited, it should be placed within the parentheses, e.g., (Robin and Reidenbach 1987, p.44). For multiple authors, use up to three names in citation. With four or more authors, use the first author's name and et al.: (Flory et al. 1992).

An alphabetical listing of references should appear at the end of the manuscript, with first author's surname first and year of publication following all authors' names. Work by the same author with the same publication year should be distinguished by lowercase letters after the date (e.g., 1987a). For authors cited more than once, substitute a one-inch line for each name that repeats. Examples are as follows:

Feyerabend, Paul (1968), "On the Improvement of the Sciences and the Arts, and the Possible Identity of the Two," Boston Studies in the Philosophy of Science, III, New York: Humanities Press, 387-415.

Schwartz, George (1963), Development of Marketing Theory, Cincinnati: South-Western Publishing Co.

Van de Ven (1989), "Nothing is Quite so Practical as a Good Theory," The Academy of Management Review, 14, (4), 486-489.

Acceptance Procedure
JMTP manuscripts are reviewed independently by members of the Editorial Review board, and their recommendations guide the Editor in his decision. The reviews are blind - neither authors nor reviewers know the identity of each other
[triple blind review process].

It is the policy of JMTP that manuscripts submitted to this journal must not be under publication consideration by another journal at the same time. Manuscripts which are substantially similar in content to articles already published or accepted for publication in this journal or elsewhere are ineligible for publication. It is the author's responsibility to abide by these provisions when submitting a manuscript for consideration to JMTP.

For additional information on editorial policy or manuscript preparation, please contact the Editor.

Page Fees
In order to keep the subscription price moderate, page fees are necessary. Contributors of articles accepted for publication will be billed page fees when they receive page proofs. The current page fee is $10.50 per page.

Journal of Ministry Marketing and Management

ADDRESS FOR SUBMISSION:

Robert Stevens, David Loudon, Co-Editors
Journal of Ministry Marketing and
   Management
University of Louisiana at Monroe
College of Business Administration
Department of Management and Marketing
Monroe, LA 71209
USA
Phone: 318-342-1186
Fax: 318-342-1209
E-Mail: mmloudon@alpha.nlu.edu
Web: www.haworthpress.com
Address May Change:

PUBLICATION GUIDELINES:

Manuscript Length: 11-15
Copies Required: Four
Computer Submission: No
Format: N/A
Fees to Review: 0.00 US$

Manuscript Style:
   See Manuscript Guidelines

CIRCULATION DATA:

Reader: Academics, Church/Ministry
   Mgrs.& Marketers
Frequency of Issue: 2 Times/Year
Copies per Issue: No Reply
Sponsor/Publisher: Haworth Press, Inc.
Subscribe Price: 45.00 US$ Individual
   65.00 US$ Institution
   75.00 US$ Library

REVIEW INFORMATION:

Type of Review: Blind Review
No. of External Reviewers: 2
No. of In House Reviewers: 0
Acceptance Rate: 21-30%
Time to Review: 1 - 2 Months
Reviewers Comments: Yes
Invited Articles: 11-20%
Fees to Publish: 0.00 US$

MANUSCRIPT TOPICS:
Advertising & Promotion Management; Business Law, Public Responsibility & Ethics; Communication; Marketing Research; Non Profit Organizations; Organizational Behavior & Theory; Organizational Development; Services; Strategic Management Policy

MANUSCRIPT GUIDELINES/COMMENTS:

About The Journal
The 90s have ushered in an era of increasing emphasis on professional development of the church and ministry management. Yet there hasn't been a scholarly journal devoted to managerial and marketing concerns of churches and ministries until the *Journal Of Ministry Marketing & Management*. This new quarterly is an applied journal devoted to providing timely and practical information on marketing and management issues in all types of church and ministry settings.

The co-editors seek contributions to the journal which demonstrate the relevance and significance of marketing and management insights to building a successful church or ministry. Each issue of this unique periodical aims to be a basic resource for all administrators of churches and ministries as well as academicians interested in this applied service area. Because it is focused on current issues, practices, and concerns of church and ministry management, the journal will examine specific marketing and management concepts, tools, cases, and methodologies useful for professionals in the ministry including

- how to write a marketing plan for your ministry
- developing strategic management and leadership
- effective decision-making processes
- how and when to use advertising and media effectively
- useful marketing research techniques
- upholding ethics in ministry marketing
- internal marketing for staff members
- ministry positioning in a competitive marketplace
- effective marketing strategies for fund raising
- managing conflict and stress
- interpersonal communication and resolving staff problems
- motivating employees and members
- recruiting and utilizing volunteers
- budgeting techniques
- organizational structure issues

1. **Original Articles Only.** Submission of a manuscript to the *Journal Of Ministry Marketing And Management* represents a certification on the part of the author(s) that it is an original work, and that neither this manuscript nor a version of it has been published elsewhere nor is being considered for publication elsewhere.

2. **Manuscript Length.** Refereed Articles--Manuscript (including references and abstract) generally should not exceed 15 double-spaced typewritten pages or approximately 4500 words (assume 300 words per page). Lengthier manuscripts maybe considered, but only at the discretion of the Editors. Sometimes, lengthier manuscripts may be considered if they can be divided up into sections for publication in successive journal issues. Practitioner's Corner Articles--manuscript should not exceed 12 pages or approximately 3600 words.

3. **Manuscript Style.** References, citations, and general style of manuscripts for this journal should follow the guidelines cited herein. Your writing style should be clear and direct and not assume that the reader is completely familiar with the buzzwords and jargon of marketing and management. Thus, ideas and terms should be fully developed for clarity to the reader.

4. **Manuscript Preparation**.
Typing: entirely double-spaced with pages numbered consecutively.

Margins: leave at least a one-inch margin on all four sides.

Paper: use white, 8-1/2" x 11" bond paper.

Number of Copies: 4 (the original plus three photocopies).

Return Envelopes. When you submit your four manuscript copies, also include:
- A regular envelope, stamped and self-addressed. This is for the Editor to send you an "acknowledgement of receipt" letter.
- Manuscripts will not be returned.

Format: Use major headings in all capital letters, centered on the page, and subheadings in capital and lower case letters, flush with the left margin.

Cover Page: Complete title of paper plus names of all authors, authors' academic degrees, professional titles, present affiliations, complete addresses, telephone numbers, fax numbrs, and any desired acknowledgment of research support or other credit. This is the only place the authors' names should appear. This page will be removed for anonymous reviewing.

Second Page: include only the paper's title (keep it short and concise) and a brief abstract of no more than 100 words to provide a substantive summary of the article giving readers a good overview of the topic.

Third Page: Begin with the title of the paper followed immediately by the body of the paper.

References: List alphabetically by surname of the first author, (author(s) complete name(s) should be given) followed by the publication date in parentheses. Type references double-spaced with a hanging indent, on a separate page at the end of the manuscript. An example style for a periodical and a book reference is shown below:

> Stevens, Robert E. and David L. Loudon (1992), Marketing for Churches and Ministries. Binghamton, NY: The Haworth Press, Inc.

> Stevens, Robert E., C. William McConkey, and David L. Loudon (1990), "A Comparison of Physicians' and Attorneys' Attitudes Toward Advertising," Journal of Professional Services Marketing, 5(2), 115-125.

Reference citations in the paper should be by the author's last name and date of publication, enclosed in parentheses, without punctuation, e.g., (Stevens and Loudon 1992). For multiple authorship of more than four authors, use the first author's name et al. If two or more works by the same author have the same publication date, they should be identified by letters after the date. The letter should also appear in the citation within the paper. EXHIBITS: All tables, charts, illustrations, etc. should be labeled "exhibits." Each exhibit must be prepared on a separate sheet of paper and must be "camera-ready." That is, they must be cleanly typed or artistically prepared so that they can be used either exactly as they are or else used after a photographic reduction in size. Always use black ink and professional drawing instruments. On the back of these items write your article title and the journal title lightly in pencil, so they do not get misplaced. In text, skip extra lines and indicate where these figures and tables are to be placed.

5. Manuscript Review Process. The journal will employ a rigorous evaluation process involving blind review by members of the editorial board. This system will protect authors and reviewers from bias and will meet desirable academic criteria. At least three reviews will be obtained for each paper. Final decisions on publication of manuscripts will be made by the Co-Editors. The review process for manuscripts should take 6-8 weeks. The editors will send an "acknowledgment of receipt" to the author listed first on the manuscript.

6. Spelling, Grammar, And Punctuation. You are responsible for preparing manuscript copy which is clearly written in acceptable scholarly English, and which contains no errors of spelling, grammar, or punctuation. Neither the Editor nor the Publisher is responsible for correcting errors of spelling and grammar: the manuscript, after acceptance by the Editor, must be immediately ready for typesetting as it is finally submitted by the author(s). Check your paper for the following common errors:
- dangling modifiers
- misplaced modifiers
- unclear antecedents
- incorrect or inconsistent abbreviations

Also, check the accuracy of all arithmetic calculations, statistics, numerical data, text citations, and references.

7. Inconsistencies Must Be Avoided. Be sure you are consistent in your use of abbreviations, terminology, and in citing references, from one part of your paper to another.

8. Preparation Of Tables, Figures, And Illustrations. All tables, figures, illustrations, etc. must be "camera-ready." That is, they must be cleanly typed or artistically prepared so that they can be used either exactly as they are or else used after a photographic reduction in size. Figures, tables, and illustrations must be prepared on separate sheets of paper. Always use black ink and professional drawing instruments. On the back of these items, write your article title and the journal title lightly in pencil, so they do not get misplaced. In text, skip extra lines and indicate where these figures and tables are to be placed (please **do not write** on face of art). Photographs are considered part of the acceptable manuscript and remain with Publisher for use in additional printings. If submitted art cannot be used, the Publisher reserves the right to redo the art and to charge the author a fee of $35.00 per hour for this service.

9. Alterations Required By Referees and Reviewers. Many times a paper is accepted by the Editor contingent upon changes that are mandated by anonymous specialist referees and members of the Editorial Board. If the Editor returns your manuscript for revisions, you are responsible for retyping any sections of the paper to incorporate these revisions (if applicable, revisions should also be put on disk).

10. Typesetting. You will not be receiving any galley proofs of your article. Editorial revisions, if any, must therefore be made while your article is still in manuscript. The final version of the manuscript will be the version you see published. Typesetter's errors will be corrected by the production staff of The Haworth Press. Authors are expected to submit manuscripts that are free from error.

11. **Electronic Media.** Haworth's in-house typesetting unit will be able to utilize your final manuscript material as prepared on most personal computers and word processors. This will minimize typographical errors and decrease overall production time lag. Please send your first draft and final draft copies of your manuscript to the journal Editor in print format for his/her final review and approval. After approval of your final manuscript, please submit the final approved version both on printed format ("hard copy") and floppy diskette.
On the outside of the diskette package write:
   A. the brand name of your computer or word processor
   B. the word-processing program that you used
   C. the title of your article, and
   D. file name

Note: Disk and hard copy must agree. In case of discrepancies, it is The Haworth Press's policy to follow hard copy. Authors are advised that no revisions of the manuscript can be made after acceptance by the Editor for publication. The benefits of this procedure are many with speed and accuracy being the most obvious. We look forward to working with you on this, knowing we will be able to serve you more efficiently in the future.

12. **Reprints.** The senior author will receive two copies of the journal issue and 25 complimentary reprints of his or her article. The junior author will receive two copies of the journal issue. These are sent several weeks after the journal issue is published and in circulation. An order form for the purchase of additional reprints will also be sent to all authors at this time. (Approximately 4-6 weeks is necessary for the preparation of reprints.) Please do not query the Journal's Editor about reprints. All such questions should be sent directly to The Haworth Press, Inc., Production Department, 21 East Broad Street, West Hazleton, PA 18201.

To order additional reprints (minimum: 50 copies), please contact the Haworth Document Delivery Center, 10 Alice Street, Binghamton, NY 13904-1580. 1-800-342-9678 or Fax (607) 722-6362.

13. **Copyright.** If your manuscript is accepted for publication, copyright ownership must be transferred officially to The Haworth Press, Inc. The Editor's acceptance letter will include a form fully explaining this. The form must be signed by all authors and returned to the Editor at that time. Failure to return the copyright form in a timely fashion will result in delay in review and subsequent publication.

Journal of Nonprofit & Public Sector Marketing

ADDRESS FOR SUBMISSION:

Donald R. Self, Editor
Journal of Nonprofit & Public Sector
  Marketing
Auburn University at Montgomery
Department of Marketing
Montgomery, AL 36117-3596
USA
Phone: 334-244-3505
Fax: 334-244-3792
E-Mail: dself@monk.aum.edu
Web: www.haworthpress.com
Address May Change:

PUBLICATION GUIDELINES:

Manuscript Length: 10-30
Copies Required: Three
Computer Submission: No
Format: N/A
Fees to Review: 0.00 US$

Manuscript Style:
  American Psychological Association

CIRCULATION DATA:

Reader: Academics
Frequency of Issue: Quarterly
Copies per Issue: Less than 1,000
Sponsor/Publisher: Haworth Press, Inc.
Subscribe Price: 60.00 US$ Individual
  120.00 US$ Institutional
  225.00 US$ Library

REVIEW INFORMATION:

Type of Review: Blind Review
No. of External Reviewers: 2
No. of In House Reviewers: 1
Acceptance Rate: 21-30%
Time to Review: 2 - 3 Months
Reviewers Comments: Yes
Invited Articles: 21-30%
Fees to Publish: 0.00 US$

MANUSCRIPT TOPICS:

Advertising & Promotion Management; Communication; Direct Marketing; Health Care Administration; Marketing Research; Marketing Theory & Applications; Non Profit Organizations; Public Administration; Purchasing/Materials Management; Sales/Selling

MANUSCRIPT GUIDELINES/COMMENTS:

About The Journal

The purpose of the *Journal of Nonprofit & Public Sector Marketing* is to provide a vehicle for the development of marketing thought and for dissemination of marketing thought and for dissemination of marketing knowledge in the nonprofit and public sectors of the economy. These sectors have recently been estimated at 25% of the wages in the U.S. economy, yet only a very small amount of the marketing literature is devoted to them.

The nonprofit and public sectors share many common denominators which separate them from the for-profit sector, including budgeting considerations, the measurement of disparate goals among various publics, and a general lack of knowledge of marketing concepts. Traditional marketers often miss these important nuances in attempting to adapt marketing strategies and concepts to these new domains. An outstanding review board has been assembled which consists of many of the scholars who have been leaders in the initial development of marketing thought in the nonprofit and public sector. Special issues are being developed in the areas of marketing for governmental services, causes and movements, leisure services, and mental health.

Instructions For Authors

1. **Original articles only.** Submission of a manuscript to this Journal represents a certification on the part of the author(s) that it is an original work, and that neither this manuscript nor a version of it has been published elsewhere nor is being considered for publication elsewhere.

2. **Manuscript length.** Your manuscript may be approximately 10-30 typed pages double-spaced (including references and abstract). Lengthier manuscripts may be considered, but only at the discretion of the Editor. Sometimes lengthier manuscripts may be considered if they can be divided up into sections for publication in successive Journal issues.

3. **Manuscript style.** References, citations and general style of manuscripts for this Journal should follow the APA style (as outlined in the latest edition of the *Publication of the American Psychological Association*). References should be double-spaced and placed in alphabetical order.

If an author wishes to submit a paper that has been already prepared in another style, he or she may do so. However, if the paper is accepted (with or without reviewer's alterations), the author is fully responsible for retyping the manuscript in the correct style as indicated above. Neither the Editor nor the Publisher is responsible for re-preparing manuscript copy to adhere to the Journal's style.

4. **Manuscript preparation.**
Margins: leave at least a one-inch margin on all four sides.
Paper: use clean white, 8-1/2" x 11" bond paper.
Number of copies: 3 (the original plus two photocopies).
Cover page: Important - staple a cover page to the manuscript, indicating only the article title (this is used for anonymous refereeing).
Second "title page": enclose a regular title page but do not staple it to the manuscript. Include the title again, plus:
- full authorship.
- an **abstract** of about 100 words.
- an introductory footnote with authors' academic degrees professional titles, affiliations, mailing addresses and any desired acknowledgement of research support or other credit.

5. **Return envelopes.** When you submit your three manuscript copies, also include:
- a 9" x 12" envelope, self-addressed and stamped (with sufficient postage to ensure return of your manuscript);
- regular envelope, stamped and self-addressed. This is for the Editor to send you an "acknowledgement of receipts" letter.

6. **Spelling, Grammar, and Punctuation**. You are responsible for preparing manuscript copy which is clearly written in acceptable scholarly English, and which contains no errors of spelling, grammar, or punctuation. Neither the Editor nor the Publisher is responsible for correcting errors of spelling and grammar: the manuscript, after acceptance by the Editor, must be immediately ready for typesetting as it is finally submitted by the author(s). Check your paper for the following common errors:

- dangling modifiers
- misplaced modifiers
- unclear antecedents
- incorrect or inconsistent abbreviations

Also, check the accuracy of all arithmetic calculations, statistics, numerical data, text citations, and references.

7. **Inconsistencies must be avoided**. Be sure you are consistent in your use of abbreviations, terminology, and in citing references, from one part of your paper to another.

8. **Preparation of tables, figures, and illustrations**. All tables, figures, illustrations, etc. must be "camera-ready." That is, they must be cleanly typed or artistically prepared so that they can be used either exactly as they are or else used after a photographic reduction in size. Figures, tables, and illustrations must be prepared on separate sheets of paper. Always use black ink and professional drawing instruments. On the back of these items, write your article title and the journal title lightly in pencil, so they do not get misplaced. In text, skip extra lines and indicate where these figures and tables are to be placed (please do not write on face of art).

9. **Alterations required by referees and reviewers**. Many times a paper is accepted by the Editor contingent upon changes that are mandated by anonymous specialist referees and members of the Editorial Board. If the Editor returns your manuscript for revisions, you are responsible for retyping any sections of the paper to incorporate these revisions (if applicable, revisions should also be put on disk).

10. **Typesetting**. You will not be receiving galley proofs of your article. Editorial revisions, if any, must therefore be made while your article is still in manuscript. The final version of the manuscript will be the version you see published. Printer's errors will be corrected by the production staff of The Haworth Press. Authors are expected to submit manuscripts, disks, and art that are free from error.

11. **Electronic media**. Haworth's in-house type-setting unit will now be able to utilize your final manuscript material as prepared on most personal computers and word processors. This will minimize typographical errors and decrease overall production time lag.

A. Please continue to send your first draft and final draft copies of your manuscript to the journal Editor in print format for his/her final review and approval;

B. Only after the journal editor has approved your final manuscript you may submit the final approved version both on:
- printed format ("hard copy")
- floppy diskette

C. Wrap your floppy diskettes in a strong diskette wrapper or holder, and write on the outside of the package:
- the brand name of your computer or word processor
- the word-processing program that you used to create your article, book chapter, or book.
- file name

The benefits of this procedure are many with speed and accuracy being the most obvious. We look forward to working with you on this, knowing we will be able to serve you more efficiently in the future.

12. **Reprints**. The senior author will receive one copy of the journal issue and 10 complimentary reprints of his or her article The junior author will receive one copy of the issue. These are sent several weeks after the journal issue is published and in circulation. An order form for the purchase of additional reprints will also be sent to all authors at this time. (Approximately 4-6 weeks is necessary for the preparation of reprints.) Please do not query the Journal's Editor about reprints. All such questions should be sent directly to The Haworth Press, Inc., Production Department, 10 Alice Street Binghamton, NY 13904-1580.

13. **Copyright**. If your manuscript is accepted for publication, copyright ownership must be transferred officially to The Haworth Press, Inc. The Editor's acceptance letter will include a form fully explaining this. The form must be signed by all authors and returned to the Editor at that time.

Journal of Nonprofit and Voluntary Sector Marketing

ADDRESS FOR SUBMISSION:

Brenda Rouse, Editor
Journal of Nonprofit and Voluntary Sector Marketing
Henry Stewart Publications
Museum House
25 Museum Street
London, WC1A 1JT
UK
Phone: 44 0171-323-2916
Fax: 44 0171-323-2918
E-Mail: brenda@hspublications.com
Web: www.henrystewart.co.uk
Address May Change:

PUBLICATION GUIDELINES:

Manuscript Length: 2,500-5,000 words
Copies Required: Three
Computer Submission: No Reply
Format: WordPerfect/MS Word
Fees to Review: 0.00 US$

Manuscript Style:
American Psychological Association

CIRCULATION DATA:

Reader: , 65% Busiess, 35% Academics
Frequency of Issue: Quarterly
Copies per Issue: 1,001 - 2,000
Sponsor/Publisher: Henry Stewart Publications
Subscribe Price: 275.00 US$ Full Rate
100.00 US$ Individual

REVIEW INFORMATION:

Type of Review: Blind Review
No. of External Reviewers: 3
No. of In House Reviewers: 2
Acceptance Rate: 50%
Time to Review: 1 - 2 Months
Reviewers Comments: Yes
Invited Articles: 31-50%
Fees to Publish: 0.00 US$

MANUSCRIPT TOPICS:
Advertising & Promotion Management; Business Education; Communication; Direct Marketing; Global Business; Marketing Research; Marketing Theory & Applications; Non Profit Organizations; Sales/Selling; Strategic Management Policy

MANUSCRIPT GUIDELINES/COMMENTS:

1. Papers should be between 2,000 and 5,000 words in length. They should be typewritten, double-spaced, on A4 paper.

2. All papers should be accompanied by a short abstract outlining the paper's aims and subject matter.

3. All papers should be accompanied by up to six keywords.

4. Papers should be accompanied by a short (about 80 words) description of the author(s) and, if appropriate, the organisation of which he or she is a member. A good quality photograph of the author(s) should also be provided.

5. Papers should be supported by actual or hypothetical examples, wherever possible and appropriate. Authors should not seek to use the Journal as a vehicle for marketing any specific product or service.

6. Authors should avoid the use of language or slang which is not in keeping with the academic and professional style of the Journal.

7. Titles of organisations etc should be written out first in full and thereafter in initials.

8. Papers should be supported by references. These should be set out in accordance with the Vancouver style--that is, they should be referred to by number in the text and set out in full at the end of the text.

9. Photographs and illustrations supporting papers should be submitted where appropriate. Photographs should be good quality positives, printed from the original negatives and in black and white only. Figures and other line illustrations should be submitted in good quality originals and a copy of the data should also be included.

10. Authors are asked to ensure that references to named people and/or organisations are accurate and without libellous implications.

11. All contributions sent to the Publisher, whether invited or not, will be submitted to the Editorial Board. Any such contribution must bear the author's full name and address, even if this is not for publication. Contributions, whether published pseudonymously or not, are accepted on the strict understanding that the author is responsible for the accuracy of all opinion, technical comment, factual report, data, figures, illustrations and photographs. Publication does not necessarily imply that these are the opinions of the Editorial Board or the Publisher, nor does the Board accept any liability for the accuracy of such comment, report and other technical and factual information. The Publisher will, however, strive to ensure that all opinion, comments, reports, data, figures, illustrations and photographs are accurate, insofar as it is within its abilities to do so. The Publisher reserves the right to edit, abridge or omit material submitted for publication.

12. All papers submitted for publication will be subject to a double-blind refereeing procedure and will be reviewed by at least two referees.

13. Papers will be published in one of two sections, Academic Papers and Practice Papers. Authors must specify for which section they are submitting their paper.

14. The author bears the responsibility for checking whether material submitted is subject to copyright or ownership rights, eg photographs, illustrations, trade literature and data. Where use is so restricted, the Publisher must be informed with the submission of the material.

15. No contribution will be accepted which has been published elsewhere, unless it is expressly invited or agreed by the Publisher. Papers and contributions published become the copyright of the Publisher, unless otherwise stated.

16. All reasonable efforts are made to ensure accurate reproduction of text, photographs and illustrations. The Publisher does not accept responsibility for mistakes, be they editorial or typographical, nor for consequences resulting from them.

Henry Stewart Publications	Henry Stewart Publications
Museum House	North American Business Office
25 Museum Street	PO Box 10812
London WC1A 1JT, UK	Birmingham, AL 35202-0812, USA
Telephone +44 (0) 171 323 2916	Telephone (800) 633-4913
Facsimile +44 (0) 171 323 2918	Facsimile (205) 995-1588

Journal of Personal Selling & Sales Management

ADDRESS FOR SUBMISSION:

Jeffrey K. Sager, Editor
Journal of Personal Selling & Sales Management
University of North Texas
Marketing Department
PO Box 311396
Denton, TX 76203-1396
USA
Phone: 940-565-3125
Fax: 940-565-3837
E-Mail: sager@cobaf.unt.edu
Web: http://mkt.cba.cmich.edu/jpssm/
Address May Change:

PUBLICATION GUIDELINES:

Manuscript Length: 21-25
Copies Required: Four
Computer Submission: No
Format: N/A
Fees to Review: 0.00 US$

Manuscript Style:
 See Manuscript Guidelines

CIRCULATION DATA:

Reader: Academics
Frequency of Issue: Quarterly
Copies per Issue: Less than 1,000
Sponsor/Publisher: Pi Sigma Epsilon/ CTC Press
Subscribe Price: 60.00 US$ Individual
 80.00 US$ Library
 80.00 US$ Company

REVIEW INFORMATION:

Type of Review: Blind Review
No. of External Reviewers: 3
No. of In House Reviewers: 0
Acceptance Rate: 21-30%
Time to Review: 2 - 3 Months
Reviewers Comments: Yes
Invited Articles: 0-5%
Fees to Publish: 0.00 US$

MANUSCRIPT TOPICS:

Business Education; Direct Marketing; Global Business; Marketing Theory & Applications; Organizational Behavior & Theory; Sales/Selling

MANUSCRIPT GUIDELINES/COMMENTS:

Description

The Journal of Personal Selling & Sales Management (JPSSM), a quarterly publication, seeks to advance the theory and practice of personal selling and sales management and thereby simultaneously bridge the gap between the academic and business communities. In essence, *JPSSM* is a forum for "cross-talk" among sales educators, researchers, and practitioners. First published in 1980, *JPSSM* offers readers high-quality research and conceptual work that spans an extensive array of topics (e.g., motivation, performance, evaluation, team selling, national account management). The associate editors and review board consist of highly regarded individuals having in-depth expertise and knowledge in personal selling and sales management.

As the only academic research-based journal in the fields of personal selling and sales management, *JPSSM* serves a diverse readership. Sales executives, professors, researchers, trainers, and students read *JPSSM* to (1) gain a broader perspective of selling and sales management beyond the boundaries of personal experience; (2) stay abreast of the knowledge explosion in selling and sales management, including the latest research findings and evolving concepts; and (3) obtain a better understanding of the thought processes and activities in which sales leaders and scholars agree.

JPSSM, in addition to publishing feature articles, has six "special sections," two of which provide a "specialized service" to readers. The Abstracts Section (published biannually) contains summaries of contemporary sales-related articles found in over sixty academic and trade publications. Abstracts are classified according to subject area. The Book Reviews Section (published each issue) offers readers synopses of recently published academic and trade texts pertaining to selling and sales management. The four other special sections are Selling and Sales Management in Action, Methods in Sales Research, Sales Technology Applications, and Sales Training and Education. These sections are designed for articles whose tone and focus are distinctly different from feature articles (see the Special Section Guidelines on this web site for information about "special section" manuscripts).

MANUSCRIPT SUBMISSION GUIDELINES
Please submit four (4) nonreturnable copies of manuscripts for publication consideration to the Editor.

Special Sections Submissions
If you have positioned your manuscript for one of the *Journal's* special sections (i.e., Selling and Sales Management in Action, Sales Technology Applications, Methods in Sales Research, or Sales Training and Education), please submit four (4) copies to the editor at the above address. Your manuscript will be forwarded to the appropriate associate editor for review. In your submission cover letter, advise the editor of your desire to have the manuscript evaluated for a special section. All manuscripts (regular article submissions and special section submissions) must conform to *JPSSM* style: word-processed, 12-point font, double-spaced (including references) on 8 1/2 by 11 inch white paper with margins of one inch on all four sides.

Letters to the Editor
Readers may send comments about previously published *JPSSM* articles, general issues concerning selling and sales management, or topics of interest to sales educators. Remarks should be double-spaced and not exceed three pages in length. The salutation should read "Dear Editor."

Order of Inclusion

A. Front Matter
First Page: Title of paper, name and position of author(s), author(s)' complete address(es), means of contact (telephone number, fax number, e-mail address), and any acknowledgment of assistance.

Second Page: A brief biographical sketch of each author, including name, degree(s) held, title or position, organization or institution, previous publications, and areas of research interest.

Third Page: Title of paper without author(s)' name(s) and a brief abstract of no more than 100 words summarizing the article. The abstract is used on the contents page and serves to generate reader interest in the article.

B. Body of Text
Text begins on the fourth page, with major headings centered and subheadings positioned flush with the left margin. All headings are in upper and lower case.
Footnotes are not to be used for reference purposes. In an extraordinary case in which a footnote is needed, it should be approved by the editor.

C. Technical Appendices
Technical appendices may be used to include mathematical or highly technical material which supports the main text but is not critical to the reader's interpretation of the text.

D. Tables and Figures
Each table or figure should be placed on a separate page and numbered consecutively beginning with Table 1 and Figure 1. A table or figure should not be included unless it is referred to in the text of the article. Placement in the text should be indicated as follows:

Place Table 2 About Here

Footnotes in tables or figures should be designated by lower case letters. Table or figure number and title should be typed on two separate lines, using upper and lower case, as follows:

Table 1
Categories of Sexual Harassment

E. References
References within the text should include the author's last name and year of publication enclosed in parentheses, e.g., (Peterson 1994). If practical, place the citation just before a punctuation mark. If the author's name is used within the text sentence, place the year of publication in parentheses, e.g., "Conclusions reached by Peterson (1994) ..." If a particular page or section is cited, it should be placed within the parentheses, e.g., (Peterson 1994, p. 68). For multiple authorship articles, use up to three names in the citation. With four or more authors, use the first author's name and et al., e.g., (Jolson et al. 1993).

A listing of references in alphabetical order should appear at the end of the manuscript (starting on a separate page), with the first author's surname first and year of publication following all authors' names. Complete names of each author are to be cited, i.e., last name, first name, middle initial. Work by the same author with the same publication year should be distinguished by lower case letters after the date (e.g., 1992a). For authors cited more than once, substitute a one-inch line for each repeated name. Examples are as follows:

Ingram, Thomas N. and Raymond W. LaForge (1992), Sales Management: Analysis and Decision Making, 2nd ed., Fort Worth: The Dryden Press.

Kotabe, Masaaki, Janet Y. Murray and Rajshekhar G. Javalgi (1995), "Global Sourcing of Services and Market Performance: Conceptual Framework and Research Propositions," in Enhancing Knowledge Development in Marketing, Barbara B. Stern and George M. Zinkhan, eds., Chicago: American Marketing Association, 277-278.

Sharma, Arun and Dan Sarel (1995), "The Impact of Customer Satisfaction Based Incentive Systems on Salespeople's Customer Service Response: An Empirical Study," Journal of Personal Selling & Sales Management, 15 (Summer), 17-29.

Special Requirements: Methods
For empirical articles there are expectations with respect to systematically documenting information about the sample(s) utilized, as well as variable relationships. With regards to the sample(s) utilized, complete information should be provided (concisely, in the text or a table) about the sampling procedure (type, selection method), method of contact (sponsorship), number in the sample frame, response rate, industries from which the sample was drawn, company characteristics, geographic scope of sampling frame, major activities/selling responsibilities represented, as well as respondent characteristics, including age, gender, tenure, experience level, and performance level. Manuscripts based on research using student samples generally will not be accepted for publication (except those directed at the Sales Training and Education section). It is expected that means, standard deviations, intercorrelations and reliability/validity indices will be provided for measures in the study.

Journal of Pharmaceutical Marketing and Management

ADDRESS FOR SUBMISSION:

Mickey C. Smith, Editor
Journal of Pharmaceutical Marketing and
    Management
University of Mississippi
Research Institute of the Pharmaceutical
    Sciences, Health Services Research
    Division, School of Pharmacy
University, MS 38677
USA
Phone: 662-915-7262
Fax: 662-915-5102
E-Mail: mcs1@olemiss.edu
Web: www.haworthpressinc.com
Address May Change:

PUBLICATION GUIDELINES:

Manuscript Length: 26-30
Copies Required: Three
Computer Submission: Yes
Format: WordPerfect
Fees to Review: 0.00 US$

Manuscript Style:
    , ASHP Guidelines in AM J. Hosp.
    Pharm.

CIRCULATION DATA:

Reader: , 50% Business, 50% Academic
Frequency of Issue: Quarterly
Copies per Issue: Less than 1,000
Sponsor/Publisher: Haworth Press, Inc.
Subscribe Price: 60.00 US$ Individual
    90.00 US$ Institution
    275.00 US$ Library

REVIEW INFORMATION:

Type of Review: Blind Review
No. of External Reviewers: 2
No. of In House Reviewers: 1
Acceptance Rate: 65%
Time to Review: 1 - 2 Months
Reviewers Comments: Yes
Invited Articles: 0-5%
Fees to Publish: 0.00 US$

MANUSCRIPT TOPICS:
Advertising & Promotion Management; Marketing Research; Marketing Theory &
Applications; Production/Operations

MANUSCRIPT GUIDELINES/COMMENTS:

About The Journal

The *Journal of Pharmaceutical Marketing & Management* is a quarterly journal devoted to solving the problems inherent in the management and marketing of pharmaceutical products and services. The journal is multidisciplinary and represents the interests of all segments of the multibillion dollar pharmaceutical industry.

The journal maintains a vigorous policy of publishing quality research reports of interest to individuals involved in the manufacturing, wholesale, institutional, retail, regulatory, organizational, and academic components of the pharmaceutical industry.

In addition to valuable research and informative book reviews, issues of the *Journal of Pharmaceutical Marketing & Management* present the "Post Papers" section, providing succinct reports of pilot studies, early results, and provocative findings from investigations and similar applications. These brief reports provide early dissemination of new and valuable professional data, informing the reader of potentially important developments.

Instructions For Authors

1. **Original articles only**. Submission of a manuscript to this Journal represents certification that none of the material in the manuscript has been previously published and that none of the material is under consideration or has been accepted for publication elsewhere.

2. **Manuscript length**. Your manuscript may be approximately 20 typed double-spaced pages (including references). Longer manuscripts may be considered at the discretion of the editor.

3. **Manuscript style**. References, citations, and general style of manuscripts for this Journal should follow ASHP guidelines (as stated in the Am J Hosp Pharm 1982; 39:1538-43 and Am J Hosp Pharm 1988; 45:177-8). References should appear at the end of the manuscript, numbered in order of appearance in the paper. Reference numbers in the text should appear in parentheses at the end of sentences.

If an author wishes to submit a paper that has been prepared in another style, he may do so. If the paper is accepted, however, the author is fully responsible for retyping the manuscript in the correct style as indicated above. Neither the Editor nor the Publisher is responsible for preparing the manuscript copy to adhere to the Journal's style.

4. **Manuscript preparation**. Submit the original manuscript and two copies. The original should include a complete title page consisting of: the author's name; the author's academic degrees, professional titles, affiliations, and mailing address; and an abstract of 100 words. The two copies should have short title pages, listing only the title of the paper.

5. **Return envelopes**. With the manuscript, submit a self-addressed and stamped envelope large enough to accommodate the manuscript if return is necessary. Also include a stamped, self-addressed business envelope for notification of receipt of the paper.

6. **Preparation of Tables, Figures, and Illustrations**. All tables, figures, and illustrations must be camera-ready. That is, they must be cleanly and artistically prepared so that they can be used either exactly as they are or in a reduced size. Figures, tables, and illustrations must be prepared on separate sheets of paper. Always use black ink and professional drawing instruments. On the back of these items, write your article title and the journal title in pencil. Indicate in the text the locations of these figures and tables.

7. **Alterations Required By Referees and Reviewers**. Many times a paper is accepted by the Editor contingent upon changes mandated by anonymous specialist referees and members of the editorial board. If the Editor returns a manuscript for revision, the author is responsible for retyping any sections of the paper to incorporate these revisions.

8. **Typesetting**. You will not receive galley proofs of their articles. Editorial revisions, if any, must be made while an article is still in manuscript. Printer's errors will be corrected by the publisher's production staff or by the editor. Authors are expected to submit manuscripts that are free from error.

9. **Reprints**. The senior author will receive one copy of the journal issue and ten complimentary reprints of the article. The junior author(s) will receive one copy of the issue. These are sent several weeks after the journal issue is published and in circulation. An order form for the purchase of additional reprints will be sent with the complimentary copies. Preparation of these reprints takes approximately ten weeks. Please do not query the Journal's editor about reprints. All such questions should be sent directly to The Haworth Press, Inc., Production Department, 10 Alice Street, Binghamton, NY 13904-1580.

10. **Copyright**. When a manuscript is accepted for publication, copyright ownership must be transferred to The Haworth Press, Inc. The editor's acceptance letter will include a form that fully explains this transferal. The form must be signed by all authors and returned to the editor before publication of the manuscript.

Journal of Problems of Theory and Practice in Reforms of Regional Economies

ADDRESS FOR SUBMISSION:

Tatiana Belkina, Editor
Journal of Problems of Theory and Practice
  in Reforms of Regional Economies
Nakhiriovskii Prospect ,47
11748 , Moscow,
Russia
Phone: 709-5422-7134
Fax:
E-Mail: belk@mail.ecfor.rsst.ru
Web:
Address May Change:

PUBLICATION GUIDELINES:

Manuscript Length: 16-20
Copies Required: Three
Computer Submission: No
Format: N/A
Fees to Review: 0.00 US$

Manuscript Style:
            American Psychological Association

CIRCULATION DATA:

Reader: Academics
Frequency of Issue: Quarterly
Copies per Issue: 1,001 - 2,000
Sponsor/Publisher: Institute of Real Estate
  Research /Russian Academy of Sciences
Subscribe Price: 10.00 US$

REVIEW INFORMATION:

Type of Review: Blind Review
No. of External Reviewers: 2
No. of In House Reviewers: 1
Acceptance Rate: 21-30%
Time to Review: 1 - 2 Months
Reviewers Comments: No
Invited Articles: 11-20%
Fees to Publish: 0.00 US$

MANUSCRIPT TOPICS:
Marketing Research; Marketing Theory & Applications; Real Estate; Small Business Entrepreneurship

MANUSCRIPT GUIDELINES/COMMENTS:

The journal is in the Russian language. All manuscripts submitted must be in Russian.

Journal of Product & Brand Management

ADDRESS FOR SUBMISSION:

Michelle Morganosky, Editor
Journal of Product & Brand Management
University of Illinois
305 Mumford Hall, MC-710
Dept. of Agricultural and Consumer Econ.
1301 West Gregory Drive
Urbana, IL 61801-3681
USA
Phone: 1 217-333-0737
Fax: 1 217-333-5538
E-Mail: morganos@uiuc.edu
Web: www.mcb.co.uk
Address May Change:

PUBLICATION GUIDELINES:

Manuscript Length: 16-20
Copies Required: Three
Computer Submission: No
Format: N/A
Fees to Review: 0.00 US$

Manuscript Style:
    See Manuscript Guidelines

CIRCULATION DATA:

Reader: Academics, Business Persons
Frequency of Issue: 6 Times/Year
Copies per Issue: No Reply
Sponsor/Publisher: MCB University Press
Subscribe Price: 799.00 US$
    2899.00 AUS$

REVIEW INFORMATION:

Type of Review: Blind Review
No. of External Reviewers: 2
No. of In House Reviewers: 1
Acceptance Rate: 40-50%
Time to Review: 1 - 2 Months
Reviewers Comments: Yes
Invited Articles: 0-5%
Fees to Publish: 0.00 US$

MANUSCRIPT TOPICS:
Advertising & Promotion Management; Brand Equity; Brand Management; Direct Marketing; Global Business; Marketing Research; Marketing Theory & Applications; Product Development; Production/Operations; Sales/Selling; Strategic Management Policy

MANUSCRIPT GUIDELINES/COMMENTS:

About the journal

The *Journal of Product & Brand Management* featuring *Pricing Strategy & Practice* offers you a direct route to worldwide research at the cutting edge of product and brand management and pricing. This internationally respected journal examines critical issues, which need to be taken into consideration when determining brand and pricing strategies and policies. Offering expert analysis and practical recommendations to aid decision making and stimulate further research activity, it provides an invaluable source of knowledge for academics and corporate practitioners. Every article published in the *Journal of Product & Brand Management* has been subject to a double blind review process to ensure its relevance and quality.

Coverage
- Brand management
- Consumer behaviour
- Pricing strategy
- Marketing research
- New product development
- International pricing
- Brand equity

Copyright
Articles submitted to the journal should be original contributions and should not be under consideration for any other publication at the same time. Authors submitting articles for publication warrant that the work is not an infringement of any existing copyright and will indemnify the publisher against any breach of such warranty. For ease of dissemination and to ensure proper policing of use, papers and contributions become the legal copyright of the publisher unless otherwise agreed. Submissions should be sent to the Editor.

Editorial objectives
The *Journal of Product & Brand Management* is an academic journal written for both practitioners and scholars. The objective of the journal is to publish articles that enrich the practice of product and brand management while simultaneously making significant contributions to knowledge of product and brand issues. Manuscripts must offer meaningful implications and recommendations for practitioners, but also must be conceptually or theoretically sound and offer significant research findings or insights.

Further, if the manuscript reports the findings of original research, the methodology and findings not only should be scientifically defensible, but also should be presented clearly and to the extent possible in a nontechnical manner such that readers with limited backgrounds in research methods and statistical analyses are not discouraged from reading the article.

However it should be noted that research is not the only basis for an acceptable article. Case analyses, book reviews, and other thought-provoking manuscripts are encouraged. Article cases of an international nature are especially welcome. The editorial goal is to create a journal of relevance to an international audience. To do this we seek articles from all parts of the world. Particularly welcome are manuscripts which address product and brand issues from the perspective of comparative international markets.

Pricing Strategy & Practice Special Section
The Editor Kent Monroe, Department of Business Administration, University of Illinois, 350 Commerce West, 1206 South Sixth Street, Champaign, IL 61820, USA.

Editorial policy
Pri*cing Strategy & Practice* provides a forum for the discussion of the real implications of pricing decisions, and will cover such issues as:
- developing and maintaining price differentials;
- discounting and other price reduction strategies;

- price and product positioning;
- price bundling;
- price comparison and advertising;
- international pricing;
- value-oriented pricing;
- organizing for price management;
- pricing for product launches;
- legal implications of pricing.

Editorial scope,
a. A brief description of the problems or issues the article will address, the basic premise of the paper, and/or the article's objective(s). This paragraph should be positioned near the front of the article.
b. Background and reference to existing, applicable literature. Articles should convince readers that authors have done their homework in reviewing and crediting relevant literature, and pointing interested readers to additional sources of information. Ordinarily, however, literature reviews need not be exhaustive. Where applicable, the background section should include an overview of the theory(ies) within which the article is couched.
c. Interesting examples that illuminate and reinforce the thrust of the article.
d. Clear presentation and discussion of the study's findings, if applicable.
e. A summary to wrap-up key ideas.

The reviewing process
Each paper is reviewed by the editor and, if it is judged suitable for this publication, it is then sent to two referees for double blind peer review. Based on their recommendations, the editor then decides whether the paper should be accepted as is, revised or rejected.

Manuscript requirements
Three copies of the manuscript should be submitted in double line spacing with wide margins. All authors should be shown and author's details must be printed on a separate sheet and the author should not be identified anywhere else in the article.

As a guide, articles should be between 3,000 and 6,000 words in length. A title of not more than eight words should be provided. A brief **autobiographical note** should be supplied including full name, affiliation, e-mail address and full international contact details. Authors must supply an **abstract** of 100-150 words. Up to six **keywords** should be included which encapsulate the principal subjects covered by the article.

Where there is a **methodology**, it should be clearly described under a separate heading. **Headings** must be short, clearly defined and not numbered. **Notes** or **Endnotes** should be used only if absolutely necessary and must be identified in the text by consecutive numbers, enclosed in square brackets and listed at the end of the article.

Figures, charts and **diagrams** should be kept to a minimum. They must be black and white with minimum shading and numbered consecutively using Arabic numerals with a brief title and labelled axes. In the text, the position of the figure should be shown by typing on a separate line the words "take in Figure 2". Good quality originals must be provided.

Tables should be kept to a minimum. They must be numbered consecutively with roman numerals and a brief title. In the text, the position of the table should be shown by typing on a separate line the words "take in Table IV".

Photos and **illustrations** must be supplied as good quality black and white original half tones with captions. Their position should be shown in the text by typing on a separate line the words "take in Plate 2".

References to other publications should be complete and in Harvard style. They should contain full bibliographical details and journal titles should not be abbreviated. For multiple citations in the same year use a, b, c immediately following the year of publication. References should be shown within the text by giving the author's last name followed by a comma and year of publication all in round brackets, e.g. (Fox, 1994). At the end of the article should be a reference list in alphabetical order as follows

(a) for books
surname, initials and year of publication, title, publisher, place of publication, e.g. Casson, M. (1979), Alternatives to the Multinational Enterprise, Macmillan, London.

(b) for chapter in edited book
surname, initials and year, "title", editor's surname, initials, title, publisher, place, pages, e.g.Bessley, M. and Wilson, P. (1984), "Public policy and small firms in Britain", in Levicki, C. (Ed.), Small Business Theory and Policy, Croom Helm, London, pp.111-26. Please note that the chapter title must be underlined.

(c) for journals
surname, initials, year "title", journal, volume, number, pages, e.g. Fox, S. (1994) "Empowerment as a catalyst for change: an example from the food industry", Supply Chain Management, Vol 2 No 3, pp. 29-33

If there is more than one author list surnames followed by initials. All authors should be shown.

Electronic sources should include the URL of the electronic site at which they may be found, as follows:

Neuman, B.C.(1995), "Security, payment, and privacy for network commerce", IEEE Journal on Selected Areas in Communications, Vol. 13 No.8, October, pp.1523-31. Available (IEEE SEPTEMBER) http://www.research.att.com/jsac/

Notes/Endnotes should be used only if absolutely necessary. They should, however, always be used for citing Web sites. They should be identified in the text by consecutive numbers enclosed in square brackets and listed at the end of the article. Please then provide full Web site addresses in the end list.

Final submission of the article

Once accepted for publication, the final version of the manuscript must be provided, accompanied by a 3.5" **disk** of the same version labelled with: disk format; author name(s); title of article; journal title; file name.

Each article must be accompanied by a completed and signed **Journal Article Record Form** available from the Editor or on http://www.literaticlub.co.uk/

The manuscript will be considered to be the definitive version of the article. The author must ensure that it is complete, grammatically correct and without spelling or typographical errors. In preparing the disk, please use one of the following formats: Word, Word Perfect, Rich text format or TeX/LaTeX. Figures which are provided electronically must be in tif, gif or pic file extensions. All figures and graphics must also be supplied as good quality originals.

Final submission requirements

Manuscripts must be clean, good quality hard copy and;
- include an abstract and keywords
- have Harvard style references
- include any figures, photos and graphics as good quality originals
- be accompanied by a labelled disk
- be accompanied by a completed Journal Article Record Form

Technical assistance is available from MCB's World Wide Web Literati Club on http://www.literaticlub.co.uk/ or contact Mike Massey at MCB, e-mail mmassey@mcb.co.uk

Journal of Promotion Management

ADDRESS FOR SUBMISSION:

Richard Alan Nelson, Editor
Journal of Promotion Management
Louisiana State University
Manship School of Mass Communication
221 Journalism Building
Baton Rouge, LA 70803-7202
USA
Phone: 225-388-6686
Fax: 225-388-2125
E-Mail: rnelson@lsu.edu
Web: www.haworthpress.com
Address May Change:

PUBLICATION GUIDELINES:

Manuscript Length: 16-20
Copies Required: Three
Computer Submission: Yes
Format: Word/WordPerfect
Fees to Review: 0.00 US$

Manuscript Style:
  American Psychological Association

CIRCULATION DATA:

Reader: Academics, Business Persons
Frequency of Issue: 2 Times/Year
Copies per Issue: Less than 1,000
Sponsor/Publisher: Haworth Press, Inc.
Subscribe Price: 40.00 US$ Individual
  65.00 US$ Institution
  95.00 US$ Library

REVIEW INFORMATION:

Type of Review: Blind Review
No. of External Reviewers: 2
No. of In House Reviewers: 1
Acceptance Rate: 21-30%
Time to Review: 1 - 2 Months
Reviewers Comments: Yes
Invited Articles: 6-10%
Fees to Publish: 0.00 US$

MANUSCRIPT TOPICS:
Advertising & Promotion Management; Direct Marketing; Global Business; Marketing Research; Marketing Theory & Applications; Non Profit Organizations; Sales/Selling; Technology/Innovation

MANUSCRIPT GUIDELINES/COMMENTS:

The *Journal of Promotion Management* focuses on applied research and planning in promotion management. It is designed for practitioners in advertising, public relations, and personal selling, as well as academicians and teachers/researchers in these areas.

This major periodical presents the latest thinking, practice, and research findings on current topics in promotion management. The broad depth of coverage provides readers with a vehicle that demonstrates theory and practice with a special emphasis on promotion management in action. JPM integrates theory and practice within its pages. Every issue attempts to demonstrate the richness of the entire area of promotion management.

The editor selects material that has direct usefulness for the advertising and promotion practitioner who needs to be up-to-date on all germane ideas, information, and trends in the field. The Journal especially emphasizes the entire scope and nature of promotional activities.

Instructions for Authors

1. Original articles only. Submission of a manuscript to this Journal represents a certification on the part of the author(s) that it is an original work, and that neither this manuscript nor a version of it has been published elsewhere nor is being considered for publication elsewhere.

2. Manuscript length. Your manuscript may be approximately 10-20 typed pages double-spaced (including references and abstract). Lengthier manuscripts may be considered, but only at the discretion of the editor. Sometimes. lengthier manuscripts may be considered if they can be divided up in to sections for publication in successive Journal issues.

3. Manuscript style. References, citations, and general style of manuscripts for this Journal should follow the APS's style (as outlined in the latest edition of the *Publication Manual of the American Psychological Association*). References should be double-spaced and placed in alphabetical order.

If an author wishes to submit a paper that has been already prepared in another style, he or she may do so. However, if the paper is accepted (with or without reviewer's alterations), the author is fully responsible for retyping the manuscript in the correct style as indicated above. Neither the Editor nor the Publisher is responsible for re-preparing manuscript copy to adhere to the Journal's style.

4. Manuscript preparation.
Margins: leave at least a one-inch margin on all four sides.
Paper: use clean white, 8 ½ " x 11" bond paper.
Number of copies: 4 (the original plus three photocopies).
Cover page: *Important* -- staple a cover page to the manuscript, indicating only the article title (this is used for anonymous refereeing).
Second "title page": enclose a regular title page but do not staple it to the manuscript. Include the title again, plus:
- full authorship
- an **abstract** of about 100 words. (Below the abstract provide 3-1 0 key words for index purposes).
- an introductory footnote with authors' academic degrees, professional titles, affiliations, mailing addresses, and any desired acknowledgment of research support or other credit.

5. Return envelopes. When you submit your four manuscript copies, also include:
- A regular envelope, stamped and self-addressed. This is for the Editor to send you an "acknowledgement of receipt" letter.
- Manuscripts will not be returned.

6. Spelling, grammar, and punctuation. You are responsible for preparing manuscript copy which is clearly written in acceptable scholarly English, and which contains no errors of

spelling, grammar, or punctuation. Neither the Editor nor the Publisher is responsible for correcting errors of spelling and grammar: the manuscript, after acceptance by the Editor, must be immediately ready for typesetting as it is finally submitted by the author(s). Check your paper for the following common errors:
- dangling modifiers
- misplaced modifiers
- unclear antecedents
- incorrect or inconsistent abbreviations

Also, check the accuracy of all arithmetic calculations, statistics, numerical data, text citations, and references.

7. Inconsistencies must be avoided. Be sure you are consistent in your use of abbreviations, terminology, and in citing references, from one part of your paper to another.

8. Preparation of tables, figures, and illustrations. All tables, figures, illustrations, etc. must be "camera-ready." That is, they must be cleanly typed or artistically prepared so that they can be used either exactly as they are or else used after a photographic reduction in size. Figures, tables, and illustrations must be prepared on separate sheets of paper. Always use black ink and professional drawing instruments. On the back of these items, write your article title and the journal title lightly in pencil, so they do not get misplaced. In text, skip extra lines and indicate where these figures and tables are to be placed (please **do not write** on face of art). Photographs are considered part of the acceptable manuscript and remain with Publisher for use in additional printings. If submitted art cannot be used, the Publisher reserves the right to redo the art and to charge the author a fee of $35.00 per hour for this service.

9. Alterations required by referees and reviewers. Many times a paper is accepted by the Editor contingent upon changes that are mandated by anonymous specialist referees and members of the Editorial Board. If the Editor returns your manuscript for revisions, you are responsible for retyping any sections of the paper to incorporate these revisions (if applicable, revisions should also be put on disk).

10. Typesetting. You will not be receiving galley proofs of your article. Editorial revisions, if any, must therefore be made while your article is still in manuscript. The final version of the manuscript will be the version you see published. Typesetter's errors will be corrected by the production staff of The Haworth Press. Authors are expected to submit manuscripts, disks, and art that are free from error.

11. Electronic media. Haworth's in-house type-setting unit is able to utilize your final manuscript material as prepared on most personal computers and word processors. This will minimize typographical errors and decrease overall production time lag. Please send the first draft and final draft copies of your manuscript to the journal Editor in print format for his/her final review and approval. **After approval of** your final manuscript, please submit the final approved version both on printed format ("hard copy") and floppy diskette. On the outside of the diskette package write:
A. the brand name of your computer or word processor
B. the word-processing program that you used

C. the title of your article, and
D. file name

Note: Disk and hard copy must agree. In case of discrepancies, it is The Haworth Press's policy to follow hard copy. Authors are advised that no revisions of the manuscript can be made after acceptance by the Editor for publication. The benefits of this procedure are many with speed and accuracy being the most obvious. We look forward to working with you on this, knowing we will be able to serve you more efficiently in the future.

12. Reprints. The senior author will receive two copies of the journal issue and 25 complimentary reprints of his or her article. The junior author will receive two copies of the journal issue. These are sent several weeks after the journal issue is published and in circulation. An order form for the purchase of additional reprints will also be sent to all authors at this time. (Approximately 4-6 weeks is necessary for the preparation of reprints.) Please do not query the Journal's Editor about reprints. All such questions should be sent directly to: The Haworth Press, Inc., Production Department, 21 East Broad Street, West Hazleton, PA 18201

To order additional reprints (minimum: 50 copies), please contact: The Haworth Document Delivery Center, 10 Alice Street, Binghamton, NY 13904-1580
1-800-342-9678 or Fax (607) 722-6362.

13. Copyright. Copyright ownership of your manuscript must be transferred officially to The Haworth Press, Inc., before we can begin the peer-review process. The Editor's letter acknowledging receipt of the manuscript will be accompanied by a form fully explaining this. All authors must sign the form and return the original to the Editor as soon as possible. Failure to return the copyright form in a timely fashion will result in delay in review and subsequent publication.

Journal of Public Policy & Marketing

ADDRESS FOR SUBMISSION:

J. Craig Andrews, Editor
Journal of Public Policy & Marketing
Marquette University
Depatment of Marketing
606 N. 13th Street
Milwaukee, WI 53233
USA
Phone: 414-288-7181
Fax: 414-288-7638
E-Mail: andrews@biz.mu.edu
Web: www.ama.org
Address May Change: 6/30/01

PUBLICATION GUIDELINES:

Manuscript Length: 26-30
Copies Required: Five
Computer Submission: No
Format: N/A
Fees to Review: 0.00 US$

Manuscript Style:
    Chicago Manual of Style

CIRCULATION DATA:

Reader: Academics, Government, Law
Frequency of Issue: 2 Times/Year
Copies per Issue: Less than 1,000
Sponsor/Publisher: American Marketing
    Association
Subscribe Price: 70.00 US$ Individual
    45.00 US$ AMA Member
    100.00 US$ Institution

REVIEW INFORMATION:

Type of Review: Blind Review
No. of External Reviewers: 3+
No. of In House Reviewers: 1
Acceptance Rate: 11-20%
Time to Review: 1 - 2 Months
Reviewers Comments: Yes
Invited Articles: 6-10%
Fees to Publish: 0.00 US$

MANUSCRIPT TOPICS:
Advertising & Promotion Management; Business Law, Public Responsibility & Ethics; Communication; Consumer Protection & Anti-trust; Global Business; Marketing Regulation; Marketing Research; Marketing Theory & Applications; Public Administration

MANUSCRIPT GUIDELINES/COMMENTS:

Mission
The *Journal of Public Policy & Marketing* (JPP&M) is the premier academic and professional journal on public policy issues and their impact on marketing. Articles feature the interpretation of the latest public policy issues and their effect on the field of marketing, as well as how marketing can be used by public policymakers.

Written for concerned marketing scholars, policymakers, government officials, legal scholars, practicing attorneys, and executives, JPP&M endeavors to comprehend the effects on marketing of public policy issues, as well as discuss marketing issues that may result in changes to public policy. Public concerns, such as ecology, health, and privacy, are also covered from the marketing perspective. JPP&M is highly respected for its topical and insightful commentary.

Primary Reader Targets
The primary audiences for JPP&M are academic scholars interested in researching the issues, public policy decision makers at all levels of government, and marketing executive faced with public policy concerns.

Relevance to Reader Group
The journal serves several different audiences: academic researchers, public policymakers, marketing managers, trade association representatives, attorneys, and consumer advocates. Therefore, every article must make a definitive contribution to at least one, and ideally several, of these audience groups. Also, because JPP&M readers differ in background and research orientation, manuscripts must be free of jargon exclusive to one discipline and discuss statistical methods and results in a nontechnical manner that can be readily understood by all readers.

Manuscript Development/Review
Articles generally are submitted to JPP&M on the basis of a refereed, double-blind review process and must be submitted in accordance with established manuscript guidelines. Criteria used by reviewers will be consistent with JPP&M's mission statement. The editor has final review and decision authority for all articles. Contributed articles from practitioners and public policymakers may be added to JPP&M at the discretion of the editor.

The Editorial Review Board represents leading scholars and thought leaders in the public policy area. Members of the Review Board are appointed by and serve at the discretion of the editor. The composition of the Review Board is consistent with and represents a balance of experience and expertise in the subjects covered.

Editorial Philosophy
JPP&M is a scholarly journal that publishes articles, thoughtful commentary, legal issues, and book reviews on marketing and public policy topics. It serves to inform readers about the influence of public policy issues on marketing practice and about the impact of marketing activity on public policy decisions. JPP&M serves as a bridge between academic researchers interested in developing new insights and practitioners concerned with solving current problems. Therefore, a JPP&M objective is to provide both scholars and practitioners with useful ideas and high-quality research.

JPP&M publishes articles that use varied research approaches. Authors are encouraged to submit empirical research papers, as well as integrative review papers, legal evaluations of case law or regulations, conceptual analyses of public policy issues, and ethical studies of social problems.

Scholarly Contribution
JPP&M's primary focus is to publish articles that contribute to knowledge by providing new perspectives, new empirical results, or new research methods. Articles accepted for publication must meet high standards for scholarship. Therefore, JPP&M publishes high-

quality empirical, conceptual, and methodological articles on marketing and public policy issues.

Varied Perspectives

JPP&M seeks manuscripts from a variety of disciplines that represent diverse perspectives. Therefore, submission of manuscripts from individuals with disparate backgrounds is encouraged. For example, prospective authors might have backgrounds in marketing, communications, economics, consumer affairs, law, public policy, sociology, psychology, anthropology, or philosophy. The journal's only requirements are that manuscripts must be well documented, well reasoned, balanced, and relevant.

Content of Published Articles

JPP&M publishes articles on (1) current public policy subjects and (2) enduring conceptual or empirical studies that have public policy implications.

First, because JPP&M publishes articles on current public policy issues, manuscripts that address topical problems are strongly encouraged. The focus of articles should be thoughtful and insightful analyses of public issues that affect the professional of marketing. Articles should be scholarly, practical, well documented, and should meet generally accepted standards for conceptual and analytical rigor appropriate for a premier professional journal. Recent issues addressed in the journal have included consumer privacy, product warnings, deregulation, the role of the FTC and the state in regulating marketing and advertising, health care, pricing, international trade, and vulnerable populations.

Second, JPP&M encourages the submission of manuscripts that advance theory development or research methods in the field. For example, manuscripts that focus on understanding consumers' processing of warning messages, developing methods for clustering products into relevant markets for antitrust analysis, or providing ethical foundations of appropriate marketing activity are suitable for publication.

Stimulating Interest in Marketing and Public Policy Research

JPP&M endeavors to inform its readers about ongoing public policy debates. Therefore, the journal encourages the submission of thoughtful statements on current controversies as a means of influencing the director of future research.

JPP&M also encourages young scholars to submit manuscripts on marketing and public policy topics. The journal will continue to play a significant role in helping emerging scholars to develop their research programs.

For manuscript guideline information, visit the JPP&M website at
http://www.ama.org/pubs/jppm/info/info3.asp
For editorial staff and publisher contact information, visit
http://www.ama.org/pubs/info/info7.asp
For subscription information on the Journal of Public Policy & Marketing, please contact: Customer Service, Subscriptions Dept., American Marketing Association, 311 South Wacker Drive, Suite 5800, Chicago, IL 60606 1-800-AMA-1150

Journal of Quality Assurance in Tourism & Hospitality

ADDRESS FOR SUBMISSION:

Sungsoo Pyo, Editor
Journal of Quality Assurance in Tourism & Hospitality
Kyonggi University
Chungjong-Ro, Seodaemoon-Ku
Department of Tourism Management
Seoul 120-702,
Korea
Phone: +82 342 703 9226
Fax: +82 342 704 1575
E-Mail: pyos@chollian.net
Web:
Address May Change:

PUBLICATION GUIDELINES:

Manuscript Length: 21-25
Copies Required: Four
Computer Submission: No
Format: N/A
Fees to Review: 0.00 US$

Manuscript Style:
American Psychological Association

CIRCULATION DATA:

Reader: Business Persons, Academic
Frequency of Issue: Quarterly
Copies per Issue: New Journal
Sponsor/Publisher: The Haworth Press, Inc
Subscribe Price: 40.00 US$ Individual
48.00 US$ Institution
75.00 US$ Library

REVIEW INFORMATION:

Type of Review: Blind Review
No. of External Reviewers: 3
No. of In House Reviewers: 0
Acceptance Rate: New J
Time to Review: 1 - 2 Months
Reviewers Comments: Yes
Invited Articles: New Journal
Fees to Publish: 0.00 US$

MANUSCRIPT TOPICS:

Business Information Systems (MIS); Communication; Direct Marketing; Labor Relations & Human Resource Mgt.; Marketing Research; Operations Research/Statistics; Organizational Behavior & Theory; Organizational Development; Production/Operations; Quality TQM; Sales/Selling; Services; Strategic Management Policy; Technology/Innovation

MANUSCRIPT GUIDELINES/COMMENTS:

Co-Editor
Eliza Ching-Yick Tse, School of Hotel Management, Faculty of Business Administratin, The Chinese University of Hong Kong, Shatin, Hong Kong. E-mail: elizatse@cuhk.edu.hk

The *Journal of Quality Assurance in Tourism & Hospitality* serves as a medium to share and disseminate information from new research findings and superior practices in tourism and find current and important information on quality planning, development, management, marketing, evaluation, and adjustments within the field. As a result, JQATH will help readers improve business practices, stay informed of successful hospitality strategies, maintain profit requirements, and increase the market share in this complex and growing field.

Comprised of conceptual and methodological research papers and case studies, JQATH offers readers examples of real world practices and experiences that involve the following areas:
- organizational development and improvement
- operational and efficiency issues
- quality policy and strategy development and implementation
- quality function deployment
- service quality improvement and customer satisfaction
- managerial issues, such as employee empowerment and benefits, quality costs, and returns on the investment
- the role and participation of private and public sectors, including residents
- international, national, and regional tourism; tourism destination sites, and systems of tourism

Manuscript Guidelines

1. Original articles only. Submission of a manuscript to this Journal represents a certification on the part of the author(s) that it is an original work, and that neither this manuscript nor a version of it has been published elsewhere nor is being considered for publication elsewhere.

2. Manuscript preparation.
Margins: leave at least a one-inch margin on all four sides.
Paper: use clean white, 8-1/2" x 11" bond paper.
Number of copies: 4 (the original plus three photocopies).
Cover page: *Important* -- staple a cover page to the manuscript, indicating only the article title (this is used for anonymous refereeing).
Second "title page": enclose a regular title page but do not staple it to the manuscript. Include the title again, plus:
- full authorship
- an **abstract** of about 100 words. (Below the abstract provide 3-1 0 key words for index purposes).
- an introductory footnote with authors' academic degrees, professional titles, affiliations, mailing addresses, and any desired acknowledgment of research support or other credit.

3. Return envelopes. When you submit your four manuscript copies, also include:
A regular envelope, stamped and self-addressed. This is for the Editor to send you an "acknowledgement of receipt" letter.

Manuscripts will not be returned.

4. Spelling, Grammar, and Punctuation. You are responsible for preparing manuscript copy which is clearly written in acceptable scholarly English, and which contains no errors of spelling, grammar, or punctuation. Neither the Editor nor the Publisher is responsible for correcting errors of spelling and grammar: the manuscript, after acceptance by the Editor,

must be immediately ready for typesetting as it is finally submitted by the author(s). Check your paper for the following common errors:
- dangling modifiers
- misplaced modifiers
- unclear antecedents
- incorrect or inconsistent abbreviations

Also, check the accuracy of all arithmetic calculations, statistics, numerical data, text citations, and references.

5. Inconsistencies must be avoided. Be sure you are consistent in your use of abbreviations, terminology, and in citing references, from one part of your paper to another.

6. Preparation of tables, figures, and illustrations. All tables, figures, illustrations, etc. must be "camera-ready." That is, they must be cleanly typed or artistically prepared so that they can be used either exactly as they are or else used after a photographic reduction in size. Figures, tables, and illustrations must be prepared on separate sheets of paper. Always use black ink and professional drawing instruments. On the back of these items, write your article title and the journal title lightly in pencil, so they do not get misplaced. In text, skip extra lines and indicate where these figures and tables are to be placed (please **do not write** on face of art). Photographs are considered part of the acceptable manuscript and remain with Publisher for use in additional printings. If submitted art cannot be used, the Publisher reserves the right to redo the art and to charge the author a fee of $35.00 per hour for this service.

7. Alterations required by referees and reviewers. Many times a paper is accepted by the Editor contingent upon changes that are mandated by anonymous specialist referees and members of the Editorial Board. If the Editor returns your manuscript for revisions, you are responsible for retyping any sections of the paper to incorporate these revisions (if applicable, revisions should also be put on disk).

8. Typesetting. You will not be receiving galley proofs of your article. Editorial revisions, if any, must therefore be made while your article is still in manuscript. The final version of the manuscript will be the version you see published. Typesetter's errors will be corrected by the production staff of The Haworth Press. Authors are expected to submit manuscripts, disks, and art that are free from error.

9. Electronic media. Haworth's in-house type-setting unit is able to utilize your final manuscript material as prepared on most personal computers and word processors. This will minimize typographical errors and decrease overall production timelag. Please send the first draft and final draft copies of your manuscript to the journal Editor in print format for his/her final review and approval. **After approval of** your final manuscript, please submit the final approved version both on printed format ("hard copy") and floppy diskette. On the outside of the diskette package write:

A. the brand name of your computer or word processor
B. the word-processing program that you used
C. the title of your article, and
D. file name

Note: Disk and hard copy must agree. In case of discrepancies, it is The Haworth Press's policy to follow hard copy. Authors are advised that no revisions of the manuscript can be made after acceptance by the Editor for publication. The benefits of this procedure are many with speed and accuracy being the most obvious. We look forward to working with you on this, knowing we will be able to serve you more efficiently in the future.

10. Reprints. The senior author will receive two copies of the journal issue and 25 complimentary reprints of his or her article. The junior author will receive two copies of the journal issue. These are sent several weeks after the journal issue is published and in circulation. An order form for the purchase of additional reprints will also be sent to all authors at this time. (Approximately 4-6 weeks is necessary for the preparation of reprints.)

Please do not query the Journal's Editor about reprints. All such questions should be sent directly to: **The Haworth Press, Inc., Production Department, 21 East Broad Street, West Hazleton, PA 18201**

To order additional reprints (minimum: 50 copies), please contact:
The Haworth Document Delivery Center, 10 Alice Street, Binghamton, NY 13904-1580
1-800-342-9678 or Fax (607) 722-6362.

11. Copyright. Copyright ownership of your manuscript must be transferred officially to The Haworth Press, Inc., before we can begin the peer-review process. The Editor's letter acknowledging receipt of the manuscript will be accompanied by a form fully explaining this. All authors must sign the form and return the original to the Editor as soon as possible. Failure to return the copyright form in a timely fashion will result in delay in review and subsequent publication.

Journal of Relationship Marketing (Journal of Customer Service in Mktg. & Mgmt.)

ADDRESS FOR SUBMISSION:

David Bejou, Founding Editor
Journal of Relationship Marketing (Journal of Customer Service in Mktg. & Mgmt.)
Virginia State University
Petersburg, VA 23806
USA
Phone: 804-524-5999
Fax: 804-524-5738
E-Mail: dbejou@vsu.edu
Web: www.haworthpress.com
Address May Change:

PUBLICATION GUIDELINES:

Manuscript Length: 16-20
Copies Required: Four
Computer Submission: No
Format: N/A
Fees to Review: 0.00 US$

Manuscript Style:
    Chicago Manual of Style

CIRCULATION DATA:

Reader: Academics, Business Persons
Frequency of Issue: Quarterly
Copies per Issue: 3,001 - 4,000
Sponsor/Publisher: Haworth Press, Inc.
Subscribe Price: 50.00 US$ Individual
    75.00 US$ Institution
    200.00 US$ Library

REVIEW INFORMATION:

Type of Review: Editorial Review
No. of External Reviewers: 3+
No. of In House Reviewers: 1
Acceptance Rate: 40%
Time to Review: 1 - 2 Months
Reviewers Comments: No
Invited Articles: 6-10%
Fees to Publish: 0.00 US$

MANUSCRIPT TOPICS:
Customer Service; Marketing Research; Marketing Theory & Applications; Quality & Value; Services

MANUSCRIPT GUIDELINES/COMMENTS:

During the next decade, there will be no greater need in the marketing of goods and services than to establish and maintain excellent customer relationships. This exciting journal provides you with:

- The cutting-edge theory, research, and practice in relationship marketing
- The latest international perspectives on relationship marketing, and
- The multidisciplinary approaches to understanding relationship marketing strategies for goods and services as applied to many different industries

The *Journal of Relationship Marketing* is a quarterly journal that publishes peer-reviewed and invited conceptual and empirical papers of original works that make serious contributions to the understanding and advancement of relationship marketing theory, research, and practice. This academic journal is interdisciplinary and international in nature. Under the editorship of Dr. David Bejou, this journal is a valuable literary resource for marketing researchers and managers in all sectors of today's ever-changing economy.

All of the articles are written by international academicians and professional with extensive experience and interest in the areas listed below. Each article is reviewed by the distinguished Editorial Board members, which are listed in each journal issue. The Journal of Relationship Marketing strives to enhance customer service, customer relationship management processes, and strategies worldwide.

Are consumers and business customers your most important assets? Are you interested in keeping your customers for life? Are you interested in developing successful long-term business relationships with your stakeholders? Would you like to be at the cutting edge of relationship marketing theories, research, and practices? If the answer is yes to any of these questions, you need to read the NEW international and multidisciplinary Journal of Relationship Marketing.

Examples of topics that may be published in the Journal:
- Evolution and life cycle of RM
- Theoretical and methodological issues in RM
- Determinants and consequences of RM
- Types of RM, networks and strategic alliances
- Internal and external customer relationship management strategies
- Psychological underpinning of RM
- Communication quality, style, and frequency in RM
- Quality, trust, commitment, satisfaction, loyalty, and dissolution in RM
- Applications of RM in different disciplines and industries
- International perspectives in RM
- Interdisciplinary nature of RM
- RM strategies in Services economy
- RM strategies in higher education
- RM strategies in e-commerce
- RM, technology, and the web
- Profitability in RM
- Case studies and best practices in RM
- Future role of RM

Instructions for Authors
1. **Original articles only**. Submission of a manuscript to this Journal represents a certification on the part of the author(s) that it is an original work and that neither this manuscript nor a version of it has been published elsewhere nor is being considered for publication elsewhere.

2. **Manuscript length**. Your manuscript may be approximately 5-50 typed pages double-spaced (including references and abstract). Lengthier manuscripts may be considered, but only

at the discretion of the Editor. Sometimes, lengthier manuscripts may be considered if they can be divided up into sections for publication in successive Journal issues.

3. **Manuscript Style**. References, citations, and general style of manuscripts for this Journal should follow the Chicago style (as outlined in the latest edition of the *Manual of Style* of the University of Chicago Press). References should be double-spaced and placed in alphabetical order.

If an author wishes to submit a paper that has been already prepared in another style, he or she may do so. However if the paper is accepted (with or without reviewer's alterations), the author is fully responsible for retyping the manuscript in the correct style as indicated above. Neither the Editor nor the Publisher is responsible for re-preparing manuscript copy to adhere to the Journal's style.

4. **Manuscript Preparation**.
Margins: leave at least a one-inch margin on all four sides.
Paper: use clean white, 8-1/2" x 11" bond paper.
Number of Copies: 3 hard copies (the original plus 2 photocopies) and 1 disk copy.
Cover Page: Important--staple a cover page to the manuscript, indicating only the article title (this is used for anonymous refereeing).
Second "Title Page": enclose a regular title page but do not staple it to the manuscript. Include the title again, plus
- full authorship
- an **abstract** of about 100 words. (Below the abstract provide 3-10 key words for index purposes).
- an introductory footnote with authors' academic degrees professional titles, affiliations, mailing addresses, and any desired acknowledgment of research support or other credit.

5. **Return Envelopes**. When you submit your three manuscript copies, also include:
- a 9" x 12" envelope, self-addressed and stamped (with sufficient postage to ensure return of your manuscript);
- a regular envelope, stamped and self-addressed. This is for the Editor to send you an "acknowledgement of receipt" letter.

6. **Spelling, Grammar, and Punctuation**. You are responsible for preparing manuscript copy which is clearly written in acceptable scholarly English, and which contains no errors of spelling grammar, or punctuation. Neither the Editor nor the Publisher is responsible for correcting errors of spelling and grammar: the manuscript, after acceptance by the Editor, must be immediately ready for typesetting as it is finally submitted by the author(s). Check your paper for the following common errors
- dangling modifiers
- misplaced modifiers
- unclear antecedents
- incorrect or inconsistent abbreviations

Also, check the accuracy of all arithmetic calculations, statistics numerical data, text citations, and references.

7. **Inconsistencies Must Be Avoided.** Be sure you are consistent in your use of abbreviations, terminology, and in citing references, from one part of your paper to another.

8. **Preparation of Tables, Figures, and Illustrations.** All tables, figures, illustrations, etc. must be "camera-ready." That is, they must be cleanly typed or artistically prepared so that they can be used either exactly as they are or else used after a photographic reduction in size. Figures, tables, and illustrations must be prepared on separate sheets of paper. Always use black ink and professional drawing instruments. On the back of these items, write your article title and the journal title lightly in pencil, so they do not get misplaced. In text, skip extra lines and indicate where these figures and tables are to be placed (please do not write on face of art). Photographs are considered part of the acceptable manuscript and remain with Publisher for use in additional printings.

9. **Alterations Required By Referees and Reviewers.** Many times a paper is accepted by the Editor contingent upon changes that are mandated by anonymous specialist referees and members of the Editorial Board. If the Editor returns your manuscript for revisions, you are responsible for retyping any sections of the paper to incorporate these revisions (if applicable, revisions should also be put on disk).

10. **Typesetting.** You will not be receiving galley proofs of your article. Editorial revisions, if any, must therefore be made while your article is still in manuscript. The final version of the manuscript will be the version you see published. Typesetters errors will be corrected by the production staff of The Haworth Press. Authors are expected to submit manuscripts, disks, and art that are free from error.

11. **Electronic Media.** Haworth's in-house type-setting unit will now be able to utilize your final manuscript material as prepared on most personal computers and word processors. This will minimize typographical errors and decrease overall production timelag.

A. Please continue to send your first draft and final draft copies of your manuscript to the journal Editor in print format for his/her final review and approval;
B. Only after the journal editor has approved your final manuscript, you may submit the final approved version both on:
   - printed format ("hard copy")
   - floppy diskette
C. Please make sure that the disk version and the hard copy (printed copy) are exactly the same.
D. Wrap your floppy diskettes in a strong diskette wrapper or holder, and write on the outside of the package:
   - the brand name of your computer or word processor
   - the word-processing program that you used to create your article, book chapter, or book
   - filename

The benefits of this procedure are many with speed and accuracy being the most obvious. We look forward to working with you on this, knowing we will be able to serve you more efficiently in the future.

12. **Reprints**. The senior author will receive one copy of the journal issue and 10 complimentary reprints of his or her article. The junior author will receive one copy of the issue. These are sent several weeks after the journal issue is published and in circulation. An order form for the purchase of additional reprints will also be sent to all authors at this time. (Approximately 4-6 weeks is necessary for the preparation of reprints.) Please do not query the Journal's Editor about reprints. All such questions should be sent directly to The Haworth Press, Inc. Production Department, 21 East Broad Street, West Hazleton, PA 18201. To order additional reprints, please contact Sample Copy Department, The Haworth Press, Inc., 10 Alice Street, Binghamton, New York 13904-1580 (607) 722-5857 (ext. 3321).

13. **Copyright**. Copyright ownership of your manuscript must be transferred officially to The Haworth Press Inc. before we can begin the peer-review process. The Editor's letter acknowledging receipt of the manuscript will be accompanied by a form fully explaining this. All authors must sign the form and return the original to the Editor as soon as possible. Failure to return the copyright form in a timely fashion will result in delay in review and subsequent publication.

Journal of Restaurant & Foodservice Marketing

ADDRESS FOR SUBMISSION:

John Bowen, Editor
Journal of Restaurant & Foodservice
  Marketing
University of Nevada, Las Vegas
William F. Harrah College of Hotel Admn.
Department of Tourism & Convention
  Admn.
Box 456023, 4505 Maryland Parkway
Las Vegas, NV 89154-6023
USA
Phone: 702-895-0876
Fax: 702-895-4870
E-Mail: bowen@ccmail.nevada.edu
Web: www.haworthpress.com
Address May Change:

PUBLICATION GUIDELINES:

Manuscript Length: 16-30
Copies Required: Three
Computer Submission: Yes
Format: Ms.Word, WdPerfect-Windows
Fees to Review: 0.00 US$

Manuscript Style:
  American Psychological Association

CIRCULATION DATA:

Reader: Academics
Frequency of Issue: Quarterly
Copies per Issue: 1,001 - 2,000
Sponsor/Publisher: Haworth Press, Inc.
Subscribe Price: 40.00 US$ Individual
  60.00 US$ Institution
  175.00 US$ Library

REVIEW INFORMATION:

Type of Review: Blind Review
No. of External Reviewers: 2
No. of In House Reviewers: 1
Acceptance Rate: 21-30%
Time to Review: 1 - 2 Months
Reviewers Comments: Yes
Invited Articles: 6-10%
Fees to Publish: 0.00 US$

MANUSCRIPT TOPICS:
Advertising & Promotion Management; Direct Marketing; Marketing Research; Marketing Theory & Applications; Sales/Selling; Services

MANUSCRIPT GUIDELINES/COMMENTS:

Manuscripts
Manuscripts should be submitted in quadruplicate to the Editor. All editorial inquiries should be directed to the Editor.

Books and software for review purposes should be submitted to H. G. Parsa, SUNY Buffalo, 1300 Elmwood Avenue, 203 Caudell Hall, Buffalo, NY 14526 (parsahg@buffalostate.edu).

A complete Instructions For Authors Form is available from the editor. Please include a stamped self-addressed envelope.

1. Original articles only. Submission of a manuscript to this Journal represents a certification on the part of the author(s) that it is an original work, and that neither this manuscript nor a version of it has been published elsewhere nor is being considered for publication elsewhere.

2. Copyright. Copyright ownership of your manuscript must be transferred officially to The Haworth Press, Inc. before we can begin the peer-review process. The Editor's letter acknowledging receipt of the manuscript will be accompanied by a form fully explaining this. All authors must sign the form and return the original to the Editor as soon as possible. Failure to return the copyright form in a timely fashion will result in delay in review and subsequent publication.

4. Manuscript Length. Your manuscript may be approximately 20-25 typed pages doublespaced (including references and abstract). Lengthier manuscripts may be considered, but only at the discretion of the Editor. Sometimes, lengthier manuscripts may be considered if they can be divided up into sections for publication in successive Journal issues.

5. Manuscript Style. References, citations, and general style of manuscripts for this Journal should follow the APA style (as outlined by the latest edition of the Publication Manual of the American Psychological Association). References should be double-spaced and placed in alphabetical order. If an author wishes to submit a paperthat had been already prepared in another style, he orshe may do so. However, if the paper is accepted (with or without reviewer's alterations), the author is fully responsible for retyping the manuscript in the correct style as indicated above. Neither the Editor nor the Publisher is responsible for re-preparing manuscript copy to adhere to the Journal's style.

6. Manuscript Preparation. Margins: leave at least a one-inch margin on all foursides. Paper: use clean, white, 8-1/2" x 11 "bond paper. Number of copies: 4 (the original plus three photocopies). Cover page: Important-staple a cover page to the manuscript, indicating only the article title (this is used for anonymous refereeing) and the ABSTRACT. Second "title page": enclose a regular title page but do not staple it to the manuscript. Include the title again, plus:
- full authorship;
- an **abstract** of about 100 words;
- 5 or 6 keywords that identify article content;
- an introductory footnote with authors' academic degrees, professional titles, affiliations, mailing addresses, and any desired acknowledgement of research support or other credit; a header or footer on each page with abbreviated title and page number of total (e.g., page 2 of 7).

7. Return Envelopes. When you submit your four manuscript copies, also include:
- a 9" x 12" envelope, self-addressed and stamped (with sufficient postage to ensure return of your manuscript);
- a regular envelope, stamped and self-addressed. This is for the Editor to send you an "acknowledgement of receipt" letter.

8. Spelling, Grammar, Punctuation And Inconsistencies. You are responsible for preparing manuscript copy which is clearly written in acceptable, scholarly English, and which contains no errors of spelling, grammar, or punctuation. Neither the Editor nor the Publisher is responsible for correcting errors of spelling and grammar: the manuscript, after acceptance by the Editor must be immediately ready for typesetting as it is finally submitted by the author(s). Also, check n the accuracy of all arithmetic calculations, statistics, numerical data, text citations, and references. **Inconsistencies must be avoided.** Be sure you are consistent in your use of abbreviations, terminology, and in citing references, from one part of your paper to another.

9. Preparation of tables, figures, and illustrations. All tables, figures, illustrations, etc., must be "camera-ready." That is, they must be cleanly typed or artistically prepared so that they can be used either exactly as they are or else used after a photographic reduction in size (Please note that dot-matrix type is often unacceptable for artwork.) Color camera-ready art reproduction is available for a fee. Restrictions may apply. Please contact journal Editor prior to submission.

10. Tables will. be printed as is and will not be typeset. If submitted art cannot be used, the Publisher reserves the right to redo the art and to charge the author a fee of $35.00 per hour for this service. The Haworth Press, Inc. is not responsible for errors incurred in the preparation of new camera-ready artwork. Figures, tables, and illustrations must be prepared on separate sheets of paper. Always use black ink and professional drawing instruments. On the back of these items, write your article title and the journal title lightly in pencil, so they do not get misplaced. In text, skip extra lines and indicate where these figures and tables are to be placed (please do not write on face of art). Photographs are considered part of the acceptable manuscript and remain with the publisher for use in additional printings.

11. Alterations required by referees and reviewers A paper may be accepted by the Editor contingent upon changes that are mandated by anonymous specialist referees and members of the Editorial Board. If the Editor returns your manuscript for revisions, you are responsible for retyping any sections of the paper to incorporate these revisions (if applicable, revisions should also be put on disk).

12. Typesetting. You will not receive galley proofs of your article. Editorial revisions, if any, must therefore be made while your article is still in manuscript. The final version of the manuscript will I be the version you see published. Typesetting errors will be corrected by the production staff of The Haworth Press, Inc. Authors are expected to submit manuscripts, disks, and art that are free from error.

13. Electronic Media Haworth's in-house typesetting unit will now be able to utilize your final manuscript material as prepared on most personal computers and word processors. This will minimize typographical errors and decrease overall production time. Please send the first draft and final draft copies of your manuscript to the journal Editor in print format for his final review and approval. After approval of your final manuscript, please submit the final approved version both on printed format ("hard copy ") and floppy diskette. On the outside of the diskette package write:

A. the brand name of your computer or word processor,
B. the word processing program that you used,
C. the title of your article, and
D. the file name.
E. NOTE: Disk and hard copy must agree.

In case of discrepancies, it is The Haworth Press' policy to follow hard copy. Authors are advised that no revisions of the manuscript can be made after acceptance by the Editor for publication. The benefits of this procedure are many with speed and accuracy being the most obvious. We look forward to working with you on this, knowing we will be able to serve you more efficiently in the future.

14. Reprints. The senior author will receive two copies of the journal issue and 25 complimentary reprints several weeks after the issue is published. The junior author will receive two copies of the journal issue. An order form will be sent to the corresponding author for the purchase of additional reprints at this time. (Approximately 4-6 weeks is necessary for the preparation of reprints.) Please do not query the Journal's Editor about reprints. All such questions should be sent directly to The Haworth Press, Inc., Production Department, 21 East Broad Street, West Hazleton, PA 18201-3809 USA. To order additional reprints, please contact The Haworth Document Delivery Service, The Haworth Press, Inc., 10 , Alice Street, Binghamton, NY 13904-1580 USA, 1-800-342-9678 or FAX 1-607-722-6362.

15. Copyright and permissions For permission to reprint articles that have appeared in Haworth journals, please contact: Copyright & Permissions Department, The Haworth Press, Inc., 10 Alice Street, Binghamton, NY 13904-1580.;

16. Library photocopying, Attention Librarians: If your library subscribes to this journal, Haworth waives all photocopying fees or any royalty payments for multiple internal library use. By "internal library use" we mean:
- photocopying multiple copies of any article for your reserve room or reference area
- photocopying of articles for routing to either students or faculty members
- multiple photocopying by students for coursework
- multiple photocopying by faculty members for passing out to students at no charge or for their own files
- other traditional internal library multiple use of journal articles

Journal of Retail Banking Services

ADDRESS FOR SUBMISSION:

Jane G. Bensahel, Editor
Journal of Retail Banking Services
1 State Street Plaza
New York, NY 10004
USA
Phone: 212-8030-8226
Fax: 212-747-1130
E-Mail:
Web:
Address May Change:

CIRCULATION DATA:

Reader: Academics, Business Persons & Bankers
Frequency of Issue: Quarterly
Copies per Issue: 2,001 - 3,000
Sponsor/Publisher: American Bankers
Subscribe Price: 225.00 US$

PUBLICATION GUIDELINES:

Manuscript Length: 8-20
Copies Required: Two
Computer Submission: Yes
Format: Mark on disk program used
Fees to Review: 0.00 US$

Manuscript Style:
　　See Manuscript Guidelines

REVIEW INFORMATION:

Type of Review: Editorial Review
No. of External Reviewers: Varies
No. of In House Reviewers: Varies
Acceptance Rate: No Reply
Time to Review: 1 Month or Less
Reviewers Comments: No
Invited Articles: Varies
Fees to Publish: 0.00 US$

MANUSCRIPT TOPICS:
Above: Within Banks & Financial Services Companies; Business Information Systems (MIS); Business Law, Public Responsibility & Ethics; Communication; Direct Marketing; Global Business; Labor Relations & Human Resource Mgt.; Marketing Research; Marketing Theory & Applications; Office Administration/Management; Operations Research/Statistics; Organizational Behavior & Theory; Organizational Development; Production/Operations; Sales/Selling; Services; Small Business Entrepreneurship; Strategic Management Policy; Technology/Innovation

MANUSCRIPT GUIDELINES/COMMENTS:

The *Journal of Retail Banking Services* welcomes the offer of unsolicited manuscripts written by practitioners and other experts in the field of retail banking services.

The journal publishes current, practical information and guidance for executives of banks and other institutions providing banking services to consumers; in both the content and tone of an article, it is important for prospective authors to keep this readership in mind. We seek material that will offer our readership new insights into, and new approaches, to success in the retail banking services business.

Manuscripts are considered for publication with the understanding that they represent original material and are offered exclusively and without fee to the *Journal of Retail Banking Services*. All accepted articles are subject to editing.

Articles must not have been published previously and may not simultaneously be submitted elsewhere.

There are no hard-and-fast rules about article length, but most published articles will range from 8-20 double-spaced manuscript pages- that is, from approximately 2,000-5,000 words.

If you are considering writing an article for the journal, you might find it helpful to query the editor before drafting the article.

If you have already written an article, please submit to the editor the article text (including a brief biography of the author) and all graphic material:
- on computer disk(s), with the program(s) used clearly marked on the disk(s)
- with two (2) hard copies, with text double-spaced and graphic material camera-ready.

Address queries or articles to: Jane G. Bensahel, Editor, Journal of Retail Banking Services, 1 State Street Plaza, New York, New York 10004; phone: 212 803-8226.

Journal of Retailing

ADDRESS FOR SUBMISSION:

Louis P. Bucklin, Editor
Journal of Retailing
University of California
Walter A. Haas School of Business
Berkeley, CA 94270-1900
USA
Phone:
Fax: 510-642-4700
E-Mail: pbucklin@haasberkeley.edu
Web: www.elsevier.nl
Address May Change:

CIRCULATION DATA:

Reader: Business Persons, Academic
Frequency of Issue: Quarterly
Copies per Issue: 2,001 - 3,000
Sponsor/Publisher: New York University/ Elsevier Science Publishing Co.
Subscribe Price: 105.00 US$ Personal
  269.00 US$

PUBLICATION GUIDELINES:

Manuscript Length: 20+
Copies Required: Five
Computer Submission: No
Format: N/A
Fees to Review: 0.00 US$

Manuscript Style:
  Chicago Manual of Style

REVIEW INFORMATION:

Type of Review: Blind Review
No. of External Reviewers: 2-3
No. of In House Reviewers: 1
Acceptance Rate: 11-20%
Time to Review: 2 - 3 Months
Reviewers Comments: Yes
Invited Articles: 0-5%
Fees to Publish: 0.00 US$

MANUSCRIPT TOPICS:
Advertising & Promotion Management; Consumer Shopping Behavior; Direct Marketing; Global Business; Marketing Research; Marketing Theory & Applications; Operations Research/Statistics; Retail Channel Management; Sales/Selling; Services; Transportation/Physical Distribution

MANUSCRIPT GUIDELINES/COMMENTS:

The Editors of the *Journal of Retailing* seek manuscripts presenting the latest in theoretical and empirical research in the field of retail marketing to an audience comprised of academicians, economists, geographers, researchers, top business executives and consultants. Retail marketing focuses upon activities supporting the sale of both services and products to householders, consumer behavior and satisfaction with respect to retail purchases, and the organization and management of retail-supply and information chains. Papers dealing with industrial marketing topics are typically not suitable unless a strong overlap with retail marketing can be observed.

JR authors demonstrate a strong knowledge of the literature of the field and rigorous logic. Accepted articles offer important new insights for theory, models, management practice, or government policy in retail and service marketing.

JR seeks articles to provide critical new understanding about the management and technology of retailing and retail/service systems as well as the environment and history in which retail institutions operate. Manuscripts that may be characterized as descriptive essays, depictions of current events or current business practices are unlikely to fit well in the journal.

Research directed toward JR's interests explores the current boundaries of our knowledge base in retail marketing. This exploration is used to design a research plan that tests whether fresh theoretical insights or valid or existing views are seriously incorrect. Authors typically employ sophisticated statistical techniques for examining data or mathematical models as means to test or evaluate ideas. Descriptive papers may be submitted where this approach is appropriate with regard to current knowledge in the special area and available data. Papers that critically review the state of the art to consolidate major themes and seek new directions are encouraged where this approach offers important new insight.

Authors who have not previously submitted manuscripts will find it useful to review recent issues of the Journal to develop an insight into the types of articles published. A review of the journal for articles upon similar topics may also provide insights.

Submission of Manuscripts and the Review Process
Authors with manuscripts to submit should send five, non-returnable copies to Louis P. Bucklin, Editor, Journal of Retailing, Haas School of Business, University of California, Berkeley, CA 94720-1900. Initial submissions may be printed on both of the paper with tables and figures located within the manuscript itself. Preparation of a final manuscript for publication is set forth below.

The editor initially scans manuscripts to determine if they generally meet the above requirements of the journal. Those accepted for review will be read by two or more reviewers in a double-blind process.

Double blind insures that readers do not know the authors of the manuscripts and vice-versa. However, authors should not leave telltale tracks in their manuscripts, such as obvious quotes from their own research or detailed reference to their unpublished papers.

The review process typically moves through two or three cycles of critique and revision before a manuscript is accepted. Though seemingly formidable, the review process plays an important role in strengthening each manuscript, a benefit of considerable value to the author(s).

In submitting a manuscript to JR, the author(s) vouch that the manuscript has neither been published, accepted for publication, nor currently under review at any other location. The author(s) also agree that the manuscript will not be placed under review elsewhere while the review process at JR is ongoing. If the JR editor accepts the manuscript or revised version for publication, the author(s) further guarantee not to withdraw it for submission elsewhere.

If the manuscript is based upon data or other materials that have been published elsewhere, or under review elsewhere, the author(s) should submit for the editor's consideration a copy of these materials.

Publication Format
In preparing the manuscript for submission, the following format should be followed.

Title Page: The title page should include the name, title, institutional affiliation, address, phone number, and e-mail address of each author. The date of the manuscript and any acknowledgments should appear on this page.

Abstract: The title of the manuscript and a 100-word summary summarizing the article should begin the numbered pages (page 1).

Text: The main text begins on the second page. A brief orientation to the focus and intended contribution of your study should introduce your paper.

Headings: Primary headings are centered in upper case. Secondary headings are flush left in upper and lower case. With the exception of initial paragraphs in primary sections, the first line of each paragraph should be indented.

Style: A concise style and minimal redundancy another enhance presentations. An emphasis upon the active tense is preferred. Issues set forth in literature review or methodology sections should be referenced subsequently only in abbreviated form. Data presented in a table or figure need not be described in detail within the text.

Equations: Special care should be taken in the presentation of equations, the capitalization and italicization of algebraic symbols in order to be clear to the typesetter. Equations should be numbered on the far right with an even margin.

Spelling: The manuscript should be subjected to both computer based grammatical and spelling review. Where spelling and hyphenation is optional, be consistent. Avoid the use of such expressions as operationalize and generalizability. Spell out numbers one through twenty in the text as well as the word percent.

References: Reference citations should be placed in the text and consist of the cited author's last name and the year of publication, enclosed in parentheses, and without punctuation, for example (Hendon 1989). If the author's name appears in the sentence, only the year of publication should appear in parentheses, for example, "...as suggested by Markin, Lillis, and Narayana (1976)." References to multiple works should occur within one set of parentheses, separated by semicolons, as in: (Mathis and Jackson 1979; Megginson 1985; Hershey 1971). Where possible, references should appear immediately before a punctuation mark.

Reference List: The list of references begins on a separate page and typed doublespaced. The first line of each entry is even with the left margin and subsequent lines are indented five spaces. Sort references by the first author's last name; multiple papers by the same author should be listed in chronological order. Use the examples below as a guide to reference style.

Book: Hall, Margaret, John Knapp and Christopher Winston (1961). Distribution in Great Britain and North America. Oxford, England: Oxford University Press.

Journal Article: Cummings, Thomas and Susan Manning (1977). "The Relationship between Worker Alienation and Work-Related Behavior," Journal of Vocational Behavior, 10 (April). 167-179.

Book Chapter: Katona, George and Eva Muller (1963). "A Study of Purchasing Decisions." Pp. 30-87 in Consumer Behavior: A Study of Purchasing Decisions. Lincoln Clark (Ed.), New York: New York University Press.

Conference Proceedings Paper: Westbrook, R. A. and Richard Oliver (1980). "Developing Better Measures of Consumer Satisfaction: Some Preliminary Results." Pp. 150-165 in Advances in Consumer Research, IX(A). Kent Monroe (Ed.), Ann Arbor, MI: Association for Consumer Research.

Unpublished Work or Working Paper: Rein, Martin and S. M. Miller, "The Demonstration Project as a Strategy of Change," Mobilization for Youth Training Institute Workshop. April 30, 1984, Columbia University, New York, NY.

Footnotes: Footnotes should be used sparingly and only for the purpose of extending or clarifying the main text with respect to an interesting, but somewhat tangential topic. Otherwise, the material should be included in the main text. Footnotes, number consecutively throughout the manuscript, should be typed, doubled spaced, and attached as a separate page.

Tables and Figures: Each table and figure is numbered consecutively in Arabic numerals. The title should be centered and in upper and lower case. Table footnotes should be indicated by a, b, c, and so forth. Tables should be limited in size while still serving the purpose of the authors. Where used, it should be as simple as possible. For example, it usually is not necessary to include both frequencies and percentages. Numerous statistical findings, such as means, scores, significance symbols of other sorts, are best relegated to the tables.

Graphics: Authors are responsible for completing professional-looking graphics. For materials such as graphs, charts, line drawings, or illustrations, we prefer that authors provide camera-ready copy. You may obtain such copy using suitable office suite programs such as Power Point and a clean, 600-dpi printer and the use of a lightly coated paper. The preparation of graphics by use of simple symbols available on word processors produces inadequate results. If you do not wish to submit camera-ready copy, a separate graphic file written in either EPS (encapsulated postscript), tiff (tagged image file format) or ps (PostScript) file may be submitted. A print from a graphics file must still be provided.

Final manuscript: If a manuscript is accepted for publication, authors should send two paper copies of their final version. These manuscripts must be printed, double-spaced on one side of

8 x 11-inch paper using one-inch margins on all sides, and 12-point type. An electronic image on diskette in either Word for Windows or WordPerfect is required.

Executive Summary: Authors must also provide an executive summary. However, this need not be included upon with the initial submission. This summary serves as an extended abstract for readers who wish to gain the flavor of an article prior to investing additional time in reading it. The review should highlight the major contributions of the article in an easily readable manner. The summary is ideally suited to point out interesting managerial, policy or social implications not touched upon within the main text. Executive summaries for all articles are printed at the front of the issue and will also appear on the journal's web page. They should be about two or three manuscript pages long.

Journal of Retailing and Consumer Services

ADDRESS FOR SUBMISSION:

Harry Timmermans, Editor
Journal of Retailing and Consumer Services
Eindhoven Univesrity of Technology
EIRASS Faculty of Architecture
Building and Planning
Postvak 20, PO Box 513
5600 MB Eindhoven,
The Netherlands
Phone: 31 0 402-472594
Fax: 31 0 402 475882
E-Mail: eirass@bwk.tue.nl
Web:
Address May Change:

PUBLICATION GUIDELINES:

Manuscript Length: 21-25
Copies Required: Three
Computer Submission: No
Format: N/A
Fees to Review: 0.00 US$

Manuscript Style:
 See Manuscript Guidelines

CIRCULATION DATA:

Reader: Academics
Frequency of Issue: Quarterly
Copies per Issue: Less than 1,000
Sponsor/Publisher: Elsevier Science
 Publishing
Subscribe Price: 127.00 US$ Personal
 362.00 US$ All except Europe & Japan
 324.00 Euro European Countries

REVIEW INFORMATION:

Type of Review: Blind Review
No. of External Reviewers: 3
No. of In House Reviewers: 0
Acceptance Rate: 11-20%
Time to Review: 2 - 3 Months
Reviewers Comments: Yes
Invited Articles: 0-5%
Fees to Publish: 0.00 US$

MANUSCRIPT TOPICS:
Advertising & Promotion Management; Business Information Systems (MIS); Consumer Behavior; Direct Marketing; Global Business; Labor Relations & Human Resource Mgt.; Marketing Research; Marketing Theory & Applications; Operations Research/Statistics; Organizational Behavior & Theory; Production/Operations; Public Administration; Purchasing/Materials Management; Sales/Selling; Services; Small Business Entrepreneurship; Strategic Management Policy; Technology/Innovation; Transportation/Physical Distribution

MANUSCRIPT GUIDELINES/COMMENTS:

Description
The journal is an international and interdisciplinary forum for research and debate in the rapidly developing - and converging - fields of retailing and services studies. Published quarterly, it focuses particularly on consumer behaviour and on policy and managerial decisions, encouraging contributions both from practitioners in the forefront of new developments in retailing and services, and from academics across a wide range of relevant disciplines. The *Journal of Retailing and Consumer Services* covers:

- the distribution and selling of goods
- the retailing of professional services such as health and law
- the retailing of consumer services such as transportation, tourism, leisure, and personal financial services.

For employers and course providers, it also addresses issues of education and training.
In addition to the main refereed articles and detailed case studies, the journal features short viewpoint pieces and state-of-the-art surveys, book and software reviews, and a calendar of events.

GUIDE FOR AUTHORS

Submission of Papers
Authors are requested to submit their original manuscript and figures plus two copies to Professor Harry Timmermans, Editor.

Submission of a paper implies that it has not been published previously, that it is not under consideration for publication elsewhere, and that if accepted it will not be published elsewhere in the same form, in English or in any other language, without the written consent of the publisher. Translated material, which has not been published in English, will also be considered. All articles are refereed to ensure accuracy and relevance, and amendments to the script may be required before final acceptance.

Types of Contribution
The journal publishes full-length research papers, case studies and book reviews. There is also a viewpoint section which exists for the expression of opinion, and allows authors to submit material not suitable for a full-length article but containing ideas worthy of publication. Full-length articles should be 4000-6000 words long, although articles longer than 6000 words will be accepted on an occasional basis, if the topic demands this length of treatment. Book reviews should be 800-1200, and viewpoints 1500-2000 words in length.

Manuscript Preparation
General: Manuscripts must be typewritten, double-spaced with wide margins on one side of white A4 paper. Good quality printouts with a font size of 12 or 10 pt are required. The corresponding author should be identified (include a Fax number and E-mail address). Full postal addresses must be given for all co-authors. Authors should consult a recent issue of the journal for style if possible. An electronic copy of the paper should accompany the final accepted version. The Editors reserve the right to adjust style to certain standards of uniformity. Authors should retain a copy of their manuscript since the Publisher cannot accept responsibility for damage or loss of papers. Original manuscripts are discarded one month after publication unless the Publisher is asked to return original material after use.

Text: Follow this order when typing manuscripts: Title, Authors, Affiliations, Abstract, Keywords, Main text, Acknowledgements, Appendix, References, Vitae, Figure Captions and then Tables. Do not import the Figures or Tables into your text. The corresponding author should be identified with an asterisk and footnote. All other footnotes (except for table footnotes) should be identified with superscript Arabic numerals. Footnotes should be grouped together in a section at the end of the text in numerical order, and double spaced. The text should be organized under appropriate section headings which, ideally, should not be more than 600 words apart. All headings should be placed on the left-hand side of the text.

Abstract: Include a self-contained abstract up to 100 words outlining in a single paragraph the aims, scope and conclusions of the paper.

Keywords: Up to three keywords or phrases (maximum 10 words in total) to facilitate access and indexing should be included.

Units: All measurements should be given in metric (SI) units.

References: All publications cited in the text should be presented in a list of references following the text of the manuscript. In the text refer to the author's name (without initials) and year of publication, e.g. "Since Peterson (1993) has shown that..." or "This is in agreement with results obtained later (Kramer, 1994)". For three or more authors use the first author followed by "et al." in the text. The list of references should be arranged alphabetically by authors' names. The manuscript should be carefully checked to ensure that the spelling of authors' names and dates are exactly the same in the text as in the reference list. References should be given in the following form:

Ratchford, B.T., Norton, D.P., 1988. A model and measurement approach for studying retail productivity. Journal of Retailing 64 (3), 241-263.

Kaplan, R.S., Norton, D.P., 1996. The Balanced Scorecard: Translating Strategy into Action. Harvard Business School Press, Boston, MA.

Sealy, K., 1992. International air transport. In: Hoyle, B.S., Knowles, R.D. (Eds.), Modern Transport Geography. Belhaven Press, London, pp. 233-256.

Illustrations: All illustrations should be provided in camera-ready form, suitable for reproduction (which may include reduction) without retouching. Photographs, charts and diagrams are all to be referred to as Figure(s) and should be numbered consecutively in the order to which they are referred. They should accompany the manuscript, but should not be included within the text. Their position should be indicated in the text. All illustrations should be clearly marked on the back with the figure number and the author's name. All figures are to have a caption. Captions should be supplied on a separate sheet.

Line drawings: Good quality printouts on white paper produced in black ink are required. All lettering, graph lines and points on graphs should be sufficiently large and bold to permit reproduction when the diagram has been reduced to a size suitable for inclusion in the journal. Dye-line prints or photocopies are not suitable for reproduction. Do not use any type of shading on computer-generated illustrations.

Photographs: Original photographs must be supplied as they are to be reproduced (e.g. black and white or colour). If necessary, a scale should be marked on the photograph. Please note that photocopies of photographs are not acceptable.

Colour: Where colour figures are required, the author will be charged accordingly.

Tables: Tables should be numbered consecutively and given a suitable caption and each table typed on a separate sheet. Footnotes to tables should be typed below the table and should be referred to by superscript lowercase letters. No vertical rules should be used. Tables should not duplicate results presented elsewhere in the manuscript, e.g. in graphs.

Electronic submission

Authors should submit an electronic copy of their paper with the final version of the manuscript. The electronic copy should match the hardcopy exactly. Always keep a backup copy of the electronic file for reference and safety. For authors using LaTeX, the document style files, as well as the instructions "Preparing articles with LaTeX" in the form of a dvi file, can be obtained free of charge from any host on the Comprehensive TeX Archive Network (CTAN) using anonymous ftp. The primary CTAN hosts are ftp.dante.de and ftp.tex.ac.uk. The Elsevier macros are in /pub/tex/macros/latex/contrib/supported/elsevier. These can also be downloaded from the Internet site: http://www.tex.ac.uk. Full details of electronic submission and other formats can be obtained from http://www.elsevier.nl/locate/disksub or from Author Services at Elsevier Science.

Proofs

Proofs will be sent to the author (first named author if no corresponding author is identified of multi-authored papers) and should be returned within 48 hours of receipt. Corrections should be restricted to typesetting errors; any others may be charged to the author. Any queries should be answered in full. Please note that authors are urged to check their proofs carefully before return, since the inclusion of late corrections cannot be guaranteed. Proofs are to be returned to the Log-in Department, Elsevier Science, Stover Court, Bampfylde Street, Exeter, Devon EX1 2AH, UK.

Offprints

Fifty offprints will be supplied free of charge. Additional offprints and copies of the issue can be ordered at a specially reduced rate using the order form sent to the corresponding author after the manuscript has been accepted. Orders for reprints (produced after publication of an article) will incur a 50% surcharge.

Copyright

All authors must sign the "Transfer of Copyright" agreement before the article can be published. This transfer agreement enables Elsevier Science Ltd to protect the copyrighted material for the authors, without the author relinquishing his/her proprietary rights. The copyright transfer covers the exclusive rights to reproduce and distribute the article, including reprints, photographic reproductions, microfilm or any other reproductions of a similar nature, and translations. It also includes the right to adapt the article for use in conjunction with computer systems and programs, including reproduction or publication in machine-readable form and incorporation in retrieval systems. Authors are responsible for obtaining from the copyright holder permission to reproduce any material for which copyright already exists.

Author Services
For queries relating to the general submission of manuscripts (including electronic text and artwork) and the status of accepted manuscripts, please contact Author Services, Log-in Department, Elsevier Science, The Boulevard, Langford Lane, Kidlington, Oxford OX5 1GB, UK. E-mail: authors@elsevier.co.uk, Fax: +44 (0) 1865 843905, Tel: +44 (0) 1865 843900. Authors can also keep a track of the progress of their accepted article through our OASIS system on the Internet. For information on an article go to this Internet page and key in the corresponding author's name and the Elsevier reference number.

Journal of Segmentation in Marketing

ADDRESS FOR SUBMISSION:

Art T. Weinstein, Editor
Journal of Segmentation in Marketing
Nova Southeastern University
School of Business and Entrepreneurship
3100 SW 9th Avenue
Fort Lauderdale, FL 33315
USA
Phone: 954-262-5097
Fax: 954-262-3965
E-Mail: art@sbe.nova.edu
Web: www.haworthpress.com
Address May Change:

PUBLICATION GUIDELINES:

Manuscript Length: 16-20
Copies Required: Four
Computer Submission: No
Format: N/A
Fees to Review: 0.00 US$

Manuscript Style:
  Chicago Manual of Style

CIRCULATION DATA:

Reader: Business Persons, Primarily
  Academics
Frequency of Issue: 2 Times/Year
Copies per Issue: No Reply
Sponsor/Publisher: Haworth Press Inc.
Subscribe Price: 60.00 US$ Individuals
  75.00 US$ Institutions
  90.00 US$ Library

REVIEW INFORMATION:

Type of Review: Blind Review
No. of External Reviewers: 2
No. of In House Reviewers: 1
Acceptance Rate: No Reply
Time to Review: 2 - 3 Months
Reviewers Comments: Yes
Invited Articles: Occasional
Fees to Publish: 0.00 US$

MANUSCRIPT TOPICS:
Direct Marketing; Marketing Research; Marketing Theory & Applications; Segmentation; Strategic Marketing; Target Marketing

MANUSCRIPT GUIDELINES/COMMENTS:

About The Journal
The *Journal of Segmentation In Marketing* is a professional, biannual journal devoted to stimulating thought and enhancing the practice of market segmentation and target marketing. The journal fills a void in the marketing literature for a cutting-edge, one-stop knowledge and action source on segmentation and related topics. As an applied, scholarly journal, it will feature a blend of conceptual pieces, articles based on empirical research, and case studies.

The goals of the *Journal of Segmentation In Marketing* are to provide scholars and marketers:
1) a rich outlet of new ideas on market segmentation;
2) an exchange forum that shares the latest methods and "best practices" relevant to customer attraction and retention, managing target markets, and researching market opportunities; and

3) an important source of segmentation knowledge/insights and industry- specific applications.

Articles will be about new segmentation methods; business, consumer, and international segmentation; demographics and psychographics; research approaches; niche marketing, strategic aspects of market identification and target market selection; computer-related applications (e.g. database marketing, census data utilization, syndicated information services, etc.); and other pertinent topics. A "Call for Papers" information sheet (available upon request) identifies more than 50 potential topics of interest to *Journal of Segmentation In Marketing* readers.

The Editor is strongly supported by a first-rate editorial review board consisting of more than 20 internationally recognized marketing/segmentation experts from leading business schools and corporations.

Instructions For Authors
1. **Original Articles Only**. Submission of a manuscript to the *Journal of Segmentation In Marketing* represents a certification on the part of the author(s) that it is an original work, and that neither this manuscript nor a version of it has been published elsewhere nor is being considered for publication elsewhere.

2. **Manuscript Length**. Your manuscript may be approximately 20 typed pages double-spaced (including references and abstract). Lengthier manuscripts may be considered, but only at the discretion of the Editor. Sometimes, lengthier manuscripts may be considered if they can be divided up into sections for publication in successive Journal issues. Shorter manuscripts (e.g. 10-15 pages) are acceptable for case studies and commentaries.

3. **Manuscript Style**. References, citations, and general style of manuscripts for the *Journal of Segmentation In Marketing* should follow the Chicago style (as outlined in the latest edition of the *Manual of Style* of the University of Chicago Press). References should be double-spaced and placed in alphabetical order.

If an author wishes to submit a paper that has been already prepared in another style, he or she may do so. However if the paper is accepted (with or without reviewer's alterations, the author is fully responsible for retyping the manuscript in the correct style as indicated above. Neither the Editor nor the Publisher is responsible for re-preparing manuscript copy to adhere to the Journal's style.

4. **Manuscript Preparation**.
Margins: leave at least a one-inch margin on all four sides.
Paper: use clean white 8 ½ x 11" bond paper.
Number of copies: 4 (the original plus three photocopies).
Cover page: **Important**--staple a cover page to the manuscript, indicating only the article title (this is used for anonymous refereeing).
Second "title page": enclose a regular title page but do not staple it to the manuscript. Include the title again, plus:
- full authorship

- an ABSTRACT of about 100-150 words. (Below the abstract provide 4-6 key words for index purposes).
- an introductory footnote with authors' academic degrees professional titles, affiliations, mailing addresses, and any desired acknowledgment of research support or other credit.

5. **Return Envelopes**. When you submit your four manuscript copies, also include:
- a 9" x 12" envelope, self-addressed and stamped (with sufficient postageto ensure return of your manuscript)
- a regular envelope, stamped and self-addressed. This is for the Editor to send you an "acknowledgement of receipt" letter.

6. **Spelling grammar, and punctuation**. You are responsible for; preparing manuscript copy which is clearly written in acceptable scholarly English, and which contains no errors of spelling, grammar, or punctuation. Neither the Editor nor the Publisher is responsible for correcting errors of spelling and grammar: the manuscript, after acceptance by the Editor, must be immediately ready for typesetting as it is finally submitted by the author(s). Check your paper for the following common errors:
- dangling modifiers
- misplaced modifiers
- unclear antecedents
- incorrect or inconsistent abbreviations

Also, check the accuracy of all arithmetic calculations, statistics, numerical data, text citations, and references.

7. **Inconsistencies must be avoided**. Be sure you are consistent in your use of abbreviations, terminology, and in citing references, from one part of your paper to another.

8. **Preparation of tables and figures**. All tables, figures, etc. must be "camera-ready." That is, they must be cleanly typed or artistically prepared so that they can be used either exactly as they are or else used after a Photographic reduction in size. Figures and tables must be prepared on separate sheets of paper. Always use black ink and professional drawing instruments. On the back of these items, write your article title and the journal title lightly in pencil, so they do not get misplaced. In text, skip extra lines and indicate where these figures and tables are to be placed (please do not write on face of art).

9. **Alterations required by reviewers**. Many times a paper is accepted by the Editor contingent upon changes that are mandated by anonymous reviewers and members of the Editorial Board. If the Editor returns your manuscript for revisions, you are responsible for retyping any sections of the paper to incorporate these revisions (if applicable, revisions should also be put on disk).

10. **Typesetting**. You will not be receiving galley proofs of your article. Editorial revisions, if any, must therefore be made while your article is still in manuscript. The final version of the manuscript will be the version you see published. Typesetter's errors will be corrected by the

production staff of The Haworth Press. Authors are expected to submit manuscripts, disks, and art that are free from error.

11. **Electronic Media**. Haworth's in-house type-setting unit is able to utilize your final manuscript material as prepared on most personal computers and word processors. This will minimize typographical errors and decrease overall production timelag. Please send the first draft and final draft copies of your manuscript to the journal Editor in print format for his/her final review and approval. After approval of your final manuscript please submit the final approved version both on printed format ("hard copy") and floppy diskette. On the outside of the diskette package write:

E. the brand name of your computer or word processor
F. the word-processing program that you used
G. the title of your article, and
H. file name

Note: Disk and hard copy must agree. In case of discrepancies, it is The Haworth Press's policy to follow hard copy. Authors are advised that no revisions of the manuscript can be made after acceptance by the Editor for publication. The benefits of this procedure are many with speed and accuracy being the most obvious. We look forward to working with you on this, knowing we will be able to serve you more efficiently in the future.

12. **Reprints**. The senior author will receive two copies of the journal issue and 10 complimentary reprints of his or her article. The junior author will receive two copies of the journal issue. These are sent several weeks after the journal issue is published and in circulation. An order form for the purchase of additional reprints will also be sent to all authors at this time. (Approximately 4-6 weeks is necessary for the preparation of reprints.) Please do not query the Journal's Editor about reprints. All such questions should be sent directly to The Haworth Press, Inc., Production Department, 21 East Broad Street, West Hazleton, PA 18201. To order additional reprints (minimum: 50 copies), please contact The Haworth Document Delivery Center, 10 Alice Street, Binghamton, NY 1 3904-1580; 1-800-342-9678 or Fax (607) 722-6362.

13. **Copyright**. Copyright ownership of your manuscript must be transferred officially to The Haworth Press, Inc. before we can begin the peer-review process. The Editor's letter acknowledging receipt of the manuscript will be accompanied by a form fully explaining this. All authors must sign the form and return the original to the Editor as soon as possible. Failure to return the copyright form in a timely fashion will result in delay in review and subsequent publication.

Journal of Selling and Major Account Management

ADDRESS FOR SUBMISSION:

Tracy Harwood, Managing Editor
Journal of Selling and Major Account
 Management
Sales Research Trust Ltd.
751 Portswood Road
Southhampton, Hampshire, S017 3SU
U.K.
Phone: +44 0 1703 677416
Fax: +44 0 1703 677416
E-Mail: kevin.wilson@dial.pipex.com
Web:
Address May Change:

PUBLICATION GUIDELINES:

Manuscript Length: 21-25
Copies Required: No Reply
Computer Submission: Yes
Format: Word for Windows
Fees to Review: 0.00 US$

Manuscript Style:
 See Manuscript Guidelines

CIRCULATION DATA:

Reader: Business Persons, Academic
Frequency of Issue: Quarterly
Copies per Issue: Less than 1,000
Sponsor/Publisher: The Sales Research
 Trust Ltd.
Subscribe Price: 190.00 US$

REVIEW INFORMATION:

Type of Review: Blind Review
No. of External Reviewers: 2
No. of In House Reviewers: 2
Acceptance Rate: 21-30%
Time to Review: 2 - 3 Months
Reviewers Comments: Yes
Invited Articles: 11-20%
Fees to Publish: 0.00 US$

MANUSCRIPT TOPICS:
Global Business; Marketing Theory & Applications; Sales/Selling

MANUSCRIPT GUIDELINES/COMMENTS:

Editor: Kevin Wilson (same address, telephone, fax, & email as given above).

Notes To Contributors
1. **Articles for consideration** should be sent to the Managing Editor Tracy Harwood, The Sales Research Trust Limited (Journal of Selling and Major Account Management), 751 Portswood Road, Southampton, 5017 3SU, United Kingdom; fax: 44+ (0)1703 586385 or by Email to kevin.wilson@dial.pipex.com. or direct to tgharwood@l ineone.net

2. **Articles in excess of 6000 words** will not normally be accepted. The Editors welcome shorter articles, case studies and reviews. Contributors should specify the length of their articles.

3. **A manuscript copy of the contribution** should be submitted if possible with a copy on 3.5" diskette in Microsoft Word 6 format, author's name(s) and short title of the article. Alternatively, the contribution may be emailed to the above address as a Microsoft Word 6 document, however contributors are advised to check submissions have been received by telephone. Neither the editors nor The Sales Research Trust accept any responsibility for loss or damage of any contributions submitted for publication in the Journal.

Outline - it is helpful to prepare and agree with an editor an outline of the article before starting work in detail.

Biographical note - supply a short biographical note giving the author(s) full name, appointment, institutions or organisation / company and recent professional attainments.

Synopsis - an abstract or resume not exceeding 100 words should be included.

Diagrams / text boxes / tables - should be submitted without shading although a copy of how the authors wishes the diagram to appear shaded may be submitted by way of illustrative example. These should be numbered consecutively and typed on separate pages at the end of the article with an indication in the text where it should appear.

References - should be cited using the Harvard method. No footnotes should be used fur references or literature citations. Wherever possible, full bibliographic details (e.g., volume number issue number or date, page numbers publisher year of publication) should be included.

Footnotes - for clarification or elaboration should be used very sparingly - they may be indicated in the text and at the beginning of the footnote by the use of asterisks and / or daggers.

4. **Any article or other contribution** submitted should be the original unpublished work of the author(s) not submitted for publication elsewhere, unless with the agreement of the editors.

5. **Manuscripts should be typewritten** using one side of A4 paper with all margins of 1" and double-spaced. Font style should be Times New Roman in 12 pitch. Footnotes should be typed at the bottom of the page and numbered consecutively throughout the text.

6. **Cross references** should not be to page numbers but to the text accompanying a particular footnote.

7 **An address for correspondence** (including Email address) should be supplied as well as a telephone and fax number at which the author may be contacted. .

8. **Authors undertake to check proofs** and to return them within the specified date. They should be free from grammatical, syntax or spelling errors. Failure to return proofs will result in the publication of the article at the editors discretion in which event the editors do not accept liability for any changes made to grammar syntax, spelling or other changes deemed necessary. The editors reserve the right not to accept any alterations or corrections made.

Copyright in all contributions is with the Sales Research Trust

Guideline For Reviewers
Thank you for agreeing to review the enclosed manuscript which is being considered for publication in the *Journal of Selling and Major Account Management*. At the request of other reviewers we have provided these notes as a guide to the review process which may be useful when added to your own experience.

Editorial Policy
The main objective of the journal is to provide a focus for collaboration between practitioners and academics for the advancement of education and research in the areas of selling and major account management. Our audience is comprised largely of practitioners in industry and academics researching in the field.

The Journal strives to enhance best practice in the field of selling and major account management. Articles that promote this will be given priority for publication. In particular, we see this as being achieved through three distinct forms of contribution: empirical papers reporting research which is concerned with testing and validating theories of sales management and selling activities; conceptual papers which develop theory as it relates to this field; and practitioner notes which provide commentaries and case studies that address key issues.

All academic papers published will contain an Executive Summary that identifies the managerial implications of the research findings.

The Role of Reviewers
We suggest that the prime responsibility of a reviewer is to assess the value of the contribution made by a paper to the aims of the Journal and to suggest ways in which this contribution may be enhanced.

A good review has three basic dimensions: *thoroughness, guidance* and *substance*. The *thoroughness* of a review reflects your knowledge of the subject matter. *Guidance* is the degree to which you provide specific written comments about how to improve the manuscript. *Substance* relates to the specificity of your comments and explanations about flaws in the manuscript. A reasonable review should take a minimum of four hours and reviewer comments to the author typically run to between one and two pages.

Format
The attached form, provided to guide you in the manuscript review process, will serve as your reporting form to the managing Editor. The evaluation categories, which appear as scales, should help you to remember to consider all aspects of the manuscript as you prepare your analysis.

Your comments to the Author
Your comments will be of great value to the author and should identify what you feel is good and what you feel could be improved within the paper. Please try to be specific and

constructive in the comments and recommendations you make, particularly where you feel that a manuscript is confusing. While many of our authors are experienced, some are just embarking on their academic career and benefit greatly from the professional advice that your review provides.

Your comments to the author should be placed on a separate piece of plain paper with nothing to identify the reviewer to the author (i.e. no letterhead, fax cover sheets, phone numbers, signatures, institution logos etc.). Some reviewers also make comments directly on the manuscript; these marked up manuscripts are returned to the authors.

Comments to the Editor
In the designated space on the review form, or in a separate letter, please also make a set of comments to the Managing Editor. You can be as candid as you please. Since the Managing Editor will read your *comments to author,* you do not need to repeat yourself. These comments to the editor will not be sent to the author, but they may be summarised in a letter to the author if pre publication changes are recommended. Please be extensive in your comments; they are particularly helpful in instructing acceptance/ rejection decisions, where papers are marginal , or where the opinions of reviewers differ significantly.

Manuscript Length
Manuscripts ordinarily should be between 4,000 and 6,000 words (about 15-25 double spaced, typewritten pages with regular size type), plus appropriate references, tables and supporting materials. Articles of a shorter length are also acceptable.

Your Recommendation
Your recommendation to the Editor regarding the final disposition of the manuscript is critical. The decision of the Editor to publish a manuscript is strongly influenced by your recommendation. The collective decisions of the individual reviewers largely shape both the editorial content and quality of the Journal. So if you like, or don't like the manuscript, please say so.

Major Revisions
You may choose to recommend major revision of a manuscript. This action is common; a significant number of the manuscripts published in the Journal have been through a major revision by the author. Recommend a major revision if you like the idea behind the manuscript and you feel the author can substantially rewrite the manuscript to make it suitable for publication in the Journal. In fairness, to both authors and reviewers, major revisions will be returned to the original set of reviewers for reconsideration. If the author meets your requirements for a major revision, there should be a high probability that you will recommend acceptance with only minor revisions.

Ethics and the Blind Review Process
The Journal uses a double-blind review process. Neither the author nor the reviewer should know the other's identify. These identities, known only to the editorial staff, are never released, even after the article has been published. If you recognise the author from something in the manuscript, have reviewed this manuscript for another journal, or have read a substantially identical version in another journal, please return the manuscript to the Managing

Editor with a note to that effect. If you have seen the article in conference proceedings please notify the editor when you return your review. Whilst we will not publish extant papers we realize that conference presentations are one means by which authors test their ideas before seeking full publication and the editor will take a view on individual cases.

Upon receipt, the Editor reviews a manuscript to ensure that its topic is within the editorial scope of the Journal and that it meets accepted professional standards as outlined in the Notes to Contributors. The Managing Editor then selects two or three reviewers on the basis of their expressed interests and expertise. If the Managing Editor has misinterpreted your knowledge, as related to the manuscript topic, please send the manuscript back to be reassigned. Under no circumstances should you turn the manuscript over to another individual for review. Certainly feel free to consult with a colleague on an issue raised in the manuscript, or for help with a technical point or two, but be sure the review represents your thoughts.

Feedback

Please feel free to contact the Managing Editor, Tracy Harwood (at the Sales Research Trust address below or direct by email to tgharwood@lineone.net), about these guidelines or any concerns you might have about other aspects of the Journal.

Journal of Services Marketing

ADDRESS FOR SUBMISSION:

Charles L. Martin, Editor
Journal of Services Marketing
Wichita State University
Dept. of Marketing & Entrepreneurship
301 Clinton Hall
Wichita, KS 67260
USA
Phone: 316-978-3367
Fax: 316-978-3276
E-Mail: martin@twsuvm.uc.twsu.edu
Web: www.mcb.co.uk
Address May Change:

CIRCULATION DATA:

Reader: Academics, Business Persons
Frequency of Issue: 6 Times/Year
Copies per Issue: No Reply
Sponsor/Publisher: MCB University Press Limited-UK
Subscribe Price: 799.00 US$
2999.00 US$

PUBLICATION GUIDELINES:

Manuscript Length: 20 Maximum
Copies Required: Four
Computer Submission: No
Format: N/A
Fees to Review: 0.00 US$

Manuscript Style:
See Manuscript Guidelines

REVIEW INFORMATION:

Type of Review: Blind Review
No. of External Reviewers: 3
No. of In House Reviewers: 1
Acceptance Rate: 21-30%
Time to Review: 2 - 3 Months
Reviewers Comments: Yes
Invited Articles: 0-5%
Fees to Publish: 0.00 US$

MANUSCRIPT TOPICS:
Advertising & Promotion Management; Business Information Systems (MIS); Communication; Consumer Behavior; Customer Service; Direct Marketing; Global Business; Health Care Administration; Marketing Research; Marketing Theory & Applications; Non Profit Organizations; Organizational Behavior & Theory; Organizational Development; Purchasing/Materials Management; Sales/Selling; Services; Small Business Entrepreneurship; Strategic Management Policy

MANUSCRIPT GUIDELINES/COMMENTS:

The objective of this Journal is to provide the practitioners of marketing with new ideas that will be applicable to their daily work. Each article must put forth recommendations as to how the material contained in the article can be utilized in business practice. The Journal should also provide teachers of marketing with actual business examples of how the theories taught in the classroom work in the "real world". We would expect that this will add meaning and "flavor" to their lectures.

The basis of an article may be research, but it is not intended that the actual research be printed. If the methodology is so unique as to warrant inclusion, it will be added as an appendix. But, research is not the only basis of an article. Cases, concepts, and industry reviews and practices may be put forth with equal acceptability. In addition, we have provided a section for Commentary, which need be little more than personal opinion.

Article content
Each article should contain:

1. Background and short references to previous articles, if they are pertinent. Specifically omit endless strings of quotations by other authors, especially if the ideas are currently well accepted. This is particularly true of citations in the literature that are five or more years old. They have generally lost their uniqueness. If previous material is pertinent, please paraphrase it and eliminate end notes and authors. Citations should be used only for significant and timely contributions. Also, standard textbooks should not be used as references. Note: With the advent of data bases, it is not possible, within the twinkling of an electronic lash, to call forth everything that has ever been written on a subject. Some authors think that all such material should be quoted and edn noted. Our readers don't. Such material may be recommended for additional reading.

2. Based premise, major thought, problem or concept.

3. A discussion of the theory incorporating any research (but not the actual research which may be added in an appendix).

4. A case example or clear argument supporting the basic premise or concept.

5. A summary to wrap-up the key ideas. Then a section title Managerial Implications and Recommendations. That is, the practical applications for the information presented in the article.

The Managerial Implications and Recommendations are the key to the entire article. Without this section no manuscript can be accepted.

Article length:
Articles should be under 8000 words. Half that amount with a few charts, graphs or side bars will also do nicely. But we will also accept articles of greater length when the topic warrants it. Also, articles in the section for Commentary can be as little as one or two pages in length, or about 800-1600 words. Here we'd like to encourage very creative writing.

Do not prepare final artwork. We will do this. Of course, if you already have artwork that can be reproduced, please advise. We would like to use it. Just make sure that what you submit is very clear.

Footnotes, end notes and references:
This journal does not follow the standard format of most other journals.

Important
References to an author's work should be handled via a number corresponding to the author's work in the alphabetized End Notes. The author's name and date (e.g. Kotler, 1984), as is the custom, should not be used; only the reference number (superscript). Thus, the reference numbers in the text will be out of numerical sequence. Other constructions such as "According to Smith..." or "(See Smith, 1983)" or "Jones describes sales as..." are not to be used. The purpose is to eliminate authors' names and extraneous words in the text that might slow down the reader's quest for the heart of the article. Other references or reading recommendations should be listed after End Notes under the title of References.

Note: Articles using the format above will be processed and reviewed in a much more expeditious manner.

Footnotes should only be used for clarification such as a definition of a term that might not be in common use, e.g. cognitive dissonance* or clarification of a point that some readers might need.

Prior exposure:
Articles that have been published elsewhere or have been submitted concurrently to other publications are generally not acceptable. However, there are exceptions such as foreign publications, conference proceedings, obscure journals, or significantly different exposure which may mitigate our policy. We are striving to have the best possible material and will, therefore, be flexible. Copyright permission for previously printed material is the responsibility of the author. On submission, we assume that such permission, where required, has been granted. (Note: Many of our authors now find that the best way to avoid copyright problems is copyright the material presented at conferences themselves. Then they can grant permission to any publication they deem worthy.)

Speeches that are rewritten into article form are generally quite acceptable.

Review Process:
The editor reviews all articles for general acceptability upon receipt. If major revisions are required at that point, the manuscript will be returned to the author with appropriate comments. If the topic is acceptable, it will be sent for review, which is double-blind to three reviewers. We ask these reviewers to return the manuscript in one month but as a practical matter it generally takes a few weeks longer.

The reviewers are asked to review for acceptability on these four points:
- Applicability to a practicing marketer
- Strong on conceptual basis or interesting case study
- Clarity of thought
- Solid summary

The last phrase, after final revision, is copy-edited for grammar, syntax, etc., which we do. Thus, a final proofing and, depending on the timing, it is always our intention to have the author see a final proof before typesetting.

The process may seem long and tedious at times but the author and we both have the same goal - excellence. Viewed from that perspective each review provides new insights and opportunities to achieve that goal. When the article is finally printed, all will agree that it was worth the trouble.

Copyright Policy:
Contents are copyrighted by this journal. All rights reserved. No part of the journal may be reproduced in any form, by microfilm, xerography or otherwise, or incorporated into any information retrieval systems, without the written permission of the copyright owner. Permission will be granted to authors desiring to republish their own articles or otherwise directly employ their articles.

Manuscript Submission:
A manuscript, abstract, and author's biography (up to 200 words) should be double spaced, with a margin on each side to facilitate comments. Also, please submit FOUR copies.

Send material to the editor.
It will be our pleasure to provide reprints of the published article and a subscription to each author.

Thank you for your interest.
Charles L. Martin, Ph.D., Editor

Journal of Sport Management

ADDRESS FOR SUBMISSION:

Trevor Slack, Editor
Journal of Sport Management
DeMontfort University, Bedford
School of Physical Education, Sport
  & Leisure
37 Lansdowne Road
Bedford, MK40 2BZ
UK
Phone: +44 1234 793313
Fax: +44 1234 350833
E-Mail: tslack@dmu.ac.uk
Web:
Address May Change: 6/30/01

PUBLICATION GUIDELINES:

Manuscript Length: 1-30
Copies Required: Five
Computer Submission: Yes
Format: MS Word
Fees to Review: 0.00 US$

Manuscript Style:
    American Psychological Association

CIRCULATION DATA:

Reader: Academics
Frequency of Issue: Quarterly
Copies per Issue: 1,001 - 2,000
Sponsor/Publisher: Human Kinetics
Subscribe Price: 42.00 US$ Individual
   126.00 US$ Institution
   26.00 US$ Student

REVIEW INFORMATION:

Type of Review: Blind Review
No. of External Reviewers: 3
No. of In House Reviewers: 0
Acceptance Rate: 11-20%
Time to Review: 1 - 2 Months
Reviewers Comments: Yes
Invited Articles: 0-5%
Fees to Publish: 0.00 US$

MANUSCRIPT TOPICS:
All Business related to Sport Management; Labor Relations & Human Resource Mgt.; Organizational Behavior & Theory; Organizational Development; Public Administration

MANUSCRIPT GUIDELINES/COMMENTS:

Editorial Policy

The *Journal of Sport Management* (JSM) publishes articles that focus on the theoretical and applied aspects of management related to sport, exercise, dance and play. Articles are evaluated on their merit for contributing to the understanding of sport management through theory development and application.

JSM publishes research and scholarly review articles short reports on replications, test development and data reanalysis (Research Notes); reports related to sport management in countries other than Canada and the United States (Beyond North America); editorials that focus on significant issues pertaining to sport management (Sport Management Perspectives) journal abstracts (Sport Management Digest); book reviews (Off the Press); and news items of interest to professionals in sport management (Management Memos). Manuscripts focusing on topics such as leadership motivation, communication, organization, professional preparation, ethics, marketing and financial administration related to sport and exercise are appropriate. Papers written from historical, psychological, philosophical, sociological, and other perspectives are encouraged. Papers focusing on sport management in n variety of settings are also desired—professional sport intercollegiate and interscholastic sport, health/sport clubs, sport arenas, and community recreational sports

JSM accepts articles that are derived from both experimental and experiential methodologies Laboratory and highly controlled field experiments may be appropriate for the study of certain sport management issues, as are field studies, surveys, case studies, observational methods and field evaluation approaches Articles submitted to JSM are judged on the appropriateness of the methods for the problem being studied rather than prescribing that certain methods are the only ones suitable for the study of sport management.

Papers investigating theoretical constructs, research that moves toward theory development, and articles that link theory with practice arc especially encouraged. JSM invites papers presenting new and/or controversial ideas ax well as those applying traditional concepts. Articles without a theoretical base arc also invited to the extent that they contribute to an understanding of sport management

Instructions to Authors
In preparing manuscripts for publication in the *Journal of Sport Management* (JSM), authors should follow the guidelines in the *Publication Manual of the American Psychological Association* (4th ed.), 1994. Copies are available in most libraries or may be obtained through the Order Dept., American Psychological Association, P.O. Box 2710, Hyattsville, MD 20784-0710.

A11 articles must be preceded by an abstract of no more than 150 words. Manuscripts must be double-spaced, including references and blocked quotations, and must be typed on standard 8 ½ - x 11-in. white paper with approximately ½ in. margins. Regular articles and reviews should not exceed 30 manuscript pages, and Research Notes should not exceed 15 pages. If footnotes are used, they should not exceed 6 lines each. All artwork must be submitted in original form and must be clean, crisp, and professional in appearance; freehand or typewritten lettering will not be accepted. PC-generated screens (i.e., dot patterns) do not reproduce well during the printing process and should not be used to create shading in figures. Stripe patterns or solids are better choices for shading. Figures can be submitted on disk if they are created in Macintosh Illustrator or Freehand or are saved in a cps, tiff, or pict format. All tables, figure captions, and footnotes must be grouped together on pages separate from the body of the text. Reference citations in the text must be accurate concerning dates of publication and spelling of author names, and they must cross-check with those in the reference list. Manuscripts will be summarily rejected if they do not follow the APA guidelines, Manuscripts will not be returned unless the authors request the return by including a self-addressed and stamped envelope.

The original manuscript and four copies should be sent to Trevor Slack, PhD, School of Physical Education, Sport & Leisure, DeMontfort University Bedford, 37 Lansdowne Road,

Bedford MK40 2BZ, UK. Manuscripts must not be submitted to another journal while they are under review by JSM. All manuscripts are evaluated by blind review. The name(s) of the authors) should not appear on the manuscript proper. The first page of the submission should include the title of the paper and the name and affiliation of each author, as well as the full mailing address, e-mail address, and fax number of the author who is to receive the galley proofs if the manuscript is accepted. The second page should show only the title at the top of the page and the running head at the bottom. Decisions regarding publication are based upon Editorial Board recommendations. Comments from reviewers concerning rejected manuscripts are made available to authors. Authors of manuscripts accepted for publication must transfer copyright to Human Kinetics Publishers, Inc.

Journal of Strategic Marketing

ADDRESS FOR SUBMISSION:

Nigel F. Piercy, Lloyd C. Harris, Editor
Journal of Strategic Marketing
Cardiff University
Cardiff Business School
Colum Drive
Cardiff, CF1 3EU
UK
Phone: 44 (0) 1228 75066
Fax: 44 (0) 1228 74419
E-Mail:
Web: www.routledge.co.uk
Address May Change:

PUBLICATION GUIDELINES:

Manuscript Length: 30+
Copies Required: Three
Computer Submission: Yes
Format: All formats, prefer Word
Fees to Review: 0.00 US$

Manuscript Style:
   Chicago Manual of Style

CIRCULATION DATA:

Reader: Academics
Frequency of Issue: Quarterly
Copies per Issue: Less than 1,000
Sponsor/Publisher: Routledge Journals
Subscribe Price: 425.00 US$ Institution
   85.00 US$ Individual
   60.00 US$ Member of Assns. Below

REVIEW INFORMATION:

Type of Review: Blind Review
No. of External Reviewers: 2
No. of In House Reviewers: No Reply
Acceptance Rate: 21-30%
Time to Review: 1 - 2 Months
Reviewers Comments: Yes
Invited Articles: 0-5%
Fees to Publish: 0.00 US$

MANUSCRIPT TOPICS:
Marketing Theory & Applications

MANUSCRIPT GUIDELINES/COMMENTS:

Subscription Price: 60 US$ for the American Marketing Association, Academy of Marketing Science, and Academy of Marketing members.

Aims and Scope:
Journal of Strategic Marketing publishes papers on key aspects of the interface between marketing and strategic management. It is a vehicle for discussing long-range activities where marketing has a role to play in managing the long-term objectives and strategies of companies. The objectives of the Journal are as follows:

1)   To bridge the disciplines of marketing and strategic management, and to address the development of knowledge concerning the role that marketing has to play in the management of strategy.

2) To provide a vehicle for the advancement of knowledge in the field of strategic marketing and to stimulate research in this area.

3) To consider the role of marketing as an orientation of management at the strategic level of organizations.

4) Explore the overall management of the marketing function within total corporate management, with particular focus on issues of concern to marketing managers, directors and vice presidents.

5) To publish state of the art papers, empirical research results, practical aspects of theory, case studies, new methodological developments, conceptual developments, and to encourage published discussion on articles.

Issues that the Journal covers include:
- Marketing philosophy in corporate management.
- The role of marketing in strategic planning.
- Marketing information systems in relation to company wide needs.
- Market and industry stakeholder needs.
- International strategies.
- SBU analysis and decision making.
- Marketing related synergies.
- Integrating marketing planning with strategic planning.
- The management of marketing-led change.
- The development and utilization of marketing plans.
- Resource allocation in strategic and marketing plans.
- HRM related to marketing personnel.
- The implementation of strategic and marketing plans.
- Marketing effectiveness at the operational and strategic levels.
- The utilization and development of control systems.
- Relationship Marketing

Articles should be between 4000-6000 words. Three copies should be sent to one of the Editors at Cardiff Business School, Colum Drive, Cardiff, CF1 3EU, UK

Submission of papers on disk
We are able to accept most common forms of disks. However, authors must also submit three hard copies of the paper for copyediting purposes. If for some reason we are unable to use the disk, the paper will be typeset in the usual manner.

Presentation
Contributions should be typed on A4 paper with double-line spacing and wide margins (at least 2.5€cm). Each article should be presented as follows:
- Title page: title, authors' names and addresses and the name, address, and telephone and fax numbers of the author to whom all correspondence concerning the article should be sent.

- Second page: title, abstract of about 150 words and up to six keywords for indexing purposes.
- Main body of the paper: presented as given below.

References
The Harvard system should be used; that is the name of the author and date of publication are cited in the text. The references are listed in alphabetical order at the end of the article in the following style:

Journal articles
Hutt, M.D., Reigen, P.H. and Ronchetto, J.R. (1988) Tracing emergent processes in marketing strategy formulation. Journal of Marketing 52, 4--19.

Articles in books, conference proceedings etc.
Wensley, J.R.C. (1987) Marketing strategy. In: M.J. Barker (ed) The Marketing Book, London: Heinemann.

Books
Jain, S.C. (1985) Marketing Planning and Strategy, 2nd Edn, Cincinnati: South-Western.

Tables and figures
Each should be numbered in the order in which they are referred to in the text and cited as Fig. 1, Figs 2--5, Table 1, Tables 1 and 2 etc.

Figures and tables should not be included in the text but accompany the manuscript on separate pages.

Figures should be originals (not photocopies), printed from a laser printer or drawn in black ink on white card. The size of any labelling should be sufficient to allow for reductions of up to 50%. Figure captions should be grouped together on a separate sheet.

Footnotes
These should not be used unless absolutely essential. If included they should be kept to a minimum, and numbered consecutively on separate sheets.

Copyright
Submission of an article to the *Journal of Strategic Marketing* is taken to imply that it presents original unpublished work which is not under consideration for publication elsewhere.

On acceptance of a paper the authors will be asked to assign copyright to the publishers, Routledge, by signing a copyright form.

Refereeing
All articles will be double-blind refereered, and comments will be communicated to the authors. Articles will only be accepted for publication when they have been modified in line with the referees' comments.

Proofs
Proofs will be sent to the corresponding author (unless otherwise specified) for correction. The author should return the proofs within three days of receipt to avoid delay to publication. Extensive alterations which were not in the original manuscript are strongly discouraged.

Journal of Targeting, Measurement, and Analysis for Targeting

ADDRESS FOR SUBMISSION:

Alexandra Davies, Asst. Pub. Editor
Journal of Targeting, Measurement, and Analysis for Targeting
Henry Stewart Publications
Museum House
25 Museum Street
London, WC1A 1JT
UK
Phone: 44 0 171-323-2916
Fax: 44 0 171-323-2918
E-Mail: alex@hspublications.co.uk
Web: www.henrystewart.co.uk
Address May Change:

CIRCULATION DATA:

Reader: , 65% Business, 35% Academic
Frequency of Issue: Quarterly
Copies per Issue: 1,001 - 2,000
Sponsor/Publisher: Henry Stewart Publications
Subscribe Price: 330.00 US$
    210.00 Pounds

PUBLICATION GUIDELINES:

Manuscript Length: 2,500 - 5,000 words
Copies Required: Three
Computer Submission: Yes
Format: MS Word/WordPerfect
Fees to Review: 0.00 US$

Manuscript Style:
    , Cambridge

REVIEW INFORMATION:

Type of Review: Blind Review
No. of External Reviewers: 3
No. of In House Reviewers: 2
Acceptance Rate: 50%
Time to Review: 1 - 2 Months
Reviewers Comments: Yes
Invited Articles: 31-50%
Fees to Publish: 0.00 US$

MANUSCRIPT TOPICS:

Advertising & Promotion Management; Business Education; Business Information Systems (MIS); Communication; Direct Marketing; Global Business; Marketing Research; Marketing Theory & Applications; Non Profit Organizations; Operations Research/Statistics; Organizational Behavior & Theory; Organizational Development; Strategic Management Policy

MANUSCRIPT GUIDELINES/COMMENTS:

1. Contributions should be between 2,000 and 5,000 words in length. All submissions should be typewritten and double spaced.

2. The Journal's Editors and Editorial Board particularly welcome submissions which present case study material, new approaches, techniques, empirical research or conceptual papers. All articles should be accompanied by a short abstract outlining the paper's aims and subject matter.

3. All articles should be accompanied by up to six keywords.

4. Articles should be accompanied by a short (about 80 words) description of the author(s) and, if appropriate, the organization of which he or she is a member.

5. Authors should not seek to use the Journal as a vehicle for marketing any specific product or service.

6. Authors should avoid the use of language or slang which is not in keeping with the professional and academic style of the Journal.

7. Titles of organizations etc should be written out first in full and thereafter in initials.

8. Articles should be supported by references. For all Henry Stewart Journals excluding Corporate Reputation Review, Tourism and Hospitality Research, Journal of Fashion Marketing and Management, Journal of Small Business and Enterprise Development, Journal of Asset Management and International Journal of Police Science Management, these should be set out in accordance with the Vancouver referencing system. References for the Journals listed above should be set out in accordance with the Harvard referencing system.

9. Photographs and illustrations supporting articles should be submitted where appropriate. Photographs should be good quality positives, printed from the original negatives and preferably in black and white only. Figures and other line illustrations should be submitted in good quality originals and a copy of the data should also be included.

10. Authors must ensure that references to named people and/or organizations are accurate, not rascist or sexist and without libellous implications.

11. All contributions sent to the Publisher, whether invited or not, will be submitted to the Journal's Editors and Editorial Board. Any such contribution must bear the author's full name and address, even if this is not for publication. Contributions, whether published pseudonymously or not, are accepted on the strict understanding that the author is responsible for the accuracy of all opinion, technical comment, factual report, data, figures, illustrations and photographs. Publication does not necessarily imply that these are the opinions of the Editorial Board, Editors or the Publisher, nor does the Board, Editors or Publisher accept any liability for the accuracy of such comment, report and other technical and factual information. The Publisher will, however, strive to ensure that all opinion, comments, reports, data, figures, illustrations and photographs are accurate, insofar as it is within its abilities to do so. The Publisher reserves the right to edit, abridge or omit material submitted for publication.

12. All Articles submitted for publication will be subject to a double-blind refereeing procedure.

13. The author bears the responsibility for checking whether material submitted is subject to copyright or ownership rights, eg photographs, illustrations, trade literature and data. Where use is so restricted, the Publisher must be informed with the submission of the material.

14. No contribution will be accepted which has been published elsewhere, unless it is expressly invited or agreed by the Publisher. Articles and contributions published become the copyright of the Publisher, unless otherwise agreed.

15. All reasonable efforts are made to ensure accurate reproduction of text, photographs and illustrations. The Publisher does not accept responsibility for mistakes, be they editorial or typographical, nor for consequences resulting from them.

16. Submissions should be sent to Henry Stewart Publications, Museum House, 25 Museum Street, London WC1A 1JT, email: submissions@hspublications.co.uk. **Please clearly state for which journal you are contributing.**

Journal of the Academy of Marketing Science

ADDRESS FOR SUBMISSION:

Rajan Varadarajan, Editor
Journal of the Academy of Marketing
 Science
Texas A&M University
Department of Marketing
4112 TAMU
College Station, TX 77843-4112
USA
Phone: 979-862-1010
Fax: 972-862-1020
E-Mail: varadarajan@tamu.edu
Web: www.bus.miami.edu/ams/
Address May Change:

PUBLICATION GUIDELINES:

Manuscript Length: 35
Copies Required: Four
Computer Submission: No
Format: N/A
Fees to Review: 0.00 US$

Manuscript Style:
 See Manuscript Guidelines

CIRCULATION DATA:

Reader: Academics
Frequency of Issue: Quarterly
Copies per Issue: 1,001 - 2,000
Sponsor/Publisher: Academy of Marketing
 Science/ Sage Publications
Subscribe Price: 85.00 US$ Individual
 265.00 US$ Institution

REVIEW INFORMATION:

Type of Review: Blind Review
No. of External Reviewers: 3
No. of In House Reviewers: 0
Acceptance Rate: 31-50%
Time to Review: 2 - 3 Months
Reviewers Comments: No Reply
Invited Articles: 0-5%
Fees to Publish: 0.00 US$

MANUSCRIPT TOPICS:
Advertising & Promotion Management; Consumer Behavior; Direct Marketing; Marketing Management; Marketing Research; Marketing Theory & Applications; Retailing; Sales/Selling; Services

MANUSCRIPT GUIDELINES/COMMENTS:

The *Journal of the Academy of Marketing Science* is the official journal of the Academy of Marketing Science. It is an international, refereed journal intended to further the science of marketing throughout the world by promoting the conduct of research and the dissemination of research results through the study and improvement of marketing as an economic, ethical, and social force.

Instructions To Contributors
Manuscripts must be double-spaced on 8 " x 11" non-erasable bond, leaving margins of at least 1". Manuscript length should be reasonable for the contribution offered. Submit four (4) clear letter-quality copies to Dr. Rajan Varadarajan, Editor, Journal of the Academy of

Marketing Science, Department of Marketing, Department of Marketing, Texas A&M University, 4112 TAMU, College Station, TX 77843-4112, (979) 862-1019. *Please proofread the manuscript very carefully.*

Manuscripts are reviewed by the editor and at least two members of the AMS Editorial Review Board or by occasional reviewers. The author's name and affiliation are removed before reviewing in order to ensure objectivity. If at all possible, please do not identify the author(s) in the body of the paper either directly or by citation. Articles accepted for publication should be accompanied by a copy of the article saved on an IBM compatible disk, preferably in WordPerfect or ASCII.

With the submission of a manuscript, the following three items should be included:

1. Cover page showing title, each author's name, affiliation, complete address, telephone and fax number, and the category of the article. Select one category from the following: Consumer and Buyer Behavior, Channels, Industrial, Marketing Management, Marketing Theory and History, Multinational (International), Research Methods, Strategic Marketing Planning, Marketing Models, Forecasting Models, Marketing Education, Promotion, Pricing, Service, Not-for-Profit, Ethics and Public Policy, Retailing, or other.

2. Information about the author(s) up to 100 words each, including terminal degree, written as a paragraph on a separate sheet to appear at manuscript end

3. Abstract of up to 150 words.

Mathematical Notation

Notations should be clearly explained within the text. Equations should be centered on the page. If equations are numbered, type the number in parentheses flush with the right margin. Unusual symbols and Greek letters should be identified. For equations that may be too wide to fit in a single column, indicate appropriate breaks.

Tables and Figures

Indicate table and figure placement within text. Each table should be typed on a separate page at the end of the article. Tables should be typed flush with the left-hand margin and have proper labeling of axes, column headings, and other notations. The table number and title should be typed on separate lines. Tables on disk should be free of cells or other dividing elements.

Figures and artwork must be high quality and camera ready, such as clean, black-and-white laser printouts. Each figure should appear on a separate page. Do not send glossies.

Endnotes and References

Use endnotes only if absolutely necessary. Endnotes should be numbered consecutively and double-spaced on a separate, attached sheet.

Reference citations within the text should consist of the author's last name and date of publication, without punctuation, enclosed within parentheses, and should be inserted before punctuation and/or at a logical break in the sentence. If several citations are needed, separate them with semicolons, and list alphabetically. Give the page number only if necessary. If the author's name has just been listed in the text, the date in parentheses is sufficient. If two or more works by an author have the same year, distinguish them by placing a, b, etc. after the year. Use et al. for works by four or more authors. For example:

Jones' latest proposal (1979) has been questioned by some (Boston 1981; Brown 1990), but is generally accepted by others (Fritz 1979; Lang 1979; Rotwang 1984). Investigators (Cockburn et al. 1985; Hodges McCollum, and Hall 1981; Lee and King 1983) have found that . . .

References should be double-spaced and attached on a separate page. Works by a single author, list chronologically; two authors, alphabetically and then chronologically; three authors, the same; four or more, list chronologically. References should be in the following format:

Books: Bagozzi, Richard P. 1980. *Causal Models in Marketing.* New York: Wiley

Journals: Singh, Jagdip. 1991. "Understanding the Structure of Consumers' *Marketing Science 19* (Summer): 223-244

Three or More Authors: Zeithaml, Valarie A., Leonard L. Berry, and A. Parasuraman. 1993. "The Nature and Determinants of Customer Experiences of Service." *Journal of the Academy of Marketing Science 21* (Winter): 1-12.

Article in a Book Edited by Another Author: Levitt, Theodore. 1988. "The Globalization of Markets." In *Multinational Marketing Management.* Eds. Robert D. Buzzell and John A. Quelch., **by** Reading MA: Addison-Wesley, 186-205.

Unpublished Dissertations: Paterson, Karen S. 1985. "The Effects of Bilingual Labels in Buyer Behavior." Dissertation. University of California at Irvine.

Journal of the Market Research Society

ADDRESS FOR SUBMISSION:

Stephen Buck
Journal of the Market Research Society
Taylor Nelson AGB plc
The Research Centre
Westgate
London, W5 1UA
UK
Phone: +44 181-967 0007
Fax: +44 181-967 4060
E-Mail:
Web:
Address May Change:

PUBLICATION GUIDELINES:

Manuscript Length: Approx. 5000 words
Copies Required: Four
Computer Submission: Yes
Format: On Acceptance/IBM Compatible
Fees to Review: 0.00 US$

Manuscript Style:
    See Manuscript Guidelines

CIRCULATION DATA:

Reader: Business Persons, Academics
Frequency of Issue: Quarterly
Copies per Issue: 2,001 - 3,000
Sponsor/Publisher: Market Research
    Society
Subscribe Price: 99.00 Pounds UK
    115.50 Pounds Overseas

REVIEW INFORMATION:

Type of Review: Editorial Review
No. of External Reviewers: 1
No. of In House Reviewers: 3
Acceptance Rate: 21-30%
Time to Review: 4 - 6 Months
Reviewers Comments: No
Invited Articles: 6-10%
Fees to Publish: 0.00 US$

MANUSCRIPT TOPICS:
Communication; Marketing Research; Marketing Theory & Applications; Production/Operations

MANUSCRIPT GUIDELINES/COMMENTS:

JRMS aims to publish papers and shorter notes concerning technical advances and practical applications, appraisals of specific problem areas, and correspondence and reviews in the broader field of marketing and social research. All main papers are refereed.

Four copies of each paper should be sent to Dr. Stephan Buck. On acceptance an IBM-compatible disk will be required in addition to hard copy.

Although there is no strict ruling on **length** of paper, main papers should be between 2000 and 5000 words. Shorter papers of less than 2000 words will be included in the Miscellany section.

Correspondence on papers which have appeared in the Journal are referred to the author of the relevant paper for comment before publication.

Tables should be typed on separate pages and prepared without vertical lines. Each table should be referred to in numerical order in the text.

References: All references to books, monographic articles and statistical sources should be identified at the appropriate point in the text by last name of author, year of publication and pagination where appropriate, all within parentheses, e.g. when the author's name is in the text: Smith (1974). References should be listed at the end of the article in alphabetical order as follows:

BUTLER, D.B. & STOKES, D. (1969). Political changes in Britain. Forces shaping electoral choice. London: Macmillan.
DIXON, L.C.W. (1971). A dynamic trend analysis of the opinion polls predicted the correct result. Journal of the Market Research Society, 13, 1, 21-24.

Footnotes should be used only for alternative observations.

Figures should be provided in a form suitable for photo reproduction.

Please avoid the use of complicated mathematical notation which requires special setting.

Each paper should be summarised by an **abstract** which is printed ahead of each paper and should enable any reader of the *Journal of The Market Research Society* to know what it is about.

A brief **biographical note** should be supplied including full name, appointment, name of organisation and address.

Overseas authors should recognise that work cited in their papers should cover British as well as overseas research in the relevant subject.

General correspondence about the JMRS should be addressed to:
Phyllis Vangelder, 17 Kenelm Close, Harrow, Middlesex HA1 3TE.
Telephone +44 181-904 2019. Fax +44 181-908 6680.

25 **reprints** of each article are provided free. Additional reprints can be purchased.

Journal of Transport Economics and Policy

ADDRESS FOR SUBMISSION:

Steve Morrison, Managing Editor
Journal of Transport Economics and Policy
University of Bath
Claverton Down
Bath
, BA2 7AY
England
Phone: +44 1225 826302
Fax: +44 1225 826767
E-Mail: mnskam@bath.ac.uk
Web: www.bath.ac.uk/academic/jourals/
Address May Change:

PUBLICATION GUIDELINES:

Manuscript Length: 20+
Copies Required: Two
Computer Submission: No
Format: N/A
Fees to Review: 0.00 US$

Manuscript Style:
  See Manuscript Guidelines

CIRCULATION DATA:

Reader: Academics, Professionals
Frequency of Issue: 3 Times/Year
Copies per Issue: 1,001 - 2,000
Sponsor/Publisher: London School of
  Economics, University of Bath
Subscribe Price: 54.00 US$ Individual
  120.00 US$ Institution
  60.00 Pounds Indv., 120.00 Pounds Inst.

REVIEW INFORMATION:

Type of Review: Editorial Review
No. of External Reviewers: 2
No. of In House Reviewers: 2
Acceptance Rate: 21-30%
Time to Review: 4 - 6 Months
Reviewers Comments: Yes
Invited Articles: 0-5%
Fees to Publish: 0.00 US$

MANUSCRIPT TOPICS:
Transportation/Physical Distribution

MANUSCRIPT GUIDELINES/COMMENTS:

Manuscript Guidelines/Comments

1. Articles range from fundamental studies making original contributions to analysis, to those exploring innovations in policy. All articles are refereed by appropriate experts, and editorial policy is assisted by a distinguished international Editorial Board. The Journal takes no sides on transport issues; the interest and academic merit of articles are the sole criteria for acceptance.

2. The Journal is distributed worldwide; it has subscribers from over 70 countries. This is reflected in its coverage, with transport practices in over 30 countries and every continent forming the basis for articles. Many aspects of urban traffic have been examined both in general and in the context of particular cites, though invariably with universal application. Topics include rail, air and motor vehicle modes, as well as shipping and infrastructure. There are regular notes on developments in government policy.

3. Contributors range from mathematicians and theoretical economists to practicing consultants, administrators and people involved in business. Their nationalities are varied as the countries about which they write.

4. At least two copies of a manuscript should be typed on one side of the paper only, in double spacing. Pages should be numbered. If the article is accepted, authors will be asked to provide a copy in DOS format.

5. Articles should contain a final section in which the author sets out his or her main conclusions in a way which will be at least broadly intelligible to the non-specialist reader. Contributors must also send two copies of an abstract, not exceeding 100 words. The abstract should state clearly (if possible in the opening sentence) the main conclusions of the article.

6. Camera-ready copy of diagrams must be provided with the manuscript; otherwise, if the article is accepted, a charge will be made to cover the cost of artwork. Diagrams should be clearly drawn and accompanied by the basic statistics that were required for their preparation; the axes must be clearly labelled; the reader must be able to understand the diagrams without hunting in the text for explanations.

7. Where mathematical arguments are used, the full working necessary for justifying each step of the argument should accompany the article, in order to assist the referee. The detailed workings will not be published. Care should be taken to ensure that all signs and symbols are clear and to avoid any possible confusion between, for example, figure 1 and letter 1.

8. Statistical tables should be clearly headed and the reader should be able to understand the meaning of each row or column without hunting in the text for explanations of symbols, etc. Units of measurement, base-dates for index numbers, geographical area covered and sources should be clearly stated. Authors are fully responsible for the accuracy of the data and for checking their proofs; whenever they feel that the referee would have difficulty in testing the derivation of their statistics, they should provide supplementary notes on the methods used, which will not be published.

9. Footnotes should be brief, as they are placed at the foot of the page. Any explanation requiring more than a very few lines should be either included in the text or placed in an appendix at the end of the article.

10. References should be carefully checked, and complete in respect of the place and year of publication. If a bibliographical list is given, it should follow the style used in the current issue. Only these works cited in the text should be included.

11. Authors are expected to read proofs expeditiously and to keep corrections down to a very low Level. If alterations are made at the proof stage, the editors reserve the right either not to give effect to them or to make a charge.

12. Because of the heavy pressure on space, the editors will give preference to articles which deal succinctly with an issue which is both important and clearly defined. The editors will not consider articles which have been submitted elsewhere.

13. **Comments on Published Articles.** Anyone wanting to submit comments on a Journal article is asked first to send a copy to the author, inviting him to send the commentator his observations and in particular to explain any points on which the commentator has misunderstood what the author was saying. The commentator is asked to allow the author a reasonable time to reply before he sends anything to the editors, and to enclose any reply which he may have received, so that the comment and rejoinder may be published together.

1. Articles range from fundamental studies making original contributions to analysis, to those exploring innovations in policy. All articles are refereed by appropriate experts, and editorial policy is assisted by a distinguished international editorial board.

2. The Journal is distributed worldwide; it has subscribers from over 70 countries. This is reflected in its coverage, with transport practices in over 30 countries and every continent forming the basis for articles. Many aspects of urban traffic have been examined both in general and in the context of particular cites, though invariably with universal application. Topics include rail, air and motor vehicle modes, as well as shipping infrastructure. There are regular notes on developments in government policy.

3. Contributors range from mathematicians and theoretical economists to practicing consultants, administrators and people involved in business. Their nationalities are varied as the countries about which they write.

4. At least two copies of manuscript should be typed on one side of the paper only, in double spacing. Pages should be numbered. If the article is accepted, authors will be asked to provide a disk copy.

5. Articles should contain a final section in which the author sets out his or her main conclusions in a way which will be at least broadly intelligible to the non-specialist reader. Contributors must also send two copies of an abstract, not exceeding 100 words. The abstract should state clearly (if possible in the opening sentence) the main conclusions of the article.

6. Camera-ready copy of diagrams must be provided with the manuscript; otherwise, if the article is accepted, a charge will be made to cover the cost of artwork. Diagrams should be clearly drawn and accompanied by the basic statistics that were required for their preparation; the axes must be clearly labelled; the reader must be able to understand the diagrams without hunting in the text for explanations.

7. Where mathematical arguments are used, the full working necessary for justifying each step of the argument should accompany the article, in order to assist the referee. The detailed workings will not be published. Care should be taken to ensure that all signs and symbols are clear and to avoid any possible confusion between, for example, figure 1 and letter 1.

8. Statistical tables should be clearly headed and the reader should be able to understand the meaning of each row or column without hunting in the text for explanations of symbols, etc.

Units of measurement, base-dates for index numbers, geographical area covered and sources should be clearly stated. Authors are fully responsible for the accuracy of the data and for checking their proofs; whenever they feel that the referee would have difficulty in testing the derivation of their statistics, they should provide supplementary notes on the methods used, which will not be published.

9. Footnotes should be brief, as they are placed at the foot of the page. Any explanation requiring more than a very few lines should be either included in the text or placed in an appendix at the end of the article.

10. References should be carefully checked, and complete in respect of the place and year of publication. If a bibliographical list is given, it should follow the style used in the current issue. Only these works cited in the text should be included.

11. Authors are expected to read proofs expeditiously and to keep corrections down to a very low level. If alterations are made at the proof stage, the editors reserve the right either not to give effect to them or to make a charge.

12. Because of the heavy pressure on space, the editors will give preference to articles which deal succinctly with an issue which is both important and clearly defined. The editors will not consider articles which have been submitted elsewhere.

13. **Comments on published articles**. Anyone wanting to submit comments on a Journal article is asked first to send a copy to the author, inviting him to send the commentator his observations and in particular to explain any points on which the commentator has misunderstood what the author was saying. The commentator is asked to allow the author a reasonable time to reply before he sends anything to the editors, and to enclose any reply which he may have received, so that the convent and rejoinder may be published together.

14. The editors will not consider articles that have been submitted elsewhere.

Journal of Transportation Law, Logistics, and Policy

ADDRESS FOR SUBMISSION:

James F. Bromley, Editor-in-Chief
Journal of Transportation Law, Logistics, and Policy
Association for Transportation Law, Logistics, and Policy
19564 Club House Road
Montgomery Village, MD 20886-3002
USA
Phone: 301-670-6733
Fax: 301-670-6735
E-Mail: ATLLP@aol.com
Web:
Address May Change:

PUBLICATION GUIDELINES:

Manuscript Length: 21-25
Copies Required: Two
Computer Submission: Yes
Format: WordPerfecct/MS-DOS
Fees to Review: 0.00 US$

Manuscript Style:
 Uniform System of Citation (Harvard Blue Book), & Chicago Manual of Style

CIRCULATION DATA:

Reader: , Legal Transport, Professionals
Frequency of Issue: Quarterly
Copies per Issue: 1,001 - 2,000
Sponsor/Publisher: Professional Association and Non-Profit Corporation
Subscribe Price: 55.00 US$
 60.00 US$ Canada
 65.00 US$ All Others

REVIEW INFORMATION:

Type of Review: Editorial Review
No. of External Reviewers: 0
No. of In House Reviewers: 1
Acceptance Rate: 70%
Time to Review: 1 - 2 Months
Reviewers Comments: No
Invited Articles: 0-5%
Fees to Publish: 0.00 US$

MANUSCRIPT TOPICS:
Business Law, Public Responsibility & Ethics; Logistics; Transportation Law, Policy and Procedure; Transportation/Physical Distribution

MANUSCRIPT GUIDELINES/COMMENTS:

The *Journal of Transportation Law, Logistics And Policy* is published by the Association of Transportation Practitioners, 19564 Club House Road, Gaithersburg, Maryland 20879. The Journal is published quarterly in the Fall, Winter, Spring, and Summer and is directed toward the needs of transportation professionals (attorney and nonattorney, traffic and distribution managers, members of faculty of post secondary educational institutions, and students) interested in transportation law, regulation, practice, and procedure.

Editorial Policy
The editorial policy of the *Journal of Transportation Law, Logistics And Policy* is to publish articles of a scholarly nature on any subject having to do with transportation --law, practice,

legislation, regulation, history, theory, economics, statistics, or any other aspect --including non-transportation subjects of interest to practitioners. Our principal concern is transportation in the United States and Canada, but we welcome also articles about transportation in other countries.

Manuscripts Accepted/Denied
No manuscript can be accepted for publication in the Journal until it has been reviewed by the Editor in Chief and Executive Editor. The Editor in Chief, in conjunction with the editorial office, will ultimately make the decision of publication.

Manuscripts are received by the Journal editorial office and, when accepted for publication, are for the "exclusive" use of the *Journal of Transportation Law, Logistics and Policy*. A manuscript that has been accepted by or that has already appeared in a book or in another periodical of general circulation, is ordinarily not acceptable for publication. There can be some exceptions, i.e., material from a forthcoming book. Publication of a series of articles to appear in successive issues of the Journal is not usual, and special permission is made with the Editor in Chief.

The Journal must be cautious against articles that are designed too directly to influence on-going litigation, as this violates ethical rules and distorts the Journal from its purpose of serving only the cause of scholarship. This concern, however, by no means prevents us from publishing articles on subjects regarding pending cases where we are satisfied that the author(s) are not acting as counsel or are not otherwise improperly attempting to influence the court or agency in the pending case.

Speeches, as such, are not published in the Journal. However, a speech may serve as the basis for an article and will be accepted when it follows the guidelines set forth in the "Manuscripts Preparation" section of this style sheet.

Manuscript submission
All correspondence regarding submission of manuscripts should be directed to James F. Bromley, Editor in Chief, *Journal of Transportation Law, Logistics and Policy*.

Manuscript preparation
Since space is at a premium in the Journal, manuscripts should be between 6,000 and 10,000 words, typically fifteen to twenty-five double spaced type-written pages. Articles of shorter or longer length will be considered.

Two copies of each manuscript should be submitted to the Editor in Chief. Since editing and page composition are done at the editorial office, we welcome and encourage manuscript submissions on 5 1/4" or 3 1/2" (MS-DOS operating system, WordPerfect 5.0, 5.1 or 6.0 formats) diskettes. If it is not possible to format your diskette to these specifications, you may submit a manuscript on a diskette of your choosing. A hard copy of the manuscript must accompany the diskette.

Manuscripts should be double-spaced with pages numbered consecutively and with margins of at least one inch at the top and bottom, and with 1 1/4" right and left margins. The editorial format of the *Journal of Transportation Law, Logistics and Policy* follows the principles of the latest edition of *A Manual of Style* and *A Uniform System of Citation*. These publications may be useful as guides in preparing your manuscript.

Author(S) Biography
Please include a brief biographical sketch on a separate sheet of paper. This may include title, company affiliation, and educational background (degrees, colleges, and dates). Other information may include admissions to practice, previous experience, and memberships in professional organizations.

Footnotes
Footnotes should be numbered consecutively throughout the manuscript and displayed on the page where they appear (rather than end notes when possibly). The Journal uses no italics in footnotes.

Every reference to an article should provide information in the following order: The author's complete name (first name, middle name or initial, last name); title of article (in quotes ["I"]); volume number; name of publication; date of publication; beginning page number of the article followed by the later page number or numbers which the author may wish to site or quote from.

Example:
Michael L. Closen, "A Proposed Code of Professional Responsibility for Law Reviews," 63 Notre Dame L. Rev. (1988), p. 55, 58.

Every reference to a book should provide specific information in the following order: The author's complete name (first name, middle name or initial, last name); the title of the book; place of publication; name of publisher, and year in parenthesis, and, where applicable, specific page references. If there is more than one volume or edition, this information should also be given.

Example:
John Guandolo, Transportation Law, 4th ed., (Dubuque, IA: William C. Brown Company, 1983), pp. 127-128.

Tables, Graphs, Charts, and Figures
Since the editorial office of the Journal supplies the printer with camera-ready copy, all tables, graphs, charts, and figures to be included in a manuscript must be originals or of good quality sufficient to be photographed. Tables, graphs, charts, and figures should be numbered consecutively through-out the manuscript. Footnotes to tables, graphs, charts, and figures should be designated by letters and should appear immediately underneath the related table, graph, chart, or figure.

Each original table, graph, chart, and figure should be put on a separate page and placed at the beginning of the manuscript. Please number all the pages that contain footnotes, references, tables, etc.

Mathematical Equations
Equations should be typed on a separate line and carry consecutive Arabic numerals in parentheses at the right-hand margin. These equations should be accurately aligned, with superscripts and subscripts properly located. References to equations in the text should be by the equation number placed in the parentheses.

Publication of Manuscript
The Editor in Chief reviews the manuscripts and edits to insure reasonable consistency of style throughout the Journal. The Editor makes the manuscript as complete and correct as possible before it goes to the editorial office for page composition. The *Journal of Transportation Law, Logistics And Policy* is copyrighted by the Association of Transportation Practitioners. After each article is accepted for publication, the author or authors are sent a notice of acceptance that includes a statement regarding copyright. This statement gives the author a choice whether to retain copyright or transfer it to the Association. Even when the author transfers the copyright, the author retains the exclusive right to prepare derivative works based upon the article.

If requests for permission to copy from or reprint an article are received they will be granted by the Journal editorial office, only upon the written concurrence of the author(s).

At the time a manuscript is accepted for publication, we cannot predict the exact issue in which it will appear. This decision is influenced by such factors as priorities of other manuscripts, timeliness of articles, number of pages, and balancing of subjects of articles.

Complimentary Copies and Reprints
Although no payment is made for articles, authors receive two complimentary copies of the issue in which their article appears. Additional (self-covered) reprints are available at cost to authors, if the editorial office is advised of such request prior to publication of the article.

Journal of Transportation Management

ADDRESS FOR SUBMISSION:

Jerry W. Wilson, Editor
Journal of Transportation Management
Georgia Southern University
College of Business Administration
Department of Marketing and Logistics
PO Box 8154
Stateboro, GA 30460-8154
USA
Phone: 912-681-0257
Fax: 912-871-1523
E-Mail: jwwilson@gsaix2.cc.gasou.edu
Web:
Address May Change:

PUBLICATION GUIDELINES:

Manuscript Length: 25 Maximum
Copies Required: Four
Computer Submission: No
Format: N/A
Fees to Review: 0.00 US$

Manuscript Style:
    See Manuscript Guidelines

CIRCULATION DATA:

Reader: Academics, Professional
Frequency of Issue: 2 Times/Year
Copies per Issue: Less than 1,000
Sponsor/Publisher: Delta Nu Alpha,
    International Transportation Fraternity
Subscribe Price: 35.00 US$

REVIEW INFORMATION:

Type of Review: Blind Review
No. of External Reviewers: 2
No. of In House Reviewers: 1
Acceptance Rate: 35%
Time to Review: 4 - 6 Months
Reviewers Comments: Yes
Invited Articles: 6-10%
Fees to Publish: 0.00 US$

MANUSCRIPT TOPICS:
Transportation/Physical Distribution

MANUSCRIPT GUIDELINES/COMMENTS:

The *Journal Of Transportation Management* (JIM) is sponsored by Delta Nu Alpha International Transportation Fraternity and published by the College of Business Administration at Georgia Southern University.

Editorial Policy
The primary purpose of the JTM is to serve as a channel for the dissemination of information relevant to the management of transportation and logistics activities in any and all types of organizations. Articles accepted for publication will be of interest to both academics and practitioners and will specifically address the managerial implications of the subject matter. Articles that are strictly theoretical in nature, with no direct application to the management of transportation and logistics activities, would be inappropriate for the JTM.

Acceptable topics for submission include, but are not limited to carrier management, modal and intermodal transportation, international transportation issues, transportation safety, marketing of transportation services, domestic and international transportation policy, transportation economics, customer service, and the changing technology of transportation. Articles from related areas, such as third party logistics and purchasing and materials management, are acceptable as long as they are specifically related to the management of transportation and logistics activities.

Submissions from industry practitioners and from practitioners co-authoring with academics are particularly encouraged in order to increase the interaction between the two groups. Authors considering the submission of an article to the JTM are encouraged to contact the editor for help in determining relevance of topic and material.

The opinions expressed in published articles are those of the authors and do not necessarily reflect the opinions of the editor, the Editorial Review Board, Delta Nu Alpha International Transportation Fraternity, or Georgia Southern University.

GUIDELINES FOR SUBMISSION/PUBLICATION
Front Matter
1. First page - Title of the paper, name and position of the author(s), author(s) complete address(es) and telephone number(s), e-mail address(es), and any acknowledgement of assistance.

2. Second page - A brief biographical sketch of each author including name, degree(s) held, title or position, organization or institution, previous publications and research interests.

3. Third page - Title of the paper without author name(s) and a brief abstract of no more than 100 words summarizing the article.

Formatting
1. Manuscripts should be typed, double-spaced (body of text only), on white 8 ½ by 11 inch paper.

2. Submit four (4) paper copies of the manuscript for review. It is not necessary to send a disk for the initial review. However, to save time and effort if accepted, the article should be prepared using either: WordPerfect for Windows or MS Word for Windows.

3. Accepted articles, in final form, are to be submitted on disk (in WPWIN or MSWORD format as described above) and in hardcopy. Note: Macintosh versions of WPWIN and MSWORD are **not** acceptable.

4. The entire manuscript should have 1" margins on all sides in Times 12-point font. Times New Roman or Century Schoolbook are both acceptable.

5. The entire manuscript must be typed **Left-Justified**, with the exception of tables and figures.

Title Page and Abstract
1. The manuscript title should be printed in Times 12-point and in all capital letters and bold print.

2. Author(s) affiliations(s) are to be printed in upper and lower case letters below the . Author(s) are to be listed with affiliation(s) only.

3. The abstract should be 100 words or less.

Body of Manuscript
1. Main headings are bolded and in all caps.

2. First level headings are upper/lower case and bolded.

3. Second level headings are upper/lower case.

4. The body is NOT indented, rather a full blank line is left between paragraphs.

5. A full blank line should be left between all headings and paragraphs.

6. Unnecessary hard returns should not be used at the end of each line.

Tables and Figures
1. **Only** Tables and Figures are to appear in camera-ready format!

2. All tables **must** be typed in WP table format or MSWORD table format. Tables should NOT be tabbed or spaced to align columns. All tables **must** be either 3 1/4 inches wide or 6 7/8 inches wide.

3. All figures **must** be created in one of the following formats: TIFF, CGM, or WPG.

4. Tables and figures are **not** to be included unless directly referred to in the body of the manuscript.

5. For accepted manuscripts, tables and figures must be included on the submitted disk and each should be on a separate page.

6. Placement of tables and figures in the manuscript should be indicated as follows:

Table or Figure About Here

Equations And Citations
1. Equations are placed on a separate line with a blank line both above and below, and numbered in parentheses, flush right. Examples:

$$y = c + ax + bx \qquad (1)$$

$$y = a + 1x + 2x + 3x + ax \qquad (2)$$

2. References within the text should include the author's last name and year of publication enclosed in parentheses, e.g. (Cunningham 1998; Rakowski and Southern 1999). For more than one cite in the same location, references should be in chronological order, as above. For more than one cite in the same year, alphabetize by author name, such as (Grimm 1998; Farris 1999; Rakowski 2000; Gibson 1994). If practical, place the citation just ahead of a punctuation mark. If the author's name is used within the text sentence, just place the year of publication in parentheses, e.g., "According to Rakowski and Southern (1996)...,". For multiple authors, use up to three names in the citation. With four or more authors, use the lead author and et al., (Mundy et al. 1999).

3. Footnotes may be used where necessary. Footnotes are in 8-point font and should appear at the bottom of the page using numbers (1, 2, etc.). Note: footnotes should be explanatory in nature if used, not for reference purposes.

4. All references should be in block style. Hanging indents are not to be used.

5. Appendices follow the body of the text but do not precede references.

6. The list of references cited in the manuscript should immediately follow the body of the text in alphabetized order, with the lead author's surname first and the year of publication following all author names. Work by the same author with the same year of publication should be distinguished by lower case letters after the date (e.g. 1999a). For author names that repear, in the same order, in subsequent cites, substitute a .5 inch underline for each name that repears. A blank line should separate each reference in the list. Do not number references.

7. All references to journals, books, etc. are italicized, NOT underlined. Examples are as follows:

Collison, Fredrick M. (1994), "Transpacific Air Service with Hong Kong: Characteristics and Issues," Journal of Transportation Management, 6(2):1-39.

Crum, Michael R. (1996), "On the Improvement of Carrier EDI Implementation Strategies," in EDI Implementation in the Transportation Industry, New York: Transportation Press, 387-404.

Johnson, James C. & Donald F. Wood (1996), Contemporary Logistics, 6th ed., Upper Saddle River, NJ: Prentice-Hall, Inc.

Manuscript Sample

TEACHING LOGISTICS STUDENTS TO TAKE OWNERSHIP OF INFORMATION INFRASTRUCTURE DEVELOPMENT

Frank W. Davis, University of Tennessee
Kenneth J. Preissler, Logistics Insights Corporation

Logistics systems, developed gradually over the past four decades, are undergoing necessary radical change in this era of increasing global competition. This article describes an approach taken by the authors to teach logistics students how to take ownership of designing their own information infrastructure and how to use it to make their organizations more flexible, providing more strategic options.

INTRODUCTION

Advances in information systems technology such as data base management systems, bar code scanning, telecommunications, and image processing have enables logistics and information managers with vision to reengineer the way the firm conducts its business. The usage of mainframe computers, personal computers, and logistics information systems has been widely studied (Gustin 1989). these studies have universally concluded that there has been rapid growth in the usage of computers and logistics information systems.

Computer Usage in the Classroom [upper/lower case and bolded]

The usage of computer applications in a logistics course has also been studied. Rao, Stenger and Wu stated that there are several approaches to integrating computers into the classroom in a business curriculum, each with its individual advantages and drawbacks (1992).

Table 1 about here

Systems Development In Practice [upper/lower case]

The study of the information systems development process of computer applications has been almost universally left up to the computer science, software engineering, and information systems educators and practitioners.

$$y = a + 1x = ax \tag{1}$$

References
Collison, Frederick M. (1994), "Transpacific Air Service with Hong Kong: Characteristics and Issues," *Journal of Transportation Management*, 6(2):1-39.

Crum, Michael R. (1996), "On the Improvement of Carrier EDI Implementation Strategies," in *EDI Implementation in the Transportation Industry*, New York: Transportation Press, 387-404.

Johnson, James C. & Donald F. Wood (1996), *Contemporary Logistics*, 6th ed., Upper Saddle River, NJ: Prentice-Hall, Inc.

Journal of Travel & Tourism Marketing

ADDRESS FOR SUBMISSION:

K. S. (Kaye) Chon, Editor
Journal of Travel & Tourism Marketing
Hong Kong Polytechnic University
Dept. of Hotel and Tourism Management
Hung Hom
Kowloon,
Hong Kong
Phone: 852-276-6638
Fax:
E-Mail: kchon@unhedu
Web: www.haworthpressinc.com
Address May Change:

CIRCULATION DATA:

Reader: Administrators
Frequency of Issue: Quarterly
Copies per Issue: 1,001 - 2,000
Sponsor/Publisher: Haworth Press, Inc.
Subscribe Price: 45.00 US$

PUBLICATION GUIDELINES:

Manuscript Length: 21-25
Copies Required: Three
Computer Submission: No
Format: N/A
Fees to Review: 0.00 US$

Manuscript Style:
     American Psychological Association

REVIEW INFORMATION:

Type of Review: Blind Review
No. of External Reviewers: 2
No. of In House Reviewers: 0
Acceptance Rate: 21-30%
Time to Review: 1 - 2 Months
Reviewers Comments: Yes
Invited Articles: 0-5%
Fees to Publish: 0.00 US$

MANUSCRIPT TOPICS:

Advertising & Promotion Management; Business Education; Business Information Systems (MIS); Business Law, Public Responsibility & Ethics; Communication; Direct Marketing; Global Business; Marketing Research; Marketing Theory & Applications; Non Profit Organizations; Operations Research/Statistics; Sales/Selling; Services; Small Business Entrepreneurship; Strategic Management Policy; Technology/Innovation; Transportation/Physical Distribution

MANUSCRIPT GUIDELINES/COMMENTS:

About The Journal

The Journal publishes empirical and conceptual articles related to research and management practice of travel and tourism marketing services. Topics could include traveler behavior, tourism industry marketing, hotel and resort industry marketing, airline industry marketing, etc.

The *Journal of Travel & Tourism Marketing* is a managerially oriented and applied journal which will serve as a medium through which researchers and managers in the field of travel and tourism can exchange ideas and keep abreast with the latest developments in the field. The journal will publish articles on travel and tourism related to marketing management practices, applied research studies, critical reviews on major issues, and business and government policies affecting travel and tourism marketing.

As an international journal, the *Journal of Travel & Tourism Marketing* will place special emphasis on submissions reflecting the perspectives of contributors from other countries and will include articles treating North American perspectives as well. Travel and tourism educators, consultants and business researchers with interests in travel and tourism marketing, and government policymakers will benefit from the timely information presented in this innovative journal.

Instructions For Authors

1. **Original articles only**. Submission of a manuscript to this Journal represents a certification on the part of the author(s) that it is an original work, and that neither this manuscript nor a version of it has been published elsewhere nor is being considered for publication elsewhere.

2. **Manuscript length**. The Journal publishes two main classes of articles: full-length articles of approximately 5,000 words (15-25 pages, double-spaced), and shorter opinion/reports/viewpoint pieces of about 1,500 words (5-10 pages, double-spaced). Longer manuscripts will be considered at the discretion of the Editor who may recommend publication as a monograph edition of the Journal or division into sections for publication in successive Journal issues.

3. **Manuscript style**. References, citations, and general style of manuscripts for this Journal should follow the APA style (as outlined in the latest edition of the *Publication Manual of The American Psychological Association*). References should be placed in alphabetical order.

4. **Manuscript preparation**.
margins: leave at least a one-inch margin on all four sides.
paper: use clean white, 8 ½ " x 11" bond paper.
number of copies: 3 (the original plus two photocopies).
cover page: Important--staple a cover page to the manuscript, indicating only the article title (this is used for anonymous refereeing).
second "title page": enclose a regular title page but do not staple it to the manuscript. Include the title again, plus:
- full authorship credits in order of seniority
- an abstract of about 100 words
- an introductory footnote with authors' academic degrees, professional titles, affiliations, mailing addresses, and any desired acknowledgement of research support or other credit.

5. **Return envelopes**. When you submit your three manuscript copies, also include:
- a regular envelope, stamped and self-addressed. This is for the Editor to send you an "acknowledgement of receipt" letter.

6. **Spelling, Grammar, and Punctuation.** You are responsible for preparing manuscript copy which is clearly written in acceptable grammar and punctuation. Neither the Editor nor the Publisher is responsible for correcting errors of spelling and grammar: the manuscript, after acceptance by the Editor, must be immediately ready for typesetting when finally submitted by the author(s).

The *APA Publication Manual* gives explicit instructions on punctuation, spelling, abbreviations, statistical formulae, etc. Check your paper for the following common errors:
- dangling modifiers
- misplaced modifiers
- unclear antecedents
- incorrect or inconsistent abbreviations

Also, check the accuracy of all arithmetic calculations statistics numerical data, text citations, and references. All cited references must be given in full, including the volume, issues, and page numbers.

7. **Inconsistencies must be avoided.** Be sure you are consistent in your use of abbreviations, terminology, and in citing references, from one part of your paper to another.

8. **Preparation of tables, figures, and illustrations.** All tables, figures, illustrations, etc. must be "camera-ready." That is, they must be cleanly typed or artistically prepared so that they can be used either exactly as they are or else used after a photographic reduction in size. Figures, tables, and illustrations must be prepared on separate sheets of paper. Always use black ink and professional drawing instruments. On the back of these items, write your article title and the journal title lightly in pencil, so they do not get misplaced. In text, skip extra lines and indicate where these figures and tables are to be placed (please do not write on face of art). Photographs are considered part of the acceptable manuscript and remain with Publisher for use in additional printings.

9. **Alterations Required By Referees and Reviewers.** Many times a paper is accepted by the Editor contingent upon changes that are mandated by anonymous specialist referees and members of the Editorial Board. If the Editor returns your manuscript for revisions, you are responsible for retyping any sections of the paper to incorporate these revisions (If applicable, revisions should also be put on disk).

10. **Typesetting.** You will not be receiving galley proofs of your article. Editorial revisions, if any, must therefore be made while your article is still in manuscript. The final version of the manuscript will be the version you see published. Typesetter's errors will be corrected by the production staff of The Haworth Press. Authors are expected to submit manuscripts, disks, and art that are free from error.

11. **Electronic media.** Haworth's in-house type-setting unit is able to utilize your final manuscript material as prepared on most personal computers and word processors. This will minimize typographical errors and decrease overall production timelag. Please send the first draft and final draft copies of your manuscript to the journal Editor in print format for his/her

final review and approval. **After approval of** your final manuscript, please submit the final approved version both on printed format ("hard copy") and floppy diskette. On the outside of the diskette package write:
A. the brand name of your computer or word processor
B. the word-processing program that you used
C. the title of your article, and
D. file name

Note: Disk and hard copy must agree. In case of discrepancies, it is The Haworth Press's policy to follow hard copy. Authors are advised that no revisions of the manuscript can be made after acceptance by the Editor for publication. The benefits of this procedure are many with speed and accuracy being the most obvious. We look forward to working with you on this, knowing we will be able to serve you more efficiently in the future.

12. **Reprints**. The senior author will receive one copy of the journal issue and 10 complimentary reprints of his or her article. Junior authors will receive one copy of the issue. These are sent several weeks after the journal issue is published and in circulation. An order form for the purchase of additional reprints will also be sent to all authors at this time. (Approximately 4-6 weeks is necessary for the preparation of reprints.) Please do not query the Journal's Editor about reprints. All such questions should be sent directly to The Haworth Press, Inc., Production Department, 21 East Broad Street, West Hazleton, PA 18201. To order additional reprints (minimum: 50 copies), please contact The Haworth Document Delivery Center, 10 Alice Street, Binghamton, New York 13904-1580 (607) 722-5857.

13. **Copyright**. If your manuscript is accepted for publication copyright ownership must be transferred officially to The Haworth Press, Inc. The Editor's acceptance letter will include a form fully explaining this. The form must be signed by all authors and the original returned to the Editor as soon as possible. Failure to return the copyright form in a timely fashion will result in delay in review and subsequent publication.

Examples of Format

Examples of References to Periodicals
1. Journal Article: One Author
Tellis, Gerald J. (1986). Beyond the many faces of price: An integration of pricing strategies. Journal of Marketing, 50 (4): 146-160.

2. Journal Article: Multiple Authors
Sheldon, Pauline J., & Mak, James (1987). The demand for package tours: A model choice model. Journal of Travel Research, 25 (3): 13-17.

3. Magazine Article
Tinnin, D.B. (1981, November 16). The heady success of Holland's Heineken. Fortune, pp. 158-164.

4. Newspaper Article: No Author
The opportunity of world brands. (1984, June 3). The New York Times, p. 6F.

5. Monograph
Franko, L.G. (1979). A survey of the impact of manufactured exports from industrializing countries in Asia and Latin America. Changing International Realities [Monograph] No. 6.

Examples of References to Books
1. Reference to an Entire Book
Urban Glen L., & Hauser, John R. (1980). Design and Marketing New Products. Englewood Cliffs, NJ: Prentice-Hall.

2. Book with a Corporate Author
Committee for Economic Development. (1981). Transnational corporations for developing countries. New York: Author.

3. Edited Book Chon, K.S. (1991). The Management of Hotel Sales and Marketing. Washington, D.C.: Hotel Sales and Marketing Association International Foundation.
4. Book with No Author or Editor.
Marketing opportunities in Japan. (1978). London: Dentsu.

5. Article or Chapter in an Edited Book.
Shostack G.L. (1986). Breaking free from product marketing. In C.W.L. Hart & D.A. Troy (Eds.), Strategic Hotel/Motel Marketing (pp. 42-50). East Lansing, Ml: Educational Institute of the AHMA.

Proceedings of Meetings and Symposia
1. Published Proceedings, Published Contributions to a Symposium

Hoistius, K. (1985). Organizational buying of airline services. In S. Shaw, L. Sparks & E. Kaynak (Eds.). Marketing in the 1990's & Beyond (pp. 262-272). Second World Marketing Congress, held at University of Stirling, Scotland, (August 28-31).

2. Unpublished Paper Presented at a Meeting
Yucelt, U. (1987). Tourism marketing planning in developing economies. Paper presented at the annual meeting of the Academy of Marketing Science, Bal Harbour, Florida.

Doctoral Dissertations 1. Published Doctoral Dissertation
Czintoka M.F. (1980). An analysis of export development strategies in selected U.S. industries. Dissertations Abstracts International (University Microfilms No. 80-15, 865).

For reference of unpublished manuscripts, publications of limited circulation, reviews and interviews, and non-print media, please refer to the latest edition of the Publication Manual of American Psychological Association.

Journal of Travel Research

ADDRESS FOR SUBMISSION:

C. R. Goeldner, Editor
Journal of Travel Research
University of Colorado at Boulder
Business Research Division
Campus Box 420
Boulder, CO 80309-0420
USA
Phone: 303-492-4267
Fax: 303-492-3620
E-Mail: goeldner@colorado.edu
Web: www.sagepub.com
Address May Change:

PUBLICATION GUIDELINES:

Manuscript Length: 11-15
Copies Required: Four
Computer Submission: Yes
Format: with 4 hardcopies
Fees to Review: 0.00 US$

Manuscript Style:
    Chicago Manual of Style

CIRCULATION DATA:

Reader: Academics, Business Persons
Frequency of Issue: Quarterly
Copies per Issue: 1,001 - 2,000
Sponsor/Publisher: Sage Publications
Subscribe Price: 145.00 US$ Individual
    160.00 US$ Institution

REVIEW INFORMATION:

Type of Review: Blind Review
No. of External Reviewers: 3
No. of In House Reviewers: 1
Acceptance Rate: 20%
Time to Review: 4 - 6 Months
Reviewers Comments: Yes
Invited Articles: 0-5%
Fees to Publish: 0.00 US$

MANUSCRIPT TOPICS:
Advertising & Promotion Management; Marketing Research; Services; Strategic Management Policy; Travel and Tourism

MANUSCRIPT GUIDELINES/COMMENTS:

Description:
Journal of Travel Research gives travel and tourism researchers, educators, and professionals up-to-date, high quality information on this ever-growing field. Founded over 35 years ago as the first scholarly journal in North America focused exclusively on travel and tourism research, JTR reflects the worldwide importance of tourism both economically and socially.
Now published by Sage Publications, an international leader in social science and business publishing, JTR will continue to bring you the most current and influential scholarship on travel and tourism available.

With its stimulating articles, reviews, and reports, JTR benefits both researchers specializing in tourism and professionals who use travel research findings to make informed decisions.

Journal of Travel Research keeps you up to date with the latest research on the most important trends and issues in travel and tourism. JTR's peer-reviewed articles not only report findings, but help you discover the right tools for conducting your own research. Topics addressed include:

- Corporate travel management
- Ecotourism
- Impact of tourism pricing
- Geographic and seasonal variation
- Measuring customer satisfaction
- Gambling and its impact
- Travel and tourism education
- Forecasting
- Heritage tourism
- Travel motivators

Journal of Travel Research enhances your work by giving you a complete picture of the travel and tourism research field. In addition to major research articles, JTR features such unique and convenient departments as:

The Travel and Research Bookshelf...an annotated, extensive listing of recent book and journal article publications on travel and tourism helps you stay current with the travel literature.

Research Notes and Communications...short articles and notes from pilot studies, innovative or exploratory research, conference reports, and announcements provide you with an exciting update of today's travel research developments and events.

Book Reviews...give you an in-depth look at the most important new books in the tourism field.

Manuscript Submission
The objective of the Journal of Travel Research is to publish articles in the field of travel research and marketing, defining this field in the broadest sense. Its purpose is to serve as a medium through which those with research interests can exchange ideas and keep abreast of the latest developments pertaining to travel research and marketing.

The journal strives to advance the level and standards used in travel research by providing readers with new, helpful information about travel research and marketing; new techniques; creative views; generalizations about travel research and marketing thought and practice; and synthesis of travel research and marketing material.

Articles are encouraged from industry practitioners as well as academics, and authors are required to include a section in their manuscripts explaining the practical application of any research technique or set of findings for industry.

The procedures guiding the selection of articles for publication in the journal require that no manuscript be accepted until it has been reviewed by the editor and several (usually three) members of the Editorial Review Board. The editor's decision to publish a manuscript is influenced considerably by the judgment of the reviewers, who are experts in their respective fields of travel. It is journal policy to remove the author's name and credentials prior to forwarding a manuscript to a reviewer to maximize objectivity and ensure that manuscripts are judged solely on the basis of their content.

Two principal criteria are used by the editor and members of the Editorial Review Board in the judgment of a manuscript:

- Does it make a significant and substantive contribution to the literature of travel research and marketing? Does it contribute to the improvement of travel research and marketing practice?

- Does it convey its message clearly and concisely? Does it communicate technical information so that it is easily understood by most readers?Manuscripts submitted to the journal can be processed expeditiously if they are prepared according to these instructions.

Manuscript Preparation
Manuscripts should be typed double-spaced, including references. Do not use single spacing anywhere. Page numbers are to be placed in the upper right-hand corner of every page. A tab indent should begin each paragraph. Manuscripts ordinarily should be between 4,000 and 6,000 words (ca.15 typewritten pages). Articles of shorter length are also acceptable and encouraged.

Submit four (4) copies of each manuscript. The author's name should not appear anywhere except on the cover page. The author should keep an extra, exact copy for future reference. Manuscripts are reviewed simultaneously by several different Editorial Review Board members who are geographically separated.

If a manuscript is based on survey research, please include a copy of the questionnaire with the manuscript.

For details of manuscript preparation not covered in the following sections, see The Chicago Manual of Style, 14th edition, Chicago and London: University of Chicago Press, 1993.

1. **What goes where?**
First Page - Name of author(s) and title; author(s) note, including present position, complete address, telephone/fax numbers, e-mail address, and any acknowledgement of financial to technical assistance. (This page will be removed prior to sending the manuscript to reviewers).

Second Page - Title of paper (without author's name)and a brief abstract of no more than 150 words substantively summarizing the article. This should be informative, giving the reader a "taste" of the article.

Body - The text, with major headings centered on the page and subheadings flush with the left margin. Major headings should use all uppercase letters; side subheadings should be typed in upper and lowercase letters. The percent sign (%) should be used.

Tables and Figures - Each table or figure should be prepared on a separate page and grouped together at the end of the manuscript. The data in tables should be arranged so that columns of like materials read down, not across. Nonsignificant decimal places in tabular data should be omitted. The tables and figures should be numbered in Arabic numerals, followed by brief descriptive titles.

When organizing tables, please keep JTR's page dimensions in mind and avoid submitting very wide tables.

Additional details should be footnoted under the table not in the title. In the text, all illustrations and charts should be referred to as figures.

Figures must be clean, crisp, black-and-white, camera-ready copies. Please avoid the use of gray-scale shading; use hatchmarks, dots, or lines instead.

References - References should be typed double-spaced in alphabetical order by author's last name (see 3).

2. Reference Citations Within Text

Citations in the text should include the author's last name and year of publication enclosed in parentheses without punctuation, for example, (Kinsey 1960). If practical, the citation should be placed immediately before a punctuation mark. Otherwise, insert it in a logical sentence break.

If a particular page, section, or equation is cited, it should be placed within the parentheses, for example, (Kinsey 1960, p.112). For multiple authors, use the full, formal citation for up to three authors, but for four or more use the first author's name with "et al." For example, use (White and Smith 1977) and (Brown, Green, and Stine 1984). For more than three authors, use (Hunt et al. 1975) unless another work published in that year would also be identified as (Hunt et al. 1975); in that case, list all authors, for example, (Hunt, Bent, Marks, and West 1975).

3. Reference List Style

List references alphabetically, principle author's surname first, followed by publication date in parentheses. The reference list should be typed double-spaced, with a hanging indent, on a separate page. Do not number references. Please examine reference lists in recent issues for specific examples. Be sure that all titles cited in the text appear in the reference list and vice versa.

4 Mathematical Notation

Mathematical notation must be clear within the text. Equations should be centered on the page. If equations are numbered, type the number in the parentheses flush with the right margin.

Unusual symbols and Greek letters should be identified by a marginal note.

For equations that may be too wide to fit in a single column, indicate appropriate breaks.

Manuscript Submission
Please send all manuscripts to C.R. Goeldner, Editor, Journal of Travel Research, Business Research Division, University of Colorado at Boulder, Campus Box 420, Boulder, CO 80309-0420; (303)492-4267.

All published material is copyrighted by Sage Publications, Inc. Every author and coauthor must sign an agreement before an article can be published.

Submission Of Final Manuscripts
Authors of final manuscripts accepted for publication should provide both a hard copy of the final version of their article and a matching version on a 3.5-inch computer disk. Please group all sections of the article in one file; do not use separate files for tables, references, and so forth. Please do not include figures on disk. Figures are acceptable as camera-ready copy only.

Journal of Vacation Marketing

ADDRESS FOR SUBMISSION:

Daryn Moody, Editor
Journal of Vacation Marketing
Museum House
25 Museum Street
London, WC1A 1JT
UK
Phone: 44 171-323-2916
Fax: 44 171-323-2918
E-Mail: daryn@hspublications.co.uk
Web: www.henrystewart.com
Address May Change:

PUBLICATION GUIDELINES:

Manuscript Length: 2,500-5,000 words
Copies Required: Three
Computer Submission: Yes
Format: MS Word/WordPerfect
Fees to Review: 0.00 US$

Manuscript Style:
  , Cambridge

CIRCULATION DATA:

Reader: , 65% Academics, 35% Business
Frequency of Issue: Quarterly
Copies per Issue: 1,001 - 2,000
Sponsor/Publisher: Henry Stewart
  Publications
Subscribe Price: 285.00 US$ Institution
  100.00 US$ Individual

REVIEW INFORMATION:

Type of Review: Blind Review
No. of External Reviewers: 3
No. of In House Reviewers: 2
Acceptance Rate: 50%
Time to Review: 2 Months
Reviewers Comments: Yes
Invited Articles: 30%
Fees to Publish: 0.00 US$

MANUSCRIPT TOPICS:
Advertising & Promotion Management; Business Education; Direct Marketing; Marketing Research; Marketing Theory & Applications; Organizational Behavior & Theory; Sales/Selling; Travel and Tourism

MANUSCRIPT GUIDELINES/COMMENTS:

1. Contributions should be between 2,000 and 5,000 words in length. All submissions should be typewritten and double spaced.

2. The Journal's Editors and Editorial Board particularly welcome submissions which present case study material, new approaches, techniques, empirical research or conceptual papers.

3. All articles should be accompanied by a short abstract outlining the paper's aims and subject matter.

4. All articles should be accompanied by up to six keywords.

5. Articles should be accompanied by a short (about 80 words) description of the author(s) and, if appropriate, the organization of which he or she is a member.

6. Authors should not seek to use the Journal as a vehicle for marketing any specific product or service.

7. Authors should avoid the use of language or slang which is not in keeping with the professional and academic style of the Journal.

8. Titles of organizations etc should be written out first in full and thereafter in initials.

9. Articles should be supported by references. For all Henry Stewart Journals excluding Corporate Reputation Review, Tourism and Hospitality Research, Journal of Fashion Marketing and Management, Journal of Small Business and Enterprise Development, Journal of Asset Management and International Journal of Police Science Management, these should be set out in accordance with the Vancouver referencing system. References for the Journals listed above should be set out in accordance with the Harvard referencing system.

10. Photographs and illustrations supporting articles should be submitted where appropriate. Photographs should be good quality positives, printed from the original negatives and preferably in black and white only. Figures and other line illustrations should be submitted in good quality originals and a copy of the data should also be included.

11. Authors must ensure that references to named people and/or organizations are accurate, not rascist or sexist and without libellous implications.

12. All contributions sent to the Publisher, whether invited or not, will be submitted to the Journal's Editors and Editorial Board. Any such contribution must bear the author's full name and address, even if this is not for publication. Contributions, whether published pseudonymously or not, are accepted on the strict understanding that the author is responsible for the accuracy of all opinion, technical comment, factual report, data, figures, illustrations and photographs. Publication does not necessarily imply that these are the opinions of the Editorial Board, Editors or the Publisher, nor does the Board, Editors or Publisher accept any liability for the accuracy of such comment, report and other technical and factual information. The Publisher will, however, strive to ensure that all opinion, comments, reports, data, figures, illustrations and photographs are accurate, insofar as it is within its abilities to do so. The Publisher reserves the right to edit, abridge or omit material submitted for publication.

13. All Articles submitted for publication will be subject to a double-blind refereeing procedure.

14. The author bears the responsibility for checking whether material submitted is subject to copyright or ownership rights, eg photographs, illustrations, trade literature and data. Where use is so restricted, the Publisher must be informed with the submission of the material.
No contribution will be accepted which has been published elsewhere, unless it is expressly invited or agreed by the Publisher. Articles and contributions published become the copyright of the Publisher, unless otherwise agreed.

15. All reasonable efforts are made to ensure accurate reproduction of text, photographs and illustrations. The Publisher does not accept responsibility for mistakes, be they editorial or typographical, nor for consequences resulting from them.

16. Submissions should be sent to Henry Stewart Publications, Museum House, 25 Museum Street, London WC1A 1JT, email: submissions@hspublications.co.uk. **Please clearly state for which journal you are contributing**

Journal of World Business

ADDRESS FOR SUBMISSION:

John W. Slocum, Jr., Editor-in-Chief
Journal of World Business
Southern Methodist University
Cox School of Business
Dallas, TX 75275-0333
USA
Phone: 214-768-3157
Fax: 214-768-4099
E-Mail: jslocum@mail.cox.smu.edu
Web:
Address May Change:

PUBLICATION GUIDELINES:

Manuscript Length: 28 Maximum
Copies Required: Four
Computer Submission: Yes
Format: MsWord or WordPerfect
Fees to Review: 0.00 US$

Manuscript Style:
    See Manuscript Guidelines

CIRCULATION DATA:

Reader: Business Persons, Academics
Frequency of Issue: Quarterly
Copies per Issue: 2,001 - 3,000
Sponsor/Publisher: JAI Press, Inc./Elsevier
   Science Inc.
Subscribe Price: 105.00 US$ Individual
   225.00 US$ Institution
   125.00 US$ Foreign Indv. & $245 Inst.

REVIEW INFORMATION:

Type of Review: Blind Review
No. of External Reviewers: 2
No. of In House Reviewers: 3
Acceptance Rate: 11-20%
Time to Review: 1 - 2 Months
Reviewers Comments: Yes
Invited Articles: 15%
Fees to Publish: 0.00 US$

MANUSCRIPT TOPICS:
Business Information Systems (MIS); Business Law, Public Responsibility & Ethics; Global Business; Labor Relations & Human Resource Mgt.; Services; Small Business Entrepreneurship; Strategic Management Policy; Technology/Innovation

MANUSCRIPT GUIDELINES/COMMENTS:

Description
Formerly the *Columbia Journal of World Business*, the journal's editors are committed to build on the past strengths to make the all new *Journal of World Business* the premier source of information on international business going into the 21st century. The scope and perspective will be to use sound theory and basic research findings as a point of departure for exciting new breakthroughs in the development and practice of international management and marketing.

With specifically designated editorial boards to recognize the importance of both the Pacific Rim and European contributions to world business, the structure of the editorial team and the new domain of *JWB* focuses on international HRM, marketing and strategic issues, broadly defined.

Mission: *Journal of World Business* seeks to publish manuscripts in the domains of international business strategy, human resource management, and marketing. Manuscripts should have relevant and concise theoretical foundations. They also need to translate their findings to professional practitioners seeking to improve their practice of management.

1. Length: Maximum of 28 pages total, double spaced, 1 1/2-inch margins and 12-point type font. Microsoft Word for windows and WordPerfect are the preferred softwares for submission. Upon final acceptance of your manuscript, you will be supplied with more specific guidelines and you will need to submit a diskette of your work.

2. The cover letter should indicate the title and the names, addresses, phone and fax numbers and e-mail address (if applicable) of two or three relevant reviewers for your paper. These may or may not be selected by the editor.

3. The title page should include the title and the names, addresses, fax, phone and e-mail of all authors. The corresponding author should be designated. A 100-word Abstract should be the second page.

4. Referencing should be generally held to a minimum and follow the *Journal of World Business* format:

In text: Put parentheses around the citation(s), use author's last name and correct date (Spender, 1995) or (Spender & Kessler, 1995). If the authors have more than one publication in a year, use the following notation (Spender, 1995, 1995a). When a work is in press, please use (Ford, in press).

End of Text:
For articles:
    Dewar, R.D., & Dutton, J.E. (1986) The adoption of radical and incremental innovations: An empirical analysis. *Management Science*, 32: 1422-1433
    Dougherty, D. (1990) Understanding new markets for products. *Strategic Management Journal*, 11:59-78.

For articles when cited journal does not publish sequential page numbers throughout a year:

    Foker, L.B. (1991). Quality: American, japanese, and Soviet perspectives. *Academy of Management Executive*, 5(4): 63-74.
    Gupta, A.K., & Wilemon, D.L. (1990). Accelerating development of technology-based new products. *California Management Review*, 32(2):24-44.

For Books:
    Hall, E.T. (1983). *The dance of life: The other dimension of time.* Garden City, NY: Anchor Press.
    Jones, J.W. (1993). *High-speed management.* San Francisco, CA: Jossey-Bass.

For articles in books:
    Katz, R. (1980). Time and Work: Toward an integrated perspective. Pp. 81-127 in L.L. Cummings & B.M. Staw (Eds.), *Research in organizational behaviour*, Vol. 3. Greenwich, CT: JAI Press.

5. Send a self-addressed, stamped return card to acknowledge receipt of the manuscript.

6. Send four copies to: John W. Slocum, Editor-in-chief
                                   Journal of World Business
                                   Cox School of Business
                                   Southern Methodist University
                                   Dallas, TX 75275-033

If From Pacific Rim/Asian countries send four copies to:
                                   Tan Hwee Hoon, Editor, Pacific Rim
                                   The National University of Singapore
                                   10 Kent Ridge Crescent
                                   Singapore 119260

If from Europe, send four copies to:
                                   Susan C. Schneider, Editor, Europe
                                   HEC University of Geneva
                                   102 Blvd. Carl Vogt
                                   CH 1211 Geneva, Switzerland

If from Latin America, send four copies to:
                                   Frank Hoy, Editor, Latin America
                                   College of Business Administration
                                   University of Texas-El Paso
                                   El Paso, TX 79968-0544

Logistics Information Management

ADDRESS FOR SUBMISSION:

Abby Day, Editor
Logistics Information Management
MCB University Press
60/62 Toller Lane
Bradford, BD8 9BY
UK
Phone: 44 1274 777700
Fax: 44 1274 785200
E-Mail: aday@mcb.co.uk
Web: www.mcb.co.uk
Address May Change:

CIRCULATION DATA:

Reader: Academics, Business Persons
Frequency of Issue: Bi-Monthly
Copies per Issue: No Reply
Sponsor/Publisher: MCB University Press
Subscribe Price: 4299.00 US$

PUBLICATION GUIDELINES:

Manuscript Length: 3,000-5,000 words
Copies Required: Three
Computer Submission: No
Format: N/A
Fees to Review: 0.00 US$

Manuscript Style:
Uniform System of Citation (Harvard Blue Book)

REVIEW INFORMATION:

Type of Review: Blind Review
No. of External Reviewers: 2
No. of In House Reviewers: 1
Acceptance Rate: 21-30%
Time to Review: 1 - 2 Months
Reviewers Comments: Yes
Invited Articles: 50% +
Fees to Publish: 0.00 US$

MANUSCRIPT TOPICS:
Business Information Systems (MIS); Production/Operations; Technology/Innovation; Transportation/Physical Distribution

MANUSCRIPT GUIDELINES/COMMENTS:

About the journal
Logistics Information Management keeps pace with the plethora of current and developing techniques and applications so that subscribers gain access to a wealth of relevant and practical material. This journal publishes a wide range of material from internationally distinguished experts. Scholarly examinations of the latest theory and practice in the world's leading teaching and research institutions are augmented by contributions from senior business managers and consultants, who report on specific logistics case histories. In addition, guest editors offer fresh perspectives and special themed issues. A lively news and reviews section keeps subscribers up to date with everything happening in a dynamic and increasingly influential field.

Coverage
- Electronic data interchange (EDI)

- Inventory management
- Just-in-time (JIT)
- Loading
- MRP II
- Scheduling
- Through lite-costs (TLC)
- Electronic point of sale (EPOS)
- Outsourcing

NOTES FOR CONTRIBUTORS

Copyright
Articles submitted to the journal should be original contributions and should not be under consideration for any other publication at the same time. Authors submitting articles for publication warrant that the work is not an infringement of any existing copyright and will indemnify the publisher against any breach of such warranty. For ease of dissemination and to ensure proper policing of use, papers and contributions become the legal copyright of the publisher unless otherwise agreed. Submissions should be sent to the Editor [at the above address].

Editorial objectives
The journal aims to publish articles which will be of value and interest to business managers, consultants, teachers and students concerned with issues of logistics information and management. In all cases, the aim is to feature practical applications.

Editorial scope
The Editor welcomes innovative and wide-ranging approaches to the area of logistics information and management, within the parameters outlined above.
Some suggestions for coverage would be:
- an evaluation of one or more techniques, such as MRPII, DRP
- case studies of logistics information management
- interfaces between logistics and other disciplines or functions
- "how to" articles, such as stocktakes
- a review of the literature on logistics information management
- implementation of systems or changes, as commentary or case study.

Whilst articles should never be superficial or trite, there is a place in *Logistics Information Management* for opinion, and for conceptual leaps which may not be able to be supported by "traditional" research or analysis. All contributions will be read and commented on by the Editor, whether successful or not.

Logistics Information Management does not publish product or service endorsements, or articles linked to or supported by advertising. Public relations offices or agencies are welcome to send well-written news releases, especially on new product information or forthcoming events which may be of interest to subscribers.

Manuscript requirements

Three copies of the manuscript should be submitted in double line spacing with wide margins. All authors should be shown and author's details must be printed on a separate sheet and the author should not be identified anywhere else in the article.

As a guide, articles should be between 3,000 and 5,000 words in length. A title of not more than eight words should be provided. A brief **autobiographical note** should be supplied including full name, affiliation, e-mail address and full international contact details. Authors must supply an **abstract** of 100-150 words. Up to six **keywords** should be included which encapsulate the principal subjects covered by the article.

Where there is a **methodology**, it should be clearly described under a separate heading. **Headings** must be short, clearly defined and not numbered. **Notes** or **Endnotes** should be used only if absolutely necessary and must be identified in the text by consecutive numbers, enclosed in square brackets and listed at the end of the article.

Figures, charts and **diagrams** should be kept to a minimum. They must be black and white with minimum shading and numbered consecutively using arabic numerals with a brief title and labelled axes. In the text, the position of the figure should be shown by typing on a separate line the words "take in Figure 2". Good quality originals must be provided.

Tables should be kept to a minimum. They must be numbered consecutively with roman numerals and a brief title. In the text, the position of the table should be shown by typing on a separate line the words "take in Table IV".

Photos and **illustrations** must be supplied as good quality black and white original half tones with captions. Their position should be shown in the text by typing on a separate line the words "take in Plate 2".

References to other publications should be complete and in Harvard style. They should contain full bibliographical details and journal titles should not be abbreviated. For multiple citations in the same year use a, b, c immediately following the year of publication. References should be shown within the text by giving the author's last name followed by a comma and year of publication all in round brackets, e.g. (Fox, 1994). At the end of the article should be a reference list in alphabetical order as follows

(a) for books
surname, initials and year of publication, title, publisher, place of publication, e.g.Casson, M. (1979), *Alternatives to the Multinational Enterprise*, Macmillan, London.

(b) for chapter in edited book
surname, initials and year, "title", editor's surname, initials, title, publisher, place, pages, e.g.Bessley, M. and Wilson, P. (1984), "Public policy and small firms in Britain", in Levicki, C. (Ed.), Small Business Theory and Policy, Croom Helm, London, pp.111-26. Please note that the chapter title must be underlined.

(c) for articles
surname, initials, year "title", journal, volume, number, pages, e.g.Fox, S. (1994) "Empowerment as a catalyst for change: an example from the food industry", Supply Chain Management, Vol 2 No 3, pp. 29-33

If there is more than one author list surnames followed by initials. All authors should be shown.

Electronic sources should include the URL of the electronic site at which they may be found, as follows:
Neuman, B.C.(1995), "Security, payment, and privacy for network commerce", IEEE Journal on Selected Areas in Communications, Vol. 13 No.8, October, pp.1523-31. Available (IEEE SEPTEMBER) http://www.research.att.com/jsac/

Notes/Endnotes should be used only if absolutely necessary. They should, however, always be used for citing Web sites. They should be identified in the text by consecutive numbers enclosed in square brackets and listed at the end of the article. Please then provide full Web site addresses in the end list.

Final submission of the article
Once accepted for publication, the final version of the manuscript must be provided, accompanied by a 3.5" **disk** of the same version labelled with: disk format; author name(s); title of article; journal title; file name.

Each article must be accompanied by a completed and signed **Journal Article Record Form** available from the Editor or on http://www.literaticlub.co.uk/

The manuscript will be considered to be the definitive version of the article. The author must ensure that it is complete, grammatically correct and without spelling or typographical errors. In preparing the disk, please use one of the following formats: Word, Word Perfect, Rich text format or TeX/LaTeX. Figures which are provided electronically must be in tif, gif or pic file extensions. All figures and graphics must also be supplied as good quality originals.

Final submission requirements
Manuscripts must be clean, good quality hard copy and;
- include an abstract and keywords
- have Harvard style references
- include any figures, photos and graphics as good quality originals
- be accompanied by a labelled disk
- be accompanied by a completed Journal Article Record Form

Technical assistance is available from MCB's World Wide Web Literati Club on http://www.literaticlub.co.uk/ or contact Mike Massey at MCB, e-mail mmassey@mcb.co.uk

Management Science

ADDRESS FOR SUBMISSION:

Hau L. Lee, Editor-in-Chief
Management Science
Stanford University
Department of Industrial Engineering
 and Engineering Management
Stanford, Ca 94305-4024
USA
Phone: 415-723-0514
Fax: 414-725-8799
E-Mail: haulee@leland.stanford.edu
Web:
Address May Change:

PUBLICATION GUIDELINES:

Manuscript Length: 32
Copies Required: Four
Computer Submission: No
Format: N/A
Fees to Review: 0.00 US$

Manuscript Style:
   See Manuscript Guidelines

CIRCULATION DATA:

Reader: Academics
Frequency of Issue: Monthly
Copies per Issue: 5,001 - 10,000
Sponsor/Publisher: INFORMS
Subscribe Price: 130.00 US$ Individual
   298.00 US$ Library/Corporate
   55.00 US$ Member

REVIEW INFORMATION:

Type of Review: Editorial Review
No. of External Reviewers: 3
No. of In House Reviewers: 0
Acceptance Rate: 11-20%
Time to Review: 4 - 6 Months
Reviewers Comments: Yes
Invited Articles: 0-5%
Fees to Publish: 0.00 US$

MANUSCRIPT TOPICS:

Accounting; Decision Analysis; Economics; Finance & Investments; Global Business; Marketing Research; Marketing Theory & Applications; Services; Supply Chain Management

MANUSCRIPT GUIDELINES/COMMENTS:

1. *Management Science* seeks to publish articles that identify, extend, or unify scientific knowledge pertaining to management. Articles must be readable, well-organized, and exhibit good writing style. Other important criteria are originality and significant contribution including the capacity to provide generalizations within the framework of application-oriented methods.

2. As much as possible, papers suitable for *Management Science* should be readable by those comfortable with undergraduate mathematics. We accept the use of graduate level mathematics only if it is essential for understanding. All articles and notes, if judged potentially suitable for *Management Science*, will be refereed by at least two competent readers.

3. Of special interest is the **methodological** approach to the implementation of real applications of *Management Science*, without losing sight of behavioral and economic realities. Papers should reflect the mutuality of interest of managers and management scientists in the total exercise of the management function. Authors seeking up-to-date information about specific Departmental Editorial Objectives should send their request to: Professor Hau L. Lee, Stanford University, Department of Industrial Engineering and Engineering Management, Stanford, CA 94305-4024.

4. The submission of a paper to *Management Science* for refereeing means that the author certifies the manuscript is not copyrighted; nor has it been accepted for publication (or published) by any refereed journal; nor is it being refereed elsewhere, at the same time. If the paper (or any version of it) has appeared, or will appear in a non-refereed publication, the details of such publication must be made known to the editor at the time of submission so that the suitability of the paper for *Management Science* can be assessed. *Management Science* requires that at least one of the authors of each accepted article sign a Copyright Transfer Agreement form. For further information write: Professor Hau L. Lee (address above).

5. *Management Science* seeks to publish significant articles that identify extend, or unify scientific knowledge pertaining to management. Submissions from all countries are welcome. TIMS is an international society of management scientists and encourages world-wide contributions.

6. Articles must be readable, well-organized and of good writing style. Additional criteria for publication are **originality and significant contribution** which provide generalizations and permit applications of *Management Science* methodology (model-building and algorithm construction.) All articles and notes, if judged potentially suitable for Management Science will be refereed by at least two competent readers. The editors will secure additional refereeing when warranted.

7. Original theory, which is not dependent on substantial mathematical content, should be submitted to *Management Science*. Theory contributions requiring a high degree of mathematical abstraction should not be submitted to *Management Science*, but should instead be directed to the joint publication of TIMS and ORSA, *Mathematics of Operations Research*.

8. Articles are expected to provide models and algorithms of well-defined structure. Descriptions of important applications of *Management Science* which do not detail the modeling structure of the system should not be submitted to *Management Science*. They should instead by directed to *Interfaces*, another joint publication of TIMS and ORSA, which publishes nonmathematical descriptions of *Management Science*.

9. In general, the mathematical methodology must be at the most accessible level of abstractness appropriate to the problem which is being discussed. As much as possible, papers suitable for *Management Science* should be readable by those comfortable with undergraduate mathematics. However, while we insist upon eliminating the unnecessary use of graduate level mathematics, if it is essential for understanding, we accept its use. State-of-the-art surveys are suitable when such reporting is warranted. Of special interest is the **methodological** approach to the implementation of real applications of *Management Science*.

497

Attention should be focused on the problems of developing and converting management theory into practice without losing sight of behavioral and economic realities. Papers should reflect the mutuality of interest of managers and management scientists in the total exercise of the management function.

10. Questions such as the following are significant in evaluating papers submitted for publication:
   1. Does the paper make original and substantive contribution to the literature of *Management Science*?
   2. Is the paper similar in whole or in part to a paper or papers published in any journal but especially in *Management Science*?
   3. Is the title concise descriptive and explicit?
   4. Does the abstract properly summarize the important content of the paper? Is it readable and usable by managers?
   5. Is the paper clear precise logical error-free and in keeping with page length requirements (see Instructions to Authors)?
   6. Is adequate credit given to other contributors in the field; are references complete?
   7. Are there revisions which will make the paper more acceptable? Is the paper more suitable for another journal?

11. *Management Science* also publishes brief articles requiring refereeing which are designated as Notes at the suggestions of the authors editors or referees. Letters and brief comments published as Communications are un-refereed. A yearly index is published. Precis appear in *Management Science* to advise readers about papers that are available from authors upon request.

12. The submission of a paper to *Management Science* for refereeing means that the author certifies the manuscript is not copyrighted; nor has it been accepted for publication (or published) by any refereed journal; nor is it being refereed elsewhere at the same time. If the paper (or any version of it) has appeared or will appear in a non-refereed publication the details of such publication must be made known to the editor at the time of submission so that the suitability of the paper for *Management Science* can be assessed.

13. Figures must be drafted in India ink on white paper in a form suitable for reduction. Lettering should be professional or uniform size and large enough to be legible when the figure is reduced to final size of 1/4 page. Special attention should be given to line weights; that is the lines of the lettering should be the same thickness as the lines of the figure. Typewritten lettering on figures is not acceptable. Figures should be designated by Arabic numerals and the captions should be typed double-spaced on a separate sheet rather than lettered on the figures themselves.

14. Manuscripts which do not conform to this format, if accepted, are subject to considerable delay pending revisions since it is not possible to have them typeset until suitable copy and art have been furnished.

15. **Submission of a paper to *Management Science* for refereeing means that the author(s) certifies that the manuscript has not been published previously nor currently submitted for publication elsewhere.**

16. Manuscripts, tentatively accepted for publication, must be accompanied by a Copyright Transfer Agreement signed by at least one of the authors (who agrees to inform the others, if any), or, in the case of "work made for hire", by the employer. The form of copyright transfer will be sent by the TIMS business office to the responsible author who must return it signed, to the Technical Editors, TIMS, 146 Westminster Street, Providence, Rhode Island 02903. Papers will not be finally accepted, nor will they begin editorial processing until the release is received. This written transfer of copyright, which previously was assumed to be implicit in the act of submitting a manuscript, is necessary under the 1978 United States of America copyright law.

17. Important: The length of papers submitted for publication in *Management Science* should be determined by author requirements. However, our objective is to insure that as many worthy papers as possible will appear in each issue. Consequently, our publication policy is to use not more pages than necessary to communicate fully the purposes, methods and applications of well-written papers that make a contribution to *Management Science* .

18. All Departments of this Journal are refereeing typewritten manuscripts of up to 32 double-spaced manuscript pages (including figures references and tables).

19. Papers exceeding 16 Journal pages (including charts, tables and figures) can be submitted as extensions of present knowledge. (Assuming 250 words per double-spaced typewritten page, 32 manuscript pages produce 16 Journal pages. Each figure constitutes about 1/4 of a Journal page.) Such papers must be accompanied by an abridged version that will satisfy the 16 Journal page constraint. The unabridged paper will be refereed. If accepted in a form exceeding 16 Journal pages, then the abridged version will be reviewed, and approved for its readability and accurate representation of the author's ideas. The satisfactory abridged version will be published. Copies of the full-length, refereed, nonabridged version will be available upon request, at cost, from: Business Office, INFORMS, 901 Elkridge Landing Road, Suite 400, Linthicum, MD, 21090-2909.

20. Manuscripts intended for publication may be sent to the appropriate Departmental Editor or to the Editor-in-Chief for the assignment. The Departmental Editor will see to it that manuscripts accepted for refereeing will be sent to at least two referees. Every effort will be made to complete refereeing in a reasonable interval. Length of time that papers requiring revision are with the author(s) is regularly published as a footnote to accepted articles.

21. All manuscripts submitted for consideration should be typed on 8-1/2" by 11" paper and should be double-spaced throughout, including references, footnotes, and abstract. We request four copies of the paper for the reviewing process. All manuscripts should be preceded by a nonmathematical abstract (as understandable to managers as possible) of not more than 500 words. Papers may be submitted in any language, but English and French are the official language of the Institute.

22. Mathematical notation should be selected so as to simplify the typesetting process. Authors should attempt to make mathematical expressions in the body of the text as simple as possible. Greek letters and unusual symbols (if handwritten rather than typed) should be labeled whenever they first appear in the manuscript, as should letter symbols "oh" and "el" (as distinguished from the numbers "zero" and "one"). Some useful alternatives to expensive notation are:

Expensive notations

$$e^{\frac{-x^2+y^2}{a}}, \quad \frac{7}{8}, \quad \frac{a+b}{c}, \quad \frac{\cos\frac{1}{x}}{\sqrt{a+\frac{b}{x}}}$$

Alternatives

$$\exp((-x^2+y^2)/a) \quad 7/8, \quad (a+b)/c, \quad \frac{\cos(1/x)}{\sqrt{a+b/x}}$$

24. Displayed material should clearly indicate the alignment that is desired. If the equations are numbered, the numbers should be given in parentheses, flush with the right margin of the page.

25. Footnotes should be numbered consecutively and typed, double-spaced, in a separate list at the end of the paper. In text, footnotes are indicated by superscript numbers alone. Footnote numbers should never be attached to mathematical symbols. Material that normally would appear as a footnote should be placed in the body of the text when it will not impair readability.

26. All references are to be listed alphabetically by author at the end of the paper and should be double-spaced. Reference callouts in the body of the text should be indicated by the year of publication in parentheses, e.g. (1960).

27. References appear in the following style:

WINDAL, PIERRE M. AND DOYLE L. WEISS, "An Interactive GLS Procedure for
    Estimating the Parameters of Models with Autocorrelated Errors Using
    Data Aggregated Over Time", J. Business, 53 (October 1980), 415-424.

28. **Submissions** Please submit four copies of each manuscript to the appropriate Departmental Editor or to the Editor-in-Chief. Departmental Editors are listed below. The Statement of Objectives for each department has been published in *Management Science*, and the issue is identified by the date following each department title.

29. **Departmental Editors:**

ACCOUNTING
Professor Bala Balachandran
Northwestern University

Kellogg Graduate School of Management
Evanston, IL 60208
847-491-2678   Fax: 847-467-1202
jpp667@nwu.edu

BUSINESS STRATEGY
Professor Rebecca Henderson
Massachusetts Institute of Technology
Sloan School of Management, E52-543
Cambridge, MA 02142
617-253-6618   Fax: 617-674-2402
rhenders@mit.edu

DECISION ANALYSIS
Professor James E. Smith
Duke University
Fuqua School of Business
Durham, NC 27708-0120
919-660-7770   Fax: 919-684-2818
james.e.smith@duke.edu

DECISION ANALYSIS
Professor Dr. Martin Weber
Universitat Mannheim
Lehrstuhl fur Finanzwirtschaft, insb.
Mannheim - Germany 68131
49-621-292-5450   Fax: 49-621-292-1168
weber@bank.bwl.uni-mannheim.de

FINANCE
Professor Phelim P. Boyle
University of Waterloo
School of Accountancy
Waterloo, Ontario, Canada N2L 3G1
519-885-1211   Fax: 519-888-7562
pboyle@uwaterloo.ca

INFORMATION SYSTEMS
Professor Chris F. Kemerer
University of Pittsburgh
278A Mervis Hall
Pittsburgh, PA 15260
412-648-1572   Fax: 412-624-2983
ckemerer@katz.business.pitt.edu

INTERDISCIPLINARY MANAGEMENT RESEARCH AND APPLICATIONS
Professor Abraham Seidmann

University of Rochester
W.E. Simon School of Business Administration
Rochester, NY 14627
716-275-5694   Fax: 716-273-1140
seidmannav@ssb.rochester.edu

MANUFACTURING, DISTRIBUTION AND SERVICE OPERATIONS
Professor Awl Federgruen
Columbia University
Graduate School of Business
New York, NY 10027
212-854-4106   Fax: 212-864-4857
afedergr@research.gsb.columbia.edu

MANUFACTURING, DISTRIBUTION AND SERVICE OPERATIONS
Professor Luk Van Wassenhove
INSEAD
Technology Management Area Boulevard de
Fontainebleau Cedex, France F77305
(1) 60 72 4326   Fax: (1) 60 72 42 42
wassenhove@insead.fr

MANUFACTURING, DISTRIBUTION AND SERVICE OPERATIONS
Professor Wallace Hopp
Northwestern University
Dept. of Industrial Engineering and Management
Evanston, IL 60208-3119
847-491-3669   Fax: 847-491-8005
hopp@nwu.edu

MARKETING
Professor Dipak Jain
Northwestern University
J. L. Kellogg Graduate School of Management
Evanston, IL 60208-2001
847-491-2840   Fax: 847-467-2747
d-jain@nwu.edu

MATHEMATICAL PROGRAMMING AND NETWORKS
Professor Thomas M. Liebling
Ecole Polytechnique Federale de Lausanne
Department of Mathematiques
Ecublens, Lausanne 1015,
41 21 693 2503   Fax: 41 21 693 22 20
thomas.liebling@epfl.ch

ORGANIZATIONAL PERFORMANCE, STRATEGY, AND DESIGN
Professor Linda Argote
Carnegie Mellon University
Graduate School of Industrial Administration
Pittsburgh, PA 15213
412-268-3683   Fax: 412-268-7064
argote@cmu.edu

PUBLIC SECTOR APPLICATIONS
Professor Bruce Golden
The University of Maryland
College of Business and Management
College Park, MD 20742
301-405-2232   Fax301-314-9157
bgolden@umdacc.umd.edu

PUBLIC SECTOR APPLICATIONS
Professor Jonathan P. Caulkins
Carnegie Mellon University
H. John Heinz III School of Public Policy
Pittsburgh, PA 15213-3890
412-268-5064   Fax: 212-268-7036
caulkins@andrew.cmu.edu

R&D/INNOVATION AND ENTREPRENEURSHIP
Professor Ralph Katz
Northeastern University
College of Business Administration
Boston, MA 02115
617-373-4724   Fax: 617-373-2491
rkatz@cba.neu.edu

STOCHASTIC MODELS AND SIMULATION
Professor Paul Wasserman
Columbia University
Graduate School of Business,
New York, NY 10027-6902
212-854-4102   Fax: 212-316-9180
pg20@columbia.edu

SUPPLY CHAIN MANAGEMENT
Professor Christopher Tang
UCLA
Anderson School of Management
Los Angeles, CA 90095
310-825-4203   Fax: 310-206-3337
ctang@anderson.ucla.edu

30. STATEMENT OF DEPARTMENTAL OBJECTIVES

Accounting

This department solicits and processes for publication papers reporting the results of high quality research that make original and significant contributions to the analysis, design development, and use of accounting systems.

Accounting Systems contributions may deal with the general area of accounting systems and the economics/ management sciences of accounting: the analysis, design and development of complex accounting choices, contracting, incentives and of communications, information processing and decision making within them. Illustrative topic areas may include financial and behavioral systems, information resource management, decision support activities, balanced scorecard and performance measures, planning and control, man-machine systems, information economics, accounting system implementation, and so on.

Accounting contributions may deal with the general areas of financial, managerial and tax accounting, as well as auditing, accounting for nonprofit organizations, social, national and environmental accounting and other related areas. Analytic or empirical investigations are welcome, as are those that rely on an economic or a behavioral paradigm. Editorial policies concern only the quality of the manuscript and its interest to the management science community.

The department encourages the submission of papers dealing with research and applications of management science in the accounting systems and accounting areas. Papers may be either theoretical or applied, but none will be published that are not both innovative and important to the development of the area. Applied research is innovative when existing models and methods of underlying disciplines are applied to a real-world situation in a creative manner, particularly when positive results are obtained in a previously "unexplored" area. Good applied research should be sensitive to the availability of empirical data, measurement and computational requirements and/or implementation issues in actual organizations.

The Department also solicits survey papers on important topic areas, provided they contribute a synthesis of the state-of-the-art in research, as well as a tutorial discussion of the subject.

To be accepted for review manuscripts should strive to meet these Departmental Objectives; they must also conform to the requirements and standards of *Management Science*. (See Editorial Policies and Instruction to Authors for further detail). Manuscripts should be submitted directly to the Departmental Editor for consideration.

Business Strategy

In the past two or three decades, research on business strategy has coalesced into a recognizable applied field. We define business strategy research to include: Theory and data on choices of actions, and plans for implementation that have long-term consequences for the firm; the study of factors which cause some firms to succeed and others to fail; and the study of how firms manage resources that are imperfectly tradeable and hence tied to the firm. All three definitions create paradigms which spawn distinct types of studies. We are eager to publish the best studies of all these types in the new Business Strategy Department of *Management Science*.

The Department will have two prejudices which reflect the traditional orientation of the journal and distinguish it from other outlets for strategy research.

First, because we believe that disciplines discipline thinking, we especially welcome business strategy papers firmly rooted in the soil of a social science. Discipline-based research might find roots in Economics (e.g. industrial organization, economics of the firm); operations (quality and delivery-time control, information technology); political science (e.g., political economy of inter- or intrafirm influence); psychology (e.g. individual and group judgments by general managers): and sociology (e.g., social networks, organizational ecology). Some of these topics overlap with the scope of the Organizational Performance Strategy and Design Department. Please consult their statement of Editorial Objectives (March 1990). or contact one or both Departmental Editors if you are unsure which Department would be more suitable for a particular submission.

Second, we encourage theorizing and empirical work closely tied to theory. We value simplicity in construction and execution of empirical work. For example we think testing a single hypothesis powerfully, and broadly, can be more valuable than testing many hypotheses simultaneously with idiosyncratic data or methods. Experimental tests are welcome, if they are carefully designed using principles established by experimenters in psychology or economics (or if they violate these principles defensibly). Case studies will be published if they show promise of replicability and achieve a particularly high standard of quality, reflecting both methodological sophistication and unique insight.

We are likely to publish articles about familiar topics, including:
- Diversification
- Economies of scale and scope
- Models of competition
- The influence of compensation and incentive systems
- The influence of top management teams
- Managerial cognition and strategic choice
- Implementation of strategies
- Corporate governance
- Acquisition and divestment
- Corporate restructuring
- Joint ventures and strategic alliances
- Introduction of new products.

(Of course, we are most eager to consider articles about topics which are *not* on this list, if they break new ground.)

Writing counts. Authors should write crisply and communicate well. Limit cumbersome notation and unfamiliar jargon. Use appendices for certain proofs technical asides, and details of data sources or computation. Ideally, tables and figures should make a sharp point with little help from the text. Write a fresh abstract summarizing the paper and enticing the reader rather than simply copying part of the paper. Be pithy; *Management Science* rarely publishes long papers.

We will strive to provide quick turnaround on papers and thoughtful constructive criticism. Some papers will be returned immediately if they are judged to be unsuitable.

Decision Analysis
The Decision Analysis Department publishes articles that create, extend, or unify scientific knowledge pertaining to decision analysis and decision making. We seek papers that describe concepts and techniques for modeling decisions as well as behaviorally oriented papers that explain or evaluate decisions or judgments. Papers may develop new theory or methodology, address problems of implementation, present empirical studies of choice behavior or decision modeling, synthesize existing ideas, or describe innovative applications. In all cases, the papers must be based on sound decision-theoretic and/or psychological principles and reasoning.

Decision settings may consist of any combination of certainty or uncertainty; competitive or non-competitive situations; individuals, groups, or markets; and applications may include personal decisions as well as decisions of firms or governments. Due to the interdisciplinary nature of the field, papers may draw upon work in a wide variety of disciplines, including management science, operations research, economics, probability and statistics, mathematics, engineering, psychology, sociology, philosophy, and political science. Moreover, the editors are open to interdisciplinary articles that use decision-theoretic principles and procedures to study decision making in areas such as marketing, finance, operations, accounting, decision support systems, medicine, and public policy. If, however, a paper fits clearly within the interests of another department of *Management Science* and its contribution is not primarily related to decision analysis or decision making, then the paper should be submitted to this other department rather than the Decision Analysis department.

The department currently has two departmental editors to cover the breadth of the field. In general, papers that are theoretically or methodologically oriented should be sent to Jim Smith. Papers that are behaviorally or descriptively oriented should be sent to Martin Weber. Papers that incorporate both elements may be sent to either editor at the author's choice; the departmental editors may however forward papers to each other if they feel the other is better suited to handle the paper. If the departmental editor finds the paper to be appropriate for consideration by the Decision Analysis department, the publication decision will be based upon its quality according to criteria that include originality, importance and significance for decision-analysis practice and/or theory, potential managerial significance, and clarity of writing style.

Finance
The Finance Department of *Management Science* seeks papers on topics that deal with the finance area broadly defined. We are looking for creative work that is innovative, significant and technically correct. Authors should clearly explain the importance of the results to a general audience. The technical level should not be too advanced; for example the

mathematical level should not stray beyond that of a good undergraduate degree in mathematics.

We welcome papers from across the field of paradigms in the finance field and encourage applications to a broad range of problems in the area. We are interested in both in the creation of new theoretical models as well as methodological extensions of existing theory. The department particularly encourages articles that lead to fresh new insights. The department is also interested in papers which conduct rigorous test of existing theories as well as empirical/quantitative studies. In particular the department welcomes submissions of papers in the area of computational finance.

Authors of empirical and quantitative papers should provide or make available enough information and data so that the results are reproducible. The paper should be written in a clear and concise manner. The author should explain the importance of the results to the non-specialist. It is our aim to provide both a speedy turnaround and constructive referees' reports.

Information Systems
The IS department at *Management Science* seeks high quality, rigorous papers that examine Information Systems in the context of the role of management in organizations. The department seeks to publish papers that will have a significant impact on research and practice. Note that all papers must address how their results should impact managerial practice.

High quality research can be done in a variety of ways, including mathematical analyses, computer simulations, laboratory experiments, field data, rigorous argument, or review of the literature. Regardless of the methodology used, it must be sufficiently rigorous that the uncommitted reader can assign high credibility to the result.

The department will support a wide variety of research topics, and it is expected that these specific topics will change over time, as the technology underlying research in this area is undergoing constant and rapid change itself. Typically, however, research will find itself focusing on research problems of either a technical, organizational, or economic nature.

Authors are reminded that their manuscripts must adhere to the *Management Science* guidelines for length. See the instructions for authors in any recent issue, or at the INFORMS publications WWW site http://www.informs.org/pubs/pubshome/html. Authors should submit five copies of their papers to the departmental editor, who will forward them to an appropriate Associate Editor.

Interdisciplinary Management Research and Applications
The multidisciplinary and interfunctional nature of the Management Science profession has been recognized since its inception. Recently, there has been increased recognition by executives for the need to implement such interdisciplinary team approaches for solving complex problems that may have a multitude of societal, political, and business dimensions. This department tries to meet the growing need for research on major management problems

that incorporate several functional perspectives, and that deal with new and nontraditional areas. Other problems and issues that will be considered include:

- business forecasting;
- compensation policies;
- electronic commerce;
- environmental policies;
- financial information systems;
- international corporate strategies
- management of quality improvement programs;
- organizational controls;
- product life-cycle management from marketing, design and manufacturing perspectives;
- project management;
- yield and revenue management; and
- other studies and applications which involve several disciplinary or cross-functional issues.

We actively solicit the submissions of original and imaginative manuscripts that are expected to be of significant interest to the Journal's readership. In particular, we are looking for manuscripts that analyze actual applications, that consolidate several functional areas of management in novel and innovative ways, and build upon several research disciplines in an original manner. Special efforts will be made by the departmental editor to provide the authors with referee reports within four months.

Manuscripts might be practice oriented or theoretical. Practice-oriented submissions should deal with real applications, not with proposed or unimplemented designs. They should provide a critical examination of the methodology and of the general value and impact of the reported application. Theoretical submissions should be problem driven, rather than motivated by hypothetical scenarios. They should exhibit scientific rigor and original analytical or conceptual frameworks that provide new and substantial managerial insights.

Submitted papers should have several attributes. First, papers should display clear evidence of synergism across several functional areas; they should not be narrowly focused. To help the departmental editor evaluate a submission, please motivate the reasons for your submission to this particular department in your cover letter. Identify the major disciplines upon which you have drawn in your paper, and explain the unique features of it. This information will be used to help select the associate editor and referees who will further evaluate your contributions. Second, authors should write manuscripts that are clear and accessible to the largest segment of the Journal readership. The use of appendices is recommended for in-depth exposition of various technical details.

Finally, given the particular nature of this department, potential contributors are strongly encouraged to communicate directly with the editor-in-chief or with the departmental editor prior to formally submitting manuscripts. This communication might verify the potential match between the paper's and the department's objectives.

Manufacturing, Distribution and Service Operations

This department encourages the publication of manuscripts which increase scientific knowledge of operations management in manufacturing, distribution and service. Papers dealing with production and/or delivery of goods and services are appropriate.

The department seeks papers that develop or use management science models and methods for problems and issues arising in the management of manufacturing, distribution and service operations. Of particular interest are papers that deal with strategic concerns such as the choice and impact of new production or information technology, and papers that may provide insight or simple models for guiding manufacturing or service policy. The department encourages papers that examine the planning and coordination of activities and resources within a manufacturing, distribution or service operation, as well as papers that consider the design, location and layout of these operations. Papers that consider the measurement of productivity, flexibility, quality or costs in some operational setting are especially welcome.

All manuscripts submitted for review will be expected to display both scientific rigor and managerial relevance. Simple analytical models will be expected to yield insight into their real world counterparts. Papers concerned with complex algorithms will be expected to address the issues of computability and implementation. Papers that extend established models need to provide significant improvements to or generalizations of the existing models and results. Papers which describe an application or system implementation will be expected to be of some general interest and have some transferable value. The design and analysis of heuristics is encouraged; however, heuristics must be analytically-based and scientifically tested (e.g., the use of analytically derived lower bounds and/or carefully controlled simulation tests).

Authors may submit their papers to any one of the three Departmental Editors.

Marketing

The Marketing Department of *Managerial Science* is interested in scientific papers which use theory, methodology, and/or measurement to address relevant marketing problems. We seek out and publish papers that make significant contributions to the development of marketing science. We suggest the following flexible guidelines:

Marketing Theory. The science of marketing is fortunate now to have 30 or more years of solid empirical evidence with respect to marketing phenomena. Recently, we have seen an explosion of research using this empirical base to derive a set of mathematical marketing theory. We encourage more theoretical papers. Such papers will be judged on relevance and creativity, as well as technical merit. The development of the theory should be supported by relevant empirical evidence. (Citations to published works are sufficient.) Furthermore, the implications of the theory should be relevant, that is, they either enable a manager to better perform his task or enable the scientist to better understand marketing phenomena. (Try to interpret all results intuitively and investigate the sensitivity of your results to changes in assumptions.)

Interface Between Marketing and Other Disciplines. One of the many strengths of *Management Science* is its interdisciplinary base. Research work that explicitly addresses issues related to the integration of the marketing management function with other functions such as R&D and operations management is particularly encouraged. Such submissions will be reviewed by experts in the relevant areas. We encourage authors to demonstrate the additional and unique insights gained from such analyses.

Methodology. Methodology papers can include decision-making models, forecasting methods or measurement techniques which are relevant primarily to marketing, but could also be of interest to other disciplines.

Decision-making models should use marketing theory and empirical evidence to provide management a usable tool for solving relevant problems. These papers will be judged on relevance, usability, and effectiveness. We encourage authors to demonstrate empirically the feasibility of their models' inputs and the usefulness of their models' outputs.

Forecasting methods can include econometrics, time-series analyses, subjective probability-based methods, as well as innovative approaches to combining them. Papers submitted should demonstrate their contribution to marketing by focusing on marketing phenomena and comparing the new method with relevant state-of-the-art marketing models. We also encourage tests of the methodology and holdout samples, predictions to new situations, predictions forward in time, etc.

Measurement techniques can include preference measurements, perceptual mapping, psychometrics, scaling procedures, etc. Measurement techniques that are employed at the individual level and then aggregated to obtain managerially relevant statistics are particularly encouraged. We also encourage explicit recognition of measurement errors and new solutions as to how they should be addressed. Papers will be judged on reliability, validity, and their managerial implications.

Behavioral Science. We encourage marketing papers which use or test theories of consumer behavior such as moods, judgements, emotional responses, and decision making. we also encourage papers addressing behavioral issues related to marketing managers' moves and responses in the context of competitive signaling, consumer dynamics, and environmental changes. Such papers should provide substantive evidence based on which new marketing theories can be developed and marketing methodologies further improved. Such papers should discuss and demonstrate relevance to marketing problems. Papers which integrate quantitative methods with behavioral theories are strongly encouraged.

Applications. We learn through experience. If *Management Science* in marketing is to be relevant, it must be applicable. We encourage papers which a apply theories, models, or methodologies which have been previously published. Such papers should include a discussion of the problem, the analyses to address the problem and an interpretation of the impact of the analyses. We view such papers as cumulative empirical experience adding to the base of marketing science. We are interested, particularly, in papers providing in-depth analyses and describing implementations of management science-based approaches in industries that have not traditionally received much attention, such as the leisure and entertainment industries.

Other. All other papers will be considered on a case-by-case basis. Our main criterion of publication is that the paper make an original and substantial contribution to the marketing literature. The paper should be written with a sufficient degree of conciseness and clarity so that it is accessible to management practitioners. For example, use active voice, write abstracts as a "report in miniature," write introductions so they can be read by all readers, highlight implications, make use of technical appendices, use clear notation, define variables unambiguously, avoid unnecessary jargon and algebra, etc.

Mathematical Programming & Networks

Papers sought by this department are those which promise noticeable improvements in managerial applications based on mathematical programming and networks. Genuine contributions to theory, algorithmic design and evaluation, modeling, and user practice are welcome. Papers whose utilitarian potential is largely speculative, however, should be directed to other journals.

We are especially interested in:

- computational studies or theoretical analyses that illuminate the *relative effectiveness* of algorithms for problems of realistic size and complexity
- contributions to the *model design process* in which real problems are confronted with available mathematical programming and artwork techniques
- well-documented *applications* teaching lessons of transferable value about the use of these techniques in supporting managerial decision making
- methodological *proposals* for the use of mathematical programming and network techniques as a source of insights and as a problem-solving tool
- expository *survey articles* that help bring important branches of the field into better focus through unifying principles or selective emphasis.

Prospective authors are advised that clarity is regarded as a virtue second only to substance. In each paper, the abstract and the introduction should spell out its contribution in nontechnical terms, without unnecessary formalisms and with clear reference to the practical problems that motivated the research.

Organizational Performance, Strategy and Design

The department encourages the publication of papers applying the analytical frameworks of the management sciences to individual, group, organizational and interorganizational behavior. A major emphasis is on papers concerned with understanding and improving organizational performance, strategy and design.

We take a broad approach to organizational performance. Examples of performance dimensions include organizational survival, productivity, quality, timeliness, profitability, flexibility, responsiveness, the development of organizational competence, employee development, and contributions to a larger system. In addition to papers that examine performance at the organizational level of analysis, we are also interested in papers focusing on the performance of the groups and departments that comprise organizations and of the networks in which organizations are embedded. Papers need not explicitly measure a performance dimension but they should have implications for organizational performance, strategy, and design.

We view organizational strategy as the means through which an organization attains its performance goals. Organizational design involves the prescription of the organization's structures and processes in order to improve its performance and survival prospects.

We wish to publish innovative papers from different disciplines, including anthropology, cognitive sciences, economics, information systems, organizational behavior, political science, psychology and sociology. Both theoretical and empirical papers are welcome. We are open to a variety of methods, including archival analyses, surveys, field studies, laboratory studies, simulations, case studies and mathematical modeling.

The editors and reviewers have three overarching questions in mind as they review research submitted to the department. First, is the research interesting and important? Second, has the paper demonstrated what it says it has? Evaluating and ruling out alternative explanations for the paper's findings will strengthen the analysis and increase confidence in the findings. Third, does the paper advance our understanding of organizational performance, strategy, and design? Papers for which the answers to these questions are judged to be yes by the editors and reviewers will be published in the journal. We want to publish the best and the most innovative papers on organizational performance, strategy, and design.

Public Sector Applications

The Public Sector Applications Department of *Management Science* seeks high-quality, well-written papers that emphasize innovative and state-of-the-art uses of management science methods in modeling and solving important decision problems encountered in the public sector. In particular, one key goal of the Department is to publish papers that describe high-impact modeling efforts. Another goal is to publish informative and comprehensive survey articles, especially those that discuss promising opportunities for future research. We take a broad view of the field and will consider papers that describe applications in such diverse areas as the environment, natural resource management (including fisheries management, forestry, wildlife management, and water resources management), energy, health care, housing, defense education, public safety, transportation, recreation, regulatory policy, regional planning, and taxation.

We are seeking to publish papers that make a significant contribution to the scholarly literature on the application of management science methods to the public sector. We envisage that most papers will strive to inform management scientists, as well as government decision makers, about interesting new ways of formulating, analyzing, and solving public sector problems. We also encourage submissions that develop new and original theories and concepts and papers that describe unusual and atypical modeling efforts.

Prospective authors should bear in mind that the departmental editors and associate editors are committed to the timely review and publication of interesting applications of management science in the public sector.

R&D/Innovation And Entrepreneurship

The management of innovative and entrepreneurial activities has become a topic of growing concern and interest within most technology-based organizations, especially in light of today's highly competitive international arena. Within the R&D/Innovation and Entrepreneurship Department, we are looking for original manuscripts that will advance our understanding of the many wide-ranging issues and problems associated with the management of research and technology. Such advancement could come from careful empirical investigations, from clear theoretical conceptualizations or models, from novel syntheses or comprehensive reviews of existing studies, or from well-argued case studies.

Our emphasis is on furthering our understanding of the management process particularly as it relates to the research, development, and engineering tasks necessary to carry out effective innovation. Manuscripts should have a clear problem focus. They should seek to extend our knowledge and perspective of important management problem areas or certain management tools and techniques. Authors submitting their work should articulate what is already known and should try to ground their study within existing streams of research theories and empirical findings. It is through the submission of interesting work that both builds on past results and stimulates future developments that we hope to establish a more coherent, cumulative, and relevant body of knowledge and understanding.

We invite all papers dealing with issues related to the management of innovation and technological activities. Because of the interdisciplinary nature of our focus, we encourage authors from a variety of disciplines to contribute to our department. Illustrative examples of relevant topics are:

- The effective utilization and management of technical professionals
- Project management including project selection. evaluation, and resource utilization
- Organizational structures and designs for enhancing innovation and entrepreneurial efforts
- Managing technological changes and discontinuities
- Managing communications and information flows
- Managing product and process innovations
- Enhancing the commercialization of new technologies
- Managing relationships and interfaces across organizational and functional areas
- Organizing and managing for faster decision-making and product development cycles
- Measuring and improving productivity and quality within R&D
- Managing the locus of innovation among R&D, manufacturing, suppliers, and customers
- Managing global technologies and multicorporate R&D centers
- Technology planning and forecasting
- Technology transfer including the diffusion and adoption of innovation and technological know-how
- Economics of R&D
- Venture capital management and new venture strategies
- Managing corporate and global alliances and joint ventures
- Patents, licensing, and intellectual property rights
- Integrating technology with strategic planning

- Public policy, government regulations, and R&D
- Management systems and rewards for innovation and entrepreneurship

Papers submitted to this department should be well written and based on sound methodological research and concepts. Both empirical and conceptual papers are welcome. Authors should keep in mind the managerial focus of our journal and should address the usefulness of their papers.

Stochastic Models and Simulation
The Applied Stochastic Models Department and the Simulation Department were recently combined into a new department of Stochastic Models and Simulation. The commonality of techniques and applications between the two areas makes the merger natural: simulation is an important tool in the study of stochastic systems, and stochastic process theory underlies much of simulation research and practice. The new Department hopes to bring together the best of the two topics and to feature new directions for both.

The Department seeks papers that contribute to the modeling, analysis, or simulation of stochastic systems through advances in methodology or application. A paper in the area may contribute through theoretical development, through algorithmic advances, or through innovative modeling and applications. Survey articles on topics of broad or growing interest are also welcome. The Department attaches particular importance to scientific rigor and to clarity of exposition.

There are currently many other outlets for publication of work on stochastic models and simulation. Compared with more specialized journals, the Department seeks papers that emphasize issues of broad interest over purely technical contributions. The mathematical level of the work should be appropriate to the contribution but excessive formalism is discouraged. Deferring necessary technical material to appendices can help make research papers accessible to a wider audience.

The Department welcomes papers in such areas as inventory and production, service operations, statistical and computational issues in simulation, telecommunications, variance reductions techniques, and all aspects of the application of probability to management science. The Department is particularly eager to attract papers in novel areas of theory and application of stochastic modeling and simulation, such as financial engineering and risk management, public health and health care operations, environmental and catastrophic risks, extremal events and insurance, new approaches to simulation efficiency, Markov chain Monte Carlo, and quasi-Monte Carlo methods.

Supply Chain Management
To compete successfully in the global market, companies need to manage the effectiveness and efficiency of the operations that manufacture and distribute their products or services to their customers. Supply chain management deals with the management of materials, information and financial flows in a network consisting of suppliers, manufacturers, distributors, retailers, and customers. Many industries have found it challenging to manage these flows efficiently and effectively.

There are three types of flows in a supply chain that require careful planning and coordination. Material flows involve both physical product flows from suppliers to customers through the chain as well as the reverse flows via product returns, servicing, recycling, and disposal. Information flows involve order transmission and delivery status. Financial flows involve credit terms payment schedules, and consignment and title ownership arrangements. These flows cut across companies and sometimes ownership arrangements. These flows cut across companies and sometimes even industries.

The Department of Supply Chain Management processes papers that focus on the coordination and integration of the flows in a supply chain consisting of multiple sites and organizations with multiple independent decision makers. (For papers that do not quite fit the above description, the author(s) should submit their papers to the Department of Manufacturing, Distribution and Service Operations.) The papers to be processed by the Department of Supply Chain Management can be:

- theoretical work motivated by real life problems and situations
- applications based on real cases
- conceptual work that provides a framework to analyze problems in industry
- empirical studies based on real data
- surveys of existing literature and industrial practice

Examples of topics include: product and process designs for supply chain management; structuring supply chains for mass customization; third party logistics; outsourcing and contract manufacturing; supplier contracting; incentive and performance measures; global supply chain management; quick response and cycle time reduction; multiproduct and multilocation production and inventory coordination; consolidation, warehousing, scheduling and coordination of transportation and production flows; and industry-wide supply chain integration.

All paper submissions should comply with the Editorial Policy and the Instructions for Authors located on the front inside cover of any issue of *Management Science*. Please submit four copies of the paper to the Departmental Editor of Supply Chain Management at the address printed above.

EDITORIAL STATEMENT

Management Science is a scholarly journal published to scientifically address the problems, interests and concerns of organizational decision-makers. Through publication of relevant theory and innovative applications, we serve the needs of both academicians and practitioners. In addition to articles from traditional fields such as operations research, mathematics, statistics, industrial engineering, psychology, sociology and political science, we publish cross-functional, multidisciplinary research to reflect the diversity of the management science profession. We also publish relevant articles and seek to stimulate research in emerging domains, such as those created by globalization of the economy, changes in public policy, and improvements in technology.

PACKING SLIP:
Amazon Marketplace Item: Cabell's Directory of Publishing Opportunities in Marketing 2001-02 (Cabell's...

Listing ID: 1008R479079
Purchased on: 05-Apr-2002 11:18:13
Shipped by: adam4splat@yahoo.com
Shipping address:

Ship to: Ted Light
Address Line 1: 3024 Kinmont Ave. #1
Address Line 2:
City: Cincinnati
State/Province/Region: OH
Zip/Postal Code: 45208
Country: United States

Buyer Name: ted light

SUBMISSIONS

The following are requirements for a manuscript submitted to *Management Science*:

- papers are not more than 32 pages including figures and tables, printed on 8 1/2" X 11" paper;
- 12-point font, and one-inch margins on all four sides;
- double-spaced throughout, including abstract, references, and footnotes;
- a nonmathematical abstract (as understandable to readers as possible) of not more than 200 words;
- four copies for the reviewing process; and
- a list of five potential referees on a separate sheet of paper with several lines describing why they would be | good reviewers, area of expertise, title, full mailing addresses, phones, fax, and e-mail. The suggested referees should not have a conflict of interest with the author(s). A person has a conflict of interest with (a) his/her major professor or a student for whom the person served as a major professor, (b) people working at the same institution, (c) coauthors on work completed or in progress _during the last four years.
- when a paper is accepted for publication, we must have a hard copy of the final version plus a disk in either Word, WordPerfect, or Tex.

Please submit manuscripts to the appropriate Departmental Editor or to the Editor-in-Chief. Departmental Editors are listed on the journal masthead.

Marketing Education Review

ADDRESS FOR SUBMISSION:

Dale A. Lunsford, Editor
Marketing Education Review
University of Texas at Tyler
Dean of Student Affairs & Ext. Relations
3900 University Boulevard
Tyler, TX 75799
USA
Phone: 903-566-7316
Fax: 903-566-7078
E-Mail: lunsford@mail.uttyl.edu
Web: cbpa.louisville.edu/mer
Address May Change:

PUBLICATION GUIDELINES:

Manuscript Length: 21-25
Copies Required: Four
Computer Submission: No
Format: N/A
Fees to Review: 0.00 US$

Manuscript Style:
    See Manuscript Guidelines

CIRCULATION DATA:

Reader: Academics
Frequency of Issue: 3 Times/Year
Copies per Issue: Less than 1,000
Sponsor/Publisher: CtC Press
Subscribe Price: 32.00 US$ Individual
    72.00 US$ Institution

REVIEW INFORMATION:

Type of Review: Blind Review
No. of External Reviewers: 2
No. of In House Reviewers: 0
Acceptance Rate: 21-30%
Time to Review: 2 - 3 Months
Reviewers Comments: Yes
Invited Articles: 0-5%
Fees to Publish: 0.00 US$

MANUSCRIPT TOPICS:
Business Education; Marketing Education

MANUSCRIPT GUIDELINES/COMMENTS:

Manuscript Preparation And Submission
Submit four (4) nonreturnable copies of manuscripts for publication consideration to Dale A. Lunsford, Editor.

All manuscripts should be typed, 11 or 12 pitch, double-spaced (including references) on 8 1/2 by 11 inch white paper with margins of at least one inch on all four sides.

Order of Material

A. Front Matter
First Page: Title of paper, name and position of author(s), author(s') complete address(es) and telephone number(s), and any acknowledgement of assistance.

Second Page: A brief biographical sketch of each author including name, degree(s) held, title or position, organization or institution, previous publications, and areas of research interest.

Third Page: Title of paper without author(s') name(s') and a brief abstract of no more than 100 words summarizing the article.

B. Body of Text

The text begins on the fourth page, with major headings centered on the page and subheadings flush with the left margin. All headings and titles should be typed with upper and lower case (Do not use all capitals).

Footnotes are not used for reference purposes. In general, footnotes are seldom needed because the text itself should be avoided. In the extreme case that a footnote is needed, it will be referred to as an endnote at the end of the article and must be approved by the editor before final submission.

C. Technical Appendices Technical appendices may be used to include mathematical or highly technical material which supports the main text but is not critical to the reader's interpretation of the text.

D. Tables and Figures

Each table or figure should be placed on a separate page and numbered consecutively beginning with Table 1 and Figure 1. A table or figure should not be included unless it is referred to in the text of the article. Placement in the text should be indicated as follows:

Table 1 about here

Footnotes in tables or figures should be designated by lower case letters. Table or figure number and title should be typed on two separate lines, using upper and lower cases, as follows:

Table 1
Prospecting Methods and Sales Force Earnings

In the event that complicated tables or figures are used within the text, please submit a high resolution print-out (preferably a ≥ 600 dot-per-inch laser copy) as the original may need to be used for printing purposes.

E. References

References within the text should include the author's last name and year of publication enclosed in parentheses, e.g. (Meddaugh 1976). If practical, place the citation just ahead of a punctuation mark. If the author's name is used within the text sentence, just place the year of publication in parentheses, e.g., "According to Meddaugh (1976)..." If a particular page or section is cited, it should be placed within the parentheses, e.g., (Meddaugh 1976, p. 48). For multiple authors, use up to three names in the citation. With four or more authors, use the first author's name and et al.; (Meddaugh et al. 1979).

An alphabetical listing of references should appear at the end of the manuscript, with first author's surname first and year of publication following all authors' names. Work by the same author with the same publication year should be distinguished by lower case letters after the date (e.g., 1983a). For authors cited more than once, substitute a one-inch line for each name that repeats. Examples are as follows:

Crissy, William J.E. and Robert M. Kaplan (1969), **Salesmanship: The Personal Force in Marketing**, New York: John Wiley & Sons.

Enis, Ben M. and Lawrence B. Chonko (1979), "A Review of Personal Selling: Implications for Managers and Researchers," In **Review of Marketing: 1978**, Gerald Zaltman and Thomas V. Bonoma, eds., Chicago: American Marketing Association, 23-32.

Ingram, Thomas N. and Danny N. Bellenger (1983),"Personal and Organizational Variables: Their Relative Effect on Reward Valences of Industrial Salespeople," **Journal of Marketing Research, 20 (May), 198-205.**

Acceptance Procedure

MER manuscripts are reviewed independently by members of the editorial review board, and their recommendations guide the Editor in his decision. The reviews are blind - neither authors nor reviewers know the identity of each other.

It is the policy of *MER* that manuscripts submitted to this journal must not be under publication consideration by another journal at the same time. Manuscripts which are substantially similar in content to articles already published or accepted for publication in this journal or elsewhere are ineligible for publication. It is the author's responsibility to abide by these provisions when submitting a manuscript for consideration to *MER*.

Marketing Educator

ADDRESS FOR SUBMISSION:

Sharon V. Thach, Editor
Marketing Educator
Tennessee State University
College of Business
Nashville, TN 37203
USA
Phone: 615-963-7139
Fax: 615-963-7133
E-Mail: sthach@tnstate.edu
Web: www.ama.org/pubs/me/info/
Address May Change:

CIRCULATION DATA:

Reader: , Professional
Frequency of Issue: Quarterly
Copies per Issue: Online Only
Sponsor/Publisher: American Marketing Association
Subscribe Price: 0.00 US$ to Members

PUBLICATION GUIDELINES:

Manuscript Length: 6-10
Copies Required: One
Computer Submission: Yes Disk
Format: Word/WordPerfect
Fees to Review: 0.00 US$

Manuscript Style:
No Reply

REVIEW INFORMATION:

Type of Review: Blind Review
No. of External Reviewers: 1
No. of In House Reviewers: 1
Acceptance Rate: 90%
Time to Review: 1 - 2 Months
Reviewers Comments: Yes
Invited Articles: 6-10%
Fees to Publish: 0.00 US$

MANUSCRIPT TOPICS:
Advertising & Promotion Management; Business Education; Business Information Systems (MIS); Business Law, Public Responsibility & Ethics; Direct Marketing; Global Business; Marketing Research; Marketing Theory & Applications; Sales/Selling; Services; Small Business Entrepreneurship; Transportation/Physical Distribution

MANUSCRIPT GUIDELINES/COMMENTS:

The *Marketing Educator* is the official publication of the Academic Council of the American Marketing Association. Articles on teaching and scholarship of interest to the members are published as well as announcements of AMA meetings, calls for papers, and awards. Brief announcements for non-AMA meetings and journals will be printed.

All materials are protected by the same laws governing intellectual property rights as the printed version of The *Marketing Educator*. Articles should be no longer than 10 printed pages.

Submissions should be sent, including a disk in either Word or WordPerfect to the editor.

Marketing Health Services

ADDRESS FOR SUBMISSION:

Richard K. Thomas, Editor
Marketing Health Services
American Marketing Association
Marketing Health Services
250 South Wacker, Suite 200
Chicago, IL 60606
USA
Phone: 1-800-262-1150
Fax: 312-648-0103
E-Mail: rthomas@ama.org
Web: www.ama.org
Address May Change:

PUBLICATION GUIDELINES:

Manuscript Length: 11-20
Copies Required: Five + 1 disk
Computer Submission: Yes
Format: Prefer MS Word
Fees to Review: 0.00 US$

Manuscript Style:
   Chicago Manual of Style

CIRCULATION DATA:

Reader: , Health Care Marketers
Frequency of Issue: Quarterly
Copies per Issue: 3,001 - 4,000
Sponsor/Publisher: American Marketing Association
Subscribe Price: 70.00 US$ Individual
   45.00 US$ AMA Member
   90.00 US$ Institution

REVIEW INFORMATION:

Type of Review: Blind Review
No. of External Reviewers: 3+
No. of In House Reviewers: 2
Acceptance Rate: 21-40%
Time to Review: 1-3 Months
Reviewers Comments: Yes
Invited Articles: 11-30%
Fees to Publish: 0.00 US$

MANUSCRIPT TOPICS:
Advertising & Promotion Management; Direct Marketing; Marketing Research; Various Marketing Areas in Health Care Field

MANUSCRIPT GUIDELINES/COMMENTS:

Editor-in-Chief: Richard K. Thomas, 1407 Union Avenue, Suite 200, Memphis, TN 38104
                Tel: (901) 726-6808, Fax: (901) 726-9028, Email: rthomas@msrg.com

Mission
Marketing Health Services is a magazine for health care marketing professionals designed to challenge current thinking and shape future decision-making. By publishing timely articles on marketing thought, research, innovation, and applications in the health care industry, the magazine promotes professional development and advances the science and ethical practice of marketing.

Editorial Approach
MHS covers topics such as strategic planning, consumer attitudes and behavior, competitor analysis, product development, pricing, distribution, promotion, health care policy, and other

management issues as they relate to marketing. A literature review is not acceptable, nor are promotional pieces for a product, person, or company. Because MHS seeks to inform our readers about cutting-edge thought and practice in health care marketing, only original material will be considered for publication.

STYLE GUIDELINES
Submission Format

- Submit five (5) hard copies of the article and one (1) copy on a computer disk. Word for Windows on a 3½-inch high-density floppy is preferred, but we can convert any common word-processing software such as Word Perfect. (Please write the format on the disk.) Hard copies should be double-spaced.

- Type on one side of the page only and use upper and lower case. On the first page include the manuscript title and name of author(s), present position, **complete** address, and telephone/fax numbers. On the second page list the title without the author's name.

- Label all charts, figures, and tables as "exhibits." Tables, figures, and charts should be submitted on a separate disk. All exhibits must be typed in Times or Helvetica and need to be done in Word or PowerPoint **only**. Please submit all exhibits on a **separate** disk. If possible, please submit in EPS or TIFF format. Use exhibits to enhance comprehension of the text, to give readers a snapshot of statistics, or to simplify/enliven complex material. They should not be used to validate methodology used to conduct a study, but to illustrate the findings (e.g., percentage of respondents who were enrolled in managed care plans. Exhibits that do not add value to the reader will be cut. There will be a limit of **four** exhibits or sidebars. Do **not** incorporate exhibits into the text file. Exhibits might be cut, depending on space availability and usefulness to the reader.

- The article text should be between 4,000 and 5,500 words.

- If the article is based on the results of a study, include details of the sample, methodology, and analysis on a separate page at the end of the article (see "Articles Based on Studies").

- Include a short biography for each author highlighting any experience that establishes expertise in the subject at hand.

Readability
MHS articles are judged not only on the depth and cope of the ideas presented, but also on their clarity and whether they can be read and understood. Keep in mind that our readers have cried backgrounds. Avoid using technical terms hat few are likely to understand; if you must use such terms, include a brief definition. Spell out acronyms on first use. **Remember: MHS is designed to be read, not deciphered.**

Articles Based on Studies
Articles based on studies should present original pinking without relying heavily on other people's research, and the study must have been conducted within the prior two years.

Interpret the findings, don't just report them; authors must clearly establish their position on an issue, even when presenting all sides of a debate. In general, the article should emphasize the findings and implications for marketers, not the methodology used to conduct the study. Some specific tips include:

- Don't wait until the end of the article to draw conclusions about a study. Create a lead using the five W's - who, what, where, when, and why - and summarize major conclusions within the first three paragraphs.

- Use a narrative writing style and avoid excessive use of passive voice. Instead of "A study was conducted on patient perceptions of hospital advertising," say "We conducted a study on ..." Passive voice often obscures the subject of the sentence, opening the door to ambiguity and possible confusion for the reader. It is also boring to read.

- Don't reference everything you've ever read on the subject. Given your background and professional standing, a certain level of knowledge and expertise is assumed. For example, citing other sources for general statements such as "Health care marketers have witnessed dynamic changes in the industry over the past decade" is like saying "The sky is blue, according to my kindergarten teacher."

Give attribution only when:

1. **Quoting someone directly**. Good quotes liven up an article if used sparingly. Write the attribution into the article as follows: "Marketing health care is no longer a 'we vs. them' approach," according to Gerald McManis and Lisa Frey in their Fall 1994 Journal of Health Care Marketing article. Whenever possible, cite the original source, not an anthology.

2. **Citing statistics**. This can be very general. Use "according to government statistics" (or press reports) when statistics are in the public domain or likely to have been widely reported. Be sure to update such data to keep the information timely. If you found Direct Marketing Association estimates in a book, cite the source, not the book, and call the DMA for an update if possible.

3. **Introducing proprietary or classic techniques**. This is often a judgment call. Give credit to A. Parasuraman, Valarie Zeithaml, and Leonard Berry for their SERVQUAL model, for example, but not if you just mention it as one of several techniques. Give the credit only once, however, and don't reference statistical methods such as LISREL.

- Use percentages when reporting survey results, rather than significance scores, eigenvalues, canonical loadings, etc. Ordinary people - not just statisticians - should be able to understand the results. Remember: Statistics should be used to make your point, not to show how thorough your research was.

References

Any necessary attribution should be written into the text (see instructions on giving attribution). Do not use reference numbers, bracketed or parenthetical notes. The goal is to have MHS read like a magazine; not like an academic journal. However, authors may provide an "Additional Reading" list of no more than 8-10 items to be included at the end of the article. The purpose of this bibliography is to steer readers to other important works on the same topic. Please follow the Journal of Marketing style when creating the list.

REVIEW PROCEDURES
The review process for a submitted article generally is completed within six to eight weeks, barring unusual circumstances. High editorial standards are maintained through use of targeted procurement of articles, an active double-blind review process, commissioned articles, and communication with members of the marketing community.

GENERAL INFORMATION
If the article is accepted for publication, we will send you a copyright form to sign. All MHS material is copyrighted by the American Marketing Association with future-use rights reserved. Articles are edited by the AMA's staff of professional editors, who generally require all titles, subtitles, abstracts, and subheads to conform to the magazine's style.

Each author will receive a complimentary copy of the issue in which his or her article appears, and reprints will be available for purchase. Send articles and correspondence to the Editor.

Marketing Intelligence & Planning

ADDRESS FOR SUBMISSION:

Michael Thomas, Editor
Marketing Intelligence & Planning
University of Strathclyde
Department of Marketing
Stenhouse Building, 173 Cathedral Street
Glasgow, G4 ORQ
Scotland
Phone: 141-552-4400 ext 3737
Fax: 141-552-2802
E-Mail: michaelt@strath.ac.uk
Web: www.mcb.co.uk
Address May Change:

PUBLICATION GUIDELINES:

Manuscript Length: 3,000-6,000 words
Copies Required: Three
Computer Submission: Yes
Format: 3.5 disk (Windows)
Fees to Review: 0.00 US$

Manuscript Style:
 Uniform System of Citation (Harvard Blue Book)

CIRCULATION DATA:

Reader: Business Persons, Academics
Frequency of Issue: Other
Copies per Issue: No Reply
Sponsor/Publisher: MCB University Press
Subscribe Price: 8749.00 US$

REVIEW INFORMATION:

Type of Review: Editorial Review
No. of External Reviewers: 1
No. of In House Reviewers: 1
Acceptance Rate: 50%
Time to Review: 4 - 6 Months
Reviewers Comments: Yes
Invited Articles: 6-10%
Fees to Publish: 0.00 US$

MANUSCRIPT TOPICS:
Advertising & Promotion Management; Business Information Systems (MIS); Direct Marketing; Global Business; Marketing Research; Marketing Theory & Applications; Organizational Development; Sales/Selling; Strategic Management Policy

MANUSCRIPT GUIDELINES/COMMENTS:

About the journal
Marketing Intelligence & Planning offers in-depth analysis of the intricate relationship between planning and implementation, plus informed opinion and critical analysis from international experts in the field. As marketing techniques and technology increase in sophistication, it is essential that marketing professionals and academics understand how to apply them effectively. As such *Marketing Intelligence & Planning* aims to provide the practical implications that will help bridge the gap between academic research and practice. Every article published in *Marketing Intelligence & Planning* has been subject to a double blind review process to ensure its relevance and quality.

Coverage
- Strategic planning
- Advertising
- Buyer behaviour
- Sales management
- Marketing research
- Information systems

NOTES FOR CONTRIBUTORS

Copyright
Articles submitted to the journal should be original contributions and should not be under consideration for any other publication at the same time. Authors submitting articles for publication warrant that the work is not an infringement of any existing copyright and will indemnify the publisher against any breach of such warranty. For ease of dissemination and to ensure proper policing of use, papers and contributions become the legal copyright of the publisher unless otherwise agreed. Submissions should be sent to: The Editor or the Assistant Editor, Keith Crosier, at the same address.

Editorial objectives
To provide a vehicle that will help practising managers translate conceptual models and market place information into usable marketing plans. Users of research need to communicate with those who undertake research about their problems. They need to know how to process that information and translate it into action plans.

General principles
a. It is our intention to encourage communications between marketing managers and researchers, to be positioned right at the academic-practitioner interface.

b. Contributors are encouraged to spell out the planning implications of their work for those involved in marketing.

c. Articles based on experiences and evidence - rather than just philosophical speculation - will receive particular encouragement.

d. A series of short articles on a linked theme appearing in successive issues would be particularly welcome.

The reviewing process
Papers are subject to a double blind review through the MCB University Press PeerNet process. Please visit http://www.peer-net.com for further information.

However, the Editor, who is a respected expert in the subject area concerned, reserves the right to select certain papers without review.

Manuscript requirements
Three copies of the manuscript should be submitted in double line spacing with wide margins, accompanied by two 3.5" disks of the same version. This should facilitate speedier reviewing. All authors should be shown and author's details must be printed on a separate sheet and the author should not be identified anywhere else in the article.

As a guide, articles should be between 3,000 and 6,000 words in length. A title of not more than eight words should be provided. A brief **autobiographical note** should be supplied including full name, affiliation, e-mail address and full international contact details. Authors must supply an **abstract** of 100-150 words. Up to six **keywords** should be included which encapsulate the principal subjects covered by the article.

Where there is a **methodology**, it should be clearly described under a separate heading. **Headings** must be short, clearly defined and not numbered. **Notes** or **Endnotes** should be used only if absolutely necessary and must be identified in the text by consecutive numbers, enclosed in square brackets and listed at the end of the article.

Figures, charts and **diagrams** should be kept to a minimum. They must be black and white with minimum shading and numbered consecutively using arabic numerals with a brief title and labelled axes. In the text, the position of the figure should be shown by typing on a separate line the words "take in Figure 2". Good quality originals must be provided.

Tables should be kept to a minimum. They must be numbered consecutively with roman numerals and a brief title. In the text, the position of the table should be shown by typing on a separate line the words "take in Table IV".

Photos and **illustrations** must be supplied as good quality black and white original half tones with captions. Their position should be shown in the text by typing on a separate line the words "take in Plate 2".

References to other publications should be complete and in Harvard style. They should contain full bibliographical details and journal titles should not be abbreviated. For multiple citations in the same year use a, b, c immediately following the year of publication. References should be shown within the text by giving the author's last name followed by a comma and year of publication all in round brackets, e.g. (Fox, 1994). At the end of the article should be a reference list in alphabetical order as follows

(a) for books
surname, initials and year of publication, title, publisher, place of publication, e.g.Casson, M. (1979), Alternatives to the Multinational Enterprise, Macmillan, London.

(b) for chapter in edited book
surname, initials and year, "title", editor's surname, initials, title, publisher, place, pages, e.g.Bessley, M. and Wilson, P. (1984), "Public policy and small firms in Britain", in Levicki, C. (Ed.), Small Business Theory and Policy, Croom Helm, London, pp.111-26. Please note that the chapter title must be underlined.

(c) for articles
surname, initials, year "title", journal, volume, number, pages, e.g.Fox, S. (1994) "Empowerment as a catalyst for change: an example from the food industry", Supply Chain Management, Vol 2 No 3, pp. 29-33

If there is more than one author list surnames followed by initials. All authors should be shown.

Electronic sources should include the URL of the electronic site at which they may be found, as follows:
Neuman, B.C.(1995), "Security, payment, and privacy for network commerce", IEEE Journal on Selected Areas in Communications, Vol. 13 No.8, October, pp.1523-31. Available (IEEE SEPTEMBER) http://www.research.att.com/jsac/

Notes/Endnotes should be used only if absolutely necessary. They should, however, always be used for citing Web sites. They should be identified in the text by consecutive numbers enclosed in square brackets and listed at the end of the article. Please then provide full Web site addresses in the end list.

Final submission of the article
Once accepted for publication, the final version of the manuscript must be provided, accompanied by a 3.5" disk of the same version labelled with: disk format; author name(s); title of article; journal title; file name.

Each article must be accompanied by a completed and signed Journal Article Record Form available from the Editor or on http://www.literaticlub.co.uk/

The manuscript will be considered to be the definitive version of the article. The author must ensure that it is complete, grammatically correct and without spelling or typographical errors. In preparing the disk, please use one of the following formats: Word, Word Perfect, Rich text format or TeX/LaTeX. Figures which are provided electronically must be in tif, gif or pic file extensions. All figures and graphics must also be supplied as good quality originals.

Final submission requirements
Manuscripts must be clean, good quality hard copy and;
- include an abstract and keywords
- have Harvard style references
- include any figures, photos and graphics as good quality originals
- be accompanied by a labelled disk
- be accompanied by a completed Journal Article Record Form

Technical assistance is available from MCB's World Wide Web Literati Club on http://www.literaticlub.co.uk/ or contact Mike Massey at MCB, e-mail mmassey@mcb.co.uk

Marketing Letters

ADDRESS FOR SUBMISSION:

Bob Meyer, Bart Weitz, Editors-in-Chief
Marketing Letters
Kluwer Academic Publishers
Journals Editorial Office
101 Phillip Drive
Norwell, MA 02061
USA
Phone: 781-871-6600
Fax: 781-871-6528
E-Mail:
Web: www.wkap.nl
Address May Change:

PUBLICATION GUIDELINES:

Manuscript Length: 11-15
Copies Required: Five
Computer Submission: No
Format: N/A
Fees to Review: 0.00 US$

Manuscript Style:
See Manuscript Guidelines

CIRCULATION DATA:

Reader: Academics
Frequency of Issue: Quarterly
Copies per Issue: Less than 1,000
Sponsor/Publisher: Kluwer Academic
   Publishers
Subscribe Price: 83.00 US$ Individual
   134.00 US$ Institution
   193.00 NLG Indv., 660 NLG Institution

REVIEW INFORMATION:

Type of Review: Editorial Review
No. of External Reviewers: 2
No. of In House Reviewers: No Reply
Acceptance Rate: 21-30%
Time to Review: 1 - 2 Months
Reviewers Comments: Yes
Invited Articles: 0-5%
Fees to Publish: 0.00 US$

MANUSCRIPT TOPICS:
Advertising & Promotion Management; Direct Marketing; Labor Relations & Human Resource Mgt.; Marketing Research

MANUSCRIPT GUIDELINES/COMMENTS:

Aims & Scope
Marketing Letters: A Journal of Research in Marketing publishes high-quality, shorter papers on marketing, the emphasis being on immediacy and current interest. The journal offers a medium for the truly rapid publication of research results. The focus of *Marketing Letters* is on empirical findings, methodological papers, and theoretical and conceptual insights across areas of research in marketing. *Marketing Letters* is required reading for anyone working in marketing science, consumer research, methodology, and marketing strategy and management. The key subject areas and topics covered in *Marketing Letters* are: choice models, consumer behavior, consumer research, management science, market research, sales and advertising, marketing management, marketing research, marketing science, psychology, and statistics.

Address For Contributors
Send five (5) copies (with cover letters) to Editors-in-Chief (address above).

Manuscript Preparation
Submitted papers should typically be less than 15 double-spaced typewritten pages, including bibliographies, tables, etc. Final versions of accepted manuscripts (including notes, references, tables, and legends) should be typed doublespaced on 8.5" x 11" (22cm x 29cm) white paper with 1" (2.5cm) margins on all sides. Sections should appear in the following order: title page, abstract, text, notes, references, tables, figure legends, and figures. Comments or replies to previously published articles should also follow this format with the exception of abstracts, which are not required.

Title Page. The title page should include the article title, authors' names and permanent affiliations, and the name, current address, and telephone number of the person to whom page proofs and reprints should be sent.

Abstract. The following page should include an abstract of not more than 100 words and a list of two to six keywords.

Text. The text of the article should begin on a new page. The introduction should have no heading or number. Subsequent section headings (including appendices) should be designated by arabic numerals (1, 2, etc.), and subsection headings should be numbered 1.1, 1.2, etc. Figures, tables, and displayed equations should be numbered consecutively throughout the text (1, 2, etc.). Equation numbers should appear flush left in parentheses and running variables for equations (e.g. $i = 1, \ldots, n$) flush right in parentheses.

Notes. Acknowledgments and related information should appear in a note designated by an asterisk after the last author's name, and subsequent notes should be numbered consecutively and designated by superscripts (1, 2, etc.) in the text. All notes should be typed double-spaced beginning on a separate page following the text.

References. References in the text should follow the author-date format (e,g. Brown (1986). Jones (1978a, 1978b). Smith and Johnson (1983)). References should be typed double-spaced beginning on a separate page following the notes, according to the following samples (journal and book titles may be underlined rather than italicized). References with up to three authors should include the names of each author, references with four or more authors should cite the first author and add "et al." It is the responsibility of authors to verify all references.

Tables. Tables should be titled and typed double-spaced, each on a separate sheet, following the references. Notes to tables should be designated by superscripted letters (a, b, etc.) within each tahle and typed double-spaced on the same page as the table. Use descriptive labels rather than computer acronyms, and explain all abbreviations. When tables are typed on oversized paper, please submit both the original and a reduced copy.

Figures. Figures for accepted manuscripts should be submitted in camera-ready form, i.e. clear glassy prints or drawn in India ink on drafting paper or high quality white paper. Lettering in figures should be large enough to be legible after half size reduction. Authors should submit one 5" x 7" (13cm x 18cm) original and two photocopies of each figure, with authors names, manuscript title, and figure number on the back of each original and copy (use gummed labels if necessary to avoid damaging originals). Figures should be enclosed in a separate envelope backed by cardboard and without staples or paper clips. Figure legends should be typed double-spaced on a separate sheet following the tables.

Page Proofs and Reprints
Corrected page proofs must be returned within three days of receipt, and alterations other than corrections may be charged to the authors. Authors will receive 25 free reprints, and may order additional copies when returning the corrected proofs.

Electronic Delivery
Important Please send only the electronic version (of accepted paper) via one of the methods listed below. Note, in the event of minor discrepancies between the electronic version and hard copy, the electronic file will be used as the final version.

Via electronic mail
Please e-mail electronic version to: KAPfiles@wkap.com
Recommended formats for sending files via e-mail:
Binary files - uuencode or binhex
Compressing files - compress, pkzip, or gzip
Collecting files - tar
The e-mail message should include the author's last name, the name of the journal to which the paper has been accepted, and the type of file (e.g., LaTex or ASCII).

Via anonymous FTP
ftp: ftp.wkap.com cd: /incoming/production
Send email to KAPfiles\@wkap.com to inform Kluwer electronic version is at this FTP site.

Via disk
Label a 3.5 inch floppy disk with the operating system and word processing program along with the authors' names, manuscript title, and name of journal to which the paper has been accepted.
Mail disk to: Kluwer Academic Publishers Desktop Department 101 Philip Drive Assinippi Park Norwell, MA 02061 USA
Any questions about the above procedures please send e-mail to: dthelp@wkap.com

Marketing Management

ADDRESS FOR SUBMISSION:

Carolyn P. Neal, Editor
Marketing Management
Georgia State University
Robinson College of Business
Department of Marketing
University Plaza
Atlanta, GA 30303
USA.
Phone: 404-651-4263
Fax: 404-651-4256
E-Mail: cneal@gsu.edu
Web: www.ama.org
Address May Change:

PUBLICATION GUIDELINES:

Manuscript Length: 4,000 words
Copies Required: Three
Computer Submission: Yes
Format: See Guidelines
Fees to Review: 0.00 US$

Manuscript Style:
American Psychological Association

CIRCULATION DATA:

Reader: Business Persons, Senior Marketing Executive
Frequency of Issue: Quarterly
Copies per Issue: 4,001 - 5,000
Sponsor/Publisher: American Marketing Association
Subscribe Price: 70.00 US$
  45.00 US$ AMA Member
  90.00 US$ Institution

REVIEW INFORMATION:

Type of Review: Blind Review
No. of External Reviewers: 3
No. of In House Reviewers: 1
Acceptance Rate: 21-30%
Time to Review: 2 - 3 Months
Reviewers Comments: Yes
Invited Articles: 50% +
Fees to Publish: 0.00 US$

MANUSCRIPT TOPICS:
Advertising & Promotion Management; Direct Marketing; Global Business; Marketing Research; Marketing Theory & Applications; Sales/Selling; Services; Strategic Management Policy; Technology/Innovation

MANUSCRIPT GUIDELINES/COMMENTS:

Mission Statement
Marketing Management (MM) packages and clearly communicates the best strategic thinking to meet the decision-making needs of knowledgeable executives managing real-world businesses.

Editorial Approach
MM provides thoughtful, timely, and useful information to senior marketing executives and other business executives whose interests lie in a compatible area. It publishes in-depth articles on functional areas of marketing, marketing management, and marketing as a philosophy of business. To help fulfill readers' professional development needs, MM provides

the cutting edge of marketing thought and presents marketing as a vital and an important element of business.

High editorial standards are maintained through the use of targeted procurement of manuscripts, an active double-blind referee process, commissioned manuscripts, solicited interviews, and communication with members of the marketing community. Whenever possible, MM takes a unique approach to the editorial product by pairing academic and practitioner authors to broaden the perspectives on a topic.

Article topics include, but are not limited to, the following categories: pricing, product development, integrated communications, logistics/distribution, marketing research, strategy/marketing management, sales management, merchandising/retailing, customer satisfaction, market-driven quality, financial issues management, societal issues, and corporate culture management.

In addition to feature articles, MM publishes a variety of departments, interviews with prominent executives, marketing classics, book reviews, and letters to the editor.

With the exception of Marketing Masters articles, MM publishes only original manuscripts. A conference speech, if edited to conform with our style, also will be considered for publication.

Review Procedure
MM employs a double-blind referee process for all except commissioned manuscripts, interviews and some departments.

MM has three editorial boards: the Editorial Policy Board, the Editorial Review Board, and the Council of Reviewers. In addition, ad hoc reviewers are enlisted for select subject matter. After reading the reviews, the editor makes all final decisions on publication. The review process should be completed within six to eight weeks, barring unusual circumstances.

Writing for MM
As senior executives, MM readers have many demands on their time. All manuscripts must, therefore, contain information essential to their professional development and/or corporate or personal interests. Try to convey that information so readers can easily and rapidly comprehend it.

All manuscripts not specifically procured by the editor will be subject to the review process. Procured manuscripts will be reviewed in a preliminary statement, as in the form of a detailed outline, and advice given for further development.

Manuscripts should comply with the style guidelines that follow.
In general, editorial content should have actual business applications and significance to the marketing profession.

Manuscripts are evaluated on a number of criteria. Generally, the manuscript must:

- Look at cutting-edge issues or topics that will affect executives in the conduct of business.

- Discuss such issues or topics in-depth, preferably with the inclusion of actual corporate experiences that point out the relevance to the reader.

- Challenge readers to look at new ideas, or perhaps old ideas in a new light and stimulate and extend their thinking, awaken their interest in, and awareness of, new approaches and options.

- Present original thinking. Avoid extensive reliance on other people's research.

- Interpret the findings of a research study, not just report them. Authors must clearly establish their position on an issue, even when presenting all sides of a debate.

- Extend ideas that are industry- or service-specific, geographically or demographically focused, or otherwise limited in scope or applicability. The information must be of value to a broad readership.

- Include a detailed description of how proposed marketing strategies can be implemented.

- Not promote a product, person, or company. Not discuss a trademarked idea or process. If a corporate story is translatable into direct benefit to other corporations, it should be written as such, not as a public relations promotion. The PR benefit is more effective when readers view the author as an expert.

In addition, reviewers will address a series of specific questions, including the following:

- Is the subject of current interest to MM's readership of senior marketing executives?
- Do you perceive any inaccuracies in the facts or data presented?
- Is the main argument clearly expressed and does the manuscript flow smoothly and logically?
- Is the writing style clear and interesting?
- Are there any new concepts or techniques presented? Are they valid and worthy of discussion?
- Does this manuscript have practical application for the business community?
- Does the supportive material – charts, graphs, and sidebars – enhance understanding of the material?

STYLE GUIDELINES
Submission Format: Please submit via electronic mail whenever possible. Otherwise, submit three (3) hard copies of the manuscript and one (1) copy on a computer disk (no Mac disks, please). Word for Windows on a 3_-inch high-density floppy is preferred, but we can convert any common word-processing software such as Word Perfect. (Please write the format on the disk.). Please use double or 1.5 spacing and do not embed graphic elements in text such as table of contents, bookmarks, and tables or boxed inserts.

Length of Manuscripts (including sidebars and exhibits): Feature article -- 3,500 to 3,800 words; Department -- 1,800 to 2,000 words.

Cover Sheet and Bios: Attach a separate sheet with author(s) name, position, and affiliation. Include address, phone, fax, and electronic mail address. This information should appear **only** on the cover sheet. Include a half-page bio for each author on a separate sheet.

Titles and Abstracts: Titles of papers should be short and concise. Executive Briefings of no more than 75 words should provide a substantive summary of the manuscript, giving the readers a good understanding of the main points.

Attribution: Avoid use of reference citation, i.e., bracketed or parenthetical notes, in the text. If attribution is absolutely necessary, such as for quoted material and statistics, write it into the text. Footnotes also should be incorporated into the text. If citations are absolutely necessary, list no more than 8 alphabetically by author on a separate page called Additional Reading at the end of the manuscript (use Journal of Marketing style to create this list).

Methodology: If the manuscript is based on a study, present only enough explanation of the methodology to establish the credibility of the study (sample frame and size, type of survey conducted, response rate); include a more detailed, but short, explanation in a separate section, possibly for use as a sidebar to the text.

Exhibits: Limit of four exhibits or sidebars. Label all charts, figures, and tables as "exhibits." Please type all exhibits in either Times or Helvetica and create them in Word or PowerPoint only. Please submit all exhibits on a separate disk, do not incorporate exhibits into the text file. Note that exhibits may have to be cut, depending on applicability and space constraints.

Readability: Do not assume that our readers are completely familiar with the concepts and terminology of the specific subject under discussion. Define acronyms and industry-specific terms. Make your text direct and clear, and use a narrative style with limited use of passive voice.

General Information
On acceptance of the manuscript, a copyright form will be sent to the authors for their signatures. Even though care will be taken with returnable material, manuscripts, photographs, and so on, we can accept no responsibility in case of loss.

Each author will receive a complimentary copy of the issue in which his or her article appears as well as information on purchasing reprints. Send all manuscripts and correspondence to the Editor.

Marketing Management Journal

ADDRESS FOR SUBMISSION:

Mike D'Amico, Editor
Marketing Management Journal
University of Akron
Department of Marketing
Akron, OH 44325-4804
USA
Phone: 330-972-7024
Fax: 330-972-5798
E-Mail: mdamico@uakron.edu
Web:
Address May Change:

PUBLICATION GUIDELINES:

Manuscript Length: 30 Maximum
Copies Required: Four
Computer Submission: No Hardcopy preferred
Format: WordPerfect
Fees to Review: 0.00 US$

Manuscript Style:
Chicago Manual of Style

CIRCULATION DATA:

Reader: Academics
Frequency of Issue: 2 Times/Year
Copies per Issue: No Reply
Sponsor/Publisher: Marketing Management Association
Subscribe Price: 45.00 US$

REVIEW INFORMATION:

Type of Review: Blind Review
No. of External Reviewers: 3
No. of In House Reviewers: 0
Acceptance Rate: 21-30%
Time to Review: 2 - 3 Months
Reviewers Comments: Yes
Invited Articles: 0-5%
Fees to Publish: 15.00 US$

MANUSCRIPT TOPICS:

Advertising & Promotion Management; Direct Marketing; Global Business; Marketing Research; Marketing Theory & Applications; Non Profit Organizations; Sales/Selling; Strategic Management Policy

MANUSCRIPT GUIDELINES/COMMENTS:

Manuscript topics:
Manuscripts reporting original, replicated, or integrative research activities; focusing on empirical, theoretical, or methodological research; and/or reviewing a broad range of marketing topics are strongly encouraged.

Manuscript guidelines:
1. Manuscripts which do not exactly follow submission guidelines will be returned to authors immediately for revision. Only submissions in the form required by the Editorial Board of the JMM will be distributed for review.

2. Manuscripts must not include any authorship identification with the exception of a separate page which should include authorship, institutional affiliation, manuscript title,

acknowledgements where required, telephone numbers for all authors, and the date of submission. The manuscript title should appear prior to the abstract on the first page of the manuscript.

Manuscripts will be reviewed through a triple-blind process.

3. The *Chicago Manual of Style* will be helpful in clarifying style relate questions. Manuscripts must be submitted on 8 ½ by 11 inch, bond paper.

Margins must be a minimum of one inch. Manuscripts should be submitted in 12 pitch type and should not exceed thirty typewritten pages inclusive of body, tables, figures, and references.

4. References used in the text should be identified at the appropriate point in the text by the last name of the author, the year of the referenced publication, and specific page identity where needed. The style should be as follows: "...Wilkie (1989)..." or "...Wilkie (1989, p. 15)." Each reference cited must appear alphabetically in the reference appendix titled "REFERENCES". References should include the author(s) full name(s). The use of "et al." is not acceptable in the reference appendix. The references should be attached to the manuscript on a separate page.

5. The Editorial Board of the JMM interprets the submission of a manuscript as a commitment to publish the manuscript in the JMM. The competition for publication in the journal requires significant commitment of time, energy, and expense in reviewing manuscripts for publication. For these reasons, the Editorial Board of the JMM regards concurrent submission of manuscripts to a professional journal while under review by another journal as unprofessional and unacceptable. Editorial policy also prohibits publication of a manuscript that has already been published in whole or in substantial part by another journal. Authors will be required to authorize copyright protection for the JMM prior to manuscripts being sent out for review. Manuscripts accepted become the copyright of the JMM.

6. The Editorial Board reserves the right for stylistic editing of manuscripts accepted for publication in the Journal. Where major stylistic editing is deemed necessary, a copy of the accepted manuscript will be provided to the author(s) for final review.

Mountain Plains Journal of Business and Economics

ADDRESS FOR SUBMISSION:

Alan R. Hamlin, Editor
Mountain Plains Journal of Business and Economics
Southern Utah University
Department of Business
351 W. Center Street
Cedar City, UT 84720
USA
Phone: 435-586-5417
Fax: 435-586-5493
E-Mail: hamlin@suu.edu
Web:
Address May Change:

PUBLICATION GUIDELINES:

Manuscript Length: 21-25
Copies Required: One
Computer Submission: Yes
Format: Microsoft Word/WordPerfect 6.1
Fees to Review: 50.00 US$

Manuscript Style:
, Same as Academy of Management

CIRCULATION DATA:

Reader: Academics
Frequency of Issue: 2 Times/Year
Copies per Issue: Less than 1,000
Sponsor/Publisher: Mountain Plains Management Association
Subscribe Price: 0.00 US$ On Line

REVIEW INFORMATION:

Type of Review: Blind Review
No. of External Reviewers: 3
No. of In House Reviewers: 1
Acceptance Rate: 21-30% (Anticipated)
Time to Review: 1 Month or Less
Reviewers Comments: Yes
Invited Articles: 0-5% (Anticipated)
Fees to Publish: 0.00 US$

MANUSCRIPT TOPICS:

Business Information Systems (MIS); Business Law, Public Responsibility & Ethics; Direct Marketing; Global Business; Labor Relations & Human Resource Mgt.; Marketing Research; Marketing Theory & Applications; Organizational Behavior & Theory; Organizational Development; Production/Operations; Public Administration; Sales/Selling; Services; Small Business Entrepreneurship; Strategic Management Policy

MANUSCRIPT GUIDELINES/COMMENTS:

Mountain Plains Journal of Business is a new journal; therefore, the percentages given for 'Acceptance Rate' and 'Invited Articles' are anticipated.

North Central Business Journal

ADDRESS FOR SUBMISSION:

James T. Noonan, Editor
North Central Business Journal
Fitchburg State College
Business Administration Department
160 Pearl Street
Fitchburg, MA 01420
USA
Phone: 978-665-3203
Fax: 978-665-3081
E-Mail: lglasgow@fsc.edu
Web:
Address May Change:

PUBLICATION GUIDELINES:

Manuscript Length: 15
Copies Required: Two
Computer Submission: Yes
Format: Microsoft Word
Fees to Review: 0.00 US$

Manuscript Style:
    See Manuscript Guidelines

CIRCULATION DATA:

Reader: Business Persons, Academics
Frequency of Issue: 2 Times/Year
Copies per Issue: Less than 1,000
Sponsor/Publisher: Fitchburg State College
Subscribe Price: No Reply

REVIEW INFORMATION:

Type of Review: Blind Review
No. of External Reviewers: 2
No. of In House Reviewers: 3+
Acceptance Rate: 50%
Time to Review: Over 6 Months
Reviewers Comments: No
Invited Articles: 50% +
Fees to Publish: 0.00 US$

MANUSCRIPT TOPICS:
Advertising & Promotion Management; Business Information Systems (MIS); Business Law; Public Responsibility & Ethics; Communication; Direct Marketing; Global Business; Health Care Administration; Labor Relations & Human Resource Mgt.; Marketing Research; Marketing Theory & Applications; Non Profit Organizations; Office Administration/Management; Operations Research/Statistics; Organizational Behavior & Theory; Organizational Development; Production/Operations; Public Administration; Purchasing/Materials Management; Sales/Selling; Services; Small Business Entrepreneurship; Strategic Management Policy; Technology/Innovation; Transportation/Physical Distribution

MANUSCRIPT GUIDELINES/COMMENTS:

1. Submit four(4) copies of your completed paper and a disk.

2. Papers should not exceed fifteen (15) double-spaced pates including text, references, and exhibits. Each paper should have a separate page with the author's name, affiliation, address and telephone number. Multiple authorship should indicate the person to be contacted.

3. Provide a self-addressed, stamped 3x5 postcard to notify you of our receipt of your paper or abstract. Please record the title of your paper on the reverse side of the postcard.

4. All papers will be blind reviewed by two outside reviewers. Papers submitted must not be presented, published, or accepted for presentation or publication elsewhere.

5. Send all correspondence to the Editor at the above address.

Operations Research

ADDRESS FOR SUBMISSION:

Lawrence M. Wein, Editor
Operations Research
MIT
Sloan School of Management
E53-343
30 Wadsworth Street
Cambridge, MA 02142-1347
USA
Phone: 617-253-6697
Fax: 617-258-7519
E-Mail: lwein@mit.edu
Web: or.pubs.informs.org
Address May Change:

PUBLICATION GUIDELINES:

Manuscript Length: Any
Copies Required: Four
Computer Submission: No
Format: N/A
Fees to Review: 0.00 US$

Manuscript Style:
     Chicago Manual of Style

CIRCULATION DATA:

Reader: Academics
Frequency of Issue: Bi-Monthly
Copies per Issue: 10,001 - 25,000
Sponsor/Publisher: Institute for Operations Research and Management Science (INFORMS)
Subscribe Price: 0.00 US$

REVIEW INFORMATION:

Type of Review: Editorial Review
No. of External Reviewers: 3
No. of In House Reviewers: 1
Acceptance Rate: 21-30%
Time to Review: 4 - 6 Months
Reviewers Comments: Yes
Invited Articles: 0-5%
Fees to Publish: 0.00 US$

MANUSCRIPT TOPICS:
Business Information Systems (MIS); Business Law, Public Responsibility & Ethics; Communication; Decision Analysis; Financial Engineering; Military; Non Profit Organizations; Operations Research/Statistics; Optimization; OR Chronicle; Production/Operations; Services; Strategic Management Policy; Transportation/Physical Distribution

MANUSCRIPT GUIDELINES/COMMENTS:

The mission of *Operations Research* is to serve the entire *Operations Research* (OR) community, including practitioners, researchers, educators, and students. Operations Research, as the flagship journal of our profession, strives to publish results that are truly insightful. Each issue of *Operations Research* attempts to provide a balance of well written articles that span the wide array of creative activities in OR. Thus, the major criteria for acceptance of a paper in *Operations Research* are that the paper is important to more than a small subset of the OR community, contains important insights, and makes a substantial contribution to the field that will stand the test of time.

General Considerations
To submit a paper to *Operations Research,* the author should send the Area Editor the entire manuscript package for review. This includes the Statement of Contribution, Copyright Transfer Agreement, a cover letter, and four copies of the manuscript. This submission can either be in hardcopy format (or in electronic form. The author must check with the appropriate Area Editor as to what electronic forms are acceptable.

Papers not in the fields covered by the Area Editors should be sent to the Editor.

Papers should not be sent to the Associate Editors.

Submission of a manuscript is a representation that the paper has neither been published nor submitted for publication elsewhere, and that, if the work is officially sponsored, it has been released for open publication.

Manuscripts will not be returned to an author unless specifically requested, or unless reviewers have provided annotations that will be of use to the author.

The text should be arranged as follows: title page, abstract, introduction, main sections, appendix, acknowledgment, and references. Appendices and an acknowledgment are optional. If a paper is accepted for publication, the Editor may request (or require) that supporting appendix material is placed online at the *Operations Research* web site. Authors should consider this either during the initial submission phase or during the final revisions of the paper and may wish to design their papers accordingly.

Personal Web Sites. Upon acceptance of a paper to *Operations Research,* the author must remove all copies of the paper from any web sites. The copyright belongs to INFORMS and placement of the paper on a web site is a violation of the copyright transfer agreement.

Observe the following points in preparing manuscripts. Papers not conforming closely to these instructions may be returned to their authors for appropriate revisions or may be delayed in the review process.

1. Statement of Contribution. A statement of contribution is required for each submitted paper. The form is available at the *Operations Research* web site. The purpose of this statement is to aid area editors and reviewers in determining if the paper a) is appropriate for the Journal and b) meets its stated objectives. Once a paper is accepted for publication, this statement will serve as the basis for the news story for the "In This Issue" column.

2. Readability. The abstract and the introduction of every paper must be free of unnecessary jargon and clearly readable by any INFORMS member. These sections should be written in an expository style that will be comprehensible to readers who are not technical experts in the subject matter.

3. Title Page. Each paper should have a title page that contains the authors' names and addresses. The usual acknowledgments should be placed in a separate section at the back of the manuscript.

4. Abstract. Preface each article with a self-contained, one paragraph abstract that summarizes the problem and the principal results and conclusions. It should not contain formulas, references or abbreviations, nor exceed 200 words.

5. Introduction. The introduction must clearly state the problem, the results to be found in the paper and their significance to the OR community. It should not contain equations or mathematical notation. Section numbering and headings begins here.

6. Main Sections. The main sections of the paper must be readable, the level of the mathematics and/or the terminology appropriate to the topic, and the material logically presented.

7. Style. The message of the paper will be enhanced if it is presented in active, forceful, and concise prose. Good writing is a craft at least as difficult as doing operations research. While the Editor and staff will correct minor lapses from good style in the manuscript, they cannot undertake wholesale revisions of poorly written papers. There is no set limit to the number of pages for a paper; however, conciseness and clarity of presentation are important publication criteria.

8. Spacing and Format. Double space manuscripts throughout, including the abstract, subsidiary matter (list of captions, for example), and references. In general, keep figures and tables to a minimum.

Each page of the manuscript should be numbered. Indent the first line of each paragraph.

9. Footnotes. *Operations Research* does not use footnotes; incorporate subsidiary material that would otherwise appear in footnotes in the main text, possibly in parentheses or brackets, or place it in a Notes section at the end of the text, before the Acknowledgment and References. Designate notes by using superscript numerals placed in serial order throughout the text.

10. Acknowledgment. Place acknowledgments of presentation, support and assistance in a final section that precedes the References, not on the title page.

11. References. List only those references that are cited in the text. References in the text should be cited by the author's surname and the year of publication-for example, Flood (1962).

If the reference has two or three authors, cite all of the authors' surnames and the year of publication—Flood, Smith and Jones (1982). If the reference has more than three authors, cite the first author's surname followed by et al. and the year of publication-Brown et al. (1985).

If there is more than one reference by the same author with the same year of publication, the first citation appearing in the text would read Flood (1962a), the second citation would read Flood (1962b), etc.

Do not use parentheses or brackets for dates when the citation is already enclosed within parentheses.

At the end of the paper list references alphabetically by the last name of the first author. Do not number the reference list. Double-space this final section.

For journal references, give the author, year of publication, title, journal name, volume, and pages for example:

FLOOD, M. M. 1962. New Operations Research Potentials. Opns. Res. 10, 423-436.

For book references, give the author, year of publication, title, publisher, city, state, and pages-for example:

MORSE, P. M., AND G. E. KIMBALL. 1951. Methods of Operations Research. John Wiley, New York, 44-65.

For references to working papers or dissertations cite the author, title, type of document, department, university, and location, for example:

ROSENWEIN, M. 1986. Design and Application of Solution Methodologies to Optimize Problems in Transportation Logistics. Ph.D. Dissertation. Department of Decision Sciences, University of Pennsylvania, Philadelphia.

12. Mathematical Expressions. Within the text, use the solidus whenever possible in preference to built-up fractions, e.g., a/(1 - b) exponentials in the form exp( ); avoid subscripts or superscripts on subscripts or superscripts; and, in general, minimize unusual typographical requirements. For displayed equations, use built-up fractions. Avoid lengthy equations that will take several lines to typeset (possibly by defining terms of the equations in separate displays).

Make subscripts and superscripts large and clear, and shown in a clearly inferior or superior position. The letter 1 and the numeral 1 and the letter O and the numeral 0, which are identical on most keyboards, should be identified. Symbols and Greek letters should be identified clearly. On their first occurrence, label unusual or ambiguous symbols by marginal notes. The difference between upper and lower case letters should be clear.

Display only those mathematical expressions that must be numbered for later reference or that need to be emphasized. Number displayed equations consecutively throughout the paper; do not number equations by section numbers. Appendix equations can be labeled A1, A2, etc. The numbers should be placed in parentheses to the right of the equation.

13. Tables. Tables should be numbered with Arabic numerals, have a title, and be referred to sequentially in the text. Column headings should be brief and not use abbreviations. Do not use vertical rules. The use of footnotes is encouraged; designate these by lower case letters. The submission of original tables suitable for reproduction is not necessary; all tables will be typeset for consistency. Each table should be on a separate sheet and not interleaved in the text.

14. Figures. Figures should be professionally drawn or laser printed and suitable for photographic reproduction. All figures must be in black and white. Color figures will be printed in black and white and do not scan properly. The author is responsible for the quality of the final form of the figure(s). Figures are scanned and corrections on page proofs are costly.

Do not clutter the figure with information that makes it difficult to read. To avoid an undesirable moiré effect when scanned, figures should be shaded with a coarse pattern rather than a fine screen. Line weights should be consistent and at least .25 points after reduction. Lettering in the body of the figure should be proportional to the graphic and be typed.

Most figures will be reduced to approximately 3 ¼ " in width. For optimal quality, please submit final figures close to that size. All details on the figures should be checked carefully because correction on proofs necessitates reshooting.

Each figure must be cited and will be placed in the order mentioned in the text. Each figure must have a caption and a number (Arabic). Do not place the caption on the original of the figure. Place captions on a separate sheet. Do not differentiate between illustrations and figures.

15. Subject Classification Scheme for the OR/MS Index. Determine the appropriate subject classifications (up to 3) and accompanying descriptive phrases for all work submitted. Choose from one to three subject categories for each manuscript. For every category chosen, write a short phrase that puts the paper in context. (The phrase can be a concise rendering of the title, or it may specify some aspect of the paper that is important but not apparent in the title.) The length of each phrase, including spaces and punctuation, should not exceed 60 characters. This information will be printed on the title page of every article, technical note, and letter that is published. The list of subject keywords can be found at the **Operations Research** web site.

Subject categories and phrases must either appear on the title page of the manuscript (this is the preferred method), or authors may use the bottom half of the Copyright Transfer Agreement.

16. Reprints. *Operations Research* does not have paper charges, nor does it supply free reprints. Authors of accepted articles may order reprints at reasonable rates at the time they submit their corrected galley proofs. Reprints of individual articles are not available from INFORMS.

Managing Editor: Joan E. Wingo
MIT Sloan School of Management

30 Wadsworth Street, E53-336
Cambridge, MA 02142-1347
617-253-6653 (phone); 617-258-7579 (fax)
jwingo@mit.edu

Area Editors
COMPUTING AND DECISION TECHNOLOGY
Dr. **Hemant K. Bhargava,** Heinz School of Public Policy and Management,
Carnegie Mellon University, 2108A Hamburg Hall, 4800 Forbes Ave., Pittsburgh, PA 15213
bhargava@computer.org
http://www.heinz.cmu.edu/~bhargava/
412-268-4408 (phone); 412-268-7036 (fax)

DECISION ANALYSIS
James S. Dyer, Department of Management Science and Information Systems, CBA 5.202,
The University of Texas at Austin, Austin, Texas 78712-1175
j.dyer@bus.utexas.edu
512-471-5278 (phone); 512-471-0587 (fax)

ENVIRONMENT, ENERGY AND NATURAL RESOURCES
Benjamin F. Hobbs, Department of Geography & Environmental Engineering, The Johns
Hopkins University, 313 Ames Hall, 3400 No. Charles St., Baltimore, MD 21218
bhobbs@jhu.edu
http://www.jhu.edu/~dogee/hobbs.html
410-516-4681 (phone); 410-516-8996 (fax)

FINANCIAL ENGINEERING
Dimitris Bertsimas, Sloan School of Management, Massachusetts Institute of Technology
30 Wadsworth Street, E53-363, Cambridge, MA 02142
dbertsim@mit.edu
http://web.mit.edu/dbertsim/www
(617)-253-4223 (phone); (617)-258-7579 (fax)

MANUFACTURING, SERVICE AND SUPPLY CHAIN OPERATIONS
Garrett van Ryzin, Graduate School of Business, 412 Uris Hall, Columbia University
New York, NY 10027
jvl @columbia.edu
212-854-4280 (phone); 212-316-9180 (fax)

MILITARY
Alan R. Washburn, Naval Postgraduate School, Code OR/WS, Monterey, CA 93943-5000
washburn@nps.navy.mil
831-656-3127 (phone); 831-656-2595 (fax)

OPTIMIZATION
Rolf H. Möhring, Department of Mathematics, Sekr. MA 6-1, Berlin University of
Technology, Strasse des 17. Juni 136, D-10623 Berlin, Germany

moehring@math.tu-berlin.de
http://www.math.tu-berlin.de/~moehring_/
+49 30 314 24594 (phone); +49 30 314 25191 (fax)

OR CHRONICLE
Frederic H. Murphy, Fox School of Business and Management, Temple University, Philadelphia PA 19122
V5256E@vm.temple.edu
(215) 204-8189 (phone); 215) 204-8029 (fax)

POLICY MODELING AND PUBLIC SECTOR OR
Edward H. Kaplan, Professor of Management Sciences and Public Health,
Yale School of Management, Box 208200, New Haven, Connecticut 06520-8200
edward.kaplan@yale.edu
203-432-6031 (phone); 203-432-9995 (fax)

SIMULATION
Michael C. Fu, The Robert H. Smith School of Business, Van Munching Hall, University of Maryland, College Park, MD 20742-1815
mfu@rhsmith.umd. edu http://www.mbs.umd.edu/DIT/faculty/fu.htm
301-405-2241 (phone); 707-897-3774 (fax)

STOCHASTIC MODELS
David D. Yao, Department of Endustrial Engineering and OR, Columbia University
New York, NY 10027-6699
yao @ieor.columbia.edu
212-854-2934 (phone); 212-854-8103 (fax)

TELECOMMUNICATIONS
Robert B. Cooper, Department of Computer Science and Engineering, Florida Atlantic University, Box 3091, Boca Raton, FL 33431-0991
bob @cse.fau.edu
http://www.cse.fau.edu/-bob/
561-297-3673 (phone); 561-297-2800 (fax)

TRANSPORTATION
Paolo Toth, DEIS, University di Bologna, Viale Risorgimento 2, 1-40136 Bologna, Italy
ptoth@deis.unibo.it
+39 051 2093028 (phone); +39 051 2093073(fax)

Pennsylvania Journal of Business and Economics

ADDRESS FOR SUBMISSION:

Kevin Roth & Carole Anderson, Co-Editors
Pennsylvania Journal of Business and
 Economics
Clarion University of Pennsylvania
Clarion, PA 16214-1232
USA
Phone: 814-393-2055
Fax: 814-393-1910
E-Mail: kroth@clarion.edu
Web:
Address May Change:

PUBLICATION GUIDELINES:

Manuscript Length: 6-10
Copies Required: One
Computer Submission: Yes if accepted
Format: WdPerfet 8, Corel, Word
Fees to Review: 0.00 US$

Manuscript Style:
 American Psychological Association

CIRCULATION DATA:

Reader: Academics
Frequency of Issue: 2 Times/Year
Copies per Issue: Less than 1,000
Sponsor/Publisher: Association of
 Pennsylvania University Business and
 Economic Faculties
Subscribe Price: No Reply

REVIEW INFORMATION:

Type of Review: Blind Review
No. of External Reviewers: 2
No. of In House Reviewers: 1
Acceptance Rate: 50%
Time to Review: 2 - 3 Months
Reviewers Comments: Yes
Invited Articles: 0-5%
Fees to Publish: 0.00 US$

MANUSCRIPT TOPICS:
Advertising & Promotion Management; Direct Marketing; Global Business; Marketing Research; Marketing Theory & Applications; Sales/Selling; Services; Small Business Entrepreneurship; Strategic Management Policy; Transportation/Physical Distribution

MANUSCRIPT GUIDELINES/COMMENTS:

The APUBEF Journal is a refereed journal aimed at publishing the papers of faculty from the business and economics disciplines within the State System of Higher Education Universities in Pennsylvania, or from business and economics faculty at comparable institutions from within Pennsylvania and from surrounding states. While theoretical works are encouraged, most published papers are empirical or pedagogical in nature.

Manuscript Style
1. Papers **must** be submitted on a 3.5" micro-computer disk using Corel, WordPerfect 8.0, or Word for DOS. Printer setup should be HP Laserjet 4. A high-quality hard copy of the paper **must** accompany your disk.

2. Use 10 point New Times Roman font for the body of the paper and all headings including the heading for **references**. Use 1" margins all around.

3. Single space the text. Double space between paragraphs and indent the first line five spaces using the tab key. Use full justification.

4. Spell-check before sending the paper and correct all grammatical errors. Also, edit the paper to address the comments and suggestions of the reviewers and editor.

Specific Requirements
1. Start the manuscript with the full title, centered in capitals, bolt print. Following a space, each author and university should be identified, one author per line. No titles (Dr., Mr., Mrs. etc.) are to be used, nor should rank be indicated. Please, no fancy type-styles other than ones specified.

2. After the last author's name and affiliation, double space, center and type the heading **abstract**, bold and all caps. All papers **must** have an abstract of no more than 150 words, which provides a brief synopsis of the paper.

3. The next heading is **introduction**, bold and all caps. Double-space before and after. All major headings MUST follow this format. Secondary headings MUST be in bold print, left justified, first letter capitalized then lower case, with a space above and below each heading.

4. Mathematical expressions and notations should be used judiciously and all symbols should be identified.

5. Tables should be arranged sequentially in the order in which the tables are first mentioned in the text and placed at the end of the manuscript. Type the word Table and its arabic numeral flush left at the top of the table, double space, then type the table title flush left above the table. The explanatory notes to a table such as probability tables, explanations of acronyms, etc. should appear below the table. Use the same 10 point New Times Roman font as used in the text and the tab function to construct the tables. If a "camera-ready" table is to be used, send the original and not a reduced copy for incorporation in the journal.

6. Figures (such as graphs, drawings, photographs, and charts) must be consecutively numbered in arabic numerals, with their captions in the order they appear in the text. All illustrations must be camera-ready;
photographs must be of professional quality, and drawings must be prepared in ink. Illustrations should be identified on the back in light pencil with the name of the author and the figure number.

7. Footnotes and end notes are permitted, but not encouraged. In most cases, the material they contain can be incorporated in the text. If footnotes are used, use the automatic footnote function (control F7) and specify a New Times Roman 10 point font for their text. End notes should be in the same 10 point Prestige Elite font as the text and placed after the references.

References

1. When citing references in the text please use parenthesis, author's named, comma and date of publication, i.e., (Wilson, 1996). For up to three authors, cite each and use the "&" for "and", i.e., (Dawes, Dowling & Peterson, 1992). For more than three authors, use the surname of the first author followed by "et al." comma and the year, i.e., (Cravens et al., l988). Multiple reference citations in a parentheses should be arranged alphabetically and a semicolon used to separate them, i.e., (Cravens et al., 1988; Dawes, Dowling & Peterson, 1992; Wilson, 1996). Text citations must correspond accurately to the references in the reference list.

2. References should be listed alphabetically at the end of the manuscript. References with the same authors in the same order are arranged according to the year of publication, the earliest first.

3. An American Psychological Association format is used for the references.

For a journal article:
Buzzell, R. D., Gale, B. T., & Sultan, R.G.M. (1975). Market share - a key to profitability. Harvard Business Review. 75-1. 97-106.

For a proceedings article:
Gronroos, C. (1983). Innovative marketing strategies and organization structures for service firms. Emerging Perspectives on Services Marketing. Berry, L.L., Shostack G.L., & Upah, G.D. eds. Chicago, IL: American Marketing Association. 9-21.

For a book:
Czepiel, J.A. (1992). Competitive Marketing Strategy. (258-263) Englewood Cliffs, NJ: Prentice-Hall.

For more information and examples please refer to the *Publication Manual Of The American Psychological Association.*

Psychology and Marketing

ADDRESS FOR SUBMISSION:

Rajan Nataraajan, Executive Editor
Psychology and Marketing
Auburn University
College of Business
Dept. of Marketing & Transportation
235 Business Building
Auburn University, AL 36849
USA
Phone: 334-844-2465
Fax: 334-844-4032
E-Mail: rnatara@business.auburn.edu
Web:
Address May Change:

PUBLICATION GUIDELINES:

Manuscript Length: 30-35
Copies Required: Five
Computer Submission: Yes
Format: Contact Editor
Fees to Review: 0.00 US$

Manuscript Style:
American Psychological Association

CIRCULATION DATA:

Reader: Academics, Business Perons
Frequency of Issue: Monthly
Copies per Issue: Less than 1,000
Sponsor/Publisher: Interscience/Wiley
Subscribe Price: 180.00 US$

REVIEW INFORMATION:

Type of Review: Blind Review
No. of External Reviewers: 3
No. of In House Reviewers: 1
Acceptance Rate: 11-20%
Time to Review: 3 Months
Reviewers Comments: Yes
Invited Articles: 0-5%
Fees to Publish: 0.00 US$

MANUSCRIPT TOPICS:
Marketing Research; Marketing Theory & Applications

MANUSCRIPT GUIDELINES/COMMENTS:

Manuscripts should be submitted in *quintuplicate* to Rajan Nataraajan, Ph.D., Executive Editor, *Psychology & Marketing*, Department of Marketing and Transportation, College of Business, 235 Business Building, Auburn University, Auburn, AL 36849-5246. Articles should be no longer than 25 double-spaced pages, comments no longer than 5 double-spaced pages. Manuscripts must adhere to the instructions on reference citations, preparation of tables and figures, and manuscript format as described in the *Publication Manual of the American Psychological Association* (4th ed.). Readers' comments on published articles must be submitted no later than one month from the date of the issue containing the article being commented on in order to ensure timeliness. All articles as well as comments are subject to editorial review. Journal policy prohibits an author from simultaneously submitting a manuscript for consideration to another journal while that manuscript is under consideration for publication in *Psychology & Marketing*.

Figures: Figures should be professionally prepared and submitted in a form suitable for reproduction (camera-ready copy). Computer-generated graphs are acceptable only if they have been printed with a good quality laser printer.

References should be compiled on a separate sheet at the end of the article. Examples follows:

Journal
Lichenstein, D. R., Bloch, P. H., & Black, W. C. (1988) Correlates of price acceptability. Journal of **Book** Consumer Research, 15, 243-252.

Lilien, G. L., & Kotler, P. (1983). Marketing decision making. New York: Harper and Row.

Article in Edited Book
Brown, E. D., & Sechrest, L. (1980). Experiments in cross-cultural research. In H. C. Triandis & J. W. Berry (Eds.), Handbook of cross-cultural psychology (Vol. 2, pp. 297–318). Boston: Allyn and Bacon, Inc.

Conference Proceeding
Schaninger, C., Buss, C., & Grover, R. (1982). The effect of sex roles on family finance handling and decision influence. In Bruce Walker (Ed.), An assessment of marketing thought and practice, Educators' Conference Proceedings, Series 48 (pp. 43–47). Chicago: American Marketing Association.

Copyright: No article can be published unless accompanied by a signed publication agreement, which serves as a transfer of copyright from author to publisher. A publication agreement may be obtained from the editor or the publisher. A copy of the publication agreement appears in most issues of the journal. Only original papers will be accepted and copyright in published papers will be vested in the publisher. It is the author's responsibility to obtain written permission to reproduce material that has appeared in another publication.

Correspondence: All other correspondence should be addressed to the Publisher, Professional/Trade Group, John Wiley & Sons, Inc., 605 Third Ave., New York, NY 10158.

DISK SUBMISSION INSTRUCTIONS

Please return your final, revised manuscript on disk as well as hard copy.
The hard copy must match the disk.
The Journal strongly encourages authors to deliver the final, revised version of their accepted manuscripts (text, tables, and, if possible, illustrations) on disk. Given the near-universal use of computer word-processing for manuscript preparation, we anticipate that providing a disk will be convenient for you, and it carries the added advantages of maintaining the integrity of your keystrokes and expediting typesetting. Please return the disk submission slip below with your manuscript and labeled disk(s).

Guidelines for Electronic Submission

Text

Storage medium. 3-1/2" high-density disk in IBM MS-DOS, Windows, or Macintosh format.

Software and format. Microsoft Word 6.0 is preferred, although manuscripts prepared with any other microcomputer word processor are acceptable. Refrain from complex formatting; the Publisher will style your manuscript according to the Journal design specifications. Do not use desktop publishing software such as Aldus PageMaker or Quark XPress. If you prepared your manuscript with one of these programs, export the text to a word processing format. Please make sure your word processing program's "fast save" feature is turned off. Please do not deliver files that contain hidden text: for example, do not use your word processor's automated features to create footnotes or reference lists.

File names. Submit the text and tables of each manuscript as a single file. Name each file with your last name (up to eight letters). Text files should be given the three-letter extension that identifies the file format. Macintosh users should maintain the MS-DOS "eight dot three" file-naming convention.

Labels. Label all disks with your name, the file name, and the word processing program and version used.

Illustrations files for full color images to be in a CMYK color space. If possible, ICC or ColorSync profiles of your output device should accompany all digital image submissions.

Storage medium. Submit as separate files from text files, on separate disks or cartridges. If feasible, full color files should be submitted on separate disks from other image files. 3-1/2" high-density disks, CD, Iomega Zip, and 5 1/4" 44- or 88-MB SyQuest cartridges can be submitted. At authors' request, cartridges and disks will be returned after publication.

Software and format. All illustration files should be in TIFF or EPS (with preview) formats. Do not submit native application formats.

Resolution. Journal quality reproduction will require greyscale and color files at resolutions yielding approximately 300 ppi. Bitmapped line art should be submitted at resolutions yielding 600-1200 ppi. These resolutions refer to the output size of the file; if you anticipate that your images will be enlarged or reduced, resolutions should be adjusted accordingly.

File names. Illustration files should be given the 2- or 3-letter extension that identifies the file format used (i.e., .tif, .eps).

Labels. Label all disks and cartridges with your name, the file names, formats, and compression schemes (if any) used. Hard copy output must accompany all files.

Qualitative Market Research: An International Journal

ADDRESS FOR SUBMISSION:

Len Tiu Wright, Editor
Qualitative Market Research: An
 International Journal
De Montfort University
Graduate School of Business
Department of Marketing
The Gateway
Leicester, LE1 9BH
UK
Phone: +44 0 1782 583424
Fax: +44 0 1162 506329
E-Mail: nrsadm@dnu.ac.uk
Web: www.mcb.co.uk
Address May Change:

PUBLICATION GUIDELINES:

Manuscript Length: 21-25
Copies Required: Three
Computer Submission: Yes
Format: MS Word 7/Windows 98
Fees to Review: 0.00 US$

Manuscript Style:
 Uniform System of Citation (Harvard
 Blue Book)

CIRCULATION DATA:

Reader: Business Persons, Academics
Frequency of Issue: Quarterly
Copies per Issue: 2,001 - 3,000
Sponsor/Publisher: MCB University Press
Subscribe Price: 299.00 US$

REVIEW INFORMATION:

Type of Review: Blind Review
No. of External Reviewers: 1 2-3
No. of In House Reviewers: 0
Acceptance Rate: 40%
Time to Review: 1 - 2 Months
Reviewers Comments: Yes
Invited Articles: 0-5%
Fees to Publish: 0.00 US$

MANUSCRIPT TOPICS:
Advertising & Promotion Management; Business Information Systems (MIS); Business Law; Public Responsibility & Ethics; Direct Marketing; Global Business; Marketing Research; Marketing Theory & Applications; Non Profit Organizations; Purchasing/Materials Management; Sales/Selling; Services; Technology/Innovation

MANUSCRIPT GUIDELINES/COMMENTS:

Copyright
Articles submitted to the journal should be original contributions and should not be under consideration for any other publication at the same time. Authors submitting articles for publication warrant that the work is not an infringement of any existing **copyright** and will indemnify the publisher against any breach of such warranty. For ease of dissemination and to ensure proper policing of use, papers and contributions become the legal copyright of the publisher unless otherwise agreed. Submissions should be sent to the Editor.

Editorial objectives
Qualitative Market Research: An International Journal aims to further the frontiers of knowledge and understanding of qualitative market research and its applications, exploring many contemporary issues and new developments in marketing. Examples of areas covered include:
- qualitative perspectives of relationships and complexities in buyer and supplier behaviour;
- commissioning and selling qualitative research;
- research design processes;
- questionaire enquiry and interviewing, focus groups, projective and enabling techniques;
- sampling techniques for qualitative research, data handling and interpretation;
- sources of bias and interviewer effect;
- applications of information technology;
- use of qualitative research to enhance quantitative work;
- stimulus material for use in research on advertising;
- packaging and new product development;
- interdisciplinary applications, e.g. sociology, economics and cultural studies;
- and from related fields in psychoanalysis, phenomenology, discourse analysis, ethnography, semiotics and grounded theory;
- analysis and case studies from public and private, profit and not-for-proft sectors;
- international marketing research;
- contemporary developments in the literature;
- ethical and legislative implications in data privacy and control.

The journal aims to break new ground by raising awareness of the dichotomy of principles and practices in research in an analytical and practical way.

Editorial scope
The content is targeted at an international readership and the areas and issues covered by the journal will be treated from cross-national and cross-cultural perspectives. The journal has the scope to cover both a breadth and depth of academic and practitioner research. Case studies and practical applications, which demonstrate the effectiveness of the methodology described, and comparative studies are also encouraged.

The reviewing process
All papers are subjected to a double-blind reviewing process and may be reviewed using the MCB University Press PeerNet process,(please visit http://www.peer-net.com for further information.)

Manuscript requirements
Three copies of the manuscript and a 3.5" disc should be submitted in double line spacing with wide margins. All authors should be shown and **author's details** must be printed on a separate sheet and the author should not be identified anywhere else in the article.

As a guide, articles should be between 4,000 and 6,000 words in **length**. A **title** of not more than eight words should be provided. A brief **autobiographical note** should be supplied including full name, affiliation, e-mail address and full international contact details. Authors must supply an **abstract** of 100-150 words. Up to six **keywords** should be included which encapsulate the principal subjects covered by the article.

Where there is a **methodology**, it should be clearly described under a separate heading. **Headings** must be short, clearly defined and not numbered. **Notes** or **Endnotes** should be used only if absolutely necessary and must be identified in the text by consecutive numbers, enclosed in square brackets and listed at the end of the article.

Figures, charts and **diagrams** should be kept to a minimum. They must be black and white with minimum shading and numbered consecutively using arabic numerals with a brief title and labelled axes. In the text, the position of the figure should be shown by typing on a separate line the words "take in Figure 2". Good quality originals must be provided.

Tables should be kept to a minimum. They must be numbered consecutively with roman numerals and a brief title. In the text, the position of the table should be shown by typing on a separate line the words "take in Table IV".

Photos and illustrations must be supplied as good quality black and white original half tones with captions. Their position should be shown in the text by typing on a separate line the words "take in Plate 2".

References to other publications should be complete and in Harvard style. They should contain full bibliographical details and journal titles should not be abbreviated. For multiple citations in the same year use a, b, c immediately following the year of publication. References should be shown within the text by giving the author's last name followed by a comma and year of publication all in round brackets, e.g. (Fox, 1994). At the end of the article should be a reference list in alphabetical order as follows

for books
surname, initials and year of publication, title, publisher, place of publication, e.g.Casson, M. (1979), *Alternatives to the Multinational Enterprise*, Macmillan, London.

for articles
surname, initials, year "title", journal, volume, number, pages, e.g.Fox, S. (1994) "Empowerment as a catalyst for change: an example from the food industry", *Supply Chain Management*, Vol 2 No 3, pp. 29-33

Final submission of the article
Once accepted for publication, the final version of the manuscript must be provided, accompanied by a 3.5" **disk** of the same version labelled with: disk format; author name(s); title of article; journal title; file name.

Each article must be accompanied by a completed and signed **Journal Article Record Form** available from the Editor or on http://www.literaticlub.co.uk/

The manuscript will be considered to be the definitive version of the article. The author must ensure that it is complete, grammatically correct and without spelling or typographical errors.

In preparing the disk, please use one of the following formats: Word, Word Perfect, Rich text format or TeX/LaTeX. Figures which are provided electronically must be in tif, gif or pic file extensions. All figures and graphics must also be supplied as good quality originals.

Final submission requirements
Manuscripts must
- be clean, good quality hard copy
- include an abstract and keywords
- have Harvard style references
- include any figures, photos and graphics as good quality originals
- be accompanied by a labelled disk
- be accompanied by a completed Journal Article Record Form

Technical assistance is available from MCB's World Wide Web Literati Club on http://www.literaticlub.co.uk/ or contact Mike Massey at MCB, e-mail mmassey@mcb.co.uk

Research in Consumer Behavior

ADDRESS FOR SUBMISSION:

Russell W. Belk, Editor
Research in Consumer Behavior
University of Utah
David Eccles School of Business
Salt Lake City, UT 84112
USA
Phone: 801-581-7401
Fax: 801-581-7214
E-Mail: mktrwb@business.utah.edu
Web:
Address May Change:

CIRCULATION DATA:

Reader: Academics
Frequency of Issue: 1 Times/Year
Copies per Issue: Less than 1,000
Sponsor/Publisher: Elsevier Science Publishing
Subscribe Price: 78.50 US$

PUBLICATION GUIDELINES:

Manuscript Length: 20+
Copies Required: Four
Computer Submission: Yes
Format: ASCII, upon acceptance
Fees to Review: 0.00 US$

Manuscript Style:
  Chicago Manual of Style, American Psychological Association

REVIEW INFORMATION:

Type of Review: Blind Review
No. of External Reviewers: 3
No. of In House Reviewers: 1
Acceptance Rate: 30%
Time to Review: 1 - 2 Months
Reviewers Comments: Yes
Invited Articles: 0-5%
Fees to Publish: 0.00 US$

MANUSCRIPT TOPICS:

Advertising & Promotion Management; Communication; Consumer Behavior; Direct Marketing; Global Business; Marketing Research; Marketing Theory & Applications; Non Profit Organizations

MANUSCRIPT GUIDELINES/COMMENTS:

RCB seeks qualitative empirical research, quantitative empirical research, theoretical papers, and methodological papers concerning any aspect of consumer acquisition, consumption, and disposition. A wide variety of theoretical and methodological perspectives will be considered. Manuscripts should be in the 25-50 page range and should be written following, approximately, *Journal of Consumer Research* style guidelines. All manuscripts will be blind reviewed. Authors will receive a copy of the volume in which their paper appears and 25 reprints of their chapter.

Author's Responsibilities

The author is responsible for correct spelling and punctuation, accurate quotations with page numbers, complete and accurate references, relevant content, coherent organization, legible appearance, and so forth. The author must proofread the manuscript after it is typed, making all corrections and changes before submitting the manuscript. Before submitting the manuscript to the editor please use the checklist on last page of pamphlet to be sure all necessary material is included.

The author is also responsible for preparing the manuscript on a word processor. Just as word processing eliminates a good amount of retyping, submitting a disk provides an opportunity to eliminate duplicate keyboarding by the typesetter. One key to success is compatibility. Therefore, the following steps should be followed closely.

1. Use a word processing program that is able to create an IBM compatible ASCII file.
2. Use 5 ¼ inch, double density disks.
3. Structure manuscript to follow guidelines.
4. Print one (1) copy for styling/copy-editing purposes.
5. Save one (1) copy of file in ASCII format.
   - Follow instructions in your word processing program.
   - Keep entire manuscript on one (1) file (no more than 75,000 characters per file).
   - Eliminate manuscript page numbers and identifying abbreviated title.
   - **Do not** use a 27 ASCII value line ending.
   - Use a 13 ASCII value at end of a paragraph.
   - **Do not** include tabular material on the file: all tabular text will be keyboarded from your printed copy.
   - **Do not** use codes for heads, bullet lists, number lists, etc.
6. Submit the file in ASCII format with your printed copy.

Volume Editor's Responsibility
The volume editor is responsible for reviewing all printed manuscripts and disks before submission for publication.

Printed manuscripts should be checked for original artwork, tables, and, where necessary, letters of permission to reprint. The manuscript checklist is a good guide to ensure a complete manuscript. The disk should be checked for proper format. If it is not a file in ASCII format. it is the volume editor's responsibility to either return the disk to the author for reformatting in ASCII or to have it done him/ herself.

GENERAL INSTRUCTIONS

Paper
Type the manuscript on one side of standard-sized (8 ½ X 11 in.) heavy white bond paper. **Do not** use onionskin or erasable paper. All pages must be of the same size. **Do not** use half sheets or strips of paper glued, taped, or stapled to the pages.

Type Element
The type must be dark, clear, and readable. A typeface that is made up of dots, as generated by some printers, is acceptable only if it is clear and legible.

Double Spacing
Double space between ALL lines of the manuscript, which includes the title, headings, footnotes, quotations, references, figure captions, and all parts of tables. Never use single-spacing or one-and-a-half spacing.

Margins
Leave uniform margins of 1 1/2 in. at the top, bottom, right, and left of every page. The length of each typed line is 5 1/2 inch. Do not justify lines; leave the right margin uneven. DO NOT hyphenate words at the end of a line; let a line run short or long rather than break a word. Type no more than 25 lines of text on a manuscript page.

Headings
Most manuscripts use from one to four headings. The four levels should appear as:

CENTERED ALL UPPERCASE HEADING

Centered Uppercase and Lowercase Heading

Flush Left, Underlined, Uppercase and Lowercase Side Heading

    Indented, underlined, lowercase paragraph heading ending with a period

Paragraphs And Indentation
Indent the first line of every paragraph and the first line of every footnote five spaces. Type the remaining lines of the manuscript to a uniform left-hand margin.

Quotations
Direct quotations must be accurate. Quotations of 40 words or less should be incorporated into the text and enclosed by double quotation marks ("). Display quotations of more than 40 words should appear as a double-spaced block with no quotation marks. DO NOT single-space. Indent 5 spaces from the left margin and 5 spaces from the right margin.

Permission To Quote
Any direct quotation, regardless of length must be accompanied by a reference citation that includes the author, year of publication, and page number(s). If you quote at length from a copyrighted work, you will also need written permission from the owner of the copyright. It is the author's responsibility to obtain permission. A copy of the letter of permission must accompany the manuscript.

Statistical And Mathematical Copy
Type all signs and symbols in mathematical copy that you can. Either type a character that resembles the symbol or draw the symbol in by hand. Identify symbols that may be hard to read or ambiguous to the copy editor or typesetter. The first time the ambiguous symbol appears in the manuscript, spell out and circle the name next to the symbol. Space mathematical copy as you would space words. Align signs and symbols carefully. Type subscripts half a line below the symbol and superscripts half a line above the symbol. Display a mathematical equation by setting it off from the text by double-spacing twice above and

below the equation. If the equation is identified by a number, type the number in parenthesis flush against the right margin. Do not underline (1) greek letters, subscripts, and superscripts that function as identifiers, and (2) abbreviations that are not variables. Mark symbols for vectors with a wavy line. Underline all other statistical symbols.

Parts Of A Manuscript
Order of manuscript pages: Number all pages consecutively. Arrange the pages of the manuscript as follows:
- title page (page 1)
- abstract (page 2)
- text (page 3)
- appendixes (start each on a separate page)
- author acknowledgement notes notes (start on a new page)
- references (start on a new page)
- tables (start each on a separate page)
- figures (start each on a separate page)

This arrangement is not the way the printed paper will appear; it is necessary for handling by the copy editor and the typesetter.

After the manuscript pages are arranged in the correct order, number them consecutively, beginning with the title page. Number ALL pages. Type the number in the upper right-hand corner using arabic numerals. Identify each manuscript page by typing an abbreviated title above the page number.

Title Page
The title page includes 4 elements:
- The title in uppercase letters.
- The Author(s) in uppercase and lowercase letters.
- An abbreviated title to be used as a running head. The running head should be a maximum of 70 characters, which includes all letters, punctuation, and spaces between words.
- Complete mailing address and phone number of each author.

Abstract
Begin the abstract on a new page. Type the word "ABSTRACT" in all uppercase letters, centered at top of page. Type the abstract itself as a single paragraph, double-spaced, indent 5 spaces from the left margin and 5 spaces from the right margin.

Text
Begin the text on a new page. The sections of the text follow each other without a break.

Appendices
Double-space the appendices and begin each on a separate page. Type the word "APPENDIX" in all uppercase letters and identifying capital letters in the order in which they are mentioned

in text, centered at the top of the page. If there is only one appendix, do not use an identifying letter.

Author Acknowledgement Notes

This note is neither numbered nor is it mentioned in text. Type the word "ACKNOWLEDGMENT" in all uppercase letters, centered at top of a new page. Type the acknowledgment itself as a double spaced single paragraph.

Notes

Notes that are mentioned in text are numbered consecutively throughout the chapter. Double-space the notes and begin on a separate page. Center the word "NOTES" in all uppercase letters at the top of the page. Indent the first line of each note 5 spaces and type the notes in the order in which they are mentioned in text.

References

Each series has it's own individual style, whether it be APA, ASA, reference notes, or a style unique to their discipline. For the style that you must follow, consult the *Publication Manual of The American Psychological Association* (THIRD Edition), *The Chicago Manual of Style* (13TH Edition), or a previous published volume in the series.

References cited in text **must** appear in the reference list; conversely, each entry in the reference list must be cited in text. It is the author's responsibility to make certain that each source referenced appears in both places and that the text citation and reference list are identical.

Important: (1) Foreign language volumes, parts, numbers, editions, and so on must be translated into their English equivalents. (2) JAI Press does not use either op. cit. or loc. cit. A short-title form is required. Ibid. is acceptable.

Items to be included in a full reference are:
Book: Author's full name
        Complete title of the book
        Editor, compiler, or translator, if any
        Series, if any, and volume or number in series
        Edition, if not the original
        Number of volumes
        Facts of publication--city where published, publisher, date of publication
        Volume number, if any
        Page number(s) of the particular citation

Article in a Periodical:
        Author's full name
        Title of the article
        Name of the periodical
        Volume (and number) of the periodical
        Date of the volume or issue
        Page number(s) of the particular citation

Unpublished Material:
>Title of document, if any, and date
>Folio number or other identifying material
>Name of collection
>Depositor, and city where it is located

Tables
Tables are numbered consecutively in the order in which they are first mentioned in text and are identified by the word "Table" and an arabic numeral. Double-space each table, regardless of length, and begin each table on a separate page. Type the short title of the manuscript and the page number in the upper right-hand corner of every page of a table. Tables are complicated to set in type and more expensive to publish than text. Therefore, they should be reserved for important data directly related to the content of the paper. Refer to every table and its data in text. Do not write "the table above/below " or "the table on p. 32" because the position and page number of a table cannot be determined until the text is typeset. In text, indicate the approximate placement of each table by a clear break in the text, inserting:

TABLE 1 ABOUT HERE

set off double-spaced above and below. Do not abbreviate table headings. Limit the use of rules to horizontal rules only. Draw all rules in pencil.

Figures
Figures are also numbered consecutively in the order in which they are first mentioned in text. Use the word "Figure" and an arabic numeral. Indicate the location of each figure by a clear break, inserting:

INSERT FIGURE 1 ABOUT HERE

set off double-spaced above and below.

All figures, charts, illustrations, halftones and chemical structures are figures and must be submitted in a form suitable for reproduction by the printer without redrawing or retouching. Careful adherence to the following instructions will ensure the high quality appearance of your paper.

1. All figures must be submitted as glossy prints or original ink drawings.

Retail Education Today

ADDRESS FOR SUBMISSION:

David J. Burns, Editor
Retail Education Today
Youngstown State University
Department of Marketing
Youngstown, OH 44555
USA
Phone: 330-742-1894
Fax: 330-742-1459
E-Mail: fr040501@ysub.ysu.edu
Web:
Address May Change:

CIRCULATION DATA:

Reader: Academics
Frequency of Issue: Quarterly
Copies per Issue: Less than 1,000
Sponsor/Publisher: American Collegiate Retailing Association
Subscribe Price: 20.00 US$

PUBLICATION GUIDELINES:

Manuscript Length: 1-5
Copies Required: Two
Computer Submission: Yes
Format: WordPerfect
Fees to Review: 0.00 US$

Manuscript Style:
    See Manuscript Guidelines

REVIEW INFORMATION:

Type of Review: Blind Review
No. of External Reviewers: 1
No. of In House Reviewers: 1
Acceptance Rate: 50%
Time to Review: 1 - 2 Months
Reviewers Comments: Yes
Invited Articles: 21-30%
Fees to Publish: 0.00 US$

MANUSCRIPT TOPICS:
Business Education; Retailing

MANUSCRIPT GUIDELINES/COMMENTS:

Papers will be reviewed in any format. Authors of accepted papers will be sent the style guidelines and will be requested to make the appropriate changes.

Service Industries Journal (The)

ADDRESS FOR SUBMISSION:

Ronald Goldsmith, Co-Editor
Service Industries Journal (The)
Florida State University
College of Business
Marketing Department
Tallahassee, FL 32306-1042
USA
Phone: 850-644-4401
Fax: 850-644-4098
E-Mail: rgoldsm@garnet.acns.fsu.edu
Web: www.frankcass.com
Address May Change:

PUBLICATION GUIDELINES:

Manuscript Length: 16-20
Copies Required: Four
Computer Submission: No
Format: N/A
Fees to Review: 0.00 US$

Manuscript Style:
, Publisher Guidelines

CIRCULATION DATA:

Reader: Academics
Frequency of Issue: Quarterly
Copies per Issue: No Reply
Sponsor/Publisher: Frank Cass and Co. Ltd
Subscribe Price: 60.00 US$ Individuals
     280.00 US$ Institutions

REVIEW INFORMATION:

Type of Review: Blind Review
No. of External Reviewers: 3
No. of In House Reviewers: 1
Acceptance Rate: 0-5%
Time to Review: 1 - 2 Months
Reviewers Comments: Yes
Invited Articles: 0-5%
Fees to Publish: 0.00 US$

MANUSCRIPT TOPICS:
Services

MANUSCRIPT GUIDELINES/COMMENTS:

Editors
Gary Akehurst, University of Portsmouth Business School, Department of Business Management, Locksway Road, Milton, Southsea Hants, UK P04 8JF.

Ronald Goldsmith, *Florida State University, USA*
Barry Howcroft, *Loughborough University Business School, UK*
Nicholas Alexander, *Bournemouth University, UK*

About the Journal
Service industries generate over two-thirds of GNP and employment in developed countries, and their importance is growing in developing countries. We must understand how they have developed, are developing and how we can improve the management of services. Services industries include retailing and distribution; financial services, including banking and

insurance; hotels and tourism; leisure, recreation and entertainment; professional and business services, including accountancy, marketing and law.

The Service Industries Journal, an international journal of service management, exists to improve our knowledge of service industries, service businesses and the effective management of services. This multidisciplinary journal was the first of its kind and has established a first class international reputation for the quality of its articles.

Manuscripts and editorial correspondence should be sent to Ronald Goldsmith in USA or Gary Akehurst in UK. (See addresses above.)

Guide to Journal Contributors

Manuscript
Articles submitted for consideration should be sent to any of the editors at the above address. Each manuscript should be submitted in triplicate (four copies would be more helpful).

Authors are asked to submit their articles presented according to the following instructions, as editors will not undertake retyping of manuscripts prior to publication.

Manuscripts must be typewritten on one side only, and **double spaced** with ample margins throughout, including pages of notes and references. All pages should be numbered consecutively.

There is no standard length for articles, but 5-6,000 words (including notes and references) is a useful target. Authors should inform the editor of the exact length of the article at the time of submission.

The article title should not exceed ten words in length. The author's name should appear on the first page, in capitals and centred underneath the title. The author's affiliation with address should appear in a footline on the first page. Acknowledgements, if any, should appear at the end of the article before the endnotes.

The article should begin with an indented and underlined summary of less than 100 words, describing the main arguments and conclusions of the article.

As no author corrections, updating or additions are allowed at proof stage, authors must make a final check of their article for content, style, proper names, quotations and references. Check especially consistency of:

> capitalisation, use of italics, hyphenation (minimal use of these is preferable), and spelling (e.g. of place names). Check for missing or duplicated numbers indicating notes.

Preparation of Diskettes
Following peer review and acceptance for publication, authors are requested to submit 3.5" computer diskettes (either IBM/PC or Macintosh-compatible) of their revised manuscripts along with a printed copy of the final manuscript. The following formats are preferred:

Microsoft Word; WordPerfect; and rich text files (RTF). Please do not embed footnotes, references, or any other text; list them in the foreground at the end of the text proper. Identify the diskette by providing lead author's name, manuscript title, name of computer file, and word-processing program, type and version number used.

Please keep at least one copy of the diskette. Diskettes will be returned after use upon request.

There is a risk that spelling mistakes, capital letters, etc. in original copy will be faithfully translated into typeset copy, so please check copy carefully before sending it.

Use the number 1, not lower case l, for numerals, and for zero use 0, not upper case O.

Print-Out
Copy presented on diskette must be accompanied by a print-out: The, print-out and the diskette must agree with each other. If corrections are made on the word processor, a new print-out must be made. The print-out must be: double spaced; in letter quality, **not draft** mode; without line-end hyphenation, and preferably unjustified; on plain paper, not greenlined computer paper.

Tables/camera-ready artwork
Tables, figures and maps should be kept to a minimum (no more than 4 per article) and should be grouped in an Appendix at the end of the article. They must be sufficiently black and clear and of good quality to be reproduced photographically. Tables should be produced on separate pages. Headings, sources and notes for tables and figures will be set by the typesetter. Tables, if created in a word processor, may appear in the main text file, but do not apply frames or tints.

The type area of a journal page is 144mm x 177mm. Please do not use more than 110 characters across (including spaces) for upright tables, or 175 characters across for landscaped ones. Avoid landscaped tables where possible, and consider reversing rows and columns to convert to an upright table. So that tables in different articles appear standard throughout the journal, please do not use more than three horizontal lines, as shown in the example, and avoid vertical lines (rules) as far as possible. Follow the style of column headings closely

Graphic elements, including tables (with the exception of those created in word processors as described above), figures, charts and photographs should be attached as separate items and saved in black and white in uncompressed TIF or JPG format. Tints should be avoided: use open patterns instead.

- As camera-ready artwork cannot be corrected at proof stage, double check for accuracy and consistency before submission.

- Do not mark up amendments or changes on any tables submitted as artwork for reproduction. This applies particularly to changes from American spelling, e.g. `labor' to `labour'. If any amendments or changes are necessary, these should be made before submission of camera-ready artwork.

- Ensure spelling is consistent with the text of an article, e.g. 'fertiliser' in text, but 'fertilizer' in table; 'defence' in text, but 'defense' in table (or vice versa).

Technical matter
- Equations, tables and diagrams should not be used unless essential to making the author's point and, where possible, should. be placed in an appendix at the end of the article.

- Symbols or Greek letters must be absolutely clear for the typesetter.

- If mathematics must be included please note that the typesetter can: turn any English or Greek letter, in upper or lower case, roman, italic or bold, into a first or second order superior; put a bar over any character but not over a group of characters.

Journal Style
Authors will be responsible for ensuring that their manuscripts correspond with the Journal style. Particular attention is drawn to the following points.

Spelling: British spelling should be used throughout, and where there is an alternative -ise (rather than -ize) endings (i.e. organise rather than organize).

Subheadings: main subheadings should be in capital letters, ranged left above the section, and sub-subheadings should have capital letters only for major words, and be underlined and ranged left above the section. Third-level subheadings should be underlined and run on as part of the paragraph (with a space above) and typed with a capital letter only for the first word.

Notes and references:
Simple references without accompanying comments: to be inserted in square brackets at the appropriate place in the text, stating author's surname, publication date of work, and (where appropriate) page numbers: [Livesey, 1979: 22-3]. If reference is made in the article to more than one work in the same year by the author, a lower case letter should be used to distinguish them: [Sparks, 1982a: 24-56].

References with comments: to appear as notes, indicated consecutively throughout the article by raised numerals corresponding to the list of notes placed at the end of the article. Notes should be kept to a minimum. Bibliographical references within the notes should follow the system described above.

A reference list should appear after the list of notes. It should contain all the works referred to, listed alphabetically by the author's surname (or name of sponsoring organisation where there is no identifiable author). Please double check that all authors mentioned in text are in the reference list, with the same spelling of names, and that they are in correct alphabetical order. Style should follow: author's surname, forename and/or initials, date of publication, title of publication (italicised), place of publication and publisher. All of this information must be provided. Thus (note especially punctuation):

Dawson, J.A. and D. Kirby, 1979, *Small Scale Retailing in the United Kingdom*, 2nd edition, Farnborough: Saxon House.

Sparks, L., 1982a, 'Female and Part-time Employment within Superstore Retailing', *European Journal of Marketing*, Vol.16, No.3, July, pp.278-94.

Sparks, L., 1982b, 'Employment in Hypermarkets and Superstores', in A.B. Smith (ed.), *Employment Trends in England and Wales*, Oxford: Basil Blackwell.

Book reviews should be preceded by full publication information in the following form:

The Business of Tourism, by J.C. Holloway. Plymouth: MacDonald & Evans, 1983. Pp.x + 246. £14.95 (paperback). ISBN 0-71210594-8.

The reviewer's name (in capital letters) and affiliation (underlined, ranged at the left) should appear at the end of the review.

While every care is taken, the Publishers cannot accept responsibility for loss of or damage to authors' manuscripts. Authors should keep at least one copy of their article.

Administrative Editor at The Service Industries Journal, Frank Cass & Co. Ltd, Newberry House, 900 Eastern Avenue, Ilford, Essex IG2 7HH, UK. Email: editors@frankcass.com

Services Marketing Quarterly

ADDRESS FOR SUBMISSION:

David Loudon, Bob Stevens, Co-Editors
Services Marketing Quarterly
University of Louisiana at Monroe
College of Business
Department of Management & Marketing
Monroe, LA 71209-0140
USA
Phone: 318-342-1186
Fax: 318-342-1209
E-Mail: mmloudon@alpha.ulm.edu
Web: www.haworthpress.inc
Address May Change:

PUBLICATION GUIDELINES:

Manuscript Length: 5-50
Copies Required: Two
Computer Submission: Yes if accepted
Format:
Fees to Review: 0.00 US$

Manuscript Style:
  Chicago Manual of Style

CIRCULATION DATA:

Reader: Academics, Business Persons
Frequency of Issue: 2 Times/Year
Copies per Issue: 3,001 - 4,000
Sponsor/Publisher: Haworth Press, Inc.
Subscribe Price: 60.00 US$ Individual
  90.00 US$ Institution
  275.00 US$ Library

REVIEW INFORMATION:

Type of Review: Editorial Review
No. of External Reviewers: 3+
No. of In House Reviewers: 1
Acceptance Rate: 50%
Time to Review: 2 - 3 Months
Reviewers Comments: No
Invited Articles: 6-10%
Fees to Publish: 0.00 US$

MANUSCRIPT TOPICS:
Marketing Research; Marketing Theory & Applications; Professional Services Marketing

MANUSCRIPT GUIDELINES/COMMENTS:

About The Journal

The *Services Marketing Quarterly* is an applied journal for marketing all types of professional services. It is devoted to supplying "how-to" marketing tools for specific sectors of the expanding service sector of the economy.

Each issue of this unique quarterly periodical is a basic resource for all service managers. Specific tools, cases, and methodologies used by other professionals in various service industries are offered for examination. The journal has covered such areas as

The distinguished practitioners and academicians share with you their experiences in developing, implementing, and evaluating their marketing campaigns and programs, and explore the latest marketing issues and methodologies.

The *Services Marketing Quarterly* demonstrates the applicability of marketing to specific professional services. It bridges a gap between theory and application by simply and clearly presenting marketing methodologies that can assist you in marketing your service.

Instructions for Authors
1. **Original Articles Only**. Submission of a manuscript to this Journal represents a certification on the part of the author(s) that it is an original work, and that neither this manuscript nor a version of it has been published elsewhere nor is being considered for publication elsewhere.

2. **Manuscript Length**. Regular articles should run between 12 and 15 pages (typewritten and double spaced). Clinical comments are illustrative case studies or brief reports of research limited to 4 pages. Reviews of books or other media should be under 2 pages.

3. **Manuscript Style**. References, citations, and general style of manuscripts for this Journal should follow the Chicago style (as outlined in the latest edition of the *Manual Of Style* of the University of Chicago Press). References should be double-spaced and placed in alphabetical order.

If an author wishes to submit a paper that has been already prepared in another style, he or she may do so. However, if the paper is accepted (with or without reviewer's alterations), the author is fully responsible for retyping the manuscript in the correct style as indicated above. Neither the Editor nor the Publisher is responsible for re-preparing manuscript copy to adhere to the Journal's style.

4. **Manuscript Preparation**.
Margins: leave at least a one-inch margin on all four sides.
Paper: use clean white, 8 ½ " x 11" bond paper.
Number Of Copies: 3 (the original plus two photocopies).
Cover Page: Important--staple a cover page to the manuscript, indicating only the article title (this is used for anonymous refereeing).
Second "Title Page": enclose a regular title page but do not staple it to the manuscript. Include the title again, plus:
- full authorship
- an **abstract** of about 100 words
- an introductory footnote with authors' academic degrees, professional titles, affiliations, mailing addresses, and any desired acknowledgement of research support or other credit.

5. **Return Envelopes**. When you submit your three manuscript copies, also include:
- a 9" x 12" envelope, self-addressed and stamped (with sufficient postage to ensure return of your manuscript);
- a regular envelope, stamped and self-addressed. This is for the Editor to send you an "acknowledgement of receipt" letter.

6. **Spelling, Grammar, and Punctuation**. You are responsible for preparing manuscript copy which is clearly written in acceptable scholarly English, and which contains no errors of

spelling, grammar, or punctuation. Neither the Editor nor the Publisher is responsible for correcting errors of spelling and grammar: the manuscript after acceptance by the Editor, must be immediately ready for typesetting as it is finally submitted by the author(s). Check your paper for the following common errors:
- dangling modifiers
- misplaced modifiers
- unclear antecedents
- incorrect or inconsistent abbreviations

Also, check the accuracy of all arithmetic calculations statistics, numerical data, text citations, and references.

7. **Inconsistencies Must Be Avoided.** Be sure you are consistent in your use of abbreviations, terminology, and in citing references, from one part of your paper to another.

8. **Preparation of Tables, Figures, and Illustrations.** All tables, figures, illustrations, etc. must be "camera-ready". That is, they must be cleanly typed or artistically prepared so that they can be used either exactly as they are or else used after a photographic reduction in size. Figures, tables, and illustrations must be prepared on separate sheets of paper. Always use black ink and professional drawing instruments. On the back of these items, write your article title and the journal title lightly in pencil, so they do not get misplaced. In text, skip extra lines and indicate where these figures and tables are to be placed (please do not write on face of art).

9. **Alterations Required By Referees and Reviewers.** Many times a paper is accepted by the Editor contingent upon changes that are mandated by anonymous specialist referees and members of the Editorial Board. If the Editor returns your manuscript for revisions, you are responsible for retyping any sections of the paper to incorporate these revisions (if applicable revisions should also be put on disk).

10. **Typesetting.** You will not be receiving galley proofs of your article. Editorial revisions, if any, must therefore be made while your article is still in manuscript. The final version of the manuscript will be the version you see published. Printer's errors will be corrected by the production staff of The Haworth Press. Authors are expected to submit manuscripts, disks, and art that are free from error.

11. **Electronic Media.** Haworth's in-house typesetting unit will now be able to utilize your final manuscript material as prepared on most personal computers and word processors. This will minimize typographical errors and decrease overall production timelag.

A. A.Please continue to send your first draft and final draft copies of your manuscript to the journal Editor in print format for his/her final review and approval

B. Only after the journal editor has approved your final manuscript, you may submit the final approved version both on:
- printed format ("hard copy")
- floppy diskette

A. Wrap your floppy diskettes in a strong diskette wrapper or holder, and write on the outside of the package:
- the brand name of your computer or word processor
- the word-processing program that you used to create your article, book chapter, or book.
- file name

The benefits of this procedure are many with speed and accuracy being the most obvious. We look forward to working with you on this knowing we will be able to serve you more efficiently in the future.

12. **Reprints**. The senior author will receive one copy of the journal issue and 10 complimentary reprints of his or her article. The junior author will receive one copy of the issue. These are sent several weeks after the journal issue is published and in circulation. An order form for the purchase of additional reprints will also be sent to all authors at this time. (Approximately 4-6 weeks is necessary for the preparation of reprints.) Please do not query the Journal's Editor about reprints. All such questions should be sent directly to The Haworth Press, Inc., Production Department 10 Alice Street, Binghamton, NY 13904-1580.

13. **Copyright**. If your manuscript is accepted for publication, copyright ownership must be transferred officially to The Haworth Press, Inc. The Editors acceptance letter will include a form fully explaining this. The form must be signed by all authors and returned to the Editor at that time.

14. **Computer Disk**. Articles require (3) hardcopies along with computer disk copy on 3 ½ " or 5 ¼ " disk in any standard word processing format.

Sloan Management Review

ADDRESS FOR SUBMISSION:

Jane Gebhart, Editor-in-Chief
Sloan Management Review
Massachusetts Institute of Technology
Alfred P. Sloan School of Management
77 Massachusetts Avenue, E60-100
Cambridge, MA 02139
USA
Phone: 617-253-7170
Fax: 617-258-9739
E-Mail: smr@mit.edu
Web: mitsloan.mit.edu/smr
Address May Change:

PUBLICATION GUIDELINES:

Manuscript Length: 16-20
Copies Required: Three
Computer Submission: Yes
Format: Microsoft Word
Fees to Review: 0.00 US$

Manuscript Style:
   See Manuscript Guidelines

CIRCULATION DATA:

Reader: Business Persons
Frequency of Issue: Quarterly
Copies per Issue: More than 25,000
Sponsor/Publisher: MIT
Subscribe Price: 79.00 US$
   125.00 US$ Foreign

REVIEW INFORMATION:

Type of Review: Blind Review
No. of External Reviewers: 2
No. of In House Reviewers: 1
Acceptance Rate: 6-10%
Time to Review: 2 - 3 Months
Reviewers Comments: Yes
Invited Articles: 11-20%
Fees to Publish: 0.00 US$

MANUSCRIPT TOPICS:

Business Education; Business Information Systems (MIS); Business Law, Public Responsibility & Ethics; Global Business; Labor Relations & Human Resource Mgt.; Marketing Theory & Applications; Operations Research/Statistics; Organizational Behavior & Theory; Organizational Development; Production/Operations; Purchasing/Materials Management; Services; Strategic Management Policy; Technology/Innovation

MANUSCRIPT GUIDELINES/COMMENTS:

Manuscript Guidelines for authors at Website: http://web.mit.edu/smr-online/

Why publish in SMR?

- Our readers. They're smart, thoughtful, influential, and successful.
- Our contributors. You'll be joining a distinguished crowd.
- Our stature. Our reprint sales and citation levels indicate that SMR articles have a long shelf life.
- Our editors. They're meticulous, accessible, and friendly.

Editorial Process

Unsolicited manuscripts are logged, acknowledged, and assigned to an in-house editor within about 10 days of receipt.

All manuscripts are read in-house. Around 20 percent are sent out for academic review. The others are turned down at this stage. Unfortunately, we cannot provide detailed comments on those manuscripts.

Manuscripts judged potentially appropriate are sent to outside reviewers. If a manuscript gets held up, it's apt to be during this step. We attempt to give authors an initial decision (accept, reject, or revise with reviewers' comments) within 10-12 weeks of receipt.

If an author has been encouraged to revise and resubmit a manuscript, we generally make an in-house decision within two weeks of receiving a revision.

Accepted articles must be submitted on disk.

Ink preparing manuscripts for publication, we do substantial but not radical rewriting and editing -- more than most academic journals and less than most magazines. We consult closely with authors along the way. Most authors are happy with the process and with the results.

Articles usually appear within 6 months of acceptance. Average time between initial submission and eventual publication is 10 months.

Editorial Tips

The ideal SMR article is both rigorous and practical. It could stand alone in a research journal, but it also helps professional managers solve real-world problems. Writing that kind of article isn't easy! We hope that the information and suggestions that follow will help:

Questions We Ask During Initial Screening

- What's this article based on? (Case study, research, consulting observations, thin air...?)
- Does it explore issues more deeply than the typical article in the popular business press?
- Does the author adequately support the claims he or she makes?
- How rich, detailed, deep, or familiar are the illustrations?
- Was I persuaded? Was I interested? Did I learn anything? Have I heard it all before?
- Was anyone trying to sell me anything?

Questions We Ask Reviewers To Answer

1. Is the paper essentially correct? If not, what changes are necessary to make it so?

2. Does the paper offer something innovative or a new insight? If not, is it, at a minimum, current with other research?

3. Would a practicing manager find the paper useful? Are there concepts, suggestions, or techniques that could be implemented immediately? If not, what changes to the paper would you recommend?

4. What parts of this paper, if any, improve your understanding of the subject matter? What new principles, applications, or ideas does the paper add to the field? Would you suggest any ways to improve the clarity or focus of the discussion?

5. How familiar is the author with the existing literature on this topic? What other sources would anchor, balance, or enhance a discussion on this topic? Is the article up to date with the management literature?

Common Problems
- Poor writing.

- General sloppiness: typos, reference to nonexistent graphics. incomplete references, etc.

- Tired examples (e.g., Wal-Mart, Southwest Airlines, J&J Code)

- Overfamiliar overview. (Can you write an introduction that doesn't even mention the pace of change in today's world or the globalization of business?)

- Too academic or too fluffy. We don't want a pure research paper unless it looks at findings from a managerial perspective. Nor do we want a series of reflections on The World As You See It (unless you're Peter Drucker).

- Tips for consultants:
  Don't oversell; wow them with your intelligence, not your aggressiveness. If the only reasonable response to reading your article would be to hire you, it isn't a good paper. Good presentations don't turn into good articles without extra time and thought. Ghostwriters are for speeches, not for journal articles.

Final Tip
Read an issue of SMR.

Manuscript Guidelines
We would rather read a completed draft than respond to an article idea or an outline.

Articles should be under 30 pages; optimal length is 20-25 pages.

We will not consider articles that have appeared elsewhere or that are being considered elsewhere. We will consider articles based on research published in a purely academic journal if the research is of broad interest and if the new treatment develops managerial perspectives thoroughly. We will consider portions of books only if they can appear in SMR before the book is published. We will consider papers that have been presented at conferences.

Authors are required to assign SMR exclusive copyright, including rights to electronic distribution.

The target audience is a mixture of academics and well-educated, sophisticated professional managers.

When you submit an article, please include the following:

1. Cover letter stating why the article should be published
2. Two double-spaced, one-sided copies of the manuscript.
3. A cover sheet that includes article title and abstract, without authors' names.
4. Numbered figures and tables, each on a separate sheet of paper.
5. Include return postage if you want rejected manuscripts returned.
6. Reference Style. Please number footnotes in the text and follow this style:
   Books
   J. March and H.J. Simon, Organizations (New York: John Wiley & Sons, 1966), pp. 413.

   Journals and Magazines
   R.E. Herzlinger and D. Calkins, "How Companies Tackle Health Care Costs," Harvard Business Review, vol. 64, January-February 1986, pp. 70-80.

   T.J. Allen and S. Cohen, "Information Flow in R&D Labs," Administrative Science Quarterly, vol. 14, December 1969, pp. 12-19.

   Article Cited in Anthology
   M. Shaw, "Communication Networks," in Advance in Experimental Social Psychology, ed. L. Berkowitz (New York: Academic Press, 1964), pp. 131-153.

   Working Papers
   C.V. Bullen, "Groupware: A Key to Managing Business Terms" (Cambridge. Massachusetts: MIT Sloan School of Management, Center for information Systems Research, Working Paper 169, May 1988).

   Dissertations
   M. Smith, "Important Topics" (Cambridge, Massachusetts: MIT Sloan School of Management, Ph.D. Diss., 1983).

   Forthcoming Books
   M. Tushman, Managing Innovation and Change (New York: McGraw-Hill), forthcoming.

   Forthcoming Articles
   M. Tushman. "An Information Processing Approach," Academy of Management Review, in press.

   Multiple References
   G. Farris, "Managing Informal Dynamics in R&D," Harvard Business Review, January-February 1986, pp. 5- 11; and F. Andrews and G. Peters, Personnel Psychology (New York: McGraw-Hill. 1986).

Contacts
Send submissions to:
The Editor
Sloan Management Review/MIT
77 Massachusetts Avenue
Cambridge, MA 02139

To inquire about a manuscript's potential suitability, e-mail Jane Gebhart at jhg@mit.edu.

To inquire about a manuscript's status, call Mary Ann Haxthausen at 617-253-3531 or e-mail her at mahaxtha@mit.edu.

Southwest Business & Economics Journal

ADDRESS FOR SUBMISSION:

V. Sivarama Kirshnan, Editor
Southwest Business & Economics Journal
Cameron University
School of Business
Business Research Center
2800 W. Gore Boulevard
Lawton, OK 73505
USA
Phone: 580-581-2805
Fax: 580-581-2253
E-Mail: sivarama@cameron.edu
Web:
Address May Change:

PUBLICATION GUIDELINES:

Manuscript Length: 11-15
Copies Required: Three
Computer Submission: Yes
Format: WordPerfect 6.0
Fees to Review: 0.00 US$

Manuscript Style:
    Chicago Manual of Style

CIRCULATION DATA:

Reader: Academics, Buiness Persons
Frequency of Issue: Yearly
Copies per Issue: 600
Sponsor/Publisher: Cameron University
Subscribe Price: 10.00 US$ Individual
    15.00 US$ Organization/Library

REVIEW INFORMATION:

Type of Review: Blind Review
No. of External Reviewers: 1
No. of In House Reviewers: 1
Acceptance Rate: 30-35%
Time to Review: 3 - 4 Months
Reviewers Comments: Yes
Invited Articles: 0-30%
Fees to Publish: 0.00 US$

MANUSCRIPT TOPICS:
Advertising & Promotion Management; Direct Marketing; Marketing Research; Marketing Theory & Applications; Sales/Selling; Services; Transportation/Physical Distribution

MANUSCRIPT GUIDELINES/COMMENTS:

The *Southwest Business and Economics Journal* provides a bridge of communication between the business community and the academia. Articles related to all business areas and regional economic development are welcome. The journal has two sections: the first consists of refereed articles from the academic community and an occasional invited article from business practitioners, and the second has abstracts of the business and economic information presented in the Cameron Business Forums. The journal is published once a year.

The target audience includes both academics and the business and professional community.

The *Southwest Business and Economics Journal* is published once a year by the Business Research Center, School of Graduate and Professional Studies, Cameron University, Lawton. OK.

Articles on applied business and economics topics related to all areas of business are invited from faculty and from business professionals.

1. All submitted work must be original work that is not under submission to another journal or under consideration for publication in another form.

2. Authors must submit three double-spaced typewritten copies of their paper.

3. The cover page shall contain the title of the paper, author's name, and affiliation. This page will be removed when the paper is sent to a referee. The first page of text should contain the title but not the name of the author.

4. A separate abstract of not more than 100 words should be included.

5. Each table and figure should be on a separate page at the end of the paper, with proper instructions about their placement in the paper.

6. Footnotes must be consecutively numbered and typed on a separate page and double-spaced.

7. Cite references in the text, placing the publication date in parentheses, e.g., "Banz (1981) was the first...

8. *Southwest Business and Economics Journal* will hold exclusive rights after acceptance.

9. Authors are advised to mention their office and residence telephone numbers and convenient times for contact.

10. Papers should be submitted to the Editor.

We accept computer submissions on 3 ½ " disk formatted in WordPerfect 6.0.

Southwestern Business Administration Journal

ADDRESS FOR SUBMISSION:

Mohamed A. Zainuba, Editor
Southwestern Business Administration
  Journal
Texas Southern University
School of Business
3100 Cleburne
Houston, TX 77004
USA
Phone: 713-313-7308
Fax: 713-313-7705
E-Mail: zainuba_ma@tsu.edu
Web:
Address May Change:

PUBLICATION GUIDELINES:

Manuscript Length: 21-25
Copies Required: Three
Computer Submission: No
Format: N/A
Fees to Review: 0.00 US$

Manuscript Style:
  See Manuscript Guidelines

CIRCULATION DATA:

Reader: Business Persons, Academics
Frequency of Issue: Yearly
Copies per Issue: 2,001 - 3,000
Sponsor/Publisher: Organizational Behavior
  Teaching Society, Texas Southern Univ.
Subscribe Price: 25.00 US$

REVIEW INFORMATION:

Type of Review: Blind Review
No. of External Reviewers: 2
No. of In House Reviewers: 1
Acceptance Rate: 31-50%
Time to Review: 2 - 3 Months
Reviewers Comments: Yes
Invited Articles: 0-5%
Fees to Publish: 0.00 US$

MANUSCRIPT TOPICS:
Advertising & Promotion Management; Business Education; Business Information Systems (MIS); Business Law, Public Responsibility & Ethics; Communication; Direct Marketing; Global Business; Labor Relations & Human Resource Mgt.; Marketing Research; Marketing Theory & Applications; Non Profit Organizations; Office Administration/Management; Operations Research/Statistics; Organizational Behavior & Theory; Organizational Development; Production/Operations; Public Administration; Sales/Selling; Small Business Entrepreneurship; Strategic Management Policy; Technology/Innovation

MANUSCRIPT GUIDELINES/COMMENTS:

The *Southwestern Business Administration Journal* is a refereed publication. The aim of this journal is to provide a forum for current thoughts, techniques, theories, issues, trends and innovations in the business administration field. All manuscripts submitted to the journal will be subject to the double-blind referee process.

FORMAT:
Manuscripts should be typed on a standard size paper (8.5 by 11) and must not exceed 25 pages, including references, appendixes, tables, and figures.

The manuscript must use Word Perfect or Microsoft Word and should be typed in a 12point font. It must be double spaced (excluding references, appendixes, tables, and figures). All margins are one inch.

Main headings should be centered and typed in all capitals. Example: INTRODUCTION.

Secondary headings should be typed flush with the left margin and in small letters, with major words beginning with capitals. Example: Learning Models.

Tables, figures, and graphs should be included where they are discussed. Do not include notations like "Insert Table 1 about here".

Do not paginate within the manuscript. Pencil in page numbers on the bottom of the hard copy.

Do not use footnotes in your manuscript.

Citations should be made in the text by inclosing the cited author's name and the year of the work cited in parentheses. Example: Several studies (Johnson, 1999; smith, 1998; Green, 1997) support this finding.

Direct quotations must give a page number(s); these follow the date of publication and are separated from it by a colon. Example: Johnson indicated that "writing is a difficult process" (1995: 6).

Periodical reference example: Johnson, C. L. 1994. The art of writing. **Academy of Management Journal,** 32: 112-125.

Book reference example: Johnson, C. L. **The art of writing.** New York: Macmillan. The title page should include the title of the manuscript and appropriate contact information (authors' names, affiliations, complete address, contact numbers, and e-mail addresses.

The second page should repeat the title of the manuscript and a brief (not to exceed 100 words) abstract. Excluding title page, the manuscript should not contain the name of the author or any affiliation which would allow the reviewer to determine authorship.

ASSUMPTIONS:
The journal assumes that:

- Authors have submitted original work and made every effort to ensure accuracy of the manuscript.

- Accepted ethical standards have been applied in the research and/or preparation of the manuscript submitted for publication.

- Authors have obtained appropriate permissions so that the publication of the manuscript would not violate any copyright or other personal or proprietary rights of others.

NOTE: Publication decisions are based on the recommendations of the journal's editorial board. Submissions are typically assigned to three reviewers for consideration. Weak or inappropriate submissions may be returned to authors without formal reviews. Authors should submit three copies of their manuscripts along with a copy on a computer disk to:

Dr. Mohamed A. Zainuba, Editor Southwestern Business Administration Journal, School of Business, Texas Southern University, 3100 Cleburne, Houston, Texas 77004. Phone (713)313-7308, Fax (713)313-7705, e-mail: zainuba ma@tsu.edu

Deadline for manuscript submission: February 15

Sport Marketing Quarterly

ADDRESS FOR SUBMISSION:

Lynn Kahle, Editor
Sport Marketing Quarterly
University of Oregon
Department of Marketing
Eugene, OR 97403-1208
USA
Phone: 541-346-3373
Fax: 541-346-3341
E-Mail: lkahle@oregon.uoregon.edu
Web:
Address May Change:

PUBLICATION GUIDELINES:

Manuscript Length: 11-25
Copies Required: Three
Computer Submission: Yes
Format: WdPerfect 5.1/6.0, Wintel
Fees to Review: 0.00 US$

Manuscript Style:
    American Psychological Association

CIRCULATION DATA:

Reader: Academics, Business Persons
Frequency of Issue: Quarterly
Copies per Issue: 1,001 - 2,000
Sponsor/Publisher: Fitness Information
    Technology
Subscribe Price: 39.00 US$ Individual
    85.00 US$ Institution
    27.00 US$ Student

REVIEW INFORMATION:

Type of Review: Blind Review
No. of External Reviewers: 2
No. of In House Reviewers: 1
Acceptance Rate: 21-30%
Time to Review: 1 - 2 Months
Reviewers Comments: Yes
Invited Articles: 6-10%
Fees to Publish: 0.00 US$

MANUSCRIPT TOPICS:

Advertising & Promotion Management; Business Education; Communication; Non Profit Organizations; Office Administration/Management; Sports

MANUSCRIPT GUIDELINES/COMMENTS:

Publisher: Fitness Information Technology
           Box 4425, University Avenue
           Morgantown, WV 26505
           For Subscription Information dial: 1-800-477-4348

Sport Marketing Quarterly represents a unique publishing concept for sport marketing practitioners and academicians. These two groups of marketing professionals will be represented in a landmark publication that will facilitate the exchange of ideas in sport marketing. For the practicing sport marketer, SMQ will provide a vehicle to share marketing successes with peers. For academicians, SMQ will provide a much-needed publishing source. For both constituencies, SMQ will provide an opportunity to work together to help professionals in the business of marketing sport.

Publishing categories for SMQ include:

    Professional   Media
    Amateur   Advertising
    Promotion   Special Events
    Facility, Arena, and/or Stadium   International
    Research   Miscellaneous

Manuscript Submission Guidelines

1. Manuscripts are to be submitted in IBM PC Word Perfect, ASCII, or Rich Text format, and marked as such directly on the d 1/2", 1.44 diskette (please inquire to SMQ if this creates a problem). Include with your diskettes 3 printed copies of the manuscript on 8 1/2 X 11 inch paper and double spaced. Margins should be 1 1/2 inches on the left side of the manuscript and 1 inch on the right side.

2. Manuscripts should be accompanied by an abstract of 150 words or less.

3. Authors are requested to follow the directions given in the *Publication Manual of the American Psychological Association* or preparing the text, tables, figures of the manuscript. All tables are to be submitted both in electronic and production quality laser output, with any screens printed in 65 Ipi. Please indicated what software was implemented to create figures (suggested software: QuarkXpress, Pagemaker, Adobe Illustrator, Coreldraw), suggested file formats are: *.tif, *.eps, *.wmf, *.pcx.

4. Manuscripts should not exceed 24 pages, including figures, tables, and reference list, if applicable.

5. Manuscripts prepared on the personal computer should be prepared in this: abstract, text, footnotes, references, and tables.

6. Evaluations of manuscripts not accepted for publication will be returned to principal author.

7. Manuscripts (and diskettes) not accepted for publication will be returned if requested by the principal author.

8. Manuscripts should not be submitted to another journal while under review by SMQ.

9. Identify on the cover letter and title page if the manuscript is derived from a master's thesis or doctoral dissertation.

10. All manuscripts go through a blind review. Therefore, the title page of the manuscript should be on a separate page from the remainder of the manuscript. The author's name(s) should not appear in the manuscript except as a reference citation.

11. Author(s) of manuscripts accepted for publication will be required to transfer copyright to Fitness Information Technology, Inc., publisher of SMQ.

12. Authors warrant that the manuscript is original except for excerpts and illustrations from copyrighted works as may be included with the permission of the copyright owner, such permission to be obtained by the authors at their expense. The hard copy and the diskett(s) submitted to the publisher must contain the appropriate credit line, if any, required by the copyright holders of the material adapted or reprinted for use.

Tourism Analysis

ADDRESS FOR SUBMISSION:

Muzzo Uysal, Co-Editor
Tourism Analysis
Virginia Polytechnic Institute and State University
Dept. of Hospitality & Tourism Mgmt.
Blacksburg, VA 24061
USA
Phone: 540-231-8476
Fax: 540-231-8313
E-Mail: samil@vt.edu
Web:
Address May Change:

PUBLICATION GUIDELINES:

Manuscript Length: 16-20
Copies Required: Three
Computer Submission: Yes
Format: Word, Text File
Fees to Review: 0.00 US$

Manuscript Style:
American Psychological Association

CIRCULATION DATA:

Reader: Academics
Frequency of Issue: Quarterly
Copies per Issue: Less than 1,000
Sponsor/Publisher: Cognitant Communication Corporation
Subscribe Price: 125.00 US$ Library
125.00 US$ Individual
40.00 US$ Professional

REVIEW INFORMATION:

Type of Review: Blind Review
No. of External Reviewers: 3
No. of In House Reviewers: 1
Acceptance Rate: 45%
Time to Review: 1 - 2 Months
Reviewers Comments: Yes
Invited Articles: 0-5%
Fees to Publish: 0.00 US$

MANUSCRIPT TOPICS:
Global Business; Services; Tourism & Hospitality Research

MANUSCRIPT GUIDELINES/COMMENTS:

Aims and Scope
The aim of *Tourism Analysis* is to promote a forum for practitioners and academicians in the fields of Leisure, Recreation, Tourism, and Hospitality (LRTH). As an interdisciplinary journal, it is an appropriate outlet for articles, research notes, and computer software packages designed to be of interest, concern, and of applied value to its audience of professionals, scholars, and students of LRTH programs the world over. The scope of the articles will include behavioral models (quantitative-qualitative), decision-making techniques and procedures, estimation models, demand-supply analysis. monitoring systems, expert systems and performance evaluation, assessment of site and destination attractiveness, new analytical tools. research methods and related areas such as validity and reliability, scale development, development of data collection instruments, methodological issues in cross-national and crosscultural studies, and computer technology and use.

Information For Contributors
Send manuscripts to the Editors: MUZAFFER UYSAL. Professor of Tourism Research, Virginia Tech, Dept. of Hospitality and Tourism Management, 355 Wallace Hall, Blacksburg, VA 24061, USA, Phone: 540-231-8426, Fax: 540-231-8313, E-mail: samil@vt.edu or RICHARD R. PERDUE Professor, College of Business and Administration, University of Colorado, Boulder, CO 80309-0419, USA, Phone: (303) 492-2923, Fax: (303) 492-5962, E-mail: Richard.Perdue@Colorado.edu

Manuscripts submitted from Europe: PROFESSOR JOSEF MAZANEC. Inst of Leisure, Recreation and Tourism, Univ. of Vienna, Augasse 2-6, A-1090 Wien, Austria, Phone: 43-1-31336-4586, E-mail: Mazanec@wu-wein.ac.at

Manuscript Submission: Manuscripts must be submitted in triplicate. They should be typewritten on one side of the paper, double spaced (including references), and should be checked carefully. All rights and permissions must be obtained by the contributor(s). These permissions should be sent upon acceptance of the manuscript for publication. Enclose a self-addressed envelope with the submitted manuscript

The title of the paper, all author names and corresponding affiliations, and name and complete mailing address for mailing proofs should be included on a separate page, because manuscripts are sent out for blind review. Include telephone and fax numbers for the designated corresponding author.

Abstract: Provide an abstract of up to 300 words. It should contain an abbreviated representation of the content of the manuscript Major results, conclusions, and/or recommendations should be given, followed by supporting details of method, scope, or purpose as appropriate. Supply 3 to 5 keywords suitable for indexing.

References should be placed at the end of the manuscript on a separate page, arranged in alphabetical order. Follow APA guidelines set forth in their Publication Manual (4th edition) for text and reference list citations, per the examples.

Text citations. (Gunn, 1990) or (Fesenmaier et al., 1994; Mazanec, 1992, 1993: Uysal & Gitelson, 1994) or (Crompton, 1979, p. 411) (for quoted material). Journal citations: Crouch, L G. (1994). The study of international tourism demand: A review of findings. Journal of Travel Research, 33(1), 12-23. Book citation: Witt, E. S., & Witt, C. A. (1992). Modeling and forecasting in tourism. London: Academic Press. Chapterlpages in edited book Frechtling, C. D. (1994). Assessing the impacts of travel and tourism: Measuring economic benefits. In 1. R. Brent Ritchie & C. R. Goeldner (Eds.), Travel, tourism, and hospitality research (2nd ed., pp. 367-391). New York: John Wiley & Sons. Please note that citations such as "personal communication" should be cited parenthetically in the text only. Do not include in the reference list.

Illustrations and diagrams should be kept to a minimum and must be suitable for direct reproduction. They should be drawn with India ink on stout paper or be laser output of 300 dpi or greater. Lettering should be large enough to be legible after reduction to printing size. Place the first author's name and figure number on the reverse side of each illustration in light pencil. Captions for illustrations should be included on separate pages at the end of the manuscript

Photographs should be submitted unmounted, on white glossy paper (slides are not acceptable).

Tables should be constructed to be intelligible without reference to the text Include a title caption and headings for columns. Avoid very wide or very long tables that would not fit printed page size. The same information should not be duplicated in tables and illustrations. Place tables on separate pages at the end of the manuscript

Computer Disk: To speed publication and ensure accuracy, authors are encouraged to submit a computer disk containing the final version of their manuscript along with the final paper version. Please observe the following criteria: I) Specify what software was used, including which release (e.g., WordPerfect 6.0). 2) Specify what computer was used 3) Include both text file and ASCII file on the disk. 4) The file should be single spaced and should use the wrap-around end-of-line feature (i.e., no return at the end of the line). All textual elements should begin flush left, with no paragraph indents. Place two returns after every element, such as title, headings, paragraphs, etc. 5) Keep a backup disk for reference and safety.

Page Proofs and Reprints: Page proofs will be sent to the designated corresponding contributor. A form for ordering reprints and copies of the journal issue in which the article appears will accompany the page proofs. Minor corrections only are allowed at proof stage.

Copyright: Publications are copyrighted for the protection of the authors and the publisher. A Transfer of Copyright Agreement will be sent to the author whose manuscript is accepted for publication. This form must be completed and returned to the Editor before the article can be published.

Although every effort is made by the publisher and editorial board to see that no inaccurate or misleading data, opinion, or statement appears in this Journal, they wish to make it clear that the data and opinions appearing in the articles and advertisements herein are the sole responsibility of the contributor or advertiser concerned. Accordingly, the publisher, the editorial board, editors, and their respective employees, officers, and agents accept no responsibility or liability whatsoever for the consequences of any such inaccurate or misleading data, opinion, or statement.

Tourism and Hospitality Research: The Surrey Quarterly Review

ADDRESS FOR SUBMISSION:

Janet Noble
Tourism and Hospitality Research: The
  Surrey Quarterly Review
Henry Stewart Publications
Museum House
25 Museum Street
London, WC1A 1JT
UK
Phone: 44 20 7323 2916
Fax: 44 20 7323 2918
E-Mail: janet@hspublications.com
Web: www.henrystewart.com
Address May Change:

PUBLICATION GUIDELINES:

Manuscript Length: 11-30
Copies Required: Three
Computer Submission: Yes
Format: MS Word
Fees to Review: 0.00 US$

Manuscript Style:
  See Manuscript Guidelines

CIRCULATION DATA:

Reader: Business Persons, Academics
Frequency of Issue: Quarterly
Copies per Issue: 1,001 - 2,000
Sponsor/Publisher: Henry Stewart
  Publications
Subscribe Price: 140.00 US$ Individual
  275.00 US$ Institution

REVIEW INFORMATION:

Type of Review: Blind Review
No. of External Reviewers: 0 2-3
No. of In House Reviewers: 1
Acceptance Rate: 21-30%
Time to Review: 1 - 2 Months
Reviewers Comments: Yes
Invited Articles: 6-10%
Fees to Publish: 0.00 US$

MANUSCRIPT TOPICS:
Advertising & Promotion Management; Communication; Global Business; Labor Relations & Human Resource Mgt.; Office Administration/Management; Operations Research/Statistics; Organizational Behavior & Theory; Organizational Development; Production/Operations; Public Administration; Purchasing/Materials Management; Services; Small Business Entrepreneurship; Strategic Management Policy

MANUSCRIPT GUIDELINES/COMMENTS:

Submission Of Papers
Authors are requested to submit three copies of each manuscript. A copy of the manuscript on disk as specified below will also be required on final acceptance. Submissions should be addressed to The Editors: Professor D. Butler or Mr. A. Lockwood, School of Management Studies for the Service Sector, University of Surrey, Guildford, Surrey, GU2 5XH, UK.

Authors submitting papers for publication should specify which section of the Journal they wish their paper to be considered for: `Academic Papers' or 'Practice Papers'. Papers submitted for publication in the 'Academic Papers' section will be subject to strict double-blind refereeing and will be reviewed by at least two referees. Those submitted for publication as a practice paper will be refereed normally by one member of the Editorial Board.

Academic papers should normally be between 4000 to 6000 words. Practice papers should be between 2000 and 4000 words in length. Papers outside these guidelines will be considered but authors should note that the review process will consider the length in relation to the content and the clarity of the writing.

They should be typewritten double-spaced on A4 paper, with a minimum of one inch margins all round and printed on one side of the paper only. Manuscripts should normally be submitted in English.

Submissions on disk should be clearly labelled with the file name, the date, the author's name and the software package used. The preferred medium is a 3.5 inch disk for Macintosh or PC. We are able to deal with most standard software packages currently available, although our preference is for Word or WordPerfect. We are also able to accept line artwork/graphics on disk. Artwork on disk is preferred on 3.5 inch PC or Macintosh format disk in a dedicated drawing package, such as Adobe Illustrator/Corel Draw/Macromedia Freehand, rather than presentation, spreadsheet or database packages. Again, each file should be carefully named, and the software package identified. Provide hard copy print out of each figure, clearly identified.

No manuscripts or figures will be returned following publication unless a request for return is made when the manuscript is originally submitted.

Normally two complimentary copies will be sent to each author. However, up to five may be supplied free to the first named author if required.

The editors and publisher will do everything possible to ensure that the manuscripts are dealt with promptly and that those which are accepted are quickly published.

All reasonable efforts are made to ensure accurate reproduction of text, photographs and illustrations. The Publisher does not accept responsibility for mistakes, be they editorial or typographical, nor for consequences resulting from them.

References
Papers should be supported by references. These should be set out according to the standard Harvard style as follows.

In the text, references should be cited by the author's name and year of publication in brackets (Jones, 1994), or "...as noted by Jones (1994)". Where there are two or more references to one author for the same year, the following form should be used: (Jones, 1993a) or (Jones, 1993b). Where references include three or more authors the form (Jones et al., 1994) should be used. A full list of references in alphabetical order should be given at the end of the paper.

All references should be written as follows: Lundberg, C. C. (1997), Widening the conduct of hospitality inquiry: toward appreciating research alternatives, Journal of Hospitality and Tourism Research, 21, 1, 1-13. Ravenscroft, N.R. (1992), Recreation Planning and Development, Basingstoke: Macmillan Press Ltd. Logan, A. (1994) Qualirv Expectations in the European Escorted Tour Sector, Guildford: University of Surrey MSc Dissertation, School of Management Studies for the Service Sector. Sheldon, P. (1994), Information technology and computer systems, in Witt, S. and Moutinho, L. (Editors), Tourism .Marketing and Management Handbook, 2nd. ed., London Prentice Hall, 126-30. Please note that references are one of the most difficult things for editors and reviewers to check and that therefore authors are requested to take extra care in their preparation. The responsibility for their accuracy rests largely with the author(s).

Copyright

No contribution will be accepted which has been published elsewhere, unless it is expressly invited or agreed by the Editors and the Publisher. Papers and contributions published become the copyright of the Publisher, unless otherwise stated.

The transfer of copyright from the author, previously implicit in the submission of the manuscript, must now be explicitly transferred to enable the publisher to ensure maximum dissemination of the author's work. A copy of the Journal Article and Copyright Agreement Form is available in the journal or from the editorial office or publisher. A signed copy of this agreement must be provided for every manuscript accepted for publication.

Papers will be accepted for publication on the understanding that they are contributed solely to this journal, that the contents have not been published in whole or in part elsewhere and that the papers are subject to editorial revision.

It is the author's responsibility to obtain written permission to quote or reproduce material that has appeared in another publication. The author bears the responsibility for checking whether material submitted is subject to copyright or ownership rights, i.e. photographs, illustrations, trade literature and data. Where use is so restricted, the Editors and the Publisher must be informed with the submission of the material.

All contributions sent to the Publisher, whether they are invited or not, must bear the author's full name and address, even if this is not for publication. Contributions, whether published pseudonymously or not, are accepted on the strict understanding that the author is responsible for the accuracy of all opinion, technical comment, factual report, data figures, illustrations and photographs. Publication does not necessarily imply that these are the opinions of the Editors, Editorial Board or the Publisher, nor does the Editor of the Board accept any liability for the accuracy of such comment, report and other technical and factual information. The Publisher will, however, strive to ensure that all opinion, comments, reports, data, figures, illustrations and photographs are accurate, insofar as it is within its abilities to do so. The Publisher reserves the right to edit, abridge or omit material submitted for publication.

Format of Submission

The first page of the manuscript should include a brief descriptive title and the author's name, affiliation, address and telephone and fax numbers, and email address. A short description of the author (about 80 words) and, if appropriate, the organisation of which he or she is a member is requested. In the case of co-authors, their full details should also be included. All correspondence will be sent to the first named author, unless otherwise indicated.

The second page should contain the title of the paper, a summary or abstract, outlining the aims and subject matter of not more than 100 words in length, and up to six key words. The summary should provide a review of the paper and not simply repeat the conclusions.

The paper should begin on the third page and need not relist the title or authors. The paper should be sub-divided into sections to aid readability as appropriate. For simplicity, section headings should be in upper case and bold, while subsection headings should be in upper and lower case and bold.

Papers should be supported by actual or hypothetical examples, wherever possible and appropriate. Authors should not seek to use the Journal as a vehicle for marketing any specific product or service. Authors should avoid the use of language or slang that is not in keeping with the academic and professional style of the Journal.

Titles of organisations etc. should be written out first in full and thereafter in initials. Authors are asked to ensure the references to named people and/or organisations are accurate and without libellous implications.

Figures and other line illustrations should be submitted in good quality originals on a separate sheet and numbered consecutively and independently of any tables in the article. Each figure should be numbered and titled. In the text, the position of figures should be indicated by typing on a separate line the words "Figure 1 about here". A copy of the data should also be included where appropriate.

Tables should be submitted on a separate sheet and numbered consecutively and independently of any figures in the article. Each table should be numbered and titled. All columns should have explanatory headings. Tables should not repeat data that are available elsewhere in the paper. In the text, the position of tables should be indicated by typing on a separate line the words "Table 1 about here".

Photographs and illustrations supporting papers may be submitted where appropriate. Photographs should be good quality positives, printed from the original negatives and in black and white only.

Tourism Management

ADDRESS FOR SUBMISSION:

Chris Ryan, Editor
Tourism Management
University of Waikato
Centre for Management Studies
Tourism Programme
Private Bag 3105
Hamilton,
New Zealand
Phone:
Fax: +64 7 8
E-Mail: caryan@waikato.ac.uk
Web: www.elsevier.com
Address May Change:

PUBLICATION GUIDELINES:

Manuscript Length: 26-30
Copies Required: Four
Computer Submission: No
Format: N/A
Fees to Review: 0.00 US$

Manuscript Style:
    American Psychological Association

CIRCULATION DATA:

Reader: Business Persons, Academics; Researchers in Commerce & Gov't
Frequency of Issue: 8 Times/Year
Copies per Issue: Less than 1,000
Sponsor/Publisher: Elsevier Science Publishing Co.
Subscribe Price: 180.00 Pounds Europe
    190.00 Pounds Overseas

REVIEW INFORMATION:

Type of Review: Blind Review
No. of External Reviewers: 3
No. of In House Reviewers: 0
Acceptance Rate: 21-30%
Time to Review: 2 - 3 Months
Reviewers Comments: Yes
Invited Articles: 6-10%
Fees to Publish: 0.00 US$

MANUSCRIPT TOPICS:
Advertising & Promotion Management; Marketing Research; Organizational Behavior & Theory; Services; Small Business Entrepreneurship; Tourism

MANUSCRIPT GUIDELINES/COMMENTS:

Tourism Management is an international journal which publishes original research in tourism, analysis of current trends, and information on the planning and management of all aspects of travel and tourism.

The journal emphasizes the broadness and interrelatedness of the tourism industry. Articles, which should take a multisectoral approach, may cover geography, economics, transportation, hotels and catering, sociology, marketing or development studies.

Tourism Management aims to publish articles that are directly relevant to its readers and of interest to both academics and practitioners. Thus, subjects covered should be treated in such a way as to appeal to as wide a range as possible, and those reporting research should attempt to draw management implications from their results. The use of examples is encouraged.

It is a condition of publication that manuscripts submitted to this Journal have not been published and will not be simultaneously submitted or published elsewhere. Translated material which has not previously been published in English will also be considered.

The editors reserve the right to edit or otherwise alter contributions but authors will receive proofs for approval before publication.

Copyright

All authors must sign the 'Transfer of Copyright' agreement before the article can be published. This transfer agreement enables Elsevier Science Ltd to protect the copyrighted material for the authors, but does not relinquish the author's proprietary rights. The copyright transfer covers the exclusive rights to reproduce and distribute the article, including reprints, photographic reproductions, microform or any other reproductions of similar nature and translations, and includes the right to adapt the article for use in conjunction with computer systems and programs, including reproduction or publication in machine-readable form and incorporation in retrieval systems. Authors are responsible for obtaining from the copyright holder permission to reproduce any figures for which copyright exists.

Submissions - Main Articles

Four copies (the original and three copies) of research papers, current issues, case studies, or responses to articles should be submitted to the Editor, Chris Ryan. Main articles should be 3000-5000 words long. All articles are double-blind refereed.

Submissions - Shorter Items

Opinion pieces, reports or responses to articles should be 800-2000 words, book reviews and news pieces 800-1000 words. These should be submitted to the Associate Editor, Stephen Page, Centre for Tourism Research, Massey University at Albany, Private Bag 102904, North Shore MSC, Auckland, New Zealand (address on inside front cover of journal).

Books for review and notices of forthcoming meetings for listing in the Calendar section should also be sent to Stephen Page. Entries must be received at least four months before date of event.

Items for inclusion as current issues, reports, bookreviews or conference reports should be typed as for major articles.

Presentation

Manuscripts must be typed in journal style, double-spaced (including footnotes; references should be triple-spaced) on one side only of International Standard Size A4 paper, with a left-hand margin of 40mm.

Manuscripts should be arranged in the following order of presentation.

First Sheet: short title (up to 40 characters including spaces), subtitle (if desired), author's name, affiliation, full postal address and telephone and fax numbers. Respective affiliations and addresses of co-authors should be clearly indicated.

Second Sheet: a self-contained abstract of not more than 150 words; acknowledgements (if any); article title abbreviated appropriately for use as a running headline.

Subsequent Sheets: main body of text; list of references; appendixes; tables (on separate sheet); footnotes (numbered consecutively); captions to illustrations (on separate sheet); illustrations. Each sheet must carry the abbreviated title of the article and the journal name.

The text should be organized under appropriate section headings, which, ideally, should not be more than 600 words apart. Section headings should be marked as follows: primary headings should be typed in capitals and underlined; secondary headings should be typed with initial capital letters and underlined. All headings should be placed on the left-hand side of the text, with a double line space above and below.

All measures should be given in metric units.

Authors are urged to write as concisely as possible, but not at the expense of clarity. Descriptive or explanatory passages, necessary as information but which tend to break up the flow of text, should be put into footnotes or appendixes.

References And Footnotes

References must be indicated (individually) in the text by use of APA system of referencing. Please use the handbook of the American Psychological Association. Footnotes should be used sparingly and indicated in the text by symbols. References and footnotes should be grouped in separate sections, in order and triple spaced, at the end of the text in numerical order and should be triple-spaced.

References should conform to current journal style.
For journals: Mellor, J. W., Food policy, food aid and structural adjustment programmes: the context of agricultural development. *Food Policy*, 1988, 13(1), 10-17.
For books: McDougall, G.H. G. and Munro, H., Slaling and attitude measurement in travel and tourism research. In *Travel Tourism and Hospitality Research, A Handbook for Managers and Researchers*, eds., J. R. B. Ritchie and C. Goeldner, Wiley, New York, 1994.
For reports: Edelstein, L. G. and Benini, C., *Meetings and Conventions*. Meetings market report, 1994 (August), pp. 60-82.

Tables

Tables should be numbered consecutively in Arabic numerals and given a suitable caption. Notes and references within tables should be included with the tables, separately from the main text. Notes should be referred to by superscript letters. All table columns should have an explanatory heading. Tables should not repeat data available elsewhere in the article, e.g. in an illustration.

Illustrations

All graphs, diagrams and other drawings should be referred to as Figures, which should be numbered consecutively in Arabic numerals and placed on separate sheets at the end of the manuscript. Their position should be indicated in the text. All illustrations must have captions, which should be typed on a separate sheet.

Illustrations should be provided in a form suitable for reproduction without retouching and should permit reduction.

Authors should minimize the amount of descriptive matter on graphs or drawings. Scale grids should not be used in the graphs, unless required for actual measurements.

Disk Submission
Authors whose papers have been given final acceptance are encouraged to submit a computer disk (5.25" or 3.5" HD/DD disk) containing the final version of the paper along with three printed copies to the Editorial Office: do not send disk with initial submission of paper.

Please observe the following criteria:
(a) Specify what software was used, including which release (e.g. WordPerfect 4.0).
(b) Specify what computer was used (either IBM compatible PC or Apple Macintosh).
(c) Include the text file and separate table and illustration files, if available.
(d) The file should follow the general instructions on style/arrangement and in particular, the reference style of this journal as given in the Notes for Contributors.
(e) The file should be single spaced and should use the wrap-around end-of-line feature (i.e. no returns at the end of each line). All textual elements should begin flush left, no paragraph indents. Place two returns after every element such as title, headings, paragraphs, figure and table callouts, etc.
(f) Keep a back-up disk for reference and safety.

Proofs
Authors are responsible for ensuring that all manuscripts (whether original or revised) are accurately typed before final submission. Manuscripts will be returned to the author with a set of instructions if they are not submitted according to our style. One set of proofs will be sent to the first-named author before publication, which should be returned promptly (by Express Air mail if outside the UK). The publishers reserve the right to charge for any changes made at the proof stage (other than printers' errors) since the insertion or deletion of a single word may necessitate the resetting of whole paragraphs..

Offprints
One copy of the journal and fifty offprints of each paper will be provided free of charge to the first-names author of main articles and current issues. Further offprints, in minimum quantities of 50, can be purchased from the Publisher.

Transportation

ADDRESS FOR SUBMISSION:

David T. Hartgen, Editor
Transportation
University of North Carolina
Department of Geography & Earth Science
Charlotte, NC 28223
U.S.A.
Phone: 704-547-4308
Fax: 704-547-3442
E-Mail: dthartge@email.uncc.edu
Web: www.wkap.nl
Address May Change:

PUBLICATION GUIDELINES:

Manuscript Length: 26-30
Copies Required: Four
Computer Submission: No
Format:
Fees to Review: 0.00 US$

Manuscript Style:
    Chicago Manual of Style

CIRCULATION DATA:

Reader: Academics,
    Government/Consulting
Frequency of Issue: Quarterly
Copies per Issue: Less than 1,000
Sponsor/Publisher: Kluwer Academic
    Publishers
Subscribe Price: 352.00 US$

REVIEW INFORMATION:

Type of Review: Editorial Review
No. of External Reviewers: 3
No. of In House Reviewers: 1
Acceptance Rate: 35%
Time to Review: 4 - 6 Months
Reviewers Comments: Yes
Invited Articles: 6-10%
Fees to Publish: 0.00 US$

MANUSCRIPT TOPICS:
Transportation/Physical Distribution

MANUSCRIPT GUIDELINES/COMMENTS:

Statement of purpose
Although the transportation needs of cities and nations around the world may differ in key details, they have much in common. By sharing research findings and practical experiences, every city and every nation can benefit.

Transportation seeks to assist in that vital exchange of information, through the publication of carefully selected papers which help to advance the international fund of knowledge.

Transportation focuses on issues of direct relevance to those concerned with the formulation of policy, the preparation and evaluation of plans, and the day to day operational management of transport systems. It is concerned not only with the policies and systems themselves, but also with their impacts on, and relationship with, other aspects of the social, economic and physical environment.

Transportation aims at being relevant to all parts of the world, industrialised, newly industrialised or developing. The journal has no modal bias, and is totally apolitical. Our mission is simply to help improve the transportation of people and goods through a better understand and appreciation of the key opportunities and constraints.

Papers published in *Transportation* are subjected to peer review in accordance with standard international practice for scholarly journals. They are only accepted for publication once the authors have adequately responded to advice given by the referees. Publication of a paper in Transportation therefore accords with the normal requirements of academic appointment and promotion panels.

Submission of manuscripts

While authors may submit manuscripts to any Editor, it is convenient if European authors send their papers to: Mr Martin G. Richards (Managing Editor), The MVA Group, MVA House, Victoria Way, Woking, Surrey, GU21 1DD, UK, tel. (0483)728051, fax (0483)755207.

Authors in Asia and the Pacific region send their papers to: Dr William Young, Monash University, Department of Civil Engineering, Clayton, Melbourne, Victoria 3168, Australia, tel. (03)565-4949, fax (03)565-4944.

Authors in the rest of the world send their papers to either: Dr David T. Hartgen, University of North Carolina, Department of Geography and Earth Science, Charlotte, NC 28223, USA, tel. 704-547-4308, fax 704-547-2767, or Prof. Ryuichi Kitamura, University of California, College of Engineering, Department of Civil Engineering, Davis, CA 95616, USA, tel. 916-752-7435, fax 916-752-7872.

Initially, authors are requested to submit their papers to any of the above editors in manuscript form. Upon acceptance, a finalized version may be submitted on floppy disk, if so desired.
No page charges are applicable, but prospective authors should condense their papers as much as possible.

Presentation and preparation of the manuscript

Manuscripts should be written in standard English and submitted in triplicate. Authors whose mother tongue is not English should have their manuscripts checked for the quality of the English before submission to the Journal. Particular attention should be given to consistency in the use of technical terms and abbreviations. For those manuscripts that may require it, language editing is available through the Journal at charge to the author.

The author should retain the original and send good, clear, legible photocopies. Manuscripts should be typed double-spaced throughout on one side of DIN A4 paper (21 x 29 cm or 8.5 x 11 inch), with wide margins 3-5 cm. All papers (including the tables, figures, legends and references) should be numbered consecutively. The manuscript should be arranged in the following order (typed cap. + lc):

Title page (page 1)

The title should be brief but informative.

A subtitle may be used to supplement and thereby shorten an excessively long main title.
Author(s) full name(s) (use "&" before the name of last author and indicate to which author correspondence should be addressed).
Affiliation(s)/Address(es) should be complete.

Key words/Abstract/Abbreviations (page 2)
Key words (a maximum of 6, in alphabetical order, suitable for indexing).
Abstract (brief and informative, not to exceed 250 words).
Abbreviations (arranged alphabetically; only those which are not familiar and/or commonly used).

Main text
The relative importance of headings and subheadings should be clear.
The approximate location of figures and tables should be indicated in the text.
New paragraphs should be clearly indented.
The use of footnotes should be avoided. However, if essential, they should be typed on the appropriate page, but clearly separated from the text with a line of space above them.

After the main text
Acknowledgements (also grants, support etc., if any) should follow the text and precede the references.
Notes (if any) should be numbered consecutively in the text with superscript numerals and listed in numerical order, after the Acknowledgements.

References
The literature references should be arranged alphabetically, typed double-spaced, and in the text referred to as: author and year of publication, e.g., (Dawson 1987; Lefebvre et al. 1986).
Citations of personal communications and unpublished data should be avoided, unless absolutely necessary; such citations should, in text, appear only as: W.D. Smith, pers. comm., C.S. Andrew, unpubl., and not in the reference list.
References should follow the style shown below:

Periodicals
Berechman J & Giuliano G (1985) Economies of scale in bus tranist. *Transportation* 12: 313-332.

Books (edited by someone other than the author of article)
Morlok EK & Viton PA (1985) Recent experience with successful private transit in large US cities. In: Lave CA (ed) *Urban Transit: The Private Challenge to Public Transportation* (pp 121-149). San Francisco: Pacific Institute for Public Policy Research.

Books (identical author and editor)
Hughes J (1979) The Philosophy of Social Research. Essex: Longman.

Tables
Each table should be typed on a separate page and numbered with Arabic numerals 'as Table x', followed by the title.

Horizontal rules should be indicated and vertical rules avoided. Table-footnotes should be marked with superscript letters.
Each table must be mentioned in the text and its location indicated in the margin.
Tables may be edited by the publisher to permit more compact typesetting.

Figures
Each figure should be mentioned in the text and numbered with Arabic numerals as 'Fig. x'.
Line drawings should be in a form suitable for reproduction without modification. Extremely small type should be avoided as figures are often reduced in size.
Photographs should be supplied as black-and-white, high contrast glossy prints. Colour plates may be inserted at the author's own expense.
Where multi-part figures are used, each part should be clearly identified in the legend, preferably with (lower case) letters.
Figures to be placed landscape should be avoided if possible.
Identify each illustration, on the back, by lightly writing author's name and figure number, also indicate the top of each figure.
Figure legends should be typed on the appropriate page after References.

Notes on contributors
Authors should include a brief summary of their professional background, together with their contact address; this will be published in the same issue of the Journal as their paper. The summary should be no longer than 40 words, including the contact address details and counting an abbreviation as a word; there will be an absolute maximum of 50 words and abbreviations.

Abbreviations and units
Only SI units and abbreviations should be used. Abbreviations should be explained when they first appear in the text. If a non-standard abbreviation is to be used extensively, it should be defined in full on page 2 as mentioned above. Whenever in doubt use SI (Système International d'Unités).

Proofs and offprints
The author will be sent an offprint order form and 2 proofs for proofreading. One set of corrected proofs together with the manuscript should be returned to the Publisher within 3 days of receipt of the material. 50 offprints will be supplied free of charge.

Transportation Journal

ADDRESS FOR SUBMISSION:

John C. Spychalski, Editor
Transportation Journal
The Pennsylvania State University
College of Business Administration
509 Business Administration Building
University Park, PA 16802
USA
Phone: 814-865-2872
Fax: 814-863-7067
E-Mail: jcs2@psu.edu
Web:
Address May Change:

PUBLICATION GUIDELINES:

Manuscript Length: 16-20
Copies Required: Four
Computer Submission: No
Format: N/A
Fees to Review: 0.00 US$

Manuscript Style:
   Chicago Manual of Style, 14th Edition

CIRCULATION DATA:

Reader: Business Persons, Academics, Government
Frequency of Issue: Quarterly
Copies per Issue: 3,001 - 4,000
Sponsor/Publisher: American Society of Transportation and Logistics
Subscribe Price: 55.00 US$ Foreign/USA

REVIEW INFORMATION:

Type of Review: Blind Review
No. of External Reviewers: 3
No. of In House Reviewers: 1
Acceptance Rate: 15%
Time to Review: 2 - 3 Months
Reviewers Comments: Yes
Invited Articles: 0-5%
Fees to Publish: 0.00 US$
                50.00 US$

MANUSCRIPT TOPICS:
Logistics; Supply Chain Management; Transportation/Physical Distribution

MANUSCRIPT GUIDELINES/COMMENTS:

1. Articles should broaden and deepen the body of theoretical and/or empirical knowledge in logistics, supply chain management and transportation.

2. **Submission**
Send manuscripts (4 copies) to: Dr. John C. Spychalski, College of Business Administration, 509 Business Administration Building, The Pennsylvania State University, University Park, PA 16802. A brief letter of transmittal should accompany the manuscript. The title page should indicate each author's academic rank or profession and affiliation, including location. The first page of the text should contain the title of the article but not the author's name. papers submitted to the Journal must be neither previously published nor submitted elsewhere for review simultaneously.

3. Format
Manuscripts should be typewritten and double spaced on one side only of medium-weight opaque bond paper. Margins should be at least one inch on all sides and pages should be numbered consecutively.

4. References
All endnotes should be numbered consecutively in the text, and the number placed as shown here.1 Notes should be single spaced and listed at the end of the article (not at the bottom of the page). Notes for books should take the following form:

1. the footnote number -- indented five spaces and slightly raised;
2. the author's names in normal order;
3. the title;
4. the facts of publication -- the city and state (followed by a colon), the publisher (followed by a comma), and the date -- all three facts enclosed in parentheses; and
5. the page or pages referred to.

Except before the parenthesis, where there is no punctuation, each item is followed by a comma, and the entire note is closed with a period. Notes for periodicals differ from notes for books in two ways:

1. the title of the article is enclosed in quotations marks and the periodical underlined, and
2. when the volume number is given, the date of publication is enclosed in parentheses and the p. included before the page number (e.g. Transportation Journal 19, No. 1 (1979), 7.). For subsequent references to a source, give the author's last name and the page rather than ibid., op., cit., or loc. cit.; add a shortened title when more than one book by that author is cited.

5. Numbers and Tabular Material
Arabic numerals should be used for quantities for 100 or greater and for percentages. The word "percent" should be used in ext material (e.g. 5 percent). Figures should be numbered consecutively in Arabic numerals. Figures should be originals and professionally drawn (i.e., camera ready) for direct reproduction by the Journal's printer.

6. Other Sources of Style Information
See the University of Chicago's *A Manual of Style*.

Transportation Research Part E: Logistics and Transportation Review

ADDRESS FOR SUBMISSION:

W. K. Talley, Editor-in-Chief
Transportation Research Part E: Logistics and Transportation Review
Old Dominion University
College of Business & Public Admin.
Department of Economics
Norfolk, VA 23529-0221
USA
Phone: 757-683-3534
Fax: 757-683-5639
E-Mail: wktalley@odu.edu
Web: www.elsevier.com
Address May Change:

PUBLICATION GUIDELINES:

Manuscript Length: 11-20
Copies Required: Four
Computer Submission: Yes w/hardcopy
Format: PC Compatible or Mac
Fees to Review: 0.00 US$

Manuscript Style:
Uniform System of Citation (Harvard Blue Book)

CIRCULATION DATA:

Reader: Academics, Business Persons
Frequency of Issue: 6 Times/Year
Copies per Issue: Less than 1,000
Sponsor/Publisher: Elsevier Science Publishing Company
Subscribe Price: 735.00 US$ Institution
  182.00 US$ Personal

REVIEW INFORMATION:

Type of Review: Blind Review
No. of External Reviewers: 2
No. of In House Reviewers: 1
Acceptance Rate: 30%
Time to Review: 4 - 6 Months
Reviewers Comments: Yes
Invited Articles: 6-10%
Fees to Publish: 0.00 US$

MANUSCRIPT TOPICS:
Transportation/Physical Distribution

MANUSCRIPT GUIDELINES/COMMENTS:

Description
Transportation Research Part E: The Logistics and Transportation Review publishes informative articles drawn from across the spectrum of logistics and transportation research. Subjects include, but are not limited to:
- transport economics including cost and production functions, capacity, demand, pricing, externalities, modal studies;
- transport infrastructure and investment appraisal;
- evaluation of public policies;
- empirical studies of management practices and performance;
- logistics and operations models, especially with application;

- logistics and supply-chain management topics.

Guide for Authors
Manuscripts should be submitted in quadruplicate to the Editor-in-Chief. They should be accompanied by a covering letter mentioning the title of the paper and the name of the corresponding author, together with mailing address, telephone and fax numbers and if available e-mail address.

Electronic Manuscripts
Authors are encouraged to submit a computer disk (5.25" or 3.5% HD/DD disk) containing the *final* version of the paper along with the *final* manuscript to the editorial office. Please observe the following criteria: (1) Send only hard copy when first submitting your paper. (2) When your paper has been refereed, revised if necessary and accepted, send a disk containing the final version with the final hard copy. Make sure that the disk and the hard copy match exactly. (3) Specify what software was used, including which release (e.g. WordPerfect 6.0) (4) Specify what computer was used (either IBM compatible PC or Apple Macintosh). (5) Text, tables and illustrations (if available on disk) should be supplied as separate files. (6) The files should follow the general instructions on style/arrangement and, in particular, the reference style of this journal as given below. (7) The file should be single-spaced and should use the wrap-around end-of-line feature (i.e. no returns at the end of each line). All textual elements should begin flush left, no paragraph indents. Place two returns after every element such as title, headings, paragraphs, figure and table call-outs. (8) Keep a back-up disk for reference and safety.

Style of Manuscript
All sections of the manuscript (abstract, text, references) should be double-spaced, using a single typeface and style. Use underlining only for definitions and subsections; do not underline for emphasis. Footnotes should be limited in number and size, and should not contain mathematical expressions.

The abstract should describe in straightforward language the contents of the paper, but not its motivation. It should explain briefly the procedures and the results, and must not contain abbreviations and acronyms.

Figures are photo-reproduced and authors will be required to furnish camera-ready artwork or glossy prints. Each figure should be placed on a separate sheet of paper, and should be typed on a separate page at the end of the manuscript.

Tables and their captions should be typed on separate sheets, numbered consecutively and indicated in the text at their approximate position.

Equations should be clearly displayed, with any unusual symbols (including Greek letters) identified in the margin.

Equation numbers should be placed in the right margin and numbered continuously, not by section.

The Harvard system of references is used: in the body of the text a paper is referred to by the author's surname with the year of publication in parentheses and at the end of the paper complete references are given alphabetically by author's surnames, journal titles should not be abbreviated, e.g.

Kanafani, A. and Abbas, M.S. (1987) Local air service and economic impact of small airports. *Journal of Transportation Engineering* 113, 42-55.

Button, K.J. (1982) *Transport Economics*. Heinemann, London.

Nash, C.A. (1988) Integration of public transport: an economic assessment. In *Bus Deregulation and Privatisation: An International Perspective,* eds J.S. Dodgson and N. Topham, pp. 17-46 Wiley, New York.

Jones, M. (1995) Cost considerations in research funding. Report of the SERC Working Group, London.

Proofs
Before publication an authors' proof will be sent to the corresponding author at the address shown on the Editor-in-Chief's covering letter. It is important that authors read the proof very carefully and answer all queries on the page proofs and return the proof to the publisher within a short time (usually 48 hours). Except for typographical errors, changes should be kept to a minimum and rewriting the text is not permitted. Authors may be charged for changes other than the correction of typographical errors. Authors are urged to check their proof carefully, since late corrections cannot be accepted. Reprints Along with page proofs, the corresponding author will receive a form for ordering reprints and full copies of the issue in which the paper appears. Twenty-five free reprints are provided; orders for additional reprints must be received before printing in order to qualify for lower prepublication rates. All co-author reprint requirements should be included on the reprint order form.

Copyright
All authors must sign the 'Transfer of Copyright' agreement before the article can be published. This transfer agreement enables Elsevier Science Ltd to protect the copyrighted material for the authors, but does not relinquish the author's proprietary rights. The copyright transfer covers the exclusive rights to reproduce and distribute the article, including reprints, photographic reproductions, microform or any other reproductions of similar nature and translations, and includes the right to adapt the article for use in conjunction with computer systems and programs, including reproduction or publication in machine-readable form and incorporation in retrieval systems. Authors are responsible for obtaining from the copyright holder permission to reproduce any figures for which copyright exists.

Transportation Science Journal

ADDRESS FOR SUBMISSION:

Gilbert Laporte, Editor
Transportation Science Journal
University de Montreal
Centre De Recherche Sur les Transports
Station Centre-ville
PO Box 6128
Montreal, H3C CJ7
Canada
Phone:
Fax: 514-343-7121
E-Mail: gilbert@crt.umontreal.ca
Web:
Address May Change:

PUBLICATION GUIDELINES:

Manuscript Length: 20+
Copies Required: Five
Computer Submission: No
Format: N/A
Fees to Review: 0.00 US$

Manuscript Style:
    See Manuscript Guidelines

CIRCULATION DATA:

Reader: Academics
Frequency of Issue: Quarterly
Copies per Issue: 1,001 - 2,000
Sponsor/Publisher: Informs/Cadmus
Subscribe Price: 35.00 US$ Individual
    100.00 US$ Institution

REVIEW INFORMATION:

Type of Review: Editorial Review
No. of External Reviewers: 3
No. of In House Reviewers: 2
Acceptance Rate: 21-30%
Time to Review: 4 - 6 Months
Reviewers Comments: Yes
Invited Articles: 0-5%
Fees to Publish: 0.00 US$

MANUSCRIPT TOPICS:
Transportation/Physical Distribution

MANUSCRIPT GUIDELINES/COMMENTS:

Editorial Policy
Transportation Science publishes original contributions and surveys on phenomena associated with all modes of transportation, present and prospective, including mainly such aspects as planning, design, economic, operational and social. Excluded are physical design aspects of such items as vehicles, highway pavements, railroad roadbeds, or other components. Contributions in related areas such as location may be of interest as long as their relevance to transportation is clearly demonstrated (e.g. papers on the location of bus depots, of airline hubs, etc.).

Contributions which advance the analytical, experimental and observational tools for the study of transportation problems are also welcome, as are critical review articles dealing with the status and direction of the above subjects. Of particular interest in scientific work on transportation processes that contribute to the understanding of the characteristics and behavior of transportation systems, and studies on Intelligent Transportation Systems (ITS).

A "Technical Notes" section contains brief articles on all of the topics mentioned above. Commentary appears in "Letter to the Editor" section. Book reviews within the scope of the Journal are also published.

All papers, notes, and letters submitted for publication are refereed and accepted solely on the basis of quality and importance. Decisions regarding the publication of papers are based, in part, on the answers to questions such as the following: Does the paper make a new and substantial contribution to the literature of the science of transportation? Does the paper provide a proper balance between text, introductory, and summary material to inform the reader of the content, importance and application of the material covered? Is the length of the paper appropriate to the subject matter and the prevailing style of the Journal? Is its character clear from the text as well as from the title and abstract? Does the paper adequately describe its relation to previously published work, and does it give proper credit and references to that work?

Information For Contributors

Manuscripts for publication and Letters to the Editor should be submitted to the Editor in five copies. Submission of a manuscript is a representation that the paper has been neither published nor submitted for publication elsewhere, and that, if the work is officially sponsored, it has been released for open publication.

Manuscripts must be double-spaced throughout with the original in typewritten or equally legible form. This journal style should be followed in the preparation of manuscripts.

Figures are required in a form suitable for photographic reproduction. Any one of a number of forms will be acceptable, e.g., original black ink drawings, or high-quality glossy prints. Lettering should be uniform in size and style and sufficiently large to be legible after reduction. Figures should be designated by arabic numbers and referred to in the text by number. Figure legends should be collectively provided on a separate sheet rather than placed on the figures themselves.

Tables may be typed on sheets separated from the text; complicated column headings should be avoided. All tables should be numbered and referred to in the text by number.

In mathematical expressions, authors are requested in general to minimize unusual or expensive typographical requirements; for example; authors are requested to use the solidus wherever possible in preference to built-up fractions, to write complicated exponentials in the form ext ( ) and to avoid subscripts and superscripts on subscripts or superscripts. Subscripts and superscripts should be shown large and clear. Greek letters and unusual symbols should be labeled on first occurrence, as should subscript "zero", to distinguish it from the letter "oh". Whether each letter is capital or lower case should be unambiguous. Equation numbers must be at the right.

Each paper must be accompanied by an abstract of about 100 to 200 works. The abstract should be adequate as an index and should summarize the principal results and conclusions.

Authors should strive for conciseness and clarity. References to related previous work should be reasonably complete, and grouped at the end of the paper. References in the text should be cited by author's surname and the year of publication, e.g.: (Jansson, 1980), (Marguier and Ceder, 1984). The following format should be used for references:

Journals: W.B. Powell and I. A. Koskosidis, "Shipment Routing Algorithms with Tree Constraints," Transportation Science 26, 230-245 (1992).

Working papers and dissertations: B. Gavish and S. C. Graves, "Scheduling and Routing in Transportation and Distribution Systems; Formulations and New Relaxations," Working Paper 8202, Graduate School of Management, University of Rochester, 1981.

Books: I. Prigogine and R. Herman, Kinetic Theory of Vehicular Traffic, Elsevier, New York, 1971.

Manuscripts will be considered for publication in this journal when copy conforming to the above instructions is furnished.

Western Journal of Communication

ADDRESS FOR SUBMISSION:

David Henry, Editor
Western Journal of Communication
University of Nevada, Las Vegas
Hank Greenspun School of Communication
4505 Maryland Parkway, Box 455007
Las Vegas, NV 89154-5007
USA
Phone: 702-895-3474
Fax: 702-895-4805
E-Mail: dhenry@ccmail.nevada.edu
Web:
Address May Change:

PUBLICATION GUIDELINES:

Manuscript Length: 15-25
Copies Required: Four
Computer Submission: No
Format: N/A
Fees to Review: 0.00 US$

Manuscript Style:
American Psychological Association, or
MLA Style Manual

CIRCULATION DATA:

Reader: Academics
Frequency of Issue: Quarterly
Copies per Issue: 2,001 - 3,000
Sponsor/Publisher: Professional Association
Subscribe Price: 70.00 US$

REVIEW INFORMATION:

Type of Review: Blind Review
No. of External Reviewers: 2
No. of In House Reviewers: 3
Acceptance Rate: 10-13%
Time to Review: 2 - 3 Months
Reviewers Comments: Yes
Invited Articles: 0-5%
Fees to Publish: 0.00 US$

MANUSCRIPT TOPICS:

Communication; International/Intercultural Communication; Interpersonal/Human Communication; Mass Communication; Organizational Behavior & Theory; Persuasion & Nonverbal Communication; Rhetorical & Applied Communication

MANUSCRIPT GUIDELINES/COMMENTS:

The *Western Journal of Communication* publishes original scholarship which advances our understanding of human communication. Research from diverse theoretical and methodological perspectives is encouraged. That diversity is reflected in WJC's history of publishing scholarship in rhetorical and communication theory, interpersonal communication, media studies, philosophy of communication, cultural and critical theory, health communication, freedom of speech, gender and communication, performance studies, and applied communication. Research accessible to both scholarly audiences and the learned public is encouraged.

Authors should submit four copies of each manuscript, double-spaced and using 10 characters per inch. Attach a separate title page which indicates:

(1) manuscript title
(2) the full name and title of each author
(3) each contributor's address, telephone number, e-mail address, and fax number, and
(4) the history of the manuscript, where appropriate.

Manuscripts must conform to either the *MLA Style Manual*, 4th Edition (1995) or the *Publication Manual of the American Psychological Association*, 4th Edition (1994).

WJC follows a policy of blind, peer review. Each manuscript is typically read by three reviewers with expertise in the study's subject matter, methodology, and theoretical perspective. Manuscripts must not be under consideration by any other publication. Manuscripts will be returned to authors. Send submissions to the Editor.

World Transport Policy & Practice

ADDRESS FOR SUBMISSION:

John Whitelegg, Editor-in-Chief
World Transport Policy & Practice
53 Derwent Road
Lancaster, LA1 3ES
UK
Phone: 44 152 4631 75
Fax: 44 152 4848 340
E-Mail:
Web: www.ecoplan.org/wtpp
Address May Change:

PUBLICATION GUIDELINES:

Manuscript Length: 6-10
Copies Required: Two
Computer Submission: Yes
Format: Word
Fees to Review: 0.00 US$

Manuscript Style:
　　See Manuscript Guidelines

CIRCULATION DATA:

Reader: , Practicioners/Academics
Frequency of Issue: Quarterly
Copies per Issue: Less than 1,000
Sponsor/Publisher: N/A
Subscribe Price: 0.00 US$ Electronic

REVIEW INFORMATION:

Type of Review: Blind Review
No. of External Reviewers: 1
No. of In House Reviewers: 1
Acceptance Rate: 40%
Time to Review: 1 - 2 Months
Reviewers Comments: Yes
Invited Articles: 21-30%
Fees to Publish: 0.00 US$

MANUSCRIPT TOPICS:
Transportation/Physical Distribution

MANUSCRIPT GUIDELINES/COMMENTS:

Mission Statement
The only practically-oriented journal dealing with the major issues in a field of international concern, the *Journal of World Transport Policy and Practice* was founded in 1995 in an attempt to provide scholars, researchers, policy makers and ordinary smart people concerned with the marked unsustainability of our current transport arrangements with a high-quality, independent medium for the presentation of original and creative ideas in world transport. The Journal appears four time a year.

In 1998 the Editorial Board came to an agreement with The commons to launch, initially on a trial basis, an electronic edition. After two years of experimentation with this new form of delivery and collaboration, the decision was made in January 2000 to move to a purely electronic publication format. One clear advantage of this is that it permits immediate, world-wide distribution at as close as one can get to zero costs.

The Journal is entirely funded by subscriptions paid in by institutions and employed professionals on a volunteer basis. Without these contributions it would not be possible for the Journal to continue. In this way the Journal is made freely available to students and those in the Third World for whom the $120.00 annual subscription poses an insurmountable obstacle.

Guidelines for Contributors

Contributions to *World Transport Policy & Practice* are welcome. Whether you are a novice author or an experienced one, the Editor would like to invite you to consider sharing your thoughts and experiences with others like yourself. We can promise a considered and constructive review of your article and, for contributions deemed suitable, publication in *World Transport Policy & Practice*. Please read through the following guidelines and feel free to contact John Whitelegg, the Editor, [mailto:ecologic@gn.apc.org], who will be pleased to offer comments on drafts, work in progress, or ideas which you believe could be made into an article.

Editorial objectives

The journal aims to provide validated information about the latest developments in transport policy to enable local authorities, governments, consultancies, NGOs and supra national organisations to speed up their policy development and implement new ideas from around the world. It aims to:
- cover all passenger and freight transport.
- deal with global as well as local issues.
- include the development of the ideas of sustainability, the design of cities and rural areas, transport corridors and international links to improve health, the economy and the environment.

Article composition

Articles should normally be between 2,000 and 4,000 words. Shorter articles can be published as "Comment" pieces. Responses to papers which have appeared in the journal, either as letters to the Editor or as response articles, will be welcomed. Submitting articles by e-mail attachment or on paper with a disk
- **By e-mail**
  Articles for publication may be submitted by e-mail attachment to Pascal Desmond [mailto:pascal@gn.apc.org] It is useful if authors indicate what software is required to read any attachments and if they include the letter combination 'zq' in the title. Please DO NOT name articles 'whitelegg', 'wtpp' or variations of these. Authors are advised that they may need to provide a version on paper and/or on 3.5" disk prepared on a Macintosh or PC system.
- **On paper**
  Articles should be typescript and double spaced with wide margins. Please send three copies. Manuscripts will not normally be returned, so you should ensure you retain a copy. Please supply the article on paper of no less than 80 gsm weight with high quality print. This will enable electronic scanning if needed. Please supply the same version of the article on a 3.5" disk prepared on a Macintosh or PC system in ASCII format. Mark the disk clearly with your name, the article title and the software you have used. Where there is ambiguity, the disk version will normally be considered definitive.

Presentation
Headings and subheadings should be used at approximately 500-750 word intervals. Please ensure that headings and subheadings are clearly identified.

Charts, diagrams and figures
These should be called "Figures" and numbered consecutively (e.g. Figure 1, Figure 2, etc.). Please make sure they are clear and can be reproduced easily. In addition, please provide the raw data so that we can redraw them, if necessary. Indicate where in the text they should appear "(Figure 1 about here)". Each figure should have a brief title (e.g. "Figure 1. Schematic of the Programme").

Tables
Tables should be numbered consecutively, independently of figures. Indicate in the text where they should appear. Give them a brief title. Please ensure that they are clear and legible. Authors should not use many tabs or spaces between columns of data normally, one tab is sufficient.

Maps
Maps are especially welcome. They should be numbered consecutively, independently of figures and tables and their location in the text should be indicated. Please ensure that they are clear, uncluttered and legible. They should have a title.

Measurements
SI units should be used throughout.

Abstracts and Keywords
Please write an abstract of 75 words or so which summarises the main points of the article. It should be sufficient for a reader to decide whether or not they want to read the whole article. Please also note up to six keywords or descriptors which describe the content of the article. These would include geographical area, if specific, industry, functions, managerial activity and process.

References
Authors should keep references to a minimum, ideally no more that ten to fifteen. References should be confined to essential items only and those that are necessary to establish key steps in an argument or key areas of support for a particular proposition. Reference citations within the text should be by the author's last name, followed by a comma and year of publication enclosed in parentheses. A reference list should follow the article, with references listed in alphabetical order in the following form: Books: Surname, Initials, (Year of Publication), Title, Publisher, Place of Publication. Articles: Surname, Initials, (Year of Publication), "Title", Journal, Volume, Number, Pages.

Originality
The author should indicate if a paper has been presented elsewhere. If the author does not do so, the Editor will assume that the paper is an original contribution. Papers appearing in World

Transport Policy & Practice should not be published elsewhere without the written consent of the Publisher of the journal.

Copyright
Authors submitting articles for publication must warrant that the work is not an infringement of any existing copyright of the publisher, unless otherwise agreed.

Written Communication

ADDRESS FOR SUBMISSION:

Deborah Brandt, Editor
Written Communication
University of Wisconsin, Madison
Department of English
6185E Helen C. White Hall
Madison, WI 53706-1475
USA
Phone: 608-263-4512
Fax: 608-263-3709
E-Mail: wrcomm@macc.wisc.edu
Web:
Address May Change:

PUBLICATION GUIDELINES:

Manuscript Length: 11-15, under 9000 wds
Copies Required: Four
Computer Submission: No
Format: N/A
Fees to Review: 0.00 US$

Manuscript Style:
    American Psychological Association

CIRCULATION DATA:

Reader: Academics
Frequency of Issue: Quarterly
Copies per Issue: 2,001 - 3,000
Sponsor/Publisher: Sage Publications, Inc.
Subscribe Price: 60.00 US$ Individual
    200.00 US$ Institution
    17.00 US$ & 52.00 US$ Single Issue

REVIEW INFORMATION:

Type of Review: Blind Review
No. of External Reviewers: 2
No. of In House Reviewers: 1
Acceptance Rate: 6-10%
Time to Review: 2 - 3 Months
Reviewers Comments: Yes
Invited Articles: 0-5%
Fees to Publish: 0.00 US$

MANUSCRIPT TOPICS:
Communication; Mass Communication; Writing

MANUSCRIPT GUIDELINES/COMMENTS:

Written Communication is an international multidisciplinary journal that publishes theory and research in writing from fields including anthropology, English, history, journalism, linguistics, psychology, and rhetoric. Among topics of interest are the nature of writing ability; the assessment of writing; the impact of technology on writing (and of writing on technology); social and political consequences of writing and writing instruction; nonacademic writing; literacy (including workplace and emergent literacy and the effects of classroom processes on literacy development); social construction of knowledge; cognition and composing; the structure of written text and written communication; relationships among gender, race, class, and writing; and connections among writing, reading, speaking, and listening. Also of interest are review essays and reviews of research on topics important to writing researchers. No worthy topic in writing is beyond the scope of the journal. Published articles will collectively represent a wide range of methodologies, but the methodology of each study must be handled expertly.

Guidelines For Submission: Prospective authors are strongly urged to acquaint themselves with previously published issues of the journal, particularly the Editors' Comments in Vol. 11, No. 1 (January 1994). Submitting an article indicates that the work reported has not been previously published, that the article - in present or revised form - is not being considered for publication in other journals or in edited volumes, and that the author(s) will not allow the article to be so considered before notification in writing of an editorial decision by *Written Communication*. Submissions should generally not exceed 9,000 words and must follow the American Psychological Association's 1994 guidelines for publication.

When submitting a manuscript:
(a) Send four copies (double-sided if possible) to Editors, *Written Communication*, in care of the University of Wisconsin-Madison, Department of English, 6185E Helen C. White Hall, 600 North Park Street, Madison, WI 53706-1475 or in care of Kent State University, Department of English, P.O. Box 5190, Kent, OH 44242.

(b) Include with each copy an abstract of 100-150 words.

(c) Provide on a separate sheet the title of the submission and the name(s), institutional affiliation(s), mailing address(es), home and office telephone number(s), fax number(s) and e-mail address(es), and a three-to-four-sentence biographical statement for each author.

(d) Include unattached postage stamps (American authors) or international postage coupons, available at local post offices (international authors) sufficient to cover separate first-class mailings of the four copies of the manuscript. Special note to international authors: Exchange value of international postage coupons need not exceed 9USD.

(e) Note that the entire manuscript should be double-spaced, including the abstract, block quotations, tables, notes, and references. Written Communication does not normally return submitted manuscripts to authors. A copy of the final revised manuscript saved on an IBM-compatible disk should be included with the final revised hard copy.

Written Communication (ISSN 0741-0883) is published four times annually - in January, April, July, and October - by Sage Publications, Inc., 2455 Teller Road, Thousand Oaks, CA 91320. Telephone: (805) 499-0721; FAX/Order Line: (805) 499-0871. Copyright 1997 by Sage Publications, Inc. All rights reserved. No portion of the contents may be reproduced in any form without written permission of the publisher.

INDEX

Journal Name	Type Review	No. Ext. Rev.	Accept. Rate	Page
Advertising & Promotion Management				
Academy of Marketing Science Review	Blind	3	11-20%	1
Academy of Marketing Studies Journal	Blind	2	21-30%	9
Agribusiness: An International Journal	Blind	2	21-30%	16
American Business Perspectives (NBDC Report)	Editorial		11-20%	22
American Demographics	N/A	0	6-10%	27
Annual Advances in Business Cases	Blind	3	30%	38
Asia Pacific Journal of Marketing and Logistics	Blind		11-20%	47
Bank Marketing Magazine	Editorial	0	50%	50
Case Research Journal	Blind	3	11-20%	64
Communications and the Law	Editorial	0	50%	73
Cornell Hotel and Restaurant Administration Quarterly	Blind	2	50%	75
European Journal of Marketing	Blind		28%	87
Global Business and Economic Review	Blind	3+	22-25%	96
Harvard Business Review	Editorial	0	0-5%	102
Industrial Marketing Management	Blind	3	20-25%	109
Interactive Marketing	Blind	2	21-30%	112
International Journal of Advertising	Blind	3+	35%	119
International Journal of Bank Marketing	Blind	2	21-30%	122
International Journal of Business	Blind	2	11-20%	127
International Journal of Hospitality & Tourism Administration	Blind	2	50%	134
International Journal of Hospitality Management	Blind	2	21-30%	138
International Journal of Research In Marketing	Blind	2	11-20%	150
International Journal of Tourism Research	Blind	2	50%	158
International Marketing Review	Blind	2	21-30%	164
Journal of Advertising	Blind	3	11-20%	179
Journal of Advertising Research	Blind	2	21-30%	182
Journal of Business and Behavioral Sciences	Blind	3	11-20%	197
Journal of Business Disciplines	Blind	3	11-20%	198
Journal of Business, Industry and Economics	Blind	2	70%	214
Journal of Communication Management	Blind	3	50%	221
Journal of Consumer Policy	Blind	3		233
Journal of Consumer Research	Blind	3	11-20%	242
Journal of Convention & Exhibition Management	Blind	3	11-20%	246
Journal of Current Issues & Research in Advertising	Blind	3	6-10%	250
Journal of Database Marketing	Blind	3	50%	254
Journal of Euromarketing	Blind	2	21-30%	260
Journal of Fashion Marketing and Management	Blind	3	50%	264
Journal of Financial Services Marketing	Blind	3	50%	267
Journal of Food Product Marketing	Blind	3	50%	270
Journal of Global Marketing	Blind	2	11-20%	276
Journal of Hospitality & Leisure Marketing	Blind	2	50%	288
Journal of Hospitality & Tourism Research	Blind	3	11-20%	292

Journal Name	Type Review	No. Ext. Rev.	Accept. Rate	Page
Journal of International Academy for Case Studies	Blind	2	11-20%	298
Journal of International Consumer Marketing	Blind	2	11-20%	301
Journal of Marketing	Blind	3	6-10%	335
Journal of Marketing Communications	Blind	2	40%	348
Journal of Marketing Education	Blind	3+	11-20%	352
Journal of Marketing Management	Blind	2	11-20%	360
Journal of Marketing Theory and Practice	Blind	3	11-20%	373
Journal of Ministry Marketing and Management	Blind	2	21-30%	377
Journal of Nonprofit & Public Sector Marketing	Blind	2	21-30%	382
Journal of Nonprofit and Voluntary Sector Marketing	Blind	3	50%	386
Journal of Pharmaceutical Marketing and Management	Blind	2	65%	393
Journal of Product & Brand Management	Blind	2	40-50%	397
Journal of Promotion Management	Blind	2	21-30%	402
Journal of Public Policy & Marketing	Blind	3+	11-20%	406
Journal of Restaurant & Foodservice Marketing	Blind	2	21-30%	418
Journal of Retailing	Blind	2-3	11-20%	424
Journal of Retailing and Consumer Services	Blind	3	11-20%	429
Journal of Services Marketing	Blind	3	21-30%	443
Journal of Targeting, Measurement, and Analysis for Targeting	Blind	3	50%	454
Journal of the Academy of Marketing Science	Blind	3	31-50%	457
Journal of Travel & Tourism Marketing	Blind	2	21-30%	475
Journal of Travel Research	Blind	3	20%	480
Journal of Vacation Marketing	Blind	3	50%	485
Marketing Educator	Blind	1	90%	519
Marketing Health Services	Blind	3+	21-40%	520
Marketing Intelligence & Planning	Editorial	1	50%	524
Marketing Letters	Editorial	2	21-30%	528
Marketing Management	Blind	3	21-30%	531
Marketing Management Journal	Blind	3	21-30%	535
North Central Business Journal	Blind	2	50%	538
Pennsylvania Journal of Business and Economics	Blind	2	50%	547
Qualitative Market Research: An International Journal	Blind	1	40%	553
Research in Consumer Behavior	Blind	3	30%	557
Southwest Business & Economics Journal	Blind	1	30-35%	578
Southwestern Business Administration Journal	Blind	2	31-50%	580
Sport Marketing Quarterly	Blind	2	21-30%	583
Tourism and Hospitality Research: The Surrey Quarterly Review	Blind	0	21-30%	589
Tourism Management	Blind	3	21-30%	593

Business Education

| Academy of Marketing Science Review | Blind | 3 | 11-20% | 1 |

INDEX

Journal Name	Type Review	No. Ext. Rev.	Accept. Rate	Page
Annual Advances in Business Cases	Blind	3	30%	38
Asia Pacific Journal of Marketing and Logistics	Blind		11-20%	47
Business Case Journal	Blind	2	21-30%	58
California Management Review	Blind	3	6-10%	61
Case Research Journal	Blind	3	11-20%	64
FIU Hospitality Review	N/A	2	21-30%	94
Global Competitiveness	Blind	2	50%	98
Global Economy Quarterly (GEQ)	Blind	2	11-20%	100
International Academy for Case Studies	Blind	3	21-30%	115
International Journal of Business	Blind	2	11-20%	127
International Journal of Business and Economics	Blind	2	11-20%	129
International Journal of Hospitality Management	Blind	2	21-30%	138
International Journal of Tourism Research	Blind	2	50%	158
Journal of Business	Blind	2	11-20%	189
Journal of Business Disciplines	Blind	3	11-20%	198
Journal of Business Education	Blind	2	11-20%	201
Journal of Communication Management	Blind	3	50%	221
Journal of Database Marketing	Blind	3	50%	254
Journal of International Academy for Case Studies	Blind	2	11-20%	298
Journal of Marketing Education	Blind	3+	11-20%	352
Journal of Nonprofit and Voluntary Sector Marketing	Blind	3	50%	386
Journal of Personal Selling & Sales Management	Blind	3	21-30%	389
Journal of Targeting, Measurement, and Analysis for Targeting	Blind	3	50%	454
Journal of Travel & Tourism Marketing	Blind	2	21-30%	475
Journal of Vacation Marketing	Blind	3	50%	485
Marketing Education Review	Blind	2	21-30%	516
Marketing Educator	Blind	1	90%	519
Retail Education Today	Blind	1	50%	563
Sloan Management Review	Blind	2	6-10%	573
Southwestern Business Administration Journal	Blind	2	31-50%	580
Sport Marketing Quarterly	Blind	2	21-30%	583

Business Information Systems (MIS)

Journal Name	Type Review	No. Ext. Rev.	Accept. Rate	Page
American Business Perspectives (NBDC Report)	Editorial		11-20%	22
Annals of Tourism Research: A Social Sciences Journal	Blind	3+	11-20%	34
Annual Advances in Business Cases	Blind	3	30%	38
Asian Journal of Business & Entrepreneurship	Blind	2	21-30%	48
Business Case Journal	Blind	2	21-30%	58
California Management Review	Blind	3	6-10%	61
Case Research Journal	Blind	3	11-20%	64
Decision Sciences (Journal of)	Blind	2	11-20%	78
Global Competitiveness	Blind	2	50%	98
Industrial Marketing Management	Blind	3	20-25%	109

Journal Name	Type Review	No. Ext. Rev.	Accept. Rate	Page
International Academy for Case Studies	Blind	3	21-30%	115
International Journal of Business	Blind	2	11-20%	127
International Journal of Business and Economics	Blind	2	11-20%	129
International Journal of Electronic Commerce (IJEC)	Blind	3	11-20%	131
International Journal of Hospitality Management	Blind	2	21-30%	138
International Journal of Physical Distribution & Logistics Management	Blind	3	21-30%	146
International Journal of Research In Marketing	Blind	2	11-20%	150
Internet Research	Blind	2	35%	174
Journal of Business and Behavioral Sciences	Blind	3	11-20%	197
Journal of Business Disciplines	Blind	3	11-20%	198
Journal of Business Education	Blind	2	11-20%	201
Journal of Business Logistics	Blind	3+	21-30%	204
Journal of Electronic Commerce	Editorial	0	21-30%	257
Journal of Global Marketing	Blind	2	11-20%	276
Journal of Hospitality & Tourism Research	Blind	3	11-20%	292
Journal of International Academy for Case Studies	Blind	2	11-20%	298
Journal of International Food & Agribusiness Marketing	Blind	2	21-30%	309
Journal of Internet Commerce	Blind	3	New J	326
Journal of Quality Assurance in Tourism & Hospitality	Blind	3	New J	409
Journal of Retail Banking Services	Editorial	Varies		422
Journal of Retailing and Consumer Services	Blind	3	11-20%	429
Journal of Services Marketing	Blind	3	21-30%	443
Journal of Targeting, Measurement, and Analysis for Targeting	Blind	3	50%	454
Journal of Travel & Tourism Marketing	Blind	2	21-30%	475
Journal of World Business	Blind	2	11-20%	488
Logistics Information Management	Blind	2	21-30%	491
Marketing Educator	Blind	1	90%	519
Marketing Intelligence & Planning	Editorial	1	50%	524
Mountain Plains Journal of Business and Economics	Blind	3	21-30%	537
North Central Business Journal	Blind	2	50%	538
Operations Research	Editorial	3	21-30%	540
Qualitative Market Research: An International Journal	Blind	1	40%	553
Sloan Management Review	Blind	2	6-10%	573
Southwestern Business Administration Journal	Blind	2	31-50%	580

Business Law, Public Responsibility & Ethics

Journal Name	Type Review	No. Ext. Rev.	Accept. Rate	Page
Academy of Marketing Studies Journal	Blind	2	21-30%	9
American Business Perspectives (NBDC Report)	Editorial		11-20%	22

INDEX

Journal Name	Type Review	No. Ext. Rev.	Accept. Rate	Page
American International College Journal of Business	Editorial	0	90%	29
Annual Advances in Business Cases	Blind	3	30%	38
Asia Pacific Business Review	Blind	3+	21-30%	44
Business Case Journal	Blind	2	21-30%	58
California Management Review	Blind	3	6-10%	61
Case Research Journal	Blind	3	11-20%	64
Communications and the Law	Editorial	0	50%	73
Family Business Review	Blind	3	21-30%	91
Global Competitiveness	Blind	2	50%	98
International Academy for Case Studies	Blind	3	21-30%	115
International Journal of Advertising	Blind	3+	35%	119
International Journal of Business and Economics	Blind	2	11-20%	129
International Journal of Hospitality & Tourism Administration	Blind	2	50%	134
International Journal of Hospitality Management	Blind	2	21-30%	138
International Research in the Business Disciplines	Blind	2	11-20%	168
Journal of Business and Behavioral Sciences	Blind	3	11-20%	197
Journal of Business Disciplines	Blind	3	11-20%	198
Journal of Business Education	Blind	2	11-20%	201
Journal of Consumer Affairs	Blind	3	21-30%	225
Journal of Consumer Marketing	Blind	3	21-27%	228
Journal of Food Product Marketing	Blind	3	50%	270
Journal of Hospitality & Tourism Research	Blind	3	11-20%	292
Journal of International Academy for Case Studies	Blind	2	11-20%	298
Journal of Macromarketing	Blind	3	11-20%	330
Journal of Marketing Education	Blind	3+	11-20%	352
Journal of Ministry Marketing and Management	Blind	2	21-30%	377
Journal of Public Policy & Marketing	Blind	3+	11-20%	406
Journal of Retail Banking Services	Editorial	Varies		422
Journal of Transportation Law, Logistics, and Policy	Editorial	0	70%	466
Journal of Travel & Tourism Marketing	Blind	2	21-30%	475
Journal of World Business	Blind	2	11-20%	488
Marketing Educator	Blind	1	90%	519
Mountain Plains Journal of Business and Economics	Blind	3	21-30%	537
North Central Business Journal	Blind	2	50%	538
Operations Research	Editorial	3	21-30%	540
Qualitative Market Research: An International Journal	Blind	1	40%	553
Sloan Management Review	Blind	2	6-10%	573
Southwestern Business Administration Journal	Blind	2	31-50%	580

Communication

Journal Name	Type Review	No. Ext. Rev.	Accept. Rate	Page
Academy of Marketing Science Review	Blind	3	11-20%	1
Bank Marketing Magazine	Editorial	0	50%	50

INDEX

Journal Name	Type Review	No. Ext. Rev.	Accept. Rate	Page
California Management Review	Blind	3	6-10%	61
Case Research Journal	Blind	3	11-20%	64
Communication Monographs	Blind	2	0-5%	67
Communication Research	Blind	3	21-30%	69
Communication Studies	Blind	3	11-20%	71
Communications and the Law	Editorial	0	50%	73
European Journal of Marketing	Blind		28%	87
Family Business Review	Blind	3	21-30%	91
Interactive Marketing	Blind	2	21-30%	112
International Academy for Case Studies	Blind	3	21-30%	115
International Journal of Advertising	Blind	3+	35%	119
International Journal of Hospitality Management	Blind	2	21-30%	138
International Journal of Research In Marketing	Blind	2	11-20%	150
Journal of Advertising	Blind	3	11-20%	179
Journal of Advertising Research	Blind	2	21-30%	182
Journal of Brand Management	Blind	3	50%	186
Journal of Business and Behavioral Sciences	Blind	3	11-20%	197
Journal of Business Disciplines	Blind	3	11-20%	198
Journal of Communication	Blind	3	11-20%	219
Journal of Communication Management	Blind	3	50%	221
Journal of Consumer Affairs	Blind	3	21-30%	225
Journal of Consumer Marketing	Blind	3	21-27%	228
Journal of Consumer Research	Blind	3	11-20%	242
Journal of Current Issues & Research in Advertising	Blind	3	6-10%	250
Journal of Database Marketing	Blind	3	50%	254
Journal of Euromarketing	Blind	2	21-30%	260
Journal of Food Product Marketing	Blind	3	50%	270
Journal of Global Marketing	Blind	2	11-20%	276
Journal of Hospitality & Leisure Marketing	Blind	2	50%	288
Journal of Interactive Marketing	Blind	2	11-20%	295
Journal of International Academy for Case Studies	Blind	2	11-20%	298
Journal of International Consumer Marketing	Blind	2	11-20%	301
Journal of International Food & Agribusiness Marketing	Blind	2	21-30%	309
Journal of Marketing Communications	Blind	2	40%	348
Journal of Marketing Education	Blind	3+	11-20%	352
Journal of Marketing Management	Blind	2	11-20%	360
Journal of Ministry Marketing and Management	Blind	2	21-30%	377
Journal of Nonprofit & Public Sector Marketing	Blind	2	21-30%	382
Journal of Nonprofit and Voluntary Sector Marketing	Blind	3	50%	386
Journal of Public Policy & Marketing	Blind	3+	11-20%	406
Journal of Quality Assurance in Tourism & Hospitality	Blind	3	New J	409
Journal of Retail Banking Services	Editorial	Varies		422

Journal Name	Type Review	No. Ext. Rev.	Accept. Rate	Page
Journal of Services Marketing	Blind	3	21-30%	443
Journal of Targeting, Measurement, and Analysis for Targeting	Blind	3	50%	454
Journal of the Market Research Society	Editorial	1	21-30%	460
Journal of Travel & Tourism Marketing	Blind	2	21-30%	475
North Central Business Journal	Blind	2	50%	538
Operations Research	Editorial	3	21-30%	540
Research in Consumer Behavior	Blind	3	30%	557
Southwestern Business Administration Journal	Blind	2	31-50%	580
Sport Marketing Quarterly	Blind	2	21-30%	583
Tourism and Hospitality Research: The Surrey Quarterly Review	Blind	0	21-30%	589
Western Journal of Communication	Blind	2	10-13%	609
Written Communication	Blind	2	6-10%	615

Direct Marketing

Journal Name	Type Review	No. Ext. Rev.	Accept. Rate	Page
Academy of Marketing Science Review	Blind	3	11-20%	1
Academy of Marketing Studies Journal	Blind	2	21-30%	9
American Business Perspectives (NBDC Report)	Editorial		11-20%	22
American Demographics	N/A	0	6-10%	27
Annual Advances in Business Cases	Blind	3	30%	38
Asia Pacific Journal of Marketing and Logistics	Blind		11-20%	47
Bank Marketing Magazine	Editorial	0	50%	50
Case Research Journal	Blind	3	11-20%	64
European Journal of Marketing	Blind		28%	87
Global Business and Economic Review	Blind	3+	22-25%	96
Harvard Business Review	Editorial	0	0-5%	102
Industrial Marketing Management	Blind	3	20-25%	109
Interactive Marketing	Blind	2	21-30%	112
International Academy for Case Studies	Blind	3	21-30%	115
International Journal of Advertising	Blind	3+	35%	119
International Journal of Bank Marketing	Blind	2	21-30%	122
International Journal of Business	Blind	2	11-20%	127
International Journal of Research In Marketing	Blind	2	11-20%	150
Journal of Advertising	Blind	3	11-20%	179
Journal of Brand Management	Blind	3	50%	186
Journal of Business and Behavioral Sciences	Blind	3	11-20%	197
Journal of Business Disciplines	Blind	3	11-20%	198
Journal of Business, Industry and Economics	Blind	2	70%	214
Journal of Communication Management	Blind	3	50%	221
Journal of Consumer Marketing	Blind	3	21-27%	228
Journal of Consumer Research	Blind	3	11-20%	242
Journal of Convention & Exhibition Management	Blind	3	11-20%	246
Journal of Current Issues & Research in Advertising	Blind	3	6-10%	250
Journal of Database Marketing	Blind	3	50%	254

INDEX

Journal Name	Type Review	No. Ext. Rev.	Accept. Rate	Page
Journal of Euromarketing	Blind	2	21-30%	260
Journal of Fashion Marketing and Management	Blind	3	50%	264
Journal of Financial Services Marketing	Blind	3	50%	267
Journal of Food Product Marketing	Blind	3	50%	270
Journal of Global Marketing	Blind	2	11-20%	276
Journal of Hospitality & Leisure Marketing	Blind	2	50%	288
Journal of Hospitality & Tourism Research	Blind	3	11-20%	292
Journal of Interactive Marketing	Blind	2	11-20%	295
Journal of International Academy for Case Studies	Blind	2	11-20%	298
Journal of International Consumer Marketing	Blind	2	11-20%	301
Journal of International Food & Agribusiness Marketing	Blind	2	21-30%	309
Journal of Marketing	Blind	3	6-10%	335
Journal of Marketing Channels	Blind	2	21-30%	344
Journal of Marketing Communications	Blind	2	40%	348
Journal of Marketing Education	Blind	3+	11-20%	352
Journal of Marketing for Higher Education	Blind	3	35%	356
Journal of Marketing Management	Blind	2	11-20%	360
Journal of Marketing Theory and Practice	Blind	3	11-20%	373
Journal of Nonprofit & Public Sector Marketing	Blind	2	21-30%	382
Journal of Nonprofit and Voluntary Sector Marketing	Blind	3	50%	386
Journal of Personal Selling & Sales Management	Blind	3	21-30%	389
Journal of Product & Brand Management	Blind	2	40-50%	397
Journal of Promotion Management	Blind	2	21-30%	402
Journal of Quality Assurance in Tourism & Hospitality	Blind	3	New J	409
Journal of Restaurant & Foodservice Marketing	Blind	2	21-30%	418
Journal of Retail Banking Services	Editorial	Varies		422
Journal of Retailing	Blind	2-3	11-20%	424
Journal of Retailing and Consumer Services	Blind	3	11-20%	429
Journal of Segmentation in Marketing	Blind	2		434
Journal of Services Marketing	Blind	3	21-30%	443
Journal of Targeting, Measurement, and Analysis for Targeting	Blind	3	50%	454
Journal of the Academy of Marketing Science	Blind	3	31-50%	457
Journal of Travel & Tourism Marketing	Blind	2	21-30%	475
Journal of Vacation Marketing	Blind	3	50%	485
Marketing Educator	Blind	1	90%	519
Marketing Health Services	Blind	3+	21-40%	520
Marketing Intelligence & Planning	Editorial	1	50%	524
Marketing Letters	Editorial	2	21-30%	528
Marketing Management	Blind	3	21-30%	531
Marketing Management Journal	Blind	3	21-30%	535
Mountain Plains Journal of Business and Economics	Blind	3	21-30%	537

INDEX

Journal Name	Type Review	No. Ext. Rev.	Accept. Rate	Page
North Central Business Journal	Blind	2	50%	538
Pennsylvania Journal of Business and Economics	Blind	2	50%	547
Qualitative Market Research: An International Journal	Blind	1	40%	553
Research in Consumer Behavior	Blind	3	30%	557
Southwest Business & Economics Journal	Blind	1	30-35%	578
Southwestern Business Administration Journal	Blind	2	31-50%	580

Global Business

Journal Name	Type Review	No. Ext. Rev.	Accept. Rate	Page
Advances in International Marketing	Blind	2	11-20%	12
American Business Perspectives (NBDC Report)	Editorial		11-20%	22
American Demographics	N/A	0	6-10%	27
American International College Journal of Business	Editorial	0	90%	29
Anatolia: An International Journal of Tourism Hospitality and Research	Blind	3	21-30%	30
Annals of Tourism Research: A Social Sciences Journal	Blind	3+	11-20%	34
Annual Advances in Business Cases	Blind	3	30%	38
Asia Pacific Business Review	Blind	3+	21-30%	44
Asia Pacific Journal of Marketing and Logistics	Blind		11-20%	47
Asian Journal of Business & Entrepreneurship	Blind	2	21-30%	48
Business Case Journal	Blind	2	21-30%	58
California Management Review	Blind	3	6-10%	61
Case Research Journal	Blind	3	11-20%	64
Family Business Review	Blind	3	21-30%	91
FIU Hospitality Review	N/A	2	21-30%	94
Global Business and Economic Review	Blind	3+	22-25%	96
Global Competitiveness	Blind	2	50%	98
Global Economy Quarterly (GEQ)	Blind	2	11-20%	100
Harvard Business Review	Editorial	0	0-5%	102
Industrial Marketing Management	Blind	3	20-25%	109
Interactive Marketing	Blind	2	21-30%	112
International Academy for Case Studies	Blind	3	21-30%	115
International Journal of Advertising	Blind	3+	35%	119
International Journal of Business	Blind	2	11-20%	127
International Journal of Business and Economics	Blind	2	11-20%	129
International Journal of Electronic Commerce (IJEC)	Blind	3	11-20%	131
International Journal of Hospitality & Tourism Administration	Blind	2	50%	134
International Journal of Hospitality Management	Blind	2	21-30%	138
International Journal of Physical Distribution & Logistics Management	Blind	3	21-30%	146
International Journal of Research In Marketing	Blind	2	11-20%	150
International Journal of Tourism Research	Blind	2	50%	158
International Marketing Review	Blind	2	21-30%	164

INDEX

Journal Name	Type Review	No. Ext. Rev.	Accept. Rate	Page
International Research in the Business Disciplines	Blind	2	11-20%	168
Journal of Advertising	Blind	3	11-20%	179
Journal of Brand Management	Blind	3	50%	186
Journal of Business	Blind	2	11-20%	189
Journal of Business and Behavioral Sciences	Blind	3	11-20%	197
Journal of Business Disciplines	Blind	3	11-20%	198
Journal of Business Education	Blind	2	11-20%	201
Journal of Business, Industry and Economics	Blind	2	70%	214
Journal of Communication Management	Blind	3	50%	221
Journal of Consumer Research	Blind	3	11-20%	242
Journal of Convention & Exhibition Management	Blind	3	11-20%	246
Journal of Database Marketing	Blind	3	50%	254
Journal of Euromarketing	Blind	2	21-30%	260
Journal of Fashion Marketing and Management	Blind	3	50%	264
Journal of Financial Services Marketing	Blind	3	50%	267
Journal of Food Product Marketing	Blind	3	50%	270
Journal of Global Marketing	Blind	2	11-20%	276
Journal of Hospitality & Tourism Research	Blind	3	11-20%	292
Journal of International Academy for Case Studies	Blind	2	11-20%	298
Journal of International Consumer Marketing	Blind	2	11-20%	301
Journal of International Food & Agribusiness Marketing	Blind	2	21-30%	309
Journal of International Marketing	Blind	2	20%	317
Journal of Marketing Communications	Blind	2	40%	348
Journal of Marketing Management	Blind	2	11-20%	360
Journal of Marketing Theory and Practice	Blind	3	11-20%	373
Journal of Nonprofit and Voluntary Sector Marketing	Blind	3	50%	386
Journal of Personal Selling & Sales Management	Blind	3	21-30%	389
Journal of Product & Brand Management	Blind	2	40-50%	397
Journal of Promotion Management	Blind	2	21-30%	402
Journal of Public Policy & Marketing	Blind	3+	11-20%	406
Journal of Retail Banking Services	Editorial	Varies		422
Journal of Retailing	Blind	2-3	11-20%	424
Journal of Retailing and Consumer Services	Blind	3	11-20%	429
Journal of Selling and Major Account Management	Blind	2	21-30%	438
Journal of Services Marketing	Blind	3	21-30%	443
Journal of Targeting, Measurement, and Analysis for Targeting	Blind	3	50%	454
Journal of Travel & Tourism Marketing	Blind	2	21-30%	475
Journal of World Business	Blind	2	11-20%	488
Management Science	Editorial	3	11-20%	495
Marketing Educator	Blind	1	90%	519
Marketing Intelligence & Planning	Editorial	1	50%	524
Marketing Management	Blind	3	21-30%	531
Marketing Management Journal	Blind	3	21-30%	535

INDEX

Journal Name	Type Review	No. Ext. Rev.	Accept. Rate	Page
Mountain Plains Journal of Business and Economics	Blind	3	21-30%	537
North Central Business Journal	Blind	2	50%	538
Pennsylvania Journal of Business and Economics	Blind	2	50%	547
Qualitative Market Research: An International Journal	Blind	1	40%	553
Research in Consumer Behavior	Blind	3	30%	557
Sloan Management Review	Blind	2	6-10%	573
Southwestern Business Administration Journal	Blind	2	31-50%	580
Tourism Analysis	Blind	3	45%	586
Tourism and Hospitality Research: The Surrey Quarterly Review	Blind	0	21-30%	589

Health Care Administration

Journal Name	Type Review	No. Ext. Rev.	Accept. Rate	Page
Business Case Journal	Blind	2	21-30%	58
Case Research Journal	Blind	3	11-20%	64
Decision Sciences (Journal of)	Blind	2	11-20%	78
Health Marketing Quarterly	Blind	2	40%	104
International Academy for Case Studies	Blind	3	21-30%	115
Journal of Business and Behavioral Sciences	Blind	3	11-20%	197
Journal of Business Disciplines	Blind	3	11-20%	198
Journal of Communication Management	Blind	3	50%	221
Journal of Hospital Marketing	Editorial	4	50%	284
Journal of International Academy for Case Studies	Blind	2	11-20%	298
Journal of Nonprofit & Public Sector Marketing	Blind	2	21-30%	382
Journal of Services Marketing	Blind	3	21-30%	443
North Central Business Journal	Blind	2	50%	538

Labor Relations & Human Resource Mgt.

Journal Name	Type Review	No. Ext. Rev.	Accept. Rate	Page
American Business Perspectives (NBDC Report)	Editorial		11-20%	22
Annual Advances in Business Cases	Blind	3	30%	38
Asian Journal of Business & Entrepreneurship	Blind	2	21-30%	48
Business Case Journal	Blind	2	21-30%	58
California Management Review	Blind	3	6-10%	61
Case Research Journal	Blind	3	11-20%	64
Communications and the Law	Editorial	0	50%	73
Family Business Review	Blind	3	21-30%	91
Global Competitiveness	Blind	2	50%	98
International Academy for Case Studies	Blind	3	21-30%	115
International Journal of Business	Blind	2	11-20%	127
International Journal of Business and Economics	Blind	2	11-20%	129
International Journal of Hospitality Management	Blind	2	21-30%	138
International Research in the Business Disciplines	Blind	2	11-20%	168
Journal of Business	Blind	2	11-20%	189
Journal of Business and Behavioral Sciences	Blind	3	11-20%	197
Journal of Business Disciplines	Blind	3	11-20%	198

Journal Name	Type Review	No. Ext. Rev.	Accept. Rate	Page
Journal of Food Product Marketing	Blind	3	50%	270
Journal of Hospitality & Tourism Research	Blind	3	11-20%	292
Journal of International Academy for Case Studies	Blind	2	11-20%	298
Journal of Quality Assurance in Tourism & Hospitality	Blind	3	New J	409
Journal of Retail Banking Services	Editorial	Varies		422
Journal of Retailing and Consumer Services	Blind	3	11-20%	429
Journal of Sport Management	Blind	3	11-20%	447
Journal of World Business	Blind	2	11-20%	488
Marketing Letters	Editorial	2	21-30%	528
Mountain Plains Journal of Business and Economics	Blind	3	21-30%	537
North Central Business Journal	Blind	2	50%	538
Sloan Management Review	Blind	2	6-10%	573
Southwestern Business Administration Journal	Blind	2	31-50%	580
Tourism and Hospitality Research: The Surrey Quarterly Review	Blind	0	21-30%	589

Marketing Research

Journal Name	Type Review	No. Ext. Rev.	Accept. Rate	Page
Academy of Marketing Science Review	Blind	3	11-20%	1
Academy of Marketing Studies Journal	Blind	2	21-30%	9
Advances in International Marketing	Blind	2	11-20%	12
American Business Perspectives (NBDC Report)	Editorial		11-20%	22
American Demographics	N/A	0	6-10%	27
American International College Journal of Business	Editorial	0	90%	29
Anatolia: An International Journal of Tourism Hospitality and Research	Blind	3	21-30%	30
Annals of Tourism Research: A Social Sciences Journal	Blind	3+	11-20%	34
Annual Advances in Business Cases	Blind	3	30%	38
Asia Pacific Journal of Marketing and Logistics	Blind		11-20%	47
Asian Journal of Business & Entrepreneurship	Blind	2	21-30%	48
Bank Marketing Magazine	Editorial	0	50%	50
California Management Review	Blind	3	6-10%	61
Case Research Journal	Blind	3	11-20%	64
Cornell Hotel and Restaurant Administration Quarterly	Blind	2	50%	75
Decision Sciences (Journal of)	Blind	2	11-20%	78
European Journal of Marketing	Blind		28%	87
FIU Hospitality Review	N/A	2	21-30%	94
Global Business and Economic Review	Blind	3+	22-25%	96
Global Competitiveness	Blind	2	50%	98
Harvard Business Review	Editorial	0	0-5%	102
Health Marketing Quarterly	Blind	2	40%	104
Industrial Marketing Management	Blind	3	20-25%	109
Interactive Marketing	Blind	2	21-30%	112

INDEX

Journal Name	Type Review	No. Ext. Rev.	Accept. Rate	Page
International Journal of Advertising	Blind	3+	35%	119
International Journal of Bank Marketing	Blind	2	21-30%	122
International Journal of Business	Blind	2	11-20%	127
International Journal of Electronic Commerce (IJEC)	Blind	3	11-20%	131
International Journal of Hospitality & Tourism Administration	Blind	2	50%	134
International Journal of Hospitality Management	Blind	2	21-30%	138
International Journal of Research In Marketing	Blind	2	11-20%	150
International Journal of Tourism Research	Blind	2	50%	158
International Marketing Review	Blind	2	21-30%	164
International Research in the Business Disciplines	Blind	2	11-20%	168
International Review of Retail, Distribution and Consumer Research	Blind	2	33%	171
Journal of Advertising Research	Blind	2	21-30%	182
Journal of Brand Management	Blind	3	50%	186
Journal of Business	Blind	2	11-20%	189
Journal of Business and Behavioral Sciences	Blind	3	11-20%	197
Journal of Business Disciplines	Blind	3	11-20%	198
Journal of Business, Industry and Economics	Blind	2	70%	214
Journal of Business-to-Business Marketing	Blind	3	21-25%	215
Journal of Communication Management	Blind	3	50%	221
Journal of Consumer Affairs	Blind	3	21-30%	225
Journal of Consumer Marketing	Blind	3	21-27%	228
Journal of Consumer Policy	Blind	3		233
Journal of Consumer Psychology	Blind	3	11-20%	240
Journal of Consumer Research	Blind	3	11-20%	242
Journal of Convention & Exhibition Management	Blind	3	11-20%	246
Journal of Euromarketing	Blind	2	21-30%	260
Journal of Fashion Marketing and Management	Blind	3	50%	264
Journal of Financial Services Marketing	Blind	3	50%	267
Journal of Food Product Marketing	Blind	3	50%	270
Journal of Global Marketing	Blind	2	11-20%	276
Journal of Hospital Marketing	Editorial	4	50%	284
Journal of Hospitality & Leisure Marketing	Blind	2	50%	288
Journal of Hospitality & Tourism Research	Blind	3	11-20%	292
Journal of International Academy for Case Studies	Blind	2	11-20%	298
Journal of International Consumer Marketing	Blind	2	11-20%	301
Journal of International Food & Agribusiness Marketing	Blind	2	21-30%	309
Journal of International Marketing	Blind	2	20%	317
Journal of Marketing Education	Blind	3+	11-20%	352
Journal of Marketing for Higher Education	Blind	3	35%	356
Journal of Marketing Management	Blind	2	11-20%	360
Journal of Marketing Research	Blind	3	11-20%	364
Journal of Marketing Theory and Practice	Blind	3	11-20%	373

INDEX

Journal Name	Type Review	No. Ext. Rev.	Accept. Rate	Page
Journal of Ministry Marketing and Management	Blind	2	21-30%	377
Journal of Nonprofit & Public Sector Marketing	Blind	2	21-30%	382
Journal of Nonprofit and Voluntary Sector Marketing	Blind	3	50%	386
Journal of Pharmaceutical Marketing and Management	Blind	2	65%	393
Journal of Problems of Theory and Practice in Reforms of Regional Economies	Blind	2	21-30%	396
Journal of Product & Brand Management	Blind	2	40-50%	397
Journal of Promotion Management	Blind	2	21-30%	402
Journal of Public Policy & Marketing	Blind	3+	11-20%	406
Journal of Quality Assurance in Tourism & Hospitality	Blind	3	New J	409
Journal of Relationship Marketing (Journal of Customer Service in Mktg. & Mgmt.)	Editorial	3+	40%	413
Journal of Restaurant & Foodservice Marketing	Blind	2	21-30%	418
Journal of Retail Banking Services	Editorial	Varies		422
Journal of Retailing	Blind	2-3	11-20%	424
Journal of Retailing and Consumer Services	Blind	3	11-20%	429
Journal of Segmentation in Marketing	Blind	2		434
Journal of Services Marketing	Blind	3	21-30%	443
Journal of Targeting, Measurement, and Analysis for Targeting	Blind	3	50%	454
Journal of the Academy of Marketing Science	Blind	3	31-50%	457
Journal of the Market Research Society	Editorial	1	21-30%	460
Journal of Travel & Tourism Marketing	Blind	2	21-30%	475
Journal of Travel Research	Blind	3	20%	480
Journal of Vacation Marketing	Blind	3	50%	485
Management Science	Editorial	3	11-20%	495
Marketing Educator	Blind	1	90%	519
Marketing Health Services	Blind	3+	21-40%	520
Marketing Intelligence & Planning	Editorial	1	50%	524
Marketing Letters	Editorial	2	21-30%	528
Marketing Management	Blind	3	21-30%	531
Marketing Management Journal	Blind	3	21-30%	535
Mountain Plains Journal of Business and Economics	Blind	3	21-30%	537
North Central Business Journal	Blind	2	50%	538
Pennsylvania Journal of Business and Economics	Blind	2	50%	547
Psychology and Marketing	Blind	3	11-20%	550
Qualitative Market Research: An International Journal	Blind	1	40%	553
Research in Consumer Behavior	Blind	3	30%	557
Services Marketing Quarterly	Editorial	3+	50%	569
Southwest Business & Economics Journal	Blind	1	30-35%	578
Southwestern Business Administration Journal	Blind	2	31-50%	580

INDEX

Journal Name	Type Review	No. Ext. Rev.	Accept. Rate	Page
Tourism Management	Blind	3	21-30%	593
Marketing Theory & Applications				
Academy of Marketing Science Review	Blind	3	11-20%	1
Academy of Marketing Studies Journal	Blind	2	21-30%	9
Advances in International Marketing	Blind	2	11-20%	12
Agribusiness: An International Journal	Blind	2	21-30%	16
American Business Perspectives (NBDC Report)	Editorial		11-20%	22
American International College Journal of Business	Editorial	0	90%	29
Anatolia: An International Journal of Tourism Hospitality and Research	Blind	3	21-30%	30
Annals of Tourism Research: A Social Sciences Journal	Blind	3+	11-20%	34
Annual Advances in Business Cases	Blind	3	30%	38
Asia Pacific Business Review	Blind	3+	21-30%	44
Asia Pacific Journal of Marketing and Logistics	Blind		11-20%	47
Asian Journal of Business & Entrepreneurship	Blind	2	21-30%	48
Bank Marketing Magazine	Editorial	0	50%	50
British Food Journal	Blind	2	50%	53
Business Case Journal	Blind	2	21-30%	58
California Management Review	Blind	3	6-10%	61
Case Research Journal	Blind	3	11-20%	64
Cornell Hotel and Restaurant Administration Quarterly	Blind	2	50%	75
Decision Sciences (Journal of)	Blind	2	11-20%	78
European Journal of Marketing	Blind		28%	87
Family Business Review	Blind	3	21-30%	91
Global Business and Economic Review	Blind	3+	22-25%	96
Global Competitiveness	Blind	2	50%	98
Harvard Business Review	Editorial	0	0-5%	102
Health Marketing Quarterly	Blind	2	40%	104
Industrial Marketing Management	Blind	3	20-25%	109
Interactive Marketing	Blind	2	21-30%	112
International Journal of Advertising	Blind	3+	35%	119
International Journal of Bank Marketing	Blind	2	21-30%	122
International Journal of Business	Blind	2	11-20%	127
International Journal of Business and Economics	Blind	2	11-20%	129
International Journal of Electronic Commerce (IJEC)	Blind	3	11-20%	131
International Journal of Hospitality & Tourism Administration	Blind	2	50%	134
International Journal of Hospitality Management	Blind	2	21-30%	138
International Journal of Physical Distribution & Logistics Management	Blind	3	21-30%	146
International Journal of Research In Marketing	Blind	2	11-20%	150
International Journal of Tourism Research	Blind	2	50%	158

INDEX

Journal Name	Type Review	No. Ext. Rev.	Accept. Rate	Page
International Marketing Review	Blind	2	21-30%	164
International Review of Retail, Distribution and Consumer Research	Blind	2	33%	171
Journal of Brand Management	Blind	3	50%	186
Journal of Business	Blind	2	11-20%	189
Journal of Business & Industrial Marketing	Blind	3	21-30%	192
Journal of Business and Behavioral Sciences	Blind	3	11-20%	197
Journal of Business Disciplines	Blind	3	11-20%	198
Journal of Business Education	Blind	2	11-20%	201
Journal of Business, Industry and Economics	Blind	2	70%	214
Journal of Business-to-Business Marketing	Blind	3	21-25%	215
Journal of Consumer Affairs	Blind	3	21-30%	225
Journal of Consumer Policy	Blind	3		233
Journal of Consumer Psychology	Blind	3	11-20%	240
Journal of Consumer Research	Blind	3	11-20%	242
Journal of Database Marketing	Blind	3	50%	254
Journal of Euromarketing	Blind	2	21-30%	260
Journal of Fashion Marketing and Management	Blind	3	50%	264
Journal of Financial Services Marketing	Blind	3	50%	267
Journal of Food Product Marketing	Blind	3	50%	270
Journal of Global Marketing	Blind	2	11-20%	276
Journal of Hospital Marketing	Editorial	4	50%	284
Journal of Hospitality & Leisure Marketing	Blind	2	50%	288
Journal of Hospitality & Tourism Research	Blind	3	11-20%	292
Journal of Interactive Marketing	Blind	2	11-20%	295
Journal of International Academy for Case Studies	Blind	2	11-20%	298
Journal of International Consumer Marketing	Blind	2	11-20%	301
Journal of International Marketing	Blind	2	20%	317
Journal of Internet Commerce	Blind	3	New J	326
Journal of Macromarketing	Blind	3	11-20%	330
Journal of Marketing	Blind	3	6-10%	335
Journal of Marketing Communications	Blind	2	40%	348
Journal of Marketing Education	Blind	3+	11-20%	352
Journal of Marketing for Higher Education	Blind	3	35%	356
Journal of Marketing Management	Blind	2	11-20%	360
Journal of Marketing Research	Blind	3	11-20%	364
Journal of Marketing Theory and Practice	Blind	3	11-20%	373
Journal of Nonprofit & Public Sector Marketing	Blind	2	21-30%	382
Journal of Nonprofit and Voluntary Sector Marketing	Blind	3	50%	386
Journal of Personal Selling & Sales Management	Blind	3	21-30%	389
Journal of Pharmaceutical Marketing and Management	Blind	2	65%	393
Journal of Problems of Theory and Practice in Reforms of Regional Economies	Blind	2	21-30%	396
Journal of Product & Brand Management	Blind	2	40-50%	397

INDEX

Journal Name	Type Review	No. Ext. Rev.	Accept. Rate	Page
Journal of Promotion Management	Blind	2	21-30%	402
Journal of Public Policy & Marketing	Blind	3+	11-20%	406
Journal of Relationship Marketing (Journal of Customer Service in Mktg. & Mgmt.)	Editorial	3+	40%	413
Journal of Restaurant & Foodservice Marketing	Blind	2	21-30%	418
Journal of Retail Banking Services	Editorial	Varies		422
Journal of Retailing	Blind	2-3	11-20%	424
Journal of Retailing and Consumer Services	Blind	3	11-20%	429
Journal of Segmentation in Marketing	Blind	2		434
Journal of Selling and Major Account Management	Blind	2	21-30%	438
Journal of Services Marketing	Blind	3	21-30%	443
Journal of Strategic Marketing	Blind	2	21-30%	450
Journal of Targeting, Measurement, and Analysis for Targeting	Blind	3	50%	454
Journal of the Academy of Marketing Science	Blind	3	31-50%	457
Journal of the Market Research Society	Editorial	1	21-30%	460
Journal of Travel & Tourism Marketing	Blind	2	21-30%	475
Journal of Vacation Marketing	Blind	3	50%	485
Management Science	Editorial	3	11-20%	495
Marketing Educator	Blind	1	90%	519
Marketing Intelligence & Planning	Editorial	1	50%	524
Marketing Management	Blind	3	21-30%	531
Marketing Management Journal	Blind	3	21-30%	535
Mountain Plains Journal of Business and Economics	Blind	3	21-30%	537
North Central Business Journal	Blind	2	50%	538
Pennsylvania Journal of Business and Economics	Blind	2	50%	547
Psychology and Marketing	Blind	3	11-20%	550
Qualitative Market Research: An International Journal	Blind	1	40%	553
Research in Consumer Behavior	Blind	3	30%	557
Services Marketing Quarterly	Editorial	3+	50%	569
Sloan Management Review	Blind	2	6-10%	573
Southwest Business & Economics Journal	Blind	1	30-35%	578
Southwestern Business Administration Journal	Blind	2	31-50%	580

Non Profit Organizations

Business Case Journal	Blind	2	21-30%	58
California Management Review	Blind	3	6-10%	61
Case Research Journal	Blind	3	11-20%	64
Global Competitiveness	Blind	2	50%	98
Harvard Business Review	Editorial	0	0-5%	102
International Journal of Hospitality & Tourism Administration	Blind	2	50%	134
International Research in the Business Disciplines	Blind	2	11-20%	168
Journal of Advertising	Blind	3	11-20%	179

Journal Name	Type Review	No. Ext. Rev.	Accept. Rate	Page
Journal of Brand Management	Blind	3	50%	186
Journal of Business and Behavioral Sciences	Blind	3	11-20%	197
Journal of Communication Management	Blind	3	50%	221
Journal of Consumer Research	Blind	3	11-20%	242
Journal of Database Marketing	Blind	3	50%	254
Journal of Hospitality & Leisure Marketing	Blind	2	50%	288
Journal of International Academy for Case Studies	Blind	2	11-20%	298
Journal of Ministry Marketing and Management	Blind	2	21-30%	377
Journal of Nonprofit & Public Sector Marketing	Blind	2	21-30%	382
Journal of Nonprofit and Voluntary Sector Marketing	Blind	3	50%	386
Journal of Promotion Management	Blind	2	21-30%	402
Journal of Services Marketing	Blind	3	21-30%	443
Journal of Targeting, Measurement, and Analysis for Targeting	Blind	3	50%	454
Journal of Travel & Tourism Marketing	Blind	2	21-30%	475
Marketing Management Journal	Blind	3	21-30%	535
North Central Business Journal	Blind	2	50%	538
Operations Research	Editorial	3	21-30%	540
Qualitative Market Research: An International Journal	Blind	1	40%	553
Research in Consumer Behavior	Blind	3	30%	557
Southwestern Business Administration Journal	Blind	2	31-50%	580
Sport Marketing Quarterly	Blind	2	21-30%	583

Office Administration/Management

Journal Name	Type Review	No. Ext. Rev.	Accept. Rate	Page
Annual Advances in Business Cases	Blind	3	30%	38
International Academy for Case Studies	Blind	3	21-30%	115
International Journal of Business	Blind	2	11-20%	127
Journal of Business and Behavioral Sciences	Blind	3	11-20%	197
Journal of Business Disciplines	Blind	3	11-20%	198
Journal of Business Education	Blind	2	11-20%	201
Journal of Hospitality & Tourism Research	Blind	3	11-20%	292
Journal of International Academy for Case Studies	Blind	2	11-20%	298
Journal of Retail Banking Services	Editorial	Varies		422
North Central Business Journal	Blind	2	50%	538
Southwestern Business Administration Journal	Blind	2	31-50%	580
Sport Marketing Quarterly	Blind	2	21-30%	583
Tourism and Hospitality Research: The Surrey Quarterly Review	Blind	0	21-30%	589

Operations Research/Statistics

Journal Name	Type Review	No. Ext. Rev.	Accept. Rate	Page
Advances in International Marketing	Blind	2	11-20%	12
Annual Advances in Business Cases	Blind	3	30%	38
Business Case Journal	Blind	2	21-30%	58
California Management Review	Blind	3	6-10%	61

INDEX

Journal Name	Type Review	No. Ext. Rev.	Accept. Rate	Page
Case Research Journal	Blind	3	11-20%	64
Decision Sciences (Journal of)	Blind	2	11-20%	78
Family Business Review	Blind	3	21-30%	91
FIU Hospitality Review	N/A	2	21-30%	94
International Journal of Business	Blind	2	11-20%	127
International Journal of Business and Economics	Blind	2	11-20%	129
Journal of Business and Behavioral Sciences	Blind	3	11-20%	197
Journal of Business Disciplines	Blind	3	11-20%	198
Journal of Communication Management	Blind	3	50%	221
Journal of Database Marketing	Blind	3	50%	254
Journal of Food Product Marketing	Blind	3	50%	270
Journal of Hospitality & Tourism Research	Blind	3	11-20%	292
Journal of International Academy for Case Studies	Blind	2	11-20%	298
Journal of Quality Assurance in Tourism & Hospitality	Blind	3	New J	409
Journal of Retail Banking Services	Editorial	Varies		422
Journal of Retailing	Blind	2-3	11-20%	424
Journal of Retailing and Consumer Services	Blind	3	11-20%	429
Journal of Targeting, Measurement, and Analysis for Targeting	Blind	3	50%	454
Journal of Travel & Tourism Marketing	Blind	2	21-30%	475
North Central Business Journal	Blind	2	50%	538
Operations Research	Editorial	3	21-30%	540
Sloan Management Review	Blind	2	6-10%	573
Southwestern Business Administration Journal	Blind	2	31-50%	580
Tourism and Hospitality Research: The Surrey Quarterly Review	Blind	0	21-30%	589

Organizational Behavior & Theory

Journal Name	Type Review	No. Ext. Rev.	Accept. Rate	Page
Advances in International Marketing	Blind	2	11-20%	12
Air Force Journal of Logistics	Blind	3	40%	21
American International College Journal of Business	Editorial	0	90%	29
Anatolia: An International Journal of Tourism Hospitality and Research	Blind	3	21-30%	30
Annual Advances in Business Cases	Blind	3	30%	38
Asia Pacific Business Review	Blind	3+	21-30%	44
Asian Journal of Business & Entrepreneurship	Blind	2	21-30%	48
Bank Marketing Magazine	Editorial	0	50%	50
Business Case Journal	Blind	2	21-30%	58
California Management Review	Blind	3	6-10%	61
Case Research Journal	Blind	3	11-20%	64
Cornell Hotel and Restaurant Administration Quarterly	Blind	2	50%	75
Decision Sciences (Journal of)	Blind	2	11-20%	78
Family Business Review	Blind	3	21-30%	91
FIU Hospitality Review	N/A	2	21-30%	94

Journal Name	Type Review	No. Ext. Rev.	Accept. Rate	Page
Interactive Marketing	Blind	2	21-30%	112
International Academy for Case Studies	Blind	3	21-30%	115
International Journal of Business	Blind	2	11-20%	127
International Journal of Business and Economics	Blind	2	11-20%	129
International Journal of Hospitality & Tourism Administration	Blind	2	50%	134
International Journal of Hospitality Management	Blind	2	21-30%	138
International Journal of Physical Distribution & Logistics Management	Blind	3	21-30%	146
International Review of Retail, Distribution and Consumer Research	Blind	2	33%	171
Journal of Business and Behavioral Sciences	Blind	3	11-20%	197
Journal of Business Disciplines	Blind	3	11-20%	198
Journal of Communication	Blind	3	11-20%	219
Journal of Communication Management	Blind	3	50%	221
Journal of Consumer Research	Blind	3	11-20%	242
Journal of Database Marketing	Blind	3	50%	254
Journal of Fashion Marketing and Management	Blind	3	50%	264
Journal of Food Product Marketing	Blind	3	50%	270
Journal of Hospitality & Tourism Research	Blind	3	11-20%	292
Journal of International Academy for Case Studies	Blind	2	11-20%	298
Journal of Marketing for Higher Education	Blind	3	35%	356
Journal of Ministry Marketing and Management	Blind	2	21-30%	377
Journal of Personal Selling & Sales Management	Blind	3	21-30%	389
Journal of Quality Assurance in Tourism & Hospitality	Blind	3	New J	409
Journal of Retail Banking Services	Editorial	Varies		422
Journal of Retailing and Consumer Services	Blind	3	11-20%	429
Journal of Services Marketing	Blind	3	21-30%	443
Journal of Sport Management	Blind	3	11-20%	447
Journal of Targeting, Measurement, and Analysis for Targeting	Blind	3	50%	454
Journal of Vacation Marketing	Blind	3	50%	485
Mountain Plains Journal of Business and Economics	Blind	3	21-30%	537
North Central Business Journal	Blind	2	50%	538
Sloan Management Review	Blind	2	6-10%	573
Southwestern Business Administration Journal	Blind	2	31-50%	580
Tourism and Hospitality Research: The Surrey Quarterly Review	Blind	0	21-30%	589
Tourism Management	Blind	3	21-30%	593
Western Journal of Communication	Blind	2	10-13%	609

Organizational Development

Advances in International Marketing	Blind	2	11-20%	12
Air Force Journal of Logistics	Blind	3	40%	21

INDEX

Journal Name	Type Review	No. Ext. Rev.	Accept. Rate	Page
Annual Advances in Business Cases	Blind	3	30%	38
Asia Pacific Business Review	Blind	3+	21-30%	44
Asian Journal of Business & Entrepreneurship	Blind	2	21-30%	48
Bank Marketing Magazine	Editorial	0	50%	50
Business Case Journal	Blind	2	21-30%	58
California Management Review	Blind	3	6-10%	61
Case Research Journal	Blind	3	11-20%	64
Family Business Review	Blind	3	21-30%	91
Global Competitiveness	Blind	2	50%	98
Interactive Marketing	Blind	2	21-30%	112
International Journal of Business	Blind	2	11-20%	127
International Journal of Electronic Commerce (IJEC)	Blind	3	11-20%	131
International Journal of Hospitality Management	Blind	2	21-30%	138
International Research in the Business Disciplines	Blind	2	11-20%	168
International Review of Retail, Distribution and Consumer Research	Blind	2	33%	171
Journal of Business and Behavioral Sciences	Blind	3	11-20%	197
Journal of Business Disciplines	Blind	3	11-20%	198
Journal of Communication Management	Blind	3	50%	221
Journal of Database Marketing	Blind	3	50%	254
Journal of Food Product Marketing	Blind	3	50%	270
Journal of Hospitality & Tourism Research	Blind	3	11-20%	292
Journal of International Academy for Case Studies	Blind	2	11-20%	298
Journal of Ministry Marketing and Management	Blind	2	21-30%	377
Journal of Quality Assurance in Tourism & Hospitality	Blind	3	New J	409
Journal of Retail Banking Services	Editorial	Varies		422
Journal of Services Marketing	Blind	3	21-30%	443
Journal of Sport Management	Blind	3	11-20%	447
Journal of Targeting, Measurement, and Analysis for Targeting	Blind	3	50%	454
Marketing Intelligence & Planning	Editorial	1	50%	524
Mountain Plains Journal of Business and Economics	Blind	3	21-30%	537
North Central Business Journal	Blind	2	50%	538
Sloan Management Review	Blind	2	6-10%	573
Southwestern Business Administration Journal	Blind	2	31-50%	580
Tourism and Hospitality Research: The Surrey Quarterly Review	Blind	0	21-30%	589

Production/Operations

Agribusiness: An International Journal	Blind	2	21-30%	16
American Business Perspectives (NBDC Report)	Editorial		11-20%	22
American International College Journal of Business	Editorial	0	90%	29
Annual Advances in Business Cases	Blind	3	30%	38

INDEX

Journal Name	Type Review	No. Ext. Rev.	Accept. Rate	Page
Asia Pacific Business Review	Blind	3+	21-30%	44
Asian Journal of Business & Entrepreneurship	Blind	2	21-30%	48
Business Case Journal	Blind	2	21-30%	58
California Management Review	Blind	3	6-10%	61
Case Research Journal	Blind	3	11-20%	64
Decision Sciences (Journal of)	Blind	2	11-20%	78
International Journal of Business and Economics	Blind	2	11-20%	129
International Journal of Logistics: Research and Applications	Blind	2	40%	143
International Journal of Physical Distribution & Logistics Management	Blind	3	21-30%	146
Journal of Business and Behavioral Sciences	Blind	3	11-20%	197
Journal of Business Disciplines	Blind	3	11-20%	198
Journal of Business Education	Blind	2	11-20%	201
Journal of Business Logistics	Blind	3+	21-30%	204
Journal of Financial Services Marketing	Blind	3	50%	267
Journal of Food Product Marketing	Blind	3	50%	270
Journal of Hospitality & Tourism Research	Blind	3	11-20%	292
Journal of Pharmaceutical Marketing and Management	Blind	2	65%	393
Journal of Product & Brand Management	Blind	2	40-50%	397
Journal of Quality Assurance in Tourism & Hospitality	Blind	3	New J	409
Journal of Retail Banking Services	Editorial	Varies		422
Journal of Retailing and Consumer Services	Blind	3	11-20%	429
Journal of the Market Research Society	Editorial	1	21-30%	460
Logistics Information Management	Blind	2	21-30%	491
Mountain Plains Journal of Business and Economics	Blind	3	21-30%	537
North Central Business Journal	Blind	2	50%	538
Operations Research	Editorial	3	21-30%	540
Sloan Management Review	Blind	2	6-10%	573
Southwestern Business Administration Journal	Blind	2	31-50%	580
Tourism and Hospitality Research: The Surrey Quarterly Review	Blind	0	21-30%	589

Public Administration

Journal Name	Type Review	No. Ext. Rev.	Accept. Rate	Page
Agribusiness: An International Journal	Blind	2	21-30%	16
Annual Advances in Business Cases	Blind	3	30%	38
California Management Review	Blind	3	6-10%	61
Case Research Journal	Blind	3	11-20%	64
International Research in the Business Disciplines	Blind	2	11-20%	168
Journal of Business	Blind	2	11-20%	189
Journal of Business and Behavioral Sciences	Blind	3	11-20%	197
Journal of Fashion Marketing and Management	Blind	3	50%	264
Journal of Hospitality & Tourism Research	Blind	3	11-20%	292

INDEX

Journal Name	Type Review	No. Ext. Rev.	Accept. Rate	Page
Journal of International Academy for Case Studies	Blind	2	11-20%	298
Journal of Nonprofit & Public Sector Marketing	Blind	2	21-30%	382
Journal of Public Policy & Marketing	Blind	3+	11-20%	406
Journal of Retailing and Consumer Services	Blind	3	11-20%	429
Journal of Sport Management	Blind	3	11-20%	447
Mountain Plains Journal of Business and Economics	Blind	3	21-30%	537
North Central Business Journal	Blind	2	50%	538
Southwestern Business Administration Journal	Blind	2	31-50%	580
Tourism and Hospitality Research: The Surrey Quarterly Review	Blind	0	21-30%	589

Purchasing/Materials Management

Journal Name	Type Review	No. Ext. Rev.	Accept. Rate	Page
Decision Sciences (Journal of)	Blind	2	11-20%	78
Global Competitiveness	Blind	2	50%	98
Industrial Marketing Management	Blind	3	20-25%	109
International Journal of Business	Blind	2	11-20%	127
International Journal of Hospitality Management	Blind	2	21-30%	138
International Journal of Logistics: Research and Applications	Blind	2	40%	143
International Journal of Physical Distribution & Logistics Management	Blind	3	21-30%	146
Journal of Business and Behavioral Sciences	Blind	3	11-20%	197
Journal of Business Disciplines	Blind	3	11-20%	198
Journal of Business-to-Business Marketing	Blind	3	21-25%	215
Journal of Food Product Marketing	Blind	3	50%	270
Journal of International Academy for Case Studies	Blind	2	11-20%	298
Journal of International Food & Agribusiness Marketing	Blind	2	21-30%	309
Journal of Marketing Management	Blind	2	11-20%	360
Journal of Nonprofit & Public Sector Marketing	Blind	2	21-30%	382
Journal of Retailing and Consumer Services	Blind	3	11-20%	429
Journal of Services Marketing	Blind	3	21-30%	443
North Central Business Journal	Blind	2	50%	538
Qualitative Market Research: An International Journal	Blind	1	40%	553
Sloan Management Review	Blind	2	6-10%	573
Tourism and Hospitality Research: The Surrey Quarterly Review	Blind	0	21-30%	589

Sales/Selling

Journal Name	Type Review	No. Ext. Rev.	Accept. Rate	Page
Academy of Marketing Science Review	Blind	3	11-20%	1
Academy of Marketing Studies Journal	Blind	2	21-30%	9
American Business Perspectives (NBDC Report)	Editorial		11-20%	22
American International College Journal of Business	Editorial	0	90%	29
Annual Advances in Business Cases	Blind	3	30%	38

INDEX

Journal Name	Type Review	No. Ext. Rev.	Accept. Rate	Page
Asia Pacific Journal of Marketing and Logistics	Blind		11-20%	47
Bank Marketing Magazine	Editorial	0	50%	50
Case Research Journal	Blind	3	11-20%	64
Cornell Hotel and Restaurant Administration Quarterly	Blind	2	50%	75
European Journal of Marketing	Blind		28%	87
Global Business and Economic Review	Blind	3+	22-25%	96
Global Competitiveness	Blind	2	50%	98
Harvard Business Review	Editorial	0	0-5%	102
Industrial Marketing Management	Blind	3	20-25%	109
International Academy for Case Studies	Blind	3	21-30%	115
International Journal of Business	Blind	2	11-20%	127
International Journal of Electronic Commerce (IJEC)	Blind	3	11-20%	131
International Journal of Hospitality Management	Blind	2	21-30%	138
International Journal of Research In Marketing	Blind	2	11-20%	150
International Journal of Tourism Research	Blind	2	50%	158
International Marketing Review	Blind	2	21-30%	164
International Research in the Business Disciplines	Blind	2	11-20%	168
Journal of Business and Behavioral Sciences	Blind	3	11-20%	197
Journal of Business Disciplines	Blind	3	11-20%	198
Journal of Business Education	Blind	2	11-20%	201
Journal of Business, Industry and Economics	Blind	2	70%	214
Journal of Consumer Marketing	Blind	3	21-27%	228
Journal of Euromarketing	Blind	2	21-30%	260
Journal of Fashion Marketing and Management	Blind	3	50%	264
Journal of Financial Services Marketing	Blind	3	50%	267
Journal of Food Product Marketing	Blind	3	50%	270
Journal of Global Marketing	Blind	2	11-20%	276
Journal of Hospitality & Leisure Marketing	Blind	2	50%	288
Journal of Hospitality & Tourism Research	Blind	3	11-20%	292
Journal of International Academy for Case Studies	Blind	2	11-20%	298
Journal of International Consumer Marketing	Blind	2	11-20%	301
Journal of International Food & Agribusiness Marketing	Blind	2	21-30%	309
Journal of Marketing	Blind	3	6-10%	335
Journal of Marketing Communications	Blind	2	40%	348
Journal of Marketing Education	Blind	3+	11-20%	352
Journal of Marketing Management	Blind	2	11-20%	360
Journal of Marketing Theory and Practice	Blind	3	11-20%	373
Journal of Nonprofit & Public Sector Marketing	Blind	2	21-30%	382
Journal of Nonprofit and Voluntary Sector Marketing	Blind	3	50%	386
Journal of Personal Selling & Sales Management	Blind	3	21-30%	389
Journal of Product & Brand Management	Blind	2	40-50%	397
Journal of Promotion Management	Blind	2	21-30%	402

INDEX

Journal Name	Type Review	No. Ext. Rev.	Accept. Rate	Page
Journal of Quality Assurance in Tourism & Hospitality	Blind	3	New J	409
Journal of Restaurant & Foodservice Marketing	Blind	2	21-30%	418
Journal of Retail Banking Services	Editorial	Varies		422
Journal of Retailing	Blind	2-3	11-20%	424
Journal of Retailing and Consumer Services	Blind	3	11-20%	429
Journal of Selling and Major Account Management	Blind	2	21-30%	438
Journal of Services Marketing	Blind	3	21-30%	443
Journal of the Academy of Marketing Science	Blind	3	31-50%	457
Journal of Travel & Tourism Marketing	Blind	2	21-30%	475
Journal of Vacation Marketing	Blind	3	50%	485
Marketing Educator	Blind	1	90%	519
Marketing Intelligence & Planning	Editorial	1	50%	524
Marketing Management	Blind	3	21-30%	531
Marketing Management Journal	Blind	3	21-30%	535
Mountain Plains Journal of Business and Economics	Blind	3	21-30%	537
North Central Business Journal	Blind	2	50%	538
Pennsylvania Journal of Business and Economics	Blind	2	50%	547
Qualitative Market Research: An International Journal	Blind	1	40%	553
Southwest Business & Economics Journal	Blind	1	30-35%	578
Southwestern Business Administration Journal	Blind	2	31-50%	580

Services

Journal Name	Type Review	No. Ext. Rev.	Accept. Rate	Page
Academy of Marketing Science Review	Blind	3	11-20%	1
Air Force Journal of Logistics	Blind	3	40%	21
American International College Journal of Business	Editorial	0	90%	29
Anatolia: An International Journal of Tourism Hospitality and Research	Blind	3	21-30%	30
Annals of Tourism Research: A Social Sciences Journal	Blind	3+	11-20%	34
Annual Advances in Business Cases	Blind	3	30%	38
Asia Pacific Journal of Marketing and Logistics	Blind		11-20%	47
Bank Marketing Magazine	Editorial	0	50%	50
California Management Review	Blind	3	6-10%	61
Case Research Journal	Blind	3	11-20%	64
Cornell Hotel and Restaurant Administration Quarterly	Blind	2	50%	75
FIU Hospitality Review	N/A	2	21-30%	94
Global Business and Economic Review	Blind	3+	22-25%	96
Global Competitiveness	Blind	2	50%	98
Harvard Business Review	Editorial	0	0-5%	102
Industrial Marketing Management	Blind	3	20-25%	109
International Academy for Case Studies	Blind	3	21-30%	115
International Journal of Business	Blind	2	11-20%	127

INDEX

Journal Name	Type Review	No. Ext. Rev.	Accept. Rate	Page
International Journal of Hospitality Management	Blind	2	21-30%	138
International Journal of Tourism Research	Blind	2	50%	158
International Research in the Business Disciplines	Blind	2	11-20%	168
International Review of Retail, Distribution and Consumer Research	Blind	2	33%	171
Journal of Advertising	Blind	3	11-20%	179
Journal of Business and Behavioral Sciences	Blind	3	11-20%	197
Journal of Business Disciplines	Blind	3	11-20%	198
Journal of Business, Industry and Economics	Blind	2	70%	214
Journal of Consumer Marketing	Blind	3	21-27%	228
Journal of Consumer Research	Blind	3	11-20%	242
Journal of Current Issues & Research in Advertising	Blind	3	6-10%	250
Journal of Euromarketing	Blind	2	21-30%	260
Journal of Financial Services Marketing	Blind	3	50%	267
Journal of Food Product Marketing	Blind	3	50%	270
Journal of Global Marketing	Blind	2	11-20%	276
Journal of Hospitality & Leisure Marketing	Blind	2	50%	288
Journal of Hospitality & Tourism Research	Blind	3	11-20%	292
Journal of International Academy for Case Studies	Blind	2	11-20%	298
Journal of International Consumer Marketing	Blind	2	11-20%	301
Journal of Marketing	Blind	3	6-10%	335
Journal of Marketing Communications	Blind	2	40%	348
Journal of Marketing Education	Blind	3+	11-20%	352
Journal of Marketing Management	Blind	2	11-20%	360
Journal of Marketing Theory and Practice	Blind	3	11-20%	373
Journal of Ministry Marketing and Management	Blind	2	21-30%	377
Journal of Quality Assurance in Tourism & Hospitality	Blind	3	New J	409
Journal of Relationship Marketing (Journal of Customer Service in Mktg. & Mgmt.)	Editorial	3+	40%	413
Journal of Restaurant & Foodservice Marketing	Blind	2	21-30%	418
Journal of Retail Banking Services	Editorial	Varies		422
Journal of Retailing	Blind	2-3	11-20%	424
Journal of Retailing and Consumer Services	Blind	3	11-20%	429
Journal of Services Marketing	Blind	3	21-30%	443
Journal of the Academy of Marketing Science	Blind	3	31-50%	457
Journal of Travel & Tourism Marketing	Blind	2	21-30%	475
Journal of Travel Research	Blind	3	20%	480
Journal of World Business	Blind	2	11-20%	488
Management Science	Editorial	3	11-20%	495
Marketing Educator	Blind	1	90%	519
Marketing Management	Blind	3	21-30%	531
Mountain Plains Journal of Business and Economics	Blind	3	21-30%	537
North Central Business Journal	Blind	2	50%	538

INDEX

Journal Name	Type Review	No. Ext. Rev.	Accept. Rate	Page
Operations Research	Editorial	3	21-30%	540
Pennsylvania Journal of Business and Economics	Blind	2	50%	547
Qualitative Market Research: An International Journal	Blind	1	40%	553
Service Industries Journal (The)	Blind	3	0-5%	564
Sloan Management Review	Blind	2	6-10%	573
Southwest Business & Economics Journal	Blind	1	30-35%	578
Tourism Analysis	Blind	3	45%	586
Tourism and Hospitality Research: The Surrey Quarterly Review	Blind	0	21-30%	589
Tourism Management	Blind	3	21-30%	593

Small Business Entrepreneurship

Journal Name	Type Review	No. Ext. Rev.	Accept. Rate	Page
Advances in International Marketing	Blind	2	11-20%	12
Agribusiness: An International Journal	Blind	2	21-30%	16
American Business Perspectives (NBDC Report)	Editorial		11-20%	22
American International College Journal of Business	Editorial	0	90%	29
Annals of Tourism Research: A Social Sciences Journal	Blind	3+	11-20%	34
Annual Advances in Business Cases	Blind	3	30%	38
Asian Journal of Business & Entrepreneurship	Blind	2	21-30%	48
Bank Marketing Magazine	Editorial	0	50%	50
Business Case Journal	Blind	2	21-30%	58
Case Research Journal	Blind	3	11-20%	64
Entrepreneurship Theory and Practice	Blind	2	11-20%	85
Family Business Review	Blind	3	21-30%	91
FIU Hospitality Review	N/A	2	21-30%	94
Global Competitiveness	Blind	2	50%	98
International Academy for Case Studies	Blind	3	21-30%	115
International Journal of Business	Blind	2	11-20%	127
International Journal of Hospitality & Tourism Administration	Blind	2	50%	134
International Journal of Tourism Research	Blind	2	50%	158
International Research in the Business Disciplines	Blind	2	11-20%	168
Journal of Business and Behavioral Sciences	Blind	3	11-20%	197
Journal of Business Disciplines	Blind	3	11-20%	198
Journal of Fashion Marketing and Management	Blind	3	50%	264
Journal of Food Product Marketing	Blind	3	50%	270
Journal of Hospitality & Tourism Research	Blind	3	11-20%	292
Journal of International Academy for Case Studies	Blind	2	11-20%	298
Journal of International Marketing	Blind	2	20%	317
Journal of Marketing Management	Blind	2	11-20%	360
Journal of Problems of Theory and Practice in Reforms of Regional Economies	Blind	2	21-30%	396
Journal of Retail Banking Services	Editorial	Varies		422
Journal of Retailing and Consumer Services	Blind	3	11-20%	429

INDEX

Journal Name	Type Review	No. Ext. Rev.	Accept. Rate	Page
Journal of Services Marketing	Blind	3	21-30%	443
Journal of Travel & Tourism Marketing	Blind	2	21-30%	475
Journal of World Business	Blind	2	11-20%	488
Marketing Educator	Blind	1	90%	519
Mountain Plains Journal of Business and Economics	Blind	3	21-30%	537
North Central Business Journal	Blind	2	50%	538
Pennsylvania Journal of Business and Economics	Blind	2	50%	547
Southwestern Business Administration Journal	Blind	2	31-50%	580
Tourism and Hospitality Research: The Surrey Quarterly Review	Blind	0	21-30%	589
Tourism Management	Blind	3	21-30%	593

Strategic Management Policy

Journal Name	Type Review	No. Ext. Rev.	Accept. Rate	Page
Advances in International Marketing	Blind	2	11-20%	12
Agribusiness: An International Journal	Blind	2	21-30%	16
Air Force Journal of Logistics	Blind	3	40%	21
American Business Perspectives (NBDC Report)	Editorial		11-20%	22
American International College Journal of Business	Editorial	0	90%	29
Annals of Tourism Research: A Social Sciences Journal	Blind	3+	11-20%	34
Annual Advances in Business Cases	Blind	3	30%	38
Asia Pacific Business Review	Blind	3+	21-30%	44
Asian Journal of Business & Entrepreneurship	Blind	2	21-30%	48
Business Case Journal	Blind	2	21-30%	58
California Management Review	Blind	3	6-10%	61
Case Research Journal	Blind	3	11-20%	64
Decision Sciences (Journal of)	Blind	2	11-20%	78
Family Business Review	Blind	3	21-30%	91
FIU Hospitality Review	N/A	2	21-30%	94
Global Business and Economic Review	Blind	3+	22-25%	96
Global Competitiveness	Blind	2	50%	98
Global Economy Quarterly (GEQ)	Blind	2	11-20%	100
Harvard Business Review	Editorial	0	0-5%	102
Industrial Marketing Management	Blind	3	20-25%	109
Interactive Marketing	Blind	2	21-30%	112
International Academy for Case Studies	Blind	3	21-30%	115
International Journal of Business	Blind	2	11-20%	127
International Journal of Business and Economics	Blind	2	11-20%	129
International Journal of Hospitality & Tourism Administration	Blind	2	50%	134
International Journal of Hospitality Management	Blind	2	21-30%	138
International Journal of Logistics: Research and Applications	Blind	2	40%	143
International Research in the Business Disciplines	Blind	2	11-20%	168
Internet Research	Blind	2	35%	174

INDEX

Journal Name	Type Review	No. Ext. Rev.	Accept. Rate	Page
Journal of Brand Management	Blind	3	50%	186
Journal of Business and Behavioral Sciences	Blind	3	11-20%	197
Journal of Business Disciplines	Blind	3	11-20%	198
Journal of Business, Industry and Economics	Blind	2	70%	214
Journal of Communication Management	Blind	3	50%	221
Journal of Database Marketing	Blind	3	50%	254
Journal of Fashion Marketing and Management	Blind	3	50%	264
Journal of Food Product Marketing	Blind	3	50%	270
Journal of Hospital Marketing	Editorial	4	50%	284
Journal of Hospitality & Leisure Marketing	Blind	2	50%	288
Journal of Hospitality & Tourism Research	Blind	3	11-20%	292
Journal of International Academy for Case Studies	Blind	2	11-20%	298
Journal of International Marketing	Blind	2	20%	317
Journal of Marketing for Higher Education	Blind	3	35%	356
Journal of Marketing Management	Blind	2	11-20%	360
Journal of Ministry Marketing and Management	Blind	2	21-30%	377
Journal of Nonprofit and Voluntary Sector Marketing	Blind	3	50%	386
Journal of Product & Brand Management	Blind	2	40-50%	397
Journal of Quality Assurance in Tourism & Hospitality	Blind	3	New J	409
Journal of Retail Banking Services	Editorial	Varies		422
Journal of Retailing and Consumer Services	Blind	3	11-20%	429
Journal of Services Marketing	Blind	3	21-30%	443
Journal of Targeting, Measurement, and Analysis for Targeting	Blind	3	50%	454
Journal of Travel & Tourism Marketing	Blind	2	21-30%	475
Journal of Travel Research	Blind	3	20%	480
Journal of World Business	Blind	2	11-20%	488
Marketing Intelligence & Planning	Editorial	1	50%	524
Marketing Management	Blind	3	21-30%	531
Marketing Management Journal	Blind	3	21-30%	535
Mountain Plains Journal of Business and Economics	Blind	3	21-30%	537
North Central Business Journal	Blind	2	50%	538
Operations Research	Editorial	3	21-30%	540
Pennsylvania Journal of Business and Economics	Blind	2	50%	547
Sloan Management Review	Blind	2	6-10%	573
Southwestern Business Administration Journal	Blind	2	31-50%	580
Tourism and Hospitality Research: The Surrey Quarterly Review	Blind	0	21-30%	589

Technology/Innovation

Air Force Journal of Logistics	Blind	3	40%	21
American Business Perspectives (NBDC Report)	Editorial		11-20%	22
American International College Journal of Business	Editorial	0	90%	29

INDEX

Journal Name	Type Review	No. Ext. Rev.	Accept. Rate	Page
Annual Advances in Business Cases	Blind	3	30%	38
Asia Pacific Business Review	Blind	3+	21-30%	44
Asia Pacific Journal of Marketing and Logistics	Blind		11-20%	47
Asian Journal of Business & Entrepreneurship	Blind	2	21-30%	48
Bank Marketing Magazine	Editorial	0	50%	50
California Management Review	Blind	3	6-10%	61
Case Research Journal	Blind	3	11-20%	64
Communications and the Law	Editorial	0	50%	73
Cornell Hotel and Restaurant Administration Quarterly	Blind	2	50%	75
Decision Sciences (Journal of)	Blind	2	11-20%	78
FIU Hospitality Review	N/A	2	21-30%	94
Global Business and Economic Review	Blind	3+	22-25%	96
Global Competitiveness	Blind	2	50%	98
Harvard Business Review	Editorial	0	0-5%	102
Industrial Marketing Management	Blind	3	20-25%	109
Interactive Marketing	Blind	2	21-30%	112
International Academy for Case Studies	Blind	3	21-30%	115
International Journal of Business and Economics	Blind	2	11-20%	129
International Journal of Electronic Commerce (IJEC)	Blind	3	11-20%	131
International Research in the Business Disciplines	Blind	2	11-20%	168
Internet Research	Blind	2	35%	174
Journal of Business and Behavioral Sciences	Blind	3	11-20%	197
Journal of Business Disciplines	Blind	3	11-20%	198
Journal of Communication	Blind	3	11-20%	219
Journal of Consumer Research	Blind	3	11-20%	242
Journal of Food Product Marketing	Blind	3	50%	270
Journal of Hospitality & Leisure Marketing	Blind	2	50%	288
Journal of Hospitality & Tourism Research	Blind	3	11-20%	292
Journal of Interactive Marketing	Blind	2	11-20%	295
Journal of International Academy for Case Studies	Blind	2	11-20%	298
Journal of Internet Commerce	Blind	3	New J	326
Journal of Marketing Education	Blind	3+	11-20%	352
Journal of Marketing Management	Blind	2	11-20%	360
Journal of Marketing Theory and Practice	Blind	3	11-20%	373
Journal of Promotion Management	Blind	2	21-30%	402
Journal of Quality Assurance in Tourism & Hospitality	Blind	3	New J	409
Journal of Retail Banking Services	Editorial	Varies		422
Journal of Retailing and Consumer Services	Blind	3	11-20%	429
Journal of Travel & Tourism Marketing	Blind	2	21-30%	475
Journal of World Business	Blind	2	11-20%	488
Logistics Information Management	Blind	2	21-30%	491
Marketing Management	Blind	3	21-30%	531
North Central Business Journal	Blind	2	50%	538

INDEX 647

Journal Name	Type Review	No. Ext. Rev.	Accept. Rate	Page
Qualitative Market Research: An International Journal	Blind	1	40%	553
Sloan Management Review	Blind	2	6-10%	573
Southwestern Business Administration Journal	Blind	2	31-50%	580

Transportation/Physical Distribution

Journal Name	Type Review	No. Ext. Rev.	Accept. Rate	Page
Agribusiness: An International Journal	Blind	2	21-30%	16
Air Force Journal of Logistics	Blind	3	40%	21
Annual Advances in Business Cases	Blind	3	30%	38
Asia Pacific Journal of Marketing and Logistics	Blind		11-20%	47
Global Business and Economic Review	Blind	3+	22-25%	96
Global Competitiveness	Blind	2	50%	98
Harvard Business Review	Editorial	0	0-5%	102
Industrial Marketing Management	Blind	3	20-25%	109
International Journal of Hospitality & Tourism Administration	Blind	2	50%	134
International Journal of Physical Distribution & Logistics Management	Blind	3	21-30%	146
International Journal of Retail and Distribution Management	Blind	2	21-30%	154
International Journal of Transport Economics	Blind	1	11-20%	162
International Marketing Review	Blind	2	21-30%	164
International Review of Retail, Distribution and Consumer Research	Blind	2	33%	171
Journal of Business and Behavioral Sciences	Blind	3	11-20%	197
Journal of Business Disciplines	Blind	3	11-20%	198
Journal of Business Logistics	Blind	3+	21-30%	204
Journal of Business, Industry and Economics	Blind	2	70%	214
Journal of Food Product Marketing	Blind	3	50%	270
Journal of International Academy for Case Studies	Blind	2	11-20%	298
Journal of International Food & Agribusiness Marketing	Blind	2	21-30%	309
Journal of Marketing Channels	Blind	2	21-30%	344
Journal of Marketing Education	Blind	3+	11-20%	352
Journal of Marketing Management	Blind	2	11-20%	360
Journal of Marketing Theory and Practice	Blind	3	11-20%	373
Journal of Retailing	Blind	2-3	11-20%	424
Journal of Retailing and Consumer Services	Blind	3	11-20%	429
Journal of Transport Economics and Policy	Editorial	2	21-30%	462
Journal of Transportation Law, Logistics, and Policy	Editorial	0	70%	466
Journal of Transportation Management	Blind	2	35%	470
Journal of Travel & Tourism Marketing	Blind	2	21-30%	475
Logistics Information Management	Blind	2	21-30%	491
Marketing Educator	Blind	1	90%	519
North Central Business Journal	Blind	2	50%	538

Journal Name	Type Review	No. Ext. Rev.	Accept. Rate	Page
Operations Research	Editorial	3	21-30%	540
Pennsylvania Journal of Business and Economics	Blind	2	50%	547
Southwest Business & Economics Journal	Blind	1	30-35%	578
Transportation	Editorial	3	35%	597
Transportation Journal	Blind	3	15%	601
Transportation Research Part E: Logistics and Transportation Review	Blind	2	30%	603
Transportation Science Journal	Editorial	3	21-30%	606
World Transport Policy & Practice	Blind	1	40%	611